S0-BUB-008

ZAGATSURVEY®

2006

TOP U.S. HOTELS, RESORTS & SPAS

Editors: Donna Marino Wilkins
with Randi Gollin

Published and distributed by
ZAGAT SURVEY, LLC
4 Columbus Circle
New York, New York 10019
Tel: 212 977 6000
E-mail: travel@zagat.com
Web site: www.zagat.com

Acknowledgments

We thank Tina Barseghian, Brian Berusch, Anne Cole, Lynn Cook, Erica Curtis, Marilyn Green, Meesha Halm, Carolyn Heller, Alice Van Housen, Rochelle Koff, Rita Kyriakides, Lori Midson, Shelley Skiles Sawyer and Ruth Tobias. We are also grateful to our editorial assistant, Josh Rogers, as well as the following members of our staff: Betsy Andrews, Reni Chin, Schuyler Frazier, Natalie Lebert, Mike Liao, Dave Makulec, Robert Poole, Robert Seixas, Thomas Sheehan, Joshua Siegel, Yoji Yamaguchi and Sharon Yates.

We are especially appreciative to the American Society of Travel Agents, thanks to whose cooperation we have had the professional input of over 900 travel agents and meeting planners.

The reviews published in this guide are based on public opinion surveys, with numerical ratings reflecting the average scores given by all survey participants who voted on each establishment and text based on direct quotes from, or fair paraphrasings of, participants' comments. Phone numbers, addresses and other factual information were correct to the best of our knowledge when published in this guide; any subsequent changes may not be reflected.

ISBN 1-57006-749-X
Printed in the United States of America

Contents

INDEXES

HOTEL TYPES

SPECIAL FEATURES

About This Survey

This *2006 Top U.S. Hotels, Resorts & Spas Survey* is an update reflecting significant developments since our last *Survey* was published. For example, we have added 53 important new hotels, as well as indicated name changes, new facilities and the like. We've also added several new icons to help readers find hotels with various features. These indicate: Dining Excellence, Historic Interest, Kitchens, Pet-Friendly, Views, Skiing and Tennis. All told, this guide now covers 1,026 of the country's best places to stay for business or pleasure.

This marks the 27th year that Zagat Survey has reported on the shared experiences of diners and travelers like you. What started in 1979 as a hobby involving 200 of our friends rating local restaurants has come a long way. Today, we have more than 250,000 active surveyors and now cover entertaining, golf, movies, music, nightlife, restaurants, shopping, theater and tourist attractions. Our guides are also available on PDAs, cell phones and by subscription at zagat.com.

By regularly surveying large numbers of avid customers, we hope to have achieved a uniquely current and reliable guide. This book's 16,413 participants are frequent travelers who stayed at hotels an average of 36 nights per year, thus this *Survey* is based on roughly 600,000 nights at hotels annually – that's 1,600 visits per night. Of these surveyors, 51% are women; 49% men; the breakdown by age is 13% in their 20s; 31%, 30s; 23%, 40s; 21%, 50s; and 12%, 60s or above.

We are especially grateful to the American Society of Travel Agents, through whom we gained the participation of over 900 travel professionals! We are proud to have their in-depth knowledge and expertise reflected in this guide. Our editors have synopsized all of these surveyors' opinions, with their comments shown in quotation marks. We sincerely thank each of these people; this book is really "theirs."

To help you locate the country's best hotels, resorts and spas, we have prepared a number of lists. See Useful Web Sites & Toll-Free Numbers (pages 9–10) and Top Ratings (pages 12–22). In addition, we have provided 44 handy indexes.

To vote in any of our upcoming *Surveys,* just register at zagat.com. Each participant will receive a free copy of the resulting guide when it is published. Your comments and even criticisms of this guide are also solicited. There is always room for improvement with your help. You can contact us at travel@zagat.com.

New York, NY
November 7, 2005

Nina and Tim
Nina and Tim Zagat

What's New

Sticker Shock: As hotels across the U.S. have seen a rise in their occupancies over the past year, room rates have followed suit. Consumers can expect to pay more across the board, both for their lodging and transportation. The disruption to the oil and gas industries from hurricanes Katrina and Rita is sending already high gas prices even higher, making the costs of popular drive destinations, such as Orlando, Las Vegas and the national parks, more expensive. Meanwhile, skyrocketing jet fuel prices will likely lead to airline ticket increases and have already contributed to the Chapter 11 bankruptcy protections sought by Delta and Northwest Airlines. How this will affect the travel industry is difficult to predict, but, for sure, it won't be good.

Outrageous Charges: Along with these rising costs, the over-the-top charges many hotels institute – including fees for phone calls, facilities usage, etc. – amount to a bait-and-switch. Even if room rates seem like a good deal, often these extra charges negate that.

Weather Weary: One of our most popular tourism destinations, New Orleans, was dealt a severe blow by both hurricanes Katrina and Rita. Despite the devastation wrought by the storms, we are optimistic that the city will be able to host its famous Mardi Gras in February. Meanwhile, the gaming destinations of Biloxi and Gulfport, Mississippi, also suffered severely, with all of the floating casinos damaged or destroyed. We join the rest of the country in our grief, and hope this region recovers as quickly as possible.

Merger Mania: It's been another big year for hotel mergers and acquisitions, from Starwood Hotels' takeover of the Le Méridien chain to the purchase of Wyndham International by the Blackstone Group. And significant management shifts occurred, e.g. New York's Pierre Hotel, once a Four Seasons, is now run by the elite India-based Taj Resorts.

More Vegas: The opening of Wynn Las Vegas this past year was just the latest in a slew of Sin City happenings. The Renaissance Las Vegas debuted, and splashy new eateries moved into the Bellagio (Fix and Sensi), the Mandalay Bay (Mix and rm) and the MGM Grand (Diego and Shibuya). The new Conrad Las Vegas will begin taking reservations next year, while actor George Clooney, along with nightclub owner Rande Gerber, are investing in a planned $3-billion resort – Las Ramblas – that is slated to break ground in 2006. Furthermore, the once-seedy Downtown area is continuing a massive revitalization.

Boutique Bonanza: Small hotels are earning big praise. The Kimpton Hotel & Restaurant Group, operator of the Hotel Monaco brand, opened San Diego's Hotel Solamar and will double the size of its company by the end of the decade. InterContinental Hotels also entered the boutique segment with its first Hotel Indigo, based in Atlanta. New offerings like Houston's Hotel Icon (with a Vongerichten restaurant) and Circa 39 in Miami Beach are also turning heads.

Tech Trends: The flat-panel TV is taking center stage in most room makeovers – Connecticut's Mayflower Inn has even added ones that look like mirrors when turned off. Taking tech a step further, New York's new Dream Hotel lends guests iPods and the Kor Hotel Group's four California locations provide Sony PlayStations. According to our surveyors, wireless Internet access is one of the most important amenities, and more hotels are rolling out the service. Some offer extra support with the addition of e-butlers or 24-hr. concierges, such as New York's Ritz-Carltons.

Pet Perks: Services and amenities for four-legged guests are getting fancier. New York's Ritz-Carlton, Central Park offers pets specially designed Burberry raincoats, Starwood hotels feature chew-toy city souvenirs and miniature bathrobes and the Peninsula Group provides walking services. We've added a pet-friendly icon to this *Survey* for hotels that allow dogs and cats.

What You're Looking For: Service is the most important factor in a good hotel stay, according to our surveyors, a finding that mirrors what our *Restaurant* and *Shopping* surveyors say. When asked what irritates them most during a visit, 59 percent cited poor service, 17 percent said dirty rooms and 12 percent pointed to noisy guests. Some 27 percent of our surveyors say personal economic factors influence their travel plans the most, and New York won the top spot as the best U.S. city to visit (chosen by 38 percent of our respondents), followed by San Francisco and Las Vegas. An overwhelming 69 percent book their travel online.

New York, NY — Donna Marino Wilkins
November 7, 2005

Travel Tips

Ask and You Shall Receive: Although occupancies and room rates are rising in most destinations, consumers who ask for special rates can still find plenty of deals, particularly by calling the on-site hotel reservationist directly rather than a toll-free operator. Hoteliers often are ready to deal, especially if your dates are flexible and it's during an off-peak time. Remember, a hotel's "rack rates" are just a jumping-off point from which to negotiate, so be sure to ask about special promotions, upgrades, etc.

Net Worth: The best bargains often reside on the Web, particularly for last-minute lodging. You can get marked-down excess inventory by booking online through individual hotels or via sites such as Expedia, Priceline and Travelocity. Sign up for automatic e-mail updates and you can get late-breaking specials sent directly to you. We've included Web Sites and Toll-Free Numbers on pages 9–10 as well as throughout the body of this guide.

Beyond a Room With a View: Make sure you know what you're getting when you book. There's a tremendous difference in room type, so ask where yours is located, what floor it's on, when it was last updated and what kind of view it has. Inquire about ongoing renovations at the hotel and find out if any planned conventions or events may disrupt your stay. Be sure to check on the specific amenities that are important to you. We've added a number of icons to help you find the hotels that offer the features you seek.

Hide-and-Seek Costs: Sometimes a deal isn't a deal once you scratch the surface, so be leery of taxes and extra charges (such as for a health club, telephone usage or parking). Some places tack on an extra mandatory daily "resort fee." To avoid nasty surprises at check-out, ask in advance about any and all extra charges, including taxes.

Use Your Own Phone: When it comes to saving money, you're always better off using your own cell phone to avoid the outrageous charges levied on most hotel phone systems. Our surveyors report that they have sometimes doubled their bill as a result of using the hotels' phones.

You've Got a Friend: Even sophisticated travelers rely on the expertise of others. A good travel agent can offer years of experience and on-property contacts that are invaluable. The key is finding a professional who understands your traveling tastes – if you do, the agent will undoubtedly save you both time and money.

Useful Web Sites & Toll-Free Numbers

HOTEL CHAIN	WEB SITE	PHONE
Adam's Mark	adamsmark.com	800-444-2326
Amanresorts	amanresorts.com	800-477-9180
Amerisuites	amerisuites.com	800-835-1516
Best Western	bestwestern.com	800-528-1234
Caesars	caesars.com	800-223-7277
Clarion	clarionhotel.com	800-252-7466
Comfort Inn	comfortinn.com	800-252-7466
Courtyard by Marriott	courtyard.com	800-321-2211
Crowne Plaza	crowneplaza.com	800-227-6963
Days Inn	daysinn.com	800-325-2525
DoubleTree	doubletree.com	800-222-8733
Embassy Suites	embassysuites.com	800-362-2779
Fairfield Inn	fairfieldinn.com	800-228-2800
Fairmont	fairmont.com	800-441-1414
Four Points	fourpoints.com	888-625-5144
Four Seasons	fourseasons.com	800-332-3442
Grand Hyatt	hyatt.com	800-233-1234
Hampton Inn	hamptoninn.com	800-426-7866
Harrah's	harrahs.com	800-427-7247
Hilton	hilton.com	800-774-1500
Hilton Garden Inn	hiltongardeninn.com	800-774-1500
Holiday Inn	holiday-inn.com	800-465-4329
Homewood Suites	homewood-suites.com	800-225-5466
Howard Johnson	hojo.com	800-406-1411
Hyatt	hyatt.com	800-233-1234
Hyatt Regency	hyatt.com	800-233-1234
InterContinental	interconti.com	800-327-0200
Joie de Vivre	jdvhospitality.com	800-738-7477
Kimpton Group	kimptongroup.com	800-546-7866
La Quinta	laquinta.com	800-531-5900
Leading Hotels	lhw.com	800-223-6800
Le Méridien	lemeridien.com	800-543-4300
Loews	loewshotels.com	800-235-6397
Luxury Collection	luxurycollection.com	800-325-3589
MainStay Suites	mainstaysuites.com	800-660-6246
Mandarin Oriental	mandarin-oriental.com	866-526-6567
Marriott	marriott.com	800-228-9290
Millennium Hotels	millenniumhotels.com	866-866-6455
Morgans Hotel Group	morganshotelgroup.com	800-606-6090
Nikko	nikkohotels.com	800-645-5687
Omni	omnihotels.com	800-843-6664
Pan Pacific	panpac.com	800-327-8585
Park Hyatt	hyatt.com	800-233-1234
Peninsula	peninsula.com	800-262-9467
Preferred Hotels	preferredhotels.com	800-323-7500
Radisson	radisson.com	800-333-3333
Ramada	ramada.com	800-272-6232
Regent	regenthotels.com	800-545-4000
Relais & Châteaux	relaischateaux.com	800-735-2478
Renaissance	renaissancehotels.com	800-468-3571
Residence Inn	residenceinn.com	800-331-3131
Ritz-Carlton	ritzcarlton.com	800-241-3333
Rosewood	rosewoodhotels.com	888-767-3966
Sheraton	sheraton.com	800-325-3535

Shoney's Inn	shoneysinn.com	800-552-4667
Small Luxury Hotels	slh.com	800-525-4800
Sonesta	sonesta.com	800-766-3782
St. Regis	stregis.com	800-598-1863
Swissôtel	swissotel.com	888-737-9477
Travelodge	travelodge.com	800-578-7878
Westin	westin.com	800-937-8461
W Hotels	whotels.com	877-946-8357
Wingate Inns	wingateinns.com	800-228-1000
Wyndham	wyndham.com	800-822-4200
AIRLINE		
AirTran	airtran.com	800-247-8726
Alaska Airlines	alaskaair.com	800-426-0333
Aloha Airlines	alohaair.com	800-367-5250
American	americanair.com	800-433-7300
America West	americawestairlines.com	800-235-9292
Continental	continental.com	800-525-0280
Delta	delta.com	800-221-1212
Frontier	frontierairlines.com	800-432-1359
Hawaiian Airlines	hawaiianair.com	800-367-5320
Hooters Air	hootersair.com	888-359-4668
JetBlue	jetblue.com	800-538-2583
Midwest Airlines	midwestairlines.com	800-452-2022
Northwest	nwa.com	800-225-2525
Song	flysong.com	800-359-7664
Southwest	southwest.com	800-435-9792
Spirit Airlines	spiritair.com	800-772-7117
Sun Country	suncountry.com	800-359-6786
United	united.com	800-241-6522
US Airways	usair.com	800-428-4322
CAR RENTAL		
Alamo	alamo.com	800-327-9633
Avis	avis.com	800-230-4898
Budget	budget.com	800-527-0700
Dollar	dollar.com	800-800-4000
Enterprise	enterprise.com	800-736-8222
Hertz	hertz.com	800-654-3131
National	nationalcar.com	800-227-7368
Payless	paylesscar.com	800-729-5377
Thrifty	thrifty.com	800-367-2277
RAILROAD/BUS		
Amtrak	amtrak.com	800-872-7245
Greyhound	greyhound.com	800-231-2222
WEB SITE/TRAVEL AGENCY		
AAA	aaa.com	800-272-2155
American Express	travel.americanexpress.com	800-346-3607
Carlson Wagonlit	carlsonwagonlit.com	763-212-1000
CheapTickets	cheaptickets.com	888-922-8849
11th Hour Vacations	11thhourvacations.com	864-331-1140
Expedia	expedia.com	800-397-3342
Hotels.com	hotels.com	800-246-8357
Hotwire	hotwire.com	877-468-9473
Liberty Travel	libertytravel.com	888-271-1584
OneTravel	onetravel.com	800-929-2523
Orbitz	orbitz.com	888-656-4546
Priceline	priceline.com	866-925-5373
Quikbook	quikbook.com	800-789-9887
Site 59	site59.com	800-845-0192
Travelocity	travelocity.com	800-249-4302
Uniglobe	uniglobetravel.com	800-999-8000
Virtuoso	virtuoso.com	800-401-4274

Ratings & Symbols

Name, Address, Phone & Fax Nos., Web Site, Rooms

Zagat Ratings

Features

	R	S	D	P	$
TIM & NINA'S INN	▽ 18	5	4	22	$110

4 Columbus Circle; 212-977-6000; fax 212-977-9760; 800-977-9000; www.zagat.com; 20 rooms, 2 suites

Despite "dazzling views" of Central Park and "lovely public spaces", surveyors are split over this "minuscule" "mini-priced" Midtown boutique hotel; fans tout its "handy location", but critics knock "rooms too small to change your mind", dining at Chez Z that's "outshone by the corner hot dog stand" and a staff that "never notices you unless they're angry."

Review, with surveyors' comments in quotes

Places with top ratings are shown in **CAPITAL LETTERS.**

The following icons are used throughout this guide to indicate hotel features:

- = Children's programs
- = Exceptional dining
- Ⓗ = Historic interest
- = Kitchens
- = Allows pets
- = Views
- = Golf courses
- Ⓢ = Notable spa facilities
- = Downhill skiing
- = Tennis

The total number of rooms per hotel is followed by the number of suites, villas, etc., e.g. 20 rooms, 2 suites.

Ratings are on a scale of **0** to **30.**

R Rooms	**S** Service	**D** Dining	**P** Public Spaces/ Facilities
18	5	4	22

0–9 poor to fair
10–15 fair to good
16–19 good to very good
20–25 very good to excellent
26–30 extraordinary to perfection
▽ low response/less reliable

Cost ($) reflects the hotel's high-season rack rate, i.e. its asking price, for a standard double room. It does not reflect frequent seasonal price changes and special rates.

A place listed without ratings is a **write-in** or **newcomer.** In the Hotel Chains section, cost is indicated as follows:

I Inexpensive, below $150
M Moderate, $150–$249
E Expensive, $250–$349
VE Very Expensive, $350 & up

For top lists, the numerical score shown is the Overall rating, i.e. the average of the hotel's scores for Rooms, Service, Dining and Public Facilities, except where noted.

Top Ratings

This list excludes chains with low voting. The numerical score to the left reflects the average of each chain's ratings for Rooms, Service and Public Facilities.

Hotel Chains

28 Four Seasons (29)

27 Ritz-Carlton (40)
Luxury Collection (10)
Relais & Châteaux (28)

26 Small Luxury Hotels (41)
Leading Hotels (55)

24 Fairmont (16)
Preferred Hotels (81)
Kimpton Group (36)
InterContinental (15)

23 Westin (66)
Renaissance (72)
W Hotels (16)

22 Sofitel (10)
Loews (18)

21 Hyatt (20)
Omni (36)
Caesars (18)
Marriott (312)
Historic Hotels (218)
Millennium (14)

20 Embassy Suites (178)
Wyndham (113)

19 Harrah's (18)
Hilton (245)
Residence Inn (482)
Sheraton (176)
Homewood Suites (150)

18 Doubletree (170)
Crown Plaza (88)

The above list includes hotel chains with at least 10 hotels in the United States. In parentheses is the number of the chain's U.S. locations. In addition, we've listed prominent marketing groups such as Relais & Châteaux and Leading Hotels of the World. Reviews for these marketing groups and other noteworthy hotel chains can be found in the Hotel Chains section on pages 23–31. Although there are excellent values among our top-rated chains, the following list features mid-range chains with the best value for the dollar.

Top Bangs for the Buck

1. Embassy Suites
2. Residence Inn by Marriott
3. Homewood Suites
4. Harrah's
5. Courtyard by Marriott
6. DoubleTree
7. Sheraton
8. Crowne Plaza

Top Hotels

(With 100 or more rooms, based on Overall score)

28 Peninsula, *Chicago*
Peninsula Beverly Hills, *Los Angeles*
27 Four Seasons, *Chicago*
Mandarin Oriental, *Miami*
Four Seasons, *New York City*
Windsor Court, *New Orleans*
Ritz-Carlton, *Chicago*
Four Seasons, *Philadelphia*
Four Seasons, *Las Vegas*
Mansion on Turtle Creek, *Dallas*
Four Seasons Beverly Hills, *Los Angeles*
Halekulani, *Oahu, HI*
Four Seasons, *Boston*
Mandarin Oriental, *New York City*
Four Seasons, *San Francisco*
Bellagio, *Las Vegas*
26 Four Seasons, *Atlanta*
Ritz-Carlton, Central Park, *New York City*
Ritz-Carlton, *San Francisco*
Four Seasons, *Miami*
Ritz-Carlton Buckhead, *Atlanta*
Ritz-Carlton Huntington, *Pasadena, CA*
St. Regis, *New York City*
Ritz-Carlton, Battery Park, *New York City*
Mandarin Oriental, *San Francisco*
Four Seasons, *Houston*
Ritz-Carlton, *Boston*
25 Park Hyatt, *Chicago*
Peninsula, *New York City*
Four Seasons, *Washington, DC*
Regent Beverly Wilshire, *Los Angeles*
Ritz-Carlton, *New Orleans*
Four Seasons, *Newport Beach, CA*
Beverly Hills Hotel, *Los Angeles*
Fairmont Olympic, *Seattle*
Ritz-Carlton Tysons Corner, *McLean, VA*
Ritz-Carlton Coconut Grove, *Miami*
Venetian, *Las Vegas*
Ritz-Carlton, *Clayton, MO*
Crescent Court, *Dallas*
New York Palace, *New York City*
St. Regis, *Houston*
Ritz-Carlton Boston Common, *Boston*
Charleston Place, *Charleston, SC*
Ritz-Carlton, *Washington, DC*
Grand America, *Salt Lake City*
Raffles L'Ermitage, *Los Angeles*
Ritz-Carlton, *Dearborn, MI*
Carlyle, *New York City*
Biltmore/Coral Gables, *Miami*

Top Resorts

(With 100 or more rooms, based on Overall score)

29 Four Seasons Hualalai, *Big Island, HI*
28 Four Seasons Wailea, *Maui, HI*
27 Ritz-Carlton, *Naples, FL*
Four Seasons Aviara, *Carlsbad, CA*
Ritz-Carlton, *Orlando*
Lodge at Koele, *Lanai, HI*
Inn at Spanish Bay, *Pebble Beach, CA*
Stein Eriksen Lodge, *Park City, UT*
Greenbrier, *White Sulphur Springs, WV*
Royal Palms, *Phoenix*
Ritz-Carlton Golf Resort, *Naples, FL*
Kahala Mandarin Oriental, *Oahu, HI*
St. Regis Monarch Beach, *Dana Point, CA*
Four Seasons at Troon North, *Scottsdale, AZ*
Montage Resort, *Laguna Beach, CA*
26 Ritz-Carlton, *Amelia Island, FL*
Phoenician, *Scottsdale, AZ*
Lodge at Pebble Beach, *Pebble Beach, CA*
Ritz-Carlton Laguna Niguel, *Dana Point, CA*
Sanctuary on Camelback Mtn., *Paradise Valley, AZ*
Ritz-Carlton, Bachelor Gulch, *Avon, CO*
Fairmont Kea Lani, *Maui, HI*
Cloister, *Sea Island, GA*
Ritz-Carlton, Lake Las Vegas, *Henderson, NV*
American Club, *Kohler, WI*
Four Seasons at Las Colinas, *Irving, TX*
Manele Bay Hotel, *Lanai, HI*
Broadmoor, *Colorado Springs*
Boulders, *Carefree, AZ*
Disney's Grand Floridian, *Orlando*
St. Regis, *Aspen*
Ritz-Carlton Reynolds Plantation, *Lake Oconee, GA*
Ritz-Carlton, *Half Moon Bay, CA*
Enchantment Resort, *Sedona, AZ*
Ritz-Carlton Key Biscayne, *Miami*
25 Four Seasons, *Palm Beach, FL*
Four Seasons Resort, *Santa Barbara, CA*
Inn on Biltmore, *Asheville, NC*
Ritz-Carlton Kapalua, *Maui, HI*
Nemacolin Woodlands, *Farmington, PA*
Mauna Lani Bay Hotel, *Big Island, HI*
Bacara, *Santa Barbara, CA*
Ritz-Carlton, *Sarasota, FL*
Fairmont Orchid, *Big Island, HI*
Breakers, *Palm Beach, FL*
Fairmont Scottsdale Princess, *Scottsdale, AZ*
Fairmont Turnberry Isle, *Aventura, FL*
JW Marriott Ihilani, *Oahu, HI*
Grand Hyatt Kauai, *Kauai, HI*
Lodge at Torrey Pines, *San Diego*

Top Small Hotels

(With less than 100 rooms, based on Overall score)

29 Lodge at Sea Island, *Sea Island, GA*
28 Blackberry Farm, *Walland, TN*
Canoe Bay, *Chetek, WI*
Twin Farms, *Barnard, VT*
Woodlands Resort, *Summerville, SC*
Château du Sureau, *Oakhurst, CA*
27 Fearrington House, *Pittsboro, NC*
Point, *Saranac Lake, NY*
Post Ranch Inn, *Big Sur, CA*
Barnsley Gardens, *Adairsville, GA*
Rancho Valencia Resort, *Rancho Santa Fe, CA*
Bel-Air, *Los Angeles*
Inn at Little Washington, *Washington, VA*
Little Palm Island, *Keys, FL*
26 Bernardus Lodge, *Carmel Valley, CA*
Gaige House Inn, *Sonoma, CA*
Sunset Key Guest Cottages, *Keys, FL*
Auberge du Soleil, *Napa, CA*
Milliken Creek Inn, *Napa, CA*
Little Nell, *Aspen*
Charlotte Inn, *Martha's Vineyard, MA*
Amangani, *Jackson, WY*
Mayflower Inn, *Washington, CT*
Maison Orleans, *New Orleans*
Meadowood, *Napa, CA*
Wauwinet, *Nantucket, MA*
Keswick Hall, *Charlottesville, VA*
Sonnenalp, *Vail, CO*
Rittenhouse Hotel, *Philadelphia*
25 San Ysidro Ranch, *Santa Barbara, CA*
Lake Placid Lodge, *Lake Placid, NY*
Blantyre, *Lenox, MA*
Simpson House Inn, *Santa Barbara, CA*
Castle Hill Inn & Resort, *Newport, RI*
Williamsburg Inn, *Williamsburg, VA*
Vintners Inn, *Santa Rosa, CA*
Willows Lodge, *Woodinville, WA*
Kenwood Inn, *Kenwood, CA*
Ritz-Carlton, Georgetown, *Washington, DC**
Bellevue Club, *Seattle*
Richmond Hill Inn, *Asheville, NC*
Fisher Island Hotel & Resort, *Miami*
Inn at Perry Cabin, *St. Michaels, MD*
Wheatleigh, *Lenox, MA**
XV Beacon, *Boston*
Castle on the Hudson, *Tarrytown, NY*
Lodge & Spa at Cordillera, *Edwards, CO*
Ventana Inn, *Big Sur, CA*
White Barn Inn, *Kennebunkport, ME*
Marquesa, *Key West, FL*

---

* Indicates a tie with hotel above

Top by Region

(Based on Overall score)

California

28 Château du Sureau, *Oakhurst*
Peninsula, *Beverly Hills*
27 Four Seasons Aviara, *Carlsbad*
Post Ranch Inn, *Big Sur*
Four Seasons, *Beverly Hills*
Inn at Spanish Bay, *Pebble Beach*
Rancho Valencia Resort, *Rancho Santa Fe*
Bel-Air, *Los Angeles*
Four Seasons, *San Francisco*
Golden Door, *Escondido*
St. Regis Monarch Beach, *Dana Point*
Montage Resort, *Laguna Beach*

Florida

27 Ritz-Carlton, *Naples*
Mandarin Oriental, *Miami*
Ritz-Carlton, *Orlando*
Little Palm Island, *Little Torch Key*
Ritz-Carlton Golf, *Naples*
26 Sunset Key Guest Cottages, *Key West*
Ritz-Carlton, *Amelia Island*
Four Seasons, *Miami*

Hawaii

29 Four Seasons Hualalai, *Big Island*
28 Four Seasons Wailea, *Maui*
27 Lodge at Koele, *Lanai*
Halekulani, *Oahu*
Kahala Mandarin Oriental, *Oahu*
26 Fairmont Kea Lani, *Maui*
Manele Bay Hotel, *Lanai*

Mid-Atlantic (DC, DE, MD, PA, VA, WV)

27 Four Seasons, *Philadelphia*
Inn at Little Washington, *Washington, VA*
Greenbrier, *White Sulphur Springs, WV*
26 Keswick Hall at Monticello, *Charlottesville, VA*
Rittenhouse Hotel, *Philadelphia*
25 Four Seasons, *Washington, DC*

Midwest (IL, IN, MI, MN, MO, OH, OK, WI)

28 Canoe Bay, *Chetek, WI*
Peninsula, *Chicago*
27 Four Seasons, *Chicago*
Ritz-Carlton, *Chicago*
26 American Club, *Kohler, WI*
25 Park Hyatt, *Chicago*

New England (MA, ME, NH, RI, VT)

28 Twin Farms, *Barnard, VT*
27 Four Seasons, *Boston*
26 Charlotte Inn, *Martha's Vineyard*
Wauwinet, *Nantucket*
Ritz-Carlton, *Boston*
25 Canyon Ranch in the Berkshires, *Lenox, MA*

New York & Environs (CT, NJ, NY)

27 Point, *Saranac Lake, NY*
Four Seasons, *New York City*
Mandarin Oriental, *New York City*
26 Ritz-Carlton, Central Park, *New York City*
Mayflower Inn, *Washington, CT*
St. Regis, *New York City*
Ritz-Carlton, Battery Park, *New York City*

Pacific Northwest (OR, WA)

25 Fairmont Olympic, *Seattle*
Willows Lodge, *Woodinville, WA*
Bellevue Club Hotel, *Seattle*
Grand Hyatt, *Seattle*

Rocky Mountains (CO, ID, MT, NV, UT, WY)

27 Four Seasons, *Las Vegas*
Stein Eriksen Lodge, *Park City, UT*
Bellagio, *Las Vegas*
26 Ritz-Carlton, Bachelor Gulch, *Avon, CO*
Ritz-Carlton, Lake Las Vegas, *Henderson, NV*
Little Nell, *Aspen*
Amangani, *Jackson, WY*
Broadmoor, *Colorado Springs, CO*

Southeast (AL, AR, GA, KY, LA, MS, NC, SC, TN)

29 Lodge at Sea Island, *Sea Island, GA*
28 Blackberry Farm, *Walland, TN*
Woodlands Resort & Inn, *Summerville, SC*
27 Fearrington House, *Pittsboro, NC*
Windsor Court, *New Orleans*
Barnsley Gardens, *Adairsville, GA*
26 Four Seasons, *Atlanta*
Cloister, *Sea Island, GA*

Southwest (AZ, NM)

27 Royal Palms, *Phoenix*
Four Seasons at Troon North, *Scottsdale, AZ*
26 Phoenician, *Scottsdale, AZ*
Sanctuary on Camelback Mtn., *Paradise Valley, AZ*
Miraval, Life in Balance, *Catalina, AZ*
Boulders, *Carefree, AZ*
Enchantment Resort, *Sedona, AZ*

Texas

27 Mansion on Turtle Creek, *Dallas*
26 Four Seasons at Las Colinas, *Irving*
Four Seasons, *Houston*
25 Crescent Court, *Dallas*
St. Regis, *Houston*
Lake Austin Spa Resort, *Austin*

U.S. Caribbean

25 Horned Dorset Primavera, *Rincon, PR*
Ritz-Carlton, *St. Thomas, USVI*
24 Caneel Bay, *St. John, USVI*
Ritz-Carlton, *Carolina, PR*

Top Rooms

(Based on Rooms score)

29 Twin Farms, *Barnard, VT*
Woodlands Resort & Inn, *Summerville, SC*
Four Seasons Hualalai, *Big Island, HI*
Lodge at Sea Island, *Sea Island, GA*
Milliken Creek Inn, *Napa, CA*
Peninsula, *Chicago*
Château du Sureau, *Oakhurst, CA*
Sunset Key Guest Cottages, *Keys, FL**
Canoe Bay, *Chetek, WI*
28 Rancho Valencia Resort, *Rancho Santa Fe, NM*
Peninsula, *Beverly Hills*
St. Regis Monarch Beach, *Dana Point, CA*
Blackberry Farm, *Walland, TN*
Post Ranch Inn, *Big Sur, CA*
Fearrington House, *Pittsboro, NC*
Four Seasons, *New York City**
Amangani, *Jackson, WY*
Four Seasons Wailea, *Maui, HI**
Point, *Saranc Lake, NY*
W Silicon Valley, *Newark, NJ*
Four Seasons, *Chicago*
Mandarin Oriental, *Miami*
Barnsley Gardens, *Atlanta*
Four Seasons, *Las Vegas*
Windsor Court Hotel, *New Orleans**

Top Service

(Based on Service score)

29 Château du Sureau, *Oakhurst, CA*
Canoe Bay, *Chetek, WI*
Four Seasons Hualalai, *Big Island, HI*
Blackberry Farm, *Walland, TN*
Lodge at Sea Island, *Sea Island, GA*
Twin Farms, *Barnard, VT**
28 Four Seasons at Wailea, *Maui, HI*
Inn at Little Washington, *Washington, VA*
Four Seasons, *Beverly Hills*
Four Seasons, *Chicago*
Four Seasons, *Las Vegas*
Ritz-Carlton, *Chicago*
Ritz-Carlton, *Naples, FL*
Peninsula, *Chicago*
Golden Door, *Escondido, CA*
Canyon Ranch in the Berkshires, *Lenox, MA*
Woodlands Resort & Inn, *Summerville, SC*
Point, *Saranac Lake, NY*
Kenwood Inn, *Kenwood, CA*
Bel-Air, Hotel, *Los Angeles*
Four Seasons, *New York City*
Peninsula, *Beverly Hills*
Halekulani, *Honolulu, HI*
Greenbrier, *White Sulphur Springs, WV*
Four Seasons, *Philadelphia*

Top Dining

(Based on Dining score)

29 Lodge at Sea Island, *Sea Island, GA*
Woodlands Resort & Inn, *Summerville, SC*
Fearrington House, *Pittsboro, NC*
Inn at Little Washington, *Washington, VA*
Blackberry Farm, *Walland, TN*

28 Château du Sureau, *Oakhurst, CA*
Chalet Suzanne Inn, *Lake Wales, FL*
Mansion on Turtle Creek, *Dallas*
Four Seasons Hualalai, *Big Island, HI*
Canoe Bay, *Chetek, WI*
Twin Farms, *Barnard, VT**
Royal Palms, *Phoenix*
Bellagio, *Las Vegas*
White Barn Inn, *Kennebunkport, ME*

27 Little Palm Island, *Little Torch Key, FL*
Ritz-Carlton, *Chicago*
Mandarin Oriental, *Miami*
Four Seasons, *Philadelphia*
Windsor Court Hotel, *New Orleans*
Inn at Langley, *Langley, WA*
Morrison House, *Alexandria, VA*
Castle on the Hudson, *Tarrytown, NY*
Homestead Inn, *Greenwich, CT*
Vintners Inn, *Santa Rosa, CA*
Peninsula, *Beverly Hills*

Top Public Facilities

(Based on Public Facilities score)

29 Lodge at Sea Island, *Sea Island, GA*
Four Seasons Hualalai, *Big Island, HI*
Barnsley Gardens, *Adairsville, GA*
Ritz-Carlton, Bachelor Gulch, *Avon, CO*

28 Blackberry Farm, *Walland, TN*
Inn at Spanish Bay, *Pebble Beach, CA*
Canyon Ranch in the Berkshires, *Lenox, MA*
Golden Door, *Escondido, CA**
Greenbrier, *White Sulphur Springs, WV*
Ritz-Carlton Reynolds Plantation, *Lake Oconee, GA*
Bellevue Club Hotel, *Seattle, WA*
Peninsula, *Chicago**
Ritz-Carlton, *Naples, FL*
Ritz-Carlton, *Orlando*
Four Seasons Aviara, *Carlsbad, CA*
Lodge at Pebble Beach, *Pebble Beach, CA*
Canyon Ranch, *Tucson, AZ*
Nemacolin Woodlands, *Farmington, PA*
St. Regis Monarch Beach, *Dana Point, CA**
Four Seasons at Las Colinas, *Irving, TX*
Park Hyatt, *Beaver Creek, CO*
Grand Hyatt Kauai, *Kauai, HI*
Grand Wailea Resort, *Maui, HI*
Boulders, *Carefree, AZ*
Phoenician, *Scottsdale, AZ*

Top Destination Spas

(Based on Overall score)

27 Golden Door, *Escondido, CA*
26 Miraval, Life in Balance, *Catalina, AZ*
Canyon Ranch, *Tucson, AZ*
25 Canyon Ranch in the Berkshires, *Lenox, MA*
Lake Austin Spa Resort, *Austin, TX*

Noteworthy Hotel Spas

American Club, *Kohler, WI*
Bacara, *Santa Barbara, CA*
Bernardus Lodge, *Carmel Valley, CA*
Enchantment Resort, *Sedona, AZ*
Four Seasons, *New York City*
Four Seasons Hualalai, *Big Island, HI*
Four Seasons Troon North, *Scottsdale, AZ*
Four Seasons Wailea, *Maui, HI*
Greenbrier, *White Sulphur Springs, VA*
Homestead, *Roanoke, VA*
JW Marriott Ihilani, *Oahu, HI*
Lake Austin Spa Resort, *Austin, TX*
Little Palm Island, *Keys, FL*
Mandarin Oriental, *New York City*
Mauna Lani Bay Hotel, *Big Island, HI*
Meadowood, *Napa, CA*
Montage Resort, *Laguna Beach, CA*
Peninsula, *Chicago*
Peninsula, *New York City*
Phoenician, *Scottsdale, AZ*
Post Ranch Inn, *Big Sur, CA*
Ritz-Carlton, *Naples, FL*
Sanctuary on Camelback Mtn., *Paradise Valley, AZ*
St. Regis Monarch Beach, *Dana Point, CA*
Venetian, *Las Vegas*

Notable Newcomers

Circa 39, *Miami*
Home Hill, *Plainfield, NH*
Icon, *Houston*
Indigo, *Atlanta*
Le Parker Méridien Palm Springs, *Palm Springs, CA*
Mansion on Forsyth Park, *Savannah, GA*
Morongo Casino, *Palm Springs, CA*
Paradisus, *San Juan, PR*
Renaissance Las Vegas, *Las Vegas*
Renaissance Ross Bridge Golf, *Birmingham, AL*
Resort at Paws Up, *Missoula, MO*
Smoke Tree Ranch, *Palm Springs*
Victor, *Miami Beach*
Vitale, *San Francisco*
Walden Country Inn, *Aurora, OH*
Whiteface Lodge, *Lake Placid, NY*

Top by Feature

Beach

Bacara, *Santa Barbara, CA*
Breakers, *Palm Beach, FL*
Caneel Bay, *St. John, USVI*
Cloister, *Sea Island, GA*
Grand Wailea, *Maui, HI*
Hapuna Beach Prince, *Big Island, HI*
Manele Bay, *Lanai, HI*
Montage Resort, *Laguna Beach, CA*
Ritz-Carlton, *Naples, FL*
Ritz-Carlton Kapalua, *Maui, HI*

Families

Disney's Animal Kingdom, *Orlando*
Disney's BoardWalk, *Orlando*
Disney's Grand Californian, *Los Angeles*
Disney's Grand Floridian, *Orlando*
Fairmont Kea Lani, *Maui, HI*
Fairmont Scottsdale Princess, *Scottsdale, AZ*
Grand Hyatt, *Seattle*
Hershey, *Hershey, PA*
Hilton Waikoloa, *Big Island, HI*
Mandalay Bay, *Las Vegas*

Golf

Boca Raton Resort, *Boca Raton, FL*
Coeur d'Alene, *Coeur d'Alene, ID*
Four Seasons Troon North, *Scottsdale, AZ*
Four Seasons Wailea, *Maui, HI*
Greenbrier, *White Sulphur Springs, WV*
Inn at Spanish Bay, *Pebble Beach, CA*
La Playa Beach, *Naples, FL*
Lodge at Koele, *Lanai, HI*
Lodge at Pebble Beach, *Pebble Beach, CA*
Lodge at Torrey Pines, *San Diego*
Pinehurst Resort, *Pinehurst, NC*
Princeville Resort, *Kauai, HI*
Ritz-Carlton Golf Resort, *Naples, FL*
Samoset, *Rockport, ME*

Historic Interest

Bel-Air, *Los Angeles*
Beverly Hills Hotel, *Los Angeles*
Blantyre, *Lenox, MA*
Castle Hill Inn, *Newport, RI*
Grand, *Mackinac Island, MI*
Inn on Biltmore, *Asheville, NC*
Keswick Hall at Monticello, *Keswick, VA*
New York Palace, *New York City*
Wheatleigh, *Lenox, MA*
Williamsburg Inn, *Williamsburg, VA*

Romance

Bel-Air, *Los Angeles*
Canoe Bay, *Chetek, WI*
Charlotte Inn, *Martha's Vineyard, MA*
Château du Sureau, *Oakhurst, CA*
Inn at Little Washington, *Washington, VA*
Inn at Perry Cabin, *St. Michaels, MD*
Little Palm Island, *Keys, FL*
Lodge at Torrey Pines, *San Diego*
Milliken Creek Inn, *Napa, CA*
Point, *Saranac Lake, NY*
Princeville Resort, *Kauai, HI*

Skiing

Charter/Beaver Creek, *Beaver Creek, CO*
Deer Valley Lodging, *Deer Valley, UT*
Goldener Hirsch Inn, *Park City, UT*
Little Nell, *Aspen*
Lodge & Spa at Cordillera, *Aspen*
Lodge at Vail, *Vail, CO*
Park Hyatt, *Beaver Creek, CO*
Ritz-Carlton, Bachelor Gulch, *Aspen*
Sonnenalp, *Vail, CO*
Stein Eriksen Lodge, *Park City, UT*
Sundance, *Salt Lake City*

Swimming Pools

Beverly Hills Hotel, *Beverly Hills*
Biltmore, *Coral Gables, FL*
Disney's Yacht Club, *Orlando*
Hyatt Regency Gainey Ranch, *Scottsdale, AZ*
Hyatt Regency Hill Country, *San Antonio, TX*
JW Marriott Desert Ridge, *Phoenix*
Le Parker Méridien, *New York City*
Pointe South Mountain, *Phoenix*
Raffles L'Ermitage, *Beverly Hills*
Raleigh, *Miami Beach*
Renaissance Esmeralda, *Indian Wells, CA*

Tennis

Caneel Bay, *St. John, USVI*
Colony Beach, *Sarasota, FL*
Four Seasons at Las Colinas, *Irving, TX*
Inn at Essex, *Essex, VT*
Lodge at Pebble Beach, *Pebble Beach, CA*
Marriott Desert Springs, *Palm Desert, CA*
Rancho Valencia, *San Diego*
Sanctuary on Camelback Mtn., *Paradise Valley, AZ*
Sandestin Golf & Beach Resort, *Sandestin, FL*
Water Color Inn, *Santa Rosa Beach, FL*
Westin Diplomat Resort, *Hollywood, FL*

Hotel Chains

Caesars 21 23 19 E

800-223-7277; www.caesars.com

The "empire is well represented" with these 18 "wonderful" properties in Las Vegas, Atlantic City, Indiana, Lake Tahoe and Tunica, Mississippi, offering casinos and restaurants, an "amenable staff" and "tasteful rooms" ("considering they go hand-in-hand with all the glitter and gambling locales"); but some say it's a "hard-to-define" brand since the chasm between each is "immense", while others fret that these were "formerly the chicest spots" but now are host to "fanny packers and salesmen."

Courtyard by Marriott 18 17 17 M

800-321-2211; www.marriott.com

It's "like the *Brady Bunch*" – "a tad cheesy but comfortable and predictable" – at these "reasonably priced" hotels (583 in the U.S.) featuring "amazingly standard rooms" "without the bells and whistles"; although they "never fail to deliver" "pleasant" service and a "nice hot breakfast to get your day started" and some even have "indoor pools and Jacuzzis, a kick factor for kids", they "can, in no way, be mistaken for resorts or luxury chains."

Crowne Plaza 19 18 17 M

800-227-6963; www.crowneplaza.com

"You'll have a good stay" at one of this chain's 88 properties that can be a "traveling salesperson's dream", especially "on the club level with its better rooms and amenities"; but most muse that rooms can be like that proverbial "box of chocolates – you never know what to expect": newer hotels or those recently renovated are "fantastic with marble bathrooms and French appointments" while older ones feel more like a "souped-up Holiday Inn."

DoubleTree 19 18 18 M

800-222-8733; www.doubletree.com

"The hospitality is as warm as the fresh" cookies at check-in at this 170-member "great value" outfit that "goes the extra mile"; business types appreciate "hassle-free" visits, while families say the large rooms "are a blessing"; still, "expect surprises from one to another" since they can vary "from plush to plebian."

Drury Inn 16 15 16 I

800-378-7946; www.druryhotels.com

"Unexpectedly impressive" vow vaunters of this "affordable" chain of 110 properties, offering "places to stay with something for everyone, including snacks" and "Quikstart breakfasts that make your day"; "the big rooms" are suitable for families, plus "free Internet service is a nice luxury in this class" (they "don't nickel and dime you with extra charges"); but doubters say some locations are "antiquated" with "somewhat shabby decor."

Embassy Suites 22 20 18 M

800-362-2779; www.embassysuites.com

Though "it's not fancy", this chain with 178 properties is the "way to go" for "budget business travelers" and can "feel like paradise if you are staying with children" thanks to "great suites with kitchenettes" ("gotta love that door between two rooms") and "home-cooked hot breakfasts"; if critics carp that facilities "vary widely" at this "ho-hum member of the Hilton family", more insist it "delivers."

FAIRMONT 24 24 24 VE

800-441-1414; www.fairmont.com

"Always" is the operative word for these 16 "divine" properties with a "European feel": "always a treat", "always dependable", "always enjoyable"; it may be the "least discussed" of the luxury chains, but when "rooms need to be fancier", service "superlative without being snobby" and "amenities superior", "this is the place to go"; however, a handful of these grande dames are "screaming for a redo."

FOUR SEASONS 29 28 29 VE

800-332-3442; www.fourseasons.com

"There's no going back" to any other after a stay amid "opulent surroundings" at one of the 29 properties of this "gold standard", rated the No. 1 Chain in this *Survey*; it's always the "classiest in town" with "ultraplush rooms", "exceptional service" (they "dote on children just the way they dote on adults"), "impeccable dining choices" and "phenomenal amenities"; if "your idea of heaven is total pampering and you understand you can't put a price on nirvana, then you're in the right place."

Grand Hyatt 23 24 22 E

800-223-1234; www.grand.hyatt.com

Like "elegant" ocean liners, these eight properties handle large numbers "extraordinarily well" offering "top-notch quality without going overboard"; a "service standard that shines", "impressive public" areas and "spacious rooms" make it a "favorite" for conventions, but nonplussed patrons find "nothing particularly grand" and advise "go out for dinner" as most of their restaurants "leave a bit to be desired."

Harrah's 19 20 19 M

800-427-7247; www.harrahs.com

"Perfect for the gambler who likes to roll out of bed and roll the dice", these 18 "glitzy casino" hotels offer "adult environments" with "surprisingly good rooms" boasting "marble bathrooms", plus they're "cheap to boot"; but grumpy gamers say "ouch to the check-in lines" and "inconsistent" quarters; N.B. the company recently acquired Caesars' properties, but temporarily lost three of its own to Hurricane Katrina.

Hilton 19 19 19 E

800-774-1500; www.hilton.com

"While it may not be luxury" this 245-unit "solid choice" is "on the upper end of the moderate chains" and can be trusted to provide "comfortable accommodations", "dependable service" and "biz-friendly" amenities, including one of the "best loyalty programs"; though "some are first-tier and others aren't", an extensive redesign for most locations in 2006 should quiet critics who cry they need to do something to improve the brand since "Paris Hilton may not be the name recognition they're looking for."

Historic Hotels of America 22 20 20 E

800-678-8946; www.historichotels.org

"Not a chain", but rather an "amalgam" of 218 "independent properties", "each with its own distinct character", this collective gives guests an "opportunity to sleep with history" as all are at least 50 years old or listed in the National Register of Historic

Places; most are a "joy to stay in" thanks to the "spirit of the staff", "interesting architecture and decor" and unique locations, but while rooms are usually "well appointed, they're sometimes tiny."

Homewood Suites 21 18 17 M

800-225-5466; www.homewood-suites.com

A residential-style, "up-and-coming" "gem in the Hilton chain", this 150-strong brand "really can be a home away from home", "complete with a kitchen" and "well-furnished" accommodations, it offers"all the amenities a business traveler needs", making it "great for long-term stays"; moreover, most maintain "it's not a bad deal for the money" – in fact, it could be the "sleeper of the whole bunch" in executing the suites trend.

Hyatt 21 22 20 E

800-223-1234; www.hyatt.com

It's "a treat to stay at" with a "staff that's ready to please", "well cared for rooms", "dramatic atrium lobbies" and "excellent food" – yes, most surveyors say these 20 properties "deliver what they promise"; whether you're looking for a "solid business" option, "restful getaway or a place to recharge the batteries", it's a "trustworthy" stop, plus the "resorts are tops"; still, a minority sighs there's "nothing above and beyond", adding "every aspect varies from hotel to hotel", ranging from "great" to "ho-hum."

INTERCONTINENTAL 24 23 24 E

800-327-0200; www.interconti.com

For a bit of "luxury", consider this chain of 15 "modern" domestic hotels that is "better than it gets recognized for" with an "efficient" staff and "stylish" quarters featuring sometimes "lush decor"; even if the rooms are "not quite top level, they're close", plus they "accommodate the business traveler", so only a few doubters declare they "try to be upscale but don't always achieve it"; N.B. a new Atlanta property recently opened in Buckhead.

KIMPTON GROUP 24 22 24 E

800-546-7866; www.kimptongroup.com

"Refreshingly different", this "non-chain chain" of 39 U.S. sites with "excellent service" "wrote the book" on "hip with a capital H" boutique hotels, such as the Monaco brand and Boston's Onyx; with plans to double the chain's size by the end of the decade, it delivers "funky" "fun" for a "grown-up getaway"– rooms are kitted out with "wild decor", "modern furnishings" and "likable quirks" (plus an over-the-top pet program); you'll "admire their efforts to revitalize historic buildings" into "witty" hotels with the added perk of complimentary local wines served nightly and "wonderful restaurants."

LEADING HOTELS OF THE WORLD 27 25 27 VE

800-223-6800; www.lhw.com

"Three words: elegant, sexy and sophisticated" apply to this "consistently superior" alliance that really seems to "choose and monitor" all 55 of its stateside members; the "rooms and service live up to the highest standards" ("everyone is treated like a VIP"), and the "food is phenomenal", in fact, if you follow this Leading outfit, you'll "feel pampered from the minute you walk through the door"; if a few feel it's "variable" property by property, most believe it's "in a league of its own"; N.B. a new loyalty program includes perks like a personal travel concierge and free stays.

Loews 22 22 21 E

800-235-6397; www.loewshotels.com

"Worth a look in any city", these 18 "classy hotels" exude "unrushed grand elegance" with "exquisite lobbies", "chic locations", "delightful" rooms and "amenities galore" along with "unmatched service"; if a few feel that the accommodations "could use a bit more imagination" ("can't describe any room I've stayed in"), most rejoin that these "premier properties" are definitely "not cookie cutter."

LUXURY COLLECTION, THE 27 27 27 VE

800-325-3589; www.luxurycollection.com

"Blown away is usually my first impression" agree admirers of Starwood's 10 "memorable" "jewels in the crown of hospitality" – a collection of "uniquely wonderful", "luxurious properties" that "aren't for the price sensitive"; expect "lots of grandeur" and "exceptional service" ("nothing is out of reach or impossible") where you have "your heart's desire" catered to.

MANDARIN ORIENTAL 28 27 28 VE

866-526-6567; www.mandarin-oriental.com

"Style, grace, modern beauty" and a "sleek Asian feel" make staying at any Mandarin "a treat" attest admirers of the seven "reliably swank" U.S. properties; "if you like to be pampered in idyllic surroundings" with "impeccable service" that "exceeds high expectations", "luxe accommodations" with "lovely linens", "fabulous spas" and "excellent views", it's "the ultimate hotel" experience, plus it fills the bill as an "expense-account favorite" and "romantic getaway"; N.B. a new Boston branch opens in 2006.

Marriott Hotels & Resorts 21 21 21 E

800-228-9290; www.marriott.com

"Consistency that's golden for a business traveler" is the byword of this "cordial" "mid-tier" chain with 312 U.S. properties that offer a "luxury feel for a moderate price"; "if you hate surprises, you'll love" the "fantastic facilities" (a push to install flat-panel HDTVs throughout its several brands over the next four years is underway) and a good rewards program, plus "you can count on them when traveling with families"; but others harrumph it's more "like an old boyfriend, reliable, but you wish you were with someone else."

Millennium Hotels 21 20 21 E

866-866-6455; www.millenniumhotels.com

"Downright astounding for the price" opine patrons of these 20 branded and non-branded U.S. hotels, a "good choice" if you're looking for a "fun, different kind of place to stay" that's a "notch more upscale than a typical chain"; the "well-appointed rooms" have "comfortable beds" and "all the new amenities", but the less impressed say the food is "expensive" and "service is not tip-top."

Morgans Hotels 19 21 18 VE

800-606-6090; www.morganshotelgroup.com

Founded by Ian Schrager, who's now moved into the luxury residential market, these six "swanky" hotels "treat mortals like celebrities"; expect "excitement, drama" and rooms with sophisticated "[Philippe] Starck decor", anchored by the "hottest nightspots"; still, a few faultfinders fume that it feels faintly "like you're shacking up in a glorified closet", adding the "hipness factor barely counterbalances indifferent service."

Omni 22 | 21 | 21 | E

800-843-6664; www.omnihotels.com

"It's always special and a little different from your average chain" concur admirers of this outfit with 36 domestic locations; the "spacious" rooms are "dependable" for business travel, "fitness centers are strong" and parents like their kids' programs, adding "how can you beat the loot bag full of candy and toys at check-in?"; but a handful see a lack of "real brand consistency."

Orient-Express ▽ 27 | 26 | 28 | VE

800-524-2420; www.orient-express.com

"Elegance and old-world charm" form the backbone of this "top-of-the line" chain with four "magnificent" hotels (plus NYC's 21 Club restaurant) offering "excellent restaurants", historic locales, "beautiful" accommodations and "great facilities" "you never want to leave"; while some are thrown by the steep prices, most retort it's "worth every penny for the service provided."

Pan Pacific ▽ 26 | 24 | 24 | E

800-327-8585; www.panpac.com

Be it for "business or leisure", "everyone should stay here at least once in a lifetime" sigh sojourners who gladly alight in this Japanese-based company's two "interesting" U.S. hotels in San Francisco and Hawaii set in "gorgeous buildings" "with all the trimmings"; completing the rosy picture are "luxurious", "classy" rooms with "super-spacious bathrooms", "always great" service and restaurants "to die for."

PARK HYATT 27 | 25 | 26 | VE

800-233-1234; www.park.hyatt.com

"Park me in one of these Hyatts" say those who fall for these eight "primo" U.S. properties that are "always a cut above in charm" and "more peaceful than the average hotel"; "guaranteed opulence" awaits – "nothing matches the attention to detail and modern (not trendy) style" of the rooms, "upscale" facilities and "European-style service as well as discretion"; P.S. the Tokyo branch was "immortalized in the film *Lost in Translation*."

Peninsula Hotels 28 | 28 | 28 | VE

800-262-9467; www.peninsula.com

"The crown jewel of the Orient", these "elegant" hotels are "not to be missed on any continent", including the U.S., where three "first-class experiences" are on offer in Beverly Hills, Chicago and New York; there's a combination of "opulence meets old-world Asian charm", the "unhurried staff" offers "service to infinity and beyond", the spa is "great" and the rooms have "amenities from mood lighting to bathrooms within bathrooms."

PREFERRED HOTELS & RESORTS WORLDWIDE 24 | 24 | 24 | VE

800-323-7500; www.preferredhotels.com

"Stay at one and you will know why they are called Preferred" opine patrons who pay homage to this marketing confederation of "unique, well-maintained properties" with 81 U.S. locales; "they're all tops" and offer "extra-special service", but "they each have their own identity" and "exacting standards that rarely slip", plus they're "in more cities than some other indie groups."

Radisson 16 | 16 | 16 | M

800-333-3333; www.radisson.com

Sure, some say that you can "stay on the cheap" in this "middle-of-the-road" chain of 212 "better than average", "well-maintained" properties with "surprisingly" good rooms and a "friendly staff", but they're in the minority; they're "not what they were, but can be a port in the storm" muse fence-sitters, but most guests gripe about "many tired hotels and workers to match."

RELAIS & CHÂTEAUX 28 | 25 | 28 | VE

800-735-2478; www.relaischateaux.com

"Who deserves it more than you?" ask fans of this membership organization with 28 "high-end", "distinctive" choices in the U.S. that are "perfect down to the smallest details"; "true respites" that are "worth a romantic getaway", they all meet exacting standards for rooms and dining, and exude "old-world charm wrapped in modern luxury"; no doubt you'll "pay dearly", but few mind since "one night makes you feel like you've been on vacation a week."

RENAISSANCE HOTELS & RESORTS 24 | 23 | 22 | E

800-468-3571; www.renaissancehotels.com

"Consistency meets varied and often better decor" at this 72-strong "top-of-the-business-class-heap" Marriott "experience" that's even "connected to the rewards program"; it's a "good place to take the family when attending a conference", plus a "weekend in a suite makes you feel like this is your renaissance" thanks to the "super-comfortable rooms" and "excellent service"; in short, it's "nothing fancy, but you get what you pay for, in a good way."

Residence Inn by Marriott 21 | 19 | 17 | M

800-331-3131; www.marriott.com/residenceinn

"You can't beat the feeling of staying in a place that has all the conveniences of home" – they even give you a "better-than-average breakfast" at these 482 properties with rooms like "little apartments"; "comfy" accommodations are kitted out with "well-outfitted" "kitchenettes suitable for cooking", plus "they'll even shop for you", making it "a perfect crash pad for workaholics on the road" and for families looking to "get a lot for the dollar."

RITZ-CARLTON 27 | 27 | 28 | VE

800-241-3333; www.ritzcarlton.com

You'll feel "like you're in another world, no matter which" of the 40 U.S. "properties you choose" from this "crème de la crème" chain where you're treated like a "VIP"; the accommodations are a "beautiful experience with amazing beds" (plus wall-mounted flat-panel LCD TVs will be standard in all rooms by the end of 2006), you're "pampered" "from the moment you step out of your car" and there are "excellent dining choices" too.

ROSEWOOD 27 | 27 | 26 | VE

888-767-3966; www.rosewoodhotels.com

"Still a paradigm of the luxury hotel", this "elegant" outfit is "outstanding in all respects", pampering patrons with five "gem"-

like U.S. properties in Dallas, New York (The Carlyle) and St. John; "they set the bar so high" that "every detail is covered", from "superb" service to "rooms to die for"; while most feel that it "strikes a balance between adult getaway and kid-friendly", a few retort "nope, no way, it's not for children": N.B. the newest hotel will open in Miami Beach in early 2006.

Sheraton 19 | 19 | 18 | M

800-325-3535; www.sheraton.com

A "typically reliable" chain "with a minimum of hoopla", this Starwood-backed group of 176 domestic hotels "doesn't knock you over with glitz and pizzazz" yet gets the job done with "good restaurant selections", "comfortable" accommodations and a "great guest program that makes it ideal for a family vacation as well as a business trip"; if the less-enthused declare "some locations excel", "others are past their prime", most are "rooting" for a "comeback."

SMALL LUXURY HOTELS OF THE WORLD 27 | 24 | 28 | VE

800-525-4800; www.slh.com

If "you want character, stay" at one of these 41 boutique properties that "feel like a charming home away from home, with a little luxury thrown in"; "synonymous with quality and reliability", they "tend to be more of a personal experience" with a "high level of service"; in short, "great for those with money who are a bit adventurous and want to escape uniformity."

Sofitel 23 | 21 | 22 | E

800-763-4835; www.sofitel.com

"Love the French spin" and "attentive service" "wherever you are" agree *amis* of this chain's 10 stateside locations, "sights to behold" with a "classy ambiance" and "gorgeous" digs (the "Euro-style minimalism" "look makes me want the designer for home", and the "beds feel like you're floating on a cloud"); a "great change of pace" from "American business hotels", they offer "appealing" "little touches" like one of the "best breakfasts around."

ST. REGIS 28 | 26 | 27 | VE

800-598-1863; www.stregis.com

"The lobby, your room and your bill will all be dripping in gold" gush guests of these eight "top go-to" hotels in the States that offer a "more mature", "luxe, plush experience" with a "twist of old-school ornateness"; "what service, what rooms and your own butler" too, not to mention "fabulous" "facilities with fantastic views" – no, it's never a wrong choice" if "you're looking for a sumptuous place to lay your head" – and, of course, "if the budget allows."

Swissôtel 23 | 21 | 22 | E

888-737-9477; www.swissotel.com

"There's something to be said for European charm" coo acolytes who feel coddled at Raffles International's U.S. branches in Chicago and New York (The Drake) as well as Raffles L'Ermitage in Beverly Hills; for those who want to settle into the "lap of luxury" – "everything you're looking for is here", including "rooms with breathtaking ambiance" and an "efficient" "staff that makes guests feel like millionaires"; most find these hotels "well worth the premium cost."

WESTIN 25 | 23 | 22 | E

800-937-8461; www.westin.com

"With simple luxury", "unexpected flair", "immaculate service" and "great all-around lodging", this chain of 66 domestic properties has "seriously upgraded in the last couple of years" with NYC's "Essex House as a prime example"; "you simply sink into the Heavenly beds" (a "stroke of genius") and "boudoir pillows" – plus the "double-headed showers are orgasmic", ensuring "you're well rested and well groomed"; "everything needed by the business traveler" is here and what's more, they "know how to treat families" and their pets.

W Hotels 24 | 23 | 22 | VE

877-946-8357; www.whotels.com

"W is for Wow" at these 16 U.S. "witty, fresh, eclectic" Starwood hotels, "each with its own personality" and "hipsters in every corner" of the "chichi lobby"; "creature comforts" abound, from "cushy" rooms with "well-stocked bathrooms" to "superb gym facilities" and "typically great restaurants"; also aesthetes swear by the "vibrant", modern interiors with the "right amount of funky" style; still, some say the "concept wears thin", carping that they're "so trendy it hurts"; N.B. designer Diane von Furstenberg has recently been enlisted to create in-room amenities.

Wyndham 20 | 20 | 20 | E

800-822-4200; www.wyndham.com

"Upscale without being upper crust", this "viable standby" with 113 U.S. locations is "best for the business squad" though its resorts are "appealing to families"; the frequent stay program perks are reminiscent of a "much more expensive hotel" with "free phone calls and Internet access to keep the kids happy on your laptop", plus the "hospitable staff" "makes you feel" like a "valuable guest"; still, a few find some spots need a "shot in the arm" along with a possible "decor overhaul."

Hotels, Resorts & Spas

Alabama

Birmingham

Renaissance Ross Bridge Golf Resort & Spa

R	S	D	P	$
–	–	–	–	$250

4000 Grand Ave.; 205-916-7677; fax 205-945-8218; www.rossbridgeresort.com; 246 rooms, 13 suites

Located on the outskirts of Birmingham, this newcomer, with a castlelike facade and 1920s styling, looks as if it's been there for years; dark woods in the grand lobby, rooms with granite counter tops and leather headboards and a Robert Trent Jones golf course attract both corporate and leisure travelers.

Wynfrey

R	S	D	P	$
▽ 20	18	17	20	$205

1000 Riverchase Galleria; 205-987-1600; 800-996-3739; www.wynfrey.com; 323 rooms, 6 suites

Just minutes away from Downtown, this "big city" destination housed in Riverchase Galleria flaunts a "super location" for "hitting the fab shops", "unlimited dining options" in the "attached food court", plus a Shula's steakhouse and a "convenient" conference center; though a few fret about "ho-hum service", most claim it's "everything you look for" in a crash pad.

Point Clear

Marriott Grand Hotel

R	S	D	P	$
20	22	19	25	$229

1 Grand Blvd.; 251-928-9201; fax 251-928-1149; 888-236-2427; www.marriottgrand.com; 374 rooms, 30 suites

A "gem of the Deep South", this "child-friendly" "destination resort" "has gone modern high-tech without losing its charm and hospitality"; with an "inspirational view" of Mobile Bay and "amazing additions" like the "great" Robert Trent Jones golf courses, "reconstructed swimming pools", "grander than grand" spa and a pier that "allows you to fish the afternoon away", it "exhibits old Alabama at its finest"; plus early-risers praise the "enormous breakfast buffet"; N.B. the property is expected to be closed for an undetermined length of time due to damage caused by Hurricane Katrina.

Alaska

Aleutian Islands

Grand Aleutian

R	S	D	P	$
–	–	–	–	$179

498 Salmon Way, Dutch Harbor; 866-581-3844; fax 907-581-7150; 800-891-1194; www.grandaleutian.com; 110 rooms, 2 suites

Set on the site of a former WWII outpost on Unalaska Island in the Aleutian archipelago, this privately owned hotel capped with a red roof reflects its surroundings with driftwood siding, native-inspired architecture, a three-story lobby with a huge stone fireplace and a fiber mural and rooms with views of the snow-capped peaks; guests can indulge in a seafood buffet and summer barbecues on the deck overlooking Margaret Bay, hike the Makushin Volcano and explore the Bering Strait.

Anchorage

Captain Cook 20 | 21 | 20 | 21 | $255

939 W. Fifth Ave.; 907-276-6000; fax 907-343-2298; 800-843-1950; www.captaincook.com; 451 rooms, 96 suites

"It's not ritzy, but" this "friendly" "treat" has an "old-world charm" akin to a "warm comforter in the cold winter"; "let this be your anchor in Anchorage" agree fans of the "spacious rooms", "great public spaces with wonderful murals", "cool bar" and "excellent dining options", including the Crow's Nest, which offers a "bird's-eye view" of the Chugach Mountain Range and a 10,000-bottle wine cellar; but it doesn't float the boat for others who muse "if Captain Cook had stayed here he wouldn't have continued his voyage."

Millennium Anchorage ▽ 17 | 18 | 19 | 18 | $260

4800 Spenard Rd.; 907-243-2300; fax 907-243-8815; 866-866-8086; www.millenniumhotels.com; 242 rooms, 6 suites

"The place to be for the Iditarod" dogsled races, this "solid" artifacts-decorated "great location" near Anchorage Airport "has a bit of the Alaska-lodge feel and the amenities of a fine hotel" including "good breakfasts"; sidewalk aviators are "fascinated by" the "views of the float planes" at the Lake Hood/Lake Spenard base, while adventurers take cruises to the face of the glacier; still, critics carp it's "like being trapped in a 1970s taxidermy shop."

Denali

Mt. McKinley Princess ▽ 16 | 16 | 14 | 16 | $179

Mile 238.5, Parks Hwy., Denali State Park; 907-683-2282; fax 907-683-2545; 800-426-0500; www.princessalaskalodges.com; 330 rooms, 4 suites

"On a clear day" you're rewarded with "an incredible view" of Mt. McKinley and the Chulitna River at this "great" Princess Alaska chain location; the bungalow-style rooms are a "bit rustic" "but comfortable", plus there's a main lodge with a stone fireplace, card tables and dramatic windows; if a few long for "more entertainment options when it rains" and find excursions like "being herded through summer camp", "all is forgiven for one glorious" afternoon in Denali National Park; N.B. open mid-May–mid-December.

Fairbanks

Pikes Waterfront Lodge – | – | – | – | $205

1850 Hoselton Dr.; 907-456-4500; fax 907-456-4515; 877-774-2400; www.pikeslodge.com; 177 rooms, 28 cabins, 3 suites

"There's nothing like watching the Northern Lights through your window" at this "friendly well-run lodge" "with great atmosphere" along the Chena River yet "close to the airport"; trophies, "historical artifacts and paintings from early Alaska fill the public spaces", plus there's "super" dining at Pike's Landing.

Girdwood

Alyeska Prince 23 | 23 | 22 | 24 | $275

1000 Arlberg Ave.; 907-754-1111; fax 907-754-2200; 800-880-3880; www.alyeskaresort.com; 296 rooms, 11 suites

Forty minutes "close to Anchorage, but a world away", this "oasis" in a "magnificent setting" offers "warm service", "spacious" accommodations and "breathtaking views from the spa and pool"; "where else can you see beluga whales from 2,300 feet above sea level", "ski in the winter and stroll the mountain tops in the summer" before "taking the gondola" to Seven Glaciers dining room "at the top" of the slopes?; still, a few find the "furnishings and bedding average for a resort in this price range."

Glacier Bay

Glacier Bay Lodge – | – | – | – | $205

179 Bartlett Cove Rd.; 907-697-4000; fax 907-697-4001; 800-229-8687; www.visitglacierbay.com; 48 rooms

A 20–30-minute jet or air taxi ride from Juneau with no road access, this rustic retreat set on Bartlett Cove and surrounded by Sitka spruce trees is the only property with overnight accommodations in Glacier Bay National Park; the main lodge boasts a huge stone fireplace, the Fairweather restaurant and a sweeping deck, and guests traverse a boardwalk to get to their rooms; during its May–September season, visitors can tour the glaciers and indulge in sea kayaking.

Wrangell-St. Elias Nat'l Park

Copper River Princess Wilderness Lodge 🏔 – | – | – | – | $179

One Brenwick Craig Rd., Copper Center; 907-822-4000; fax 907-822-4480; 800-426-0500; www.princesslodges.com; 85 rooms

One of the "most beautiful – and secluded – of the Princess Alaska resorts", this "incredible" "rustic" "surprise" is set on a bluff at the junction of the Klutina and Copper Rivers near the Wrangell-St. Elias National Park; "funky but fun", this red lodge boasts two stories of windows offering mountain views plus "large, cabin-style rooms", "good" regional food and a tour desk that books whitewater rafting and salmon fishing excursions.

Arizona

★ Tops in State

27 Royal Palms, *Phoenix*
Four Seasons at Troon North, *Scottsdale*
26 Phoenician, *Scottsdale*
Sanctuary on Camelback Mountain, *Paradise Valley*
Miraval, *Catalina*
Boulders, *Carefree*
Enchantment Resort, *Sedona*
Canyon Ranch, *Tucson*
25 Fairmont Scottsdale Princess, *Scottsdale*
24 Arizona Biltmore, *Phoenix*

Grand Canyon

El Tovar Ⓗ🏔 17 | 19 | 19 | 20 | $144

South Rim, Grand Canyon Nat'l Park; 303-297-2757; fax 303-297-3175; 888-297-2757; www.grandcanyonlodges.com; 66 rooms, 12 suites

"Nothing compares to waking up" with the Grand "Canyon at your doorstep" agree admirers awed by the "location, location, location" of this "rustic" 1905 lodge "loaded with historic charm";

it's "cool to stay" "right on the South Rim" so "reserve a balcony suite" and saddle up a "rocking chair on the porch" to feast on the "breathtaking views" – and don't forget to "book dinner reservations" way in advance; N.B. major renovations were completed in April 2005.

Phoenix/Scottsdale

Arizona Biltmore | 23 | 24 | 23 | 26 | $445

2400 E. Missouri St., Phoenix; 602-955-6600; fax 602-381-7600; 800-950-0086; www.arizonabiltmore.com; 637 rooms, 101 suites

"Brimming with history", this "living tribute to Frank Lloyd Wright's" design style offers "plenty to do without leaving" the premises; "kids love running around" the "immaculate grounds", and the whole family can relax in the "plush rooms", lounge by one of eight pools or soak up the spa's "subdued luxury"; if some feel it does "not fulfill its promise", others retort "you couldn't ask for more, except maybe winning the lottery to pay for it."

BOULDERS, THE | 27 | 26 | 23 | 28 | $699

34631 N. Tom Darlington Dr., Carefree; 480-488-9009; fax 480-488-4118; 800-553-1717; www.wyndham.com; 160 casitas, 55 villas

"Huge natural boulders", the "kind of setting that becomes more enchanting with each day", provide a "breathtaking" backdrop for this "sprawling" Wyndham-owned resort "away from the bustle of Scottsdale" that makes you "feel like the *Flintstones*" upon arrival, but more like "royalty" once ensconced; it's the "modern West done right" with a staff that attends to "every whim", casitas reminiscent of "mountain retreats with roaring fireplaces", "delicious" food, "top-notch golf" and the Golden Door "spa as great as the views."

Caleo Resort & Spa | – | – | – | – | $300

(fka SunBurst Resort)

4925 N. Scottsdale Rd., Scottsdale; 480-945-7666; fax 480-946-4056; 800-528-7867; www.caleoresort.com; 204 rooms, 8 suites

Set "in the heart of Scottsdale", this inviting hideaway (formerly the SunBurst Resort) is a "great alternative to larger resorts in the area", especially after a $6-million renovation that includes a new ocean-inspired restaurant, BALEENscottsdale; rooms have private terraces overlooking the McDowell Mountains and are decorated in earth and sky colors and Native American fabrics, the palm-flanked lagoon-style pools sport outdoor fireplaces and SpaTerre features Indonesian treatments; concierges can arrange tours by jeep, horse or even hot-air balloon.

CopperWynd Resort & Club | ▽ 26 | 24 | 24 | 23 | $425

13225 N. Eagle Ridge Dr., Fountain Hills; 480-333-1900; fax 480-333-1901; 877-707-7760; www.copperwynd.com; 32 rooms, 8 villas

"Stunning views" of the "beautiful" Sonora desert can be had from this "simply outstanding" mountain vantage point in northern Scottsdale, a member of Small Luxury Hotels of the World in an "ideal environment that's outdone itself" with "friendly" service that's "always there to help", a "great spa and gym facilities", courts for "tennis buffs" and "delicious food" at Alchemy – the "not

to be missed" restaurant with "floor-to-ceiling windows", and duffers have privileges at many local "challenging" golf courses.

FAIRMONT SCOTTSDALE PRINCESS 25 | 24 | 23 | 27 | $499

7575 E. Princess Dr., Scottsdale; 480-585-4848; fax 480-585-0091; 800-254-7544; www.fairmont.com; 458 rooms, 2 suites, 72 villas, 119 casitas

"Finally found out what a real resort is like" applaud admirers awed by this "truly deluxe", Spanish Colonial–style "gorgeous property" framed by the McDowell Mountains with "wonderfully manicured" grounds "for romping with children", the "one-in-a-million Willow Stream spa", "classy pools", a golf course "where the big boys play", "fine dining" and a "staff that can't do enough for you"; the "casita rooms are worth the splurge", especially when you see the "deep, soaking tubs" in the "luxurious bathrooms."

FOUR SEASONS RESORT SCOTTSDALE AT TROON NORTH 27 | 28 | 24 | 27 | $595

10600 E. Crescent Moon Dr., Scottsdale; 480-515-5700; fax 480-513-5599; 888-207-9696; www.fourseasons.com; 188 rooms, 22 suites

Whether "spritzing you with Evian, delivering frozen grapes and cold treats" poolside or "serving sumptuous" meals, the staff will "do almost anything to please you" at this "desert paradise" at the base of Pinnacle Peak where the "dramatic setting envelopes your soul as much as the spa pampers your mind and body"; the "modern" "adobe-style casitas" make up a small village with "perfectly manicured", "funky cacti", "but if you've got money to burn, request a suite with a private plunge pool and outdoor shower"; N.B. a new kids' activities complex was recently added.

Hermosa Inn 23 | 23 | 25 | 21 | $299

5532 N. Palo Cristi Rd., Paradise Valley; 602-955-8614; fax 602-955-8299; 800-241-1210; www.hermosainn.com; 17 rooms, 11 casitas, 3 haciendas, 4 villas

"If you want a true Phoenix experience", this "charming inn" "tucked in a residential neighborhood" with an "unsurpassed view of Camelback Mountain" "may be the place"; "lounge by the pool and you'll think you're in a scene out of *Bambi*", then relax in "stylish casitas" before checking out the "outstanding" LON restaurant, named for the cowboy artist who built this "romantic spot" in the 1930s.

Hyatt Regency at Gainey Ranch 22 | 23 | 22 | 27 | $425

7500 E. Doubletree Ranch Rd., Scottsdale; 480-444-1234; fax 480-483-5550; 800-554-9288; www.scottsdale.hyatt.com; 440 rooms, 32 suites, 18 casitas

"Pools, pools and more pools" – 10, actually – "with a lagoon, a waterslide and a man-made beach" "raise lounging to an art form" at this "great getaway" with "magnificently landscaped", "picture-perfect grounds" offering "just about everything a family could want"; from the "gondola ride that's a must" ("who'da thunk it?") and "incredible golf" to the "plush rooms", "inspired Southwestern cuisine" and "bars good for mingling", it "exceeds expectations"; still, a few frown it's "crowded with conventioneers" and confide "expected more enchantment."

James Hotel ▽ 19 20 24 20 $269

7353 E. Indian School Rd., Scottsdale; 480-308-1100; fax 480-308-1200; 866-505-2637; www.jameshotels.com; 177 rooms, 17 suites

It's "about time Phoenix put together a trendy hotel" applaud admirers of NYC restaurateur Stephen Hanson and Equinox Fitness Clubs' co-founder Danny Errico's "starkly modern" newcomer, a former Downtown conference center that's now as "hip as could be", "generating good word of mouth" via the Fiamma Trattoria restaurant, "delicious room service", "first-rate pools and gym" and a "cool bar" ("not an old fuddy duddy"); "at this price, you couldn't ask for a better spot."

JW Marriott Camelback Inn 24 25 21 26 $489

5402 E. Lincoln Dr., Scottsdale; 480-948-1700; fax 480-951-8469; 800-582-2169; www.camelbackinn.com; 426 casitas, 27 suites

This nearly 60-year-old, "lavishly landscaped" "grande dame" with "jovial service", a "real desert feel" and a "charm all its own" offers a "touch of the Old West" along with a "gorgeous new spa" ("decompression heaven"), "great golf", "excellent food" and "lots of activities for children"; the "comfortable" casitas provide "stellar views" – "sipping morning coffee on the private patio with a Camelback Mountain backdrop is a delight" – prompting some to consider "moving in for the winter."

JW Marriott Desert Ridge Resort & Spa 23 23 22 27 $589

5350 E. Marriott Dr., Phoenix; 480-293-5000; fax 480-293-3600; 800-835-6206; www.jwdesertridgeresort.com; 869 rooms, 81 suites

"Checked in and didn't want to leave", admit admirers of this "spacious resort" with "indulgent" service and "beautiful views" of the McDowell Mountains; "if you've got a conference", "bring your family" to enjoy the lazy river pool ("looks like a mirage in the desert"), the "fantastic spa, "challenging golf courses" and "lots of dining choices"; but detractors declare it's too "mammoth", adding "skip it if you don't like badges."

PHOENICIAN, THE 26 26 25 28 $625

6000 E. Camelback Rd., Scottsdale; 480-941-8200; fax 480-947-4311; 800-888-8234; www.thephoenician.com; 474 rooms, 66 suites, 107 casitas, 7 villas

"Starwood fires on all cylinders" at this "ultimate resort" in Scottsdale offering "grand" "opulence" "with Southwestern charm and a billionaire's ambiance"; expect the "Midas touch when it comes to service", "glorious grounds", "manicured golf courses", an "out-of-this-world spa", "sublime pools" ("how many ritzy hotels have a waterslide for kids?"), "delicious cabanas" and "excellent restaurant choices" including the "awesome" Mary Elaine's (voted No. 1 for Decor in our *Phoenix/Scottsdale Restaurant Survey*); this one is "worth every gold coin."

Pointe Hilton Squaw Peak 20 20 17 23 $299

7677 N. 16th St., Phoenix; 602-997-2626; fax 602-997-2391; 800-685-0550; www.pointehilton.com; 433 suites, 52 rooms, 78 casitas

"Can't be beat for family fun" applaud locals and out-of-towners who "stay and play at the fabulous water park" at this resort in the Phoenix Mountain Preserve where you can "float down the lazy river pool and leave your worries behind", "beat the heat" at "so many pools you lose track" – one with a 130-ft. waterslide, "one for playing basketball and one with a waterfall" – and enjoy "lots of other activities" like horseback riding; P.S. children also "really like the Western-themed restaurants and shops."

Pointe Hilton Tapatio Cliffs 19 19 19 23 $239

11111 N. Seventh St., Phoenix; 602-866-7500; fax 602-993-0276; 800-876-4683; www.pointehilton.com; 585 suites

"Take the family for wet fun" to this "hilly", all-suite resort "set atop" a nature preserve boasting the "outstanding" Falls Water Village, a sprawling area with a 138-ft. waterslide and "lots of pools to splash around in", a "challenging golf course" and horseback riding; the rooms are "comfortable" and "dinner at the top of the hotel is worth it for the view", but a few feel service runs "hot and cold" and snipe "you need a Sherpa to navigate your way" around.

Pointe South Mountain 21 19 17 24 $325

7777 S. Pointe Pkwy., Phoenix; 602-438-9000; fax 602-431-6535; 877-800-4888; www.pointesouthmountain.com; 640 suites

A "terrifically fun family destination" set against the backdrop of the South Mountain Preserve, this "vast" resort has "something for everyone", from "great grounds for a walk around the golf course" to an "amazing pool" and "huge water park"; the "rooms are small suites" with "excellent amenities", plus the "staff is super nice"; but others complain the sprawling layout "makes it hard to find what's offered" and "conventions dominate."

Ritz-Carlton, The 23 26 22 21 $359

2401 E. Camelback Rd., Phoenix; 602-468-0700; fax 602-468-0793; 800-241-3333; www.ritzcarlton.com; 269 rooms, 12 suites

"When you want to be pampered in Phoenix but can't take the time to be tempted by traditional resort facilities" head to this "city-style" high-rise "businessman's Ritz" in the Camelback Corridor; the "superb" suites, "convenient" location near "great shops" at the "swanky Biltmore Fashion Park", a "top-notch" staff and "delightful" dining at Bistro win points, but detractors dis it as "dependable, but not spectacular, except for the service."

ROYAL PALMS HOTEL & CASITAS 27 27 28 26 $405

5200 E. Camelback Rd., Phoenix; 602-840-3610; fax 602-840-6927; 800-672-6011; www.royalpalmshotel.com; 34 rooms, 44 casitas, 5 villas, 34 suites

"Much more homey than" your typical mega resort, this historic mansion offers a "distinctly different" "experience in the desert"; it's "worth staying at this" "enchanted" "sanctuary" "for the dining at T. Cook's and the spa alone", plus the "genuine staff" "provides you with everything" from chocolates to fresh fruit every morning ("ask for a room with a patio view of Camelback Mountain"); factor in a "beautiful pool area" and a "classy" "old Hollywood feel" and it spells "fabulous with a capital F."

SANCTUARY ON CAMELBACK MOUNTAIN 27 | 26 | 26 | 27 | $415

5700 E. McDonald Dr., Paradise Valley; 480-948-2100; fax 480-483-7314; 800-245-2051; www.sanctuaryoncamelback.com; 98 casitas, 4 private houses

"From the moment you leave the desert sun" and enter the "cool lobby" of this "stylish Zen retreat" with "gorgeous Asian-inspired decor", "you're treated like no other guests exist" sigh admirers of this Small Luxury Hotels of the World member, who come for the "privacy and breathtaking views of Camelback", "sumptuous" food, "tasteful bar" and "exquisite" spa "pampering" ("don't miss the treatments in the Sanctum"); "relax and renew" in the "casitas designed for romance and fun" or "tubs with bath salts and natural sponges" – it's like "heaven on earth."

Sheraton Wild Horse Pass Resort & Spa 25 | 22 | 22 | 27 | $429

5594 W. Wild Horse Pass Blvd., Phoenix; 602-225-0100; fax 602-225-0300; 888-218-8989; www.wildhorsepassresort.com; 474 rooms, 26 suites

"Relax all day and play all night" at this resort on the Gila River Indian Community's land 11 miles south of Phoenix airport that "pays homage to its Native American heritage"; "retreat from city life" with a "golf course that retains the desert's natural landscaping", an "amazing spa" and equestrian center, an "upscale restaurant featuring herbs and grains from the reservation" or a boat ride on the lazy river to the nearby casino; still, some feel "way the heck away from everything" here.

Wigwam Resort 22 | 21 | 22 | 23 | $235

300 E. Wigwam Blvd., Litchfield Park; 623-935-3811; fax 623-935-3737; 800-327-0396; www.wigwamresort.com; 259 casitas, 72 suites

Once owned by Goodyear Tire, Starwood's "high-end", "historic resort" in the Sonoran Desert feels "quite a ways from civilization" (about 25 minutes from Phoenix airport) "but quite civilized itself" with "super courses" for duffers, a "gorgeous pool", a "considerate staff and delectable food"; its "old-world charm is apparent" so "make certain you stay in one of the original casitas" then "wander the halls and examine the curios"; still, it's not everyone's cup of teepee – some find it "inconvenient for non-golfers"; N.B. a new spa opens in December 2005.

Wyndham Buttes Resort 20 | 19 | 17 | 22 | $229

2000 Westcourt Way, Tempe; 602-225-9000; fax 602-438-8622; 800-843-1986; www.wyndhambuttes.com; 344 rooms, 9 suites

"The delightful" "dual pools with waterfalls" and "hot tubs nestled in the rocks are one of a kind" and so are the "gorgeous views from the mountaintop restaurant" at this "lovely location" overlooking Phoenix; "with Tempe Diablo stadium behind the property" there's "not much more an Angel fan could ask for", plus it's "great for the family" with "lots of activities to keep kids entertained"; still, detractors snap it's "showing its age" and conclude the vistas are "not enough to balance marginal food"; N.B. the new full-service Sasura Spa by Golden Door opened in September 2005.

Prescott

Hassayampa Inn Ⓗ ▽ 18 | 24 | 23 | 18 | $189

122 E. Gurley St.; 928-778-9434; fax 928-445-8590; 800-322-1927; www.hassayampainn.com; 55 rooms, 12 suites

"Travel back in time to the early Southwest" at this "beautifully restored" 1927 historic landmark "with lots of character", "friendly, efficient service" and a "wonderful Downtown location" close to "many sights"; "spare" rooms are "on the small side", but "they make up for it with ambiance", especially in the "rustic" lobby with fireplace; P.S. the Peacock Dining Room is "excellent", and "breakfast is an unexpected plus."

Sedona

Canyon Villa – | – | – | – | $189

125 Canyon Circle Dr.; 928-284-1226; fax 928-284-2114; www.canyonvilla.com; 11 rooms

Walk "inside the front door" of this "warm, comfortable" inn "adjacent to the huge Red Rocks" and "you are in heaven"; each of the rooms (decorated in Early American, Native American or Santa Fe styles) is "different", some with gas fireplaces, Jacuzzis and "fantastic views of magnificent scenery", and the "living and dining rooms are so homey."

ENCHANTMENT RESORT 26 | 25 | 24 | 28 | $395

525 Boynton Canyon Rd.; 928-282-2900; fax 928-282-9249; 800-826-4180; www.enchantmentresort.com; 160 rooms, 60 suites

This "astounding" member of Small Luxury Hotels of the World, with "awe-inspiring grounds", a "pampering staff" and "exemplary food", offers a "blissful" "bit of heaven in the Red Rocks" of "wondrous" Boynton Canyon; "bring on an instant release of stress" with a visit or "stay at the attached", "Zen-like" Mii amo spa, "indulge in a massage in a private hut open to the sky", "hike in every direction" and wake up to "juice and a paper at your casita door" – "ah, to return!"

Hilton Sedona Resort 22 | 20 | 17 | 22 | $229

90 Ridge Trail Dr.; 928-284-4040; fax 928-284-6940; 877-273-3762; www.hiltonsedona.com; 171 suites, 48 rooms

"Views of the Red Rocks abound" at this "good choice for families" a few miles from the main tourist area at the edge of Oak Creek where some of the "spacious suites" have "modern gas fireplaces and Jacuzzis"; wander around the "beautiful hotel grounds", "indulge in a guilty-pleasure tan" by the two-tiered pool, visit the "nice spa", work out at the 2,500-sq.-ft. fitness center or tee off at the "very good golf course" steps away.

L'Auberge de Sedona 23 | 24 | 25 | 21 | $419

301 L'Auberge Ln.; 928-282-1661; fax 520-282-2885; 800-272-6777; www.lauberge.com; 33 cottages, 21 rooms, 2 suites, 1 house

"Red Rocks and Provence merge" at this "absolutely mystic" resort "nestled by the banks of Oak Creek" with "lush grounds", a "gracious staff" and a "gourmet restaurant" offering "superb" French fare; "to appreciate the special quietness" of this "idyllic setting", "get a posh cabin" by the stream (they're "not modern, but roughing it has never been so charming") and "eat breakfast with the ducks" – it's like having "your own country estate."

Los Abrigados ▽ 19 | 20 | 18 | 22 | $225

160 Portal Ln.; 928-282-1777; fax 928-282-2614; 800-258-2899; www.losabrigados.com; 187 suites, 3 private houses

"Beautiful grounds" are the draw at this "lovely", "upscale but not pretentious" property that also boasts "spacious rooms (many offer private hot tubs)" and a "convenient location for shoppers" "interested in visiting the quaint Tiaquepaque" "artists' colony/mall" next door; admirers appreciate the "daily activities" for kids and multiple restaurants, and suggest "don't skip the spa!"; still, detractors deride it as "nothing special" finding the "rooms are not up to snuff."

Tucson

Arizona Inn 21 | 26 | 24 | 23 | $289

2200 E. Elm St.; 520-325-1541; fax 520-881-5830; 800-933-1093; www.arizonainn.com; 66 rooms, 20 suites

It's the "cat's pajamas" purr supporters of this "utterly charming", family-owned 1930 "classic" "in the center of town" run by a staff that "genuinely cares about your comfort"; for those "looking for the Arizona back in the day", this "serene oasis" exudes a "desert elegance" with "fine rooms" (some with fireplaces and patios), "wonderful complimentary high tea", "excellent dining", a "great" pool, "peaceful" landscaped grounds and even a "lovely piano bar."

CANYON RANCH 22 | 27 | 25 | 28 | $747

8600 E. Rockcliff Rd.; 520-749-9000; fax 520-749-1646; 800-742-9000; www.canyonranch.com; 155 rooms, 33 casitas

"You only have to think it, and your wish will be granted" at this "rejuvenating", "upscale coed" "boot camp in heaven", the "perfect retreat" where you can "hang your hat for a few active days" and "regroup"; it's "the ultimate for fitness buffs" thanks to "abundant classes", "superior hiking guides" and "excellent" "healthy food", and for "pampering" there's the "spa to end all spas" with "top-notch facilities"; "you get what you pay for and you pay a lot" – but "you leave feeling like a million bucks"; N.B. the per-night rate is based on a required four-night minimum stay.

Hacienda del Sol 21 | 22 | 24 | 20 | $245

5601 N. Hacienda del Sol Rd.; 520-299-1501; fax 520-299-5554; 800-728-6514; www.haciendadelsol.com; 22 rooms, 5 suites, 3 casitas

"If you like vintage, you'll like this" "classic" hacienda, formerly an all-girls school in the 1930s, a dude ranch for Hollywood stars in the 1940s and now a "terrific place to stay" with a "lovely setting", "friendly service" and "some of the best dining in Tucson"; still, a few feel the "rooms need updating" and surmise if "older adobe" buildings "aren't your bag" you may want to ride on.

Hilton El Conquistador 19 | 20 | 18 | 21 | $199

10000 N. Oracle Rd.; 520-544-5000; fax 520-544-1222; 800-325-8131; www.hiltonelconquistador.com; 328 rooms, 100 suites

"Not as swank as some, but very comfortable for a midrange meeting hotel" and "family-oriented resort", this "golf locale" formerly under the Sheraton flag in the Santa Catalina foothills is "trying to improve everything", offering "accommodating" service, "fun casitas" and "spacious rooms", "lovely pools" with a new 143-ft. waterslide, plus "nearby stables" and tennis courts; but a few find that while it "has great potential" it can feel "like a perpetual Shriner's convention."

Lodge at Ventana Canyon 22 22 18 23 $549

6200 N. Clubhouse Ln.; 520-577-1400; fax 520-577-4065; 800-828-5701; www.thelodgeatventanacanyon.com; 50 suites

This "great small hotel with big service" in the foothills of the Santa Catalina Mountains is a "place to enjoy nature and luxury accommodations at the same time"; the "two Tom Fazio–designed golf courses are definitely a draw" for duffers, plus the "private" "huge" suites boast "enormous bathrooms"; however, a few "disappointed" patrons deem dining options "poor" and declare that the "interiors could use a little help" – "even the pleasant staff can't compensate."

Loews Ventana Canyon 24 24 23 26 $350

7000 N. Resort Dr.; 520-299-2020; fax 520-299-6832; 800-234-5117; www.loewshotels.com; 377 rooms, 21 suites

It's "the *crème* of the resort crop in Tucson" crow acolytes who head to this "terrific oasis from the dog-eat-dog world" "nestled into" the "cactus-covered foothills" of the "dramatic" Catalina Mountains; the "beautifully manicured" setting, "breathtaking golf courses", "gorgeous spa", "unparalleled food" and "large rooms with awesome bathtubs", plus "all the amenities for those who want to be pampered" prompt patrons to pledge "I would raise my kids here if I could."

MIRAVAL, LIFE IN BALANCE 24 27 26 28 $695

5000 E. Via Estancia Miraval, Catalina; 520-825-4000; fax 520-825-5163; 800-232-3969; www.miravalresort.com; 106 rooms

The "ne plus ultra of spas" agree guests who "feel completely removed from the stressful real world" after a few hours at this "incredible getaway" north of Tucson; embark on a "desert hike at sunrise", "climb a rock wall", "go mountain biking", indulge in an "amazing hot stone massage", then dine on "healthful" food "in your spa bathrobe if you want" and "enjoy wine with dinner" (the "availability of alcohol puts it over the top"); even "an assertive Manhattan woman can become spiritual" here – "truly, there's no place like it."

Starr Pass Resort & Spa – – – – $179

3645 West Starr Pass Blvd.; 520-792-3500; fax 520-670-0427; www.starrpasstucson.com; 40 rooms, 40 suites

This long-awaited JW Marriott resort just south of downtown Tucson has everything a starry-eyed vacationer could want: 27 holes of golf on an Arnold Palmer–designed course, the 20,000-sq.-ft. Hashani spa, seven restaurants, a tennis complex, a fitness center, hiking in Tucson Mountain Park, and rooms that incorporate a Southwestern modern styling; beautiful sunset views are just the icing on the cake.

Westin La Paloma 23 | 22 | 21 | 25 | $429
3800 E. Sunrise Dr.; 520-742-6000; fax 520-577-5878; 800-228-3000; www.westinlapalomaresort.com; 462 rooms, 25 suites
"The big pool with a 177-ft. waterslide is a treat for kids and those who want to be kids" (there's also an adult freeform pool and swim-up bar) at this "resort favorite" "where your cares slip away" thanks to "postcard views of the Santa Catalina Mountains" from the "posh" rooms and "lovely casitas"; "it's a great place to kick back or hold a conference", plus the "top-notch" Jack Nicklaus golf course, the Elizabeth Arden Red Door spa and dining at Janos are all "unbelievable" experiences.

Westward Look Resort ∇ 22 | 21 | 21 | 23 | $289
245 E. Ina Rd.; 520-297-1151; fax 520-297-9023; 800-722-2500; www.westwardlook.com; 242 rooms, 2 suites
"Beautiful walking paths", "natural landscaping" and abundant "bird life are the best parts" of this "affordable resort with all the amenities", including a spa, set high in the Santa Catalina foothills overlooking Tucson; wranglers relish the Gold Room restaurant's "excellent food", and the "extremely comfortable" suites are "decorated in true Southwestern style"; still, a handful find the "rooms a little tired."

Arkansas

Little Rock

Capital Hotel ∇ 23 | 25 | 23 | 21 | $226
111 W. Markham St.; 501-374-7474; fax 501-370-7091; 800-766-7666; www.thecapitalhotel.com; 121 rooms, 5 suites
"Among the best Arkansas has to offer", this "quaint", "restored" 1876 classic brimming "with character and history" struts its stuff with "fine suites", an "elegant", "top-notch" New American restaurant and a "great location in the heart of Downtown" offering "easy access to wonderful bars" and eateries; the elevator, reportedly built wide to accommodate President Ulysses Grant, who preferred to ride his horse to his room, now boasts the "great touch" of cushion-filled benches.

Peabody Little Rock ∇ 22 | 21 | 21 | 23 | $199
3 Statehouse Plaza; 501-906-4000; fax 501-375-4721; 800-732-2639; www.peabodylittlerock.com; 396 rooms, 22 suites
"Top of the heap" pronounce proponents of this "conveniently" located property "near great restaurants and nightlife" in the Rivermarket district; a "friendly staff" and "nice views" of the Arkansas river are superseded only by the march of the Peabody ducks, "a ceremony very well" orchestrated in the hotel lobby twice daily by a master, followed by five North American mallards, four hens and one drake; while a few frustrated folks flap about "average, average, average" digs, most agree "it's all very comfortable"; N.B. a multimillion-dollar refurbishment may not be reflected in above ratings.

California

★ **Tops in State**

28 Château du Sureau, *Oakhurst*
Peninsula, *Beverly Hills*
27 Four Seasons Aviara, *Carlsbad*
Post Ranch Inn, *Big Sur*
Four Seasons, *Beverly Hills*
Inn at Spanish Bay, *Pebble Beach*
Rancho Valencia, *Rancho Santa Fe*
Bel-Air, *Los Angeles*
Four Seasons, *San Francisco*
Golden Door, *Escondido*

Carmel Area

BERNARDUS LODGE | 27 | 26 | 27 | 26 | $485 |

415 Carmel Valley Rd., Carmel Valley; 831-658-3400; fax 831-659-3529; 888-648-9463; www.bernardus.com; 55 rooms, 2 suites

What "sybaritic satisfaction" sigh acolytes who dub this "oasis of fine food and wines" "about 10 miles from the Carmel hubbub" "nirvana"; "surrounded by vineyards, horses and hills", it's a "place to pamper all the senses", from the "heaven-on-earth spa" to "complimentary goody baskets" to "luxurious rooms" with feather "beds you never want to leave" and "bathtubs big enough to swim laps in"; the "romantic" Marinus restaurant is "top-notch" and the "incredible" staff "makes you feel like a VIP."

Carmel Valley Ranch | 25 | 22 | 20 | 24 | $579 |

1 Old Ranch Rd., Carmel; 831-625-9500; fax 831-624-2858; 800-422-7635; www.wyndhamcarmelvalleyranch.com; 144 suites

Not far from Carmel-by-the-Sea, this "dreamy", Wyndham-flagged getaway "out of the fog belt" offers guests "genteel country club charm" "amid rolling hills" and the Santa Lucia Mountains; "wild turkeys greet you" and "deer roam peacefully" about the "lush" grounds while the "staff waits on your every whim"; the "spacious" quarters overlooking the "incredible" golf course "make you feel at home" with in-room treatments, "huge tubs and a fireplace", prompting sensualists to "demand wine and a roaring fire even on warm days."

Casa Palmero at Pebble Beach | – | – | – | – | $705 |

1518 Cypress Dr., Pebble Beach; 831-622-6650; fax 831-622-6655; 800-654-9300; www.pebblebeach.com; 7 rooms, 9 rooms, 3 suites, 5 studios

A Mediterranean motif characterizes this posh Pebble Beach resort, from its mustard-colored plaster walls and archways to the fountains scattered throughout the grounds; some rooms have French doors that lead to private patios and whirlpools, while others feature dining areas facing the famous fairways; guests have full access to the newly remodeled Beach and Tennis Club, with its clay and hard-surface courts, and to the forest-shrouded Spa at Pebble Beach, while a dozen eateries give plenty of options.

Centrella Bed and Breakfast Inn ▽ 19 22 16 18 $165
612 Central Ave., Pacific Grove; 831-372-3372; fax 831-372-2036; 800-233-3372; www.centrellainn.com; 26 rooms
"Lovely" with "unparalleled hospitality", this 1892 "gem" of a B&B is a "short walk to the beach" and "anything and everything" on Monterey Peninsula, including Cannery Row's "quaint shops and restaurants" (let the "staff help you plan your day's adventures"); the accommodations, ranging from cottages to Victorian rooms to attic suites, some with claw-foot tubs, potbelly stoves and Jacuzzis, offer a "good value", while the "common area provides endless enjoyment on misty gray days."

Cobblestone Inn 20 21 16 18 $155
Junipero, bet. 7th & 8th Sts., Carmel; 831-625-5222; 800-833-8836; www.foursisters.com; 24 rooms
A "charming atmosphere" prevails at Four Sisters Inns' English country–style B&B that's "very near Ocean Avenue's shops" yet manages to stay "quiet and relaxing"; guests can take breakfast on the patio or have it brought to their rooms, and enjoy afternoon wine and hors d'oeuvres by the roaring fire in the dining room; the "quaint" quarters boast four-poster beds, jetted tubs and fireplaces, though a few deem them "fine, but not fabulous."

Cypress Inn 20 22 19 19 $195
Lincoln & 7th St., Carmel; 831-624-3871; fax 831-624-8216; 800-443-7443; www.cypress-inn.com; 45 rooms
"Woof!" – what "doggy heaven" purr pet lovers of this "cozy little Spanish-style inn" in Carmel-by-the-Sea where co-owner Doris Day welcomes canines and cats and the staff dispenses "thoughtful touches like sherry and fruit baskets"; "admire the ocean" from your "lovely room", then have a drink or tea in the Library Bar filled with photos from the movie star's films; but "if you don't like" furry friends, you may be "barking up the wrong tree."

Green Gables Inn 21 23 20 21 $260
301 Oceanview Blvd., Pacific Grove; 831-375-2095; fax 831-375-5437; 800-722-1774; www.foursisters.com; 11 rooms
The Four Sisters Inns' "delightful", restored 1888 Queen Anne Victorian B&B with an "ideal setting" overlooking the rocky coast of Monterey Bay draws "knickknack lovers and Victoriana buffs" alike with its "wonderful" rooms, some with canopy beds, mahogany furniture and fireplaces; the "hearty" breakfasts are "lovely" and the views "amazing" – all that, and "games in the parlor" and hors d'oeuvres in the evening – "what more can you ask" from a "charming seaside getaway"?

Highlands Inn, Park Hyatt 25 24 26 23 $510
120 Highlands Dr., Carmel; 831-620-1234; fax 831-626-1574; 800-682-4811; www.highlandsinn.hyatt.com; 37 rooms, 8 townhouses, 5 suites
"R&R is carried to the nth" degree at this Carmel oasis offering "first-class" cliffside "romance"; "wake to sea lions", have an AM "soak in your double tub with a view of the ocean" and crawl back under the covers to "capture the vista from bed" too in your "cabinlike" room with a fireplace, balcony, kitchenette and decor of "Oriental simplicity"; "beautiful common spaces", a "lush pool" and "sumptuous" fare at Pacific's Edge restaurant complete the high.

Inn at Depot Hill ▽ 25 | 24 | 20 | 20 | $240

250 Monterey Ave., Santa Cruz; 831-462-3376; fax 831-462-3697; 800-572-2632; www.innatdepothill.com; 12 suites

"All the rooms have themes", and they're all "well thought out" and "done with class, not kitsch" at this "pleasant" "little gem" of a B&B in Santa Cruz; "witty personal service" from a "delightful" staff, "breakfast to die for", the "best Japanese soaking tub ever" in the Railroad Baron room and a whirlpool for two on the Côte d'Azur deck add up to "luxurious comfort."

INN AT SPANISH BAY Ⓢ 27 | 27 | 25 | 28 | $505

2700 17-Mile Dr., Pebble Beach; 831-647-7500; fax 831-644-7960; 800-654-9300; www.pebblebeach.com; 252 rooms, 17 suites

"Enjoy the breathtaking", "unequalled views of the setting sun" and "incredible ocean" while listening to the "mournful sound of a bagpiper" "as he strolls the course" sigh those swept away by this "secluded" "paradise" near the Del Monte Forest; it's an "unforgettable" "golf heaven", but even for non-duffers it's an "experience" "to be savored", so "light a fire, curl up with a loved one" in a "modern room" and "luxuriate" in the "outstanding spa", "fabulous service" and "delicious food" at Roy's.

La Playa Hotel Ⓗ Ⓢ 19 | 20 | 20 | 21 | $200

Camino Real at 8th St., Carmel; 831-624-6476; fax 831-624-7966; 800-582-8900; www.laplayahotel.com; 73 rooms, 2 suites, 5 cottages

A few "easy" "blocks from the heart of shopping and the beach", this "charming" 100-year-old Mediterranean-style hotel on the National Register of Historic Places is "centrally located" and "utterly delightful", with "handsome public rooms", a "romantic" restaurant, "prompt" service, "lush gardens" and a "tranquil courtyard pool area"; the "comfortable" rooms can be "small" so supporters suggest staying in one of the "unique cottages."

L'Auberge Carmel Ⓗ – | – | – | – | $495

Monte Verde St., Carmel; 831-624-8578; fax 831-626-1018; www.laubergecarmel.com; 20 rooms

A newcomer in the heart of Carmel-by-the-Sea, this European-style inn (and member of Small Luxury Hotels of the World) is set in a restored 1929 home where individually designed guestrooms feature fine linens and bathrooms with soaking tubs and floor heating; the intimate 12-table restaurant, with its 4,500-bottle underground wine cellar and a contemporary Californian menu from executive chef Walter Manzke (also of Bouchée), is a highlight.

LODGE AT PEBBLE BEACH, THE Ⓢ 26 | 27 | 25 | 28 | $580

1700 17-Mile Dr., Pebble Beach; 831-647-7500; fax 831-644-7960; 800-654-9300; www.pebblebeach.com; 150 rooms, 11 suites

"Paradise is two hours from San Francisco" at this "granddaddy of all golf resorts", a "legendary" "old-school" lodge that's "an oasis of perfect service"; everything "oozes class", from the "luxurious" suites (many with fireplaces and balconies) to the "world-class dining", and "the views overlooking the course and the ocean are a hole in one"; if the links aren't your thing, there are tennis courts, a pool, a spa and shops, so for a "dream weekend" that will "put the spark back into any relationship", "this is the place to be."

Mission Ranch 21 | 21 | 20 | 21 | $200

26270 Dolores St., Carmel; 831-624-6436; fax 831-626-4163; 800-538-8221; www.missionranchcarmel.com; 29 rooms, 2 cottages

Owned by actor Clint Eastwood, this "piece of old California" – a "refurbished sheep ranch" turned "laid-back" B&B – "may not be for everyone", but it's a "peaceful" escape from Carmel's "throngs of tourists"; among the "comfortable rooms" (some with fireplaces), regulars recommend those "overlooking the fields and ocean", and though you can "walk to town", after "sunset drinks" in the "great piano bar", you may "never want to leave."

Monterey Plaza Hotel & Spa 23 | 22 | 19 | 22 | $290

400 Cannery Row, Monterey; 831-646-1700; fax 831-646-0285; 800-334-3999; www.woodsidehotels.com; 280 rooms, 10 suites

"Wake to the sea lions barking", "watch the otters frolic" "with the surf at your feet", then "walk out the door" to "the heart of Cannery Row, near the aquarium, restaurants and shopping" when you stay at this "fabulous perch over the Pacific"; the "staff is eager to please", and though a minority maintains that the place feels "more corporate than cozy", admirers advise reserve an "ample-size" "room with an ocean view, and you've booked the ultimate Monterey vacation."

Pacific, Hotel ∇ 24 | 21 | 15 | 20 | $239

300 Pacific St., Monterey; 831-373-5700; fax 831-373-6951; 800-554-5542; www.hotelpacific.com; 105 suites

"Try to get a room facing the patio and fountains" if you're looking for "a romantic place to hole up with someone" say sensualists who sequester themselves at this "luxuriously appointed" all-suite hotel; in the "charming old adobe" building, the "cozy" accommodations with fireplaces and balconies boast "wonderful beds that you can sink into", and though there's "no restaurant" on-site, they serve a "great" continental breakfast buffet; P.S. there are plenty of dining "options within a block or two" too.

POST RANCH INN 28 | 27 | 27 | 27 | $525

Hwy. 1, Big Sur; 831-667-2200; fax 831-667-2512; 800-527-2200; www.postranchinn.com; 30 cottages

Big spenders are willing to "mortgage the house to stay" at this "architecturally striking inn" (a member of Small Luxury Hotels of the World) where "ecotourist meets luxurious romantic getaway" – and if prices are "over the top, so is the view" from the "amazing cliff-top cottages and treehouses with very private balconies"; the "comfortable", "rustic" rooms are furnished with fireplaces and "granite tubs for two", and after a day of yoga or hiking, "book a sunset meal" at the "wonderful" Sierra Mar (rated No. 1 for Decor in our *San Francisco Bay Area Restaurant Survey*).

Quail Lodge 23 | 22 | 22 | 24 | $395

8205 Valley Greens Dr., Carmel; 831-624-2888; fax 831-624-3726; 888-828-8787; www.quaillodge.com; 79 rooms, 14 suites, 4 villas

After a $25-million renovation, this "serene" "golfer's paradise" located in "sunny Carmel Valley" is "beautiful all over" according to duffers and others, with "palatial" suites furnished with "private hot tubs" that invite you to "relax with a glass of Chardonnay"; service is "very caring", and the "Covey restaurant is outstanding."

Seven Gables Inn | 24 | 21 | 22 | 20 | $175

555 Ocean View Blvd., Pacific Grove; 831-372-4341; www.pginns.com; 13 rooms, 1 suite

"Perfect for a honeymoon or a getaway", this "delightful B&B", a family-owned Victorian 1886 landmark with "amazing views" of Monterey Bay, has a "wonderful staff" and "cozy" rooms with "nooks and crannies" and "antiques that defy belief"; further making for a "marvelous" experience, guests are treated to "excellent breakfasts" and afternoon hors d'oeuvres.

Spindrift Inn | 26 | 24 | 16 | 20 | $269

652 Cannery Row, Monterey; 831-646-8900; fax 831-646-5342; 800-841-1879; www.spindriftinn.com; 42 rooms

A "luxurious" "canopy bed, paned-glass windows overlooking the sea, an overstuffed slipper chair nestled near a fireplace, seals on the rocks" – yes, a "retreat" to this "enchanting" "private haven" on McAbee beach is like a "dream" come to life; with "views down Cannery Row or across the bay" ("you can't get much closer to the Pacific"), a "terrific staff" and "breakfast delivered on a silver tray", this "charming" inn is "really worthy of a romantic retreat."

Stonepine | 25 | 24 | 23 | 24 | $1200

150 E. Carmel Valley Rd., Carmel Valley; 831-659-2245; fax 831-659-5160; www.stonepinecalifornia.com; 4 houses, 8 rooms

"Don't come here if you'd find heaven boring" joust jesters who feel like "lord and lady of the manor" presiding over this "Carmel Valley dreamscape" on "magnificent grounds" with a staff that "treats you like royalty"; said to be the oldest working equestrian farm west of the Mississippi, it's especially "great if you like horseback riding", and the Mediterranean-style château and guest cottages feel like the "lap of luxury"; if a few find it "disappointing", most sigh "we'd live here if we could"; N.B. rates are per night for a two-bedroom house.

Tickle Pink Inn | 23 | 21 | 16 | 19 | $289

155 Highland Dr., Carmel; 831-624-1244; fax 831-626-9516; 800-635-4774; www.ticklepinkinn.com; 23 rooms, 11 suites, 1 cottage

"What a fun, romantic name" exclaim enthusiasts "charmed" by this "amazing little place" four miles from Carmel-by-the-Sea, the site of the former home of Senator and Mrs. Edward Tickle whose passion was growing pink flowers; "comfort reigns" in the "spacious rooms" with "magnificent" Pacific views, and guests are treated to "lovely amenities" like fireplaces, a terrace hot tub and a "fantastic complimentary wine and cheese hour."

VENTANA INN | 25 | 25 | 24 | 25 | $459

Hwy. 1, Big Sur; 831-667-2331; fax 831-667-0573; 800-628-6500; www.ventanainn.com; 13 villas, 27 suites, 22 rooms

"Cast your fate to winding Highway 1" to get to this "rustic" "hedonistic paradise" in an "achingly beautiful location" on a "cliff overlooking the Pacific"; expect "instant peace and tranquility" as you "cuddle up in front of your fireplace" in your townhouse suite, settle into one of the "carefully arranged cottages" with a "hot tub on the deck" or just "watch the whales go by" from your room, then "follow the footpath through the woods to the fabulous restaurant"; talk about a "romantic getaway" – it's enough to "make you want to be a famous recluse."

Dana Point

Marriott Laguna Cliffs Resort 21 | 21 | 17 | 21 | $249

25135 Park Lantern; 949-661-5000; fax 949-661-5358; 800-533-9748; www.marriott.com; 362 rooms, 15 suites

At this "restful" resort "high on a bluff" "overlooking the Pacific", it's important to "get the right room" – so choose one with a "breathtaking view of the beach" or the "rolling hills"; this "quiet hideaway" is a relative "bargain compared to" other "high-end hotels on the coast", and the "proximity to shops and restaurants is a plus", as is the "helpful staff"; it may "not be in the same league" as more posh properties, but it's still "a lovely place to while away a few days."

RITZ-CARLTON LAGUNA NIGUEL 26 | 27 | 26 | 27 | $425

1 Ritz-Carlton Dr.; 949-240-2000; fax 949-240-0829; 800-241-3333; www.ritzcarlton.com; 363 rooms, 30 suites

Perched "on a bluff overlooking the Pacific", this "elegant and stately" hotel offers "coastal views that make an adjective like 'breathtaking' completely inadequate"; not to be overlooked are the "exquisite service from the surf to the spa", "beautiful landscapes and gardens", two "gorgeous" outdoor pools, "wonderful rooms" and "excellent food" (a new regional Californian restaurant, 162, opened in mid-2005); for many, there's simply "no need to leave" because it "has it all."

ST. REGIS MONARCH BEACH 28 | 25 | 25 | 28 | $525

1 Monarch Beach Resort; 949-234-3200; fax 949-234-3201; 800-722-1543; www.stregis.com; 326 rooms, 74 suites

"Fantastic on all counts", this "over-the-top" Tuscan-style "must-stay" on "stunning grounds" with "regal fountains" overlooking the ocean feels like a "fancy cruise ship on land"; it's a "spectacularly relaxing place" with "superb" service, "sumptuous" rooms graced with balconies offering "coastal views", "bathrooms loaded with marble" and "every imaginable amenity", a "beautifully run spa" ("so decadent"), a Robert Trent Jones, Jr. golf course and an "impressive gym"; while all of the restaurants are "outstanding", most agree it feels like a "bonus" to have Aqua on-site.

Eureka

Carter House Hotel and Restaurant Ⓗ ▽ 20 | 22 | 23 | 16 | $193

301 L St.; 707-444-8062; fax 707-444-8067; 800-404-1390; www.carterhouse.com; 11 suites, 21 rooms, 1 cottage

"Makes a stop in Eureka worthwhile", especially if you're "en route to Oregon" insist enthusiasts who head five hours north of San Francisco to this enclave of four "charming" Victorian inns and cottages on Humbolt Bay for a "taste of the past" coupled with an "excellent dinner" at Restaurant 301; part "historic B&B", part "contemporary hotel", it's a "wonderful gem" with a staff that "couldn't be nicer" and quarters boasting four-poster beds, whirlpools and marble fireplaces.

Huntington Beach

Hyatt Regency Huntington Beach Resort & Spa | 26 | 22 | 20 | 27 | $275

21500 Pacific Coast Hwy.; 714-698-1234; fax 714-845-4990; 800-233-1234; www.huntingtonbeach.hyatt.com; 460 rooms, 57 suites

For a tubular stay, "spring for an ocean view" from your "comfy room with a balcony" at the "favorite new hotel" for vacationers hanging ten across the street from "the famous surfing beach"; with "music piped in" through submerged speakers, the "refreshing" salt-water pool is "cool" in more ways than one, and the "s'mores offered for the open fire pit" are "a hit with kids"; since the staff is "warm and accommodating", perhaps the only drawback is the "south-facing ugly power plant" vista.

Inverness

Manka's Inverness Lodge | 22 | 22 | 25 | 20 | $215

30 Callendar Way; 415-669-1034; fax 415-669-1598; www.mankas.com; 4 cabins, 1 suite, 1 house, 8 rooms

"You feel like you're a million miles from San Francisco" in this "woodsy setting" where the "outstanding kitchen" serving creative Californian cuisine makes it worth the hour's drive from the city just "for the food"; "for anyone needing a little peace and quiet", though, arrange to stay in the "luxuriously rustic rooms" with "big tubs, decks and outdoor showers" "under the 100-ft.-tall trees" – the "hunting-cabin style" "transports you to an earlier time", while the emphasis is on "natural well-being."

Laguna Beach

MONTAGE RESORT & SPA | 26 | 26 | 26 | 27 | $795

30801 S. Coast Hwy.; 949-715-6000; fax 949-715-6100; 866-271-6953; www.montagelagunabeach.com; 262 rooms, 51 suites, 37 bungalows

A "Craftsman-style" "knockout", this "architectural wonder" in Laguna Beach is "one of the most beautiful resorts in California"; it's blessed with "God's choice of location", offering up "amazing" "Big Sur–style views of rocks, heavy surf, cliffs and crescents of gorgeous sand", and from the "delightful lobby" with a "roaring fire" to the "opulent" rooms to the "first-class spa", this "top-notch" place "defines beach classy"; "service is out of this world" too, and if you "splurge on dinner at Studio" (voted No. 1 for Decor in Orange County in our *LA Restaurant Survey*), "you won't be disappointed" with the "impeccable" Cal-French cuisine.

Surf & Sand Resort | 21 | 21 | 22 | 21 | $490

1555 S. Coast Hwy.; 949-497-4477; fax 949-494-7653; 888-869-7569; www.surfandsandresort.com; 152 rooms, 13 suites

The "real joy" at this "cozy retreat" is "being rocked to sleep by the sound of the surf" with the "crashing waves" "literally lapping at the wall below your balcony"; the "atmosphere is refined but unpretentious" and "very conducive to relaxation" with "every bright, airy room" offering a "stunning view" – you can even "watch the dolphins swim by"; add in "fabulous breakfasts" and brunch on the terrace at Splashes restaurant and a "lovely" spa and you've got a "true California experience."

Lake Tahoe Area

Nakoma Resort & Spa | – | – | – | – | $249 |

343 Bear Run Rd., Clio; 877-418-0880; fax 530-832-0884; 800-446-5368; www.nakomaresort.com; 10 villas

What an "awesome place" sigh the contented who escape the daily grind at this member of Small Luxury Hotels of the World in Clio with just 10 villas, a clubhouse originally designed for a never-built Frank Lloyd Wright project in Wisconsin, a spa that's "so relaxing" and the added perk of the Dragon golf course; the amenities-laden suite-size rooms are kitted out with Frette linens, Jacuzzi tubs and wood-burning fireplaces.

PlumpJack Squaw Valley Inn | 19 | 19 | 23 | 20 | $375 |

1920 Squaw Valley Rd., Olympic Valley; 530-583-1576; fax 530-583-1734; 800-323-7666; www.plumpjack.com; 56 rooms, 5 suites

Just "steps from the slopes", this property is a "happening place to be in ski season", offering "exceptional" dining and "hip", "quirkily designed" rooms sporting "crazy deep color tones and court jester decor" (cognoscenti counsel "try to get a room on the top floor" as it can be "noisy" down below); some complain the staff is "not well trained", but others point out the location is the "real reason to stay here."

Resort at Squaw Creek | 19 | 20 | 17 | 24 | $514 |

400 Squaw Creek Rd., Olympic Valley; 530-583-6300; fax 530-581-5407; 800-327-3353; www.squawcreek.com; 203 rooms, 200 suites

Set at "the base of California's best ski mountain", this resort is "more like a ski village than a hotel", with "shops, restaurants and a spa" in addition to "ski-in-and-out facilities" and "its own chairlift to the slopes"; "incredible views" and a staff that provides "drink service to the outdoor hot tubs, even during snowstorms", help make up for "standard" rooms that "lack space or charm"; P.S. there's also an "amazing golf course."

Los Angeles

★ **Tops in City**

28 Peninsula Beverly Hills
27 Four Seasons at Beverly Hills
Bel-Air, Hotel
Montage Resort
26 Ritz-Carlton Huntington
25 Regent Beverly Wilshire
Beverly Hills Hotel & Bungalows
Raffles L'Ermitage
Shutters on the Beach
24 Casa Del Mar

Argyle, The ⒽⓈ | 20 | 19 | 19 | 19 | $350

8358 Sunset Blvd., West Hollywood; 323-654-7100; fax 323-654-1004; 800-225-2637; www.argylehotel.com; 20 rooms, 44 suites

"You can't get closer to the Hollywood spirit" of the '30s than this "dreamy art deco" tower "smack dab on the Sunset Strip", a "masterpiece of architecture" that's "loaded with atmosphere", from the "luxurious rooms" to the "fun roaring '20s revival club scene" and dining at Tower Bar to the "glamorous pool", site of a scene from Robert Altman's *The Player*; the less starry-eyed who snap that she's "an aging actress" may be appeased by extensive upgrade plans by owner Jeff Klein.

BEL-AIR, HOTEL ✕Ⓗ | 27 | 28 | 26 | 27 | $395

701 Stone Canyon Rd., Bel Air; 310-472-1211; fax 310-476-5890; 800-648-4097; www.hotelbelair.com; 52 rooms, 39 suites

"The Bel of any ball", this "swanky, seriously expensive" Bel-Air "sanctuary" spells "unrepentant luxury", from the "inconspicuous service" that "takes care of every whim" to the "opulent" rooms to the impressive pool area and bar (voted No. 1 for overall Appeal and Service in our *LA Nightlife Survey*); "wave hello to your favorite celeb as you nosh" on the "fab" fare at the "superb" restaurant (voted No. 1 for Decor in our *LA Restaurant Survey*), "take a walk to see the swans" and "lush gardens" with "someone special" and give in to the "elegant pampering"; "go without the kids" and you may have more.

BEVERLY HILLS HOTEL & BUNGALOWS ⒽⓈ | 26 | 26 | 24 | 26 | $425

9641 Sunset Blvd., Beverly Hills; 310-276-2251; fax 310-887-2887; 800-283-8885; www.beverlyhillshotel.com; 135 rooms, 37 suites, 31 bungalows

"Step back into a bygone era of glitz and glamour" at this "icon" "nestled amongst lush palms" and "marvelous grounds" "like a perfectly preserved movie set"; whether you stay in an "oh-so-private bungalow" or a "plush" room with a "canopy bed and huge bathroom", the "pink palace never ceases to amaze"; the "pool is legendary", La Prairie spa and the work-out room are "pluses" and dinner or "a drink in the Polo Lounge" where you can "view stars in their natural habitat" is "unforgettable."

Casa Del Mar, Hotel ✕Ⓢ | 25 | 24 | 23 | 25 | $420

1910 Ocean Way, Santa Monica; 310-581-5533; fax 310-581-5503; 800-898-6999; www.hotelcasadelmar.com; 118 rooms, 11 suites

Defines "luxury by the sea" swoon admirers of this "gorgeous" "palazzo" on Santa Monica beach where you "feel like a star" just "entering the splendid lobby"; loyalists "love" the "amazing bar" where you can "sip generous libations" and "watch the sunset" and the "waves crash as people blade by"; the "well-appointed" rooms, "terrific service", a "gorgeous terrace pool", "beautiful restaurant" (a post-*Survey* chef change may outdate the above score) and updated spa "make it hard to leave."

Century Plaza Ⓢ | 21 | 21 | 19 | 22 | $419

2025 Ave. of the Stars, Century City; 310-277-2000; fax 310-551-3355; 800-835-3535; www.westincenturyplaza.com; 687 rooms, 41 suites

A "favorite among business travelers", this "dramatic" Westin property with "gracious service" boasts a "huge, enticing lobby", a "prime" West LA location "convenient to shopping", restaurants and movie theaters, a "fantastic spa", plus "totally cool pools" and "commendable dining"; the rooms offer "exceptional views", plus "sinfully comfortable beds"; but for many the "convention throngs" are off-putting and the space "way too big to enjoy."

Chateau Marmont 20 21 20 21 $370

8221 Sunset Blvd., Hollywood; 323-656-1010; fax 323-655-5311; 800-242-8328; www.chateaumarmont.com; 11 rooms, 32 suites, 9 cottages, 4 bungalows

"Old Hollywood is alive and well in the bungalows", suites and rooms of this "celebrity retreat" "hidden away from the bustle of the Strip"; whether you're "avoiding the paparazzi, cheating on your spouse" or just a "hip guest", it's still the "perfect choice for a secluded stay"; the "wildly varying rooms" are "charming in a vintage way" and chef Mohammad Islam (ex NYC's Mercer Kitchen) creates "sophisticated" fare, plus there's "stargazing galore" in the "ever-popular bar"; if cynics snipe it's "not worth the fuss", loyalists lash back "you can see why it's a legend."

Disneyland Hotel 17 21 16 22 $270

1150 Magic Way, Anaheim; 714-778-6600; fax 714-956-6597; www.disneyland.com; 925 rooms, 55 suites

There's "nothing like an original" agree kid-toting touters of this "old Mouse standby", a "delightful family hotel" just "footsteps from Downtown Disney and the two Disney parks"; the room fixtures are "emblazoned with Mickey", "the Never Land pool and slides are lots of fun" and you can "walk downstairs and have breakfast in Goofy's kitchen" – what a "great way to add to the magic"; those who squeak it's due for a sprinkling of some "pixie dust" may be appeased by recent renovations.

Disney's Grand Californian 23 24 23 26 $275

1600 S. Disneyland Dr., Anaheim; 714-635-2300; fax 714-300-7300; www.disneyland.com; 713 rooms, 38 suites

"Even Sleeping Beauty didn't have a place this magical to crash" crow acolytes of this "architecturally stunning" "treasure" with "incredible hospitality", an "Old West Coast–lodge" ambiance and "woodsy, rustic decor"; with "Disneyland in your backyard", "it's a grand place" for both kids and adults "to park" and enjoy the "fun waterslide", "gourmet food" at the Napa Rose restaurant and "gorgeous lobby with extravagantly large hearths" made for storytelling sessions.

Fairmont Miramar 22 22 18 22 $389

101 Wilshire Blvd., Santa Monica; 310-576-7777; fax 310-458-7912; 866-540-4470; www.fairmont.com; 208 rooms, 62 suites, 32 bungalows

What a "beach beauty" bellow believers, convinced that this historic property dating back to 1921 "has it all", from that "special glow of a hotel that's seen the likes of presidents and movie stars" à la Jean Harlow and Marilyn Monroe to a location "right at the doorstep of Santa Monica's Third Street Promenade" to "gorgeous grounds" and "ocean views that can't be beat"; rooms in the old wing are "lush and plush – you truly feel pampered", but the "lovely" "private" "bungalows are the way to go here", and are especially "superb for families."

Farmer's Daughter | – | – | – | – | $144 |

115 S. Fairfax Ave.; 323-937-3930; fax 323-932-1608; 800-334-1658; www.farmersdaughterhotel.com; 64 rooms, 2 suites

A little bit country, a little bit rock 'n' roll: that's about the gist of this quirky hotel with proximity to sites both historical – including LA's oldest farmer's market and the La Brea tar pits – and hip (hello, Hollywood); with its wink-wink down-home decor (think his-and-hers room schemes decked in gingham and denim), all the amenities urbanites require and an on-site orchard for nature lovers, this is one daughter worth adopting.

FOUR SEASONS HOTEL LOS ANGELES AT BEVERLY HILLS | 27 | 28 | 26 | 27 | $375 |

300 S. Doheny Dr., Beverly Hills; 310-273-2222; fax 310-859-3824; 800-332-3442; www.fourseasons.com; 179 rooms, 106 suites

If not for its "high celeb quotient" ("be mindful of the paparazzi"), this "idyllic setting" near Rodeo Drive with "magnificent views" and "restorative powers" might "make you forget you're in the midst of LA"; expect "extravagant floral arrangements in the lobby and exquisite gardens", "tranquil rooms" "with all the comforts you can imagine" and a staff that "coddles you" with so much "attention", "you feel like one of Hollywood's elite" – especially at the "blissful pool" and "amazing spa" or while enjoying an "intimate dinner" at the "outstanding" Gardens restaurant.

Le Méridien at Beverly Hills | 23 | 21 | 18 | 20 | $335 |

465 S. La Cienega Blvd., Beverly Hills; 310-247-0400; fax 310-247-0315; 800-645-5624; www.lemeridien.com; 245 rooms, 55 suites

This "chic hotel on the outskirts of Beverly Hills" is a "business traveler's dream"; the "quiet, cavernous rooms" are done in a "modern Asian style" (with some "French additions"), and with the "deep soaking tubs and huge showers", you could "be happy" "staying in the bathroom"; service is "professional", particularly in the "lobby bar" (it's "staffed with fun people who take care of their customers"), and while the "bathtub-sized" "pool is a bit embarrassing", the spa is a nice diversion.

Le Merigot Beach Hotel & Spa | 23 | 23 | 20 | 23 | $359 |

1740 Ocean Ave., Santa Monica; 310-395-9700; fax 310-395-9200; 800-228-9290; www.lemerigothotel.com; 160 rooms, 15 suites

"Every question is answered, every need is met" by the staff at this "sophisticated" Marriott-owned hotel in Santa Monica that's just "steps from the beach"; it's "thoughtfully appointed in a hip California way", and the vistas are "fabulous", particularly "if you're lucky enough to snag an ocean-view room"; you can sample spa services that range from yoga, to meditation, to body wraps, and the "open-air gym keeps you going", at least till it's time to indulge in well-regarded French fare at Le Cézanne restaurant.

Loews Beverly Hills | 20 | 21 | 16 | 17 | $229 |

1224 S. Beverwil Dr., Beverly Hills; 310-277-2800; fax 310-277-5470; 800-235-6397; www.loewshotels.com; 124 rooms, 13 suites

The extremely "comfortable" "beds are the attraction" at this hillside high-rise in Beverly Hills, where some of the "stylish" "spacious rooms" have "beautiful" views of the Santa Monica mountains, the city or the famed Hollywood sign; the "above-average" staff tries hard, but the setting is not quite in the thick of things (at least "the reasonable prices reflect this"), and detractors decry the 1960s "motel feel" of a "business hotel that's trying to be groovy."

Loews Santa Monica Beach Hotel 20 | 20 | 18 | 23 | $399

1700 Ocean Ave., Santa Monica; 310-458-6700; fax 310-458-6761; 800-235-6397; www.loewshotels.com; 323 rooms, 19 suites

"If your kids like sand and surf", this "family-friendly resort" has a "location that can't be beat" – "convenient to the sea and to the delights of Santa Monica", it's "walking distance to the pier" too; among the "stylish" accommodations, the best are the ocean view quarters "higher than the 3rd floor" ("otherwise you could end up sleeping with your head just a few feet from the Ocean Avenue traffic"); but a handful find some rooms are "cramped", and grumble that the "dining reaches new 'loews'", leading critics to counsel "put your relatives up" here, but stay elsewhere yourself.

Maison 140 15 | 18 | 10 | 13 | $265

140 S. Lasky Dr., Beverly Hills; 310-281-4000; fax 310-281-4001; 800-670-6182; www.maison140.com; 43 rooms

"Done up like a French brothel", this "intimate" boutique hotel – all "rich reds" and "black lacquer" – is a "sexy" "boîte" with a "cool bar" set in a 1930s former apartment building "in the heart of Beverly Hills"; design divas fancy the "small but stylish rooms", complete with DVD players and high-speed Internet access, and appreciate the "personal service", but food options are "limited" ("no pool" either), and overall, there's "no feeling of luxury" here.

Millennium Biltmore 18 | 20 | 20 | 21 | $259

506 S. Grand Ave.; 213-624-1011; fax 213-612-1545; 800-245-8673; www.millennium-hotels.com; 637 rooms, 46 suites

"Step back in time to the days when they knew how to decorate" at this "classy" 1923 hotel, a "wonderful reminder of what LA used to be" "combined with modern-day conveniences" (an indoor pool, high-speed Internet access), and service that's "only a finger snap away"; "some rooms are fabulous", while others, unfortunately, "are like closets with a bed", and modernists maintain that this "fading – but still glam – queen" is "old school, with a capital old."

Mondrian 20 | 18 | 22 | 22 | $375

8440 Sunset Blvd., West Hollywood; 323-650-8999; fax 323-650-5215; 800-525-8029; www.morganshotelgroup.com; 53 rooms, 185 suites

"You'll feel like a rock star at this" "totally hip, totally LA" Ian Schrager boutique hotel where you'll always "see plenty of celebs"; guests get "access to Asia de Cuba" (where the "superb" Latin-Asian fusion fare is among "the most eclectic" in town) and to the "hard-to-get-into Skybar", which buzzes with "beautiful people till the break of dawn"; the "spare" rooms with "panoramic city views" are awash in a "sea of white", but the staff "has some serious attitude", and in these "ultracool surroundings", "if you're over a certain age, the bustle may make you nuts."

Mosaic Hotel | – | – | – | – | $275

125 S. Spalding Dr., Beverly Hills; 310-278-0303; fax 310-278-1728; 800-463-4466; www.mosaichotel.com; 44 rooms, 5 suites

This three-year-old boutique in Beverly Hills is steps from the prime shopping scene and features a sleek, clean style and a high-tech approach; expect warm colors, floral art and garden ponds along with flat-screen plasma TVs, high-speed Internet access, feather beds and goose-down comforters; a Continental menu is served in a candlelit dining room off the courtyard pool area.

Omni Hotel | 21 | 19 | 17 | 19 | $259

251 S. Olive St.; 213-617-3300; fax 213-617-3399; 800-843-6664; www.omnilosangeles.com; 440 rooms, 13 suites

At this "solid" option "for a business trip" (particularly "if you need to be Downtown"), the best features, aside from the "convenient" location near the Pacific Stock Exchange, the county courthouse and MoCA (the contemporary art museum), are the "enormous", "comfortable" rooms and "beautiful outdoor pool"; in the morning, the staff provides "a courtesy car for local errands", though the unimpressed insist that the "lackluster" building "needs a good LA face-lift."

Paradise Pier Hotel | ∇ 19 | 20 | 16 | 19 | $255

1717 S. Disneyland Dr., Anaheim; 714-999-0990; fax 714-776-5763; www.disneyland.com; 347 rooms, 20 suites

"Definitely not Mickey Mouse", this "moderately priced option" is a "good value" when you want to "stay at Disneyland"; the "character breakfast buffet is a blast for kids", as is the rooftop pool, particularly since it's all managed by a "friendly" "well-trained" crew; some of the rooms have "great views of the California Adventure" park next door but are otherwise "standard", to which frugal fans retort, a "Disney vacation is not about the hotel" anyway.

Park Hyatt | 23 | 24 | 19 | 21 | $345

2151 Ave. of the Stars, Century City; 310-277-1234; fax 310-785-9240; 800-233-1234; www.hyatt.com; 178 rooms, 189 suites

A business travelers' "home away from home", this "beautifully appointed" hotel in Century City boasts a staff that "will move heaven and earth to accommodate any request"; the "modern" rooms are "quietly luxe", with fax machines, complimentary mineral waters and your choice of pillow, there's a new spa and the "cool lobby bar" is graced with occasional "celeb sightings"; "close to key attractions", it's still an "elegant respite from Downtown LA", so if only they "could upgrade the dining", it would be a "standout."

PENINSULA BEVERLY HILLS | 28 | 28 | 27 | 28 | $425

9882 S. Santa Monica Blvd., Beverly Hills; 310-551-2888; fax 310-788-2319; 800-462-7899; www.peninsula.com; 144 rooms, 36 suites, 16 villas

Small wonder the scene's "wall-to-wall celebs" at this "perfect" "jewel" in Beverly Hills, for it's "what every urban hotel should be" – "luscious", "exquisitely" decorated rooms, a "staff that knows what you need and gets it done almost without asking", a rooftop "pool area that can't be any more romantic and heavenly", "outstanding dining" and perhaps the "best afternoon tea in LA"; in sum, it's a "grand experience from check-in to check-out."

RAFFLES L'ERMITAGE 27 | 25 | 22 | 25 | $498

9291 Burton Way, Beverly Hills; 310-278-3344; fax 310-278-8247; 800-800-2113; www.raffles.com; 119 rooms, 4 suites

The "quiet, almost sleepy residential location belies the hip, urban space inside" this "excellent European-style hotel" where "enormous rooms" sport "sleek, sophisticated decor" and "stars get treated like real people, and real people feel like stars" thanks to a staff that treats "everyone special, without sniveling or kissing up"; you can drink in the sun at the "divine rooftop pool" by day and watch the "lights of the whole city" after dark.

Rancho Bernardo Inn 20 | 22 | 23 | 23 | $269

17550 Bernardo Oaks Dr., Rancho Bernardo; 858-675-8500; fax 858-675-8501; 877-517-9342; www.ranchobernardoinn.com; 276 rooms, 12 suites

A "quiet" "inland getaway" from the "hustle of Downtown", this "self-contained" "oasis of calm" offers "championship caliber golf and tennis facilities", "fabulous" French fare from its "excellent restaurant", El Bizcocho, and "competent" service; the "rooms are variable" – some are "spacious" with "nice architectural features", while others are "small" and "in need of renovation" – but the "beautiful setting" is "relaxing" and "peaceful."

REGENT BEVERLY WILSHIRE 26 | 27 | 24 | 25 | $425

9500 Wilshire Blvd., Beverly Hills; 310-275-5200; fax 310-274-2851; 800-545-4000; www.fourseasons.com; 280 rooms, 115 suites

"Elegance is everywhere" at this "ageless" "grand old dame" that's "more than just the *Pretty Woman* hotel"; "everything" "screams luxury" here, from "unparalleled service" to the "well-appointed rooms" (some feel those in the Wilshire wing "have more class and style"), and you "can't beat the location" "just steps away from Rodeo Drive"; after you "max out your credit cards", you can unwind at the "swanky bar" or in the "rooftop pool."

Renaissance Hollywood 22 | 20 | 18 | 21 | $319

1755 N. Highland Ave., Hollywood; 323-856-1200; fax 323-856-1205; 800-468-3571; www.renaissancehotels.com; 604 rooms, 33 suites

Blessed with a "perfect central location" "next to the Hollywood-Highland shopping complex", this "funky modern" hotel is a "very satisfactory place to stay", boasting "large", "'50s retro" ("but not cheesy") rooms, some with "spectacular views of the hills"; the staff manages to stay "hip" "without any service lapses", but "enough with the 'my pleasure'" business snap curmudgeons, who also grouse about the "tourist" influx from the adjacent mall.

RITZ-CARLTON HUNTINGTON HOTEL & SPA 26 | 26 | 25 | 27 | $310

1401 S. Oak Knoll Ave., Pasadena; 626-568-3900; fax 626-568-3700; 800-241-3333; www.ritzcarlton.com; 358 rooms, 26 suites, 8 cottages

"Nestled in an upscale, old-money Pasadena neighborhood", this "California classic" boasts "gorgeous grounds", an "elegant old-world atmosphere" and "plush" facilities, including a "state-of-the-art work-out room and spa", complemented by "charming" cottages and "spectacular, lavishly appointed" guestrooms; "celebrities aren't the only ones receiving five-star service" from an "attentive" staff that's "like no other", and the dining is "tasty and creative", all of which "make it a special destination."

Ritz-Carlton Marina del Rey 24 | 26 | 23 | 24 | $350

4375 Admiralty Way, Marina del Rey; 310-823-1700; fax 310-823-2403; 800-241-3333; www.ritzcarlton.com; 281 rooms, 23 suites

A "lovely choice for those wanting to stay on the city's west side", this "delightful" property wins praise for "flawless service" by an "accommodating" staff (particularly on the "concierge level") that "goes out of its way to be helpful"; the "rooms are spacious", "comfortable and relaxing", and the "spectacular view of the Marina is something you'll never forget."

Shutters on the Beach 25 | 25 | 24 | 25 | $445

1 Pico Blvd., Santa Monica; 310-458-0030; fax 310-458-4589; 800-334-9000; www.shuttersonthebeach.com; 180 rooms, 12 suites

"How can you lose with a beach and a carnival outside your door" ask admirers of this "posh" oceanfront "jewel" near the Santa Monica pier that's "more New England summer than LA glitz"; "if it's pampering you want, it's pampering you'll get", from the "pleasant spa" to the "charming lobby" bar "great for star spotting" to the "wonderful" dining at One Pico to the "divine" quarters; "open the shutters and everything is tops" with the Pacific below and a room kitted out with "incredible beds", Jacuzzis and "sweet touches" like "your own rubber ducky."

Sofitel 22 | 24 | 20 | 21 | $369

8555 Beverly Blvd., West Hollywood; 310-278-5444; fax 310-657-2816; 800-521-7772; www.sofitel.com; 297 rooms, 13 suites

Offering a "little bit of Provence across from the Beverly Center", this "elegant hotel" with a "friendly, attentive staff" makes you feel like you just returned from "visiting the Eiffel Tower"; the "cozy" rooms have "funky French decor" and "whimsical touches" that prompt *amis* to say 'ah, *oui*', while the "fine bar scene" and "wickedly" good breakfasts at the "decent brasserie" add to its cachet; but a few just say *non,* convinced it "could use updating."

Viceroy 20 | 17 | 19 | 20 | $389

1819 Ocean Ave., Santa Monica; 310-260-7500; fax 310-260-7515; 800-670-6185; www.viceroysantamonica.com; 145 rooms, 18 suites

"Retro hipster chic" is the byword at the Kor Hotel Group's "trendy spot" "by the beach" that truly "makes a statement" thanks to Kelly Wearstler's "cool" interior design that's "like no other"; "love every bit of staying here" sigh those smitten by the "crisp, luxurious" rooms, the "lobby-as-party concept" and "late-night drinks by the pool"; but it's not everyone's cup of vice: cynics snap "rooms are lacking", like a "cake with pretty icing, and no taste inside."

W Westwood 24 | 21 | 20 | 23 | $550

930 Hilgard Ave., Westwood; 310-208-8765; fax 310-824-0355; 877-946-8357; www.whotels.com; 258 suites

"Even after the initial buzz" from the "funky lobby with black-clad attendants", this "class act" near Westwood's shops and theaters "feels special"; the "stylish rooms" with "brilliant beds", a "swanky pool that's LA hip", the new Nine Thirty restaurant (opened post-*Survey*) under the direction of chef Travis Lett and the "absolutely gorgeous bars" – it all "makes you feel like a VIP."

Wyndham Bel Age | 22 | 21 | 20 | 20 | $349

1020 N. San Vicente Blvd., West Hollywood; 310-854-1111; fax 310-854-0926; 800-822-4200; www.wyndham-belage.com; 200 suites

"Expansive and not expensive" "way cool" balconied rooms with "top-rate amenities" and an "incredible rooftop pool" with "amazing 360-degree views of LA" make you feel "like a member of Aaron Spelling's *90210* at this all-suite hotel behind Sunset Strip; you can't help but "enjoy the hospitality" and Diaghilev, the French-Russian restaurant that's "in a class by itself"; but a few fret that the "large quarters need more personality."

Mendocino

Stanford Inn by the Sea | 25 | 24 | 21 | 25 | $295

Hwy. 1 & Comptche-Ukiah Rd.; 707-937-5615; fax 707-937-0305; 800-331-8884; www.stanfordinn.com; 32 rooms, 9 suites

A "unique property" in "magical" Mendocino, this "home away from home" is "far enough from the village to feel isolated, but close enough to walk – and you get to bring" Fido too; the "rugged-style rooms come with fireplaces" and "drop-dead views of the ocean", the "facilities are lovely" ("don't miss the greenhouse pool or the organic garden") and there's "great vegetarian chow" and a "friendly staff."

Napa

AUBERGE DU SOLEIL | 26 | 26 | 27 | 26 | $550

180 Rutherford Hill Rd., Rutherford; 707-963-1211; fax 707-963-8764; 800-348-5406; www.aubergedusoleil.com; 31 rooms, 19 suites, 2 cottages

"Perched on a hillside overlooking olive trees" and a "magnificent valley" along the Silverado Trail, Relais & Châteaux's "crème de la crème" "idyllic" "oasis" feels like "Provence in California"; with a "decadent" monastery-inspired spa, "blissful" accommodations", a "sublime wine list" and "superb food" via chef Robert Curry (ex Greystone Restaurant), you "never have to leave the premises"; get up early to spot hot-air balloons "rising in the mist" or "have a drink on the terrace at sundown."

Calistoga Ranch | – | – | – | – | $550

580 Lommel Rd., Calistoga; 707-254-2800; fax 707-254-2888; 800-942-4220; www.calistogaranch.com; 46 cottages

With 140 of of its 157 acres devoted to hiking and wellness, this Auberge Resorts Napa Valley retreat surrounded by majestic oak trees, natural spring-fed soaking tubs and, of course, vineyards makes it easy to get with the program; freestanding cottages have fireplaces, down duvets, entertainment centers and high-speed Internet access, while the on-site Bathhouse Spa utilizes geothermal springs in its treatments; Californian cuisine is served at the Lakehouse and Wine Cave restaurants – both open only to guests and owners.

Carneros Inn | – | – | – | – | $400 |

4048 Sonoma Hwy.; 707-299-4900; fax 707-299-4950; 888-400-9000; www.thecarnerosinn.com; 106 cottages

"High-wired meets farmhouse" is the vibe at this "up-and-comer" between Napa and Sonoma where "impeccably designed" guest cottages are outfitted with flat-screen TVs, DVD players and "every new wave amenity", along with heated patios, private gardens and outdoor showers; the "food is fantastic at the Hilltop" restaurant with a "Tuscany-like" view of the Carneros region, and they've added a new American restaurant, The Farm, as well; the whole affair, along with an "awesome spa" is enough to make "you feel like you're at someone's private estate"; N.B. post-*Survey* changes include a new kids' pool, yoga studio and fitness center.

Inn at Southbridge | 21 | 22 | 21 | 21 | $450 |

1020 Main St., St. Helena; 707-967-9400; fax 707-967-9486; 800-520-6800; www.innatsouthbridge.com; 20 rooms

"Conveniently located in St. Helena", this "charming" member of Small Luxury Hotels of the World "framed in wisteria" is "within walking distance of super restaurants", a "well-stocked wine shop" and its "terrific" affiliated spa next door; "start the day right" with a "fantastic breakfast" and finish it with "excellent pizzas" at the "built-in" restaurant; in between, relax in the "spacious" second-floor rooms with skylights, "vaulted ceilings" and fireplaces.

La Résidence | 22 | 22 | 21 | 19 | $295 |

4066 Howard Ln.; 707-253-0337; fax 707-253-0382; 800-253-9203; www.laresidence.com; 17 rooms, 8 suites

"Stay in one of the larger suites – you will thank yourself over and over again" agree admirers of this "quaint, comfy" "French-inspired B&B", a "perfect wine country setting" "right off the main drag and close to everything"; "breakfast is to die for" and "afternoon wine and cheese is a great time to meet interesting" guests – yes, the "owners care about making you comfortable"; P.S. the manageable rate "won't set you back a mortgage payment."

MEADOWOOD NAPA VALLEY | 26 | 26 | 24 | 27 | $625 |

900 Meadowood Ln., St. Helena; 707-963-3646; fax 707-963-3532; 800-458-8080; www.meadowood.com; 74 rooms, 11 suites

"Like summer camp with the Rockefellers", this "feel-good" Relais & Châteaux resort in a "bucolic private" setting is "first class in every way"; the "secluded" "cabins nestled on the hillside" – with "lovely", "spare" "New England–style" decor, "cozy comforters" and "marble bathrooms" – are ever so "romantic", the staff manages to be "both polished and" West Coast "casual", the Californian cuisine is "outrageously wonderful" and you can "play croquet or swim a few laps in between vineyard adventures"; sure, you'd better "have the checkbook ready", but hedonists hold that it's "worth the splurge."

MILLIKEN CREEK INN | 29 | 27 | 24 | 26 | $395 |

1815 Silverado Trail; 707-255-1197; fax 707-255-3112; 888-622-5775; www.millikencreekinn.com; 12 rooms

It's "all the little touches" that "make you feel so pampered" at this "romantic", "intimate" Napa inn where "sultry music greets you" en route to your "luxuriously minimalist room" and "breezes waft in from your private deck overlooking the river"; there's a nightly "fabulous"wine tasting and, since "no kids are allowed", it's the perfect "place to celebrate an anniversary."

Mount View Ⓢ | 18 | 20 | 18 | 19 | $195 |

1457 Lincoln Ave., Calistoga; 707-942-6877; fax 707-942-6904; 800-816-6877; www.mountviewhotel.com; 29 rooms, 3 cottages

In this "simple country house with a wonderful spa" in Calistoga, the "charming rooms are filled with antiques" and the "friendly staff" helps create a "peaceful environment" – just the thing for a wine country getaway; some say the interior "needs some updating", but the in-town location makes it a handy spot "to hang out and soak up the local color" and the post-*Survey* opening of the vino-centric Stomp Restaurant may increase its appeal.

Napa River Inn Ⓗ Ⓢ | – | – | – | – | $179 |

500 Main St.; 877-251-8500; fax 707-251-8504; 877-251-8500; www.napariverinn.com; 66 rooms, 1 suite

With a unique setting in three buildings within the Historic Napa Mill, this luxury boutique melds the old and the new, offering rooms that capture the spirit of the 1800s, yet have WiFi access, goose-down comforters and CD players (some boast fireplaces and views of the river); it's within walking distance of 10 tasting rooms and several award-winning restaurants, and offers complimentary breakfasts by Sweetie Pies Bakery.

Napa Valley Lodge | 21 | 20 | 15 | 19 | $332 |

2230 Madison St., Yountville; 707-944-2468; fax 707-944-9362; 800-368-2468; www.woodsidehotels.com; 50 rooms, 5 suites

For foodies, the main advantage of this "comfortable", "reliable" hotel is its "convenient" position "down the street" from the acclaimed French Laundry, and since it's "centrally located in Yountville", it's also a "great base" from which "to explore Napa Valley"; "well-decorated rooms", all with balconies and some with fireplaces, are a plus, though a handful huff it "looks like a motor lodge from the outside" and is a bit too "near the highway."

Silverado Ⓢ | 18 | 19 | 18 | 22 | $175 |

1600 Atlas Peak Rd.; 707-257-0200; fax 707-257-2867; 800-532-0500; www.silveradoresort.com; 140 rooms, 280 suites

Offering a "happy oasis from which to sample" Napa Valley wines, this "sprawling property" offers "homelike accommodations in a country-club setting" with two "wonderful" 18-hole golf courses, a "stellar spa", 17 tennis courts and eight swimming pools; the "plantation-style" mansion houses two restaurants, while the "lovely" cottages, many with "terrific fireplaces", are "privately owned condos maintained by the resort"; still, foes lament it's been "undone by" "'70s-style" rooms in "need of a major face-lift"; N.B. there's a new Asian fusion–Californian seafood restaurant.

Villagio Inn & Spa Ⓢ | 25 | 23 | 18 | 24 | $330 |

6481 Washington St., Yountville; 707-944-8877; fax 707-944-8855; 800-351-1133; www.villagio.com; 86 rooms, 26 suites

"What a find" fawn fans of this "sweet Tuscan-style inn" with "lovely grounds" and "gracious service" in "the heart of Yountville";

the "cheerful" quarters boast "delicious beds, bathtubs big enough for two", fireplaces and decks, and there are complimentary breakfasts ("we were met with a feast each morning"), afternoon "poolside wine tastings" and the "added bonus" of a recently renovated spa; P.S. be sure to "get a room far from the highway."

Vintage Inn 23 | 22 | 16 | 19 | $365

6541 Washington St., Yountville; 707-944-1112; fax 707-944-1617; 800-351-1133; www.vintageinn.com; 68 rooms, 12 suites

"A bit of Europe" is on offer at this "intimate", "serene property" "convenient to Yountville's Restaurant Row", providing guests with an "amazingly romantic experience" and an "excellent" "base for exploring wine country"; the "huge" rooms with "magnificent bathrooms and fireplaces" are done up in "vintage colors" and even allow pets, plus the "personable" service and "champagne breakfast" make you feel "wonderfully spoiled"; N.B. guests can use the spa facilities at sister property Villagio.

Newport Beach

Balboa Bay Club & Resort Ⓢ – | – | – | – | $425

1221 West Coast Hwy.; 949-645-5000; fax 949-630-4215; 888-445-7153; www.balboabayclub.com; 122 rooms, 10 suites

"Very elegant" (Bogie and Bacall, and even the Duke, frequented this Newport Beach destination back in the day), this "totally redone" resort pampers guests with huge tropical-style rooms boasting oversized bathrooms and outdoor patios overlooking Balboa Bay, plus an on-site gym, spa and Olympic-size pool; nearby activities include shopping galore at South Coast Plaza and Fashion Island Mall, golfing, yachting and hiking; still, a few are miffed that the adjoining club is "exclusive", so resort guests can't access the private beach and other members-only facilities.

Fairmont Newport Beach 18 | 21 | 19 | 19 | $209

4500 MacArthur Blvd.; 949-476-2001 ; fax 949-476-0153 ; 800-441-1414; www.fairmont.com; 411 rooms, 24 suites

A "great value in Orange County" that's recently been taken over by the Fairmont chain, this "convenient" "launching pad" for those who "need to be close to John Wayne Airport" or want to "play golf at the area's championship courses" has "well-maintained rooms", an "accommodating staff", a "wonderful pool" and a notable Sunday brunch; while some say it's "pretty vanilla", a post-*Survey* $23-million refurbishment may change all that for the better.

FOUR SEASONS Ⓢ 26 | 27 | 24 | 24 | $365

690 Newport Center Dr.; 949-759-0808; fax 949-759-0568; 800-332-3442; www.fourseasons.com; 212 rooms, 83 suites

"Always fabulous" insist touters of this "longtime favorite" nestled "next door to the fabulous shopping and restaurants of Fashion Island" mall; it's the "ultimate in class", with "plush rooms", especially the "spacious and airy corner" ones, "top-drawer" service, a "gorgeous pool" with a 17-ft. open fireplace that's lit at night, an "elegant spa" and a "lively" bar that draws "a good mix of both locals and out-of-towners"; plus, the "wonderful" Pavilion restaurant was voted No. 1 for Service in Orange County in our *LA Restaurant Survey.*

Palm Springs Area

★ Tops in Area

23 La Quinta Resort
22 Lodge at Rancho Mirage
Renaissance Esmerelda
Marriott Desert Springs
21 Hyatt Grand Champions

Ballantines ▽ 18 | 21 | 11 | 19 | $159

1420 N. Indian Canyon Dr., Palm Springs; 760-320-1178; fax 760-320-5308; 800-485-2808; www.ballantineshotels.com; 8 rooms, 4 suites, 1 studio

The "ultimate in Palm Springs retro chic", this "fun, kitschy" hotel is "adored by anyone who appreciates" modernized 1950s design; each room has a theme, ranging from Pretty in Pink for the blush-colored digs where Marilyn Monroe stayed in the late 1940s to the Rebel Studio named for James Dean, and most have "patios where you can take in the amazing sunsets"; don't miss breakfast and cocktails at the "sleek pool with the mountains in the distance."

Hyatt Grand Champions 22 | 21 | 18 | 24 | $335

44-600 Indian Wells Ln., Indian Wells; 760-341-1000; fax 760-568-2236; 800-233-1234; www.grandchampions.hyatt.com; 426 rooms, 35 suites, 19 villas

Palm Springs visitors need pools, and this "spread out" resort has "lots of them", some "family-friendly" with waterslides and one "much-appreciated" for adults only; as for other activities, the "spa is killer", but putters sink the "rather ordinary" golf courses and say it's "no longer a prime tennis center"; still, for "relaxation and enjoyment", rooms with "huge bathtubs", "sunken living rooms and balconies" are "spacious" and "elegant", and the "cozy casitas" "with butler service and private whirlpools are the best."

La Quinta Resort & Club 22 | 23 | 21 | 25 | $415

49-499 Eisenhower Dr., La Quinta; 760-564-4111; fax 760-564-5768; 800-598-3828; www.laquintaresort.com; 700 rooms, 27 suites, 193 casitas

"You can imagine the old movie stars hanging out" at this "classic vintage" Palm Springs retreat that "combines the grandeur" of bygone "Hollywood days with modern" perks including a "superb spa", "expansive" fairways and "equally great" tennis courts; "heavenly" describes the "manicured grounds" and "sprawling casitas at the base" of the Santa Rosa Mountains with private pools and a staff "attuned to your needs", plus the dining experience is "over-the-top" thanks to the addition of Azur by Le Bernadin; still, a few counter it "needs a face-lift."

Le Parker Méridien Palm Springs – | – | – | – | $425

4200 East Palm Canyon Dr., Palm Springs; 760-770-5000; fax 760-324-2188; 800-543-4300; www.palmsprings.lemeridien.com; 131 rooms, 12 villas, 1 village house

There's a hint of '50s styling along with California cool at this 13-acre oasis set beneath an umbrella of palm trees and featuring white brick detailing, indoor fire pits and faux fur rugs; accommodations are in one-bedroom villas or a two-bedroom Gene Autry residence with hidden patios draped behind bougainvillea, and there are pools and an extensive spa on-site.

Lodge at Rancho Mirage 22 | 22 | 22 | 23 | $229

68-900 Frank Sinatra Dr., Rancho Mirage; 760-321-8282; fax 760-321-6928; 866-518-6817; www.lodgeatranchomirage.com; 219 rooms, 21 suites
"What a place to get stranded!" sigh those who've sequestered themselves at this "high desert" "oasis", a "magical" "secluded" resort outside of Palm Springs that's "highly recommended for an adult getaway" since the service is "superlative" and the best of the "classy" rooms have "spectacular" views of the mountains and the valley below; after indulging in the "excellent" Californian cuisine or "in every kind of wrap, massage and facial treatment" at the Avanyu spa, "your body and mind will thank you."

Marriott Desert Springs 21 | 21 | 21 | 26 | $225

74855 Country Club Dr., Palm Desert; 760-341-2211; fax 760-341-1872; 800-228-9290; www.marriott.com; 833 rooms, 51 suites
There's "something for everyone" at this "massive" "self-contained resort" set on "pristine grounds" in Palm Desert; with "swimming, tennis, golf and a spa", even "a gondola ride", families can find "plenty to do" (it resembles "Disneyland" when the "humongous property" is "filled with kids"), but there's a "singles scene" too (the "big party at the main pool" is "like spring break for adults"); dining choices are "varied" and the "courteous staff" does its best to overcome the "impersonal" feel, but some snipe the "standard Marriott" "rooms are nothing to write home about."

Marriott Rancho Las Palmas 19 | 20 | 16 | 21 | $350

41000 Bob Hope Dr., Rancho Mirage; 760-568-2727; fax 760-568-5845; 800-458-8786; www.marriott.com; 432 rooms, 22 suites
"Manicured grounds and the hacienda-style architecture are the strengths of this" "dependable" resort that is family friendly given its "miniature water park", pools and Kids' Club activities; there's a "pretty good golf course" for mom and dad, too, and "mission-style buildings" "perfect for the desert"; the "rooms are good-sized", but "nothing fancy", so "save your cash" if you expect luxurious.

Morongo Casino, Resort & Spa – | – | – | – | $305

49500 Seminole Dr., Cabazon; 951-849-3080; fax 951-755-5736; 800-252-4499; www.casinomorongo.com; 272 rooms, 32 suites, 6 casitas
Not your average casino resort, this new 27-story hotel from the Morongo Band of Mission Indians boasts mountain or canyon views from every room and secluded VIP casitas with private pools and gardens; expect a dramatic entry canopy with swirling lights, a casino with a private poker room, rooftop Italian dining and a full-service spa, plus a swimming area with a water slide.

Renaissance Esmeralda 22 | 22 | 20 | 25 | $229

44-400 Indian Wells Ln., Indian Wells; 760-773-4444; fax 760-773-9250; 800-214-5540; www.renaissancehotels.com; 538 rooms, 22 suites
The "openness" of this "huge resort" "lends itself to the Palm Springs lifestyle", and its "elegant setting" is highlighted by

"beautiful common areas", including two "top-notch" golf courses and a "fabulous pool" with a "sandy beach"; the service is "friendly" and the remodeled lodgings are "well appointed", though critics say the walk to some rooms can "take 20 minutes."

Smoke Tree Ranch – – – – $395

1850 Smoke Tree Lane, Palm Springs; 760-327-1221; fax 760-327-9490; 800-787-3922; www.smoketreeranch.net; 37 studios, 18 cottages, 2 cottages

Bring a compass if you plan to wander through the wildflowers that blanket the grounds of this meal-inclusive resort just a few minutes from Downtown Palm Springs that covers 375 historic acres in the San Jacinto Mountains; one- and two-room plantation-shuttered private cottages have kitchens, cable TV and private patios (most have wood-burning fireplaces), and activities include on-site stables, tennis, biking, nearby golfing and in-room spa services.

Two Bunch Palms 16 22 18 23 $260

67-425 Two Bunch Palms Trail, Desert Hot Springs; 760-329-8791; fax 760-329-1317; 800-472-4334; www.twobunchpalms.com; 23 rooms, 6 suites, 16 villas

"All you need is a bathing suit and robe" at this "tranquil, funky" "hideaway" for the "Hollywood crowd" where the "hot springs are a pure delight" – "don't miss the mud baths" – and "the sublime occurs when you have your cocktail" in the "exotic nature pool"; while "the rooms are not lavish" and "dining is so-so, the spa facilities are quite phenomenal" and the "unparalleled treatments" do "wonders for your hair, skin and frame of mind."

Viceroy Palm Springs 20 20 18 20 $199

415 S. Belardo Rd., Palm Springs; 760-320-4117; fax 760-323-3303; 800-670-6184; www.viceroypalmsprings.com; 50 rooms, 12 villas, 6 suites

"Oh-so-chic" with "lovely gardens" and "plenty of pools", the Kor Hotel Group's "intimate" spa resort is "smartly designed" by Kelly Wearstler in a "swanky" yellow-and-black Hollywood Regency style to evoke a "retro Palm Springs" feel; "fantastic bungalows" and "postmodern" "rooms that seem like they're from some wild dream" offer a sip of "champagne for those on a beer budget"; still, a few cynics find it all a smidgen "tacky."

Westin Mission Hills 23 20 18 24 $450

71333 Dinah Shore Dr., Rancho Mirage; 760-328-5955; fax 760-770-2199; 800-236-2427; www.westin.com; 450 rooms, 40 suites

"Golf is the name of the game" at this "luxury resort" with Spanish-Moorish architecture set in a "breathtaking" Rancho Mirage desertscape a short drive from Palm Springs; but if that's not your mission, you can enjoy "lots of pools" as well as "slick" rooms ("take an extra day to enjoy their beds – just sleep, sleep, sleep"); but others harrumph it's "pedestrian."

Willows Historic Palm Springs Inn, The ▽ 28 29 24 26 $295

412 W. Tahquitz Canyon Way, Palm Springs; 760-320-0771; fax 760-320-0780; 800-966-9597; www.thewillowspalmsprings.com; 8 rooms

"Exclusive and private despite being steps from the main drag", this "tranquil" "paradise" with "personal service" and "incredible breakfasts" once drew the likes of Albert Einstein, Carole Lombard and Clark Gable and still "evokes Palm Springs in its previous golden age"; the "1920s glamour pervades", from the "gorgeous" "character-filled" rooms with claw-foot tubs and pewter fixtures to the "phenomenal" desert gardens with views of Coachella Valley to the "pool and gazebo, real havens of relaxation."

Riverside

Mission Inn Ⓗ Ⓢ 20 | 21 | 22 | 23 | $190

3649 Mission Inn Ave.; 951-341-6760; fax 951-341-6730; 800-843-7755; www.missioninn.com; 211 rooms, 28 suites

It's "a delight to tour" this "classic hotel" with a "marvelous Spanish mission ambiance"; "every room is different", and there are "historical surprises around every corner" (not only is it a National Historic Landmark, there's even a museum on-site); carnivores are content with the "heavenly" steaks at Duane's Restaurant (or try the new Las Campanas Mexican eatery) so if you're in Riverside, it's "the only place to stay."

Sacramento

Sheraton Grand 22 | 21 | 14 | 21 | $339

1230 J St.; 916-447-1700; fax 916-447-1701; 800-325-3232; www.sheraton.com; 477 rooms, 26 suites

"Modern and efficient", this "much-needed" Sacramento hotel in the "attractively converted" Public Market Building is set in a "great location next to the Capitol", offering the "politically connected", along with "frequent travelers", "everything they need"; "spacious rooms", a fitness center, a staff that "makes you feel at home" and a "hopping" lobby bar with views of the open atrium prompt patrons to pledge "would definitely stay here again on business."

San Diego

★ **Tops in Area**

27 Four Seasons Aviara
Rancho Valencia Resort
Golden Door
25 Lodge at Torrey Pines
23 W San Diego

Barona Valley Ranch Resort & Casino ⛳ Ⓢ ▽ 18 | 19 | 16 | 22 | $249

1932 Wildcat Canyon Rd., Lakeside; 619-443-2300; fax 619-443-8186; 888-722-7662; www.barona.com; 364 rooms, 33 suites

"Not for the die-hard Vegas lover but an easy weekend getaway" "in the middle of East County", this former 1930s cattle ranch–turned–rustic, suburban gambling resort, run by the Barona Band of Mission Indians and designed by Caesars Palace's architect, "gets an 'A' for trying", with 2,000 slot machines, "great golf and good grub"; but the less game snipe it's simply "ho-hum."

Cal-a-Vie Ⓢ – | – | – | – | $785

2249 Somerset Rd., Vista; 760-945-2055; fax 760-630-0074; 866-772-4283; www.cal-a-vie.com; 24 rooms

"Off-the-charts amazing", this "gem" set on 200 acres 40 miles north of San Diego is the "ultimate spa experience" especially since the addition of a 17,000-sq.-ft. fitness facility; guests "lose weight and get pampered, all in one week", hike trails by the nearby golf course, play tennis, then "rejuvenate" with hydrotherapy in the Provence-style bathhouse; there's a "terrific staff/patron ratio", and rates include three daily treatments (there's a three-night minimum stay required).

del Coronado, Hotel 20 23 22 25 $300

1500 Orange Ave., Coronado; 619-435-6611; fax 619-522-8262; 800-582-2595; www.hoteldel.com; 600 rooms, 80 suites, 7 cottages, 1 house

"Enjoy what resort life was like way back when" at this "19th-century wonder" "packed with architectural uniqueness"; a "family-friendly destination" with "impeccable service" and "abundant" amenities, this is "where the true beach vacation lives" and where "history hides in every corner", from the "haunted rooms" to the Marilyn Monroe photos; even if a few feel it's "living off its laurels", most say "spring for an oceanfront" room or just "take the ferry over from San Diego for the champagne brunch."

FOUR SEASONS AVIARA 27 27 26 28 $495

7100 Four Seasons Point, Carlsbad; 760-603-6800; fax 760-603-6801; 800-332-3442; www.fourseasons.com; 285 rooms, 44 suites

"Feel the grandeur when you enter the lobby" of this "heavenly", "first-class family resort" "in the hills of Carlsbad" about 30 minutes north of San Diego with "awesome views and scenery"; it has "all the touches one expects" – from "bath sponges spelling out kids' names and personalized cookies" ("children feel like kings and queens"), to "elegant rooms", an "enormous health club with the latest equipment", a "lovely golf course", "yummy" bar drinks and "delectable food" – clearly it's the "benchmark from which to compare others."

GOLDEN DOOR 25 28 25 28 $929

777 Deer Springs Rd., San Marcos, Escondido; 760-744-5777; fax 760-471-2393; 800-424-0777; www.goldendoor.com; 40 rooms

Open the door to a "soul-searching respite in a stress-filled world" at this "well-run", "quintessential California health" resort 40 miles northeast of San Diego, voted the No. 1 Destination Spa in this *Survey*, with its "Zen-like atmosphere", on-site nutritionist, "incredible cuisine" and "fabulous packages", it offers "pricey pampering for princesses" (and 'princes' too, four times a year) for one-week minimum stays; the "staff-to-guest ratio ensures" "excellent service", and with a meditation sanctuary and bevy of gyms, tennis courts and pools, sojourners are "encouraged to do as much or as little as they wish."

Grande Colonial 21 21 20 18 $259

910 Prospect St., La Jolla; 858-454-2181; fax 858-454-5679; 800-826-1278; www.thegrandecolonial.com; 58 rooms, 17 suites

Set near the coast "in the heart of La Jolla's shopping district" 15 miles northwest of San Diego Airport, the "central location" of this "sweet little" circa-1913 boutique hotel is "great" "for walking to local attractions"; the "charming" oceanview rooms "score big on comfort", and the staff is truly "interested in guests' well being";

P.S. the "wine pairings" and "fabulous" fare at chef Jason Knibb's Nine Ten restaurant is a "must for foodies."

Hilton La Jolla Torrey Pines | 19 | 20 | 17 | 21 | $329

10950 N. Torrey Pines Rd., La Jolla; 858-558-1500; fax 858-450-4584; 800-762-6160; www.hilton.com; 349 rooms, 8 suites

"If golf is your bag, this is the place" to caddie your habit; some "preferred tee times" as well as "comfortable" rooms with balcony vistas onto the "world-famous", oceanside course (site of the 2008 U.S. Open) "obviate" the "chain ambiance", while the spa, "fabulous" nearby beach and "great brunch" help complete the round; though "monstrous walks" along "sprawling" corridors have duffers huffing worse than on the links, the "attentive" staff helps with an otherwise "relaxing" stay.

Hyatt Regency La Jolla at Aventine | 21 | 20 | 18 | 22 | $294

3777 La Jolla Village Dr.; 858-552-1234; fax 858-552-6066; 800-233-1234; www.hyatt.com; 325 rooms, 24 suites

A "visually striking" Michael Graves "high-rise" in a "beach resort town", this "business-class hotel" is "a fish out of water", literally and figuratively; it's "stylish", "with adjoining restaurants and clubs" (including the "trendy" Cafe Japengo), and "convenient to Legoland, Sea World" and UCSD, but it's "too far" from the ocean and thus "not extremely relaxing"; look toward the "well-maintained" rooms, the "nice" pool with "beyond-luxurious" private cabanas, the "terrific" gym and the happening, "noisy" bar scene if you want to unwind.

Inn at Rancho Santa Fe, The | 21 | 23 | 22 | 22 | $295

5951 Linea de Cielo, Rancho Santa Fe; 858-756-1131; fax 858-759-1604; 800-843-4661; www.theinnatrsf.com; 70 rooms, 16 suites, 1 cottage

"Kick back in the genuine comfort" of "a time gone by" at this Roaring '20s "grande dame" "nestled in the hills" of "beautiful North San Diego County", a "real throwback to the days when its stand-alone villas were rented by LA's elite for a weekend retreat"; the "inviting" inn might be a bit "tired" for modernists, but with a "quaint" air, "gracious" rooms, an "inspired" restaurant and a pet-friendly policy, you and your pooch will be "livin' like old money."

La Casa del Zorro Desert Resort | 23 | 23 | 19 | 23 | $325

3845 Yaqui Pass Rd., Borrego Springs; 760-767-5323; fax 760-767-5963; 800-824-1884; www.lacasadelzorro.com; 48 rooms, 12 suites, 19 casitas

"Not what I'd call fancy, but the total experience is enticing" at this refurbished "delightful resort" in the Anza-Borrego Desert State Park where there's "no pretension, just comfort"; it's a "good alternative to Palm Springs, if you don't mind the isolation" but "still want modern conveniences and attentive service", "beautiful grounds", a "Spanish villa landscape" and "wide range of accommodations" including "unique" casitas with private pools or spas.

La Costa 19 20 19 23 $325

2100 Costa Del Mar Rd., Carlsbad; 760-438-9111; fax 760-438-3758; 800-854-5000; www.lacosta.com; 402 rooms, 77 suites

Following a "lovely" $140-million "makeover", this "something-for-everybody resort" appeals to "tennis, golf and gym rats alike" with "memorable" facilities, along with "attentive service"; the "generous rooms" are "designed to the max" but still steeped in "character" while the full-service "spa is fabulous, darling", as is the "added treat" of the Chopra Center, offering Ayurvedic therapies, yoga and meditation; those who scoff the "food isn't special" may be appeased by the addition of BlueFire Grill, offering coastal Californian cuisine.

L'Auberge Del Mar 22 23 21 22 $365

1540 Camino Del Mar, Del Mar; 858-259-1515; fax 858-755-4940; 800-245-9757; www.laubergedelmar.com; 112 rooms, 8 suites

A "favorite couples' place", this "tranquil" resort and spa in "demure" Downtown Del Mar is an "intimate" setting "to recharge your batteries"; "retreat" to your "tasteful" "beachy-casual" room (some have "views of the Pacific"), luxuriate in a body scrub or massage, or lounge by the "lovely" pool, and the "fabulous" "staff will cater to your every need"; you're "within walking distance of a great beach", near "all the chic boutiques and restaurants" and "just a stone's throw from the race track."

La Valencia Hotel 22 24 24 21 $350

1132 Prospect St., La Jolla; 858-454-0771; fax 858-456-3921; 800-451-0772; www.lavalencia.com; 89 rooms, 12 suites, 15 villas

"Quick! over your shoulder . . . is that Douglas Fairbanks?" – yes, you feel you're among the "glamorous movie stars from the golden age of Hollywood" at this "updated classic" in La Jolla Village with "impeccable" "service of yesteryear"; like a "lovely" 1926 "masterpiece" "dipped in bronze", this "place to treasure" has "lost none" of its "luster" or "old California character" with "cozy", "smallish rooms" offering "magnificent views" of the Pacific and gardens, "outstanding oceanfront villas" and "wonderful food at The Sky Room and Whaling Bar."

LODGE AT TORREY PINES 25 25 24 26 $450

11480 N. Torrey Pines Rd., La Jolla; 858-453-4420; fax 858-550-3908; 800-656-0087; www.lodgetorreypines.com; 166 rooms, 9 suites

"From the kilt-clad valets to the antique Stickley furniture to the championship golf out the front door", this "amazing Craftsman-style" resort gets it right; the staff treats you "royally" – as if you were visiting "your rich uncle's hunting lodge" – and their "attention to detail is superb"; the rooms are "a visual treat", there's a "fabulous spa" and the "fresh, inspired" Californian cuisine is "some of the best hotel dining in the area"; P.S. "bring your hiking shoes for walks" through neighboring Torrey Pines State Park.

Loews Coronado Bay Resort 22 21 20 23 $325

4000 Coronado Bay Rd., Coronado; 619-424-4000; fax 619-424-4400; 800-235-6397; www.loewshotels.com; 403 rooms, 37 suites

"If you're traveling with your kids and your dog", there may be "no more welcoming hotel" than this "family-oriented property" on Coronado Island; it's run by "lovely folks" who treat pets "as well as two-legged guests", and the rooms, done in "breezy colors", "feel like a Nantucket cottage"; the "location is a little out of the way", but with so "many activities" to keep little ones occupied, including "the drive-in movie nights and s'mores on the beach", you "hardly need to go anywhere else."

Manchester Grand Hyatt 21 | 20 | 18 | 23 | $270

1 Market Pl.; 619-232-1234; fax 619-233-6464; 800-233-1234; www.manchestergrand.hyatt.com; 1530 rooms, 95 suites

With "fantastic views from nearly every room" and a handy "location on the waterfront" "next to Seaport Village", these two towers make a "comfortable" base for exploring San Diego's Downtown; "professionally run", it's "perfect for a conference or large event", with tennis courts, pools and a fitness center to blow off steam when work is done; some surveyors are pleasantly surprised that a place "this enormous could feel so welcoming", but for others, it's just a "big, impersonal convention hotel."

Marriott Coronado Island 21 | 20 | 19 | 23 | $269

2000 Second St., Coronado; 619-435-3000; fax 619-435-4183; 800-228-9290; www.marriott.com; 273 rooms, 27 suites

Swimming, tennis and a spa, plus a "great location" for "biking or walking along the bay", make this "unpretentious" resort on Coronado Island "over the bridge from Downtown San Diego" a "good spot for family trips"; though the rooms are "pretty standard", the best ones have "balconies overlooking" the water.

Marriott Del Mar 20 | 20 | 20 | 19 | $238

11966 El Camino Real; 858-523-1700; fax 858-523-1355; 800-228-9290; www.marriott.com; 281 rooms, 3 suites

Respondents "can't believe they're eating in a Marriott" when they dine at Arterra, the Bradley Ogden–designed restaurant where the New American fare "shines"; otherwise, this "functional" Del Mar "hotel is geared toward business people", with "tastefully appointed rooms", a "great exercise facility" and a "helpful staff"; it's surprisingly "quiet inside", given that it's "adjacent to the freeway" – you "must have a car" to get anywhere.

Marriott San Diego & Marina 19 | 19 | 17 | 22 | $375

333 W. Harbor Dr.; 619-234-1500; fax 619-234-8678; 800-228-9290; www.marriott.com; 1305 rooms, 55 suites

Offering plenty of "amenities to pamper you" ("and impress your kids"), this "big resort on San Diego Bay" is a "solid" choice for business or pleasure; the "pool area is a tropical paradise", and if you snag a room "on the upper floors", you'll enjoy "panoramic" "harbor views"; it's an "easy walk to Seaport Village and the Gaslamp Quarter", and "the staff does a good job, considering the number of guests" they have to deal with, but "God help you if you're here when a big convention is in town."

Parisi, Hotel ▽ 25 | 21 | 14 | 20 | $325

1111 Prospect St., La Jolla; 858-454-1511; fax 858-454-1531; www.hotelparisi.com; 7 rooms, 13 suites

"Beautifully decorated" accommodations "in the heart of La Jolla" near the coastline make this "quiet" boutique "jewel" (a member of Small Luxury Hotels of the World) "perfect for weekend escapes"; loyalists "love the feng shui design" that brings on a "Zen, Zen, Zen" state of mind (you can even push a button on your phone for a therapy session with a psychologist); while there's room service from nearby Tapenade restaurant, a few find it "disappointing to walk" two blocks down to eat out.

RANCHO VALENCIA RESORT 28 27 26 27 $550

5921 Valencia Circle, Rancho Santa Fe; 858-756-1123; fax 858-756-0165; 800-548-3664; www.ranchovalencia.com; 36 rooms, 12 suites, 1 hacienda

"Paradise must be like this" "beyond-excellent" Relais & Châteaux resort where the "sense of privacy and luxury is incredible" in "lush, spacious" casitas with "bathrooms bigger than a typical New York City hotel room"; the staff is "trained to give only the best" (the "amazing room service" includes "fresh juice at your doorstep when you awake"), the "gorgeous grounds" feature 18 "immaculate" tennis courts and two outdoor swimming pools, and a "wonderful dining experience" awaits at the "romantic" restaurant; it may be "expensive", but once you're here, "you don't want to leave."

Solamar, Hotel – – – – $399

435 Sixth Ave.; 619-531-8740; fax 619-531-8742; 877-536-0508; www.kimptonhotels.com; 235 rooms

One block from the Padres' Petco Park and three blocks from the convention center, this quirky Kimpton hotel in the Gaslamp area boasts a vibrant palette of pink, green and blue, with polka dots and stripes in its pet-friendly rooms; a 13,000-sq.-ft. pool deck overlooks the baseball field and Californian-Global fare is served at Jsix and Jbar.

Westgate Hotel Ⓢ 22 23 21 20 $365

1055 Second Ave.; 619-238-1818; fax 619-557-3737; 800-221-3802; www.westgatehotel.com; 215 rooms, 8 suites

"Holy gilding! – there's "gold" and "beautiful antiques" all around; you feel like you're in Versailles at this "Downtown oasis of refinement" where "palatial rooms" have a "lovely European feel", the "staff is informative" and the Fontainebleu Restaurant "holds its own" for "special-event meals", plus, this is "*the* place" to "take your daughter to high tea"; but the froufrou weary find it "too opulent."

W San Diego Ⓢ 24 24 21 23 $300

421 W. B St.; 619-231-8220; fax 619-231-5779; 866-837-4147; www.whotels.com; 238 rooms, 21 suites

"Not your usual W style"-wise, this Downtown "hip, happening" "haunt" with a "marvelous staff" makes you feel like you're staying "in an upscale beachside cabana"; awash in "seaside colors", the "cheerful" "rooms are trendy without being gaudy" – they "even have disposable cameras in the minibar" – while the "ridiculously fun" "sandy rooftop bar is a great place to unwind" and "enjoy the sunset" along with "eye candy galore", excellent cocktails and a fire pit; but others opine "go for the service and location, not for the amenities", especially the "puddle they call a pool."

San Francisco Bay Area

★ **Tops in Area**

27 Four Seasons
26 Ritz-Carlton
Mandarin Oriental
25 Vintners Inn
24 Campton Place Hotel
23 Park Hyatt
Albion River Inn
Palomar, Hotel
Huntington Hotel
22 Palace Hotel

Adagio Hotel ▽ 19 | 20 | 22 | 19 | $259

550 Geary St., San Francisco; 415-775-5000; fax 415-775-9388; 800-228-8830 ; www.jdvhospitality.com; 169 rooms, 2 suites

This "modern, funky" boutique hotel two blocks from Union Square is a hit with hipsters and sophisticates who give the rooms with "comfy beds", "great linens, Aveda bath products" and business center a thumb's up; the "fabulous bar", "innovative" Med fare and "cool surroundings" at the new Cortez restaurant truly "make it worth the visit", especially for a "getaway weekend."

Albion River Inn 24 | 23 | 24 | 20 | $235

3790 Hwy. 1 N., Albion; 707-937-1919; fax 707-937-2604; 800-479-7944; www.albionriverinn.com; 16 rooms, 6 cottages

A "Mendocino Coast tour is not complete without a stay" at this "secluded spot" overlooking the Pacific Ocean and Albion River at the Albion Cove; the "light-filled cottages" offer "stunning sea views" and "wonderfully stocked fireplaces" – some even have private yards running "to the edge of the cliff" – and the "excellent service" includes "breakfast shuttled to your door in a basket"; P.S. the "scotch tastings are unbelievable."

Archbishop's Mansion Ⓗ 25 | 22 | 16 | 19 | $315

1000 Fulton St., San Francisco; 415-563-7872; fax 415-885-3193; 800-543-5820; www.thearchbishopsmansion.com; 9 rooms, 6 suites

You almost "feel like you've stepped into a novel" at the former Archbishop of San Francisco's 1904 mansion, now an "upscale B&B" on Alamo Square Park near the famous Painted Ladies Victorians; "if you're looking for a romantic weekend getaway, go no further" say fans aflutter over the "heavenly rooms", each named for an opera and many "deliciously furnished" with "armoires big enough to live in" and "plush canopied beds" (little wonder "couples slip in late to wine hour" . . .); the less faithful find it "out of the way", but WiFi access thoughout helps.

Argent Hotel 22 | 21 | 17 | 20 | $249

50 Third St., San Francisco; 415-974-6400; fax 415-543-8268; 877-222-6699; www.argenthotel.com; 642 rooms, 24 suites

"Very chic" with an "arty feel" that's "perfect" for its "premier location" near "the gorgeous San Francisco Museum of Modern Art", this "find" is "usually priced right" with a "staff that's knowledgeable about SF"; the "sleek rooms" (many in "unusual, comment-worthy shapes") bewitch with "extraordinary city views" from "fantastic floor-to-ceiling windows", but a handful find the "food just ok, which is sad, given everything else."

Argonaut Hotel-Fisherman's Wharf | 22 | 22 | 16 | 20 | $329

495 Jefferson St., San Francisco; 415-563-0800; fax 415-563-2800; 866-415-0704; www.argonauthotel.com; 239 rooms, 13 suites

"Ahoy, there!" – Kimpton's "funky, nautical-themed" boutique hotel in a renovated 1907 warehouse is "a welcome addition to Fisherman's Wharf" and especially "friendly for families, including pets"; the "luxuriously appointed rooms" sport original brick walls or wooden beams, "comfy beds" and "great views of the Golden Gate Bridge", while the "convivial" "nightly wine reception" and restaurant's chowders are a "treat"; if a few mates find the maritime motif a "little too themey", most salute the "change of pace."

Campton Place Hotel | 24 | 25 | 26 | 22 | $475

340 Stockton St., San Francisco; 415-781-5555; fax 415-955-5536; 800-288-0502; www.camptonplace.com; 100 rooms, 10 suites

A "choice stay in the city", this restored, "pet-friendly" "class act" dating back to the early 1900s "feels like your wealthy relatives' home"; the "can't-be-beat location off Union Square" is "fab" for a "shopping spree ('deliver to Campton Place, darling')", plus there's "outstanding dining" at the "divine" restaurant, along with an "intimate bar" and a rooftop gym; "everything is top-shelf", from the "luxurious", "Euro-spare–design" rooms with soaking tubs, "tremendously fluffy comforters and towels" to a "staff that always goes the extra mile."

Casa Madrona Ⓢ | 23 | 21 | 18 | 20 | $255

801 Bridgeway, Sausalito; 415-332-0502; fax 415-332-2537; 800-567-9524; www.casamadrona.com; 55 rooms, 4 suites

It's the "quintessential Sausalito hotel: funky, perfectly charming" and "peaceful" declare admirers who "love the diversity" of room options "spread all over the hillside" as well as Poggia restaurant, a "dream right out of Tuscany", and the "excellent spa" on-site; the original 1885 Victorian mansion boasts "quaint", "individually designed suites" and "views of the ocean wherever you turn" while accommodations in the new wing and cottages are "beautifully furnished" in a contemporary California style.

Claremont Resort Ⓢ | 20 | 22 | 20 | 24 | $299

41 Tunnel Rd., Berkeley; 510-843-3000; fax 510-843-3229; 800-551-7266; www.claremontresort.com; 269 rooms, 10 suites

"Rock on!" rave supporters of this "stately" "grande dame of the East Bay" "tucked in the foothills of Berkeley" with a "castlelike setting" dating back to 1915, "fairy-tale"-esque grounds, "great tennis courts" and pools, and a "top-notch" European-style spa with a "unique menu of services and knowledgeable attendants"; "don't miss" Jordan's restaurant or the bar at sunset (an "'it' spot, even among locals"), but be sure to "ask for a bay view" room.

Clift | 20 | 20 | 21 | 20 | $325

495 Geary St., San Francisco; 415-775-4700; fax 415-441-4621; 800-606-6090; www.morganshotelgroup.com; 337 rooms, 26 suites

Beneath the "shiny", "trendy" veneer "beats the heart of a wonderfully run hotel" concur Clift-hangers convinced that this Morgans Hotel property "delivers a sensory experience", from its "old-money–elegant setting" and Philippe Starck furniture to the "fun-filled Asia de Cuba restaurant" and Redwood Room lounge;

the "cool, chic digs" have "amazing linens", plus there's an "excellent spa", but cynics say the staff "is too cool for guests" and sum it up: "wow for the surroundings, *ciao* for the room space."

Fairmont San Francisco Ⓢ 22 | 23 | 20 | 22 | $289

950 Mason St., San Francisco; 415-772-5000; fax 415-772-5013; 800-441-1414; www.fairmont.com; 529 rooms, 62 suites

"Remember the way it was" at this "timelessly chic", "majestic hotel" "atop Nob Hill" that "retains its inimitable cachet, even for seasoned road warriors"; the "tower rooms are a must, with unsurpassed views" of Union Square and the Bay, the "white-glove service" is "delightfully hospitable" and there's "old-world charm" at Laurel Court restaurant, but "for a dash of camp, complete with cheesy fake thunderstorms, don't miss cocktails at the Tonga Room."

FOUR SEASONS SAN FRANCISCO Ⓢ 27 | 28 | 26 | 27 | $469

757 Market St., San Francisco; 415-633-3000; fax 415-633-3001; 800-332-3442; www.fourseasons.com; 231 rooms, 46 suites

One of the "poshest hotels to call SF home", this "spectacular" "retreat" in the Yerba Buena district near the San Francisco Museum of Modern Art boasts "breathtakingly contemporary architecture", "sublime service" and a "canny concierge desk"; a "beautiful lobby awaits your arrival" along with "rooms so quiet and incredibly appointed you wish you lived there", an "über-cool bar", "excellent food", a "terrific spa" and access to the Sports Club/LA downstairs.

Griffon, Hotel – | – | – | – | $169

155 Steuart St., San Francisco; 415-495-2100; fax 415-495-3522; www.hotelgriffon.com; 54 rooms, 8 suites

If you have a penchant for bay views, the low hum of foghorns and the booming Downtown SF Financial District, this slightly South of Market hotel is an urban chic option; exposed brick, marble vanities, mahogany headboards, simple furnishings and a solid downstairs restaurant make for a well-rounded stay.

Huntington Hotel & Nob Hill Spa Ⓗ Ⓢ 21 | 25 | 23 | 21 | $320

1075 California St., San Francisco; 415-474-5400; fax 415-474-6227; www.huntingtonhotel.com; 100 rooms, 35 suites

With a "discreet" "staff that strives to help you in any way", this "understated" Nob Hill member of Small Luxury Hotels of the World feels like a "gracious private club" where each "spacious", "luxury" room is "different" but all evoke "old-school gentility", and the restaurant/lounge's "amazing food", "classic cocktails", "music and ambiance remind you of another era"; if it's all "a little frayed at the edges", the same can't be said for the "fabulous spa" featuring "wonderful" skyline views from the infinity pool.

Hyatt Vineyard Creek Hotel & Spa Ⓢ ▽ 22 | 15 | 16 | 23 | $249

170 Railroad St., Santa Rosa; 707-636-7100; fax 707-636-7130; 800-233-1234; www.vineyardcreek.hyatt.com; 135 rooms, 20 suites

Set in the Historic Railroad Square a stone's throw from shopping, galleries and wine country, this Med-style boutique, which came under Hyatt management post-*Survey,* charms business folk and vacationers alike; rooms are "small but comfortable", plus there's an on-site spa and Seafood Brasserie restaurant worth making tracks for; but others feel up a creek with "*très ordinaire*" digs.

Inn Above Tide 25 | 23 | 16 | 22 | $265

30 El Portal, Sausalito; 415-332-9535; fax 415-332-6714; 800-893-8433; www.innabovetide.com; 26 rooms, 3 suites

"Shhh, don't tell anyone" about this "fabulous" "secret" on the water in Sausalito "a stone's throw from the ferry" where "all the rooms face Alcatraz, the Oakland hills, the Bay Bridge and the San Francisco skyline"; "the Inn offers a wine-and-cheese get-together at the end of the day", but a sip all alone "on your private deck is one of life's little pleasures", and "should the weather turn chilly", just crank up the gas fireplace.

Lafayette Park Hotel & Spa Ⓢ ∇ 23 | 19 | 18 | 20 | $249

3287 Mt. Diablo Blvd., Lafayette; 925-283-3700; fax 925-284-1621; 800-368-2468; www.lafayetteparkhotel.com; 136 rooms, 12 suites

"Off the beaten path and a great alternative", this "lovely" East Bay hotel with French Norman architecture and a three-story domed lobby has "comfortable, well-appointed rooms", a European-style spa, fully equipped fitness center and restaurant; but the less-impressed find the food "ok, no better than that" and mutter it's "in the middle of nowhere, not Napa, not San Francisco, just nearby."

Majestic Hotel Ⓗ 21 | 24 | 22 | 17 | $150

1500 Sutter St., San Francisco; 415-441-1100; fax 415-673-7331; 800-869-8966; www.thehotelmajestic.com; 49 rooms, 9 suites

Built in 1902 as a railroad magnate's home, this "cozy" Pacific Heights boutique hotel has "tons of character" and "Victorian charm"; the "great staff" helps "you feel at home", and chain-o-phobes cheer for "rooms that can't be found anywhere else", with their four-poster beds, claw-foot tubs and antiques; despite the "old San Francisco" ambiance, there are plenty of "up-to-date amenities", too (WiFi access, complimentary morning limo service), and the Avalon Bar is an urban "oasis."

MANDARIN ORIENTAL ✕ 27 | 27 | 24 | 24 | $505

222 Sansome St., San Francisco; 415-276-9888; fax 415-276-9600; 800-622-0404; www.mandarinoriental.com; 154 rooms, 4 suites

In these "heavenly rooms" "in the sky", "you'll want to stand at the windows all night", savoring the "breathtaking views" of the Golden Gate Bridge (there are even "killer" vistas "from the whirlpool tubs" in the "stunning bathrooms" almost big enough to have "their own zip code"); "service is a differentiating factor" here – well trained" and "super polite" – and Silks restaurant serves "excellent" Asian-Californian cuisine; while the Downtown location "near the Financial District" is convenient for business people, the starry-eyed swear that this "luxurious" tower is "romance writ large."

Mark Hopkins InterContinental Ⓗ 22 | 23 | 20 | 21 | $329

1 Nob Hill, San Francisco; 415-392-3434; fax 415-421-3302; 800-662-4455; www.markhopkins.net; 340 rooms, 40 suites

"If you're feeling swanky", head for this "grand lady" "on top of Nob Hill", a "class act" that's been "a favorite for a weekend getaway" since 1926; "ditch the kids", "go upstairs to the Top of the Mark" to "watch the sunset" and sip "great martinis", then retreat to your "posh room" (the "corner" ones have "sensational views") and if there's anything you need, just ask the "tip-top staff"; even if "the facilities aren't cutting-edge", you'll still be "on top of the world."

Monaco, Hotel ⓢ 22 | 22 | 21 | 20 | $289

501 Geary St., San Francisco; 415-292-0100; fax 415-292-0111; 866-622-5284; www.monaco-sf.com; 168 rooms, 33 suites

"What a fun hotel!" exclaim enthusiasts of this "sleekly designed" Kimpton Group boutique property, where the many "witty touches" make it a "charmer"; there's a "nightly wine reception, with munchies, massages and fortune tellers", "colorful" "eclectic furnishings" and an "attentive" staff that's "not overly in your face"; but beware the "teeny-weeny rooms" that are "too small for two adults to move around in."

Nikko, Hotel 21 | 22 | 20 | 20 | $365

222 Mason St., San Francisco; 415-394-1111; fax 415-394-1106; 800-645-5687; www.hotelnikkosf.com; 510 rooms, 22 suites

"Heaven for the business traveler" may be this "cosmopolitan" hotel near Union Square where "everything works"; you can "escape the rat race" by relaxing in the coolly "modern" "Japanese minimalist" rooms, "soaking in water up to your neck" in the oversized bathtubs and stopping into the sushi bar for "better-than-expected" fin fare; sure, the property may be "unremarkable", but the "staff does everything" "to make your stay pleasant", and the location "is central to all of Downtown San Francisco."

Omni ⓢ 24 | 23 | 19 | 23 | $335

500 California St., San Francisco; 415-677-9494; fax 415-677-4107; 800-843-6664; www.omnisanfrancisco.com; 347 rooms, 15 suites

From the "gorgeous lobby" to the "traditional" rooms with "high-ceilinged marble baths", this "gem in the Financial District" retains the "classy" feel of its former life as a 1920s bank; the "respectful staff" pays "attention to detail", and Bob's Bar is a "fun" spot to hang out (the restaurant serves respectable steaks, too); since it's "within walking distance to everything", it's a "great choice for business travelers."

Palace Hotel ⓗⓢ 22 | 22 | 22 | 23 | $539

2 New Montgomery St., San Francisco; 415-512-1111; fax 415-543-0671; 888-625-5144; www.sfpalace.com; 518 rooms, 34 suites

"It's not called the Palace for nothing", laud loyalists of this "well-preserved historic hotel", an 1875 "grande dame" that's "as elegant as it gets"; your "jaw will drop" at the "gorgeous public spaces", "especially the Garden Court" dining room with its "glass ceiling"; the staff gives you the "royal treatment", so sink into the "sumptuous beds", and you'll "feel like a mogul" at this "Bay Area classic."

Palomar, Hotel 24 | 22 | 26 | 19 | $409

12 Fourth St., San Francisco; 415-348-1111; fax 415-348-0302; 866-373-4941; www.hotelpalomar.com; 182 rooms, 16 suites

At this "swank" boutique hotel south of Market that "attracts those in-the-know", be sure to check out the "divine" Fifth Floor

Restaurant, an "epicurean dream come true" serving "fabulous" New French fare; after dinner, head to your "hip, stylish room" done up with "dark mahogany wood", "faux leopard-skin carpets" and complimentary WiFi access; there aren't a ton of amenities, but "what they do have is good", and the surprisingly "friendly staff" keeps things "upbeat."

Pan Pacific San Francisco, The 24 23 20 22 $369

500 Post St., San Francisco; 415-771-8600; fax 415-398-0267; 800-327-8585; www.panpac.com; 296 rooms, 33 suites

"Bring the Rolls around" sigh surveyors who savor the "top-notch service" at this "elegant", "modern" hotel, where conveniences include "complimentary chauffeured cars", in-room "butler call buttons" and "central location" near Union Square that's ideal "for business travelers and tourists alike"; "everyone from the doorman to the room-service staff is polite", and guests revel in "luxurious amenities" that range from Bose radios to "oversized marble bathrooms" to your choice of pillows.

Park Hyatt 25 25 21 22 $315

333 Battery St., San Francisco; 415-392-1234; fax 415-421-2433; 800-233-1234; www.parksanfrancisco.hyatt.com; 342 rooms, 18 suites

The "caring staff" that "treats guests with genuine interest" "makes business travel special" at this "clublike hotel at the edge of the Financial District" where the contemporary rooms have a certain "masculine elegance" with "lots of marble everywhere"; the Park Grill serves up "reliable" New American fare, and there's a "state-of-the-art fitness center" too, so the "low glitz, high efficiency" style makes this a road warriors' "favorite."

Petite Auberge 20 24 20 14 $199

863 Bush St., San Francisco; 415-928-6000; fax 415-673-7214; 800-365-3004; www.petiteaubergesf.com; 25 rooms, 1 suite

A "respite from the hustle and bustle of the city", this "homey" inn is a "welcome change of pace from the big venues" (though "not if you're looking for a hip hangout"), offering "killer breakfasts" and "small" rooms with "lots of teddy bears" that make you "feel like you're home"; while some makeover mavens feel a "renovation is needed", others marvel at how "well maintained" it is.

Prescott Hotel, The 20 25 26 18 $189

545 Post St., San Francisco; 415-563-0303; fax 415-563-6831; 866-271-3632; www.prescotthotel.com; 132 rooms, 32 suites

"You can't beat the food" at this "European-style" boutique property attached to Wolfgang Puck's "marvelous" restaurant, Postrio, "right in Union Square"; the Club Floor is "especially worth it" for the "free drinks and hors d'oeuvres" ("be sure to get a pizza!") and the service is "impeccable"; though some grouse about the "smallish" guestrooms ("not enough room to swing a cat"), they "serve their purpose."

Rex 20 21 15 19 $229

562 Sutter St., San Francisco; 415-433-4434; fax 415-433-3695; 800-433-4434; www.thehotelrex.com; 92 rooms, 2 suites

Those who "prefer funk over formality" are drawn to this very "affordable" "European flavored" hotel "perfectly located in the Theater District right near Union Square"; "abstract art covering the walls", "well-kept, cool and arty rooms" and "friendly, personal small-town service", as well as "little touches" such as "free nightly wine and cheese", all lend it "great personality and style."

RITZ-CARLTON, THE 26 | 27 | 26 | 26 | $395

600 Stockton St., San Francisco; 415-296-7465; fax 415-291-0288; 800-241-3333; www.ritzcarlton.com; 194 rooms, 100 suites, 42 suites

"Everything is first-rate" at this "superb" hotel full of English "old-world charm"; it exemplifies "what a Ritz should be" with "subdued rooms" and "suites that are a treat", "fabulous food" and an "impeccable" staff at the Ritz-Carlton Dining Room; though the "killer walk up and down the hill to get anywhere" is as "steep" as its prices, the location offers "easy access to shopping and Fisherman's Wharf, Chinatown and fantastic restaurants."

Serrano Hotel 21 | 21 | 17 | 17 | $339

405 Taylor St., San Francisco; 415-885-2500; fax 415-474-4879; 866-289-6561; www.serranohotel.com; 217 rooms, 19 suites

"Small rooms with big style", a "fun lobby" where guests gather for wine tastings, an "ever-helpful staff" and the convenience of Ponzu, the "lively Asian" restaurant next door, make Kimpton's "cute boutique hotel" in the Theater District a "cool" choice for a "weekend getaway"; admirers delight in the colorful decor that's "hip" in a Spanish revival "baroque sort of way" and given the "reasonable rates" suggest "spring for the suite or corner room."

Stanford Court Renaissance Hotel, The 20 | 21 | 19 | 20 | $189

905 California St., San Francisco; 415-989-3500; fax 415-391-0513; 800-468-3571; www.renaissancehotels.com; 371 rooms, 22 suites

"Clang, clang" go the cable cars at this "sentimental favorite" in an "ideal" Nob Hill location at the "intersection of two trolley lines"; "bask in the understated elegance" enhanced by a "magnificent Tiffany stained-glass" dome in the lobby and "spacious rooms" with "all the amenities of a well-run hotel" along with "personable service"; but the less courtly feel it's "not what it used to be."

VINTNERS INN 26 | 25 | 27 | 23 | $275

4350 Barnes Rd., Santa Rosa; 707-575-7350; fax 707-575-1426; 800-421-2584; www.vintnersinn.com; 38 rooms, 6 suites

"Who doesn't want to have breakfast outside overlooking a beautiful vineyard?" query the contented who find this inn with an "amazing location" "better than staying with the Napa Valley crowds"; the "lovely" rooms, in-room spa services, nearby tennis and golf and "outstanding food" at John Ash & Co. win over wine-loving patrons, but a few still pop their corks over the lack of a pool.

Vitale, Hotel – | – | – | – | $270

8 Mission St., San Francisco; 415-278-3700; fax 415-278-3750; 888-890-8688; www.hotelvitale.com; 8 suites, 191 rooms

Opened in March 2005, this tranquil urban hotel sits in the now hot Embarcadero and features muted earth tones and a very easygoing vibe; expect those ubiquitous flat-screen TVs, along with sweeping Bay views (from some rooms), a penthouse yoga studio, American cuisine utilizing ingredients from the local Farmer's Market at chef Paul Arenstam's Americano restaurant and a circular cocktail lounge with 180-degree vistas.

Westin St. Francis, The 21 | 21 | 19 | 21 | $409
335 Powell St., San Francisco; 415-397-7000; fax 415-774-0124; 888-625-5144; www.westin.com; 1130 rooms, 65 suites
"The common rooms hearken back to San Francisco's golden age" at this "old, stately", "lush" "legend" with "all the bells and whistles", but guests are split over which part to stay in: nostalgists "prefer the older section, overlooking Union Square" – the "rooms are smaller, but have a connection to the hotel's legacy" – while modernists like the "chic charm" of the tower rooms; still, "views from the glassed-in elevator", a "perfect location" and a "classy afternoon tea" are appreciated by most.

White Swan Inn 24 | 23 | 17 | 16 | $179
845 Bush St., San Francisco; 415-775-1755; fax 415-775-5717; 800-999-9570; www.whiteswaninnsf.com; 23 rooms, 3 suites
It's "rare to find a cozy B&B in a big city" muse admirers who swan about this "very English", "magical" "gem" atop Nob Hill with a "Victorian atmosphere", advising "stay here for a taste of the good life"; "charming, quaint" rooms with working fireplaces, "wine and appetizers at dusk", "homemade items on the breakfast" menu and a renovated parlor all add up to an "absolutely lovely" experience that "far exceeds expectations."

W San Francisco 24 | 21 | 21 | 22 | $429
181 Third St., San Francisco; 415-777-5300; fax 415-817-7823; 877-946-8357; www.whotels.com; 414 rooms, 9 suites
"Imaginative furniture and use of color" "straight out of a Picasso painting" make this "super-chic hotel" as "fresh and hip as the San Francisco Museum of Modern Art" next door; the "Zen-like", "ultraplush" accommodations boast "intoxicatingly comfortable beds" ("beg, borrow and steal your way into a corner room") and "good times will no doubt be had" at the "always bumpin'" XYZ bar, "awesome restaurant" and "fitness room accessible 24/7"; if a few pout "cool, yes, comfortable, no", most just "want to move in"; N.B. a Bliss spa was added post-*Survey*.

San Jose

De Anza, Hotel 21 | 21 | 19 | 18 | $399
233 W. Santa Clara St.; 408-286-1000; fax 408-286-0500; 800-843-3700; www.hoteldeanza.com; 91 rooms, 9 suites
A "lovely, handsomely restored" hotel, this Downtown "gem" "with its own character" is a "refreshing respite" from the "cookie-cutter chains"; loyalists "love the feel of its historic past" re-created through "unique" details in the lobby and in the "hip", "well-decorated rooms" with several different layouts; other benefits include an "efficient" staff, an "excellent restaurant" and a 'Raid the Pantry' late-night amenity that's a "lifesaver when arriving in the wee hours."

Fairmont San Jose 24 | 21 | 21 | 23 | $259
170 S. Market St.; 408-998-1900; fax 408-287-1648; 800-866-5577; www.fairmont.com; 731 rooms, 74 suites
"Stay here when you're in SJ for business and you may never go home" attest admirers of this Silicon Valley Downtown "favorite" with "amazing rooms" in the newer tower that feature "large marble bathrooms"; the "popular lobby lounge is great for casual

meetings", the "pool could be at a Caribbean resort" and "dining and service are excellent"; but insiders confide watch out for "outrageous crowds when a convention is in town."

Lodge at Cordevalle – – – – $575

One CordeValle Club Dr., San Martin; 408-695-4500; fax 408-695-4578; 877-255-2626; www.cordevalle.com; 28 rooms, 5 suites, 3 houses

This Auberge Resorts property 30 minutes south of San Jose spares no expense: it features a championship, Robert Trent Jones, Jr. golf course and modern bungalows and fairway homes, complete with Frette linens, flat-screen TVs, DVD/CD players, leather couches and fireplaces; there's an on-site spa that offers treatments utilizing locally grown herbs and ingredients, and several restaurants from fine dining to casual.

San Luis Obispo

Apple Farm 21 22 18 18 $149

2015 Monterey St.; 805-544-2040; fax 805-544-2513; 800-255-2040; www.applefarm.com; 104 rooms

"Very charming and folksy", this "country-themed", "relaxing escape on the Central Coast" provides "an oasis for the modern traveler" with a "small spa", "good ol' homestyle" "hearty dining" and "spacious", "quaint" Victorian rooms with canopy beds, fireplaces, robes and apple cider ("you can't help but fall in love"); but it's a "little too cutesy-pie" and "corny" "for some tastes", in fact, the frill-resistant say it "screams Laura Ashley" and consider the restaurant "nothing more than a glorified diner."

Santa Barbara

Andalucia, Hotel – – – – $325

31 West Carrillo St.; 805-884-0300; fax 805-884-8153; www.andaluciasb.com; 77 rooms, 20 suites

Spanish Mediterranean meets modern boutique (read: heavy wooden beams, subdued pastels and wrought-iron chandeliers) at this Downtown Santa Barbara inn, which touts its impressive contemporary (and local) fine art collection; El Cielo – the name of both the rooftop pool and the lounge – might be the best spot in town for a sunset cocktail, with commanding views of the Pacific Ocean, Channel Islands and Santa Ynez mountains.

BACARA RESORT & SPA, THE 27 24 23 27 $425

8301 Hollister Ave.; 805-968-0100; fax 805-968-1800; 877-422-4245; www.bacararesort.com; 311 rooms, 49 suites

"Synonymous with tranquility, indulgence and luxury", this "sparkling white" "dreamy resort" overlooking the ocean north of Santa Barbara is the "ultimate" escape for Angelinos, movie stars and anyone looking to "truly relax"; a "million little touches make it unforgettable", including the "luxuriant grounds", "spectacular" Spanish-style rooms with "comfy feather beds under mounds of pillows" and Frette linens, the "elegant pool" made for "basking in chaise lounges", "out-of-this-world spa" and "great cuisine" at Miró restaurant; still, a few find the "beach not as picturesque" as expected.

El Encanto Hotel 18 22 23 19 $269

1900 Lausen Rd.; 805-687-5000; fax 805-687-3903; 800-346-7039; www.elencantohotel.com; 59 rooms, 15 suites, 10 villas

"The true essence" of town can be found at this "classic" with "panache" "perched on a hillside" overlooking the Mission Santa Barbara where "rambling gardens" "make you feel like a celebrity getting away from it all"; a recent takeover by Orient-Express Hotels prompts a 10-month shuttering of the property for major renovations beginning in fall 2006; until then, guests can enjoy the "fantastic" Cal-French restaurant, "spacious suites" and "Craftsman-style bungalows with sweet porches."

FOUR SEASONS RESORT SANTA BARBARA 24 27 25 26 $550

1260 Channel Dr.; 805-969-2261; fax 805-565-8323; 800-332-3442; www.fourseasons.com; 148 rooms, 13 suites, 46 cottages

This "fabulous" Spanish Colonial hacienda near the beach is "truly a playground paradise" complete with "luxurious" bungalows, "cloud"-like mattresses, "gorgeous grounds", a "sparkling spa", "fantastic" dining (it was voted No. 1 for Decor in Santa Barbara in our *LA Restaurant Survey*) and a "lovely kids' program"; "face spritzers by the poolside keep you fresh", and "just when you thought it couldn't get any better, you experience the lavish" oceanside Sunday brunch – "so decadent!"; P.S. "if you're a light sleeper, avoid the cottages near the train tracks."

Montecito Inn 18 21 21 17 $225

1295 Coast Village Rd.; 805-969-7854; fax 805-969-0623; 800-843-2017; www.montecitoinn.com; 51 rooms, 10 suites

"Like Charlie Chaplin" (the original owner), this "charming" inn run by a "gracious" staff is "a classic"; guests love the "gem of a location", "walking distance to the town and beach", and The Café, which "caters to the Santa Barbara ladies-who-lunch crowd" with "upscale" Californian cuisine; though the suites "with huge marble baths" are "superb" "for a rendezvous", critics complain that other rooms are cursed with "paper-thin walls."

SAN YSIDRO RANCH 26 26 25 24 $339

900 San Ysidro Ln.; 805-565-1700; fax 805-565-1995; 800-368-6788; www.sanysidroranch.com; 40 rooms

"Honeymoon here as often as you can" coo lovebirds who alight at this "legendary" "hideaway of JFK and Jackie", now a Relaix & Châteaux retreat in the Montecito foothills, where everyone's "treated like millionaires"; while "famous for its secluded cottages" that "fit like an elegant glove", this "romantic", "luxuriously exclusive camp" also offers "gorgeous large rooms" with "oodles of pillows and a fireplace too", a "quiet-on-weekdays pool", "nearby hiking trails" and horseback riding.

SIMPSON HOUSE INN 26 27 24 25 $585

121 E. Arrellaga St.; 805-963-7067; fax 805-564-4811; 800-676-1280; www.simpsonhouseinn.com; 15 rooms

Reminiscent of a "Merchant Ivory film" sigh those smitten by this "predictably enchanting", "picturesque B&B", an East-lake–style 1874 Victorian estate with "wonderful" English gardens "near the center of town", "superb breakfasts" on the porch and "warm, attentive service"; rooms "range from small and cute to large and grand, but the deluxe experience is to take one of the cottages in the back" – it's "so cozy and offers such a nice change from a regular hotel" you can't help but "wish nobody else knew about it."

Upham Hotel 20 | 21 | 22 | 17 | $250

1404 De La Vina St.; 805-962-0058; fax 805-963-2825; 800-727-0876; www.uphamhotel.com; 41 rooms, 9 cottages

"Lovely" and "distinctive", this recently renovated 1871 Victorian inn near the State Street shops is said to be California's longest continuously running hotel; the "European-style" rooms are "small, but the charming antiques and unique touches make up for the lack of space", and it's worth getting up for breakfast.

Solvang

Alisal Guest Ranch & Resort 20 | 23 | 21 | 27 | $435

1054 Alisal Rd.; 805-688-6411; fax 805-688-2510; 800-425-4725; www.alisal.com; 36 rooms, 37 suites

Providing a "rustic getaway" with "terrific service", this "classy dude ranch" 35 miles northwest of Santa Barbara offers "lots of activities to keep everyone" busy; dating back to 1946, with no TVs or phones, it's a "wonderful time warp" and the "perfect" place to "make believe you're a cowboy"; saddle up for a ride through the Santa Ynez Valley, head to the "petting zoo" or enjoy the "great golf" and tennis.

Fess Parker's Wine Country Inn & Spa Ⓢ 20 | 20 | 19 | 20 | $360

2860 Grand Ave., Los Olivos; 805-688-7788; fax 805-688-1942; 800-446-2455; www.fessparker.com; 19 rooms, 2 suites

It's "just a delight" attest admirers of this "romantic getaway" in a "quaint town" in Santa Ynez Valley about five miles from Solvang (28 miles north of Santa Barbara), "near many wineries, including, of course, Mr. Parker's"; the "restaurant tries hard to please", even offering guests free breakfast and dinner, "masseuses are first-rate" (you can even "treat Fido" to a rubdown) and the "grounds are lovely"; still, a few shrug it's in "need of an interior overhaul."

Sonoma

Applewood Inn Ⓗ 20 | 21 | 23 | 20 | $185

13555 Hwy. 116, Guerneville; 707-869-9093; fax 707-869-9170; 800-555-8509; www.applewoodinn.com; 18 rooms

"Incredibly classy and beautiful", this "wonderful retreat" with a "dreamy" setting in a historic house dating back to 1922 on the Russian River is also the home of the La Buona Forchetta cooking school; the "terrific restaurant" features Chef Gabrielle Dery's "excellent" Continental fare and core enthusiasts "like the layout" of the redwood tree–filled property with accommodations facing a terraced garden courtyard.

Bodega Bay Lodge and Spa Ⓢ 21 | 21 | 19 | 21 | $255

103 Coast Hwy., Bodega Bay; 707-875-3525; fax 707-875-2428; 800-368-2468; www.bodegabaylodge.com; 76 rooms, 8 suites

"Wonderfully restful" with a "gorgeous setting" and a "small spa", this "friendly" oceanfront resort in a "rustic" fishing village "feels worlds away from San Francisco", even though it's only one hour north; "start a fire in the fireplace" of your "delightful room" or "stately suite with private patio", then take in the "awesome views" of the Pacific and the Bay, so "romantic it makes snuggling easy"; P.S. the "wine tastings are a plus" at the "excellent" restaurant.

Fairmont Sonoma Mission Inn & Spa 22 | 23 | 21 | 25 | $299

100 Boyes Blvd.; 707-938-9000; fax 707-938-4250; 800-862-4945; www.fairmont.com/sonoma; 166 rooms, 60 suites

Feel "pampered" at this "sanctuary" where the "staff excels" and the "rejuvenating spa" boasts "fantastic treatments" including a "virtual Roman bath house" and "honest-to-goodness" mineral baths, plus an "athletic crew to take you on bike rides through wine country"; "enjoy champagne in your room" ("stay in a romantic suite with a fireplace!"), then go to Santé for a "wonderful dinner."

GAIGE HOUSE INN 27 | 27 | 26 | 25 | $300

13540 Arnold Dr., Glen Ellen; 707-935-0237; fax 707-935-6411; 800-935-0237; www.gaige.com; 9 rooms, 11 suites, 4 cottages

"There are 1,000 reasons to stay" at this "luxurious" Asian-influenced inn in Sonoma, but chef Charles Holmes' "scrumptious" "breakfasts are worth it alone" agree gourmands, who even wake up in time "after too much wine tasting the night before"; the setting near Calabasas Creek with a "beautiful pool area" and whirlpool spa is "absolutely idyllic", the "incredible rooms" are "design masterpieces" ("splurge on a suite separate from the main building" or a "relaxing cottage") and service is "fabulous."

Healdsburg, Hotel 24 | 21 | 24 | 22 | $395

25 Matheson St., Healdsburg; 707-431-2800; fax 707-431-0414; 800-889-7188; www.hotelhealdsburg.com; 49 rooms, 6 suites

At this "chic", "minimalist masterpiece", stylists so adore the rooms that they "want to steal the furnishings", gourmands go gaga for the "fantastic complimentary breakfast" and for Charlie Palmer's "superb" culinary "homage to Sonoma" at Dry Creek Kitchen, and sun-worshipers wallow in the "great little pool area"; but oenophiles probably love this member of Small Luxury Hotels of the World the most because it's in "an ideal location to visit wineries."

Honor Mansion ▽ 22 | 26 | 24 | 26 | $220

14891 Grove St., Healdsburg; 707-433-4277; fax 707-431-7173; 800-554-4667; www.honormansion.com; 5 rooms, 8 suites

"This place is just toooo romantic – so don't go alone" coo canoodlers who insist that this Sonoma County inn, comprised of an 1883 mansion, cottages and suites, "gets better each time"; the "detail-oriented owners think of everything to make you feel at home", from rooms boasting antiques, claw-foot tubs, European linens and secluded porches to "ridiculously rich, delicious breakfasts"; rose gardens and a "koi pond add a soothing touch", plus guests can play croquet and bocce ball.

KENWOOD INN 27 | 28 | 20 | 27 | $400

10400 Sonoma Hwy., Kenwood; 707-833-1293; fax 707-833-1247; 800-353-6966; www.kenwoodinn.com; 27 rooms, 3 suites

"Adam and Eve in paradise is what comes to mind" at this "serene", "little spot" 15 minutes from Sonoma with a center "secret garden", "great pool", a "unique spa" and "fresh fruit and great local wine everywhere you turn"; the "warm hosts" proffer "polite service" while the "romantic" rooms in the Italian-style buildings boast "lovely fireplaces"; since "only breakfast is available", the only interruption to "your dreamy stay" is "having to get other meals."

MacArthur Place 26 | 24 | 18 | 24 | $349

29 E. MacArthur St.; 707-938-2929; fax 707-933-9833; 800-722-1866; www.macarthurplace.com; 33 rooms, 29 suites, 2 cottages

"Bring us back to Sonoma" if we can return to this "perfect B&B" assert surveyors of this "peaceful" wine-country estate that "hits all the right notes"; in the "sumptuous rooms", "the decor says country, but the DVD players, flat-screen TVs and glorious baths are all that modern city-dwellers could ask for", and the staff "bends over backwards to make your stay special"; with "beautiful grounds" and a "luxurious spa", only the Saddles Steakhouse may not live up to the otherwise "outstanding" accolades.

Madrona Manor 23 | 22 | 26 | 21 | $250

1001 Westside Rd., Healdsburg; 707-433-4231; fax 707-433-0703; 800-258-4003; www.madronamanor.com; 22 rooms, 5 suites

Some of "the best dining" in the "Sonoma wine country" may be found at this "quintessential Victorian inn" that's "just like your grandmother's house – if she's a gourmet cook with her own herb garden"; "old-world charm abounds" in this "elegant mansion atop a hill" where you can "hide" in the "tasteful" rooms (some "with fireplaces and Jacuzzi tubs"), and fortunately, the "staff is available" only when you need them; N.B. no kids under 12.

St. Orres 19 | 20 | 26 | 15 | $220

36601 Coast Hwy. 1, Gualala; 707-884-3303; fax 707-884-1840; www.saintorres.com; 8 rooms, 13 cottages

With its "whimsical" Russian-inspired onion-shaped domes, "rustic rooms" with communal bathrooms and "lovely" "detached cabins", this Northern coast "compound" has a "great eclectic feel" akin to a "little enchanted village"; you're "among the redwood trees and stars, but with every creature comfort", from "private hot tubs" to "creative food" at the "outstanding restaurant" (which some say is the "real joy of St. Orres – aside from the flocks of wild turkeys").

Whale Watch Inn 25 | 23 | 16 | 19 | $180

35100 Hwy. 1, Gualala; 707-884-3667; fax 707-884-3100; 800-942-5342; www.whalewatchinn.com; 18 rooms

"How can you resist" an "architecturally fascinating enclave of buildings" "offering both a warm fireplace" and "million-dollar views" of the Pacific with "whales frolicking in the sea" ponder patrons of this "sublime" escape on the Mendocino Coast; there are "no TVs", "so bring your lover or a great book" and relax in your "rustic" rooms; P.S. an "excellent breakfast" is included.

South Bay

Cypress Hotel, The – | – | – | – | $219

10050 S. De Anza Blvd., Cupertino; 408-253-8900; fax 408-253-3800; 800-499-1408; www.thecypresshotel.com; 196 rooms, 28 suites

What a "creative interior" agree guests agog over the "oh-so-hip atmosphere" at the Kimpton Group's Mediterranean villa–style boutique hotel near San Jose with its playful mix of polka dots and patterns along with "leopard-print carpets"; prized for its WiFi access (this is Silicon Valley, after all), wine receptions, an Olympic-sized pool and Helios restaurant, it's a "find in a sea of mediocrity."

Garden Court Hotel 21 | 22 | 17 | 18 | $339

520 Cowper St., Palo Alto; 650-322-9000; fax 650-324-3609; 800-824-9028; www.gardencourt.com; 48 rooms, 14 suites

"Kiss-your-feet service" is the siren call of this "charming" "model for an excellent small-city hotel", located in a "unique spot" in Downtown Palo Alto; though "great for pleasure", it's also "home away from home for business travelers", with high-speed Internet, a "gorgeous courtyard for events" and Il Fornaio restaurant, which "crackles with deal making" ("this is where the venture capital world" holds court); still, a few knock the "amateur" service.

RITZ-CARLTON HALF MOON BAY 26 | 26 | 24 | 27 | $345

1 Miramontes Point Rd., Half Moon Bay; 650-712-7000; fax 650-712-7070; 800-293-0524; www.ritzcarlton.com; 239 rooms, 22 suites

You feel "like you're on the craggy coast of Scotland", with "bagpipes playing on the knoll at sunset" and the "Half Moon Bay fog" rolling in over this "magnificent property" that "sits like a castle on a bluff overlooking the Pacific"; "location, location, location" provides it with "gorgeous views" and an "awe-inspiring cliffside golf course", while the "spectacular" rooms, "excellent" service, "beautiful people and a bountiful bill" are "everything you expect from a Ritz."

Seal Cove Inn ∇ 27 | 25 | 23 | 22 | $325

221 Cypress Ave., Moss Beach; 650-728-4114; fax 650-728-4116; 800-995-9987; www.sealcoveinn.com; 10 rooms

"Beautiful and relaxing", this "romantic" B&B "getaway" owned by guidebook writer Karen Brown and her husband, Rick, is tucked in a seaside village outside Half Moon Bay near secluded beaches, tide pools and those namesake seals, who sun on the rocks of Fitzgerald Marine Reserve (a "haunting scene in black and white"); the "cute" Euro-style rooms are decorated with antiques, plus guests enjoy breakfast, evening wine and hors d'oeuvres.

Stanford Park Hotel 22 | 21 | 17 | 19 | $295

100 El Camino Real, Menlo Park; 650-322-1234; fax 650-322-0975; 800-368-2468; www.stanfordparkhotel.com; 154 rooms, 9 suites

"Homey", "quaint and quiet", this four-story English Colonial and European-style hotel "very close to Stanford University" is a "convenient oasis for business or pleasure"; the "lovely lobby with a big roaring fireplace" feels as "welcoming" as the "friendly staff", "huge" accommodations and "attractive common areas", plus the "food at the Duck Club is quite good"; but some say "beware" of "rooms just inches" from the "noisy train tracks."

W Silicon Valley 28 | 23 | 17 | 21 | $349

8200 Gateway Blvd., Newark; 510-494-8800; fax 510-794-3001; 877-946-8357; www.whotels.com; 172 suites

"So cool, so modern, so cheap on the weekends", this "unique" Silicon Valley location "way off the beaten path" is "worth it if you don't mind" the "15-minute drive from Palo Alto"; the "spacious" fully wired suites have "full kitchen setups", plus there's an outdoor heated pool and a "very helpful" staff; but insiders caution "don't expect the nightlife action the other Ws enjoy", and remember, there are "fine restaurants across Dumbart Bridge."

Yosemite

Ahwahnee, The Ⓗ 20 | 21 | 21 | 25 | $379

Yosemite National Park, Yosemite National Park; 209-372-1407; fax 209-372-1463; www.yosemitepark.com; 93 rooms, 6 suites, 24 cottages

"Lodgelike with that sense of lux" and "down-home service", this "sumptuous wooded retreat" "fits with Yosemite's grandeur" while "hearkening back to a more gracious era"; opt for a "cushy" cottage or a "balcony room for an unequalled view" ("elicits a gasp every time"), and if you can, get dinner tickets for the Bracebridge Christmas celebration – the "U.S. National Park's delicious version of a state lottery"; if a few feel the accommodations and menu "haven't kept up with the times", most shrug, where else can you "dine while watching deer nibble and waterfalls tumble"?

CHÂTEAU DU SUREAU Ⓢ 29 | 29 | 28 | 25 | $550

48688 Victoria Ln., Oakhurst; 559-683-6860; fax 559-683-0800; www.chateaudusureau.com; 12 rooms, 1 villa

"If you can't get to Europe", hotelier/chef Erna Kubin-Clanin's "expensive but amazing" Provençal-style château is "the next best thing!" declare devotees who voted the "unobtrusive" staff that "can't do enough for you" No. 1 for Service in this *Survey*; "nestled in the foothills" of the Sierra Nevada Mountains 20 minutes from Yosemite's southern gate, it's one of the "most romantic spots in the world" – or at least the "ultimate hideaway" with "exquisite" antiques-filled rooms straight "out of Architectural Digest" and "superlative dining" at the Relais Gourmand restaurant; N.B. Spa Sureau opens in September 2006.

Tenaya Lodge Ⓢ 18 | 20 | 18 | 20 | $319

1122 Hwy. 41, Fish Camp, Fish Camp; 559-683-6555; fax 559-683-6147; 800-635-5807; www.tenayalodge.com; 224 rooms, 20 suites

A "wonderful spot" from which to explore Yosemite agree guests who like this "hideaway's" "great proximity" to the park's southern entrance; it's a "relief from the too rustic accommodations nearby" with "not fancy but" "comfy rooms", a "charming lobby" and "pleasant facilities" like "hot tubs that are great to come back to after a day of hiking"; naysayers nix the "non-interesting pool, scarcely there" spa treatments and "blah cuisine."

Colorado

★ **Tops in State**

26 Ritz-Carlton, Bachelor Gulch, *Avon*
Little Nell, *Aspen*
Broadmoor, *Colorado Springs*
St. Regis, *Aspen*
Sonnenalp, *Vail*
25 Lodge & Spa at Cordillera, *Edwards*
23 Teatro, Hotel, *Denver*
Monaco, Hotel, *Denver*

Aspen

Jerome, Hotel 23 | 24 | 23 | 22 | $835

330 E. Main St.; 970-920-1000; fax 970-920-2784; 800-331-7213; www.hoteljerome.com; 76 rooms, 15 suites

Many "notable visitors have stayed" at this "Victorian"-style "treasure" that's "ideally located in the heart" of things and is an "elegant" base "winter or summer"; the "concierge is excellent", the staff "pampers you" and chef Slossberg's food "pleases even the most discriminating" epicures, who recommend a "drink at the J-Bar and climbing into bed" in one of the "spacious" quarters; you might think you "bought the room, not rented it" when you get the bill, but most feel "it's worth it."

LITTLE NELL, THE 27 | 26 | 26 | 26 | $645

675 E. Durant Ave.; 970-920-4600; fax 970-920-4670; 888-843-6355; www.thelittlenell.com; 77 rooms, 15 suites

"Classy, understated" and fortuitously located "at the base of Ajax", this Relais & Châteaux affiliated "European-style gem" is a perennial magnet for "chichi" folk who appreciate the "world-class dining", "top-notch" amenities like the "relaxing pool", staff that "goes beyond the call of duty" and the fact that you can "walk down the hall, put on your boots and get on the gondola"; the "luxury rooms" are "well stocked" and "properly organized for skiers", so despite "super-expensive" tabs, most are ready to "move in and call it home."

LODGE & SPA AT CORDILLERA, THE 25 | 25 | 23 | 27 | $549

2205 Cordillera Way, Edwards; 970-926-2200; fax 970-926-2486; 800-877-3529; www.cordilleralodge.com; 55 rooms, 10 suites

Even before a recent multimillion-dollar renovation, this "top-of-the-line" resort in a "top-of-the-world location" near Vail has had globe-trotters rhapsodizing over the views that go on "for miles", "amazing service", "terrific golf" and "intimate, romantic" quarters; expanded bathrooms, pool and fitness makeovers, furniture and room updates, private patios, a 20,000-sq.-ft. destination spa and a European bistro should distract those who complain "there's nothing going on" in its "middle-of-nowhere" location.

RITZ-CARLTON, BACHELOR GULCH 27 | 26 | 23 | 29 | $575

0130 Daybreak Ridge, Avon; 970-748-6200; fax 970-748-6300; 800-576-5582; www.ritzcarlton.com; 208 rooms, 29 suites

If you "want to avoid the crowds and hype of Beaver Creek and Vail", consider this "luxury" resort that resembles a "log cabin on steroids"; perks include "excellent" ski valets, an "amazing" spa, a "lively bar" and "great golf" at the Red Sky Club; if a few say the "secluded site" is "inconvenient for die-hard skiers" and dining is "not up to Ritz standards", they're overshadowed by loyalists who insist it's a "can't-miss treat."

Sky Hotel ∇ 15 | 14 | – | 18 | $329

709 E. Durant St.; 970-925-6760; fax 970-925-6778; 800-882-2582; www.theskyhotel.com; 84 rooms, 6 suites

"Small and very hip", this pet-friendly boutique hotel betrays the "trademark quirky style" of the Kimpton Group in its "cozy" "medium-size" rooms stocked with Frette linens and Aveda bath products and in the "great bar, lounge" and lobby, which hosts "wine tastings nightly"; while there's no on-site dining, morning coffee is offered and although it's a relative "value in a killer location", its assets are undercut by "nonexistent service" and what design-snobs deem a "cobbled-together" look.

ST. REGIS 26 | 26 | 25 | 26 | $850

315 E. Dean St.; 970-920-3300; fax 970-925-8998; 888-454-9005; www.stregisaspen.com; 156 rooms, 23 suites

"Superb in every way", this "rustic-luxury" resort at the base of Aspen Mountain welcomes guests with its "beautiful" lobby warmed by a "roaring fire", "thoughtful concierge", "gracious" service and "plush" accommodations furnished with "perfect beds"; after hitting the slopes or following a workout in the "enormous" gym, head to the new Remede spa or for a "great" dinner at Olives followed by drinks at the "amazing" bar; yes, it's "expensive, but what in this town isn't?"; N.B. a post-*Survey* refurbishment may outdate some of the above scores.

Beaver Creek

Beaver Creek Lodge 23 | 22 | 19 | 26 | $409

26 Avondale Ln.; 970-845-9800; fax 970-845-8242; 800-525-7280; www.beavercreeklodge.net; 72 suites

Nestled amid the "spectacular surroundings", this "absolutely beautiful place" is "fun" snow or sun, as there's "lots to do nearby" including skiing and skating, swinging your clubs on the "fun mountainside golf course" and "upscale shopping"; the "terrific amenities" encompass an indoor/outdoor pool (bolstered by access to the Charter at Beaver Creek's spa), and service is "top-notch", with the only weakness being the "thin" on-site dining options; N.B. post-*Survey* upgrades include the addition of new LCD, flat-screen TVs and a rock climbing wall.

Charter at Beaver Creek, The ▽ 24 | 19 | 19 | 23 | $450

120 Offerson Rd.; 970-949-6660; fax 970-949-4667; 800-525-6660; www.thecharter.com; 65 rooms, 115 condos

Boasting a "fabulous setting", this "relaxed vacation spot" comprises a "variety of condo suites" "so close" to the slopes that "you can almost roll out of bed and onto the lifts"; while most "love the staff and spa" and agree that rooms are a "solid value", eagle eyes warn accommodations "don't always resemble those in the brochures" as "furnishings vary depending on the unit's owners"; still, it's all about the "ski-in/ski-out" location.

Inn at Beaver Creek ▽ 25 | 23 | 21 | 23 | $518

10 Elk Track Ln.; 970-845-7800; fax 970-845-5279; 800-859-8242; www.vbcrp.com; 45 rooms, 1 condo

"It just doesn't get any better" than having doorstep access to the Strawberry Park Express chairlift say die-hard skiers who praise this intimate, "expensive" lodge located within walking distance to shops and restaurants in the village; assets include concierge service, fitness facilities, a heated outdoor swimming pool and use of a Robert Trent Jones Jr. golf course as well as the facilities at its sister properties.

Park Hyatt | 23 | 22 | 20 | 28 | $700

136 E. Thomas Pl.; 970-949-1234; fax 970-827-6796; 800-233-1234; www.beavercreek.hyatt.com; 269 rooms, 36 suites
"Just a snowball throw from the lift" is this "family"-oriented resort featuring a "fantastic" Allegria spa, a "storybook setting" and "pampering at every turn" from the "friendly" staff that sees that your "boots are warmed" and "skis waiting"; rooms are "tasteful", if "standard Hyatt", and those with a fireplace "worth the extra buck", and while dining is "marginal", the "great lobby for après-activity drinks" and the outdoor fire pit are pluses.

Pines Lodge | ∇ 26 | 25 | 26 | 23 | $629

141 Scott Hill Rd.; 970-845-7900; fax 970-845-7809; 866-605-7625; www.pineslodge.com; 60 rooms
Located on the "fringe of Beaver Creek Village", this rustic retreat "has it all", including ski-in/ski-out mountain access; most notably, it also has the highly regarded Grouse Mountain Grill, a "super" regional American restaurant that "serves everything you could ever want"; if some pout that the accommodations "need an update" and the "hot tub facilities could use a face-lift", most opine that the staff is "attentive" and deem it an overall "great value."

Clark

Home Ranch | – | – | – | – | $350

54880 RCR 129; 970-879-1780; fax 970-879-1795; www.homeranch.com; 6 rooms, 8 cabins
Bunking at this Relais & Châteaux–affiliated ranch in a "beautiful part of northwest Colorado" near Steamboat Springs is "fun for the whole family, especially if you horseback ride"; but there are also plenty of non-equine activities like hiking, cross-country skiing, relaxing in private hot tubs outside the well-appointed cabins or in the sauna and pool off the main lodge, and enjoying "great food" at the on-site, guests-only restaurant.

Colorado Springs

BROADMOOR, THE | 25 | 26 | 25 | 28 | $325

1 Lake Ave.; 719-634-7711; fax 719-577-5700; 800-634-7711; www.broadmoor.com; 593 rooms, 107 suites
"Premium comfort" and the "glory of the Rockies" are in abundance at this Colorado Springs "lap of luxury" whose "sprawling" grounds include "world-class" tennis and golf facilities and an "excellent" renovated spa that "keep you occupied for days" and permit "conventioneers and leisure travelers to coexist" in harmony; each one of the "incredible restaurants" is "better than the next" and the staff is "gracious", but "pampering has its cost."

Cliff House at Pikes Peak | ∇ 26 | 23 | 26 | 22 | $199

306 Canon Ave., Manitou Springs; 719-685-3000; fax 719-685-3913; 888-212-7000; www.thecliffhouse.com; 17 studios, 38 suites
So, this boutique hotel in historic Manitou Springs "doesn't have a pool and on-demand movies", but the "lovely grounds" and "superb" in-room perks like "VCRs, spa tubs and gas fireplaces" in some make this "*the* place" for a "romantic, comfortable, relaxing weekend away from it all"; P.S. the dining room dishes out "some of the best food in Colorado", with "breakfasts that can't be beat."

Denver

Boulderado, Hotel Ⓗ 20 21 22 19 $195

2115 13th St., Boulder; 303-442-4344; fax 303-442-4378; 800-433-4344; www.boulderado.com; 139 rooms, 21 suites

"Is that Wyatt Earp in the lobby" quip those "charmed" by this "beautifully restored" National Landmark hotel "in the heart of Downtown Boulder" that may not offer the level of "luxury" found at some of its neighbors but is a "memorable" place to "dine, drink beer and hang out"; "one-of-a-kind" trademarks include the "knockout lobby" and "historic rooms" that may entail "carrying your luggage through a labyrinth" of corridors but nonetheless are preferable to the "motel"-like "newer rooms."

Brown Palace Hotel ⒽⓈ 21 24 23 21 $289

321 17th St.; 303-297-3111; fax 303-312-5900; 800-321-2599; www.brownpalace.com; 190 rooms, 51 suites

Enter a "Victorian daydream" via this circa-1892 "grande dame" where guests alight in a "spectacular" lobby that's the backdrop for "afternoon tea rivaling the best in London" and the pervading "regal" vibe means it's "not a place for toddlers"; service is "accommodating", and even if a couple of nitpickers note the "rooms vary widely", most agree it's "aging well."

C Lazy U Ranch – – – – $311

3640 Colorado Hwy. 125, Granby; 970-887-3344; fax 970-887-3917; www.clazyu.com; 43 rooms

Since 1947, this 8,000-acre dude ranch west of Denver has coddled little cowpokes and their parents with a wealth of family-friendly activities ranging from riding programs and fly fishing to paddle-boating; accommodations feature Southwestern-style furnishings, plush robes, fresh fruit baskets and luxurious bath amenities, and most even have fireplaces; regional specialties are served in the rustic restaurant, followed by fireside entertainment; N.B. per-night rates are based on a required minimum weeklong stay.

Inverness Hotel ∇ 20 22 21 24 $309

200 Inverness Dr., W, Englewood; 303-799-5800; fax 303-799-5874; 800-832-9053; www.invernesshotel.com; 284 rooms, 18 suites

An "excellent place to work and play" is the word on this resort south of Denver that has "very good convention facilities" and prime access to the Inverness golf course onto which some of the rooms look; non-duffers might find the "location boring", but they can at least enjoy the "awesome suites", "free broadband" and "efficient" service.

JW Marriott Denver at Cherry Creek Ⓢ – – – – $209

150 Clayton Ln.; 303-316-2700; fax 303-316-4697; 800-228-9290; www.jwmarriottdenver.com; 191 rooms, 5 suites

Smack in the middle of Cherry Creek, Denver's trendiest area for well-heeled scenesters, this elegant, pet-friendly boutique-style hotel sports oversized rooms equipped with flat-screen TVs, DVD/CD players and kaleidoscopic color schemes, and many offer views of the Rocky Mountains and Downtown skyline; Mirepoix restaurant showcases chef Bryan Moscatello's creative American cuisine, and the European spa delivers luxe treatments.

Marriott South, Denver ▽ 20 | 22 | 15 | 19 | $179
10345 Park Meadows Dr., Littleton; 303-925-0004; fax 303-925-0005; 800-228-9290; www.marriott.com; 276 rooms, 3 suites
It's "very un-Marriott" note corporate types of this "beautifully decorated" "business stop" "stuck in the midst of the Tech Center" south of Denver; location aside, it's a "wonderful building" and a "terrific value" with a "great bar and restaurant", "spacious lobby" and "good service"; amenities include an indoor pool, fitness center and in-room high-speed Internet for those who can't leave their laptops at home.

Monaco, Hotel Ⓢ 26 | 24 | 23 | 21 | $289
1717 Champa St.; 303-296-1717; fax 303-296-1818; 800-990-1303; www.monaco-denver.com; 157 rooms, 32 suites
The "resident Jack Russell Terrier adds her own welcome" at this "centrally located" and "wonderfully quirky, pet-friendly" Kimpton Group hotel that dispenses complimentary wine during its "fun" evening get-togethers; "business and personal travelers" on the same "funky" wavelength dig the "big" rooms' "Moroccan whorehouse-fantasy" trappings and "fantastic beds" and praise the Aveda spa and Panzano restaurant.

Omni Interlocken Ⓢ ▽ 21 | 24 | 19 | 22 | $230
500 Interlocken Blvd., Broomfield; 303-438-6600; fax 303-438-7224; 800-843-6664; www.omnihotels.com; 378 rooms, 12 suites
"Convenient for both Boulder and Denver", this chain hotel has "expansive views" of the Rockies, a 27-hole championship golf course, a new pool and nearby hiking and biking trails that help negate the pervading "corporate feel"; expect an "efficient" staff and "above-average", "comfortable rooms", with leisure-seekers urging "check out the spa" and cruise the "neighboring mall", which has both shops and restaurants.

Oxford Hotel Ⓗ Ⓢ 19 | 22 | 22 | 19 | $209
1600 17th St.; 303-628-5400; fax 303-628-5413; 800-228-5838; www.theoxfordhotel.com; 79 rooms, 1 suite
Revel in "19th-century charm" at this "quaint" boutique address that "makes you imagine you're a guest at the home of a wealthy aunt" and is the oldest continuously operating hotel in Denver; if a few feel it's "time to refurbish", most find it has "lots of personality", with "charming antiques", one of "the best martini bars in the Rockies", a neighboring spa and a "good" McCormick's seafood restaurant – in short, it "deserves its spot on the National Register of Historic Places."

Teatro, Hotel ✕ 25 | 23 | 24 | 22 | $235
1100 14th St.; 303-228-1100; fax 303-228-1101; 888-727-1200; www.hotelteatro.com; 103 rooms, 8 suites
Located "right next to the Denver Center for the Performing Arts", this "high-class" yet "funky" boutique hotel (a member of Small Luxury Hotels of the World) pleases theater-buffs with its "many luxury touches" like "aromatherapy baths, yoga-on-demand", down comforters and pillow preferences; a "helpful staff" ministers to guests and their pets, while foodies feast on New American at Restaurant Kevin Taylor.

Westin Tabor Center 21 20 17 20 $299

1672 Lawrence St.; 303-572-9100; fax 303-572-7288; 800-937-8461; www.westin.com; 421 rooms, 9 suites

This "sophisticated" "business-travelers' standby" has a "superb location right on the 16th Street pedestrian mall" and "many fun things to do within walking distance"; while some call it "sterile"-looking, others counter "it's wonderfully comfortable" and has service that "makes you feel right at home"; a word of advice: "skip the on-site dining as there's much better in Denver."

Keystone

Keystone Resort 21 20 19 24 $330

22010 Hwy. 6; 970-496-4000; fax 970-496-4215; 888-222-9298; www.keystone.snow.com; 255 rooms, 1173 condos

"A very solid place for a family ski trip" or a "summer vacation" centered on "trail rides", hiking and "walking along the Colorado River", this resort features a range of different lodging options plus a "gorgeous conference center"; the "rustic" rooms are "large", "neat" and "well equipped", if "a bit shopworn" (some updating is planned), and the "varied dining choices" get a mixed billing; still, most appreciate the "relaxed" feel and the ski-in/ski-out access.

Montrose

Elk Mountain Resort – – – – $350

97 Elk Walk; 970-252-4900; 877-355-9255; www.elkmountainresort.com; 21 rooms, 18 cottages

Expect to keep busy at this 275-acre resort, where a vast array of activities – fishing, rock climbing, tennis, mountain bike riding, canoeing, skiing, zooming around on ATVs – is available; but some choose to head right for the Valhalla Shooting Club, where guests can play James Bond for a day, learning proper shooting methods and self-defense tactics; accommodations incude rooms with wood walls, 450-thread-count linens and soaking tubs as well as individual 2,600-sq.-ft. cottages; the main eatery, Tarragon, serves regional and Alpine Pyrenee fare.

Snowmass

Snowmass Club ∇ 21 22 19 26 $650

0239 Snowmass Club Circle, Snowmass Village; 970-923-5600; 800-525-0710; www.snowmassclub.com; 54 villas

"Convenient to the Aspen mountains" and blessed with "great views", this private residence complex offers various membership and accommodation options; the affiliated facilities, like the athletic club, tennis courts and James Engh golf course, are "terrific" and those in-the-know claim "it's a great bargain off season" when, "for the price of a room, you might get a luxury condo."

Stonebridge Inn ∇ 18 20 15 21 $249

300 Carriage Way, Snowmass Village; 970-923-2420; fax 970-923-5889; 800-213-3214; www.stonebridgeinn.com; 87 rooms, 5 suites

For a "family vacation" near Snowmass Village, this "cozy, friendly hotel with a pleasant staff" does the trick; just "don't expect any special services" caution high-maintenance critics who lament that it's "not luxurious" and the "rooms are rather average" (a renovation was completed post-*Survey*); still, complimentary breakfast and après-ski soup, a "heated outdoor pool and happenin' hot tub make up" for shortcomings.

Steamboat Springs

Steamboat Grand Resort ▽ 22 | 22 | 17 | 26 | $303

2300 Mt. Werner Circle; 970-871-5500 ; fax 970-871-5501 ; 877-306-2628; www.steamboatgrand.com; 31 studios, 296 rooms

Square footage is what counts at this "perfect family hotel" in a "fantastic" Steamboat location "on the slopes", so make sure to ask for one of the "apartment-sized" suites or else you might get stuck with a "minuscule" "standard" room with "no space for a suitcase"; dining isn't tops, but after a day swishing through powder, you can "relax" in the "great Jacuzzi and bar."

Telluride

Ice House Lodge – | – | – | – | $430

310 S. Fir; 970-728-6300; fax 970-728-6358; 800-544-3436; www.icehouselodge.com; 28 rooms, 16 condos, 8 suites

Set in a "breathtaking locale" and "convenient to town and the gondolas", this Southwestern-themed hotel entices sore-muscled skiers with its heated pool, hot tub and steam room and satisfies business-types with its conference room facilities and high-speed Internet; although there's no gym or on-site dining other than for breakfast, there's a well-stocked après-ski bar plus La Marmotte French restaurant next door.

Inn at Lost Creek – | – | – | – | $625

119 Lost Creek Ln.; 970-728-5678; fax 970-728-7953; 888-601-5678; www.innatlostcreek.com; 19 rooms, 8 suites, 3 studios

Patrons of this Western-style boutique hotel laud its "beautiful setting", highly regarded 9545 restaurant and "spacious" rooms that are variably equipped with jetted tubs, stereos, WiFi, stone fireplaces, kitchens and balconies with mountain views; a "top-notch" place to stay "anytime of the year", it's in its prime in winter when snowflakes fall upon the rooftop's outdoor spas and the easy gondola access is a boon.

Telluride, Hotel – | – | – | – | $429

199 N. Cornet St.; 970-369-1188; fax 970-369-1292; 866-468-3501; www.thehoteltelluride.com; 54 rooms, 4 suites

If Ralph Lauren needed a place to crash in Telluride, he might choose this rustic-chic boutique hotel (a member of Small Luxury Hotels of the World) whose accommodations come equipped with custom furnishings, refrigerators, Aveda spa amenities, down comforters and balconies opening to the San Juan Mountains; a full-service spa, bistro and bar are all on the premises.

Wyndham Peaks 24 | 21 | 21 | 26 | $285

136 Country Club Dr.; 970-728-6800; fax 970-728-6175; 800-789-2220; www.thepeaksresort.com; 136 rooms, 38 suites, 10 cabins, 14 resort homes

Expect "Rocky Mountain highs" at this resort with a "simply stunning" setting, ski-in/ski-out convenience, loads of facilities like squash and racquetball courts, a climbing wall and "lovely suites" and private cabins that capture "wonderful views"; the "concierge recommends activities that we wouldn't have found on our own", and if its restaurants "can't keep up with the local dining scene, that's probably better if you're spending time" at the on-site branch of the Golden Door spa.

Vail

Lodge at Vail, The 22 | 22 | 22 | 23 | $529

174 E. Gore Creek Dr.; 970-476-5011; fax 970-476-7425; 877-528-7625; www.lodgeatvail.com; 120 rooms, 46 suites

Lazybones love being "so close to the slopes that you can ski out and then stumble back in" for an "excellent" meal at the Wildflower or to unwind at the "great piano bar" at this "grand" lodge; the "newer rooms" are "lovely", but others are "too small for the price" and in need of "refurbishment"; still, compensation is found in the outdoor pool, hot tubs and Vail Valley golf; N.B. an expansion is planned for spring 2006.

SONNENALP 26 | 27 | 23 | 27 | $750

20 Vail Rd.; 970-476-5656; fax 970-476-1639; 866-284-4141; www.sonnenalp.com; 88 suites

Fans of this "true alpine experience" "in the center of Vail Village" "want to yodel" about its "lovely" Bavarian-style decor, "top-notch spa for après-ski massages", "good fitness center", "incredible" service and one of the "best breakfast buffets anywhere"; although all are "comfy" and have baths with heated floors, "streetside rooms can be noisy" so request one facing "burbling" Gore Creek; "you can't ski in and ski out but who cares" when the "atmosphere is this magnificent."

Vail Cascade Resort & Spa 21 | 23 | 20 | 26 | $529

1300 Westhaven Dr.; 970-476-7111; fax 970-479-7020; 800-282-4183; www.vailcascade.com; 266 rooms, 25 suites, 72 condos

It "couldn't be more convenient" say snow-fiends of this resort on Gore Creek as the "ski concierge stores your equipment and a private lift whisks you to the top of the mountain"; other assets include the "classy" lobby with "fireplace nooks", the "primo" Aria spa and "amiable" staff, all of which help overcome the "drawbacks" of being a bit "far from Vail nightlife" and "mediocre" dining; N.B. renovations were completed post-*Survey*.

Connecticut

Greenwich

Delamar, The 25 | 23 | 25 | 23 | $435

500 Steamboat Rd.; 203-661-9800; fax 203-661-2513; 866-335-2627; www.thedelamar.com; 74 rooms, 9 suites

An "opulent", Mediterranean-style "jewel box" (and member of Small Luxury Hotels of the World) with a "fabulous waterfront location", this getaway is "just a stone's throw" from "chic shopping and dining" and the train station; aesthetes adore the "plush" suites overlooking the harbor, 450-thread-count sheets, coral marble vanities and hand-painted furniture as well as the

Provençal food at the "superb" L'Escale restaurant; if some deem the staff "amateur", others feel "management is working on it."

Homestead Inn ✕Ⓗ 21 | 24 | 27 | 19 | $495
420 Field Point Rd.; 203-869-7500; fax 203-869-7502; 800-735-2478; www.homesteadinn.com; 11 rooms, 7 suites
"In a word: divine" declare admirers of Relais & Châteaux's "beautiful old manse" dating back to 1799 and decorated with rich textiles and "charming" furniture from around the world; "it's a treat" to stay in the "exquisite", "romantic" chambers and suites with antiques, Frette linens and heated bathroom floors, but it's the Thomas Henkelmann restaurant, where the co-owner/chef himself presides, that lures locals and visitors alike – it was voted Most Popular and No. 1 for Decor in our *Connecticut Restaurant Survey.*

Hyatt Regency Ⓢ 20 | 21 | 18 | 21 | $169
1800 E. Putnam Ave., Old Greenwich; 203-637-1234; fax 203-637-2940; 800-233-1234; www.hyatt.com; 361 rooms, 12 suites
The "place smells of old money", from the moment you pull up to the "majestic hotel on top of a hill" with "curb appeal" and enter the four-story atrium lobby "filled with trees and a stream" – a "beautiful place to have a drink or dinner"; although the quarters are "well kept", a handful huff it's "nothing fancy" just "decent."

Hartford

Goodwin Hotel Ⓗ ▽ 19 | 19 | 18 | 18 | $249
1 Haynes St.; 860-246-7500; fax 860-247-4576; 800-922-5006 ; www.goodwinhotel.com; 100 rooms, 24 suites
"Hey, is that the governor?" – yes, "elegance abounds" at this "well-restored" "old-world charmer" near the Civic Center; the historic setting makes it a "great place for drinks" and dinner, and a "gem" to stay in, with rooms boasting turn-of-the-century decor and a newly refurbished meeting space; but doubters shrug there are "almost no facilities" and advise eating elsewhere.

Ledyard

Foxwoods Resort Ⓢ 20 | 19 | 18 | 22 | $315
39 Norwich Westerly Blvd., Mashantucket; 860-312-3000; fax 860-312-5044; 800-369-9663; www.foxwoods.com; 1216 rooms, 200 suites
Like a "glitzy Oz rising out of the rural landscape", this "one-stop 'shopping'" destination "for fun and games" "looks like the Emerald City at the end of the yellow brick road" – or at least like a "modern", "Vegas-style" hotel in "beautiful forest surroundings"; "gamblers flock here for the convenience" of the "huge casino" ("a shuttle bus is provided"), dining options galore, the spa and nearby golf course, rather than the "small rooms" and "crowded" atmosphere.

Mystic

Inn at Mystic 21 | 18 | 19 | 18 | $185
Rtes. 1 & 27; 860-536-9604; fax 860-572-1635; 800-237-2415; www.innatmystic.com; 67 rooms
"Canopy beds, fireplaces, great food and WiFi access – that's what I call romance" say admirers of this "quaint inn in a quaint town"

comprised of five buildings, including the circa-1904 Haley Mansion; it's "close to everything", with many rooms offering "scenic views of the Long Island Sound" and Mystic Harbor.

Mystic Marriott Ⓢ 20 | 20 | 18 | 21 | $239

625 North Rd.; 860-446-2600 ; fax 860-446-2601; 800-228-9290; www.mysticmarriott.com; 281 rooms, 4 suites

"A fine place to stay when going to Mystic and the casinos", this "well-run", "surprisingly pleasant" "alternative to older" options is "worth it alone" for the Elizabeth Arden Red Door Spa in the lobby; even though it's a Marriott, it's somewhat of a "sleeper", though those in-the-know reveal that the "rooms are comfortable" and service is "efficient", plus there's a "large pool", "great work-out facilities" and an "innovative restaurant."

New Preston

Boulders Inn, The Ⓢ 20 | 21 | 22 | 19 | $350

Shore Rd.; 860-868-0541; fax 860-868-1925; 800-455-1565; www.bouldersinn.com; 17 rooms, 3 suites

"The experience is like a memory of a warm sunny day from days gone by" wax nostalgists who make haste for this "restful oasis", a "romantic", recently renovated 1890 Dutch Colonial mansion about 45 minutes west of Hartford with spa and gym facilities; "sit on rocking chairs looking over Lake Waramaug at tea time", enjoy "fantastic dinners" on the hillside terrace or in the "excellent dining room with a view", then bed down in "cozy" rooms in the main lodge, the carriage house or hillside cottages.

Norwich

Spa at Norwich Inn, The Ⓢ 21 | 23 | 22 | 25 | $250

607 W. Thames St.; 860-886-2401; fax 860-886-9483; 800-275-4772; www.thespaatnorwichinn.com; 49 rooms, 4 suites, 52 villas

"Tranquil, comfortable and relaxing", this "absolute joy" "has it all", from a "top-shelf spa" with "heavenly" treatments and "well-trained therapists" to a location "close to the Mohegan Sun casino"; "spacious rooms", villas with fireplaces and kitchens and a "lovely, intimate restaurant" where you can dine alfresco overlooking the reflecting pool all make it the "perfect weekend getaway" "when you want to be pampered"; P.S. "it's not uncommon to see the bar packed with people in bathrobes."

Old Saybrook

Saybrook Point Inn & Spa Ⓢ 22 | 22 | 21 | 23 | $359

2 Bridge St.; 860-395-2000; fax 860-388-1504; 800-243-0212; www.saybrook.com; 65 rooms, 16 suites

"A wonderful place for young and old alike", this pet-friendly "charming waterside property" coddles guests with "lovely rooms" boasting working fireplaces and balconies; "try their Sunday brunch" at the Terra Mar Grille – it's a "marvelous way to see" the "fabulous views" of the Long Island Sound and Connecticut River, plus they've done a "major do over" of the "divine" spa; still, a few gripe the "public areas are taken up by weddings" during the "busy summer season."

Uncasville

Mohegan Sun Casino Hotel 23 | 22 | 23 | 25 | $175

1 Mohegan Sun Blvd.; 860-862-8000; fax 860-862-7419; 888-226-7711; www.mohegansun.com; 1020 rooms, 180 suites

"Everything is splendid" at this "whimsical", "polished" "modern palace" "reminiscent of Alice's Wonderland" with "more than enough to amuse"; the rooms are "stylish", the "diverse group" of restaurants vary "from fast food to elegant dining" and there's even a shopping mall with a seven-story waterfall; "you truly forget whatever may exist in the outside world when in the architecturally unique casino", with its sky dome planetarium, while "top-line entertainment" and a "gorgeous" spa add to the "glamour."

Washington

MAYFLOWER INN 27 | 27 | 25 | 25 | $450

118 Woodbury Rd.; 860-868-9466; fax 860-868-1497; www.mayflowerinn.com; 17 rooms, 7 suites

"The pilgrims never had it so good" but you will at this "dreamy", "picturesque inn" "nestled in the middle of the woods" with a "wonderful pool", fitness center and spa services; it's "upscale all the way", with accommodations that make you feel "like you're staying in an aristocratic British country house without the annoyance of eccentric hosts" but with "unparalleled" service ("how do they know who you are when you pull up?!"), and the cuisine is "marvelous" too; just be prepared for that "serious dent in your wallet."

Westport

INN AT NATIONAL HALL, THE 26 | 26 | – | 20 | $350

2 Post Rd. W.; 203-221-1351; fax 203-221-0276; 800-628-4255; www.innatnationalhall.com; 8 rooms, 8 suites

Offering "elegance and comfort where you least expect it", Relais & Châteaux's "over-the-top" circa-1873 luxury hotel on the National Register of Historic Places is "chic to the point of distraction" – it's come a long way since its former incarnation as a furniture factory; each "room is completely unique" with "attention to detail" evident at every turn, plus the Downtown "location on the other side of the bridge from Main Street" near "shopping and fine dining couldn't be better", especially since there's no longer an on-site restaurant.

Delaware

Wilmington

du Pont, Hotel 26 | 25 | 25 | 23 | $409

11th & Market Sts.; 302-594-3100; fax 302-594-3108; 800-441-9019; www.hoteldupont.com; 206 rooms, 10 suites

Oozing with "stately" "old-world posh", this "queen of the Mid-Atlantic" is "the pride of Wilmington"; the "ballrooms are magical" enough to "throw a wedding", the Sunday brunch "must be experienced to be believed" and the "to dress for" Green Room has service so "extraordinary" they'd "grind up a filet mignon to make a hamburger" for a picky youngster; the suites' "outstanding" details include "huge Jacuzzis", fireplaces, "see-thru showers" and "the most comfortable beds", while a show in the on-site Victorian theater is a "must."

Inn at Montchanin, The ✕Ⓗ | 25 | 23 | 25 | 21 | $169

Kirk Rd. & Rte. 100, Montchanin; 302-888-2133; fax 302-888-0389; 800-269-2473; www.montchanin.com; 12 rooms, 16 suites

The "outstanding" restaurant, Krazy Kat's ("one of the best in the state"), and the "charming", "individually decorated" country rooms are the draws of this restored 19th-century inn three miles from Downtown Wilmington that's listed on the National Register of Historic Places and also a member of Small Luxury Hotels of the World; a "lovely getaway from New York City" (about two hours), especially in the spring "when the whole area is blooming" with "fabulous horticulture", it's "a pricey but creative" option for touring the Brandywine Valley.

District of Columbia

★ **Tops in District**

25 Four Seasons
Ritz-Carlton, Georgetown
Ritz-Carlton
24 Hay-Adams
Willard InterContinental
23 St. Regis
22 Fairmont Washington
Jefferson

Washington, DC

Fairmont Washington, The Ⓢ | 24 | 23 | 19 | 23 | $279

2401 M St., NW, Washington; 202-429-2400; fax 202-457-5089; 800-257-7544; www.fairmont.com; 415 rooms, 30 suites

Snuggled in a "great pocket" in the West End "a little away from all the DC noise" but "close to everything", this "luxurious" property with an "impressive", "airy lobby" and "wonderful staff" offers "spacious rooms", with many overlooking a "gorgeous central courtyard", an "awesome health club" and a "high-end" Sunday champagne brunch in The Colonnade; "check out the Gold level, an even more amazing hotel within a hotel" boasting "secluded deluxe rooms" and "all the amenities."

FOUR SEASONS ✕Ⓢ | 25 | 27 | 25 | 25 | $480

2800 Pennsylvania Ave., NW, Washington; 202-342-0444; fax 202-944-2055; 800-332-3442; www.fourseasons.com; 211 rooms, 51 suites

"Still the old faithful for" "VIPs", "CEOs and rock stars alike", this "ultraluxe", "child-friendly" "class act" in "trendy Georgetown" offers a "gracious" experience with "beds that feel like heaven", "delightful afternoon tea" and a "hopping bar" in the lobby, plus Seasons, an "astonishingly good restaurant"; it's "everything you expect" from "incomparable service" to the "enjoyable spa" and three-level gym.

George, Hotel 22 21 24 18 $350

15 E St., NW, Washington; 202-347-4200; fax 202-347-4213; 800-576-8331; www.hotelgeorge.com; 136 rooms, 3 suites

"By George, I think they've got it!", deadpan devotees of the Kimpton Group's "avant-garde" "chic boutique" that's "really funky for straight-laced Capitol Hill" and characterized by "super-comfortable beds" and "stylishly decorated rooms" with "extra touches" like "wonderful" pillow-top mattresses and "white noise machines" that mask the "bleating traffic sounds"; "don't miss Bistro Bis", the "affordable", "out-of-this-world" French restaurant downstairs – it's "worth the stay alone", plus there's a "lively bar."

Grand Hyatt Washington 19 19 16 21 $370

1000 H St., NW, Washington; 202-582-1234; fax 202-637-4781; 800-233-1234; www.hyatt.com; 850 rooms, 38 suites

"Nothing frilly, but right on for biz or pleasure" with a "very friendly staff" to boot echo enthusiasts of this Downtown hotel opposite the convention center with a Metro "connection in the basement", a "soaring atrium" and "great views from your room"; those who carp it "doesn't distinguish itself" may find more luxury after post-*Survey* renovations that aren't fully reflected in above scores.

Hay-Adams, The 24 27 24 23 $575

16th & H Sts., NW, Washington; 202-638-6600; fax 202-638-2716; 800-424-5054; www.hayadams.com; 125 rooms, 20 suites

"A beautiful redo" has raised this "historic" "DC classic" "beyond criticism", especially if you "ask for a room facing the White House" ("makes you feel like a head of state"); it "sets the standard" with "unforgettable views from the rooftop deck", "flawless service" and "breathtaking" rooms sporting "amazing" linens; "dining here is a must", and "if you hang around long enough" over your "power cocktail" in the Off the Record bar "you're sure to catch an earful" of West Wing "gossip."

Helix, Hotel 24 19 15 19 $239

1430 Rhode Island Ave., NW, Washington; 202-462-9001; fax 202-332-3519; 800-706-1202; www.hotelhelix.com; 160 rooms, 18 suites

Squeeze into your "hip huggin' bell bottoms and say yeah, baby!" to this "energetic", "outrageous" "Austin Powers comes to DC" "hot spot extraordinaire"; the "kitschy", "NYC-style" "apartment-type" boutique quarters are "imaginatively decorated" with "faux fur bedspreads", "shimmery curtains", "lava lights" and "great shower heads", plus the minibar is stocked with "wax lips and Pop Rocks"; "if you long to sip a Cosmopolitan" and "mingle with the young, trendy crowd", head to the "lively" lounge.

Jefferson, The 22 24 22 20 $299

1200 16th St., NW, Washington; 202-347-2200; fax 202-331-7982; 866-270-8118; www.thejeffersonwashingtondc.com; 68 rooms, 32 suites

For a "romantic, in-city getaway with a view of the Washington Monument" this "historic", "dog-friendly" beaux arts–inspired former apartment building, a "favorite of diplomats", delivers "a European feel" with "genteel facilities", "fantastic canopy beds and every amenity you can think of" coupled with "impeccable comfort" and "true white-glove service"; it's a "treat" for tea, and dinner at the "charming" Restaurant at the Jefferson "must be the only well-kept secret in town."

Madera, Hotel ✗ ⌂ ▽ 22 | 22 | 25 | 16 | $309

1310 New Hampshire Ave., NW, Washington; 202-296-7600; fax 202-293-2476; 800-430-1202; www.hotelmadera.com; 82 rooms

An apartment building back in the 1940s, this Dupont Circle spot has been transformed into "an incredibly modern", "trendy" Kimpton boutique property offering a "hip, Euro-chic" experience with "nicely furnished" "funky rooms" replete with Aveda bath amenities (but "the smallest bathrooms on earth") and "an informal, but grown-up staff"; Firefly, the "fabulous" restaurant, offers a "creative" New American menu and is also "popular" with locals.

Madison Hotel, The ⌂ 22 | 25 | 20 | 20 | $379

15th & M Sts., NW, Washington; 202-862-1600; fax 202-785-1255; 800-424-8577; www.themadisondc.com; 311 rooms, 42 suites

"Beautiful renovations" have "vastly improved" this "lovely" fortysomething "classic businessperson's" "bargain" "centrally located" near the White House that fittingly "bills itself as the hotel of diplomats and presidents" (you may see "secret service agents roaming the hallways"); the "super-friendly staff" complements the "huge", "old-style" rooms kitted out with "quality" Frette duvets, "comfy beds" and American Empire and Georgian furniture; culinary cronies coo over the "Palette, which offers great food and ambiance", and the "wonderful Sunday brunch" in The Federalist restaurant.

Mandarin Oriental ⓢ ▽ 25 | 27 | 22 | 25 | $350

1330 Maryland Ave., SW, Washington; 202-554 8588 ; fax 202-554 8999 ; 888-888-1788; www.mandarinoriental.com/washington/; 347 rooms, 53 suites

The Chinese marble "bathrooms are like palaces" at this "polished" "jewel" that just may "force everyone to rediscover southwest DC"; guests gush over the 16 types of "lush rooms" and "superb suites", state-of-the-art televisions, "outstanding service", "wonderful spa" and "free limo transportation and boat rides to Georgetown"; with a "pretty view of the water", the Empress Lounge is "a hot spot for cocktails", plus the "food is quite good" at Café MoZU.

Monaco, Hotel ⌂ 23 | 21 | 22 | 20 | $409

700 F St., NW, Washington; 202-628-7177; fax 202-628-7277; 800-649-1202; www.monaco-dc.com; 168 rooms, 16 suites

"If leopard print robes" are "your cup of tea", then pounce on this "funky" Kimpton "outpost" in the "beautifully renovated" 1839 Tariff Building next to the Spy Museum in Penn Quarter, now the "epicenter" of DC's "'it' spots"; get a "good jolt of hipness" as you "walk down the majestic hallways" toward your "big-on-the-cool-quotient" room with vaulted "high ceilings" and "lovely lighting" or head to the "chic" Poste-Modern Brasserie.

Morrison-Clark Inn ✗ ⓘ 18 | 21 | 24 | 13 | $229

1015 L St., NW, Washington; 202-898-1200; fax 202-289-8576; 800-222-8474; www.morrisonclark.com; 41 rooms, 13 suites

"Step back in time" at this "beautiful old inn" built from 1864-era townhouses with "quaint", albeit "small rooms", "wine and nuts in the evening" and "one of the best dining rooms" in DC for indulging in a "*très* luxe dinner"; regulars recommend the Victorian quarters where "the sitting areas and private bedroom" are "good for separating teenagers from parents" and suggest that you "sleep in" since "breakfast is a non-event."

Park Hyatt – – – – $450

1201 24th St., NW, Washington; 202-789-1234; fax 202-419-6795; 800-633-7313; www.hyatt.com; 92 rooms, 131 suites

Fans have always found "service beyond the call of duty" and a "concierge with an answer to every question" at this Georgetown "gem" that's closed for a $24-million major renovation until spring 2006; rooms designed by Tony Chi will feature limestone bathrooms with rain showers, WiFi connections, flat-screen satellite TVs and cordless phones, and a new farm-to-table, open-kitchen restaurant, a lobby bar and a salon with a tea cellar are also planned.

Renaissance Mayflower Ⓗ 21 22 20 21 $499

1127 Connecticut Ave., NW, Washington; 202-347-3000; fax 202-776-9182; 800-228-7697; www.renaissancehotels.com; 583 rooms, 74 suites

"Rich in history", this "classy", "quintessential DC" "grande dame" "takes you back to another time" with its "beautiful marble lobby" and "old-world sophistication"; the bar is "great" for "people-watching", "the restaurant is the place to be seen" and "breakfast is a must" – "you understand why presidents" and celebs stay here (Monica Lewinsky was put up in the presidential suite during the Starr investigation); P.S. it's undergoing a $10-million renovation.

RITZ-CARLTON 26 25 24 25 $399

1150 22nd St., NW, Washington; 202-835-0500; fax 202-835-1588; 800-241-3333; www.ritzcarlton.com; 267 rooms, 33 suites

More than any amenity at this "posh DC spot", fitness fans fawn over the "cavernous", "second to none" Sports Club/LA on premises, but it hits "all the high notes" in other ways too, from its "superb location" "within walking distance to the Kennedy Center, Metro and Rock Creek Park" to its "luxurious" quarters, "amazing" bathrooms", "top-notch service" and "excellent restaurants"; insiders advocate bunking on the private Club Floor.

RITZ-CARLTON, GEORGETOWN Ⓢ 27 26 24 24 $650

3100 South St., NW, Washington; 202-912-4100; fax 202-912-4199; 800-241-3333; www.ritzcarlton.com; 54 rooms, 34 suites

"What a beauty!" coo cosmopolitans bowled over by this "brilliant" "converted incinerator" in "the heart of Georgetown" boasting "unique architecture" that reminds you "this is power player central", "not your grandmother's Ritz"; "predictably superb service", "big, comfy rooms", a "wonderful fitness center" and "great views of the Potomac" are coupled with a spa that takes "pampering to new heights", plus you can "savor the surroundings" of Fahrenheit restaurant and the "hot scene" at the bar, Degrees.

Rouge, Hotel 23 19 16 17 $279

1315 16th St., NW, Washington; 202-232-8000; fax 202-332-6257; 800-738-1202; www.rougehotel.com; 137 rooms

Flaunting a "free-spirited funkiness" that the "young and young at heart" "get a kick out of", Kimpton's "swanky", "sexy", "romantic" boutique "getaway" on Embassy Row seduces with a "rock star feel", "affordable", "spacious, creative" accommodations ("who can resist the red and leopard" decor?), "decadent room-service menus", a "fun" bar and a "complimentary brunch of cold pizza and Bloodies that's pure fun."

Sofitel Lafayette Square ▽ 26 | 22 | 20 | 22 | $480

806 15th St., NW, Washington; 202-730-8800; fax 202-730-8500; 800-763-4835; www.sofitel.com; 220 rooms, 17 suites

Exuding a "bit of French class in the nation's capital", this "reasonably priced" "gem" in a "good Downtown location" proffers up "incredibly comfortable rooms" that are "*très jolie*" with some of the "best beds ever", plus "fabulous bathrooms" stocked with "fantastic bath amenities"; *amis* applaud the "friendly" "front desk staff that remembers you by name" and concur that the dining options are "tasty", if "expensive", and the "lobby bar is great for after-work drinks."

St. Regis 24 | 25 | 22 | 21 | $550

923 16th St., NW, Washington; 202-638-2626; fax 202-638-4231; 888-627-8087; www.stregis.com\washington; 179 rooms, 14 suites

"If you can't stay at the White House, spend the night in luxury right down the block" at this "pampering" "epitome of swank", "characteristic of St. Regis excellence" all the way "from the butler service to the clubby lobby bar" to the "outstanding dining"; the "elegantly decorated" rooms sport "bedding so luxurious you may skip the early morning appointment"; still, a few critics snipe it's "a bit stodgy."

Watergate Hotel Ⓗ 22 | 19 | 19 | 19 | $325

2650 Virginia Ave., NW, Washington; 202-965-2300; fax 202-337-7915; 800-289-1555; www.thewatergatehotel.com; 106 rooms, 144 suites

"Where were you in '72?" – yes, this site of the Nixon/Watergate scandal "is still worth it for the notoriety alone" profess history buffs who extol the "luxury suites with spectacular views" of the Potomac, "wonderful location" with "access to the Kennedy Center" and a "beautiful lobby bar"; but, a few deem it a "tattered belle" in "need of a refurb" and frown over "snooty service."

Westin Embassy Row 21 | 20 | 16 | 18 | $300

2100 Massachusetts Ave., NW, Washington; 202-293-2100; fax 202-293-0641; 800-228-3000; www.westin.com; 174 rooms, 32 suites

Admirers of this "former home of the Gore family", an "elegant", "stately, old" hotel "tucked into Embassy Row" say "it adds a bit of character to normal business stays" thanks to an "attentive staff" that "makes you feel welcome", "Heavenly beds and showers", an "above-average work-out facility" and a "wonderful neighborhood to explore"; dissenters, however, find it "jaded and faded" and claim that "it takes an act of Congress to get breakfast in a time."

Westin Grand 23 | 19 | 17 | 20 | $339

2350 M St., NW, Washington; 202-429-0100; fax 202-429-9759; 800-228-3000; www.westin.com; 260 rooms, 3 suites

Offering a "slice of Europe" in the West End, this "well-kept" "classic" "steps from where the action is" showcases "superb rooms" ("try to snag one with a balcony") and some of the "most comfortable beds in the world" coupled with "decadent soaking tubs" in the "huge marble bathrooms"; if a finicky few fume about "room service with limited hours" and "subpar dining options", other patrons retort "when you're in the heart of Washington, who needs them?"

Willard InterContinental Ⓗ 25 | 25 | 23 | 24 | $575

1401 Pennsylvania Ave., NW, Washington; 202-628-9100; fax 202-637-7326; 800-327-0200; www.interconti.com; 299 rooms, 42 suites

"Old-world civility is updated in a new-world way" at this "magnificently restored", "elite" "residence of presidents" near the Smithsonian "oozing sophistication and history"; it's a "must-do experience at least once in your life" thanks to "superb" meals in the Willard Room Restaurant, "top-drawer service" and "fantastic beds" in "lavish" rooms revealing "great views" of the White House; join the flocks at the Round Robin Bar and "eavesdrop on" the "bigwigs."

Florida

★ **Tops in State**

27 Ritz-Carlton, *Naples*
Mandarin Oriental, *Miami*
Ritz-Carlton, *Orlando*
Little Palm Island, *Little Torch Key*
Ritz-Carlton Golf Resort, *Naples*

26 Sunset Key Guest Cottages, *Key West*
Ritz-Carlton, *Amelia Island*
Four Seasons, *Miami*
Disney's Grand Floridian, *Lake Buena Vista*
Ritz-Carlton, *Key Biscayne*

Amelia Island

Amelia Island Plantation 20 | 21 | 18 | 24 | $341

6800 First Coast Hwy.; 904-261-6161; fax 904-277-5945; 800-874-6878; www.aipfl.com; 249 rooms, 418 villas

This "relaxed" resort near JAX has "everything a family could ask for" from a full spa, three golf courses and clay tennis courts, to "lovely shops", "gorgeous" beaches and "an amazing bike path"; if some are "disappointed by the spartan rooms" and "spotty condos" and cite "disconnected service" and "average" dining, more praise the activities that will "keep a kid out of your hair for hours."

RITZ-CARLTON, THE 26 | 27 | 26 | 27 | $349

4750 Amelia Island Pkwy.; 904-277-1100; fax 904-277-1145; 800-241-3333; www.ritzcarlton.com; 400 rooms, 49 suites

"Tai chi at sunrise", "the ocean whispering in the background" – what a "way to start the day" at this "secluded" "oasis" on a barrier island off northeast Florida where "service is king" and "everything is at your fingertips"; with a "lovely setting" on a "perfect stretch of beach", "airy" rooms overlooking the water, an 18-hole golf course, nine tennis courts, a "unique kiddie pool" and fine dining choices, it's an "excellent resort, but at these prices it should be."

Destin

Hilton Sandestin Beach, Golf Resort & Spa | 19 | 20 | 19 | 24 | $259 |

4000 Sandestin Blvd. S.; 850-267-9500; fax 850-267-3076; 800-367-1271; www.sandestinbeachhilton.com; 576 rooms, 22 suites

"A gem on the Emerald Coast" about 65 miles east of Pensacola, this "beautifully maintained" property on "one of Florida's most beautiful beaches" is "great for golfers and families"; the "staff is accommodating" and the rooms are "big", plus there's a "wonderful" spa, fitness center and children's programs, all in a setting so "relaxing" "there's no reason to leave."

Ft. Lauderdale

Atlantic, The | – | – | – | – | $429 |

601 N. Ft. Lauderdale Beach Blvd.; 954-567-8020; fax 954-567-8040; 800-325-3589; www.starwood.com; 92 rooms, 32 suites

When it comes to amenities and service at this beachfront Starwood Luxury Collection property, the numbers speak for themselves, starting with 124 modern rooms and facilities that operate 24/7, including the business center, gym, room service and even the concierge; the spa emphasizes European-style treatments inspired by the locale, the pool area sports a hot tub, cafe and private cabanas, and the restaurant, Trina, is a hot spot.

Boca Raton Resort & Club | 23 | 23 | 22 | 26 | $250 |

501 E. Camino Real, Boca Raton; 561-447-3000; fax 561-447-3183; 800-327-0101; www.bocaresort.com; 849 rooms, 132 suites, 60 villas

Enjoy "unbelievable golf", "excellent" tennis, a full-service marina and "pampering" too in the "decadent" Palazzo Spa at this "perfectly pink" resort whose 1926 Addison Mizner–designed core continues to be expanded; "room quality is uneven" with some whispering "the best are those in the Beach Club", although all guests can cross the Intracoastal by ferry to the hotel's private stretch of sand.

Lago Mar Resort & Club | 21 | 23 | 21 | 23 | $285 |

1700 S. Ocean Ln.; 954-523-6511; fax 954-524-6627; 800-524-6627; www.lagomar.com; 40 rooms, 164 suites

"Elegant" and "uncommercialized", this is "old Florida, the way you remember it" attest nostalgists who return year after year to this "kid-friendly" family-owned "home away from home" on "gorgeous grounds" in exclusive Harbor Beach; whether you watch the "ocean liners glide by" from your "private" stretch of sand, revel in your "ample-sized suite" or "visit the soda shop" and the spa, it's an "ideal place to relax."

Marriott Harbor Beach Resort & Spa | 21 | 22 | 19 | 25 | $339 |

3030 Holiday Dr.; 954-525-4000; fax 954-766-6152; 800-222-6543; www.marriottharborbeach.com; 602 rooms, 35 suites

"One of the few Ft. Lauderdale hotels right on the beach", this "standout" affords "views of the ocean" and "cruise ships heading into port"; "outstanding service", an "excellent" spa, an "awesome pool" and "delicious" seafood make it "perfect for a business meeting" or a "weekend getaway", though it's "pricey."

Pillars at New River Sound ∇ 25 | 23 | – | 23 | $210

111 Birch Rd.; 954-467-9639; fax 954-763-2845; 800-800-7666; www.pillarshotel.com; 18 rooms, 5 suites

"Hopefully one to keep a secret" confide insiders who "love" this "intimate getaway", a tiny British Colonial–inspired member of Small Luxury Hotels of the World on the Intracoastal Waterway that's "unobtrusive in every way"; "classy" and "quiet", it "charms" from the outset with oak floors, a grand piano, wine bar and a library in the lobby, plus a freshwater pool and "cozy" plantation-style rooms; there's "no dining" but you can "catch the water taxi" to "see how the rich and famous live."

Seminole Hard Rock Hotel & Casino Hollywood – | – | – | – | $250

1 Seminole Way, Hollywood; 954-327-7625; 866-802-7529; www.seminolehardrock.com; 437 rooms, 63 suites

Indulgence to the max seems to be the rock 'n' roll credo at this sprawling, Mediterranean-style gaming resort in Hollywood; night-owls (and early birds) flock to the casino open round the clock, plus it boasts a pool-gone-wild with waterfalls and hot tubs, and there's a golf course, gym and spa; add in an entertainment complex filled with 15 restaurants, eight nightclubs and live music venues, and chances are you may never even make it to your room.

Westin Diplomat Resort & Spa 26 | 21 | 21 | 25 | $325

3555 S. Ocean Dr., Hollywood; 954-602-6000; fax 954-602-7000; 888-627-9057; www.diplomatresort.com; 900 rooms, 100 suites

"Magnificent" ocean views add the "wow" factor to this "architectural wonder" that works for "business and pleasure", exuding "elegance" with a "stunning" 60-ft. atrium and "extremely cool" glass-bottomed infinity pool; it feels like a "cruise ship on land" with multiple restaurants and well-designed "dream rooms with plenty of amenities"; for golf, tennis and an "enjoyable spa", head to the nearby Diplomat Country Club.

Ft. Myers

Casa Ybel Resort 21 | 20 | 20 | 21 | $435

2255 W. Gulf Dr., Sanibel; 239-472-3145; fax 239-472-2109; 800-276-4753 ; www.casaybelresort.com; 114 condos

Truly a "place you want to return to", this "charming" resort with "lovely manicured lawns" is "great for families" thanks to kitchen-equipped suites that are "nothing fancy but spacious" and an "active kids' club" with a "pleasant" staff; with a "large pool" near the sugar-white beach, volleyball, bike rentals and six tennis courts, everyone "can enjoy their own activity."

Sanibel Harbour Resort & Spa – | – | – | – | $299

17260 Harbour Pointe Dr.; 239-466-4000; fax 239-466-2150; 800-767-7777; www.sanibel-resort.com; 278 rooms, 69 suites, 54 condos

Since its $40-million renovation this 85-acre plantation retreat overlooking Sanibel and Captiva Islands is a top choice for families;

there's a plethora of activities and amenities: an extensive kids' club, fishing, sailing, sunset dinner cruises on a private yacht, seven eateries and a 40,000-sq.-ft. on-site spa and fitness center; accommodations include rooms and waterfront condominiums with antique bamboo furnishings.

Hutchinson Island

Hutchinson Island Marriott ▽ 19 | 20 | 17 | 21 | $269

555 N.E. Ocean Blvd.; 772-225-3700 ; fax 772-225-0003 ; www.marriott.com; 214 rooms, 70 suites

"A great spot for a weekend getaway" or business meetings, this "sprawling" 200-acre oceanfront resort "has a lot of island in its soul"; with an 18-hole executive golf course, tennis, mini spa, 77-slip marina and a "superb beach and pool", it's "worth the extra money" to get a "room with a view"; but a few grumble it's "slightly run-down" and wish "the food was better."

Jacksonville

Lodge & Club, The 25 | 21 | 20 | 25 | $360

607 Ponte Vedra Blvd., Ponte Vedra; 904-273-9500; fax 904-273-0210; 800-243-4304 ; www.pvresorts.com; 20 suites, 44 rooms

"Roll out of bed and into the ocean" at this Mediterranean-inspired getaway, about 20 miles southeast of Jacksonville, built on the site where the Innlet, an inn dating back to 1940, once stood; they "did a great job on renovations" reveal admirers who delight in the "spacious rooms" with fireplaces and Jacuzzis or Roman-style tubs and "cozy window seats" for those "beautiful views"; N.B. while there is a fitness center, this location shares some facilities with nearby larger sibling Ponte Vedra Inn & Club.

Ponte Vedra Inn & Club 23 | 23 | 22 | 26 | $270

200 Ponte Vedra Blvd., Ponte Vedra Beach; 904-285-1111; fax 904-285-2111; 800-234-7842; www.pvresorts.com; 250 rooms, 45 suites

The "grounds are beautiful" at this "wonderful resort" spread over 300 acres "on a beautiful stretch" of "pristine, talcum powder sand beaches" near sibling Lodge & Club; it's "great for golf and tennis", horseback riding, sailing, biking and swimming (there are four pools, including an adults-only pool and children's wading pool), plus regulars recommend you "book the spa prior to arrival – spots fill up quickly" – and "opt for suites if you can afford it"; N.B. a new spa is under construction.

Keys

Cheeca Lodge & Spa 21 | 22 | 22 | 24 | $319

81801 Overseas US Hwy. 1, Islamorada; 305-664-4651; fax 305-664-2893; 800-327-2888; www.rockresorts.com; 129 rooms, 63 suites, 9 bungalows

Those "in search of Kokomo" can find a piece of it at this "upscale" yet "laid-back" and "kid-friendly" RockResort that's a member of Small Luxury Hotels of the World and worth "robbing a bank" to stay in; despite its "beautiful location on the Atlantic", some swimmers find the "beach is a disappointment", but there are "hot tubs under tropical trees", two pools and saltwater lagoons "to lounge in", plus golf, fishing and the Avanyu Spa.

Gardens Hotel ▽ 24 | 22 | 14 | 22 | $285
526 Angela St., Key West; 305-294-2661; fax 305-292-1007; 800-526-2664; www.gardenshotel.com; 12 rooms, 4 suites, 1 cottage
With "lush" tropical botanical gardens, as befits this former private estate's name, this "incredibly romantic" retreat is "just close enough to the craziness of Duval Street" while remaining "secluded" thanks to all that "jungle foliage"; even without a long list of resort services admirers admit it's a "beautiful place to stay" thanks to its Old Town Conch architecture (providing sojourners shell-ter since the 1870s); a "soothing pool" and complimentary "European-style breakfast" make it one of the "best in Key West."

Hawk's Cay Resort 21 | 20 | 18 | 23 | $260
61 Hawk's Cay Blvd., Duck Key; 305-743-7000; fax 305-743-5215; 888-445-6393; www.hawkscay.com; 161 rooms, 16 suites, 300 villas
Fans of the "natural beauty of the Keys" where "the fish practically jump in your lap" flip over the "fantastic views" at this "classic family resort" that feels like a "step back to the *Wonder Years*"; the "numerous amenities", including a "terrific swim with the dolphins" program, a "super pirate-ship pool" for tykes, teen and adult spa and "relaxing bar", "make you think you're in the Carribean"; even those who snipe the rooms "need updating" find the "location wonderful."

Hilton Key West Resort & Marina 24 | 22 | 19 | 23 | $496
245 Front St., Key West; 305-294-4000; fax 305-294-4086; 800-445-8667; www.hilton.com; 147 rooms, 31 suites
The big plus for this Victorian-style resort overlooking the Gulf is its setting "in the heart" of Margaritaville, a "nice stumbling distance" from the "madness" of Duval Street "without the noise"; "it's hard to imagine the sun ever setting at this lovely property" but it does, and the views are "priceless", so head to the dock or take the short boat ride to Sunset Key across the bay.

Hyatt Key West Resort & Marina 21 | 20 | 18 | 21 | $325
601 Front St., Key West; 305-296-9900; fax 305-809-4050; 800-233-1234; www.hyatt.com; 110 rooms, 10 suites
"Location, location, location definitely counts" at this "intimate", "relaxing resort" "right at the dock" "within walking distance to the bars and restaurants on Duval Street" but "far enough away for some peace and solitude"; while it lacks the "feel of old Key West", the "rooms are well appointed", plus the staff "remembers your name" and it even has its own "tiny beach" and golf and tennis clubs nearby.

LITTLE PALM ISLAND 27 | 27 | 27 | 25 | $1145
28500 Overseas Hwy., Little Torch Key; 305-872-2524; fax 305-872-4843; 800-343-8567; www.littlepalmisland.com; 30 bungalows
"If you can afford it", this "exclusive", "ultimate private island getaway", accessible only by boat or seaplane, delivers "South Pacific paradise in the Florida Keys"; "no phones, no television" and "no children under age 16" enhance the "incredibly romantic"

feel, with "fine dining" (the restaurant was voted No. 1 for Food, Decor and Service in the Keys section of our *Miami/So. Florida Restaurant Survey*), "thatched-roof bungalows" with outside showers (a "rustic palace where you're treated like royalty") and "luxurious amenities"; yes, "this is your chance to get away from the world and experience true tranquility."

MARQUESA HOTEL, THE 25 | 26 | 25 | 23 | $285

600 Fleming St., Key West; 305-292-1919; fax 305-294-2121; 800-869-4631; www.marquesa.com; 27 rooms, 13 suites

"Truly an enjoyable", "charming" "retreat from the norm", this Old Town inn comprised of four clapboard houses, including an 1880s building on the National Historic Register, offers a "quiet location" in a "tropical garden setting" "within walking distance of Duval Street"; the "divine rooms" are "romantic" (kids under 12 aren't allowed) and most have "balconies overlooking the beautifully landscaped courtyard", service is "excellent" and there's even a "pool area that feels like an oasis"; P.S. the "attached Café Marquesa is superb."

Ocean Reef Club 21 | 22 | 20 | 25 | $475

35 Ocean Reef Dr., Key Largo; 305-367-2611; fax 305-367-5909; 800-741-7333; www.oceanreef.com; 320 rooms, 17 suites, 70 condos

"Be sure to rent a golf cart" to putt around this sprawling, "luxury resort", with guestrooms, suites and villas on 4,000 acres on the northernmost tip of Key Largo, about 50 miles south of Miami where the "scenery is like heaven on earth"; it's akin to a "self-contained" "private club" community with "its own post office, church, school", 175-slip marina, two 18-hole golf courses, 10 tennis courts, croquet courts, cooking school, theater, spa – there's even a landing strip for private planes, "a few happening bars" and "good food everywhere."

Pier House Resort & Caribbean Spa 21 | 21 | 21 | 22 | $290

1 Duval St., Key West; 305-296-4600; fax 305-296-9085; 800-327-8340; www.pierhouse.com; 126 rooms, 16 suites

"You can't beat a hotel with a topless sunbathing area" say feisty fans of this "nifty" Old Town "home base from which to venture forth into the wilds of Key West" in an "enviable location in the heart of Duval Street"; the rooms are "private and pretty", plus the "teeny, tiny" man-made beach, Caribbean spa, and restaurant and bar options "add to the illusion of being on a tropical island", helped along by a "deck where you can sip frozen drinks, listen to live music and watch the sunset."

Sheraton Suites Key West ▽ 20 | 23 | 14 | 19 | $359

2001 S. Roosevelt Blvd., Key West; 305-292-9800; fax 305-294-6009; 800-325-3535; www.sheratonkeywest.com; 180 suites

A "comfy" "place to spend a holiday", this all-suites chain link is set across the street from Key West's largest public beach; the "rooms are huge with full-sized bathrooms" and the "staff is laid-back", but the "real center of the universe here is the very inviting" lagoon-style pool with cascading waterfalls and a bar; still, foes frown that it's "lukewarm" and the "food is just tolerable", advising take the shuttle service to "all of the action" on Duval Street.

SUNSET KEY GUEST COTTAGES | 29 | 26 | 24 | 28 | $725

245 Front St., Key West; 305-292-5300; fax 305-292-5395; 888-477-7786; www.sunsetkeyisland.com; 37 cottages

It's "just a short ride from the craziness of Duval Street", yet this "island paradise", accessible only by launch service, seems like "another world", with "graceful white cottages", complete with "large wraparound porches boasting ceiling fans"; you "feel like the rich and famous" with a "great breakfast delivered to your room", two tennis courts, a pool and "palm-fringed beaches", and when you've had your fill of "relaxing time", "take the boat to town for the sunset party" at Mallory Square.

Wyndham Casa Marina Resort | 21 | 22 | 22 | 25 | $429

1500 Reynolds St., Key West; 305-296-3535; fax 305-296-4633; 800-626-0777; www.wyndham.com; 236 rooms, 75 suites

For a "taste of grandeur", guests alight at this former Henry Flagler mansion, a "classic" 1920 resort on the National Register of Historic Places within walking distance of local "treats"; it "captures" yesteryear "in a marvelous way", so "get a room in the older part overlooking the water" – it will "quickly charm you" – then head to one of the "best beaches in beach-starved Key West", or the "memorable pools"; P.S. the "great food may keep you in the hotel, which is saying a lot" in this town.

Miami

★ **Tops in City**

27 Mandarin Oriental
26 Four Seasons
Ritz-Carlton Key Biscayne
25 Ritz-Carlton Coconut Grove
Fisher Island Hotel
Fairmont Turnberry Isle
Biltmore Hotel
24 Tides, The
23 Delano
Grove Isle Club & Resort

Astor, Hotel | 20 | 21 | 24 | 17 | $140

956 Washington Ave., Miami Beach; 305-531-8081; fax 305-531-3193; 800-270-4981; www.hotelastor.com; 17 rooms, 23 suites

The "best-kept secret in Miami" might be this 1936 South Beach "luxe boutique hotel" whose "low-key glamour" and "perfect location" "away from the beach but close to the action" attract "abundant" crowds of "beautiful people"; although there's no pool or on-site gym (there's a Crunch nearby), rooms are "well appointed" and Metro restaurant is "perfect for dates" or an "extraordinary" gospel brunch.

Bentley Beach Hotel | – | – | – | – | $500

101 Ocean Dr., Miami Beach; 305-938-4600; fax 305-938-4601; www.thebentleyhotels.com; 109 suites

Located on the southern tip of Ocean Drive in South Beach, this new all-suite hipster offers accommodations with kitchenettes, marble flooring, nine-ft. ceilings, hand-sewn rugs and sweeping Atlantic Ocean views; expect poolside cabanas and chic beach beds, a branch of the European Caroli Health Club and Spa and two upscale eateries via chef Tom Billante (of Bal Harbour's Carpaccio).

BILTMORE HOTEL, THE 23 | 24 | 25 | 27 | $399

1200 Anastasia Ave., Coral Gables; 305-445-1926; fax 305-913-3152; 800-727-1926; www.biltmorehotel.com; 280 rooms, 6 suites

"Wow" gasp first-timers "blown away" by the "grandeur" of this Mediterranean-style "pearl of Coral Gables" that "takes you back to a time when travel meant elegance"; the "small", "well-appointed" rooms seem "ordinary" compared with the "ornate" lobby and "breathtaking", "lushly" landscaped 23,000-sq.-ft. pool where Johnny Weissmuller and Esther Williams once made waves; the "spectacular" "country club"–like grounds also encompass a remodeled golf course, fitness center, spa, lighted tennis courts and fine dining at the "superb" Palme d'Or and 1200 restaurant.

Circa 39 – | – | – | – | $199

3900 Collins Ave., Miami Beach; 305-538-4900; fax 305-538-4988; 877-8-247-2239; www.circa39.com; 67 rooms, 15 suites

Minimalist chic rules at this South Beach hotel where the fashion-conscious stay, work and play – there's poolside WiFi access, massage cabanas and a fitness room; score a suite with a kitchenette and let the waves lull you to sleep, and it should be a peaceful slumber since the pulsating clubs of Collins Road are a bit of a stroll away.

Conrad Miami – | – | – | – | $449

1395 Brickell Ave.; 305-503-6500; fax 305-533-7177; www.conradmiami.com; 14 suites, 189 rooms, 47 apartments

Hilton's upscale cousin offers both hotel rooms and private residences in its concave glass tower rising above Downtown Miami; there are sweeping views of Biscayne Bay, a 25th-floor bar and restaurant, rooftop pool, comprehensive business center, fitness club with tennis courts and full-service spa.

Delano 21 | 22 | 24 | 26 | $745

1685 Collins Ave., Miami Beach; 305-672-2000; fax 305-532-0099; 800-555-5001; www.delano-hotel.com; 184 rooms, 24 suites, 8 bungalows

"It's not just a hotel but a destination" say those seduced by this "ageless" South Beach Morgans Hotel where "billowing" double-height white curtains in the lobby transport you to "another realm"; if some smirk the "postage stamp–size" rooms are "hospital"-like and are irked by the "buff", "arrogant" staff, more are preoccupied by the "pool that never quits", "wonderful beach", "endless eye-candy parade" at the "jammin' bar" and "expensive but exquisite" Blue Door restaurant; just "don't forget to bring your bling" and try "not to have a bad hair day."

Doral Golf Resort & Spa 19 | 20 | 18 | 24 | $299

4400 NW 87th Ave.; 305-592-2000; fax 305-594-4682; 800-713-6725; www.doralresort.com; 493 rooms, 200 suites

"If you've got the next Tiger Woods-in-training", take the "little ones", otherwise, just "take the honey for a weekend of relaxation", including 90 holes at five "challenging golf courses", featuring the "must-play" famed Blue Monster, and a "top-notch spa" where you can "pamper yourself" with "luxurious" treatments; with other perks like the Arthur Ashe Tennis Center and an "impressive pool", guests rationalize that perhaps food, "service and accommodations don't need to be impeccable."

Eden Roc, Renaissance 19 | 20 | 17 | 22 | $349

4525 Collins Ave., Miami Beach; 305-531-0000; fax 305-674-5555; 800-327-8337; www.renaissancehotels.com; 349 rooms, 63 suites

A 1956 "throwback to Miami Beach's heyday", this oceanfront "Rat Pack favorite" is the bee's knees in contemporary "retro cool" thanks to a $10-million "face-lift" (which may not be reflected in the above ratings); "where better to live like Secret Agent 007 in *Goldfinger*" with "plush amenities" like an "awesome spa and health club", a rock climbing wall, squash courts, a "fabulous pool with cabanas, beachfront dining and a social bar"; still, it can be far from Eden "for individuals who want to be in the heart of the scene."

FAIRMONT TURNBERRY ISLE RESORT & CLUB 25 | 25 | 23 | 26 | $559

19999 W. Country Club Dr., Aventura; 305-932-6200; fax 305-933-6560; 800-327-7028; www.turnberryisle.com; 351 rooms, 41 suites

"Pamper yourself at the Willow Stream Spa" and at the two golf courses and 19 tennis courts on this "exquisitely appointed" resort with 300 "luscious" acres "that's close enough to Miami" "but just far enough away"; guests "luxuriate in the marble bathrooms with whirlpool tubs and TVs" and "spacious rooms" with "European-inspired furnishings", revel in the "lighthearted atmosphere" and "venture out only when they need to refuel at restaurants ranging from gourmet to casual chic" or rev up wardrobes at Bal Harbour or Adventura Mall.

FISHER ISLAND HOTEL & RESORT 25 | 25 | 23 | 26 | $575

(fka Inn at Fisher Island)

1 Fisher Island Dr., Miami Beach; 305-535-6080; fax 305-535-6003; 800-537-3708; www.fisherisland.com; 2 rooms, 49 suites, 7 villas, 3 cottages

"Take the ferry to paradise" aka this former 1928 Vanderbilt mansion converted into an "expensive" but "gorgeous" resort encompassing cottages, villas, seaside suites and condos on a 216-acre private island with the "Miami skyline as the backdrop"; "fun golf carts" take you where you need to go, whether it's the "superb spa", tennis courts, a golf course (currently being renovated) or boating; "you can't go wrong for a weekend getaway, though you won't have enough time to enjoy the amenities."

FOUR SEASONS MIAMI 27 | 26 | 24 | 27 | $375

1435 Brickell Ave.; 305-358-3535; fax 305-358-7758; www.fourseasons.com/miami; 182 rooms, 39 suites

If you're "looking for a respite from South Beach", "this is the place", a "gorgeous" "urban oasis" in Downtown Miami that's near the financial district ("perfect for the business traveler") and "convenient to everything"; "true Four Seasons charm" is on display via "complimentary frozen grapes" and "handy Evian mists" as you tan, and there's plenty of "glitz" too, with "magnificent rooms", a "terrific" gym and a "fabulous" spa – little wonder "drinks Friday night by the pool are the hottest ticket in town."

Grove Isle Club & Resort 23 | 23 | 26 | 21 | $350

4 Grove Isle Dr., Coconut Grove; 305-858-8300; fax 305-858-5908; 800-884-7683; www.groveisle.com; 49 rooms

Escape from the "Miami hustle" and head "off the beaten path" to this "romantic", "hidden castaway treasure" with "amazing service" on a "secluded", "tiny island" right off the coast of Coconut Grove; it's "worth the trek" even if just to savor the "outstanding" seafood and "beautiful setting" at the "upscale" Baleen's restaurant, plus the "exotic rooms" with a Caribbean Colonial decor, tennis and a 111-slip marina make it all the more "idyllic"; N.B. a new spa opened in 2005.

Hotel, The 19 | 21 | 26 | 20 | $205

801 Collins Ave., Miami Beach; 305-531-2222; fax 305-531-3222; 877-843-4683; www.thehotelofsouthbeach.com; 48 rooms, 4 suites

What a "cool SoBe" "classic" concur acolytes of this boutique property transformed by fashion designer Todd Oldham into a "funky" haunt with the "hippest lobby bar" around; the "artful" rooms are "gorgeous" (though "tiny"), but "why spend time there" when the "wonderful rooftop pool" with a "to-die-for view" "beckons"?; "be sure to eat at Wish" – from the "spectacular" outdoor terrace to the "delicious" fare, it's just "awesome"; N.B. the Spire Bar & Lounge opened post-*Survey*.

Hyatt Regency Coral Gables 22 | 21 | 17 | 20 | $285

50 Alhambra Plaza, Coral Gables; 305-441-1234; fax 305-441-0520; 800-233-1234; www.coralgables.hyatt.com; 242 rooms

"If you want to avoid the hubbub of South Beach", head to this "pick of Downtown Coral Gables", a "great business location" "just a short stroll to the local gourmet restaurants and boutique shops" of Miracle Mile and "convenient to the University of Miami"; inspired by Spain's Alhambra Palace, the building has a "Mediterranean feel" and "beautiful ceilings", plus boosters also give the "big comfortable rooms", health club and pool and "nice Sunday brunch" a thumb's up.

InterContinental Miami 20 | 19 | 18 | 20 | $229

100 Chopin Plaza; 305-577-1000; fax 305-577-0384; 800-327-0200; www.interconti.com; 607 rooms, 34 suites

A "first-class business hotel in Downtown Miami" that also offers "good meeting facilities", this appealing choice is "more for an adult crowd" though "there are lots of shops and restaurants" at the nearby "popular tourist area", Bayside Marketplace, "to make older kids happy"; the "comfortable rooms", casual Blue Water Cafe and "fabulous poolside deck" "provide beautiful views" of the bay and "ships in the harbor", plus it's "convenient" to American Airlines Arena, home of the Miami Heat.

JW Marriott Hotel Miami ▽ 24 | 22 | 19 | 23 | $229

1109 Brickell Ave.; 305-329-3500; fax 305-371-8820; 800-228-9290; www.marriott.com; 296 rooms, 22 suites

Set in a "perfect Downtown location", this "popular place for business travelers" is perhaps what other hotels "should model themselves after"; the "lovely" accommodations come equipped with computers and "very good amenities", plus there are 14 on-site meeting rooms; at the end of the day wind down in "a modern, elegant" setting with "divine beds", "beautiful artwork" and "a great view of Biscayne Bay."

Loews Miami Beach 21 21 20 24 $399

1601 Collins Ave., Miami Beach; 305-604-1601; fax 305-604-3999; 800-235-6397; www.loewshotels.com; 739 rooms, 51 suites

Surrounded by "lush palms", this "behemoth's" "great location" in the heart of SoBe's art deco district "can't be beat"; it may "not be as chic" as some of the smaller boutique properties in the area, but pragmatic patrons find it "convenient" and "accommodating" – "you request it and you've got it – from a yoga ball to a baby bottle" to "ices served poolside" – plus the fitness center, spa and "facilities on the beach are dazzling", and Emeril's restaurant is "quite a perk."

MANDARIN ORIENTAL 28 26 27 28 $525

500 Brickell Key Dr.; 305-913-8288; fax 305-913-8300; 866-888-6780; www.mandarinoriental.com; 327 rooms, 31 suites

"Are we in Tokyo or Miami" muse acolytes of this "multicultural" "major wow" "outpost on Brickell Key" that packs a "definite cool factor" especially for those who "don't want to be surrounded by the South Beach crowd" but still want "decadent R&R"; it's all about "Zen and the art of luxury", from the "superb restaurant, Azul", with "unbelievable views" of Biscayne Bay to the "glorious rooms" with "spacious soaking tubs" and "gorgeous amenities" to the "pampering" 15,000-sq.-ft. spa and "world-class service."

Mayfair Hotel & Spa 21 20 16 18 $219

3000 Florida Ave., Coconut Grove; 305-441-0000; fax 305-447-9173; 800-328-8880; www.mayfairhousehotel.com; 179 suites

"A glass of champagne" is served at check-in at this "quirky" but "sexy" art nouveau "getaway" in a "great location" by CocoWalk and the Streets of Mayfair; though the hot tubs are a "great" touch and the "building is beautiful", the facilities are "dated", so it's a good thing new owners plan a major upgrade, adding a 13,000-sq.-ft. rooftop area with plasma TVs, private spa and cocktail lounge.

Mutiny ▽ 22 18 16 20 $299

2951 S. Bayshore Dr., Coconut Grove; 305-441-2100; fax 305-441-2822; 888-868-8469; www.themutiny.com; 118 suites, 2 penthouses

Located on Sailboat Bay with "outstanding views of the waterfront" or "the city", this 12-story tower in Coconut Grove offers a mix of private condos and "spacious" deluxe suites and penthouses with private rooftop spas, plus features like a poolside waterfall, on-site restaurant and fitness center; N.B. WiFi has recently been added to all rooms.

Nash, Hotel – – – – $250

1120 Collins Ave., Miami Beach; 305-674-7800; fax 305-538-8288; 800-403-6274; www.hotelnash.com; 37 rooms, 18 suites

"If you're looking for cheap(er) and chic in a prime" art deco district location, this "trendy" boutique hotel, restored to its '30s glamour, "fits the bill", with the added perk of Mark's South Beach, featuring star chef Mark Militello's Floribbean fare; seductive comfort rules, whether at the three spa pools and courtyard garden or in rooms, colored in soothing sage and ivory and sporting "great showers with lots of toys" like Dornbracht bath fixtures.

Omni Colonnade ▽ 26 | 22 | 17 | 23 | $289

180 Aragon Ave., Coral Gables; 305-441-2600; fax 305-445-3929; 800-843-6664; www.omnicolonnade.com; 134 rooms, 23 suites

From the "glass of champagne" at check-in to the "bathrobes and ice bucket service, they really take care of you" at this "mostly modern" "classic" landmark in Downtown Gables, "well situated" "near trendy boutiques", eateries and area attractions; "marble, high ceilings and a colonnade add to the lofty effect", plus the "rooms are nicely furnished" with "comfy beds" (go for the "kickin' duplex room") and the rooftop sundeck and "nice pool" offer "great views"; N.B. there's on-site dining at Tula.

Pritikin Longevity Center & Spa Ⓢ – | – | – | – | $750

19735 Turnberry Way, Aventura; 305-935-7131; fax 305-935-7371; 800-327-4914; www.pritikin.com; 75 rooms, 8 suites

Most guests immerse themselves for two to four weeks in diet revolutionary Nathan Pritikin's lifestyle-changing program at this medically focused facility located midway between Miami and Ft. Lauderdale; despite deluxe waterfront suites offering whirlpool tubs and therapeutic spa treatments (for a supplemental fee), the goal here is to permanently improve one's health via monitored exercise programs, extensive lectures and a heart-healthy eating regimen; N.B. above nightly rates are per person, based on a required one-week minimum stay.

Raleigh, The 16 | 19 | 17 | 21 | $325

1775 Collins Ave., Miami Beach; 305-534-6300; fax 305-538-3140; www.raleighhotel.com; 105 rooms

"André Balazs gets it right again at this charming" art deco "golden nugget", "one of the hottest spots" "nestled amid the hustle-bustle of South Beach"; "can't get enough of the palm-shaded" "fabulous, famous pool" – it's "reason enough to stay here" – plus the "beach area rocks", so "put on your bikini and strut your stuff" among the "beautiful people"; afterwards, relax in your "incredibly comfortable bed" and try to forget that your room is "ridiculously small"; N.B. a multimillion-dollar renovation is underway, which may impact the above ratings.

RITZ-CARLTON COCONUT GROVE ✕Ⓢ 26 | 27 | 24 | 25 | $399

3300 SW 27th Ave., Coconut Grove; 305-644-4680; fax 305-644-4681; 800-241-3333; www.ritzcarlton.com; 98 rooms, 17 suites

"It's not your father's Ritz", rather, it's a "hip, sexy" Italian Renaissance–style "boutiquey" destination with a "beautiful lobby" where "every detail is thought of", from the location in "the heart of the Grove" within "walking distance of shops and the harbor" to the "fantastic dedicated staff" that "waits on you hand and foot" to the "great spa and gym"; the "classy, comfortable rooms" are "inviting" with "pretty white marble bathrooms", plus the Bizcaya Grill restaurant is "breathtaking" – try the "amazing" Sunday brunch, "it's definitely worth the splurge."

RITZ-CARLTON KEY BISCAYNE | 26 | 26 | 24 | 27 | $389 |

455 Grand Bay Dr., Key Biscayne; 305-365-4500; fax 305-365-4505; 800-241-3333; www.ritzcarlton.com; 342 rooms, 60 suites

"It's just a bridge away from Downtown Miami", nevertheless this "lavish" Key Biscayne oceanfront resort feels like a "wonderfully landscaped" "tropical" "paradise" with "deliciously appointed rooms" offering "gorgeous views of the ocean", "excellent dining" at Cioppino and "stellar service" with "loads of personnel to attend to every whim"; it's a "delightful place for just about anything" with a "to-die-for" oceanview spa sporting 21 treatment rooms, a "first-class beach" and an 11-court tennis garden, the largest of any Ritz, that's "terrific" for racquet "buffs."

Ritz-Carlton South Beach | 24 | 21 | 21 | 24 | $409 |

1 Lincoln Rd., Miami Beach; 786-276-4000; fax 786-276-4001; 800-241-3333; www.ritzcarlton.com; 376 rooms, 41 suites

"On the surface" this newly restored 1953 Morris Lapidus–designed art deco retreat "exudes the cool style of SoBe while deep down it's all Ritz Carlton", a "swoonworthy" oceanfront destination with $2 million worth of original artwork; "calm and classy", it "delivers" "magnificent rooms" with "luxurious decor" and "spacious bathrooms", an "incredible lobby" and "excellent service"; N.B. a David Bouley restaurant is slated to open in October 2005.

Setai, The | – | – | – | – | $900 |

2001 Collins Ave., Miami Beach; 305-520-6000; fax 305-520-6111; www.setai.com; 125 suites

This Miami Beach one-year-old from Amanresort co-founder Adrian Zecha sports a sleek, Asian-inspired silhouette and muted color scheme that just may toy with guests' sense of place; the all-suite accommodations are decked out with daybed seating, Acqua di Parma toiletries and in-room tubs for treatments without having to don a bathrobe; in addition to the spa itself, a restaurant, several bars and a pool offer distractions from all that sand and sea.

Shore Club, The | 20 | 19 | 25 | 24 | $545 |

1901 Collins Ave., Miami Beach; 305-695-3100; fax 305-695-3299; 877-640-9500; www.shoreclub.com; 332 rooms, 19 suites, 8 bungalows

"Talk about who's who" – this "swanky" "oasis" from the Morgans Hotel Group is the "scene to end all scenes" with celebs ("ah, there's Derek Jeter" . . .), "scantily clad hipsters" and "beautiful people all around you", whether you're parked at the "incredible pool" "that goes on forever" with its "Moroccan fantasy bar area", Skybar's "hectic night parties" or the "*très* chic" Nobu and Ago (co-owned by actor Robert De Niro); "service is up to par with what you would expect" from a "trendy" South Beach property, and while accommodations are "spare" "they do the trick" – you "don't stay in your room anyway."

Sonesta Beach Resort Key Biscayne | 21 | 20 | 19 | 22 | $300 |

350 Ocean Dr., Key Biscayne; 305-361-2021; fax 305-361-3096; 800-766-3782; www.sonesta.com; 281 rooms, 12 suites

A "respite from the frenzy of Miami Beach", this oceanfront resort near the Miami Seaquarium is "where romancing couples and families" can vacation "in harmony"; "nothing beats breakfast on the balcony while watching the ocean", unless, of course, you're "pampering yourself" at the "excellent" Euro-style spa or "just relaxing" at the "great beach" or Olympic-size pool.

Tides, The | 25 | 24 | 23 | 22 | $550 |

1220 Ocean Dr., Miami Beach; 305-604-5070; fax 305-503-3275; 800-439-4095; www.thetideshotel.com; 42 rooms, 3 suites

A "sublime" "oasis of hip civility", this art deco "charmer" designed by architect L. Murray Dixon in 1936 sports a "sizzling beach location" "in the heart" of SoBe, an "amazing staff" and an interior that's as "modern", and "minimalist, as the outside, with white the only color" evident in the "lovely large rooms", complete with telescopes and "gorgeous ocean views"; it's "incredibly romantic to dine alfresco" "across from the water", but a handful fume it's "party central" and wave away the pool as a "non-event."

Victor, Hotel | – | – | – | – | $335 |

1144 Ocean Drive, Miami Beach; 305-428-1234; fax 305-421-6281; www.hotelvictorsouthbeach.com; 40 rooms, 34 rooms, 8 bungalows, 8 suites

Who'd expect the newest South Beach hipster, within a perfume's whiff of the famed Versace mansion, to be managed by Hyatt Hotels?; it features 1930s Parisian styling via Jacques Garcia, SoBe hip outlets – restaurant Vix, seviche bar Vue and lounge V Bar are *the* places to see and be seen – and infinity-edge soaking tubs; rooms with outdoor showers make for a rather cool stay, but if it's not quite breezy enough, just talk to the on-site 'Vibe Manager' or resident DJ.

Wyndham Grand Bay - Coconut Grove | 22 | 22 | 20 | 19 | $300 |

2669 S. Bayshore Dr., Coconut Grove; 305-858-9600; fax 305-859-2026; 866-269-4915; www.wyndhamcoconutgrove.com; 130 rooms, 47 suites

"Still treats you as if you are a king or queen" with the kind of "service you hope for" opine patrons of this "quiet" "concierge-type" Grove hotel offering a "great location for an easy overnight" stay and a "fabulous view" of Biscayne Bay; the "beautiful foyer and bar" along with the on-site Bistro "add to its delights"; but grumblers gripe that this "once glittering symbol" is a "little worn around the edges."

Naples

Hyatt Regency Coconut Point Resort & Spa | 23 | 23 | 20 | 25 | $375 |

5001 Coconut Rd., Bonita Springs; 239-444-1234; fax 239-390-4277; 800-233-1234; www.coconutpoint.hyatt.com; 420 rooms, 30 suites

It's a "really neat place to stay in the Naples area" plus the exclusive "beach makes it feel like a real getaway" agree admirers who go nuts over this "secluded" spot with an "airy lobby" and "attentive service"; it's "just delightful", with a 5,000-sq.-ft. lagoon and "awesome" corkscrew waterslide (a kid "favorite"), "lavish surroundings", plus an "excellent spa" and golf course and "very good" dining options; but cynics snap it's "quite a trek" to take the boat to the private island.

La Playa Beach & Golf Resort 24 | 23 | 24 | 23 | $525

9891 Gulf Shore Dr.; 239-597-3123; fax 239-597-8283; 800-237-6883; www.laplayaresort.com; 180 rooms, 9 suites

Offering the "feel of a boutique hotel with the amenities of a large one", this refurbished "gem" has an "unbeatable setting right on the Gulf"; "can't say enough about the beautifully decorated rooms", "delightful public spaces" and "friendly service", and it's "spectacular to eat dinner as the sun sets into the water"; add in "fantastic golf" and the SpaTerre and fitness center and most are more than game to "get away here and relax."

Marco Beach Ocean Resort ∇ 23 | 23 | 23 | 26 | $239

480 S. Collier Blvd., Marco Island; 239-393-1400; fax 239-393-1401; 800-260-5089; www.marcoresort.com; 100 suites

Overlooking the Gulf "on Marco's sugar-white Crescent Beach", this "lovely", "sophisticated" all-suites Mediterranean-style boutique hotel "exudes charm" and a "wonderful European feel", prompting romantics to envision "a wedding on the sand" or at least "soaking in granite tubs" – when not soaking up "great views"; "luxurious" amenities include a full spa and fitness center, king-size beds, full and mini kitchens and balconies.

Marco Island Marriott Golf Resort & Spa 21 | 21 | 17 | 23 | $390

400 S. Collier Blvd., Marco Island; 239-394-2511; fax 239-642-2672; 800-438-4373; www.marriott.com; 629 rooms, 92 suites, 6 penthouses

"The grounds are lush and inviting, as are the green waters of the Gulf", while the updated rooms at this "great family place" "pick up some Florida flavor while keeping the best of Marriott's predictability" – no "we did not want to leave" reveal admirers; it has "one of the prettiest stretches of famous Crescent Beach", so "get up early and waste the day away" on the sugary sand or at the "lovely pools", then head to the "terrific pool spa" or redesigned golf course – you just "can't go wrong here."

Registry Resort, The 23 | 23 | 21 | 23 | $439

475 Seagate Dr.; 239-597-3232; fax 239-594-6777; 800-247-9810; www.registryresort.com; 474 rooms, 29 suites, 49 villas

A "jewel among the mangroves", this Gulfside family resort boasts "beautiful grounds" and "gorgeous rooms" with Tuscan-inspired decor; with five pools and a "fun" 100-ft. waterslide, 15 tennis courts, kids' camp, a health club and affiliation with the Naples Grande Golf Course "you want for nothing", plus the "long boardwalk to the beach" allows for a "flora and fauna lesson", and if "you'd rather not stroll" through the swamp there's the trolley; but chair potatoes harrumph it's "too far away."

RITZ-CARLTON GOLF RESORT 27 | 27 | 25 | 27 | $329

2600 Tiburon Dr.; 239-593-2000; fax 239-254-3300; 800-241-3333; www.ritzcarlton.com; 257 rooms, 38 suites

"If golf is your passion, this is the place to be", but even non-duffers deem this "absolutely stunning" retreat an "instant classic"; loyalists "love" the "long driveway that makes you feel like you are riding up to your castle", the "cookies and lemonade at check-in", the "impeccable service" and the "exquisite rooms" with "luxurious bathrooms stocked with perfect amenities"; it's a "wonderful low-key alternative" to Ritz-Carlton Naples, but if you want a spa and sand, you must take the shuttle "down the road" to the "big sister on the beach."

RITZ-CARLTON NAPLES 27 | 28 | 27 | 28 | $550

280 Vanderbilt Beach Rd.; 239-598-3300; fax 239-598-6690; 800-241-3333; www.ritzcarlton.com; 441 rooms, 22 suites

The "ultimate" "luxury escape", this "heavenly" "crown jewel" in the "Ritz resort empire" seduces sybarites with "sweeping" Gulf sunset views, an "extraordinary" three-story spa, four tennis courts, "elegant" rooms and club floor, a "divine" white sand beach, "luscious grounds" and an "incredible staff"; the selection of restaurants, including an all-you-can-eat breakfast, "leaves nothing to be desired" – and the whole place will be renovated head to toe in 2005; N.B. shuttle service is available to its nearby sister golf resort.

Orlando

★ **Tops in City**

27 Ritz-Carlton
26 Disney's Grand Floridian
25 Disney's Animal Kingdom
JW Marriott
24 Disney's BoardWalk Resort
Loews Portofino Bay
Disney's Wilderness Lodge
Hyatt Regency Grand Cypress
Disney's Beach Club
23 Disney's Yacht Club

Celebration Hotel 22 | 22 | 19 | 21 | $225

700 Bloom St., Celebration; 407-566-6000; fax 407-566-6001; 888-499-3800; www.celebrationhotel.com; 115 rooms

Within "close proximity to Disney parks", golf and a spa, this resort set in the "picture-perfect" planned community of Celebration is both a "business hotel for adults" and a "place for fun, sun and family"; the decor has a "very Pottery Barn feel", and while on-site "dining is adequate", the "bar is comfortable" and "it's an easy walk to rather good" restaurants.

Disney's Animal Kingdom Lodge 24 | 25 | 23 | 27 | $324

2901 Osceola Pkwy., Lake Buena Vista; 407-938-3000; www.disneyworld.com; 1274 rooms, 19 suites

"What could be better than waking up to real zebras, giraffes" and other exotic animals "roaming right outside your window" (if you "pay the extra bucks" for a savannah view) at this African-themed resort that despite being "far from other attractions" is "one of Disney's best"; although "accommodations are small, the safari-inspired decor makes you forget" the constraints, as do the "high-quality" Jiko and Boma restaurants, "enormous pool", "fire pit that's a perfect place to wind down" and "wonderful" staff; so "the only problem here is getting the kids to leave."

Disney's Beach Club Resort | 23 | 24 | 20 | 27 | $415
1800 Epcot Resorts Blvd., Lake Buena Vista; 407-934-8000; fax 407-934-3850; www.disneyworld.com; 520 rooms, 56 suites
Offering a "beachy feel right in the middle of Orlando" is this "gorgeous" resort where "there's something for young and old" and that's "just steps from Epcot and MGM Studios"; highlights include the "amazing" Stormalong Bay water park that's "a child's dream", a "sandy-bottomed wading pool for the little ones", "casual restaurants" plus an ice-cream parlor and "excellent Disney-quality service."

Disney's BoardWalk Resort | 24 | 25 | 22 | 26 | $415
2101 N. Epcot Resorts Blvd., Lake Buena Vista; 407-939-5100; fax 407-939-5150; www.disneyworld.com; 372 rooms, 383 resort homes
"Step back to the 1920s" at this "whimsical" hotel, notable for its "very friendly staff", "fun atmosphere" and "huge, bright" "welcoming rooms" in a "fantastic" Boardwalk location where guests find "penny candy, radio dramas", arcades, "face painting", "lovely shops and restaurants", and entertainment reminiscent of the "Atlantic City and Coney Island of yesteryear"; while it's just "a short stroll to Epcot" it can be "a long walk" to your room unless you stay "in the center of the resort."

DISNEY'S GRAND FLORIDIAN RESORT & SPA | 26 | 26 | 24 | 28 | $459
4401 Floridian Way, Lake Buena Vista; 407-824-2421; fax 407-824-3186; www.disneyworld.com; 668 rooms, 90 suites
Happily ever after endings seem possible at this "magical" "Victorian gem", a "real tonic" to the world of make-believe, especially "if you want to do Disney in style"; there's "Mickey marvelousness" everywhere, from the high tea and "stellar rooms" ("swanky" enough for adults) to "gorgeous grounds" to "traveling on the Monorail to the Magic Kingdom"; parents further praise the kid-friendly character breakfasts, themed rooms, "great view of fireworks" and the "impeccable" staff."

Disney's Polynesian Resort | 21 | 24 | 20 | 24 | $419
1600 Seven Seas Dr., Lake Buena Vista; 407-824-2000; fax 407-824-3174; www.disneyworld.com; 821 rooms, 32 suites
"Don't miss the luau" at this "laid-back" yet "deluxe resort", a "tropical" "oasis when you've had enough" of the Kingdom and "where you can hula" the night away in a "fantasyland" of "lush" palms and white sand beach (the "hammocks are very inviting"); it's one of Mickeyland's most "romantic, relaxing" settings yet kid-friendly, with a volcano pool, sailboats and arcades, plus the "Monorail makes Park hopping a breeze"; while some complain the rooms are "dated", others counter it "hides its age well."

Disney's Wilderness Lodge | 23 | 25 | 21 | 27 | $289
901 Timberline Dr., Lake Buena Vista; 407-824-3200; fax 407-824-3232; www.disneyworld.com; 700 rooms, 27 suites
"Disney's answer to the great outdoors", this family resort exudes "rustic charm" in a woodsy setting that feels "like the great Northwest only in Florida", where you can "relax in rocking chairs by the stone fireplace" in a "beautiful", split-log lobby ("take the free hotel tour for loads of information"); kids "love the faux Old Faithful" (a "geyser of all things!"), sand-bottomed pool

and bunk beds while carnivores of all ages adore the "ever-rowdy Whispering Canyon Cafe."

Disney's Yacht Club Resort | 23 | 25 | 19 | 27 | $404 |

1700 Epcot Resorts Blvd., Lake Buena Vista; 407-934-7000; fax 407-934-3450; www.disneyworld.com; 610 rooms, 11 suites

Patrons praise "this more sedate" "deluxe" destination with "easy access to Epcot" that's like a "New England experience in Orlando" with a "nautical-themed" lobby and environs "that make you want to put on a blue blazer and deck shoes"; it's a "more adult getaway" (even the "Yachtsman Steakhouse serves decidedly grown-up food") but it's also a "kids' paradise", with a "fantastic" pool shared with Disney's Beach Club on Stormalong Bay; a very "attentive staff" and "elegant facilities" make for smooth sailing.

Gaylord Palms | 23 | 20 | 18 | 24 | $200 |

6000 W. Osceola Pkwy.; 407-586-0000; fax 407-586-1999; www.gaylordpalms.com; 1275 rooms, 125 suites

"It's like Vegas" at this "massive" "theme park", a convention hotel that's "close enough to Disney"; there's a "grand atrium" with waterfalls, a "Canyon Ranch spa and adults-only pool" and "lots of kids' activities", plus "excellent dining" and entertainment and "spacious, well-appointed rooms reminiscent of the Biosphere"; but naysayers scoff that it "draws from the 'more is more' school of design" and "makes up in hokey what it lacks in class."

Hard Rock Hotel Orlando | 25 | 22 | 20 | 26 | $284 |

5800 Universal Blvd.; 407-503-2000; fax 407-503-7655; 800-232-7827; www.universalorlando.com/hardrock; 621 rooms, 29 suites

"Rock 'n' roll, baby!", yeah, this "funky", "fun" "family vacation spot" with a "boutique" feel is "as hip as it gets in Orlando"; it's a "memorable experience" for "young rockers, grown-up hippies" and teens alike, with CD players in the "amazing" rooms, an "awesome guitar-shaped pool" with "groovy underwater stereo speakers", a "modern lounge" and dining that reaches "far beyond expectations"; the "best perk", however, is the Express pass "that lets guests bypass lines" at Universal.

Hyatt Regency Grand Cypress | 23 | 24 | 22 | 27 | $349 |

1 Grand Cypress Blvd.; 407-239-1234; fax 407-239-3800; 800-233-1234; www.hyatt.com; 676 rooms, 74 suites

An "elegant escape from the tourist world" for the "Disney-ed-out", this 1,500-acre Lake Buena Vista conventioneers- and "kid-friendly" "oasis" feels like a "self-contained island of relaxation" with a "beautiful atrium" boasting "lush vegetation, sculptures and running water" where "children are captivated" by "parrots flying around"; once outside, explore the "amazing" grounds", from the free-form pool with "grottos, caves and waterfalls" to the "wonderfully challenging" Jack Nicklaus–designed golf courses.

JW Marriott Orlando, Grande Lakes | 25 | 24 | 23 | 27 | $249 |

4040 Central Florida Pkwy.; 407-206-2300; fax 407-206-2301; 800-228-9290; www.marriott.com; 934 rooms, 64 suites

"Sit in the lap of luxury" at this "first-class" hotel on 500 "beautiful" acres with "very comfortable rooms", a "high level of service" and "superb dining"; it's "close enough to the parks" yet – close your ears Mickey – "far enough to maintain your sanity and de-Disney your senses", with "plenty of options" for everyone, be it "hanging out at the massive pool and lazy river", or "to-die-for spa" or teeing off at the nearby Ritz-Carlton Golf Club; N.B. the 28,000-sq.-ft. exhibition hall, Coquina, is now open.

Loews Portofino Bay 25 | 23 | 22 | 26 | $320

5601 Universal Blvd.; 407-503-1000; fax 407-503-1010; 800-232-7827; www.loewshotels.com; 711 rooms, 39 suites

"While it ain't Italy" it sure "feels like it" maintain *amici* of this "*magnifico*" family resort that strives to duplicate the seaside village of Portofino with "Vespas in the courtyard" and "plush rooms" with "*molto bene* beds", yet still manages to be "less cloying" than other thematic destinations; "send the kids away so you can play" at the "wonderful spa" and "incredible pool" and enjoy the "great" dining, then "take a ferry to Universal."

Marriott Orlando World Center Resort & Convention Center 20 | 20 | 18 | 24 | $219

8701 World Center Dr.; 407-239-4200; fax 407-238-8777; 800-228-9290; www.marriott.com; 1892 rooms, 111 suites

Even though it's a "gigantic resort", the staff "does a good job" at this "wonderful facility" with a "fantastic" free-form pool, hot tubs and a "great" 18-hole golf course and a spa; a few taunt it's "too damn big" with "generic rooms", but more profess it provides an "exceptional family experience" or business destination.

Peabody Orlando, The 22 | 22 | 21 | 22 | $395

9801 International Dr.; 407-352-4000; fax 407-351-0073; 800-732-2639; www.peabodyorlando.com; 891 rooms, 57 suites

"Forget Donald! here's where the cool ducks hang out" confirm fans who flock to see the "twice daily march of the mallards" by the lobby fountain, a "tradition that endures" at this chain's "elegant" retreat; no wonder it lures expense-accounters: you "can't beat the location if you're going to the convention center", the "rooms are swank and the staff ain't snobby"; "hit the B-Line for diner food" and treat yourself to high tea weekday afternoons.

Renaissance Orlando Resort at SeaWorld 21 | 20 | 16 | 20 | $219

6677 Sea Harbor Dr.; 407-351-5555; fax 407-351-9991; 800-468-3571; www.renaissancehotels.com; 778 rooms, 64 suites

"Walk to SeaWorld" from this "comfortable resort", a "good choice" "for those who like the big hotel feel"; the "atrium, with its koi ponds and birdcage, sets a relaxing tone" while the "lobby is light and airy", the "rooms impressive" and the "breakfast buffet comprehensive"; but "otherwise, the food is just good" shrug critics who consider this property "something of a cookie-cutter."

RITZ-CARLTON ORLANDO, GRANDE LAKES 27 | 27 | 26 | 28 | $349

4012 Central Florida Pkwy.; 407-206-2400; fax 407-206-2401; 800-576-5760; www.ritzcarlton.com; 518 rooms, 66 suites

"Ooo-la-la!" this Ritz two-year-old two miles from SeaWorld is "starting out great" agree admirers who find it a real "escape", "especially if you wish a nighttime reprieve from the world of

Mickey"; "service is superlative", the rooms are "gorgeous" and you can "make a day of the incredible pool area", "phenomenal" spa with 40 treatment rooms, 18-hole golf course and three tennis courts; while dining options abound, Norman's, featuring the fare of celebrity chef Norman Van Aken, is the "epitome of *magnifique*."

Royal Pacific Resort 22 20 21 24 $234

6300 Hollywood Way; 407-503-3000; fax 407-503-3166; 800-232-7827; www.loewshotels.com; 949 rooms, 51 suites

"South Pacific in the '30s" – that's the inspiration for Loews' "perfect location near all the Universal Studio attractions" evident in its wood carvings, totems, orchids, waterfalls and Saturday luaus; the "smartly decorated rooms" and "beautiful greenery" exude a "quiet elegance – what a relief after a hard day of fun" – plus the "phenomenal" lagoon-style pool area, kids' buffet, delectable treats at Emeril's Tchoup Chop and sprawling fitness center "make it a must for families"; N.B. guests have access to the spa at nearby Loews Portofino Bay Hotel.

Villas of Grand Cypress, The ▽ 28 24 22 27 $450

1 N. Jacaranda St., Lake Buena Vista; 407-239-4700; fax 407-239-7219; 800-835-7377; www.grandcypress.com; 73 suites, 96 villas

"Convenient to all things Disney", this sprawling Lake Buena Vista resort also offers a "peaceful getaway from the frenzy"; "it's a treat to stay" in the "lovely", "spacious" Med-style villas with sunken Roman tubs and patios "overlooking the lagoons" and fairways; duffers delight in the "outstanding" Jack Nicklaus–designed courses, plus the "excellent golf instruction", equestrian center, tennis courts, spa, marina, seven restaurants and "other facilities please" plenty; N.B. renovations are currently underway.

Walt Disney World Dolphin 19 21 19 23 $325

1500 Epcot Resorts Blvd., Lake Buena Vista; 407-934-4000; fax 407-934-4880; 800-227-1500; www.swandolphin.com; 1373 rooms, 136 suites

"Be amazed by Michael Graves'" "whimsical" "architecture while feasting like royalty at Todd English's bluezoo" restaurant or Shula's Steakhouse" at this "O-town" location that's a "little less Mickey"; the rooms are "cheery", "service bends over backwards" and the "cool beach" and "wonderful pool area" make it a "good choice" for families and the "convention set"; but the disappointed deem the decor "tacky" and bristle at the "conference hotel atmosphere"; N.B. a spa opened post-*Survey*.

Walt Disney World Swan 20 21 18 22 $325

1500 Epcot Resorts Blvd., Lake Buena Vista; 407-934-3000; fax 407-934-4499; 800-248-7926; www.swandolphin.com; 668 rooms, 90 suites

"Pick your animal" – the Dolphin's sister resort with "awesome architecture" graced with swan statues is a "solid choice" and also "just a stone's throw from Epcot" and MGM; it's a tad "goofy", but still "classy" with a "tranquil atmosphere", five pools, a grotto beach and several restaurants, all of which "makes you feel like an adult"; biz types confer it's also "convention world done right" with "terrific meeting accommodations."

Westin Grand Bohemian 26 23 22 22 $499
325 S. Orange Ave.; 407-313-9000; fax 407-313-9001; 888-472-6312; www.grandbohemianhotel.com; 214 rooms, 36 suites
"What a hotel would look like if designed by Cirque du Soleil" quip patrons of this "classy", "chic", boutique experience, a "must see for art lovers" with more than 150 original pieces on display, and a Downtown alternative for the "more sophisticated traveler"; "bohemians and epicures alike enjoy the luxurious trappings" including "rooms that are plum gorgeous (unless you get a red one)", "fine dining" at Boheme and a "surprisingly fun", "hip velvet lounge"; P.S. "stay here once and you're theirs forever."

Wyndham Palace Resort & Spa 19 20 18 21 $289
1900 N. Buena Vista Dr., Lake Buena Vista; 407-827-2727; fax 407-827-3364; 800-996-3426; www.wyndhampalaceresort.com; 888 rooms, 124 suites
"Take me away from Mickey and spoil me rotten" sigh weary parents who hightail it to the "lovely" European-style spa at this "super-convenient" location an "easy stroll" from Downtown Disney; "comfortable" quarters with "private balconies" "coupled with outstanding dining" and a "wonderful pool" "make this a must"; N.B. cynics may be pleased by post-*Survey* renovations.

Palm Beach

Brazilian Court 20 22 23 18 $550
301 Australian Ave.; 561-655-7740; fax 561-655-0801; 800-552-0335; www.thebraziliancourt.com; 40 rooms, 40 suites
"A welcome change from too-large, impersonal hotels", this "quaint" boutique retreat built in 1926 and frequented by Palm Beach personalities like Marjorie Merriweather Post is having its "shabbily genteel" persona refreshed into a condo property with upgraded decor and furnishings, a Frédéric Fekkai spa and the Manhattan import Café Boulud, which offers "romantic" alfresco dining and was voted No. 1 for Decor in the Palm Beach section of our *Miami/So. Florida Restaurant Survey*; but best, perhaps, is its timeless location near the ocean and steps from Worth Avenue.

BREAKERS, THE 23 25 24 27 $470
1 S. County Rd.; 561-655-6611; fax 561-659-8403; 800-833-3141; www.thebreakers.com; 503 rooms, 57 suites
"Now you're talking" say fans of this oceanfront "playground" that's been the "buckle in Palm Beach's belt" for over a century, combining "kid-friendliness" with adult "sophistication" and "service fit for royalty"; compared with the "robber baron–baroque" public areas, the "small" rooms seem "underwhelming" (although a recent renovation may have changed things), but "great golf" on the newly reopened Rees Jones–designed Breakers West, a spa and dinner at L'Escalier make this "budget-buster" "worth a visit"; N.B. it's currently adding bungalows and a new restaurant and pools.

Chesterfield 19 23 19 19 $250
363 Cocoanut Row; 561-659-5800; fax 561-659-6707; 800-243-7871; www.chesterfieldpb.com; 41 rooms, 11 suites, 1 penthouse
This "charming, European-style" boutique, a member of Small Luxury Hotels of the World, might be "limited in facilities", but it

enjoys a "prime location within walking distance to Worth Avenue and the beach" and has a "very friendly staff" that can organize passes to nearby gyms and spas; although some feel it's "time to redecorate" the "too small" rooms, others appreciate their pet-friendliness and note the real "cat's meow" is the Leopard Lounge, which offers live entertainment.

Colony Hotel 20 | 21 | 19 | 21 | $440

155 Hammon Ave.; 561-655-5430; fax 561-659-8104; 800-521-5525; www.thecolonypalmbeach.com; 68 rooms, 16 suites, 7 villas

"Sun-bathing can be an art" at the pool areas of this "quiet", "civilized" hotel with a "perfect location" near posh Worth Avenue; the redesigned Polo restaurant is alternately described as "superb" and "disappointing", while the "very small rooms'" "outdated" decor will likely be enhanced by a post-*Survey* renovation; if some nostalgists lament "it was better in the 1960s and '70s", others happily detect a whiff of "Old Florida" and claim the bar still hosts a "very Palm Beach scene."

FOUR SEASONS 25 | 26 | 25 | 25 | $495

2800 S. Ocean Blvd.; 561-582-2800; fax 561-547-1374; 800-432-2335; www.fourseasons.com; 194 rooms, 13 suites

"You're treated like a king" at this "crown jewel", where "every need is attended to", from "fresh fruit and a spray of mist on your face as you lie" at the oceanfront pool (like "having your own Palm Beach mansion") to "excellent children's programs" to the "best massages" at the full-service spa; "the rooms are beautiful, the grounds spectacular and the restaurant serves awesome fish" (and was voted No. 1 for Service in the Palm Beach section of our *Miami/So. Florida Restaurant Survey*); but a handful find being three miles south of Worth Avenue too "removed."

PGA National Resort & Spa 17 | 18 | 17 | 24 | $399

400 Ave. of the Champions, Palm Beach Gardens; 561-627-2000; fax 561-227-2595; 800-633-9150; www.pga-resorts.com; 339 rooms, 59 villas

"It's all about the golf" opine putters who dream of playing the "first-rate" Fazio, Litten, Nicklaus and Palmer–designed courses at this home of the PGA of America golf tournament that also boasts a resort and cottages with "huge rooms" overlooking the fairways; the "great" health and racquet club with 19 tennis courts, a "pretty darned good" "luxurious spa", "beautiful walkways and a man-made beach" ensure there's plenty for non-duffers to do; still, cynics snipe "it's nothing special."

Ritz-Carlton Palm Beach 25 | 25 | 23 | 25 | $560

100 S. Ocean Blvd., Manalapan; 561-533-6000; fax 561-588-4202; 800-241-3333; www.ritzcarlton.com; 214 rooms, 56 suites

"Wake up to the sounds of the ocean" at this "smallish" property that "lacks the grand scale of other Ritz resorts" despite its seven acres of beach; "fond memories" are created with "magnificent suites" ("splurge on the club floor"), the "upscale" champagne Sunday brunch at the "wonderfully plush" Soleil restaurant, seven tennis courts and a "lovely" spa; still, the less-smitten mutter this is "no Palm Beach" – it's "off the beaten path" about 10 minutes south.

Sandestin

Sandestin Golf & Beach Resort ▽ 23 | 22 | 22 | 28 | $168

9300 Emerald Coast Pkwy. W.; 850-267-8150; fax 850-267-8222; 800-277-0800; www.sandestin.com; 343 rooms, 1276 villas

"Everything you could want in a beach vacation" can be found at this "expansive resort" on 2,400 acres between the Gulf of Mexico and Choctawhatchee Bay, eight miles east of Destin, where "white sand, blue water" and five accommodation areas await; "ride jet skis to catch views of stingrays", and once on shore, take advantage of the four golf courses and "fabulous lessons", 15 tennis courts and spa before exploring the boutiques at Village of Baytowne Wharf; N.B. 650 rooms are currently being added.

Santa Rosa Beach

Water Color Inn ▽ 28 | 26 | 25 | 26 | $395

34 Goldenrod Circle, Seagrove Beach; 850-534-5000; fax 850-534-5001; 888-775-2545; www.watercolorinn.com; 60 rooms, 66 cottages, 69 townhouses

"Just what the Panhandle needed", this "amazing undiscovered gem" (a member of Small Luxury Hotels of the World) with "beautiful architecture" designed by David Rockwell is comprised of a separate hotel and vacation cottages and set on a "fantastic stretch" of white Gulf Coast beach; "now this is a first-rate resort" – "it's relaxation to a T" attest admirers awed by the "excellent" accommodations, "gorgeous pool and spa", five tennis courts, biking and "great Fish Out of Water restaurant"; N.B. there's also a Tom Fazio–designed golf course six miles east.

Sarasota

Captiva Beach Resort 21 | 20 | 19 | 23 | $175

6772 Sara Sea Circle, Siesta Key; 941-349-4131; fax 941-349-8141; 800-349-4131; www.captivabeachresort.com; 3 bungalows, 6 apartments, 7 suites, 4 villas

"Ship-wreck me here anytime" say those who make a habit of "relaxing and resting" at this inn steps from the sugary sands of Crescent Beach on Siesta Key near Sarasota; owners Robert and Jane Ispaso make vacationing easy for families, with cooking facilities in all rooms and suites (and restaurants "within walking distance"), a pool and "attentive service"; P.S. post-*Survey* renovations should quiet critics who claim it "needs a makeover."

Colony Beach & Tennis Resort, The 20 | 22 | 22 | 24 | $400

1620 Gulf of Mexico Dr., Longboat Key; 941-383-6464; fax 941-383-7549; 800-426-5669; www.colonybeachresort.com; 234 suites

While "tennis rules" at this coastal resort, it's also a "wonderful vacation spot for everyone" thanks to a "gorgeous stretch of beach", a spa, activities for children in a "secure environment where they can roam free" and a restaurant whose "views cannot be beat"; some are "disappointed" by the "tired" rooms, but having a "glass of champagne while overlooking the Gulf is a daily highlight."

Resort at Longboat Key Club, The 22 | 20 | 19 | 23 | $310

301 Gulf of Mexico Dr., Longboat Key; 941-383-8821; fax 941-383-0359; 800-237-8821; www.longboatkeyclub.com; 205 rooms, 180 suites

"All the creature comforts of home in a beachfront setting" can be found at this "lovely" resort in a "perfect location" on a barrier island in the Gulf, just off the coast of Sarasota; it's "just what a resort should be", with "suitelike rooms", a "great spa", fitness center, a 45-hole golf course "in great shape" and 38 tennis courts; still, the disappointed tut it's just "so-so – I expected more."

RITZ-CARLTON 25 | 26 | 24 | 25 | $300

1111 Ritz-Carlton Dr.; 941-309-2000; fax 941-309-2100; 800-241-3333; www.ritzcarlton.com; 244 rooms, 22 suites

"Plush with a capital P" applaud patrons of the "over-the-top" facility in "the heart of Sarasota" boasting a "staff that makes you feel like you live there"; the "stunning" $30-million Members Beach Club with "every amenity and activity one could hope for", including a Gulf-front pool, "great outdoor patio restaurant" and kids' recreation on Lido Key is just a "short van ride" away and should "help overcome its urban location"; guests also revel in the "world-class" spa and "rooms with all the needed accoutrements", plus a golf course opens in December 2005.

St. Augustine

Casa Monica Hotel Ⓗ ▽ 24 | 24 | 22 | 22 | $169

95 Cordova St.; 904-827-1888; fax 904-827-0426; 800-648-1888; www.casamonica.com; 124 rooms, 14 suites

It's "unlike anything else in St. Augustine" sigh surveyors about this "delightful" 1888 hotel on the National Register of Historic Places that's like "staying in a castle" thanks to its "romantic" Moorish-revival architecture, "amazing" suites and "small rooms furnished very well" with wrought-iron beds and a pervading "old-world charm"; although it's not on the sands, it has a "superb Downtown location within walking distance to everything", access to a beach club, a "wonderful pool", "terrific bar" and "top-notch" restaurant.

Renaissance Resort at World Golf Village, The ▽ 20 | 20 | 15 | 21 | $189

500 S. Legacy Trail; 904-940-8000; fax 904-940-8008; 888-740-7020; www.worldgolfrenaissance.com; 271 rooms, 30 suites

"Golf heaven" awaits at this "great setting", home of the World Golf of Fame, two 18-hole championship courses, with one designed by Arnold Palmer and Jack Nicklaus, the Murray Bros. Caddyshack restaurant created by actor Bill Murray and a 10-story hotel with an atrium lobby; non-duffers take to the tennis courts and swimming pools or access the Serenata Beach Club in nearby Ponte Vedra Beach, but others say "forget it" if you're not on the green team.

Tampa/St. Petersburg

Belleview Biltmore Ⓗ Ⓢ 18 | 20 | 19 | 20 | $179

25 Belleview Blvd., Clearwater; 727-373-3000; fax 727-441-4173; 800-237-8947; www.belleviewbiltmore.com; 198 rooms, 40 suites

Opened in 1897, this "large", "grande dame" nicknamed the 'White Queen of the Gulf' is undergoing a "much-needed" major restoration to upgrade rooms and add such features as high-speed Internet service; but the "gorgeous" coastal setting is still intact, and the Donald Ross–designed golf course, red-clay tennis courts, spa and fitness center, three dining areas and an off-site beach club are there for the asking.

Chalet Suzanne Inn ✕Ⓢ 20 | 24 | 28 | 17 | $169

3800 Chalet Suzanne Dr., Lake Wales; 863-676-6011; fax 863-676-1814; 800-433-6011; www.chaletsuzanne.com; 26 rooms

Whether for a "memorable" American meal or a "romantic" weekend getaway, those with a "funky" sensibility favor this "charming" family-owned Central Florida inn and restaurant; each of the "quaint" rooms is "uniquely designed" and furnished with "eclectic antiques", and activities include use of the pool and private lake, tours of its gourmet soup-canning plant and enjoying "drinks and nibbles in the wine cellar while waiting to have dinner."

Clearwater Beach Marriott Suites on Sand Key ∇ 23 | 24 | 22 | 24 | $189

1201 Gulf Blvd., Clearwater Beach; 727-596-1100; fax 727-595-4292; www.marriott.com; 220 suites

An aquatic playground featuring a 35-ft. waterfall and a year-round children's program help make this "suite retreat" with "unbeatable" views of Clearwater Bay and the Gulf of Mexico a "marvelous" family getaway; while its Sand Key locale can be "a bit sleepy", the resort keeps guests busy with "white-sand beaches", water sports, tennis and a health club, plus there's always Busch Gardens about 35 miles away.

Don CeSar Beach Resort, A Loews Hotel ⒽⓈ 22 | 24 | 22 | 24 | $200

3400 Gulf Blvd., St. Petersburg Beach; 727-360-1881; fax 727-367-7597; 800-282-1116; www.doncesar.com; 235 rooms, 40 suites, 2 penthouses

"The pink lady is quite a dame" agree admirers of this "well-restored" Spanish-style "luxury hotel" that once attracted guests like F. Scott Fitzgerald and today, under the Loews banner, "stands out from the boxie chains"; "anyone can be Cinderella at this enchanting" resort on St. Pete's "pristine sugar-white beach" where "sunset is like living in a postcard" with "perfect drinks and dolphins leaping"; "plush", "small rooms" and "excellent" food enhances the "fairy tale" for all but a few who say it "misses on service, especially for such palatial prices"; N.B. new spa construction is planned for 2006.

Grand Hyatt Tampa Bay 23 | 22 | 23 | 22 | $225

6200 Courtney Campbell Cswy., Tampa; 813-874-1234; fax 813-207-6790; 800-233-1234; www.hyatt.com; 421 rooms, 24 suites

A "great escape" just five minutes from the airport, this "Tampa oasis" is set on a 35-acre wildlife resort where you can "spot the occasional dolphin in the bay" and even go for "excellent nature walks"; rooms are done up in "bright" coastal colors ("for comfort and privacy, ask for a casita" – they're "excellent for a romantic getaway") while Armani's, the "fantastic" rooftop restaurant, sports "awesome views" and "pleasant service"; just a couple complain it's a "bland business" bunker.

Hyatt Regency Tampa Bay ▽ 21 | 20 | 23 | 22 | $215

211 N. Tampa St., Tampa; 813-225-1234; fax 813-273-0234; www.tamparegency.hyatt.com; 503 rooms, 18 suites

"Conveniently located" in the business district near the Port of Tampa, this "comfortable" "quality property" boasts a five-story atrium, site of the "surprisingly good" Avanzare bistro, recently renovated rooms decorated with contemporary flair and a heated outdoor pool with a rooftop deck and whirlpool; guests can work out at the on-premises health club and also access the YMCA next door, plus there are 17 golf courses nearby to satisfy duffers.

Renaissance Vinoy 23 | 24 | 23 | 25 | $349

501 Fifth Ave., NE, St. Petersburg; 727-894-1000; fax 727-894-1970; 888-303-4430; www.vinoyrenaissanceresort.com; 344 rooms, 16 suites

This restored 1925 "grande dame" with a Mediterranean Revival design on the National Register of Historic Places "overflows" with "panache" and "old-world elegance" evident in its "superior service", afternoon tea and "fantastic" Sunday brunch; sure, it's "not on the beach, but you can walk to the St. Pete pier, the Salvador Dali museum, galleries, shops and restaurants", the "lounge/pool area is fabulous" and the complex includes five eateries, 12 tennis courts, a spa and a golf course.

Saddlebrook Resort 18 | 19 | 16 | 23 | $327

5700 Saddlebrook Way, Wesley Chapel; 813-973-1111; fax 813-973-4504; 800-729-8383; www.saddlebrookresort.com; 130 rooms, 414 suites

A "spacious resort" north of Tampa, this 480-acre property is also a "golfer's paradise" acknowledge guests who take to the two "excellent" 18-hole Arnold Palmer signature courses before moving on to the "great" 45-court tennis center, "refreshing" spa and "spacious" accommodations; but dissenters declare it's "nice for a day, not a stay" with rooms in "need of updating" and "restaurants that aren't good enough to eat at every night."

Vero Beach

Disney's Vero Beach Resort ▽ 22 | 21 | 17 | 24 | $300

9250 Island Grove Terrace; 772-234-2000; fax 772-234-2030; www.disneyvacationclub.com; 175 apartments

It's "Disney charm without the characters" at this "relaxing", "child-friendly location" with the feel of a Northeastern seaside setting from the early 1900s; there are "tons of family-oriented" things to do, like "campfires complete with sing-alongs and s'mores", an ocean learning center, volleyball and swimming; the villas "are especially beautiful" and the "restaurant's a delight", but partiers pout it's rather "subdued."

Georgia

★ **Tops in State**

29 Lodge at Sea Island, *Sea Island*
27 Barnsley Gardens, *Adairsville*
26 Four Seasons, *Atlanta*
Cloister, *Sea Island*
Ritz-Carlton Buckhead, *Atlanta*
Ritz-Carlton Reynolds Plantation, *Greensboro*

Atlanta

BARNSLEY GARDENS | 28 | 26 | 26 | 29 | $285

597 Barnsley Gardens Rd., Adairsville; 770-773-7480; fax 770-877-9155; 877-773-2447; www.barnsleyresort.com; 70 cottages

For a "fabulous escape" an hour north of Atlanta, travelers head for this "romantic" country "oasis", a member of Small Luxury Hotels of the World that "boasts the most beautiful grounds short of heaven", including a "challenging" golf course, "a favorite fly-fishing pond" and turn-of-the-century "moonlit ruins"; no matter where you're from, you'll feel "hundreds of miles away from home" "relaxing" in a "wonderful" "individual cottage" and treated to "remarkable personal service" from a "friendly staff."

Crowne Plaza Ravinia | ∇ 18 | 20 | 20 | 22 | $200

4355 Ashford Dunwoody Rd.; 770-395-7700 ; fax 770-392-9503 ; www.crowneplaza.com/atl-ravinia; 475 rooms, 20 suites

"Strong Southern-style hospitality reigns supreme" at this "first-rate" business hotel in Dunwoody; the "comfy" confines are touted for "great amenities for the price", "pretty public areas" and La Grotta, the "superb" Italian restaurant, but those who call it "just ordinary" say "no one thing" "raises the overall impression."

FOUR SEASONS | 26 | 27 | 26 | 26 | $315

75 14th St.; 404-881-9898; fax 404-873-4692; 800-332-3442; www.fourseasons.com; 226 rooms, 18 suites

The "pampering staff" "goes overboard" at this "elegant" entry where the "first-rate guestrooms" are "large and well appointed", with "marble bathrooms that hit the spot"; work off the "exceptionally creative" Park 75 restaurant's "top-notch food" in the "state-of-the-art" gym, lounge on the "breathtaking deck" of the "beautiful, sun-lit indoor pool" or take an "easy walk to fun Midtown sites" from an "awesome" hotel that prompts visitors to exclaim "if I could, I would have moved in."

Georgian Terrace | 22 | 20 | 20 | 21 | $119

659 Peachtree St.; 404-897-1991; fax 404-724-9116; 800-651-2316; www.thegeorgianterrace.com; 319 suites

Visitors to this "absolutely beautiful" "circa-1911 grande dame" sigh a collective "ahhhh" over its "perfect" Midtown location across from the Fox Theater and "gorgeous skyline views" from an expansive "terrace that overlooks Peachtree Street and all that flies by"; the property is renovating into condo units over the next two years, but visitors can still enjoy "spacious suites" and a "good brunch buffet" at The Savoy Bar and Grill, courtesy of a "well-trained and energetic staff."

Grand Hyatt | 22 | 22 | 18 | 22 | $245

3300 Peachtree Rd., NE; 404-365-8100; fax 404-233-5686; 800-233-1234; www.hyatt.com; 439 rooms, 22 suites

"Business travelers demanding a cut above" report a "positive experience" at this "upscale hotel", while "shopping enthusiasts" buy into the "tip-top" "heart-of-Buckhead" location near Lenox Square and Phipps Plaza; the "well-maintained" facility sports a lobby with a "boutique feel" and "funky" elements from the former Nikko hotel, including a Japanese garden with three-story waterfall; the rooms are "surprisingly luxurious", the dining is "good" and the staff "goes the extra mile", literally – the "decent limo service" "will take you anywhere you'd like to go."

Indigo, Hotel – | – | – | – | $144

683 Peachtree St. NE; 404-874-9200; fax 404-873-4245; www.hotelindigo.com; 140 rooms

A hip newcomer that makes bold use of its namesake color, this Midtown pet-friendly boutique brand from InterContinental Hotels blends Southern classic style with minimalist chic; rooms have high-speed Internet access, satellite TV and coffeemakers, there's a basic fitness center and you can grab a Starbucks coffee in the morning at the on-site casual eatery, Golden Bean.

InterContinental Buckhead – | – | – | – | $329

3315 Peachtree Rd. NE; 404-946-9000; fax 404-946-9001; www.intercontinental.com; 401 rooms, 21 suites

Modern, Southern charm is on tap at this towering new hotel in Buckhead where rooms boast pillowtop bedding and marble baths, there's an in-house French brasserie, Au Pied de Cochon, and nightly jazz livens things up at XO bar (both have outdoor seating); business types can take advantage of versatile meeting space.

JW Marriott Hotel Lenox 23 | 22 | 19 | 23 | $309

3300 Lenox Rd., NE; 404-262-3344; fax 404-262-8689; 800-228-9290; www.marriott.com; 367 rooms, 4 suites

For "location, location, location", this "excellent hotel" in Buckhead "can't be beat" since it's "connected to one of Atlanta's premier shopping malls" and offers access to public transportation as well as "several great restaurants within an easy walk"; boosters brag about "good bargains to be had" in the form of "lovely, large rooms" "done in rich fabrics" with "amazing baths", matched by "well-maintained" public spaces including "excellent bar and dining facilities" serviced by a "wonderful staff."

Renaissance Waverly ∇ 22 | 20 | 21 | 19 | $219

2450 Galleria Pkwy.; 770-953-4500; fax 770-953-0740; www.renaissancehotels.com; 497 rooms, 24 suites

"Quiet" quarters with "nice bathrooms" off a "distinctive" vaulted atrium make this "solid conference hotel" "attached to the Galleria" "comfortable for business or personal" matters "outside the congestion of Downtown Atlanta"; though an "accommodating staff" delivers "efficient service", they can't do anything about "nightmare traffic", so "if you have meetings in the city", make sure to give yourself extra time to get there.

Ritz-Carlton, The 24 | 25 | 23 | 23 | $299

181 Peachtree St., NE; 404-659-0400; fax 404-688-0400; 800-241-3333; www.ritzcarlton.com; 422 rooms, 22 suites

Business travelers appreciate this "highly competent" "oasis" "in the heart of Downtown" where "subdued surroundings", "beautiful rooms" and "top-notch suites" "well stocked with amenities" offer a "civilized" "haven" from "convention corridor" madness; a "courteous staff" delivers "first-class" service, including in the "elegant" Grill, but they still can't satisfy finicky guests who find that, relative to its Buckhead sib, this link "lacks the Ritz magic."

RITZ-CARLTON BUCKHEAD ✕ 26 | 27 | 26 | 26 | $425

3434 Peachtree Rd., NE; 404-237-2700; fax 404-239-0078; 800-241-3333; www.ritzcarlton.com; 524 rooms, 29 suites

"Everything a wonderful hotel should be and then some", this "heaven on earth" "sandwiched between two of the South's ritziest malls" is the "only place to stay in Buckhead" say "coddled shoppers", business types and weekenders looking for "total luxury"; the "elegant" "treasure" "doesn't miss a step": the "exquisite" rooms are adorned in "plush furniture", perhaps one of "the best lobby lounges in America" delivers "great people-watching", the "magical" Dining Room serves "glorious food" and high tea is "unforgettable."

W Atlanta 23 | 21 | 19 | 20 | $249

111 Perimeter Ctr. W.; 770-396-6800; fax 770-394-4805; 800-683-6100; www.whotels.com; 121 rooms, 154 suites

It's "hip", it's "trendy", it's "in the boondocks" – the "big", "awesome rooms with every amenity" radiate a "Zen" kind of "warmth", the staff is "responsive to the smallest needs" and the "chichi nightclub lobby" of this link in the "contemporary" boutique chain is the place to "kick back" for cocktails "after a great day of shopping" at Perimeter Mall; still, "unless you have business" in Dunwoody, it's "out of the way."

Westin Buckhead ∇ 24 | 20 | 20 | 22 | $389

3391 Peachtree Rd. NE; 404-365-0065; fax 404-365-8787; www.westin.com; 365 rooms

"Recently rebranded", this former Swissôtel in an "excellent location" adjacent to popular malls is one of "Buckhead's best-kept secrets and values" with "beautiful appointments" and "sleek, comfortable rooms" featuring the brand's "wonderful" Heavenly beds; the "club level shines" for breakfast, cocktails and the "shouldn't-be-missed" dessert bar, while suits "eating on the company dime" say the Palm steakhouse is "a nice touch"; better still, the "accommodating staff" offers a "free limo to local spots."

Westin Peachtree Plaza 22 | 19 | 15 | 21 | $385

210 Peachtree St., NW; 404-659-1400; fax 404-589-7424; 800-937-8461; www.westin.com; 1028 rooms, 40 suites

"Breathtaking views" out the "huge" windows of your "lovely", "comfortable room" high up in Downtown's cylindrical "landmark" make you "feel you're in the heavens", as you "melt" into the "wonderful linens" on your "dreamy bed"; a "must" is the "fun glass elevator" ride from the "urban-chic lobby" to Sun Dial, the revolving restaurant where the fare "does not measure up to the rest" of the northern hemisphere's tallest hotel, though the faithful feel it might improve under the new chef.

Braselton

Château Élan Ⓢ 20 | 21 | 19 | 23 | $189

100 Rue Charlemagne; 678-425-0900; fax 678-425-6000; 800-233-9463; www.chateauelan.com; 288 rooms, 8 villas

Fans "feel like they're in a fairy tale" at this "beautiful" resort "nestled in the vineyards" an hour north of Atlanta, where "tremendous golf" and a "luxurious", "serene spa" make for a "fine weekend" getaway; the "charming" staff "tries hard", the rooms are "simple" yet "spacious" and the fare can be "divine", but oenophiles opine that the wine is "not to be mistaken for Napa" – nor is the "hokey" "faux château" to be confused with Europe sniff snobs.

Georgia Coast

CLOISTER, THE | 25 | 28 | 25 | 27 | $425

100 Hudson Pl., Sea Island; 912-638-3611; fax 912-638-5823; 800-732-4752; www.seaisland.com; 177 rooms, 32 suites, 150 bungalows

"Southern luxury is defined" at Georgia's "grande dame" of "island destination resorts", a "romantic" "time warp to the era of gracious living" that "segues into the modern era" with an ongoing $200-million renovation; rooms, suites and bungalows are "beautifully appointed", the "many dining choices" offer "excellent food" and an "unparalleled" staff oversees "a bevy of activities for the whole family", plus there's a "gorgeous" private beach, "world-class golf" and a "fabulous spa."

Jekyll Island Club Hotel | 22 | 25 | 23 | 24 | $209

371 Riverview Dr., Jekyll Island; 912-635-2600; fax 912-635-2818; 800-535-9547; www.jekyllclub.com; 142 rooms, 13 suites, 2 cottages

"Wish you were related to the Carnegies?" – vacation "like a robber baron" at this "state treasure", an 1887 "millionaires'" "escape" on an "island paradise" off the southern Georgia coast where the "lovely rooms" are part of the "unique charm"; partake in "excellent activities" such as croquet, biking, swimming and horse-drawn carriage rides through town, "take your pick from several restaurants", including a cafe "under the stars", or just "relax" and let the staff help you "do nothing."

King and Prince Beach & Golf Resort | – | – | – | – | $205

201 Arnold Rd., Little St. Simons Island; 912-638-3631; www.kingandprince.com; 140 rooms, 40 suites, 6 villas

A recent multimillion-dollar renovation enhanced this low-key Georgian island hotel where dark woods, wrought iron and plantation-style ceiling fans adorn the historic main building's new guestrooms (there are also two- and three-bedroom beach villas); tennis courts, a championship golf course and a solarium, with an indoor and four outdoor pools, round out the picture.

LODGE AT SEA ISLAND, THE | 29 | 29 | 29 | 29 | $700

100 Retreat Ave., Sea Island; 912-638-3611; fax 912-634-3909; 800-732-4752; www.seaisland.com; 40 rooms, 2 suites

"Georgeous", "luxurious", "magnificent" – raves abound for this No. 1 Small Hotel in our *Survey,* which also won the Top spot for "fabulous" dining; a mansionlike Georgia "jewel" of a "golfer's paradise", it delivers the "height of luxury" with a "terrific staff", 54 holes of golf and "outstanding" rooms with personal butlers who serve "warm cookies and milk before bed", draw a rose petal bath and "wow" travelers ("never had better service"); a complete spa and a "great bar that invites lingering" add to an "elegant" experience that's "worth every cent."

Lodge on Little St. Simons Island ∇ 23 24 25 24 $650

Little St. Simons Island, Little St. Simons Island; 912-638-7472; fax 912-634-1811; 888-733-5774; www.littlestsimonsisland.com; 7 rooms, 2 suites, 4 houses

"Like summer camp for adults", this resort on 10,000 acres of a "secluded island" in the Atlantic is a "great place to relax" or to get busy with "lots of activities" likes water sports, shelling and exploring the seven miles of pristine beaches with "unbelievable wildlife"; the "rustic atmosphere" is spiced up with "fantastic" Low Country fare, and a "great staff" oversees it all.

Lake Oconee

RITZ-CARLTON REYNOLDS PLANTATION Ⓢ 27 24 23 28 $375

1 Lake Oconee Trail, Greensboro; 706-467-0600; fax 706-467-0601; 800-241-3333; www.ritzcarlton.com; 251 rooms, 22 suites, 6 cottages, 1 house

"Ninety minutes from Atlanta" "surrounded by Georgia red clay" is this "magical hideaway" in the "wilderness" where "luxury is redefined" in the form of "amazing golf", an "outstanding spa", "very good food", "gracious suites" and "lovely rooms" with "every amenity"; visitors can "truly relax" in "elegant" "hunting lodge" digs set in "hilly, wooded", "landscaped grounds" that include a "perfect infinity-edge pool" overlooking the "beautiful lake."

Savannah

Ballastone Inn Ⓗ ∇ 28 26 18 23 $255

14 E. Oglethorpe Ave.; 912-236-1484; fax 912-236-4626; 800-822-4553; www.ballastone.com; 13 rooms, 3 suites

In an "excellent location" in the "heart of historic Savannah", this "charming" B&B "sets the bar" with its "gorgeous rooms", boasting lavender-scented sheets, and "welcoming" ways with "wonderful afternoon tea and snacks and evening hors d'oeuvres"; guests are treated like "Southern gentility" by a "helpful" staff in an 1838 home complete with a live oak–lined courtyard and koi pond.

Gastonian, The Ⓗ ∇ 28 25 20 21 $215

220 E. Gaston St.; 912-232-2869; fax 912-232-0710; 800-322-6603; www.gastonian.com; 13 rooms, 3 suites, 1 carriage house

With comments ranging from "lovely" to "lovely" to "lovely!", it's clear that this "romantic" B&B in Savannah's historic district is, well, "really a lovely place to stay"; "step back into old times" across the threshold of a "large", antique-strewn room where a "big, deep bathtub" and "to-die-for linens" add to the 1868 "charm"; with the "wonderful help" serving "great food", including happy-hour snacks, "what else do you need?" – how about a place to put up your kids under 12, who aren't allowed here.

Mansion on Forsyth Park, The ⓗ Ⓢ – – – – $335

700 Drayton St.; 912-238-5158; fax 912-238-5146; 888-711-5114; www.mansiononforsythpark.com; 120 rooms, 6 suites

Set in an 1888 mansion in the heart of Savannah, this National Historic Landmark is now a brand-new hotel blending modern

European style with top-notch cuisine – there's an on-site state-of-the-art cooking school (700 Kitchen) and the 700 Drayton restaurant serving Eclectic cuisine in eight private dining rooms, two lounges and an outdoor terrace overlooking Forsyth Park; the Poseiden Spa has a full lineup of pampering treatments and yoga and tai chi classes.

Mulberry Inn ∇ 22 | 23 | 18 | 20 | $189
601 E. Bay St.; 912-238-1200; fax 912-236-2184; 877-468-1200; www.savannahhotel.com; 123 rooms, 22 suites
"Perfectly located for walking around Downtown" and "getting to all the fun at River Street", this "standby favorite" offers a "good value" for a "comfortable" stay in the historic district; regulars who "love" the daily afternoon tea and the landscaped courtyard with its cafe, pool and hot tub marvel "you'd never believe this is a Holiday Inn property."

River Street Inn ∇ 23 | 24 | 18 | 21 | $209
124 E. Bay St.; 912-234-6400; fax 912-234-1478; 800-253-4229; www.riverstreetinn.com; 86 rooms
For a "unique place to stay in Savannah" surveyors veer toward the waterfront and this "quaint" boutique hotel lodged in "historic buildings" organized around a five-story atrium, with guestrooms that are each individually and "wonderfully furnished" with period antiques; be sure to "get a river view", but "avoid" being lodged directly "over the bar next door", and do let the "attentive staff" help make it the kind of "memorable stay" you'll "always come back" for.

Westin Savannah Harbor Resort 23 | 20 | 20 | 25 | $309
1 Resort Dr.; 912-201-2000; fax 912-201-2001; www.westinsavannah.com; 390 rooms, 13 suites
On "incredible" island grounds across the river from the historic district is Savannah's "new standard" for "full-service luxury golf hotels"; after a morning on the "great" links, devour a "fabulous jazz Sunday brunch", dip into the "delightful spa", descend into a hammock around the "nice pool", disembark from the "fun" (if "unpredictable") water taxi for a night in town and retire to a "to-die-for bed" amid "beautiful decor"; just note that the bugs don't share the "hospitable" staff's "wonderful Southern charm", so "avoid mosquito season."

Hawaii

★ **Tops in State**

29 Four Seasons Hualalai, *Big Island*
28 Four Seasons at Wailea, *Maui*
27 Lodge at Koele, *Lanai*
Halekulani, *Oahu*
Kahala Mandarin Oriental, *Oahu*
26 Fairmont Kea Lani, *Maui*
Manele Bay Hotel, *Lanai*
25 Ritz-Carlton Kapalua, *Maui*
Mauna Lani Bay Hotel, *Big Island*
Fairmont Orchid, *Big Island*
JW Marriott Ihilani, *Oahu*
Grand Hyatt Kauai, *Kauai*

Big Island

FAIRMONT ORCHID, THE 25 | 25 | 23 | 27 | $469

1 N. Kaniku Dr., Kohala Coast; 808-885-2000; fax 808-885-1064; 800-845-9905; www.fairmont.com/orchid; 486 rooms, 54 suites

A sunset "beachside massage" watching "turtles do water ballet" is "too dreamy to be real" report regulars who relish the "extremely solicitous staff" at this "uncrowded" resort with an "immense" pool and a gorgeous beach "safe for snorkeling"; add in "world-class" golf and "terrific" dining at Brown's Beach House where they'll "sashimi a tuna you catch", and it's heaven for all but those who cry over decor "lacking an authentic Polynesian" feel.

FOUR SEASONS RESORT HUALALAI 29 | 29 | 28 | 29 | $560

100 Ka'upulehu Dr., Kaupulehu-Kona; 808-325-8000; fax 808-325-8200; 800-332-3442; www.fourseasons.com; 212 rooms, 30 suites, 1 villa

"Perfection, utter perfection" rhapsodize reviewers who've once again rated this "honeymooners' paradise" the No. 1 Resort in this *Survey* – and why not? "the outdoor lava rock showers are a blast", the spa is "voluptuous", "dining by the ocean in the moonlight" is "truly special" (try Alan Wong's Pacific Asian cuisine), the "most amazing fitness center" allows you to exercise outdoors and it all "never feels crowded, even when completely full"; as if that weren't enough, the "classy staff" "recognizes you by name" and is filled with "Aloha spirit."

Hapuna Beach Prince Hotel 24 | 23 | 21 | 25 | $399

62-100 Kauna'oa Dr., Kohala Coast; 808-880-1111; fax 808-880-3142; 866-774-6236; www.princeresortshawaii.com; 314 rooms, 36 suites

You're greeted with passion fruit juice and a scented wash towel in the "open-air lobby" of this "elegant" resort where a "relaxing" stay means time on the "amazing Arnold Palmer golf course", strolls on the "long beach" and access to the facilities of sister property Mauna Kea next door; the service is "excellent" and dining options are "very good", but the multilevel resort is "difficult to navigate."

Hilton Waikoloa Village 20 | 21 | 20 | 27 | $369

425 Waikoloa Beach Dr., Waikoloa; 808-886-1234; fax 808-886-2900; 800-445-8667; www.hiltonwaikoloavillage.com; 1159 rooms, 57 suites, 25 cabanas

Families ask "what more could you want" from "Disney World, Hawaiian style" than this "fairy-tale place" with "whales frolicking" and "dolphins swimming up to you"?; most love getting around the "massive" resort by taking the "tram one way" and a boat the other, or just walking through the "excellent art" collections; water buffs "wallow in waterslide pools" or snorkel alongside sea turtles, and though most applaud the "informative staff" and "great spa" others are irritated it "doesn't have its own beach."

Kona Village Resort 25 | 25 | 23 | 25 | $530

Kaupulehu Dr., Kailua-Kona; 808-325-5555; fax 808-325-5124; 800-367-5290; www.konavillage.com; 125 bungalows

Paradise lovers claim "total bliss" at this "Eden of lagoons and flowers" with "no electronic distractions (phone, TV, radio)", where you'll get "spoiled rotten" by both an "incredible staff" and the "modern thatched huts" with private Jacuzzis and ocean views; it's all about relaxation, so snorkel with free equipment ("turtles everywhere") then head to the "famous luau" or the "fine" eatery; most agree "this is what vacations should be"; N.B. Marriott took over management post-*Survey* and plans to add a two-story spa.

Mauna Kea Beach Hotel | 22 | 24 | 22 | 26 | $370 |

62-100 Mauna Kea Beach Dr., Kohala Coast; 808-882-7222; fax 808-882-5700; 800-882-6060; www.princeresortshawaii.com; 300 rooms, 10 suites

For the "best beach and golf" on the Big Island, loyalists laud this "older" property whose "spectacular" setting on the Kohala Coast's white sands is only matched by its "incredible service"; it may be "outclassed by newer resorts" with bigger, more modern rooms, but "excellent tennis facilities", "fantastic" golf and a "superb swimming pool" have that "tried and true" appeal.

MAUNA LANI BAY HOTEL | 24 | 25 | 25 | 26 | $430 |

68-1400 Mauna Lani Dr., Kohala Coast; 808-885-6622; fax 808-885-1474; 800-367-2323; www.maunalani.com; 324 rooms, 14 suites, 5 bungalows

A "tropical heaven" with "outstanding spa treatments" ("try the underwater massage"), this "divine" hotel on the Kohala Coast has a "killer golf course" and "superb" service; though some say it "hits high notes in all areas" from the service to the "spacious rooms", others insist the "dated" decor has "seen better days."

Waikoloa Beach Marriott | 17 | 20 | 17 | 23 | $239 |

69-275 Waikoloa Beach Dr., Waikoloa; 808-886-6789; fax 808-886-3604; 800-922-5533; www.waikoloabeachmarriott.com; 508 rooms, 17 suites, 20 cabanas

It's "old Hawaii style" at this "much improved" property that's a "good value" in an "excellent location"; a "beautiful open-air lobby", "sensational snorkeling" and a "staff that tries to please" make up for "plain", "small" rooms and merely "decent" fare (there are "lots of restaurants nearby" including Roy's); N.B. a spa will open in June 2006.

Kauai

GRAND HYATT KAUAI RESORT | 24 | 24 | 23 | 28 | $455 |

1571 Poipu Rd., Koloa; 808-742-1234; fax 808-742-1557; 800-233-1234; www.hyatt.com; 565 rooms, 37 suites

Alight on Kauai's "sunniest location" at this "sprawling" property that completely renovated its rooms and has an "infectious Aloha spirit"; you'll find an entryway that's "absolutely breathtaking", rooms "bedecked with orchids" – some "opening up to gardens" and outdoor lava rock showers – and "excellent" food; regulars also rave about the lazy river pools and float-in grottos and a staff that "knows your name", but celeb-spotters just like being "down the hall from Harrison Ford and Calista Flockhart" or "watching Tiger Woods play golf."

Hanalei Bay Resort 19 19 21 23 $185

5380 Honoiki Rd., Princeville; 808-826-6522; fax 808-826-6680; 800-827-4427; www.hanaleibaykauai.com; 280 rooms

"The perfect spot for romance" on Kauai is "overlooking the beach from *South Pacific*" – an "ideal location" complete with "lush gardens and sweeping rainbows"; while some say don't miss "sunset dinner at the Bali Hai Restaurant", they're not so keen on rooms in this "mostly timeshare" resort.

Marriott Kauai Resort & Beach Club 21 21 19 25 $339

3610 Rice St., Lihue; 808-245-5050; fax 808-245-5049; 800-220-2925; www.marriott.com; 334 rooms, 11 suites

"That pool!" exclaim enthusiasts enamored by the "huge" size and "lush landscaping" of the water facility at this "lovely" "family-friendly property"; while most appreciate the "breathtaking open-air lobby", "stunning artwork" throughout and "spectacular views" from oceanfront rooms, a good portion pout over "mediocre" food and "dated looking" quarters.

Princeville Resort 26 24 23 26 $465

5520 Ka Haku Rd., Princeville; 808-826-9644; fax 808-826-1166; 800-826-4400 ; www.princeville.com; 201 rooms, 51 suites

When you get a load of the "incredible" Bali Hai sunsets at this "outrageous" resort you may think you've found "the most beautiful place on earth"; from a lobby with "marble everything" to an infinity pool to service "without a hint of pretentiousness" to the junior suites' "ingenious" liquid crystal shower windows for ocean viewing, this is where "the rich and famous get away from it all"; unfortunately, a few expected more than "adequate" food.

Lanai

LODGE AT KOELE 27 27 26 27 $400

1 Keomuku Hwy., Lanai City; 808-565-7300; fax 808-565-3868; 800-321-4666; www.lanai-resorts.com; 88 rooms, 14 suites

Imagine a "first-class British hunting lodge" in the "misty highlands" and you've got this "absolutely superb" property (soon to be a Four Seasons) that sits amid pine trees and cooler temperatures ("take a sweater"); there's "stellar" service and "top-notch" food, plus clay shooting, croquet, horseback-riding and "wonderful" golf, but if you want to swim or snorkel you must "take the [complimentary] shuttle down to the beach" at its sister property, Manele Bay; some "can't believe they're in Hawaii" when they're playing "backgammon by the fire", but it's all so "unbelievably romantic" it must be.

MANELE BAY HOTEL 26 26 24 27 $400

1 Manele Bay Rd., Lanai City; 808-565-7700; fax 808-565-2483; www.islandoflanai.com; 222 rooms, 27 suites

Gaga guests step into "the *Lifestyles of the Rich & Famous*" when they stay at this "hideaway" (soon to be a Four Seasons) where the staff "magically" appears when you need them and is "hidden when you don't"; rooms have "unbelievable" marble baths with "enough space to roller skate", the golf and "fabulous dining" "alone would make it one of the best [resorts] in the world" and there's access to all the amenities at the Lodge at Koele; P.S. if it's "too expensive" to stay, "take a day trip over from Lahaina", Maui, for snorkeling or dining.

Maui

FAIRMONT KEA LANI 28 26 24 27 $385

4100 Wailea Alanui Dr., Wailea; 808-875-4100; fax 808-875-1200; 800-441-1414; www.fairmont.com; 413 suites, 37 villas

If it's "absolute paradise" you seek, head to this "romantic" Wailea all-suite hotel featuring "luxurious" accommodations (some with private plunge pools), "bathrooms as big as a bedroom" and service "beyond comparison"; arrive to "chilled guava juice", then head to "separate adult and children's pools" (guess which one has the swim-up bar?); dine "beyond belief" at Nick's Fishmarket or barbecue on your villa lanai (room service delivers "meat and fish to grill") – indeed, most would understand "if you never left."

FOUR SEASONS AT WAILEA 28 28 27 27 $385

3900 Wailea Alanui, Wailea; 808-874-8000; fax 808-874-2244; 800-334-6284; www.fourseasons.com; 300 rooms, 73 suites

"Pinch me, I'm in heaven" sigh pampered patrons "spritzed with Evian" as they lounge poolside ("stake your claim on a cabana early") at this "Eden"-like resort where "quiet elegance" prevails; if you check into the "club level, you'll never leave" unless it's to golf on the "amazing" Wailea courses, have a "couples massage on the beach" or eat at the "excellent" Spago; better still, the always "attentive staff" provides such "impeccable" service you'll "feel like Hawaiian royalty."

Grand Wailea Resort 24 24 23 28 $515

3850 Wailea Alanui Dr., Wailea; 808-875-1234; fax 808-879-4077; 800-888-6100; www.grandwailea.com; 728 rooms, 52 suites

"Sell the house and stay until the money runs out" at this resort "as grand as its name" that's "kid heaven" due to nine pools, "the only water elevator in Hawaii" and a "Disneyesque" Tarzan swing where you can "forget being grown up"; you'll also find "the most indulgent" spa treatments imaginable, with "post cocktails on the terrace at sunset", a "not-to-be missed" restaurant (Humuhumu), private poolside cabanas where "lovely young men spritz you with Evian" and rooms so "gorgeous you could sleep in the marble bathroom"; though critics cry it's "very big, like a public market" and not exactly peaceful.

Hana-Maui, Hotel 27 25 22 25 $395

5031 Hana Hwy., Hana; 808-248-8211; fax 808-248-7202; 800-321-4262; www.hotelhanamaui.com; 47 cottages, 10 rooms, 7 suites

Secretive sorts are "almost afraid to let the word out" on this lush resort with "million-dollar views" and a "setting you dream about" at the end of the Hana Highway; fans "highly recommend" the Sea Ranch cottages with outdoor Jacuzzis and "bathrooms as large as a New York apartment" and tout the "entertainment performed by an in-house staff" ("better than hearing the *Hawaiian Wedding Song* for the umpteenth time"); while a few complain "mealtime can be boring", others find this member of Small Luxury Hotels of the World a good bet for a few nights' stay.

Hyatt Regency 22 | 23 | 23 | 26 | $400

200 Nohea Kai Dr., Lahaina; 808-661-1234; fax 808-667-4714; 800-233-1234; www.hyatt.com; 775 rooms, 31 suites
Calling this "the most fanciful hotel" ever, loyalists love the lobby filled with "lush palm trees, exotic animals, including penguins", the miles of pools with a "grown-up waterslide", the Spa Moana offering outdoor massages and the "hammocks by the beach", not to mention rooms with "views of ocean, beach and mountains"; a few grouch about the "rocky beach", however, and admit it's "hard to drag the kids out of the pools" once they get in.

Kapalua Bay Hotel 22 | 24 | 22 | 25 | $435

1 Bay Dr., Kapalua; 808-669-5656; fax 808-669-4690; 800-367-8000; www.kapaluabayhotel.com; 191 rooms, 5 suites, 14 villas
A "real Hawaiian experience" can be had at this "tranquilizing hotel" where "swimming with the sea turtles", "great golf" and whale-watching are part of the experience; there's "not too much to do" beyond this, but "that could be a good thing"; though some complain it "needs a face-lift", most just concentrate on the "breezy, open rooms" and the "marvelous breakfast buffet."

Kapalua Villas 22 | 17 | 21 | 24 | $209

500 Office Rd., Kapalua; 808-669-8088; fax 808-669-5234; 800-545-0018; www.kapaluavillas.com; 290 villas
Duffers are delighted by "the best golfing trip" they've ever had at this "beautiful home away from home" where condos with full kitchens mean "saving money on meals" yet you get "charge privileges" at two nearby five-star resorts (Ritz-Carlton Kapalua and the Kapalua Bay Hotel); the units are showing "wear and tear" snipe some, but overall it's a good choice for families.

RITZ-CARLTON KAPALUA 25 | 26 | 24 | 26 | $365

1 Ritz-Carlton Dr., Kapalua; 808-669-6200; fax 808-665-0026; 800-262-8440; www.ritzcarlton.com; 490 rooms, 58 suites
A "tremendous" resort on "sprawling, tropical" grounds, this Big Island outpost delivers most of what you'd expect from a Ritz: "elegant" rooms with "huge marble bathrooms" and "plush robes", "pampering" service, "over-the-top golf", a newly renovated spa and "isolation from the real world" in an "incredible" location; still, a handful of harsher critics find it "a little too large and impersonal" and say the "rainy side of Maui" makes it "unpredictable."

Sheraton Maui 21 | 20 | 19 | 23 | $370

2605 Kaanapali Pkwy., Lahaina; 808-661-0031; fax 808-661-0458; 800-782-9488; www.sheraton.com/maui; 464 rooms, 46 suites
The "awesome" beach ("best on the island" say some) is the stand-out feature of this otherwise "average" hotel since it's got "great snorkeling" and it's "not as frantic as some others"; "be sure to get an oceanview room" though, and don't expect much from the "limited" dining or the somewhat "disinterested" service.

Westin Maui 21 | 22 | 19 | 24 | $390

2365 Kaanapali Pkwy., Lahaina; 808-667-2525; fax 808-661-2469; 800-937-8461; www.westin.com; 731 rooms, 27 suites
It's no wonder there are so many "kids running amok" at this Kaanapali resort since it has such "heavenly" pools featuring

slides, waterfalls and lagoons, plus "lots of activities" including a Keiki Kamp for little ones – "great" for families but "too crowded and noisy" for non–tot-toters; luckily, there's a new spa, an adult-only swim area and a "tremendous" beachfront location with "fantastic ocean views", so the lackluster dining is forgiven.

Molokai

Molokai Ranch & Lodge | 20 | 20 | 17 | 23 | $285 |

100 Maunaloa Hwy., Maunaloa; 808-552-2741; fax 808-552-2773; 888-627-8082; www.molokai-ranch.com; 22 rooms, 40 bungalows

If "roughing it in paradise" is your idea of fun, you'll find "rustic luxury" to spare at this ranch-style country lodge (a member of Small Luxury Hotels of the World) that includes bungalowlike 'tentalos' with four-poster beds and solar-heated water; you can horseback ride, kayak, hike or "do nothing" but enjoy "great views" of this quiet, less-developed island; it's "all you need for an active, relaxing vacation."

Oahu

HALEKULANI Ⓢ | 27 | 28 | 27 | 26 | $415 |

2199 Kalia Rd., Honolulu; 808-923-2311; fax 808-926-8004; 800-367-2343; www.halekulani.com; 415 rooms, 40 suites

For "magical calm in the heart of the Waikiki hurricane" head to this enclave of "luxury and beauty" where there are "incredible" rooms (a new suite is designed by Vera Wang) with "terrific views", "marvelous service", the "divine La Mer" oceanside restaurant (voted No. 1 for Decor and Service in our *Honolulu Restaurant Survey*) and the "best tropical drinks, Hawaiian music and hula at sunset" at the waterside House Without a Key; don't expect much of a beach (it's "pretty narrow"), but if you "leave the munchkins with grandma" and go with the one you love, you'll find it "wonderful in every way."

Hawaii Prince Hotel Waikiki Ⓢ | 22 | 23 | 21 | 21 | $325 |

100 Holomoana St., Honolulu; 808-956-1111; fax 808-946-0811; 800-321-6248; www.princeresortshawaii.com; 464 rooms, 57 suites

Waikiki's "best bargain" is "off the strip" but convenient to the "convention center and shopping" with rooms "overlooking the harbor" featuring "floor to ceiling glass" and "large, luxurious baths"; still, it loses points for a "small pool" and the fact that you must board a shuttle to the beach or the Arnold Palmer golf course; P.S. if you've got teenagers in tow, they may "run away with your credit card at the nearby Ala Moana Mall."

Hilton Hawaiian Village Ⓢ | 20 | 20 | 19 | 24 | $199 |

2005 Kalia Rd., Honolulu; 808-949-4321; fax 808-947-7898; 800-774-1500; www.hilton.com; 2655 rooms, 345 suites

There are "excellent facilities" at this "small town" of a resort that's "busier than a mall the day before Christmas"; "endless" kid-friendly activities, a "lobby with parrots, orchids" and fun-to-watch "penguins and flamingos", the "best [spacious] beaches on Waikiki", torch-lightings, weekly fireworks, a luxe spa and rooms with "phenomenal" views win fans; but though food options are plentiful, they don't impress, and the sheer size results in a "touristy" feel with "impersonal" service.

Hyatt Regency Waikiki Resort & Spa 20 | 22 | 18 | 21 | $275
2424 Kalakaua Ave., Honolulu; 808-923-1234; fax 808-923-7839; 800-233-1234; www.hyatt.com; 1212 rooms, 18 suites
Enthusiasts ask "how can you not like a hotel with a waterfall in the middle?", praising the central "heart of Waikiki" location of this business-oriented property directly "across the street from the beach" and "smack in the middle of the action"; while some love the "awesome views from the high floors", others say it's "too touristy" with "limited dining choices."

JW MARRIOTT IHILANI RESORT & SPA 27 | 25 | 21 | 26 | $425
92-1001 Olani St., Ko Olina, Kapolei; 808-679-0079; fax 808-679-0080; 800-626-4446; www.marriott.com; 351 rooms, 36 suites
With four "gorgeous man-made" lagoons far from the "hustle and bustle of Waikiki", this "amazing resort impresses" with "great golf" on a Ted Robinson–designed course, "world-class" spa treatments and child-friendly marine activities like swimming with stingrays; have "the best meal ever" at Azul (check out the "magnificent breakfast buffet") and relax on "gigantic" lanais with teak furniture.

KAHALA MANDARIN ORIENTAL 26 | 27 | 26 | 27 | $395
5000 Kahala Ave., Honolulu; 808-739-8888; fax 808-739-8800; 800-367-2525; www.mandarinoriental.com; 333 rooms, 33 suites
"Can former presidents and heads of movie studios be wrong?" ask admirers who "relax away from the craziness of Waikiki" at this "quiet gem"; "nothing beats the Dolphin Quest" encounters for kids or "one of the best" restaurants in town (Hoku's), and "sublime" service makes it all run smoothly; add in a spa with suites for "fabulous treatments" and rooms with "breathtaking views" and you've found a "sensational" spot where "old money comes to relax."

Marriott Waikiki Beach 20 | 20 | 15 | 19 | $219
2552 Kalakaua Ave., Honolulu; 808-922-6611; 800-367-5370; www.marriott.com; 1295 rooms, 15 suites
"Beautiful ocean and Diamond Head views", an "ideal location" and "friendly" service make this renovated chainster a "pleasant" option, especially for families who appreciate the "relatively informal dining options", the rooftop swimming pool and the nearby "quiet" portion of Waikiki Beach; it's a short walk to the Honolulu Zoo, but a few grumble over having to "cross a major street" to get to the sand.

Royal Hawaiian, The 20 | 23 | 21 | 23 | $395
2259 Kalakaua Ave., Honolulu; 808-923-7311; fax 808-931-7098; 888-488-3535; www.royal-hawaiian.com; 528 rooms, 35 suites
It's "like stepping through a time warp into the '20s" when you pay a visit to this "world-famous pink lady" on Waikiki Beach where you can head for the "classic Mai Tai Bar" for "great Hawaiian music" and the "courteous staff" attends to you; but non-nostalgics sigh that this "old girl" "could use a tuck or two."

Sheraton Moana Surfrider 19 | 22 | 19 | 22 | $310

2365 Kalakaua Ave., Honolulu; 808-922-3111; fax 808-924-4799; 800-325-3535; www.sheraton.com; 753 rooms, 46 suites

Get a dose of "new and old" at this "grand" centurian where the more recent towers have "larger rooms and balconies" but "those in the original section have more charm"; "sit on a porch rocking chair" or head for the "best sunset hula" by the courtyard's "sprawling banyan tree" then enjoy dinner overlooking the ocean – it may be "standard", but if you like history, "this one's for you."

Waikiki Parc Hotel ▽ 20 | 23 | 20 | 17 | $229

2233 Helumoa Rd., Honolulu; 808-921-7272; fax 808-931-6638; www.waikikiparchotel.com; 297 rooms

What a surprise to find "W quality with logical prices" in Waikiki; this "quaint" boutique with "prompt" service and complimentary buffet breakfasts (from Japanese miso soup to pancakes) is an "incredible value" in a "convenient location"; "ask for a room" with a "gorgeous view of the ocean" and be ready to walk to the beach.

W Honolulu - Diamond Head 23 | 21 | 23 | 16 | $430

2885 Kalakaua Ave., Honolulu; 808-922-1700; fax 808-923-2249; 800-325-3535; www.whotels.com; 47 rooms, 2 suites

For most it's all about the "spectacular" "views of Diamond Head" at this "hip" boutique with a slightly "out-of-the-way location" at the end of the Waikiki strip; a "favorite of high-profile visitors" fond of privacy, it offers a "fabulous restaurant and bar" and "sleek" rooms; but some grumble over the lack of a pool and say if "you're looking for lots of amenities, this isn't the place."

Idaho

Coeur d'Alene

Coeur d'Alene, The 22 | 23 | 22 | 26 | $199

115 S. Second St.; 208-765-4000; fax 208-664-7278; 800-688-5253; www.cdaresort.com; 337 rooms, 15 suites

"Amazing to find" this "high-rise" "mountain lake jewel" "in the middle of nowhere" exclaim enthusiasts of this "down-to-earth" escape in northern Idaho with "world-class service"; tee off at the "impeccable golf course" "featuring a floating green", indulge in an "evening boat ride" and the "consistently good Sunday brunch", then take in the "unbeatable view" from the "awesome" rooms ("upgrade to a suite"); N.B. spa renovations are underway.

Ketchum

Knob Hill Inn – | – | – | – | $210

960 N. Main St.; 208-726-8010; fax 208-726-2712; 800-526-8010; www.knobhillinn.com; 22 rooms, 4 suites

Located in a "quaint setting" ringed by gardens, this "wonderful" Relais & Châteaux chalet dispenses "charm" and "thoughtful service" along with complimentary breakfast; suites and rooms boast marble baths and balconies with views of Bald Mountain and Griffin Butte, and there's a lap pool, sauna, Jacuzzi and exercise

room on-site with skiing, shopping and golf available in nearby Sun Valley, Ketchum and Elkhorn.

Sun Valley

Sun Valley Lodge 19 | 22 | 22 | 24 | $189

1 Sun Valley Rd.; 208-622-2001; fax 208-622-2030; 800-786-8259; www.sunvalley.com; 242 condos, 191 rooms, 85 suites, 7 houses

"Simultaneously elaborate and quaint", this recently renovated, "incredible" resort strikes the "right balance of old-school charm and ski resort chic" with accommodations ranging from standard rooms to cottages and condos; acolytes tout the hot tub, a "steamy must, the over-the-top Sunday brunch", "outstanding golf courses" and the "bowling alley, a lovable oddity"; Bing Crosby, Gary Cooper, even Hemingway stayed here (just take a look at the "star-studded photos lining the hallways"), and this "favorite" still attracts the likes of "Arnold, Maria and the kids."

Illinois

Chicago

★ **Tops in City**

28 Peninsula
27 Four Seasons
Ritz-Carlton
24 Park Hyatt
23 Fairmont
Sofitel

Burnham, Hotel 22 | 22 | 22 | 19 | $229

1 W. Washington St.; 312-782-1111; fax 312-782-0899; 866-690-1986; www.burnhamhotel.com; 103 rooms, 19 suites

A "tasteful, worthy tribute to the great fin de siècle architect" Daniel Burnham, the Kimpton Group's "lovingly restored" Reliance building landmark is now a pet-friendly "neat" boutique "treasure" in the Loop that's "walkable to everything"; the European-style "rooms are small" but "splendidly furnished", and "comfortable" with "whimsical" touches, the concierge makes "interesting recommendations", and there's "surprisingly good dining" in the Atwood Cafe and complimentary "wine in the evening."

Deer Path Inn 16 | 22 | 21 | 18 | $220

255 E. Illinois Rd., Lake Forest; 847-234-2280; fax 847-234-3352; 800-788-9480; www.dpihotel.com; 25 rooms, 31 suites

Opened in 1929, this "charming" Tudor-style retreat less than a mile from Lake Michigan in "posh Lake Forest" "takes you back in time to an English countryside inn" with "gracious" service, antique furniture, a courtyard garden and Continental dining in The English Room; those who deem it a trifle "tired" and find the "average amenities" less than endearing may be appeased by upcoming renovations; N.B. there's a golf course nearby.

Drake, The 21 | 23 | 21 | 22 | $249

140 E. Walton Pl.; 312-787-2200; fax 312-787-1431; 800-553-7253; www.thedrakehotel.com; 463 rooms, 74 suites

Loyalists love this 1920 "veteran of distinction" for its "old-school luxury", "ideal" Magnificent Mile location, a "non-intrusive" staff and "gorgeous centerpiece lobby", site of "amazing tea service"; the "classic" Cape Cod Room (and new Drake Bros.' Steaks Chicago) is "where you take your visiting rich relatives to dinner" and the "lake-facing" suites or "huge club level rooms" "where you put them up"; the few who deem it a "dated" "dowager" will happily note there's a $15-million renovation planned.

Fairmont Chicago 25 | 23 | 22 | 23 | $339

200 N. Columbus Dr.; 312-565-8000; fax 312-565-1032; 800-441-1414; www.fairmont.com; 626 rooms, 66 suites

"Modern, yet still classy, this "luxe" chain link near Millennium Park is a "little off the beaten track but still close enough to the action" with "marvelous rooms" offering "stunning views of the lake" and the Navy Pier; the "fantastic" staff "caters to every whim", the "roomy bathrooms" are "pampering", the "food is super" and the "next-door athletic club is a palace" (though you must "pay extra"); but a few faultfinders sigh "if only it were on Michigan Avenue" and quibble that quarters "could use updating."

FOUR SEASONS 28 | 28 | 27 | 27 | $555

120 E. Delaware Pl.; 312-280-8800; fax 312-280-1748; 800-332-3442; www.fourseasons.com; 175 rooms, 168 suites

Enjoy "life lived at its best" in this "plush" "haven of tranquility" that "has it all for families and business", including "a fantastic location", "excellent dining" in Seasons ("Sunday brunch is an over-the-top foodfest" and "afternoon tea a treat"), a "top-drawer spa" and an "outstanding pool"; the "gracious lobby" is "exquisitely decorated", "rooms are large with lovely furnishings" (many with "stunning views up Michigan Avenue") and "impeccable service" "caters to your every need."

Hard Rock Hotel Chicago ▽ 20 | 17 | 15 | 17 | $199

230 N. Michigan Ave.; 312-345-1000; fax 312-345-1012; 877-762-5468; www.hardrockhotelchicago.com; 368 rooms, 13 suites

An "excellent place for music lovers", this "cool" first urban Hard Rock Hotel, set in the Loop's historic Carbide & Carbon building (built in 1929 to resemble a champagne bottle), rocks according to guests who get in the boutique hotel groove with "small, nicely decorated rooms" and a "hoppin' bar"; "concierge service can't be beat, service is knowledgeable" and it offers "good value" for the buck; N.B. the on-site China Grill restaurant opened post-*Survey*.

Hilton Chicago 18 | 19 | 17 | 20 | $184

720 S. Michigan Ave.; 312-922-4400; fax 312-922-5240; 800-774-1500; www.hilton.com; 1544 rooms

A "reliable", "fine old hotel" in the Grant Park/museum district, this "huge", "convention-oriented" property with a "spectacular ballroom" and an "array of in-house restaurants and bars" is a "good business bunk", with many double rooms sporting two baths and "gorgeous lake views"; loyalists laud the "location, location, location" but others find it "a bit out of the way."

House of Blues Hotel 22 | 20 | 19 | 20 | $250

333 N. Dearborn St.; 312-245-0333; fax 312-923-2444; 877-569-3742; www.loewshotels.com; 347 rooms, 20 suites

"Cool, dude", yes, this "trendy, funky" River Norther offers a "refreshing change from the mundane" with "super-comfortable rooms" done up in "wild, wacky colors" and a "harmonica in the mini-fridge"; part outsider/folk art museum, part night club, with "live nightly music acts" and a lobby bar that "resembles an opium den" (plus a brand-new bowling lounge), it's "one of the more fun places to stay in Chi-town", and "they couldn't be more welcoming" to pets and kids; if a few sing the blues about the "nightmare"-inducing decor, most say that's what "keeps you interested."

InterContinental Ⓗ 21 | 21 | 19 | 22 | $300

505 N. Michigan Ave.; 312-944-4100; fax 312-944-1320; 800-628-2112; www.interconti.com; 735 rooms, 72 suites

The "splendid restoration" "did wonders" for this "gorgeous" 1929 landmark "with exotic details" and a "wonderful lobby"; "request a room in the historic tower" "with more character" or stretch out in the "spacious new wing", dunk in the Roman-style tiled indoor pool – "worth admiring even if you don't swim" – and revel in the "old-world service"; if a few deem the digs "small", others concur the "tremendous location", "lovely food" at Zest and "amazing lounges" "make up for any demerits."

Le Méridien 26 | 23 | 18 | 22 | $359

521 N. Rush St.; 312-645-1500; fax 312-645-1550; 800-543-4300; www.lemeridien.com; 278 rooms, 33 suites

Noted for its "cosmopolitan decor and ambiance", this "sleek, stylish" "nice surprise in a big city" boasts a very "convenient skybridge" to the Northbridge Mall, "comfortable", "quiet rooms" with "modern furnishings", "spacious, elegant bathrooms" ("bigger than my New York City living room"), a "more than adequate gym" and an "attentive staff"; "you can usually get a great rate" "for shopping and business alike" ("high-tech rooms delight!"), plus the Gold Coast location is "surrounded by nightlife" and some of "the best restaurants around."

Monaco, Hotel 24 | 22 | 18 | 20 | $209

225 N. Wabash Ave.; 312-960-8500; fax 312-960-1883; 800-397-7661; www.monaco-chicago.com; 170 rooms, 22 suites

"A bit zany" with "lovely" accommodations kitted out with "plush furniture" and a "pet goldfish", Kimpton's "beautiful boutique hotel", set in a former hat factory, comes "highly recommended", especially "if you need to stay closer to the Loop rather than Michigan Avenue shopping"; "the attention to detail is above and beyond", from the "leopard print terry robes" to the "super-friendly" staff to the "wine happy hour" – little wonder the awed declare "we had a blast!"

Omni Ambassador East Ⓗ 19 | 21 | 21 | 19 | $229

1301 N. State Pkwy.; 312-787-7200; fax 312-787-4760; 800-843-6664; www.omniambassadoreast.com; 239 rooms, 46 suites

Situated "in a real neighborhood" (as in the tony Gold Coast, "close to the Magnificent Mile"), this "lovely", "old-school" landmark with an "elegant lobby" and "exceptionally friendly staff" makes "you feel like you are part of the Rat Pack", especially when ensconced in the Pump Room restaurant ("can't beat it for atmosphere"); the less-impressed who decry "small rooms and minute bathrooms" in "need of refurbishment" may be appeased by the renovations planned for 2006.

Omni Chicago 23 21 18 21 $349

676 N. Michigan Ave.; 312-944-6664; fax 312-266-3015; 800-843-6664; www.omnihotels.com; 347 suites

"Visit the Mag Mile from the mid mile" at this "well-located but unpretentious" "perfect executive's hotel" that's also "close to many family attractions" like the "Navy Pier and American Girl store" ("walk out to all the shopping you could dream of"); "love that every room" is a "beautifully styled suite" and all now have 37-inch plasma TVs, plus the food at Cielo is "good enough not to wander outdoors", the "staff is child-friendly" and there are "warm touches throughout"; just a few label it "plain vanilla."

Palmer House Hilton Ⓗ 18 21 18 19 $199

17 E. Monroe St.; 312-726-7500; fax 312-917-1707; 800-774-1500; www.hilton.com; 1639 rooms

"Experience a bygone era" at this "old-school, corporate meeting" chain link so "huge it could be a city in itself" with a "lavish", intricately detailed lobby and "elegant ballrooms"; its Loop address is "ideally located for a weekend jaunt" to the museums, theater and shopping, plus the "gym and pool are great"; "rooms range from comfortable to broom closets" "small enough to fit in your palm", though the renovations may not be reflected in the outpouring of opinions deeming accommodations "outdated."

PARK HYATT Ⓢ 26 26 24 26 $455

800 N. Michigan Ave.; 312-335-1234; fax 312-239-4000; 800-778-7477; www.parkhyatt.com; 196 rooms, 8 suites

"Get ready to be spoiled" at this "sleek, modern" "over the top at every stop" Gold Coast site that "screams sexy" with "high-design rooms" that are "complete bliss" ("Eames chairs!"), offering "superb views" of the lake and Water Tower "that will bring a tear to your eye", "high-tech gadgets" and bathrooms boasting "luxury amenities" like "extra-deep tubs with candles"; NoMi restaurant and the adjacent bar are "hip and happening", the "health club is spiffy" and the staff is "incredible."

PENINSULA Ⓢ 29 28 27 28 $445

108 E. Superior St.; 312-337-2888; fax 312-751-2888; 866-288-8889; www.peninsula.com; 256 rooms, 83 suites

"Absolutely the best Chicago" "has to offer" – in fact, this "seamless experience" of "luxury on steroids" is the No. 1 Hotel in this *Survey*, a bastion of "comfort and tranquility" with "impeccably appointed", "technologically savvy rooms", "decadent bathrooms with in-tub TVs" and "top-notch amenities", "opulent public areas", "exquisite service" and four "diverse dining" options "to die for" (special kudos for Avenues and Shanghai Terrace); there's also the "elegant" 14,000-sq-ft. spa and "ideal location" with "Chicago's playground just outside your door."

Renaissance Chicago 23 21 18 21 $239

1 W. Wacker Dr.; 312-372-7200; fax 312-372-0093; 800-468-3571; www.renaissancehotels.com; 513 rooms, 40 suites

A "perfect jumping-off place for Chicago's attractions" such as "shopping, theater, restaurants – everything you want to see and do" – and "convenient for business", this "elegant" "respite" "with a small hotel feel" in the inner Loop gives "all the amenities without the Mag Mile attitude"; the "beautifully furnished", "nice-size rooms" offer "comfort with a view" of the river and lake, and the "helpful" staff "treats you with respect."

RITZ-CARLTON (A FOUR SEASONS HOTEL) 27 | 28 | 27 | 26 | $375

160 E. Pearson St.; 312-266-1000; fax 312-266-9498; 800-621-6906; www.fourseasons.com; 344 rooms, 91 suites

"Still on its game", this "world-class" pet-friendly "special treat" set above Water Tower Place off the "Boul Mich" promises the "pure pampering" of "polished service", "wonderful room layouts", "antiques-filled decor", a "beautiful lobby" and "great lap pool", plus the "outstanding" Ritz-Carlton Dining Room, which welcomed a new chef, Kevin Hickey, post-*Survey*, and was voted No. 1 for Decor and Service in our *Chicago Restaurant Survey*; it's "perfect for the business traveler" but also "quite solicitous of kids", and "the best shopping is right out the door."

71, Hotel – | – | – | – | $239

71 E. Wacker Dr.; 312-346-7100; fax 312-346-1721; www.hotel71.com; 422 rooms, 32 suites

The Loop's former Executive Plaza, given a $20-million face-lift, presents a modern, steel and blue-tinted glass exterior housing large guestrooms that were originally designed as apartments, with panoramic skyline and river views; it has the latest business amenities and luxurious touches like 300-thread-count linens (plus eight executive boardroom suites with in-room meeting space), a high-tech lounge with WiFi capabilities and Porter's steakhouse.

Sheraton Chicago Hotel & Towers 19 | 19 | 17 | 21 | $149

301 E. North Water St.; 312-464-1000; fax 312-464-9140; 877-242-2558; www.sheratonchicago.com; 1176 rooms, 52 suites

"Rambling" and "classy", this "solid" Loop "convention hotel" "located at the confluence of Lake Michigan and the Chicago River" "a short cab ride from everything" has "bright open public spaces" and "ample-size", "minimalist" accommodations with "super-cool views" of the skyline or water; bored businessmen bemoan it as "bland" and "impersonal", reporting "rooms too small, hotel too big", and ruing that it's "off the beaten path."

Sofitel Chicago O'Hare 22 | 21 | 20 | 20 | $179

5550 N. River Rd., Rosemont; 847-678-4488; fax 847-678-4244; 800-233-5959; www.sofitel.com; 288 rooms, 12 suites

A "Gallic respite in the O'Hare wasteland" agree *amis* of this "refreshing change of pace from a typical airport property" that even offers a "park and fly package" with "covered parking"; the "staff brings 'your wish is my command' to a new level", the "excellent restaurant" has a "French ambiance" and the "plush" surroundings coddle with "lots of comforts"; if a few grumblers grouch it's a "workmanlike" way station that "doesn't live up to other Sofitels", most find it "invigorating."

Sofitel Chicago Water Tower 25 | 23 | 22 | 23 | $339

20 E. Chestnut St.; 312-324-4000; fax 312-324-4026; 877-813-7700; www.sofitel.com; 382 rooms, 33 suites

"Business oriented" with "lots of international guests", this "hip and comfy" Gold Coast "architectural gem" with a "French twist" is both "modern-looking and exciting"; the "large, soothing", "blond-wood rooms" boast "bold color accents", "sumptuous beds" you "sink into" and "just plain luxurious bathrooms", plus they've got "all the amenities, from stereo to high-speed Internet"; the "always busy bar" is "the best": "very chic, very black clothes", and what's more, the food in Café des Architectes is "delicious."

Sutton Place 22 21 17 20 $305

21 E. Bellevue Pl.; 312-266-2100; fax 312-266-2103; 800-606-8188; www.suttonplace.com; 206 rooms, 40 suites

Set "on the edge of the Rush Street entertainment area" with "sleek", "avant-garde", art deco–inspired rooms that "fit the vibe of the surroundings", this "funky" boutique hotel is a "fun place to stay" (they even put up the Chicago Blackhawks); an "excellent connection with a local gym facility", the on-site Whisky Bar & Grill and "lots of amenities" make it "great for business trips"; but others fault the "uneven" accommodations and "inattentive" staff.

Swissôtel 24 23 20 21 $479

323 E. Wacker Dr.; 312-565-0565; fax 312-565-0315; 888-737-9477; www.swissotel.com; 596 rooms, 36 suites

"Nice-size", "elegant rooms" with "sweeping views" of the city, the lake and Navy Pier, "comfy beds" and "mini-spa"–like baths draw devotees to this Loop "sleeper" run with "Swiss efficiency"; it's "great for the business traveler", with a "wonderful rooftop pool" and work-out room (though "you have to pay for using" the latter) and "fine dining at the Palm"; but the more neutral say it "just blends in" and the "pricey" restaurant is "not worth it."

W City Center 21 21 19 20 $299

172 W. Adams St.; 312-332-1200; fax 312-917-5771; 888-627-8280; www.whotels.com; 368 rooms, 12 suites

"Score another win for the W chain" with this "chic, sleek, sexy" pet-friendly boutique hotel with a "business and financial driven" Loop location (there's "not much happening in the neighborhood"), "contemporary", "funky" rooms, a "hipper-than-thou", "fun, Gothic, music-filled lobby and chic bar" for "people-watching" and "courteous, professional staff"; but naysayers note it's not only "noisy" and "uppity", but "so minimalist it hurts", crowing "you're not cool enough to stay here."

Westin River North 23 20 17 20 $399

320 N. Dearborn Ave.; 312-744-1900; fax 312-527-2650; 877-866-9216; www.westinchicago.com; 407 rooms, 17 suites

"Not your typical Westin", "the former Hotel Nikko still has that Far East feel to it", along with "spacious", "well-appointed rooms", a "wide-open lobby lounge", a "great fitness center" (for an "extra charge") and a River North location "for business travel", "surrounded by hot restaurants" – all this and "service with a smile"; still, some lukewarm respondents reckon the "rooms could use a little updating" and note "it lacks that special" something.

Whitehall Hotel, The Ⓗ 21 23 18 18 $279

105 E. Delaware Pl.; 312-944-6300; fax 312-944-8552; 800-948-4255; www.thewhitehallhotel.com; 213 rooms, 8 suites

"You feel like you're in a little world away from the city" at this "sophisticated refuge", a circa-1928 "charming European-style hotel" with "old-world" "character" ("more like a pied-à-terre"); nestled in a "fantastic" Gold Coast setting, it's "suited for business travelers" and also "a wonderful place to spend a weekend" with "inviting and comfortable rooms" and "unpretentious service" that "knows how to make guests feel welcome"; nonplussed patrons pout it's "lost its edge."

W Lakeshore Ⓢ 22 | 20 | 19 | 20 | $429

644 N. Lake Shore Dr.; 312-943-9200; fax 312-255-4411; 877-946-8357; www.whotels.com; 525 rooms, 31 suites

"Hip and upscale", this "rock 'n' roll business hotel – go figure" – with a "helpful, oh-so-cool staff" – is also "the place to be" for couples, "boomers and younger" (and their pets); admirers are awed by the "awfully tony", "modern decor" and "typical W swank", the "great lobby bar" "with a lot of action" and the "amazing Whiskey Blue" rooftop lounge where you can "watch the sunset over Lake Michigan"; but weary travelers whine it's "too dark, too trendy" and they "can do without the attitude"; N.B. a Bliss spa opened in 2005.

Galena

Eagle Ridge Resort & Spa Ⓢ 22 | 21 | 18 | 24 | $199

444 Eagle Ridge Dr.; 815-777-2444; fax 815-777-5609; 800-892-2269; www.eagleridge.com; 78 rooms, 2 suites, 375 resort homes

"An outstanding getaway", this "secluded", "well-groomed" resort "with rolling hills and beautiful grounds" six miles from historic Downtown offers "wonderful views of wildlife" and Lake Galena, a "lovely staff" and "Sunday brunch that's a must"; whether you "rent a beautiful house", a "group-friendly townhouse" or a room in the inn, it's a "great family" "escape", so indulge in 63 holes of "golf, golf, golf" and "a full array of activities", including paddle boat rentals, horseback riding, hiking, tennis, fishing and skiing.

Gilman

Heartland Spa Ⓢ ▽ 17 | 20 | 19 | 21 | $1030

1237 E. 1600 North Rd.; 815-683-2182; fax 815 683-2144; 800-545-4853; www.heartlandspa.com; 16 rooms

"If you're looking for luxury, try an alternative" since this "stress-free" Gilman getaway 90 miles south of Chicago is "rather spartan"; set on 32 rural acres with a secluded lake, it offers nutrition counseling, exercise classes, yoga, spa treatments, hiking and wintertime cross-country skiing "at reasonable prices"; unsatiated guests are advised to "take advantage of the policy that allows you to ask for extra" low-fat food.

Indiana

Indianapolis

Canterbury Hotel Ⓗ 20 | 22 | 19 | 18 | $275

123 S. Illinois St.; 317-634-3000; fax 317- 685-2519; www.canterburyhotel.com; 74 rooms, 25 suites

Offering "a cute" "alternative to the chains" Downtown, this European-style boutique hotel with a "marvelous, unpretentious

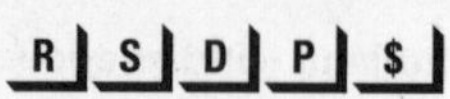

restaurant" "is well placed next to" the Circle Center shopping mall; "it's very quaint", as befits its lodging lineage dating back to the 1850s, with "unusual, top-drawer duplex suites", "rooms with four-poster beds", a lobby with "abundant fresh flowers and antiques" and a staff "dedicated" to "exceeding expectations"; if a few find it "a tired throwback to another era", most insist it's still "charming."

Westin | 23 | 20 | 20 | 21 | $289

50 S. Capitol Ave.; 317-262-8100; fax 317-231-3928; www.westin.com/indianapolis; 533 rooms, 40 suites

"Convenient to the RCA Dome" and connected by sky bridge to the Indiana Convention Center, this "great Downtown location" has "everything to offer", from "large rooms" with "soft feathery comforters", "the most comfortable beds in Indianapolis" and "modern decor" to "terrific dining" at Shula's Steakhouse to an "excellent" "staff that impresses"; still, a few grouchers gripe "service lowered my delight", deeming this chain link a "no-frills" "cookie-cutter property."

Kansas

Overland Park

Sheraton Overland Park Hotel | ∇ 23 | 20 | 18 | 22 | $209

6100 College Blvd.; 913-234-2100; fax 913-234-2111; 866-478-2777; www.sheraton.com; 412 rooms, 18 suites

"Unexpectedly upscale", this "sparkling" tower "attached to the Overland Park Convention Center" boasts plenty of "business savvy", from the "refreshingly unique public areas" (the stylish lobby lounge is a perfect place to meet) to the solicitous staff; rooms are quite "comfortable", if "predictably appointed", and though the in-house eateries earn no particular praise, the hotel is "close to a wealth of shopping and dining options."

Wichita

Inn at the Park Ⓗ | – | – | – | – | $160

3751 E. Douglas Ave.; 316-652-0500; fax 316-652-0525; 800-258-1951; www.innatthepark.com; 10 rooms, 2 suites

Fireplace lovers take note: many of the hearths in this 1909 English-style manor in residential College Hill are "spectacular"; sybarites swoon over the antiques-filled rooms, stained-glass windows and intimate gardens, and for even more privacy, "ask for a room in the century-old carriage house" with its own hot tub; N.B. a chef in residence can whip up dinners *à deux.*

Kentucky

Louisville

Camberley Brown Hotel, The Ⓗ | ∇ 21 | 23 | 23 | 19 | $265

335 W. Broadway; 502-583-1234; fax 502-587-7006; 888-888-5252; www.thebrownhotel.com; 293 rooms, 6 suites

"Better than a tray of mint juleps", this "lovely" 1927 Theater Square landmark on the National Register of Historic Places is as

"Louisville should be": "full of Southern charm and Northern efficiency", with a "beautiful lobby", rooms sporting Italian marble bathrooms and "incomparable service"; the English Grill restaurant still lures loyalists with its "national treasure" – the legendary Hot Brown sandwich (turkey, cheese and bacon) – "you must eat it where it was invented."

Seelbach Hilton Ⓗ🏌👓Ⓢ | 20 | 23 | 23 | 20 | $219 |

500 Fourth Ave.; 502-585-3200; fax 502-585-9240; 800-445-8667; www.seelbachhilton.com; 291 rooms, 30 suites

"Storied in history" ("check out Al Capone's escape route during Prohibition"), this "classy" Downtown destination on the National Register of Historic Places that inspired the backdrop of F. Scott Fitzgerald's flapper-era *Great Gatsby* makes you "feel like you're in the 1920s with all the amenities of the 2000s", augmented by "gracious" service, the "excellent Oak Room" restaurant and a bar that's a "bourbon-lover's paradise"; still, while some are smitten by "rooms with plenty of old-world charm", grumpy critics growl "I believe mine was a former closet."

Louisiana

At press time, New Orleans was just beginning its recovery from Hurricane Katrina's devastation. We are publishing these reviews of its top hotels in the faith that they will be operational in the near future.

New Orleans

★ **Tops in City**

27 Windsor Court
26 Maison Orleans
25 Ritz-Carlton
23 Monaco, Hotel
Le Pavillon

Bienville House, Hotel 👓 | ▽ 17 | 21 | 19 | 17 | $235 |

320 Decatur St.; 504-529-2345; fax 504-525-6079; 800-535-7836; www.bienvillehouse.com; 80 rooms, 3 suites

"You'll love this hotel right in the middle of the French Quarter" say most fans, especially after a pricey renovation a few years back; but others counter, although "the pool is a joy for toddlers", the family might feel like they're in detention if booked in a "prisonlike" interior room "with no windows"; N.B. for a self-made taste of the Big Easy, go in for a lesson at its Louisiana Heritage Café & School of Cooking.

Bourbon Orleans - Wyndham Ⓗ👓 | 19 | 20 | 17 | 19 | $349 |

717 Orleans St.; 504-571-4622; www.wyndham.com; 170 rooms, 50 suites

"If the Quarter is your taste, then this facility will sate your hunger" for N'Awlins "history well preserved", particularly given the Wyndham's "very nice" $14-million restoration of the "gorgeous" 1817 building, along with updates like a new restaurant, a martini bar and a gym; you'll "feel like Laura Ashley" in a "fabulously" "quaint" yet "reasonably priced" townhouse suite with a "huge balcony", but "light sleepers" should avoid rooms overlooking the "24/7 Mardi Gras" on the Bourbon Street side.

Chateau Sonesta 22 | 21 | 17 | 21 | $249

800 Rue Iberville; 504-586-0800; fax 504-586-1987; 800-766-3782; www.chateausonesta.com; 226 rooms, 25 suites

For low-key "charm on a budget", this "quiet oasis in the middle of NOLA insanity" is "a wonderful place to stay"; its rooms are "generous in size", its "pool area is nice" and its Red Fish Grill is justifiably popular; "possibly the best concierge on the planet" can also reserve a table for you at one of the many "top restaurants an easy five-minute walk away."

Fairmont New Orleans Ⓗ 19 | 21 | 18 | 20 | $289

123 Baronne St.; 504-529-7111; fax 504-522-2303; 800-441-1414; www.fairmont.com; 615 rooms, 85 suites

"Imagine Scarlett" sweeping through "the spectacular lobby" or Huey P. Long sipping a Sazerac in the bar, "the birthplace of the cocktail", at this "grande dame" of the CBD; though she's "beautifully decorated" at Christmas, she's otherwise "showing her age", with "spotty" dining and "small", "threadbare" rooms.

Iberville Suites Ⓢ ∇ 24 | 23 | 19 | 23 | $310

910 Rue Iberville; 504-523-2400; fax 504-524-1320; 866-229-4351; www.ibervillesuites.com; 230 suites

As the "polite", "happy employees" might tell you, it's "very cool" that you can stay in these "comfortable" Quarter suites "sharing some facilities" and "amenities of the Ritz-Carlton" (it's in the same building) but with "less costly" tabs; indulge in the "fab spa services and charge them to your room" or partake of the "free-for-all" at the "great breakfast buffet", even if snobs say the "garage-sale leftovers" of the luxury chain can be "depressing."

InterContinental 21 | 21 | 16 | 19 | $425

444 St. Charles Ave.; 504-525-5566; fax 504-523-7310 ; www.new-orleans.intercontinental.com; 458 rooms, 21 suites

Perhaps "a little off the beaten path but swank and safe" in the CBD "with a streetcar running in front", this "clean", "quiet", "conventionlike hotel" is "not very glamorous", but it's "convenient enough for business people" who can rest easy on an "incredible bed" in a "spacious" room after conferencing in the "exceptional meeting facilities"; it houses a "bakery serving good pastries", and its jazz-and-champagne "Sunday brunch is a local favorite."

International House Ⓢ 24 | 25 | 19 | 22 | $279

221 Camp St.; 504-553-9550; fax 504-553-9560; 800-633-5770; 116 rooms, 3 suites

"Fun, funky" and "super-chic" with a "popular" candlelit lobby bar, a "trendy" French-Vietnamese eatery and a surprisingly "friendly staff", this "sleek" CBD boutique stands out in "a town with a dearth of them"; the "small" rooms might be akin to "sophisticated" "closets", but "the bathtubs are the deepest ever", the "glass showers are fantastic", the private "penthouse balconies" are "great" and "CD players with jazz" discs amp up the "sexy" vibe.

Le Pavillon Hotel 24 | 25 | 21 | 23 | $259

833 Poydras St.; 504-581-3111; fax 504-620-4130; 800-535-9095; www.lepavillon.com; 219 rooms, 7 suites

"A touch of true France", this "opulent" CBD "belle" boasts "a royal feel in every room", where you can make "like a bon vivant" nibbling on "gratis peanut butter and jelly" for a pre-snooze snack amid "old-fashioned" "puffy beds, curtains and towels"; "when the parades are rolling on the street below", a staff "without parallel" will direct you to the rooftop pool where "the view is magical."

Loews New Orleans ▽ 25 | 25 | 21 | 23 | $249

300 Poydras St.; 504-595-3300; fax 504-595-3310; 800-235-6397; www.loewshotels.com; 273 rooms, 12 suites

"Hip and fun", this two-year-old with an "elegant atmosphere" is set in a "fabulous" Downtown location in the former Lykes Building near the convention center and across the street from Harrah's Casino; it's a "great experience", from the spacious rooms offering panoramic views of the Mississippi River, city skyline or the French Quarter, amenities like WiFi access and the "excellent Brennan family restaurant" Café Adelaide, plus "service is so attentive the staff seems to trip over one another."

Maison de Ville & the Audobon Cottages Ⓗ ▽ 24 | 25 | 24 | 19 | $249

727 Rue Toulouse; 504-561-5858; fax 504-528-9939; 800-634-1600; www.hotelmaisondeville.com; 14 rooms, 2 suites, 7 cottages

"With slanted floors, lots of history" and "very good service", this "small" Vieux Carré inn, organized around "a lovely central courtyard with a fountain" where Tennessee Williams put the final blush on Blanche DuBois, is both "charming and convenient"; for a "private villa" experience, "ask for the Audobon Cottages", the "less well-located but more modern" bungalows where the namesake naturalist conjured his *Birds of America*; N.B. for an excellent French feast, dine at Bistro at Maison de Ville.

Maison Dupuy 18 | 21 | 21 | 19 | $219

1001 Rue Toulouse; 504-586-8000; fax 504-525-5334; 800-535-9177; www.maisondupuy.com; 187 rooms, 12 suites, 1 cottage

There's a "warm Southern hospitality bordering on the flirtatious" by the "helpful, friendly staff" at this "cute" French Quarterite "a little out of the way" of "the noise and smell of Bourbon Street"; if your room is a bit too "intimate", escape to the "lovely interior courtyard" with its heated pool, Jacuzzi and fountain, and don't miss the "great Sunday jazz brunch" or dinner at Dominque's, the hotel's fine French-Caribbean restaurant.

MAISON ORLEANS Ⓢ 27 | 24 | 26 | 26 | $509

904 Rue Iberville; 504-670-2900; fax 504-670-2910; 800-241-3333; www.maisonorleans.com; 74 rooms, 1 suite

Looking for "your own private mansion tucked in an out-of-the-way section of the Quarter"? – "keep the kiddies at home" and go in for "one of the most romantic" experiences in New Orleans, this "amazing boutique hotel" where guests have signing privileges at the adjacent Ritz-Carlton; after a "great soak" in the "enormous bath fit for two", lounge in your "beautiful room with hardwood floors, antiques and faux fireplace."

Monaco, Hotel 25 | 23 | 23 | 23 | $334

333 St. Charles Ave.; 504-561-0010; fax 504-310-2777; 866-685-8359; www.monaco-neworleans.com; 227 rooms, 23 suites

If "your friend Mr. Goldfish (a nice companion in your room)" could talk he'd tell you it's "hip, diddy, hip" to stay at this "quirky", "delightful" boutique housed in a former Masonic temple on a Biz District streetcar line "a few blocks from the riffraff"; there's "funky" yet "sumptuous" "safari" decor and an "energetic atmosphere" in which to enjoy a complimentary "happy-hour massage and glass of wine" followed by dinner at David English's "swanky" Cobalt.

Monteleone, Hotel Ⓗ Ⓢ — | – | – | – | $200

214 Rue Royale; 504-523-3341; fax 504-681-4491; 800-535-9595; www.hotelmonteleone.com; 459 rooms, 63 suites, 51 studios

Walk into a page of history at this French Quarter literary landmark that's played host to famous writers like Ernest Hemingway and William Faulkner and offers specialized suites bearing the authors' names; expect rooms with marble and granite baths, plush robes and upscale amenities, a rooftop pool, a revolving bar and an on-site Aria spa, plus a blend of Cajun and Creole favorites in three restaurants – the Hunt Room, Le Café and the Aft Deck Oyster Bar.

Omni Royal Orleans — 20 | 22 | 22 | 22 | $279

621 St. Louis St.; 504-529-5333; fax 504-529-7089; 800-843-6664; www.omniroyalorleans.com; 330 rooms, 16 suites

"Within walking distance of everything legal and illegal" stands the "epitome of New Orleans elegance", where the staff "goes out of its way to justify the $$$ outlay"; "splurge for a lovely suite" with Quarter views (other rooms are "small), "have a drink and watch the river flow" at the rooftop pool, dine at the "popular" Rib Room amid the "locals" and sigh "*très magnifique*"; just don't include the kids – "let them come alone, when they're over 21."

RITZ-CARLTON NEW ORLEANS Ⓢ — 26 | 26 | 24 | 26 | $419

921 Canal St.; 504-524-1331; fax 504-524-7675; 800-241-3333; www.ritzcarlton.com; 452 rooms, 37 suites

What is "decadence with character"? – a combination of "splendid" accommodations ("the concierge floor rocks!"), a "sinfully relaxing" spa and "top-notch" service striking just "the right balance of security and freedom"; so "get away from the party atmosphere" to an "outstanding" Quarter-adjacent "haven" that covers all the bases, with "great jazz in the lobby bar", "exquisite" afternoon tea and an attitude that even lets "kids be king."

Royal Sonesta — 20 | 21 | 20 | 20 | $250

300 Bourbon St.; 504-586-0300; fax 504-586-0335; 800-766-3782; www.royalsonestano.com; 478 rooms, 22 suites

"Bourbon Street is a no-no" for children, but freewheeling "adults love" the wrought-iron "balcony views" of "ground zero" for strip clubs, "drunks" and "characters"; "light sleepers" should get a room overlooking the "serene" courtyard, but don't expect a "warm welcome" – "the staff seems unconcerned with repeat business."

Soniat House Ⓗ — 25 | 25 | 18 | 22 | $265

1133 Chartres St.; 504-522-0570; fax 504-522-7208; 800-544-8808; www.soniathouse.com; 23 rooms, 10 suites, 1 cottage

"Behind a simple green door" lies a "romantic", "little" boutique "hideaway" with a "French Quarter–sans-Vegas" vibe; ensconced in a "fabulous" room in a trio of "old townhouses" steeped in antiques, "Louisiana charm" and "sophisticated" "hospitality", you'll feel like "the guest in the home of a friend" "in the early

1800s" at this member of Small Luxury Hotels of the World; stay "upstairs with street views", and "breakfast in bed" on "delicious biscuits in a basket with a hot stone to keep them warm and the best coffee on the planet."

W French Quarter 21 | 21 | 18 | 19 | $505

316 Chartres St.; 504-581-1200; fax 504-523-2910; 877-946-8357; www.whotels.com/frenchquarter; 96 rooms, 2 suites

This "fantastic success fuses old French Quarter buildings into a sleek modern hotel" with "hipster rooms", "party parts" and "swanky" "quiet areas" off "mood-lit" "hallways smelling of magnolia" and leading to a "pretty courtyard" with a "splendid little pool"; it offers "everything Ws are known for, including feather beds" in which to "indulge" in "room service from Bacco."

WINDSOR COURT HOTEL 28 | 28 | 27 | 26 | $450

300 Gravier St.; 504-523-6000; fax 504-596-4513; 800-262-2662; www.windsorcourthotel.com; 324 suites

"If Cinderella ever needed a new design for her happily-ever-after castle, this would be the prototype"; you "get what you pay for" in "pomp and circumstance" (but with "great off-season deals") from the "superbly decorated rooms" to the "baroque music"–filled lobby to the "phenomenal" New Orleans Grill (voted No. 1 for Decor and Service in our *New Orleans Restaurant Survey*); if a few feel it's "too snooty for families", most retort that the "wonderful" "staff falls all over itself" to make children happy.

W New Orleans 22 | 21 | 19 | 21 | $469

333 Poydras St.; 504-525-9444; fax 504-581-7179; 877-946-8357; www.whotels.com; 400 rooms, 23 suites

It's "bangin'!" boast the "young and trendy" about this "hip, happening and wired" spot where "great games", a "chic bar" and "comfy sofas" in a lobby that "exudes energy" are all part of the scene; the "slick" staff is "reminiscent of *Men in Black,* but their mission is to host your stay" in the CBD "within walking distance of the Quarter", which might be "too far if you're stone drunk" say all the imbibing "beautiful people."

Wyndham at Canal Place 22 | 21 | 17 | 23 | $219

100 Rue Iberville; 504-566-7006; fax 504-553-5133; 800-822-4200; www.wyndham.com; 398 rooms, 40 suites

"Huge windows" in a "gigantic" lobby provide "phenomenal" sightings of "passing ships and barges" on the Mississippi at this "great place for business meetings" "within walking distance to the French Quarter and Riverwalk" and "practically next door to the aquarium"; "convention"-goers gush that you "must get a high floor" for "romantic" exterior views "at sundown", despite interiors that "could stand to be updated."

White Castle

Nottoway Plantation ▽ 24 | 19 | 15 | 19 | $145

30970 Hwy. 405 (The Great River Rd.); 225-545-2730; fax 225-545-8632; 866-527-6884; www.nottoway.com; 11 rooms, 3 suites

Have yourself "transported in time" to the era of "*Gone With the Wind*" at this "authentically restored" 1859 plantation home "filled with antiques" (many from the original antebellum owner) that's an hour and a half from New Orleans along "the flowing Mississippi"; the "elegant" edifice and "beautiful grounds" are open to the public, but "stay in the master suite", and you'll "have a run of the house after the tours leave."

Maine

Bar Harbor

Bar Harbor Inn Ⓗ 22 | 21 | 20 | 21 | $239

Newport Dr.; 207-288-3351; fax 207-288-8454; 800-248-3351; www.barharborinn.com; 149 rooms, 4 suites

It's a "trip worth making" for the "commanding harbor view" of Frenchman's Bay declare devotees of this "relaxing", "old-world" inn, a former social club dating to 1887 boasting "elegant facilities" that include rooms with balconies or fireplaces and a staff that does an "awesome job of helping plan things to do in Bar Harbor"; eat a complimentary breakfast in the lobby or a "wonderful lobster lunch" at the Terrace Grille before heading "Downtown for shopping" or to Arcadia National Park a few miles away.

Brunswick

Captain Daniel Stone Inn Ⓗ – | – | – | – | $170

10 Water St.; 207-725-9898; fax 207-725-9898; 877-573-5151; www.captaindanielstoneinn.com; 30 rooms, 4 suites

Historians designate Brunswick's coastal community as the area where the Civil War began and ended so guests at this "charming", "reliable" expanded and restored 1819 Federal-style inn with "differently decorated" rooms can't help but grasp a glimpse of the past; keep cozy next to the fireplace in the Narcissa Stone restaurant during the winter and when weather turns warm, dine alfresco on the veranda.

Cape Elizabeth

Inn by the Sea 24 | 22 | 20 | 24 | $339

40 Bowery Beach Rd.; 207-799-3134; fax 207-799-4779; 800-888-4287; www.innbythesea.com; 43 suites

"Make your base" at this retreat with "wonderful service" on the Southern Maine coast and you'll "come home to a great ocean view" in duplexes with "enormous bathrooms" or in "rooms like condos"; it's "fabulous for families", especially if you're "traveling with man's best friend" ("they treat your dog like a king"), and a "romantic spot" for a "New England honeymoon" since there's "a beautiful beach for sunset strolls" and "lovely" meals at the Audubon, a New American restaurant.

Freeport

Harraseeket Inn 22 | 24 | 24 | 20 | $215

162 Main St.; 207-865-9377; fax 207-865-1684; 800-342-6423; www.harraseeketinn.com; 84 rooms, 6 suites, 8 townhouses

"Shop till you drop" at the Freeport outlets, then head "down the road" to this "lovely inn" with "Yankee charm" that "captures the feel of old New England" "in the middle of the Downtown hubbub";

"say ahhh" as you step into "comfortable rooms, many with fireplaces", and indulge in the "fantastic breakfast" and "great afternoon tea" ("complimentary treats"), and dinner featuring organic fare; while there's "not much rock 'n' roll" flavorwise, it does offer a "calm" respite "for summer camp parents' weekend" or an "off-season getaway."

Kennebunkport

Captain Lord Mansion 25 | 22 | 19 | 19 | $239

6 Pleasant St.; 207-967-3141; fax 207-967-3172; 800-522-3141; www.captainlord.com; 19 rooms, 1 suite

Get "away from the noise" and be "a few blocks from the ocean" at this 1812 buttercup-yellow inn in residential Kennebunkport where the "owners are hands on and it shows"; "attention to detail prevails" with "incredible" antiques-filled rooms featuring "heated bathroom floors", "waterfall showers" and "two-person Jacuzzis with candles"; rates include a family-style breakfast in a country kitchen and you can take "a lovely walk to Dock Square where restaurants abound" for other meals.

Cliff House, The 🅜Ⓢ🎾 16 | 19 | 19 | 22 | $310

Shore Rd., Ogunquit; 207-361-1000; fax 207-361-2122; www.cliffhousemaine.com; 192 rooms, 2 suites

"You cannot beat" the "drop dead view from a lofty perch" above Bald Head Cliff "overlooking the Atlantic" at this "tranquil" spot that "keeps on growing and adding amenities" like the "beautiful" spa, plus the ampitheater and connector from hotel to fitness center; the 70-acre property is "well run" by an "attentive staff", "Sunday brunch is not to be missed" and while a few find the rooms "charming", most insist they "beg for a makeover" and suggest "spending extra" on spa accommodations.

WHITE BARN INN, THE ✕🅜Ⓢ 24 | 26 | 28 | 22 | $345

37 Beach Ave.; 207-967-2321; fax 207-967-1100; www.whitebarninn.com; 20 rooms, 12 suites

"The ultimate" in a "romantic getaway", this "unbelievably luxurious" venue is set in "warm, wonderful" 19th-century "restored barns" a "short walk from Kennebunkport's village"; they'll make you "feel totally pampered", from the staff's "New England hospitality" to the "outstanding" Relais Gourmand restaurant boasting "breathtaking flowers" and "exemplary" seafood that's "worth the trip from wherever"; rooms range from "small and comfortable with all the amenities" to "particularly attractive luxury suites", plus there's a "fabulous pool" and spa services; it's the "last word", so "come – and bring money."

Mount Desert Island

Asticou Inn Ⓗ🎾 ▽ 19 | 23 | 23 | 23 | $225

15 Peabody Dr., Northeast Harbor; 207-276-3344; 800-258-3373; www.asticou.com; 31 rooms, 17 suites

"A gracious, weather-worn inn delightfully perched on the edge" of Acadia National Park and "at the head of the Northeast Harbor", this 1883 "trip back to Victorian vacationing" also offers quarters at three other lodgings, all awash in "old-fashioned quaintness" and "charm"; take in the "beautiful gardens", tee off at nearby courses and be sure to "bring a good book and a loved one" for "entertainment as there's no radio or TV" in most rooms.

Prouts Neck

Black Point Inn 20 | 22 | 21 | 22 | $420

510 Black Point Rd., Scarborough; 207-883-2500; fax 207-883-9976; 800-258-0003; www.blackpointinn.com; 71 rooms, 13 suites

"Homey" and "peaceful for a quasi-romantic getaway", this "preppy" 1878 inn sits on the tip of Prouts Neck, with a "gorgeous" "oceanfront vista on the rocky Maine coast"; acolytes adore the "unobtrusive staff" and "excellent amenities" including croquet, indoor pool, golf, tennis and kayaking, and agree it's a "beautiful spot" to take afternoon tea on the sun porch or eat "lobster three times a day"; N.B. room rates include some meals.

Rockport

Samoset Resort 18 | 19 | 19 | 23 | $299

220 Warrenton St.; 207-594-2511; fax 207-594-0722; 800-341-1650; www.samosetresort.com; 156 rooms, 22 suites

You can't help but be "enamored" by this "picturesque golf resort" with "beautiful views of Penobscot Bay" that include "white sails dotting" the water, sigh admirers who settle into "comfortable rooms" and "massive suites" for "summer stays"; from "very good" dining and "cocktails on the balcony" to "great golfing", tennis courts and facilities, it "has something to offer everyone"; P.S. a $10-million renovation may help sway the handful who fret it "feels more like a Florida resort."

York Harbor

York Harbor Inn 20 | 20 | 20 | 19 | $139

Rte. 1A; 207-363-5119; fax 207-363-7151; 800-343-3869; www.yorkharborinn.com; 47 rooms, 1 suite

Drive an hour north of Boston to find this "romantic" inn in a "breathtaking setting" in York Harbor where you can sit on the "lovely porch and look out to the ocean" or in the 300-year-old common room decorated with historical mementos; luxury quarters feature decks, fireplaces and/or Jacuzzi tubs while many standard rooms are done up with period decor, plus there's "great dining" in the seaside restaurant; but grouchers give the rooms "mixed reviews" and bemoan "tight parking."

Maryland

Baltimore

Admiral Fell Inn 21 | 21 | 21 | 19 | $199

888 S. Broadway; 410-522-7377; fax 410-522-0707; 800-292-4667; www.admiralfell.com; 76 rooms, 4 suites

Boasting a colorful past dating back two centuries, this "former sailors'" boarding house "on the water" "in historic Fell's Point" is now a "nicely appointed", Euro-style "urban" boutique oasis with "wonderfully charming" rooms in "odd serpentine hallways that can make finding yours an adventure"; dining is limited to the lounge and raw bar, but there's a "delicious free breakfast and afternoon refreshments", and "accommodating employees" help find the "best restaurants within walking distance."

Antrim 1844 ⒽⓂ🎾 — | — | — | — | $235

30 Trevanion Rd., Taneytown; 410-756-6812; fax 410-756-2744; 800-858-1844; www.antrim1844.com; 19 suites, 10 rooms
Vacationers to nearby Gettysburg can opt for this renovated country mansion, recently remodeled by owners Richard and Dorothy Mollett, and located on 24 acres of manicured gardens in Maryland's Catoctin Foothills; expect rooms with wood-burning fireplaces, antiques, marble tubs and canopy feather beds, and hearty dinners served in various dining spaces within the house.

Harbor Court Hotel ✕ⓂⓈ🎾 25 | 24 | 24 | 23 | $335

550 Light St.; 410-234-0550; fax 410-659-5925; 800-824-0076; www.harborcourt.com; 173 rooms, 22 suites
Offering an "elegant" "European feel" and "convenient" to all attractions, this "hideaway" with "spectacular views" feels like a "sanctuary amid the madness" of the Inner Harbor; "attention to detail" is evident from the "top-notch rooms" to a "staff that's friendly toward children" to a fitness center and a "pool that provide nice diversions"; you also "gotta love" the Explorer's Lounge with its "fabulous" drinks and atmosphere and the Hampton's restaurant, serving one of the "best crab soups" (and voted No. 1 for Decor and Service in our *Baltimore Restaurant Survey*).

Hyatt Regency Ⓜ🎾 21 | 20 | 18 | 20 | $299

300 Light St.; 410-528-1234; fax 410-685-3362; 800-233-1234; www.hyatt.com; 461 rooms, 25 suites
"Ideal for the business traveler" and an "easy walk" "to all the tourist spots", this "centrally located" "Baltimore icon" offers skywalk access to the convention center, an "attentive staff" that includes a "nice concierge", "well-appointed" rooms, a fitness center and a rooftop pool along with Pisces, a seafood restaurant "with a lovely view" of Inner Harbor; still, disappointed visitors are vexed that it's "more of a road warrior's hotel."

Loews Annapolis 🐕Ⓜ 20 | 21 | 18 | 19 | $239

126 West St., Annapolis; 410-263-7777; fax 410-263-0084; 800-526-2593; www.loewshotels.com; 207 rooms, 10 suites
Defined by "polite, prompt service", this "pleasant", pet-friendly hotel has a "small feel that works great with all families", along with a "good restaurant" called Breeze "where kids fit in", a "decent fitness room" and "great conference center" that's "fine for meetings"; but there are literally two sides to this site "within walking distance of Annapolis' historic district": take "one step in the wrong direction" and the location can feel "questionable."

Marriott Waterfront Baltimore ⓂⓈ 20 | 20 | 18 | 20 | $349

700 Aliceanna St.; 410-385-3000; fax 410-895-1900; 800-228-9290; www.marriott.com; 729 rooms, 22 suites
With an "international staff" "that goes the extra mile" "to give it flavor", the "king of conference hotels" easily "manages the swelling convention crowd" from its "convenient location" on the edge of Inner Harbor; most of the "modern yet sophisticated rooms" share "postcard-perfect views", plus there's a "terrific bar",

"Sunday brunch is a steal" and "banquet areas are beautiful"; all in all, it's a "solid" choice, with "no fatal flaws."

Renaissance Harborplace 23 | 21 | 18 | 22 | $249

202 E. Pratt St.; 410-547-1200; fax 410-539-5786; 800-535-1201; www.renaissancehotels.com; 582 rooms, 36 suites

"Lovely for sleep, scenery and nearby" activities, this "ideally located", "Marriott-owned" "better choice for commercial hotel stays" offers "proximity to sporting venues" and is "directly connected to" Harborplace, "a huge mall" – "you don't even have to go outside!"; "the indoor pool in a glass atrium is a treat" and "highly kid-friendly" (hint: "dad can take the kids swimming while mom shops"), and the restaurant is a "welcome surprise."

Cambridge

Hyatt Regency Chesapeake Bay 24 | 22 | 21 | 27 | $289

2800 Ocean Gateway; 410-901-1234; fax 410-901-6302; 800-233-1234; www.chesapeakebay.hyatt.com; 379 rooms, 21 suites

Like a "Caribbean resort on the Chesapeake", this "grand" "getaway" "in the middle of nowhere (almost)", complete with a "fabulous golf course", 150-slip marina, the "top-notch" Stillwater spa, "good dining", a wildlife refuge and kids' camp, "takes care of the whole family" ("they even show movies at the indoor pool!"); there are "great organized events" "during summer months", while on "blustery winter weekends, the view is spectacular with the river frozen", and you can make s'mores in the lobby's fireplace.

St. Michaels

INN AT PERRY CABIN 27 | 24 | 26 | 23 | $345

308 Watkins Ln.; 410-745-2200; fax 410-745-3348; 877-340-2617; www.perrycabin.com; 49 rooms, 33 suites

"Expecting a bucolic cabin? it's not, in fact", following Orient-Express' $20-million renovation, this "weekend destination" in "a charming little town on the Chesapeake" is like "Laura Ashley on steroids" with "impeccable service"; from the "heaven-on-earth suites" to the Molton Brown toiletries, they "spare no expense", plus "dining is an event" (there's even a "doggy menu"); just a few fret it's "lost its intimacy"; N.B. spa construction is underway.

Massachusetts

Boston

★ **Tops in City**

27 Four Seasons
26 Ritz-Carlton
25 Ritz-Carlton Boston Common
XV Beacon
23 Boston Harbor Hotel
Nine Zero Hotel
22 Langham Hotel
Seaport Hotel
Charles Hotel
Eliot Hotel

Beacon Hill Hotel 22 22 21 17 $285

25 Charles St.; 617-723-7575; fax 617-723-7525; 888-959-2442; www.beaconhillhotel.com; 12 rooms, 1 suite

You "can't beat the location of this little nook" on Beacon Hill, where rooms are "a bit cramped" but "comfortable" and "well appointed" with flat-screen TVs; and while it's short on facilities and "needs a bar", there's a "lovely roof deck", a "terrific" French bistro and "a certain charm because of its size" to compensate.

Boston Harbor Hotel 24 23 22 24 $320

70 Rowes Wharf; 617-439-7000; fax 617-951-9307; 800-752-7077; www.bhh.com; 204 rooms, 26 suites

"Spoil yourself" at this hotel with a "spectacular location right on the harbor where there's lots of activity day and night"; while most praise the "ornate" lobby, chef David Bruce's "awesome" food in the Meritage restaurant and "discreet" service, others only find "standard stuff."

Charles Hotel 22 22 23 22 $599

1 Bennett St., Cambridge; 617-864-1200; fax 617-864-5715; 800-882-1818; www.charleshotel.com; 248 rooms, 45 suites

"What this hotel has in spades is its location to everything" that makes it a "sensible" choice for "parents of Harvard students" and businessmen alike; fans praise the rooms stocked with Bose radios and "cloud"-like beds as "Swiss in functionality, New England in comfort", but others complain they have a "dormitory quality"; still, sybarites love the "excellent" spa, music mavens dig Regattabar's "top jazz" and "foodies" flip for the "fantastic" Rialto restaurant.

Colonnade 19 18 19 20 $375

120 Huntington Ave.; 617-424-7000; fax 617-425-3222; 800-962-3030; www.colonnadehotel.com; 276 rooms, 9 suites

"Late-night dinners at on-site Brasserie Jo are like eating at a Parisian bistro" enthuse nostalgic guests of this otherwise "typical urban hotel" near shopping, the symphony and the Common; families find it's "a great choice in summer, thanks to the fun rooftop pool", though sanctuary-seekers counter "busloads of tourists" can make for "noisy" nights in "mediocre" digs and few warm to the "ordinary" service.

Commonwealth, Hotel – – – – $300

500 Commonwealth Ave.; 617-933-5000; fax 617-266-6888; www.hotelcommonwealth.com; 149 rooms, 1 suite

If you're hankering to be near the Red Sox or simply want a plush stay, this newcomer two blocks from Fenway Park is calling you to the plate; slide into a room with a view of the stadium or swing for a suite with L'Occitane bath amenities, wireless phones that work anywhere in the hotel, imported Italian linens and down comforters; when it's time to eat, head to the award-winning Great Bay, or, come May, to an alfresco table at Eastern Standard.

Eliot Hotel 24 22 24 18 $400

370 Commonwealth Ave.; 617-267-1607; fax 617-536-9114; 800-443-5468; www.eliothotel.com; 16 rooms, 79 suites

Reminiscent of "old hotels in Europe", this "posh" boutique property in the Back Bay contains "classically furnished" rooms and suites offering an "excellent value"; facilities are "limited", which is why some feel it's "not for families", but "adults who love gracious living" appreciate Ken Oringer's "superb" Clio restaurant and Uni sashimi bar, plus "nearby Newbury shopping"; N.B. the entire hotel will undergo renovations this year.

Fairmont Copley Plaza | 21 | 23 | 21 | 21 | $315 |

138 St. James Ave.; 617-267-5300; fax 617-375-9648; 800-441-1414; www.fairmont.com; 307 rooms, 76 suites

From its "opulent" marble-clad lobby to the Oak Room (voted No. 1 for Decor in our *Boston Restaurant Survey*) "that makes it worth the stay" alone, this "landmark" situated "near all major attractions and transportation" "evokes the age of railroads and steamships", and though not "family-oriented" per se, makes "kids feel like Eloise"; service "varies" between "excellent" and "lacking", and while it's "starting to age", ongoing renovations are "bringing the luster out" of its "dated" rooms.

XV BEACON | 26 | 26 | 25 | 22 | $395 |

15 Beacon St.; 617-670-1500; fax 617-670-2525; 877-982-3226; www.xvbeacon.com; 57 rooms, 3 suites

It's the "extra touches that count" at this "shelter magazine"–ready "urban sanctuary" that's "easily among Boston's elite" properties; the "cozy", "haute-moderne" though somewhat "dark" rooms are "small but space is well utilized", incorporating fireplaces and "every electronic geegaw" (like LCD TVs in the baths) all triggered by remote controls; the "top-notch" Federalist restaurant, "free limo service" that "takes you anywhere in the city" and "competent staff" all make this place "worth the splurge."

FOUR SEASONS | 27 | 27 | 27 | 26 | $425 |

200 Boylston St.; 617-338-4400; fax 617-423-0154; 800-332-3442; www.fourseasons.com; 202 rooms, 72 suites

Fresh from extensive renovations (with more to come), this "epitome" of "luxury" overlooking the Common draws an "upscale crowd" and "mega-celebs" with its "sumptuous rooms" stocked with "world-class appointments", "outstanding" Aujourd'hui restaurant (voted No. 1 for Service in our *Boston Restaurant Survey*) and a lounge known for its "lovely afternoon tea"; the "caring" staff "can accomplish anything", so "if you can afford it, it's not to be missed."

Hotel @ MIT | ▽ 21 | 20 | 17 | 20 | $319 |

20 Sidney St., Cambridge; 617-577-0200; fax 617-494-8366; 800-222-8733; www.hotelatmit.com; 197 rooms, 13 suites

"Geeks rule" at this "quiet" and "high tech–themed" hotel whose "quirky" lobby's filled with robots from MIT labs; fittingly, the "spacious, trendy" accommodations have "equations on the sheets, circuit-board lamps", plus WiFi, ergonomically designed furniture and Bose stereos, and there's an "always pleasant" staff to help "you understand what to do" with it all.

Hyatt Regency Boston | 19 | 19 | 17 | 18 | $245 |

1 Avenue de Lafayette; 617-912-1234; fax 617-451-2198; 800-233-1234; www.hyattregencyboston.com; 475 rooms, 26 suites

Formerly a Swissôtel, this chain link might be "off the beaten path for tourists" but is "very convenient to the Financial District"; rooms are "big and comfortable", but many complain about the "tired" decor, a fitness center the "size of a closet" and pool that "needs to be fixed", and are hopeful they'll be remedied by renovations that are currently underway.

Jacob Hill Inn | – | – | – | – | $245 |

120 Jacob St., Seekonk; 508-336-9165; 888-336-9165; www.inn-providence-ri.com; 8 rooms, 2 suites

A 10-minute drive from Downtown Providence, Rhode Island, and an hour from Boston, this 1722 B&B-style inn surrounded by wooded land features rooms with fireplaces and Jacuzzi tubs, a swimming pool, tennis courts and a new billiard room with plasma TV; N.B. a minimum stay of two nights (three on holiday weekends) is required.

Jurys | – | – | – | – | $235 |

350 Stuart St.; 617-266-7200; fax 617-266-7203; www.jurys-boston-hotels.com; 222 rooms, 3 suites

Owned by the Dublin-based outfit Jury Doyle Hotels, this newish addition to the Back Bay is set on the former site of the Boston Police Headquarters, near the Common and Copley Square; a $60-million renovation has returned the landmark back to its 1920s glory with a modern edge, bringing along Emerald Isle touches like Cuffs, an Irish bar, and Stanhope Grille, serving a traditional Irish breakfast; the amenities-laden rooms have marble baths and free WiFi access, plus there's also a fully equipped business center.

Langham Hotel | 22 | 22 | 24 | 21 | $325 |

250 Franklin St.; 617-451-1900; fax 617-423-2844; 800-791-7764; www.langhamhotels.com; 308 rooms, 18 suites

Now owned by the London-based Langham chain, this erstwhile Le Méridien "catering to high-end business travelers" is still the "venerable lady of the Financial District"; some of the facilities are "looking tired", like the "too tiny" gym, but "small" rooms "have every amenity"; loyalists are pleased that the signature restaurant, Julien, is still what "others aspire to be", Café Fleuri's chocolate buffet is ever "excellent" and the staff "helpful."

Lenox, The | 21 | 22 | 19 | 19 | $328 |

61 Exeter St.; 617-536-5300; fax 617-267-1237; 800-225-7676; www.lenoxhotel.com; 199 rooms, 13 suites

Revered by fans as "the Algonquin of Boston", this "cozy", "quirky" yet "elegant" hotel even has its own Round Table of sorts: City Bar, a "cool" "local nightspot" that "attracts all the hipsters", as well as the "cozy" Sólás pub and "trendy" Azure restaurant; and when you're ready to tuck in for the night, the "small" rooms have fireplaces and "comfortable beds."

Marlowe, Hotel | 25 | 21 | 21 | 20 | $309 |

25 Edwin Land Blvd., Cambridge; 617-868-8000; fax 617-868-8001; www.hotelmarlowe.com; 222 rooms, 14 suites

The Kimpton Group's "funky-chic" aesthetic permeates this pet-friendly boutique hotel near the Charles River, where "wild fabrics abound" in the "sexy" lobby and "colorful" rooms have "leopard-print robes"; equally pervasive is "friendliness" toward guests and their pets, with the complimentary wine hour seen as a "nice touch"; although there are "few restaurants or places of interest within walking distance", there's a "lively bar" and Bambara eatery on-site, with "Harvard Square a quick cab ride" away.

Marriott Copley Place 20 20 18 22 $499

110 Huntington Ave.; 617-236-5800; fax 617-236-5885; 888-236-2427; www.marriott.com; 1100 rooms, 47 suites

Set "right in the heart of the Back Bay" and connected to two malls, this "busy", "conventioneer"-oriented hotel is particularly "convenient" in "bad weather when you can shop and dine without having to go outside"; the rooms, some of which have "great Charles River views", come with "very comfortable beds", and the "accommodating" staff, including a "superior concierge", ensures that "there are few disappointments."

Millennium Bostonian Hotel 21 21 21 20 $259

26 North St.; 617-523-3600; fax 617-523-2454; 866-866-8086; www.millennium-hotels.com; 193 rooms, 8 suites

"Innlike" yet "contemporary", this hotel across from Quincy Market and Faneuil Hall boasts "attractive" rooms with French doors onto balconies – although business travelers should request one with high-speed Internet access; while the "gym could use an upgrade" and it gets a "little loud at night because of the area", it still offers "good value for the money"; N.B. an Aveda spa is next door.

Nine Zero Hotel 24 22 22 22 $309

90 Tremont St.; 617-772-5800; fax 617-772-5810; 800-434-7347; www.ninezerohotel.com; 185 rooms, 4 suites, 1 penthouse

"Finally, a boutique hotel in Boston that isn't Colonial" say those whose sensibilities jibe with this "slick", "ultramodern" property "within walking distance of the Common and Faneuil Hall"; the same "clean lines" found in the lobby carry into the rooms, with pros "asking for one on a high floor as Tremont Street gets noisy"; meanwhile, there's a "hip scene" at Spire restaurant and "friendly", if sometimes "lacking", service.

Onyx Hotel – – – – $209

155 Portland St.; 617-557-9955; fax 617-557-0005; www.onyxhotel.com; 110 rooms, 2 suites

Opened in May 2004, this Kimpton hotel near North Station and the Fleet Center flashes contemporary cool in a decor scheme using granite, aluminum and suede in bold black, reds and taupes; wine gatherings are held in the lobby nightly, the pet-friendly rooms are technologically up to speed, passes are provided for a nearby gym and the Ruby Room restaurant serves breakfast, dinner and drinks.

RITZ-CARLTON, BOSTON, THE Ⓢ 25 27 26 24 $495

15 Arlington St.; 617-536-5700; fax 617-536-1335; www.ritzcarlton.com; 230 rooms, 43 suites

Now restored to a level of "opulence" "ideal for discriminating travelers and business folk on expense accounts", this landmark with the "Public Garden at its front door" seems to "only get better with age"; the "elegant" rooms contain some of the "world's most comfortable beds", the Lounge's high tea is a "decadent afternoon indulgence", "romantic" French dinners unfold in the main dining room and the staff "treats you like long-lost relatives", "going out of their way over the littlest things."

RITZ-CARLTON BOSTON COMMON 26 | 26 | 24 | 25 | $495

10 Avery St.; 617-574-7100; fax 617-574-7200; 800-241-3333; www.ritzcarlton.com; 150 rooms, 43 suites

Although it shares the chain's "signature" "superb" service, Boston's second Ritz has a more "contemporary" look and "laid-back feel than the original"; also, certain "spacious", "high-tech" quarters have a view of the Common, some of the "best facilities possible" await (for a fee) at the adjacent Sports Club/LA, there's a "trendy bar scene" and "sophisticated" dining at Blu Cafe, although "room service is so good you don't need to leave" your perch.

Royal Sonesta 20 | 20 | 19 | 20 | $299

5 Cambridge Pkwy., Cambridge; 617-806-4200; fax 617-806-4232; 800-766-3782; www.sonesta.com/boston; 377 rooms, 23 suites

Offering proximity to the Museum of Science, MIT and more, this Cambridge hotel also earns admiration for its "interesting modern art collection" and "great" pool with a retractable roof; the Internet-wired rooms feature "gorgeous views of the Charles River" while "fab" restaurant Davio's serves up Italian steakhouse fare, all "without the high costs" of local counterparts.

Seaport Hotel 23 | 23 | 21 | 22 | $279

1 Seaport Ln.; 617-385-4000; fax 617-385-4001; 877-732-7678; www.seaportboston.com; 402 rooms, 24 suites

It's somewhat "off the beaten path" in the "revitalized" Seaport district, but this hotel, a quick skip from the airport, is "fantastic if you're attending meetings at the adjacent convention center" or WTC and is "worth the trip for its clean, modern facilities" that include a spa, "nice fitness club" and indoor pool; additionally, the staff's "courteous" despite the no-tipping policy, and rooms are "large and very comfortable", so do "ask for one with a view."

Westin Copley Place 23 | 21 | 19 | 22 | $449

10 Huntington Ave.; 617-262-9600; fax 617-424-7483; 800-937-8461; www.westin.com; 754 rooms, 49 suites

"Perfectly placed" "in the center of everything", this "high-rise" sports skyway connections to the Hynes Center and two malls, providing "endless shopping and dining options" so parents and conventioneers can "sneak out" for a break; "rooms are standard Westin fare, but there's nothing wrong with that", especially with those "incredible Heavenly beds" and "panoramic views" from some; though it's "too large for personalized attention", the staff's nonetheless "amenable" and facilities are "high-quality."

Cape Cod & The Islands

Century House – | – | – | – | $195

10 Cliff Rd., Nantucket; 508-228-0530; www.centuryhouse.com; 13 rooms, 1 suite

If you can tear yourself away from 'Gerry's Berry Buffet' breakfast or afternoon cookies and cream on the veranda, you might consider touring the surrounding area where this charming 1830s B&B is located; classic styling is met with luxurious modern amenities (Molton Brown bath products) at this cliffside spot frequented by TV producers scouting locations and soaking up works of the former artists-in-residence.

CHARLOTTE INN, THE 27 26 26 25 $495

27 S. Summer St., Edgartown; 508-627-4751; fax 508-627-4652; 800-735-2478; 23 rooms, 2 suites

So "serene" is this Relais & Châteaux "oasis in the heart of Edgartown" and away from the water that you might feel you're "in the presence of ghosts"; with "very comfortable" rooms steeped in "Yankee charm", "beautiful grounds", a "staff that bends over backwards for you" and a no-kids policy, it's ideal for "romantic weekends"; it's also "always booked", although you can try for a table at the "fantastic" L'Etoile restaurant, aka "the poor man's way to enjoy the place."

Chatham Bars Inn 22 23 22 25 $320

297 Shore Rd., Chatham; 508-945-0096; fax 508-945-6785; 800-527-4884; www.chathambarsinn.com; 163 rooms, 42 suites

"Like a large family beach house", this resort bustles with "ample activities" including tennis, swimming and kids' programs and is a "quick walk from town" ("a true gift when summer traffic comes to a standstill"); the "nautically styled" inn and cottage accommodations have "lovely amenities", and some guests dream of "pulling up a rocking chair at sunset" for cocktails on the "Kennedy-esque front porch."

Dan'l Webster Inn 23 23 22 20 $199

149 Main St., Sandwich; 508-888-3622; fax 508-888-5156; 800-444-3566; www.danlwebsterinn.com; 37 rooms, 16 suites

With its relaxed "romantic" air, this "quaint" Cape inn "makes you slow down, pause and reflect on New England life" of yore as you "grab a pint in the great tavern" or sample the dining room's "delicious" Traditional American and Asian-Fusion fare (the menu changes every month); though some find it "a little too rustic" and say there's "not much to do in the area", an on-site spa and a "welcoming" staff help compensate.

Harbor View Hotel 18 20 17 20 $330

131 N. Water St., Edgartown; 508-627-7000; fax 508-627-8417; 800-225-6005; www.harbor-view.com; 118 rooms, 9 suites, 2 townhouses

"The view of the Edgartown lighthouse alone is worth the price" of a stay at this harbor-side inn within "walking distance" of the action but "without the traffic of Main Street"; of course, there are also "well-kept" rooms, "lovely grounds", a pool "kids love to swim in" but adults might find too "*Romper Room*"–like, a "picturesque" porch and The Coach House restaurant, which serves up "above-average food" along with "unbeatable" vistas.

Ocean Edge Resort & Golf Club 21 20 18 24 $378

2907 Main St., Brewster; 508-896-9000; fax 508-896-9123; 800-343-6074; www.oceanedge.com; 90 rooms, 245 villas

"It's like having a summer home for a week" sigh guests of this "active person's dream" resort on a 400-acre former estate on the Cape that has a "very playable golf course", "plenty of pools" and "access to great walking and cycling trails", plus "bonfires and other fun family events"; dining options are "adequate", and the "basic", "comfortable" "cookie-cutter condos could be anywhere, but the beach with its changing tides is fantastic."

WAUWINET, THE | 25 | 26 | 26 | 25 | $700 |

120 Wauwinet Rd., Nantucket; 508-228-0145; fax 508-228-6712; 800-426-8718; www.wauwinet.com; 35 rooms, 9 cottages

"Far from the maddening crowds" of Nantucket Town and bordering a nature preserve is this "elegant, Waspy" Relais & Châteaux–affiliated inn that offers adults a "quiet" "respite"; while "not the most opulent", the rooms are "welcoming" with views of the garden or water; but aside from the "beautiful beaches", the real highlight's the "masterful" Topper's restaurant, whose ingredients "take the prize for freshness"; you might need an "extra credit card" to swing it here, but most think "it's worth it."

Wequassett Inn | 21 | 23 | 23 | 24 | $400 |

Rte. 28, Pleasant Bay, Chatham; 508-432-5400; fax 508-430-3131; 800-225-7125; www.wequassett.com; 98 rooms, 6 suites

You'll find "all the New England charm you're looking for" at this Pleasant Bay inn where "breathtaking views" enhance the "classy" yet "low-key atmosphere" and the staff "understands service"; but some feel the "rooms don't live up to the rest of the experience", which includes dining on some of the "freshest shellfish" at any of four "outstanding" eateries and playing on the "gorgeous" neighboring Cape Cod National Golf Club course.

White Elephant | 24 | 26 | 24 | 24 | $525 |

50 Easton St., Nantucket; 508-228-2500; fax 508-325-1195; 800-475-2637; www.whiteelephanthotel.com; 23 rooms, 30 suites, 11 cottages, 1 house

"Simple elegance is the key" appeal of this "perfectly manicured jewel overlooking Nantucket Harbor" and within walking distance of town, where guests go for "salt-air relaxation", "top-notch" seafood and steak at Brant Point Grill or just "sitting outside in rocking chairs", "drinking champagne and watching the sunset"; while some sigh "if only they had a pool" and other recreational facilities, more appreciate the "much-improved" service.

Deerfield

Deerfield Inn Ⓗ | ∇ 20 | 22 | 19 | 17 | $255 |

81 Old Main St.; 413-774-5587; fax 413-775-7221; 800-926-3865; www.deerfieldinn.com; 23 rooms

Those looking for a "truly New England" experience should consider this "small", "rustic" 1884 inn in the village of Deerfield, whose "unique history is not to be missed"; befitting the setting, the slightly "tired" rooms are "well appointed" with "lots of antiques" and have orchard or village views; "lovely" owners and "special-event meals" add to the charm.

Lenox

Blantyre ⒽⓈ | 25 | 26 | 26 | 24 | $450 |

16 Blantyre Rd.; 413-637-3556; fax 413-637-4282; www.blantyre.com; 13 rooms, 8 suites, 4 cottages

For a "luxurious getaway in the Berkshires", consider this "remarkable" century-old Relais & Châteaux resort with "beautiful grounds" encompassing tennis and croquet courts, a pool and walking trails and a location ideal for "enjoying all the festivals", including Tanglewood; pros advise "you're missing it all if you don't stay in the main house", which evokes a "grand English estate", but all guests receive the same "impeccable" service and can dine on "world-class food" in the "very formal" restaurant.

CANYON RANCH IN THE BERKSHIRES 22 | 28 | 24 | 28 | $733

165 Kemble St.; 413-637-4400; fax 413-637-0057; 800-326-7080; www.canyonranch.com; 104 rooms, 22 suites

"You'll feel fab" at this "sybaritic" Berkshires spa where there's "lots to do" like visiting "excellent medical providers", attending "informative cooking demonstrations" and "impressive lectures", taking "fitness classes tailored to every level" and then "being rewarded for your hard work with a scrub massage"; the food's also "very good considering it's so healthy", and the staff "has customer service down to a science", "catering to your every whim" except those barred by the no-alcohol rule.

Cranwell Resort 21 | 20 | 20 | 24 | $265

55 Lee Rd.; 413-637-1364; fax 413-637-4364; 800-272-6935; www.cranwell.com; 79 rooms, 26 suites

"A curious mix of new spa and old resort", this Tudor-style inn on the former Berkshire Hunt and Country Club grounds provides a "wonderful alternative" to its better-known neighbors, whether for playing the "fun golf course", taking an exercise or yoga class, cross-country skiing in winter or getting a "hot-stone massage that's sheer bliss"; "rooms vary in size" but "are nicely appointed", the staff's "friendly" and there's a "high-end restaurant" and pub.

WHEATLEIGH 25 | 26 | 26 | 23 | $575

11 Hawthorne St.; 413-637-0610; fax 413-637-4507; www.wheatleigh.com; 10 rooms, 9 suites

"Italy in the Berkshires" is what this "exceptional" property set in a Renaissance-redux 1893 mansion evokes for "luxury"-seekers and music-lovers thrilled to have "Tanglewood within walking distance"; "elegantly understated" accommodations, "spectacular grounds", "innovative, delicious" French fare from a "chef willing to take chances" and "superior but non-obtrusive service" add up to a "very romantic" experience.

Rockport

Emerson Inn by the Sea – | – | – | – | $179

1 Cathedral Ave.; 978-546-6321; fax 978-546-7043; 800-964-5550; www.emersoninnbythesea.com; 36 rooms

Set along a stretch of "beautiful New England coastline" in Cape Ann, this inn maintains traces of its earlier incarnation as a resort favored by namesake Ralph Waldo Emerson, and his kind; many of the "small" but "rustic and comfortable" rooms overlook Sandy Bay, and the Grand Café offers views from its sprawling veranda; N.B. the place is BYO (Rockport is a dry town).

Williamstown

Orchards, The 21 | 20 | 21 | 18 | $215

222 Adams Rd.; 413-458-9611; fax 413-458-3273; 800-225-1517; www.orchardshotel.com; 48 rooms, 1 suite

A "perfect place to stay between Williams College and MASS MoCA", this "European"-style inn is "best in fall when Berkshires foliage is at its height" and guests might still be able to dine on the patio, but the "very cozy" rooms and "gratis high tea" are available year-round; if some deem it a "glorified motel", more are charmed by the "gracious, old-world" service and "warm chocolate-chip cookies on your pillow, which make everything ok."

Michigan

Bay Harbor

Inn at Bay Harbor, A Renaissance Golf Resort ▽ 26 | 24 | 19 | 25 | $294

3600 Village Harbor Dr.; 231-439-4000; fax 231-439-4094; 800-462-6963; www.innatbayharbor.com; 75 rooms, 77 suites

Those looking to "unwind" in a "beautiful setting" along Lake Michigan head to this "upscale" resort with a "first-class spa" and a golf course whose "spectacular views" mitigate "overpriced" green fees; rooms are "spacious" and some have balconies, and if service alternates between being "charming" and in need of "training", most concede "life doesn't get any better" than at this "superior" place.

Detroit

Dearborn Inn, The 20 | 21 | 21 | 21 | $199

20301 Oakwood Blvd., Dearborn; 313-271-2700; fax 313-271-7464; 800-228-9290; www.marriott.com; 200 rooms, 17 suites, 5 houses

Take a "step back to a more genteel time" at this "classic" Georgian-style property "built by Henry Ford" and now owned by Marriott; some note there's a "variance in accommodations" and recommend staying in the "excellent main hotel" rather than the "charming" cottages to avoid the "walk in the cold Michigan winters"; in summer, the "manicured lawn and gazebo are popular for weddings" and the "epic brunch is worth the room – maybe even the flight" – anytime of year.

RITZ-CARLTON, THE 25 | 26 | 25 | 23 | $305

300 Town Center Dr., Dearborn; 313-441-2000; fax 313-253-4418; 800-241-3333; www.ritzcarlton.com; 293 rooms, 15 suites

"If you have to go to Detroit", this Dearborn address is a "first-class" choice, even if frequent Ritz-Carlton guests say it lacks the "usual glitz and glamour" of the chain's other properties; the staff is "very attentive" and it's home to "one of the better restaurants" in the area, so even if "your comptroller will hate" the "pricey" tabs, most agree "it's worth every penny."

Royal Park Hotel – | – | – | – | $399

600 East University Dr., Rochester; 248-652-2600; fax 248-652-8900; www.royalparkhotel.net; 128 rooms, 15 suites

Just outside of Detroit sits this old-world English countryside–style estate with furnishings of marble, slate and cherry wood and a high tea served in the lobby; it's all set up for relaxation, with fly-fishing available in nearby Paint Creek, the cozy Brookshire restaurant with seasonal terrace dining and an impressive wine list, and a library where cigars are on offer.

Townsend Hotel, The | 25 | 24 | 24 | 23 | $350

100 Townsend St., Birmingham; 248-642-7900; fax 248-645-9061; 800-548-4172; www.townsendhotel.com; 92 rooms, 58 suites

Fans of this "classy" "little jewel" north of Detroit in "upscale" Birmingham say everything's "superb", from the "great bedding and baths" to "fine" service and "very good but very expensive dining"; there's no on-site spa, but shops and restaurants are within walking distance, and there's "plenty of star wattage" courtesy of "celebs who stay here."

Westin Detroit Metropolitan Airport | ∇ 25 | 19 | 18 | 24 | $269

2501 Worldgateway Pl.; 734-942-6500; fax 734-942-6600; www.westin.com; 404 rooms, 10 suites

"I'm in an airport?" quip jet-setters who alight in the "bamboo-forested" lobby of this "unexpectedly luxurious" hotel in the Midfield Terminal where a "good staff" then checks them into "chic, Asian-style" rooms with "soundproofed" windows "overlooking the tarmac"; "convenient for meetings", it's a "top choice for those who need to fly-in, fly-out and still retain their sanity."

Grand Rapids

Amway Grand Plaza Ⓗ | 21 | 22 | 20 | 20 | $215

187 Monroe NW; 616-774-2000; fax 616-458-6641; 800-253-3590; www.amwaygrand.com; 626 rooms, 36 suites

Incongruously set in "woefully blue-collar" Grand Rapids, this "ritzy" hotel wows guests with its "amazing" circa-1913 building sporting a "top-floor restaurant that makes for a romantic evening"; claustrophobes book the "larger", newer rooms as the quarters on the old side of the property "are the size of a bed", but the "staff makes you feel welcome" no matter where you sleep.

Mackinac Island

Grand Hotel ✕ⒽⓈ | 22 | 26 | 24 | 27 | $470

Mackinac Island; 906-847-3331; fax 906-847-3259; 800-334-7263; www.grandhotel.com; 348 rooms, 37 suites

The "quintessence of Midwest romanticism" is this "historic" hotel on car-free Mackinac Island where guests partake of "horse-drawn carriage rides", "terrific" dining, and "rocking chairs and lakeside views on the front porch"; the "rooms are fine but not great", and if casual types harrumph that "they're sticklers for jackets and ties" in the evenings, most like the "upper-class feeling", which is also sustained by the tip-free service.

Traverse City

Great Wolf Lodge Ⓢ | – | – | – | – | $279

3575 N. US 31 S.; 231-941-3600; 866-478-9653; www.greatwolflodge.com; 281 suites

Parents praise this frontier-themed "great family resort", offering "tons of activities" like in-room movies, an arcade and 3-D theater, plus an immense slide-filled "kids' paradise" water park; grown-ups appreciate the "spacious rooms", "helpful staff", Aveda spa and "work-out room that rivals any professional gym."

Minnesota

Minneapolis/St. Paul

Grand Hotel 24 24 22 25 $359

615 Second Ave. S, Minneapolis; 612-288-8888; fax 612-373-0407; 866-843-4745; www.grandhotelminneapolis.com; 123 rooms, 17 suites

"An unexpected find", this "very elegant" "charmer" set in a 1911 building in the "heart of Minneapolis" offers "tastefully appointed" rooms that include "great beds" and "bizarrely large" baths with marble tubs, color TVs and Aveda products; other pluses include the "state-of-the-art fitness center", an "excellent" restaurant and a "concierge who will do just about everything for you."

Graves 601 Hotel ▽ 27 21 23 23 $349

(fka Le Méridien Hotel)

601 First Ave., N, Minneapolis; 612-677-1100; fax 612-677-1200; 800-543-4300; www.graves601hotel.com; 251 rooms, 4 suites

"Cool comes to Minneapolis" via this "gorgeous" property whose "ultramodern" decor scheme and "dim lighting" make some think they're "walking into the film *The Matrix*"; rooms outfitted with "comfortable beds", plasma TVs, high-speed or WiFi access, baths with Hermès soap and "awesome" rain showers, and the "great bar" at Cosmos restaurant, are all "*très bien*" and offset "so-so service", "poor work-out facilities" and "pricey" rates.

Marquette Hotel 21 20 17 19 $319

7th St. & Marquette Ave., Minneapolis; 612-333-4545; fax 612-288-2188; 800-328-4782; www.marquettehotel.com; 266 rooms, 14 suites

Guests "love the central location" of this Hilton-managed property whose adjoining mall "gives easy access to shopping", not to mention the freedom to "bar-hop in the dead of winter"; rooms reveal a "modern Scandinavian sensibility" and have "good-sized baths"; if a few mark the staff "inexperienced" they're at least "energetic" and can direct you to the 50th-floor Windows on Minnesota restaurant to take in panoramic views.

Nicollet Island Inn ▽ 21 21 24 15 $240

95 Merriam St., Minneapolis; 612-331-1800; fax 612-331-6528; www.nicolletislandinn.com; 24 rooms

What's "unique" about this "cute", "compact" inn housed in a 19th-century factory building is its location on an island in the Mississippi River yet "within blocks of Downtown" Minneapolis; such a situation affords "woodsy shore" and skyline views from the on-site restaurant, which features an "excellent Sunday brunch"; still, while its locale and size are "pluses", a disappointed few feel it's beginning to "look a little dowdy."

Saint Paul Hotel, The 24 25 23 22 $249

350 Market St., St. Paul; 651-292-9292; fax 651-228-9506; 800-292-9292; www.stpaulhotel.com; 224 rooms, 32 suites

It might be a "grand old hotel", but this 1910 property has "kept up with modern times", and now has WiFi throughout; guestrooms (renovated post-*Survey*) are "quiet like a tomb, but in a good way", and "turndown service with a bottle of water is excellent"; the St. Paul Grill is "always dependable", making it one of the "best places for brunch or dinner before a performance at the Ordway Center."

Sofitel ▽ 21 | 20 | 23 | 19 | $229

5601 W. 78th St., Bloomington; 952-835-1900; fax 952-835-2696; 800-876-6303; www.sofitel.com; 276 rooms, 6 suites

Shop till you drop at the Mall of America and then be revived by "tasty French-American" food at Chez Colette and La Fougasse restaurants at this "nice suburban getaway" that "doesn't have anything within walking distance" but is "one of the better places close to the airport"; "massive renovations" currently underway should improve the "large" but "tired" rooms and lobby and pump up the France-based chain's "European flair."

Mississippi

Biloxi

Beau Rivage Resort & Casino 22 | 19 | 20 | 24 | $229

875 Beach Blvd.; 228-386-7111; fax 228-386-7414; 800-567-6667; www.beaurivage.com; 1645 rooms, 95 suites

"Las Vegas–style, Southern hospitality", yes even "Atlantic City could take a lesson" from the "Bellagio's little sister", an "amazing resort right on the Mississippi Gulf Coast" offering "gambling and excellent shows", "good dining" and "lush greenery that makes you feel as if you've been whisked away to paradise"; an "inviting lobby", "well-equipped work-out facilities with a pool and spa" (and a new Tom Fazio golf course in 2006), plus "gorgeous rooms with spectacular views" of the Beau Rivage Bay seal the deal; N.B. it was expected to be closed for at least several months due to major damage from Hurricane Katrina.

Natchez

Monmouth Plantation ▽ 24 | 27 | 27 | 24 | $195

36 Melrose Ave.; 601-442-5852; fax 601-446-7762; 800-828-4531; www.monmouthplantation.com; 14 rooms, 16 suites

"The Old South rises up and charms" at this "unique" National Historic landmark and member of Small Luxury Hotels of the World – an "incredibly romantic" restored antebellum 1818 mansion that feels "like a step back in time" to "plantation life" with "outstanding service" and candlelit dinners (no kids under 14 allowed); 26 landscaped acres are filled with moss-covered oaks, and "lovely rooms" are furnished with period pieces.

Missouri

Branson

Chateau on the Lake Resort ▽ 22 | 20 | 19 | 22 | $164

415 N. State Hwy.; 417-334-1161; fax 417-339-5566; 888-333-5253; www.chateauonthelakebranson.com; 244 rooms, 57 suites

Even if you find Branson itself "a little cheesy", when you stay at this "all-class" château with "gorgeous" views of "giant" Table Rock Lake, you'll find yourself "peacefully isolated" in the "amazing country"; "kids love the in-house movie theater" and outdoor pool, while adults appreciate a full-service marina and the spa, but even if the "standard rooms are quite comfortable", some find the food and service just a little "hillbilly."

Kansas City

Fairmont Kansas City | 21 | 21 | 19 | 21 | $229

401 Ward Pkwy.; 816-756-1500; fax 816-756-1635; 800-441-1414; www.fairmont.com; 346 rooms, 20 suites

For a little bit of Europe in the Midwest, head to this city property with "awesome views" of the Country Club Plaza awash in Spanish architecture, European art and lots of boutiques and restaurants; while workaholics wallow in the WiFi world (there's public area access and a 24-hour business center) and leisure-lovers linger at the "civilized" swimming pool and full-service spa, both say service can be "spotty" and rooms are in need of a "big-time renovation" – which it's in the process of receiving.

Phillips, Hotel Ⓗ | ▽ 24 | 24 | 21 | 20 | $189

106 W. 12th St.; 816-221-7000; fax 816-221-3477; 866-701-8218; www.hotelphillips.com; 215 rooms, 2 suites

Sentimentalists savor the "stunning lobby" and "fine rooms" of this "charming" 1931 art deco landmark; it may be in a "run-down part of town", but it's just two blocks from the convention center, has one of "the most friendly staffs" in town and houses the "reliable Chophouse restaurant" for a further "touch of the old KC."

Raphael, The | 21 | 22 | 21 | 19 | $189

325 Ward Pkwy.; 816-756-3800; fax 816-802-2131; 800-821-5343; www.raphaelkc.com; 35 rooms, 88 suites

Quaintly "romantic", this "regal gal" smiles with "understated", "old-fashioned" European grace in a "terrific Country Club Plaza location" (there are views of "lovely holiday lights" in December); even though her "tiara may need polishing" at this point to correct "dramatically" varying rooms, loyalists allow that with just a few more royal funds invested, she'd be "booked solid."

Osage Beach

Tan Tar A Resort Ⓢ | 18 | 19 | 16 | 22 | $149

State Road KK, mile marker 26; 573-348-3131; 800-826-8272; www.tan-tar-a.com; 820 rooms, 169 suites

One look at the "great indoor waterpark" at this Lake of the Ozarks 420-acre "compound" in the "middle of nowhere", and you'll never get your kids to leave say families who find that the "crazy maze of passages, rooms, arcades, bowling alleys and restaurants" literally makes them "dizzy"; add in golf, horseback riding and all that "walking up and down the resort's hills" and you'll work up an appetite – it's just too bad "there's only one restaurant that serves halfway decent food."

St. Louis

Hyatt Regency Ⓗ | 22 | 21 | 19 | 23 | $249

1 St. Louis Union Station; 314-231-1234; fax 314-923-3970; 800-233-1234; www.hyatt.com; 538 rooms, 20 suites

Train buffs travel "back in time" when they disembark at this "architectural wonder" set in "historic" Union Station, where the "breathtaking" lobby features vaulted ceilings and Tiffany glass and the restaurant is "usually jam-packed with businessmen on power lunches"; if you choo-choose the "lovely rooms" in the older building, you'll find lots of "character", and when it's time to refuel your engine, take advantage of the eateries (along with theaters and shops) at the adjoining marketplace; sure it's a bit "quirky", but most climb right aboard.

Renaissance Grand Hotel ▽ 21 | 20 | 16 | 21 | $189

800 Washington Ave.; 314-621-9600; fax 314-621-9601; 800-468-3571; www.renaissancehotels.com; 875 rooms, 43 suites

A "particularly elegant restoration of the old Statler", this business hotel in a "not so great neighborhood" has "excellent access" to America's Center for large-scale meetings and a "how-can-I-help-you?" staff; but cranky critics find "odd-shaped rooms" and a "convention-style" property "ridiculously dressed up" to look older and grander than it is.

RITZ-CARLTON, THE 26 | 26 | 25 | 24 | $269

100 Carondelet Plaza, Clayton; 314-863-6300; fax 314-863-3525; 800-241-3333; www.ritzcarlton.com; 269 rooms, 33 suites

"Is there really another choice?" ask comfort-seekers of the "only hotel in town worth mentioning", truly an "ultimate luxury" outpost in upscale Clayton; almost every "cavernous" room has a balcony (some with "amazing views" of the city and Arch), the Grill restaurant is an area "favorite" and the concierge level offers the "the best lounge food" around; while just a few Ritz regulars report this one is "not as polished as those in other cities", most admit even a "standard" specimen of this brand stands way above the Gateway City's other offerings.

Roberts Mayfair, The Ⓗ ▽ 21 | 21 | 16 | 19 | $169

806 St. Charles St.; 314-421-2500; www.wyndham.com; 182 suites

The briefcase brigade may fare better at this 1925 "predominately business" Wyndham property that "can feel empty on weekends", but offers WiFi access in public spaces, high-speed Internet in rooms and a "great Downtown location"; while service is uneven – "above and beyond" to some, "inept" to others – and the dining gets few raves, this historic spot once played host to notables like Irving Berlin and Cary Grant, and it still has "lots of potential."

Montana

Big Sky

Big Sky Resort Ⓢ ▽ 23 | 21 | 20 | 24 | $276

1 Lone Mountain Trail; 406-995-5000; fax 406-995-5001; 800-548-4486; www.bigskyresort.com; 370 rooms, 130 suites, 150 condos

Located 18 miles from Yellowstone National Park, this sprawling multifaceted retreat with "beautiful views" of Love Peak is a skiers dream; even off the slopes the sky seems to be the limit, with options ranging from condos to the three-story Huntley Lodge, named for the resort's late founder, former NBC newscaster Chet Huntley; most of the other accommodations, including Summit at Big Sky, a 10-story luxury hotel, and the recently restored Shoshone and Powder Ridge Cabins, have ski-in/ski-out access.

Darby

Triple Creek Ranch | – | – | – | – | $510 |

5551 W. Fork Rd.; 406-821-4600; fax 406-821-4666; 800-654-2943; www.triplecreekranch.com; 19 cabins

"Hot tub under the stars – it's a Western fantasy even without the horses" say sojourners who indeed soak and saddle up at this Relais & Châteaux "secluded", amenity-laden vacation spot about 78 miles south of Missoula airport; "life on a ranch doesn't get much better than this", so take in the "gorgeous surroundings" of West Fork Valley, "pamper yourself" with "wonderful food" and bed down in "rustic yet luxurious" log cabins; "it's pricey, but worth every penny", plus there's "personable service" to boot.

Missoula

Resort at Paws Up | – | – | – | – | $370 |

40060 Paws Up Rd., Greenough; 406-244-5200; fax 406-244-5201; 800-473-0601; www.pawsup.com/resort; 18 houses, 3 tents

Even the tent rooms along the river banks have electricity and art at this super-luxe hotel (a member of Small Luxury Hotels of the World) in the foothills of the Garnet Mountains 25 miles from Missoula whose accommodations also include vacation homes with feather beds, hot tubs and flat-screen TVs, as well as additional rooms in a restored farmhouse; the 37,000 acres are a veritable playground for shooting sporting clays, fly fishing, boating, rafting and tubing (plus dog sledding in the winter), and a spa opens in 2006.

Pray

Chico Hot Springs Resort ▽ | 15 | 24 | 26 | 25 | $49 |

1 Old Chico Rd.; 406-333-4933; www.chicohotsprings.com; 112 rooms, 15 suites, 2 chalets, 7 cabins

Caution: "gazing at mountains as steam rises from two full-sized hot spring–fed pools" could cause "absolute contentment" say travelers who happen upon this "hidden" resort in a "remote locale" 60 miles from Bozeman's airport; accommodations abound, from the historic main lodge with a newer wing, to cabins, cottages and chalets, plus the "food is delicious", hospitality is "outstanding" and you may "run into celebrities along with locals"; chances are most are thinking the same thing: "with a little more attention to the decor this place could be incredible."

Whitefish

Grouse Mountain Lodge ▽ | 18 | 21 | 18 | 20 | $199 |

2 Fairway Dr.; 406-862-3000; fax 406-862-0326; 800-321-8822; www.grousemountainlodge.com; 125 rooms, 12 loft rooms, 8 suites

"A lovely stop en route to Yellowstone" in Flathead Valley, this upscale Western lodge with a "nice log feel to it" allows the Glacier National Park–bound a place to "relax and deflate between busy city lives and the wilderness"; with two outdoor spas, "lovely grounds", "large comfortable rooms", "excellent dining" at three venues, plus swimming, horseback riding, rafting and skiing at nearby Big Valley, it's also a "great getaway" destination in and of itself – "what more could you ask for in the middle of nowhere?"

Nevada

Incline Village

Hyatt Regency Resort & Casino | 19 | 21 | 19 | 24 | $330 |

111 Country Club Dr.; 775-832-1234; fax 775-831-7508; 800-553-3288; www.laketahoe.hyatt.com; 390 rooms, 10 suites, 24 cottages

With its makeover "finally completed – thank goodness!" this "real resort" in a "dreamy setting" with a private beach, an on-site spa (Tahoe's largest), a golf course and nearby downhill and cross-country skiing is "dramatically improved" opine its patient patrons; while a few faultfinders feel the dining may be "weak", the top-shelf pool with heated decking and swim-out access from inside help compensate.

Las Vegas

★ **Tops in City**

27 Four Seasons
Bellagio
26 Ritz-Carlton, Lake Las Vegas
25 Venetian
24 Mandalay Bay
Green Valley Ranch, *Henderson*
23 Hyatt Regency Lake Resort, *Henderson*
JW Marriott

BELLAGIO HOTEL | 27 | 25 | 28 | 28 | $359 |

3600 Las Vegas Blvd. S.; 702-693-7111; fax 702-693-8546; 888-987-6667; www.bellagiolasvegas.com; 3421 rooms, 512 suites, 9 villas

The "sophisticated" exception in a "desert of trashiness", this "mega" monument "wows" with a "spectacular water show", "out-of-this-world spa" and staff that "treats everyone like a Rockefeller"; you might have to elbow through "hordes" at check-in to get to your "phenomenal" suite, but at least you can eat at "top-notch" spots like Picasso (rated Most Popular and No. 1 for Decor and Service in our *Las Vegas Restaurant Survey*) or at the new Sensi with a 3,000-sq.-ft. open kitchen and score tickets to the "incredible" 'O'; N.B. a new spa tower opened post-*Survey*.

Caesars Palace | 22 | 21 | 22 | 24 | $200 |

3570 Las Vegas Blvd. S.; 702-731-7110; fax 702-866-1700; 800-634-6661; www.caesarspalace.com; 3348 rooms

A "classic" that's "coming back to life", this center Strip spot is "extravagant" in a "Vegas cheesy way" (you half "expect to see Wayne Newton in a toga"); even if a few find it "fallen like Rome", loyalists point to the expanded Forum Shops (with new restaurants Sushi Roku, BOA Steakhouse and Bradley Ogden) and a "pro" staff to explain why they often return to this "cool" "old-schooler"; N.B. the new Augustus Tower added almost 1,000 rooms this year.

FOUR SEASONS HOTEL LAS VEGAS | 28 | 28 | 26 | 27 | $350 |

3960 Las Vegas Blvd. S.; 702-632-5000; fax 702-632-5195; 877-632-5000; www.fourseasons.com; 338 rooms, 86 suites

Yes, you can find "tasteful", "peaceful" surroundings in Sin City – if you're willing to pay the price for this "piece of heaven" on the

35th to 39th floors of the Mandalay Bay where pool attendants "spritz Evian" and deliver chilled towels to your complimentary cabana and you can dine at the "superb" Charlie Palmer Steak; rooms with "huge marble" baths filled with L'Occitane toiletries are so "sumptuous", "you'll never miss the sound of the slots"; even though a few seek more "pizzazz", regulars relish in "relief from the Vegas glare"; N.B. there's full access to the 11-acre beach/pool complex at the Mandalay.

Green Valley Ranch Resort & Spa 24 | 23 | 22 | 25 | $350

2300 Paseo Verde Pkwy., Henderson; 702-617-7777; fax 702-617-7778; 866-782-9487; www.greenvalleyranchresort.com; 425 rooms, 73 suites

For a "high roller look" with "prices that won't break the house", roll the dice on Vegas' "best-kept secret" (at least before the Discovery Channel's *American Casino* started filming there): a three-year-old "sprawling" Med-style resort seven miles from Downtown with a "hip and happening pool area" sporting private cabanas and a "see-and-be-seen" bar (Whiskey Beach); there's also a "chic spa", six restaurants, a retail complex and "terrific" rooms, some with views of the Strip, as well as the requisite casino; N.B. a major expansion will add more than 300 rooms.

Hard Rock Hotel & Casino 19 | 18 | 21 | 23 | $429

4455 Paradise Rd.; 702-693-5000; fax 702-693-5010; 800-473-7625; www.hardrockhotel.com; 583 rooms, 64 suites

Be among the other "sexy people" at this off-the-Strip themester with "a pool that cannot be beat", "hip music" and a "perennial spring break" atmosphere; sure "the lobby gets packed on concert nights" and you "can't always carry on a conversation in the restaurant", but it's all a "blissful frenzy" for the "under-30" "pierced" set who don't mind the "halfway-decent rooms"; "if you don't have a fake tan, fake boobs or a fake attitude", just go for an "incredible" dinner at Nobu.

Hyatt Regency Lake Resort 23 | 24 | 21 | 26 | $269

101 Montelago Blvd., Henderson; 702-567-1234; fax 702-567-6103; 800-233-1234; www.hyatt.com; 446 rooms, 47 suites

A "warm Moroccan motif", "gorgeous grounds" and "helpful service" make this resort half an hour from Downtown the perfect "hideout" from the Strip's "glitz"; there's a "tiny" casino ("not for serious gamblers"), "fabulous" sushi at Japengo and a "wonderful" golf course, but type A's tsk it's "too far away from anywhere to be considered a Vegas hotel."

JW Marriott Las Vegas Resort, Spa & Golf 26 | 22 | 19 | 23 | $389

221 N. Rampart Blvd.; 702-869-7777; fax 702-869-7771; 877-869-8777; www.marriott.com; 464 rooms, 77 suites

"Away from the hustle and bustle" but "still close enough to lose money" on the Strip (there's a free shuttle back and forth), this high-end Marriott "feels more like it's in Rancho Mirage than Vegas", with "fabulous rooms" sporting "enormous" baths, a "luxurious" gym and spa and "professional, if a bit uppity", service; while some say this former Regent is "less polished than other JWs" and you may want to go elsewhere for dinner, overall it's "trying very hard."

Mandalay Bay Hotel 24 21 25 27 $259

3950 Las Vegas Blvd. S.; 702-632-7777; fax 702-632-7328; 877-632-7000; www.mandalaybay.com; 3200 rooms, 1120 suites

You "can't beat the man-made beach" wager water-wallowers wooed by the "amazing" lazy river and wave pool complex at this family resort – just "rent a cabana" to escape the "*Romper Room*"–like atmosphere during school vacations; there's also a "luxe" spa, "incredible" dining options including chef Rick Moonen's rm and "spread out" gaming tables to "avoid that cramped feeling"; those few who find the rooms "plain" and the facility starting to "age" may appreciate the brand-new "swanky" all-suite addition, THEhotel, with chef Alain Ducasse's new venture Mix and rooms with "lots of perks" including plasma TVs.

MGM Grand Hotel 19 18 21 22 $329

3799 Las Vegas Blvd. S.; 702-891-7777; fax 702-891-1030; 800-929-1111; www.mgmgrand.com; 4254 rooms, 751 suites, 29 villas

"Huge – no *really* huge" sums up this mammoth "monstrosity" that's "too big to navigate with youngsters" unless they're up for "mile-long" walks or you "put them on a leash"; still, it has "everything you want under one roof": "airy rooms" (stick with the luxury Skylofts on the top two floors), lots of "eclectic" dining options, a "gigantic" pool and a lion in the casino; too bad the "fun little amusement park" is gone, but it now houses three nightclubs.

Mirage Hotel 20 20 20 23 $499

3400 Las Vegas Blvd. S.; 702-791-7111; fax 702-891-1030; 800-627-6667; www.mirage.com; 2770 rooms, 279 suites

"If you can forge your way through the jungle in the lobby" you'll find a "tropical" interior and "nicely decorated rooms" at this "mainstay" on the Strip; although if it's "been overshadowed by glitzier" properties and hipsters snap it's "so 1990s", fans can't get enough of the erupting volcano, the "kid-pleasing" dolphin habitat, the white tigers (minus Siegfried and Roy) and Renoir restaurant.

Palms Casino Hotel 21 20 21 22 $329

4321 W. Flamingo Rd.; 702-942-7777; fax 702-942-7001; 866-942-7777; www.palms.com; 389 rooms, 41 suites

It's about the clubbing "scene", especially at the "lively nightspots" Rain and Ghostbar (50 stories above the city), at this "funky" off-Strip hotel that's "another hip place for twentysomethings" and "celebrities galore"; the "staff has more attitude than a one-hit wonder" and cranky critics claim if it hadn't hosted MTV's *Real World,* it would be "so far in the Hard Rock's rearview mirror, it'd be in California", but most maintain if you're a "hottie" wearing the "latest styles" you'll feel right at home.

Paris Las Vegas 21 20 21 22 $299

3655 Las Vegas Blvd. S.; 702-946-7000; fax 702-967-3836; 888-266-5687; www.parislasvegas.com; 2916 rooms, 295 suites

The casino is a "work of art" at this Paris-themed resort fronted by a replica of the Eiffel Tower where the service is "more friendly" than in the namesake city and you can book a room ("do yourself a favor and get a suite") with a view of the nearby Bellagio's dancing fountains; if you can fight the "herds", the pool is "fabulous" and the restaurants and shops "suit every taste", but to really enjoy it, you must "embrace the kitsch" – every last "plastic" "tacky" piece.

Renaissance Las Vegas | – | – | – | – | $169 |

3400 Paradise Rd.; 702-733-6533; fax 702-735-3131; www.renaissancelasvegas.com; 518 rooms, 30 suites

There's never been a hipper or more modern place to stay near a convention center than this value-laden hotel melding a club atmosphere with soft in-room colors, bold patterns and serenity enough to get the job done in a city that never works; there's no gaming on-site, but its ENVY Steakhouse is the off-Strip spot to get carnal with a T-bone and a scotch, so who needs a casino anyway?

Rio All-Suite Hotel & Casino Ⓢ | 23 | 19 | 20 | 21 | $370 |

3700 W. Flamingo Rd.; 702-777-7777; fax 702-777-2360; 888-746-7482; www.playrio.com; 2551 suites

Kid-toting travelers tout "lots of room to spread out" at this all-suiter with daily Mardi Gras parades, "colorful" decor and a "vast selection of food" including an "awesome" seafood buffet; though the "views from the Voodoo Lounge" and decent comps win adult accolades, it's a bit "noisy", "tired" and "tattered" for some and a "drag" to be a 10-minute walk from the Strip's "excitement."

RITZ-CARLTON, LAKE LAS VEGAS Ⓢ | 27 | 26 | 24 | 27 | $339 |

1610 Lake Las Vegas Pkwy., Henderson; 702-567-4700; fax 702-567-4777; 800-241-3333; www.ritzcarlton.com; 314 rooms

If you need "an oasis in the middle of the desert", head to this "elegant" new Tuscany-inspired outpost 30 minutes from the neon where "fantastic" facilities include two golf courses, a "full view of the Strip's lights at night", an "exceptional" spa and "luxurious rooms."

VENETIAN HOTEL Ⓢ | 27 | 23 | 25 | 26 | $899 |

3355 Las Vegas Blvd. S.; 702-414-1000; fax 702-414-1100; 877-283-6423; www.venetian.com; 4036 suites

It's "a little cheaper than flying to Italy" when you stay at this "drop-dead" "gorgeous" re-creation complete with "opera-singing gondoliers", a fake nightly sunset in St. Mark's Square and a "wonderfully romantic" vibe; immerse yourself in the "best" of the city's "pricey" faux worlds – get pampered in the "sublime" Canyon Ranch spa, view "amazing" works of art, eat at one of the 16 "outstanding restaurants", sink into a "decadent suite" that's "bigger than your first studio apartment" and then yell "*bravissimo!*" at the top of your lungs.

Wynn Las Vegas Casino Resort Ⓢ | – | – | – | – | $299 |

3131 Las Vegas Blvd. S; fax 702-770-1510; 888-320-9966; www.wynnlasvegas.com; 2108 rooms, 608 suites

The latest megaresort to open in Vegas, this Steve Wynn property has just about everything: a 111,000-sq.-ft. light-filled casino, a dozen restaurants from top chefs including Daniel Boulud, a collection of upscale boutiques, an art gallery of masterworks by the likes of Picasso and Van Gogh, an 18-hole Tom Fazio/Steve Wynn golf course, a full-service spa, a man-made mountain with a five-story waterfall and two showrooms (one housing a new aquatic show by Cirque du Soleil founder Franco Dragone); accommodations include Fairway Villas facing the greens and a VIP tower with a separate entrance.

New Hampshire

Bretton Woods

Mount Washington Hotel & Resort, The | 17 | 22 | 19 | 24 | $340 |

Rte. 302; 603-278-1000; fax 603-278-8838; 800-314-1752; www.mtwashington.com; 271 rooms, 13 suites, 66 townhouses

"Even jaded East Coasters return year after year" to this 1902 "family retreat" "in the heart of the Presidential Range" lured by its all-inclusive plan, "friendly staff" and "phenomenal facilities" that include "vast and exciting" cross-country ski trails and nearby downhill slopes; while a handful feel that the rooms "need refurbishment" and dining is merely "acceptable", everyone adores the "huge wraparound porch"; N.B. a new spa opened in 2005.

Dixville Notch

Balsams, The | 19 | 26 | 26 | 25 | $289 |

Rte. 26, Lake Gloriette; 603-255-3400; fax 603-255-4221; 800-255-0600; www.thebalsams.com; 193 rooms, 11 suites

"Regardless of the season", "there's something for everyone" to do at this "grand", family-oriented "oldie but goodie" with a "secluded location" in the Great North Woods and "beautiful" White Mountain views; while the "hotel itself could use an update", dining is "great" and the array of all-inclusive facilities, including a "fabulous golf course" and cross-country ski trails, is "amazing", making it "one of the best for the money."

Newcastle

Wentworth by the Sea by Marriott | ▽ 24 | 21 | 21 | 23 | $279 |

588 Wentworth Rd.; 603-422-7322; fax 603-422-7329; 866-240-6313; www.wentworth.com; 161 rooms

"A gem is reborn" say fans of this "great weekend escape" on New Castle Island that was built in 1874 but "extensively renovated" and reopened by Marriott; the "tasteful" rooms and "amazing" baths "successfully blend the old with the new" and though tennis and an on-site beach beckon guests outside, some confess the "beds are too comfy to leave."

Plainfield

Home Hill | – | – | – | – | $235 |

703 River Rd.; 603-675-6165; fax 603-675-5220; www.homehillinn.com; 8 rooms, 2 suites, 1 cottage

Have a European vacation at this Relais & Châteaux–affiliated French-inspired inn in Plainfield (12 miles from Dartmouth College) set in an 1818 home with accommodations in two separate buildings; most of the restored rooms have fireplaces or terraces, and in-room furnishings include canopy beds, Victorian loveseats and antiques, while a seasonal private cottage is available for rental; guests have access to the courses at the nearby private Montcalm Golf Club, and foodies will want to dine in chef Victoria du Roure's Provençal restaurant.

New Jersey

Atlantic City

Bally's 17 17 18 19 $299

Boardwalk & Park Pl.; 609-340-2000; fax 609-340-1725; 800-772-7777; www.ballys.com; 1646 rooms, 100 suites

"Make sure you get a Tower room" at this "dated" Boardwalk property, and then focus on the good points: "one of the best" buffets and Jewish-style delis in the area, "efficient" management and an "outstanding pool" and spa; but others just can't ignore the need for "a complete overhaul" from the "blinding carpets" to the "smoky smell" to a theme that "needs rethinking."

Borgata Hotel Casino & Spa 27 21 24 26 $249

1 Borgata Way; 609-317-1000; 866-692-6742; www.theborgata.com; 1600 rooms, 402 suites

"At last, Vegas comes East" say fans of "by far the best" hotel in the city; with 11 "sophisticated" restaurants including Susanna Foo's Suilan, "tasteful" rooms with "huge" baths, an "impressive" spa and pool, "stunning artwork" and a "bright, energetic" casino with smoke-free areas, it "sets a new standard" as "the only place to be"; too bad popularity means "god-awful" lines and spotty service.

Caesars Atlantic City 21 19 20 20 $400

2100 Pacific Ave.; 609-348-4411; fax 609-441-2261; 800-443-0104; www.caesars.com; 960 rooms, 17 suites

"Ask for the Ocean or Centurion Towers" or else you'll be playing "room roulette" say friends and countrymen of this "Roman extravaganza" with a "great position on the boardwalk" and "plenty to offer" gaming gladiators; there's "prompt" service, a "really cool lobby", a "to-die-for" spa and "excellent" dining options; still, this ruler is "showing his age" and he's no spring chicken.

Sands Hotel ▽ 15 14 17 14 $225

Indiana Ave.; 609-441-4000; 1-800-227-2637; www.sandsac.com; 370 rooms, 30 suites

Head here if you're looking for "just a place to sleep" say those who come for the "lowest rates", an "excellent value" buffet and the "interesting casino clientele"; otherwise it's "on the seedy side for AC" and there are "much better places than this."

Seaview Marriott Resort & Spa 18 20 17 22 $209

401 S. New York Rd., Galloway; 609-652-1800; fax 609-652-2307; 800-205-6518; www.marriott.com; 297 rooms, 57 suites

If you like golfing or pampering, this resort works for a "weekend getaway" since it has "the best spa in Jersey" (an Elizabeth Arden facility) plus two "awesome" courses – all a "short enough drive from the casinos"; the "terrific ocean setting" and the "excellent Sunday brunch" win praise, but others dis it as a "used-to-be."

Tropicana – – – – $399

S. Brighton Ave.; 609-340-4000; 800-843-8767; www.tropicana.net; 2030 rooms, 100 suites

A taste of old Havana is now on tap for guests of this veteran hotel that recently opened The Quarter dining and entertainment complex with three floors of shopping, restaurants (including Jeffrey Chodorow's Red Square), a spa, 500 new rooms and Jersey's only IMAX theater; other highlights include beachside cabana service, three concierge desks and a deluxe bi-level suite.

Trump Marina 20 18 18 20 $429
Huron Ave. & Brigantine Blvd.; 609-441-2000; 800-777-1177; www.trumpmarina.com; 570 rooms, 150 suites
With "wonderful views of the ocean" "away from the tumult", this casino hotel with "typical Trump" decor (meaning "tacky" to some) is a "great stop for boaters" who can tie up the skiff before shuffling the cards; while mariners maintain it's "better than the boardwalk hotels" thanks to "recently remodeled rooms" and "competent service", others find it a "bit depressing."

Trump Plaza 17 16 16 18 $250
The Boardwalk at Mississippi Ave.; 609-441-6000; fax 609-441-6679; 800-677-7378; www.trumpplaza.com; 764 rooms, 142 suites
The suites have "sweeping views of the boardwalk and ocean", but reviewers have mixed feelings about the rest of this hotel: there are "lots of places to eat" and "the Donald runs a tight ship" say some, but others snap it has "lost its edge", with "standard" rooms that look like they "haven't been fixed up since it opened" and too much "typically overrated Trump glitz."

Trump Taj Mahal 19 17 18 20 $375
1000 Boardwalk; 609-449-1000; fax 609-449-6818; 800-825-8786; www.trumptaj.com; 1130 rooms, 120 suites
An Indian-themed palace awaits its subjects at this 17-acre boardwalk city-within-a-city, where seven two-ton elephant statues guard the entrance, there's Carrera marble and German crystal chandeliers everywhere and suites feature ocean views, individual spas and butler services; other amenities include the casino's newly renovated private Bengal Club, a health and fitness center with an Olympic-size pool and nine restaurants.

Bernardsville

Bernards Inn 19 22 26 18 $179
27 Mine Brook Rd.; 908-766-0002; fax 908-766-4604; 888-766-0002; www.bernardsinn.com; 16 rooms, 4 suites
Come to this 1907 Mission-style inn "only for the restaurant" rave reviewers – though a new chef, Corey Heyer, was appointed post-*Survey,* the New American menu still features dishes like a grain-fed veal chop with morel mushrooms and spring pea flan, along with an 8,000-bottle wine collection; while the staff is "friendly" and the setting "quaint", the "incredible" dining steals the show.

Cape May

Congress Hall ▽ 22 19 18 23 $335
251 Beach Ave.; 609-884-8421; fax 609-884-6094; 888-944-1816; www.congresshall.com; 101 rooms, 5 suites
A "beautifully renovated Victorian classic", this "combination of elegance and seaside informality" has an "exceptional location" overlooking the Atlantic, "ocean-facing rockers you could spend hours in" and "fabulous original baths" with deep '20s tubs right "off

the pages of *Martha Stewart Living*"; though food is "just ok" and the service "could be better", the Blue Pig Tavern is "a must" and it's "one of the few Cape May hotels with a pool."

Inn of Cape May Ⓗ ▽ 19 | 23 | 23 | 19 | $210

7 Ocean St.; 609-884-5555; fax 609-884-3871; 800-582-5933; www.innofcapemay.com; 51 rooms, 16 suites

The wraparound porch and Victorian decor will "make you feel like donning a girdle and hoop dress" at this "quaint" "treasure" in the heart of the historic district and across the street from the beach; an antiques shop and the oceanfront seafood restaurant, Aleathea's, win praise – "who doesn't love Cape May?"

Virginia, The ✕Ⓗ 20 | 23 | 26 | 19 | $145

25 Jackson St.; 609-884-5700; fax 609-884-1236; 800-732-4236; www.virginiahotel.com; 24 rooms

For an "extremely romantic" stay in Cape May, head to this "classy" turn-of-the-last-century inn boasting "one of the best restaurants in town" (the Ebbitt Room) with a "fabulous wine list"; most of the quarters are "not so roomy", though four have terraces overlooking Jackson Street, but you'll "forget the claustrophobia after that fine meal"; N.B. renovations were completed this past year.

Short Hills

Hilton ⓈⓈ 23 | 25 | 25 | 25 | $199

41 JFK Pkwy.; 973-379-0100; fax 973-379-6870; 800-445-8667; www.hilton.com; 272 rooms, 32 suites

"Who would think there existed" a "first-rate hotel in the middle of NJ" and "close to a great mall" as well?; there's "nothing fancy about the architecture", but inside, the rooms are "fabulous" with marble baths, the staff makes you feel "special" and the pool is an "exotic Grecian temple"; with an "excellent" spa and an "amazing Sunday brunch", you'll "swear you stepped into a Ritz-Carlton."

Spring Lake

Normandy Inn Ⓗ ▽ 24 | 23 | 19 | 19 | $295

21 Tuttle Ave.; 732-449-7172; 800-449-1888; www.normandyinn.com; 15 rooms, 2 suites, 1 carriage house

This "well-decorated" 19th-century inn near the beach in a "great shore town" has a certain "understated elegance" and "charm"; listed on the National Register of Historic Places, it has "lovely rooms" with "huge beds" (some boasting fireplaces) and antiques; chefs from the French Culinary Institute prepare the "delish" breakfasts, and free bikes are provided.

New Mexico

Albuquerque

Hyatt Regency Tamaya Ⓢ 24 | 23 | 21 | 27 | $215

1300 Tuyuna Trail, Santa Ana Pueblo; 505-867-1234; fax 505-867-1400; 800-554-9288; www.hyatt.com; 327 rooms, 23 suites

"Superb and unexpected", this "magnificent", pueblo-style resort "practically in the middle of nowhere" about 30 miles north of

Albuquerque airport is "worth going out of the way for"; "it has a Zen feel" that transcends everything from the "beautifully situated" colorful rooms looking out on the Sandia Mountains to the "out-of-this-world" spa ("get the pedicure – heck, get everything"); "pretty pools", horseback riding and an "excellent golf course" seal the deal.

Santa Fe

Bishop's Lodge Resort & Spa 21 | 21 | 20 | 23 | $325

1297 Bishop's Lodge Rd.; 505-983-6377; fax 505-983-0832; 800-419-0492; www.bishopslodge.com; 101 rooms, 10 suites

It's the "Wild West" at this "recently renovated, but not fancy", "charming" "escape" with an "incomparable setting" in the Sangre de Cristo Mountains; "if you're ok with being a little ways out of town", this "semi-secluded" lodge offers "Santa Fe without the commercialism" with rooms with exposed beams, hiking trails and a nature-inspired "pleasant" spa; but a few deem the staff "inattentive."

Eldorado Hotel 21 | 20 | 21 | 20 | $279

309 W. San Francisco St.; 505-988-4455; fax 505-995-4555; 800-988-4455; www.eldoradohotel.com; 214 rooms, 5 suites

"The location can't be beat" attest admirers of this "lovely" pueblo-revival style "favorite" "on the square" with "cultural destinations within walking distance" and a "small rooftop pool that's a great escape"; some of the Southwestern-style rooms boast Kiva fireplaces and "great views" of the Sangre de Cristo Mountains (the penthouse terrace "begs for a pitcher of margaritas and a vat of guacamole"), plus there's "attentive butler service"; but the dissatisfied deem it "generic" and "overpriced."

Houses of the Moon 18 | 22 | 13 | 24 | $215

3451 Hyde Park Rd.; 505-982-9304; fax 505-989-5077; www.tenthousandwaves.com; 12 rooms

"Your tensions disappear into the surrounding mountains" at this "serene" spot "hidden" "on your way to the ski resorts of Santa Fe"; the "exquisite" on-site Japanese spa – Ten Thousand Waves – where "you can hot tub under the stars" "in the desert", "enjoy couples massage" and "unwind in the beauty of the New Mexico wilderness" is a perfect retreat before heading to your minimalist-style casita; still, most advise "it's all about the Zen aura" of the services – the "rooms are secondary."

Inn of the Anasazi 25 | 25 | 25 | 21 | $259

113 Washington Ave.; 505-988-3030; fax 505-988-3277; 800-688-8100; www.innoftheanasazi.com; 57 rooms

The "quintessential pueblo living experience for the modern traveler", this "enchanting" hotel (a member of Small Luxury Hotels of the World) is "steps away from the square" and "romantic to the nth degree"; "every detail appears to have been chosen by an art lover and environmentalist", with the "charming architecture" inspired by the mud and stone dwellings of the ancient Anasazis; the "rooms are on the small side, but beautifully appointed" with a "great New Mexico look" (some with gaslit Kiva fireplaces), and the dining room is "excellent."

Inn of the Five Graces – | – | – | – | $360

150 E. DeVargass St.; 505-992-0957; fax 505-955-0549; www.fivegraces.com; 22 suites

Tibet lands in Santa Fe at this boutique where everything from the Far East–influenced upholstery and kilim rugs to the silk pillows strewn over curtained four-poster beds, stone fireplaces and hand-painted tiled bathrooms evoke the mystical country that its original owner, Ira Seret (a rug and antique importer), was fond of; the Garrett Hotel group took over management in 2002 and its name refers to the five graces of Tibetan culture or the five human senses.

Inn on the Alameda 21 | 21 | 16 | 18 | $205

303 E. Alameda; 505-984-2121; fax 505-986-8325; 888-984-2121; www.innonthealameda.com; 59 rooms, 10 suites

"Quirky and original" accommodations are the backbone of this "lovely, quaint" adobe-walled "inn in the heart of Santa Fe" within "walking distance of Canyon Road and the Plaza"; it's a "mercifully quiet" place where you can take "comfortable refuge after a long day" ("be sure to get a room with a Kiva fireplace so you can listen to it while you sleep"), plus "nice public rooms" and an "awesome breakfast and wine reception" "add to the whole experience."

La Posada de Santa Fe ⒽⓈ 22 | 22 | 20 | 23 | $239

330 E. Palace Ave.; 505-986-0000; fax 505-986-9646; 866-331-7625; www.laposadadesantafe.com; 117 rooms, 40 suites

"If you want to stay in a historic place", go to this "enchanting", Southwestern retreat with a "gorgeous pueblo village feel" near the town square, "where you can be entertained by local musicians and shop the sidewalk vendors", browse in "galleries and eat at extraordinary spots" and return to "beautiful" "New Mexico–style lodgings", some of which feature Kiva fireplaces; guests also gush over the "outrageous" Avanyu spa and a "to-die-for" restaurant.

Taos

EL MONTE SAGRADO ✕Ⓢ ▽ 28 | 25 | 26 | 27 | $325

317 Kit Carson Rd.; 505-758-3502; fax 505-737-2985; 800-828-8267; www.elmontesagrado.com; 24 suites, 12 casitas

"New-age baroque meets green consciousness" at "newspaper magnate Tom Worrell's" "eco-friendly" boutique resort at the foot of the Sangre de Cristo Mountains, a "perfect lovers' hideaway" that's "top of the line at every level"; the "rooms are palatial" and decorated in Native American motifs or with artifacts from local artists, and the "wonderful spa" (with new steam and sauna rooms) has "everything" a massage-and-treatment "fan would want", plus the restaurant and Anadonda bar are "amazing places."

New York

Adirondacks

Elk Lake Lodge – | – | – | – | $150

Blue Ridge Rd., North Hudson; 518-532-7616; fax 518-532-9262; www.elklakelodge.com; 6 rooms, 8 cottages

A "spectacular location" on 12,000 acres in the Adirondacks (a five-hour drive from NYC) makes this 1904 lakeside resort equally "wonderful" for romantics and nature lovers; guests can stay in the main lodge or cabins and enjoy birdwatching, boating, swimming, canoeing and hiking – but the "pristine" setting (described by *National Geographic* as the "pearl of the Adirondacks") is really "why you come"; open May–October only.

Friends Lake Inn ▽ 21 | 28 | 27 | 21 | $325

963 Friends Lake Rd., Chestertown; 518-494-4751; fax 518-494-4616; www.friendslake.com; 17 rooms

The chef "brings food and wine pairings to a new high" in the "fantastic" dining room (with a "wonderful wine cellar") of this Adirondack inn – an "oasis in the middle of nowhere" that's a "perfect romantic hideaway"; go kayaking, snowshoeing and hiking, or just enjoy the "cute", "comfortable" rooms and the "charming" staff.

LAKE PLACID LODGE 27 | 27 | 23 | 25 | $300

Whiteface Inn Rd., Lake Placid; 518-523-2700; fax 518-523-1124; 877-523-2700; www.lakeplacidlodge.com; 14 rooms, 3 suites, 17 cabins

You may need "a mountain of cash" to stay at this "elegant" Relais & Châteaux "gem" (it's also a member of Small Luxury Hotels of the World), but it's such a "romantic" "heaven" you'll soon be "dreaming of a return"; "stay in a cottage by the lake", marvel at the "gorgeous details" and enjoy the "fabulous meals", "stunning" grounds and "outstanding service" ("they're even lovely to your pooch"); one word sums it up: "wow."

Mirror Lake Inn 23 | 24 | 24 | 25 | $235

5 Mirror Lake Dr., Lake Placid; 518-523-2544; fax 518-523-2871; www.mirrorlakeinn.com; 110 rooms, 18 suites

Reminiscent "of what Lake Placid once was", this lakeside retreat is "lovely" "anytime of year" with its "elegant" common rooms, "top-notch spa" and "wonderful tea" (try the chocolate-chip cookies); fit folks find plenty of skiing, hiking, golfing and fishing, but even if you just aim to "enjoy the mountain air", this one comes "highly recommended."

POINT, THE 28 | 28 | 26 | 27 | $1250

Upper Saranac Lake, Saranac Lake; 518-891-5674; fax 518-891-1152; 800-255-3530; www.thepointresort.com; 10 rooms, 1 suite

"Say good-bye to Junior's trust fund" and "live like a Rockefeller" at this "poshly rustic" Relais & Châteaux "gem" that's "as close to perfect as you can get"; "leave the kids at home" and revel in its "over-the-top" service and romantic private rooms with fireplaces and antiques, then "bring a big appetite" and "be ready to meet new people" at the "best" communal dinners; there's "nothing quite like it", leaving some with just one complaint: "can't afford to return."

Sagamore, The 21 | 22 | 21 | 25 | $269

110 Sagamore Rd., Bolton Landing; 518-644-9400; fax 518-743-6036; 800-358-3585; www.thesagamore.com; 174 rooms, 176 suites

A "divine" setting "away from it all" on "breathtaking" Lake George sets this "well-run" Adirondacks landmark apart, especially "in the fall when the leaves are changing" and in winter when "the boughs of the evergreens are bent with snow"; "stay in the newer condos" to avoid "mediocre" rooms, visit the "awesome spa" and "don't expect gourmet fare."

Whiteface Lodge – – – – $290

7 Whiteface Inn Ln., Lake Placid; 518-523-2133; fax 518-523-8010; 800-523-3387; www.thewhitefacelodge.com; 85 suites

Cozy up to this new Grand Adirondack lodge with a three-story Great Room, two restaurants, a lounge and suite accommodations in both the main lodge or the more luxurious Pavillion, with indoor/ outdoor pools and hot tubs, a BBQ bistro and outdoor fireplaces; activities include hiking, skating in a year-round rink, boating and relaxing in the on-site spa; N.B. one-, two- and three-bedroom residences are available in full or partial ownership options.

Buffalo

Mansion on Delaware, The ∇ 27 27 17 24 $159

414 Delaware Ave.; 716-886-3300; fax 716-883-3923; www.mansionondelaware.com; 25 rooms, 3 suites

Who would have thought you could have a "faux millionaire's life" in "a real millionaire's row mansion" in Buffalo? – apparently you can at this "elegant boutique" originally built in the 1860s with "fabulous [Second Empire] architecture"; "a favorite when celebs come to town", it's also a "perfect alternative to a chain" for business types who like the "personalized" service, "superior rooms" and complimentary breakfasts, early evening cocktails and sedan service to Downtown.

Catskills

Kate's Lazy Meadow Motel – – – – $175

5191 Rte. 28, Mt. Tremper; 845-688-7200; www.lazymeadow.com; 7 suites

You'll find a little love shack up in the Catskills thanks to former B-52's member Kate Pierson, who restored these 1950s cabins 10 minutes from Woodstock on Esopus Creek with the help of artist buddies; she's retained the era's vibe in turquoise kitchens and colorful, quirky decor, but has also added modern amenities like cable TV and high-speed Internet, plus it's pet-friendly and there's a video library that includes a campy collection of films.

MIRBEAU INN & SPA ∇ 27 26 28 28 $395

851 W. Genesee St., Skaneateles; 315-685-5006; fax 315-685-5150; 877-647-2328; www.mirbeau.com; 34 rooms, 4 cottages

Those who've found this "charming" French country–style inn in the Finger Lakes region "can't say enough" about it; first, there's the restaurant's "excellent" tasting menu in which "each item is more delicious than the last" and the "presentation is as gorgeous as the property's setting"; then there's the "wonderful" spa with treatments like an orange parfait wrap; finally, there are the rooms with fireplaces and "incredible beds" ("our son is a constant reminder of the incredible trip we had"); it all adds up to a "perfect place to enjoy the sights of central New York."

Mohonk Mountain House 19 22 18 26 $439

1000 Mountain Rest Rd., New Paltz; 845-255-1000; fax 845-256-2161; 800-772-6646; www.mohonk.com; 240 rooms, 11 suites, 4 cottages

The "spectacular setting" is what "you'll always remember" at this Victorian "treasure" in the Shawangunk Mountains where "pristine grounds" afford "breathtaking views", "excellent" hiking and outdoor exploring "anytime of year" (in winter you can "return to a lit fireplace in your room" and fall brings glorious foliage); while there are no TVs or AC, and critics find "bland" food, it's still "a great family place"; N.B. a new fitness center and spa opened in 2005.

New Age Health Spa 13 | 20 | 19 | 24 | $244

Rte. 55, Neversink; 845-985-7600; fax 845-985-2467; 800-682-4348; www.newagehealthspa.com; 37 rooms

It's a "whole 'nother world" at this "down-to-earth" destination spa that's "like summer camp for adults"; it's more "rustic than luxurious" ("you don't come for the rooms"), but the "tranquil location so near the city", a "knowledgeable staff", "unpretentious" facilities, spa cuisine that can be "delicious" and the Cayuga Yoga & Meditation Center make it "*the* place" to "get healthy."

Cooperstown

Otesaga, The 20 | 22 | 19 | 23 | $380

60 Lake St.; 607-547-9931; fax 607-547-9675; 800-348-6222; www.otesaga.com; 115 rooms, 20 suites

Yes, it's "still the turn of the last century" at this "gorgeous" hotel nestled on the lakefront and near the Baseball Hall of Fame; they're pitching a solid game with "large rooms", a "veranda to rock on" with a sunset cocktail, an outdoor whirlpool and "substantial meals" crafted by executive chef David Lockwood (his post-*Survey* appointment may outdate the above Food score); too bad they're not batting a thousand with the "dated" decor.

Hudson Valley

Beekman Arms & Delamater House 18 | 19 | 21 | 16 | $250

6387 Mill St., Rhinebeck; 845-876-7077; fax 845-876-7077; 800-361-6517; www.beekmandelamaterinn.com; 67 rooms, 2 suites

How lovely to get "a decanter of sherry" in your room at this "charming" "getaway from NYC madness"; set in 13 separate buildings, the quarters "vary greatly", with some more "shabby" than "historic", and "for the price, one would expect better service", but "delicious" food and a central location within walking distance of "quaint" Rhinebeck make it "worth a weekend drive."

Inn at Bullis Hall – | – | – | – | $325

88 Hunns Lake Rd, Stone Ridge; 845-868-1665; fax 845-868-1441; www.bullishall.com; 3 suites, 2 rooms

You might expect to run into Camilla Parker Bowles when you stay at this distinguished country inn situated in prime fox hunting country 90 minutes north of NYC, where running with the hounds is as common as playing polo and backgammon; built in 1832, this Relais & Châteaux property boasts rooms adorned with oak-paneled walls, antiques, Frette linens and Marsona sleep machines.

Le Chambord 19 | 22 | 20 | 19 | $155

2732 Rte. 52, Hopewell Junction; 845-221-1941; www.lechambord.com; 9 rooms, 16 suites

Set in an 1863 Georgian Colonial mansion, this "truly romantic inn" boasts a main building that "looks like Tara from *Gone With the*

Wind" and a French restaurant that admirers say is "well worth the trip" (75 minutes from Manhattan); the staff is "earnest" and the grounds are especially suitable "for a weekend wedding", but the less-charmed chirp that "rooms need a redo."

Old Drovers Inn Ⓗ 18 | 23 | 24 | 15 | $210

196 E. Duncan Hill Rd., Dover Plains; 845-832-9311; fax 845-832-6356; 800-735-2478; www.olddroversinn.com; 4 rooms

"Hear the history in the squeaky floorboards" of this tiny, "very romantic" inn where "friendly owners" set the tone for a "charming" country weekend; there's "excellent" American fare in the historic restaurant and they "bring dessert to your room", just "watch your head" in the dining area since the "ceilings are low."

Roselawn – | – | – | – | $250

113 Roselawn Rd., Highland Mills; 845-928-1440; fax 845-928-1410; www.roselawninn.com; 5 rooms

Just 50 miles north of New York, this tiny Hudson Valley resort offers five distinct rooms, from a master suite with its own fireplace, sauna, steam bath and Jacuzzi to the Blue Room done up in Philippe Starck style; public spaces include a central great room with fireplace, bar, flat-screen TV and stereo, as well as an outdoor pool, a private dining room (organic breakfasts are served) and 17 acres of grounds; N.B. guests can rent out the entire property.

Long Island

American Hotel Ⓗ 18 | 23 | 25 | 16 | $335

25 Main St., Sag Harbor; 631-725-3535; fax 631-725-3573; www.theamericanhotel.com; 8 rooms

This "historic" 1846 Long Island hotel "steps from everything" in Sag Harbor boasts some of "the best food" out East, with an "incredible" Sunday brunch and an "alluring" wine list ("plan not to drive" afterward); though the rooms are "tiny" and the facilities "very limited", overall it's "absolutely charming", especially in summer when you can sit on the porch ("in a Ralph Lauren ad") and watch the "pretty people", including literary types with nearby vacation homes.

Garden City Hotel Ⓢ 24 | 24 | 23 | 24 | $225

45 Seventh St., Garden City; 516-747-3000; fax 516-747-1414; 877-549-0400; www.gchotel.com; 260 rooms, 20 suites

Long Island locals consider this "luxury" hotel "a must for Sunday brunch" (the restaurant, Polo, was voted No. 1 for Service in our *Long Island Restaurant Survey*) and for the "great bar that turns into a club" on weekends, but business travelers are more attuned to its "extraordinary" staff, "yesteryear elegance" and "large rooms" with "wonderful thick robes"; yes, "everything is expensive", but "worth every dollar"; N.B. there's a train to Manhattan right across the street.

Gurney's Inn Resort & Spa Ⓢ 18 | 19 | 18 | 21 | $310

290 Old Montauk Hwy., Montauk; 631-668-2345; fax 631-668-3576; 800-848-7639; www.gurneys-inn.com; 65 rooms, 30 suites, 5 cottages

The "magnificent" beach setting and "wonderful" spa are the best reasons to consider a stay at this property on the tip of Long Island that has undergone major renovations over the past few years, which include a new spa and the Sea Grill restaurant; though most agree it's "restful", it's "a bit pricey" for what you get.

New York City

★ Tops in City

27 Four Seasons
Mandarin Oriental
26 Ritz-Carlton, Central Park
St. Regis
Ritz-Carlton Battery Park
25 Peninsula
New York Palace
Carlyle
Pierre
Trump International
24 Plaza Athénée
Lowell
Mark
23 W Union Square

Alex Hotel ▽ 22 | 22 | 20 | 20 | $299

205 E. 45th St., Manhattan; 212-867-5100; fax 212-867-7878; www.thealexhotel.com; 73 rooms, 133 suites

David Rockwell is the designer behind this contemporary Midtown boutique with "au courant tech" amenities including LCD flat-panel TVs in every room ("a luxury in the bathroom") and WiFi in public areas, plus Frette linens and suites with kitchens; "on-the-ball" service and chef Marcus Samuelsson's modern Japanese cuisine at Ringo further the appeal of this "sure hit."

Algonquin Hotel Ⓗ 17 | 21 | 19 | 17 | $279

59 W. 44th St., Manhattan; 212-840-6800; fax 212-944-1419; 888-304-2047; www.algonquinhotel.com; 174 rooms, 24 suites

"Curl up in the lounge with a martini and some Dorothy Parker poetry" and "dream" of the literary Roundtable (which met here in the '20s) at this "classic" piece of "old NY" in a "terrific" Theater District location; so what if the "rooms are a bit tiny" – the place "exudes warmth" and is "steeped in history", from the Blue Bar, with waiters "almost as old as the hotel itself", to the Oak Room, "one of the best cabarets in town"; P.S. "renovations have increased its vintage feel."

Benjamin, The Ⓢ 23 | 22 | 16 | 19 | $319

125 E. 50th St., Manhattan; 212-715-2500; fax 212-715-2525; 888-423-6526; www.thebenjamin.com; 115 rooms, 94 suites

You'll "definitely get your zzzs" thanks to a pillow concierge and 11 types to choose from (down, buckwheat, jelly neckroll, etc.) coupled with Frette linens at this "classy" Midtown suite hotel; there's an on-site wellness center, a "courteous" staff that "knows guests' names" and "reasonable rates", but the rooms are "nothing to brag about"; N.B. a new restaurant, Ocean 50, opened in 2005.

Blakely, The – | – | – | – | $265

136 W. 55th St., Manhattan; 212-245-1800; fax 212-582-8332; www.blakelynewyork.com; 58 rooms, 42 suites

The hoteliers behind the Chambers and the Maritime take credit for this Midtown spot with classic cherry furnishings, in-room

WiFi, flat-screen TVs and DVD players, marble bathrooms, Frette cotton robes and complimentary *New York Times* delivery; a slick Italian restaurant, Abboccato (operated by owners of the well-known Molyvos), occupies a lobby-level spot.

Bryant Park, The 22 21 22 21 $335

40 W. 40th St., Manhattan; 212-869-0100; fax 212-869-4446; 877-640-9300; www.bryantparkhotel.com; 86 rooms, 42 suites

It's still a "fashionista hangout" with a "casually hip bar scene in the Cellar", but even non-cutting-edge types appreciate this Midtowner that's "close to everything" and lets you "live like a NYer" – or even better than most NYers, since it has loftlike spaces with "beautiful views of Bryant Park", "brilliant" marble bathrooms and "butlers on standby"; if you really get lucky, you might "see a Victoria's Secret show" during Fashion Week or snag reservations at the trendy new Japanese eatery, Koi.

CARLYLE, THE 25 27 24 23 $595

35 E. 76th St., Manhattan; 212-744-1600; fax 212-717-4682; 888-767-3966; www.thecarlyle.com; 122 rooms, 57 suites

Step into "a Cole Porter song" at this "aristocratic" Upper Eastsider that's "certain to impress" with its "gracious" staff, "tony" location and "residential feel" that "screams sophistication"; it's "great for star sighting" or "stashing your visiting girlfriend", and there's luxe French dining (brunch is "not to be missed") plus "top-class entertainment" – though the late Bobby Short is surely missed in Bemelmans Bar.

Chambers 22 22 25 20 $425

15 W. 56th St., Manhattan; 212-974-5656; fax 212-974-5657; 866-204-5656; www.chambersnyc.com; 72 rooms, 5 suites

You "feel like you're in a magazine ad" when you step into the "killer lobby" of this David Rockwell–designed Midtown boutique "where all the action is" – especially at chef Geoffrey Zakarian's "fantastic" New American restaurant, Town; "great attention to detail" extends to the "cool", "minimalist" rooms, which sport rain shower fixtures, Bumble & Bumble bath products and wireless Internet, and the "very sexy" late-night scene guarantees a truly "trendy NY experience."

City Club Hotel 19 19 22 16 $265

55 W. 44th St., Manhattan; 212-921-5500; fax 212-944-5544; www.cityclubhotel.com; 65 rooms

The "phenomenal" on-site restaurant, Daniel Boulud's db Bistro Moderne, is a big draw, but beyond that this three-year-old Midtown boutique draws mixed notices; critics cite "tiny" rooms that stress "form over function" and also knock "amateurish" service from a staff "obviously hired for looks"; nothing wrong with that, respond Gen-Xers who also like the "sexy bathrooms", "cool" TVs hidden in the mirror ("click and it appears") and "chic" color scheme.

Dream Hotel Ⓢ – – – – $429

210 W. 55th St., Manhattan; 212-247-2000; fax 212-974-0595; www.dreamny.com; 208 rooms, 20 suites

There's plenty of places to relax, maybe even daydream, at this Midtown newcomer from hotelier Vikram Chatwal and fashion surrealist David LaChapelle, since it's got an eclectic lobby lounge with a two-floor circular aquarium (largest in the Northeast), a separate colorfully striped bar, a rooftop respite, Ava Lounge, with 1950s French Riviera–inspired decor and the attached David Rockwell–designed Serafina restaurant with lots of outdoor seating; rooms have 300-thread-count Egyptian cotton linens, H2O toiletries, flat-screen plasma TVs and iPods to use around town, and the Chopra Center New York will open shortly.

Elysée, Hotel Ⓗ 21 | 24 | 18 | 19 | $225

60 E. 54th St., Manhattan; 212-753-1066; fax 212-980-9278; 800-535-9733; www.elyseehotel.com; 85 rooms, 16 suites

"If only home were so elegant" sigh old-schoolers smitten by this "romantic" European boutique built in the '20s in an "excellent" Midtown location; "gorgeous" interiors, complimentary breakfasts and evening hors d'oeuvres, a staff that "couldn't be nicer" and the "fun" Monkey Bar add up to an "exceptionally comfortable" stay; only a few sticklers suggest it's time for "another restoration."

Embassy Suites Hotel 23 | 21 | 16 | 21 | $209

102 North End Ave., Manhattan; 212-945-0100; fax 212-945-3012; 800-362-2779; www.newyorkcity.embsuites.com; 463 suites

"Spacious rooms with breathtaking views of the Hudson" and the Statue of Liberty are the highlight of this Battery Park City all-suite that's "one of the best values" for families (there's complimentary breakfast) and convenient for corporate types doing business "way Downtown"; access to the New York Sports Club facility "is a plus" and Bath & Body Works toiletries are a nice touch, just "beware" the multitude of "tour groups" and the "costly" cabs to Midtown.

Essex House Ⓢ 21 | 22 | 22 | 21 | $599

160 Central Park S., Manhattan; 212-247-0300; fax 212-315-1839; 800-937-8461; www.essexhouse.com; 469 rooms, 32 suites

It "feels like a private residence" if you stay at the St. Regis Club in this "old-school" hotel where the "views of Central Park are amazing" and the butler service is "too posh for words"; while a few find the regular rooms "dungeonlike", the location makes up for it, plus you can enjoy "some of the finest" dining in the city at Alain Ducasse, a bar that's straight out of a "'40s movie" and proximity to shopping at the new Time Warner Center.

FOUR SEASONS Ⓢ 28 | 28 | 26 | 27 | $625

57 E. 57th St., Manhattan; 212-758-5700; fax 212-758-5711; 800-487-3769; www.fourseasons.com; 305 rooms, 63 suites

"Towering above all the rest", this "stunning" I.M. Pei–designed "power" palace "in the center of the world" "sets the standard" as the No. 1–rated New York hotel in this *Survey*; seasoned travelers insist it's "nearly flawless" – "every need is quickly addressed", you'll "get the best sleep of your life" in the "unbelievably large" rooms (just don't "get lost in" the "exquisite" baths with Bulgari toiletries), and you'll find a celeb-studded "hopping bar scene" and "ultra-gourmet" fare at Fifty Seven Fifty Seven.

Gansevoort, Hotel Ⓢ ▽ 23 | 21 | 20 | 24 | $495

18 Ninth Ave., Manhattan; 212-206-6700; fax 212-255-5858; 877-426-7386; www.hotelgansevoort.com; 187 rooms, 20 suites, 1 duplex

A "fantastic location in Manhattan's hottest neighborhood" – the Meatpacking District – gives this "trendster" an edge; it's certainly "trying to be cool" with a "swanky design" featuring back-lit glass in changing colors, plasma TVs (even in the elevator), a "sleek" Japanese eatery, Ono, and that "amazing" landscaped rooftop lounge with a heated pool and 360-degree views (look down at the once-private goings-on atop the exclusive Soho House nearby); the only quibbles are "small" rooms and "noise" from the area's many hot restaurants; N.B. a spa opens in fall 2005.

Helmsley Park Lane 17 | 18 | 15 | 16 | $325

36 Central Park S., Manhattan; 212-521-6640; fax 212-750-7279; 800-221-4982; www.helmsleyparklane.com; 400 rooms, 195 suites

It's a good thing this "fabulously located" Midtown dowager has "out-of-this-world Central Park views" for a "great price" because many guests must avert their eyes from the "tattered" "shabbiness" of this "sagging" old girl that's so obviously in "need of a face-lift"; it may still have some "charm" despite "uptight" service, however, and you can expect "occasional sightings of Leona [Helmsley]."

Hudson 15 | 17 | 19 | 20 | $310

356 W. 58th St., Manhattan; 212-554-6000; fax 212-554-6001; 800-606-6090; www.morganshotelgroup.com; 773 rooms, 30 suites

There's a "continuous party" at this "throbbing" Columbus Circle hipster in the shadow of the new Time Warner Center, where the "starlike" clientele gravitates to the "hot scene" in the bar and "rooftop terrace"; though the "dramatic" modern design and "affordable" rates win fans, critics who are "so over renting a tiny closet from black-clad models" who act as though "the hotel got in the way of their nightclub" say this "thump-thump-thumper" is all about "fashion over function" for "extreme people-watchers."

Inn at Irving Place Ⓗ 26 | 26 | 18 | 19 | $330

56 Irving Pl., Manhattan; 212-533-4600; fax 212-533-4611; 800-685-1447; www.innatirving.com; 6 rooms, 5 suites

A "lovely inn" on one of Manhattan's most "elegant" streets, this Gramercy Park charmer set in a pair of 1834 townhouses is "perfect" for a "romantic weekend"; a "world-class" staff, one of the "best high teas" and proximity to great restaurants (Pure Food and Wine, Casa Mono) and historic bars (Pete's Tavern) help make this an "exquisite" member of Small Luxury Hotels of the World.

Iroquois 19 | 21 | 20 | 19 | $259

49 W. 44th St., Manhattan; 212-840-3080; fax 212-398-1754; 800-332-7220; www.iroquoisny.com; 105 rooms, 9 suites

Sometimes you just want to stay in the big city "without all the big city noise" and this "intimate" Midtown boutique in the Theater District (a member of Small Luxury Hotels of the World) does the trick with a "friendly" staff that's always "available to answer questions", a "great French restaurant, Triomphe", and a bar that serves up a mean Cosmopolitan; extras like free Internet service and morning coffee win points, but you'll have to "bring a shoehorn to get yourself into the small rooms."

Kitano, The 23 | 25 | 23 | 20 | $480

66 Park Ave., Manhattan; 212-885-7000; fax 212-885-7100; 800-548-2666; www.kitano.com; 131 rooms, 18 suites

Serenity-seekers applaud this "understated" Murray Hill "oasis" where the staff "treats you with fabled Japanese hospitality" and the overall "Zen" feeling is an antidote to "hectic Manhattan"; rooms have complimentary green tea, soundproofed windows and towel-warmers, and the main restaurant features kaiseki cuisine; business types "highly recommend it for off-site meetings", especially the rooftop space with views.

Le Parker Méridien ✗ Ⓢ 22 | 20 | 22 | 22 | $460
118 W. 57th St., Manhattan; 212-245-5000; fax 212-708-7471; 800-543-4300; www.parkermeridien.com; 510 rooms, 221 suites
"Wonderfully tasteful", "spacious" rooms, modern decor with "lots of flair" and "the best hotel gym in NYC" (with an enclosed rooftop pool boasting a "stunning" Central Park view) make this "well-run" Midtown choice "worth returning to"; maybe some hotels rate higher, but how many have "cartoons entertaining you in the elevator" and a $1,000 omelet on the "stand-out" breakfast menu (at Norma's)? P.S. "hidden in a corner" off the front desk is the "best little" "funky burger joint" around.

Library Hotel 22 | 25 | 19 | 23 | $315
299 Madison Ave., Manhattan; 212-983-4500; fax 212-499-9099; 877-793-7323; www.libraryhotel.com; 57 rooms, 3 suites
Finally, a Midtowner that "isn't cookie-cutter, yet affordable": this "bookish" boutique near the New York Public Library is a "bibliophile's heaven" with "really interesting decor" – floors are identified by Dewey Decimel System categories (e.g. philosophy, poetry) and the "quaint" if small rooms are filled with literary works related to that floor's theme; add a staff that "cares", complimentary evening wine and cheese and a "peaceful reading room" with fireplace, and you've found yourself a novel place to stay.

Lowell, The 26 | 28 | 23 | 20 | $555
28 E. 63rd St., Manhattan; 212-838-1400; fax 212-319-4230; 800-221-4444; www.lowellhotel.com; 21 rooms, 47 suites
The "discreet staff" provides stand-out service at this "small European" "classic" in a "quiet" East Side residential area; "don't be surprised" to see celebs enjoying an "anonymous" stay here, drawn by the "blue-blood" atmosphere, the "very good" Post House restaurant and the "wonderful" suites featuring fireplaces and "the best linens" (it's a "great place to have an affair").

MANDARIN ORIENTAL ✗ Ⓢ 27 | 26 | 26 | 28 | $655
80 Columbus Circle, Manhattan; 212-805-8800; fax 212-805-8882; 866-801-8880; www.mandarinoriental.com; 203 rooms, 48 suites
A "stupendous" hotel "befitting a world-class city", this "shining" Columbus Circle two-year-old in the Time Warner Center has all the makings of a "power" paragon: "priceless views" overlooking Central Park from the 35th-floor lobby lounge, a "spectacular" spa with private treatment suites, sleek "high-tech" rooms with plasma TVs in bedrooms and baths, the "fabulous", "sceney" Asiate restaurant and, of course, "extremely steep" prices; most agree it's already become a "must-see stop for the ultrachic."

Maritime Hotel, The Ⓗ 21 | 21 | 23 | 21 | $345
363 W. 16th St., Manhattan; 212-242-4300; fax 212-242-1188; www.themaritimehotel.com; 125 rooms, 4 suites
Scenesters dock at this "shipshape" Chelsea spot known for its "cool" nightlife and first-class "people-watching", whether in the

outdoor garden, the rooftop lounge, the lobby bars, the "fantastic" downstairs club, Hiro, or the "superb" Japanese restaurant, Matsuri; while the 1960s yacht look strikes some mates as "a little kitschy", most salute the "effortless elegance" in a design featuring porthole windows, teak furnishings and ocean-themed fabrics.

Mark, The 24 26 24 22 $510

25 E. 77th St., Manhattan; 212-744-4300; fax 212-744-2749; 800-843-6275; www.mandarinoriental.com; 124 rooms, 54 suites

Experience "classic elegance" at this Upper Eastsider that's a "low-key" respite from the city's mean streets; "top-notch service", "luxurious" neoclassical Italian rooms with "heated bathroom floors", a new chef, Jean-Pierre Bagnato, and a "wonderfully convenient" location turn this into "a favorite", at least for those on a "Rockefeller budget."

Marriott Brooklyn 20 20 18 21 $239

333 Adams St., Brooklyn; 718-246-7000; fax 718-246-0563; 800-843-4898; www.marriott.com; 355 rooms, 21 suites

Bridge hoppers attest to a "glorious" "alternative to Manhattan" at this "more affordable" borough hotel close to historic Brooklyn Heights; there are "comfortable" accommodations, a "spacious dining room with ethnic specialties" and decent service – and it's all a "quick cab" or "easy subway" ride to Downtown.

Marriott Marquis 19 18 17 20 $299

1535 Broadway, Manhattan; 212-398-1900; fax 212-704-8930; 800-843-4898; www.marriott.com; 1896 rooms, 50 suites

It's "bright lights, big city" at this Times Square colossus with a lobby that's as "bustling" as the "crowded" sidewalks outside; the location is prime "for tourists", especially Broadway buffs (there's even a theater inside), and the glass elevators provide a bit of a show (watch out for "legendary slow rides"); though it's "too big to get great service" and often turns into a "zoo"-like "convention central", you can't beat those "gorgeous views."

Mercer, The 23 21 26 20 $450

147 Mercer St., Manhattan; 212-966-6060; fax 212-965-3838; 888-918-6060; www.mercerhotel.com; 60 rooms, 15 suites

"The awesome food" at Jean-Georges Vongerichten's French-American Mercer Kitchen gets high marks at this "sleek" SoHo spot where "stylish" Hollywood hipsters and other lovers of "the luxe life" are attended to by a staff that "seems to know it's better dressed than you are"; "modern simplicity" reigns in rooms with Face Stockholm toiletries, and the "amazing" location is "smack in the middle" of the area's arty action, but doubters find "too much flash, trash and attitude" for the price.

Michelangelo, The 25 24 18 20 $395

152 W. 51st St., Manhattan; 212-765-1900; fax 212-541-6604; 800-237-0990; www.michelangelohotel.com; 143 rooms, 35 suites

The namesake artist "would be proud" of this "quiet" Italian-style "overlooked gem" in an "ideal location for Midtown theater and shopping"; it earns high marks from families for its "amazingly spacious rooms" with imported fabrics and cherry woods, and the complimentary breakfasts and "wonderful staff" are pluses, but the restaurant doesn't quite live up to the rest.

Millenium Hilton 23 | 20 | 16 | 21 | $199

55 Church St., Manhattan; 212-693-2001; fax 212-571-2316; www.hilton.com; 465 rooms, 100 suites

The "marvelous" rooms at this Downtown business hotel have "the most updated facilities" including 42-inch plasma TVs and wireless Internet access as well as "breathtaking views of the East River and Midtown" from higher floors, and the efficient staff "goes out of its way" to please; even though the restaurant needs help and a few are put off by the vendors and gawking tourists at the adjacent Ground Zero, this Hilton is staging "a great comeback."

Millennium UN Plaza 22 | 20 | 16 | 21 | $239

1 United Nations Plaza, Manhattan; 212-758-1234; fax 212-702-5051; 866-866-8086; www.millennium-hotels.com; 383 rooms, 44 suites

Bump into "ambassadors and United Nations staffers" at this "very hushed and refined" Eastsider that may be somewhat "out of the way" from major sights but has "knockout" city and river views from most rooms; the indoor pool and health club are "tops", there's an on-site tennis court and the staff couldn't be "more welcoming", but naysayers note a "frayed elegance" that makes it seem "a millennium old."

Muse, The 22 | 23 | 20 | 20 | $299

130 W. 46th St., Manhattan; 212-485-2400; fax 212-485-2900; 877-692-6873; www.themusehotel.com; 182 rooms, 18 suites

"Trendy" *and* "friendly"? – it's possible when you stay in this "unique" boutique in the Theater District where you're "part of the cool crowd" but there's "none of the New York attitude" from the "young, eager staff"; "small" rooms have "fabulous appointments" like feather beds (some have balconies), and there's a decent eatery, District – plus they even "welcome your four-legged friends."

NEW YORK PALACE Ⓗ Ⓢ 26 | 25 | 25 | 25 | $595

455 Madison Ave., Manhattan; 212-888-7000; fax 212-303-6000; 800-697-2522; www.newyorkpalace.com; 825 rooms, 73 suites

Royalists relish "old-world" style "done right" at this "flawlessly maintained" Midtown art deco palace that's "one of Manhattan's most elegant properties"; views of St. Patrick's Cathedral from the upper floors are "magnificent" (Tower rooms are "worth the splurge"), the full-service gym is "awesome" and the "exceptional concierge staff" makes "you want to return again and again" – just "bring the treasury" to settle the bill or look for weekend specials; N.B. the new on-site restaurant, Istana, offers room service.

Paramount 13 | 17 | 16 | 16 | $279

235 W. 46th St., Manhattan; 212-764-5500; fax 212-354-5237; 888-741-5600; www.solmelia.com; 582 rooms, 12 suites

The "cool" vibe is still there, even if Ian Schrager isn't (he's left the helm of Morgans Hotel Group), at this Theater District "rocker" with a "sleek" no-name entrance, "sceney bar" and "glam" lobby for "people-watching"; unfortunately, the staffers "think they're too cool to serve you" and when you see your "prison cell–size" quarters that critics find "more dated than funky" (they "belong back in 1995"), you may think "it's a joke" – but many patrons "like laughing along with them."

Park South Hotel ▽ 21 | 22 | 19 | 20 | $215

122 E. 28th St., Manhattan; 212-448-1024; fax 212-448-0811; www.parksouthhotel.com; 141 rooms

It's "one of those little secrets that's getting out" whisper fans of this "chic", "friendly" Murray Hill hotel where the "sophisticated" "matchbox"-size rooms have "great linens and amenities" and are "priced right"; it's "somewhat out of the way" for major sightseeing, but there's a "don't-miss" bar for fireside drinks at the on-site Black Duck restaurant.

PENINSULA, THE 26 | 26 | 23 | 26 | $625

700 Fifth Ave., Manhattan; 212-956-2888; fax 212-903-3949; 800-262-9467; www.peninsula.com; 185 rooms, 54 suites

For a "taste of the good life", check into this "exclusive" Midtown hotel with an "amazing spa", health club and pool as well as "plush", "state-of-the-art" rooms with bedside consoles to operate the TV, air-conditioning and lights; "outstanding", "understated" service means it's "excellent for business travelers" as well as celebs seeking anonymity, but if you can't take the "steep prices", just go for a rooftop cocktail at the Pen-Top Bar & Terrace – there's "nowhere better for sunset drinks" and views up Fifth Avenue.

Pierre New York, The 25 | 27 | 24 | 23 | $595

2 E. 61st St., Manhattan; 212-838-8000; fax 212-940-8109; 800-223-6800; www.tajhotels.com; 150 rooms, 52 suites

Soak up the "opulence" at this European "grande dame" with a "rich" address (across from Central Park) and "prices to match"; a post-*Survey* management switch from Four Seasons to the luxury India-based chain Taj Resorts will include a substantial renovation to what some have called the "antiquated beauty", but request a room on the park and you'll have an "excellent" stay.

Plaza Athénée, Hôtel 25 | 27 | 23 | 23 | $515

37 E. 64th St., Manhattan; 212-734-9100; fax 212-772-0958; 800-447-8800; www.plaza-athenee.com; 115 rooms, 35 suites

"Responsive" yet "understated" service is the highlight of this "discreet" Upper Eastsider, a "perfect-size" "gem"; "wonderfully luxurious" rooms with Belgian linens on the "most comfortable beds" win praise, and the on-site restaurant, Arabelle, is deemed "a hidden treasure" by admirers; Francophiles say it's "almost as good as being at its Paris sister" property.

Regency, The 25 | 23 | 20 | 21 | $419

540 Park Ave., Manhattan; 212-759-4100; fax 212-826-5674; 800-233-2356; www.loewshotels.com; 266 rooms, 85 suites

"Best for the business traveler" who can catch the legendary "power breakfast" and end the day "having a drink at the famous bar" ("a haunt for actors"), this Upper Eastsider is "unassuming" yet offers a "touch of elegance"; assets include "huge rooms" with "fluffy pillows", "consistent" service and a "gourmet menu for your pet", but light sleepers long for "thicker walls."

Renaissance 22 | 23 | 20 | 20 | $419

714 Seventh Ave., Manhattan; 212-765-7676; fax 212-765-1962; 800-468-3571; www.renaissancehotels.com; 305 rooms, 5 suites

"How rare to have a normal-size room in Times Square" say sojourners surprised by this property "hidden behind a wall of advertising" that's "much nicer inside than outside"; though it "overlooks the bright lights" and crowded streets, it's a "quiet" "oasis away from it all" and the restaurant "has views" of the neon.

Rihga Royal | 26 | 23 | 18 | 21 | $539

151 W. 54th St., Manhattan; 212-307-5000; fax 212-765-6530; 800-937-5454; www.rihgaroyalny.com; 504 suites

The "spacious" accommodations at this "economical" all-suite property are "perfect for families" who want to "spread out", and the Midtown location offers city views and convenience to theater and shopping; briefcase toters tout "solid concierges" and starstruck fans will find "lots of TV folks" to ogle, but critics contend "time has not been good" to this Royal and the want of a real restaurant ("Halcyon doesn't cut it") makes it a "near miss at true luxury"; N.B. a post-*Survey* ownership and management change to The Blackstone Group may have outdated some of the scores.

RITZ-CARLTON, BATTERY PARK Ⓢ | 27 | 27 | 23 | 25 | $475

2 West St., Manhattan; 212-344-0800; fax 212-344-3801; 800-241-3333; www.ritzcarlton.com; 254 rooms, 44 suites

Sure, it's "out of the way" for tourists ("as far south as you can go") unless they pine for "cool Statue of Liberty vistas" and proximity to Ellis Island ferries, but financial folks say this "classy" addition to Downtown has "everything you'd expect from a Ritz": "perfect service", "superb rooms" with Frette linens, aromatic bath menus and telescopes in the harborview category, a "spectacular rooftop terrace and raw bar" and a "delectable brunch"; P.S. "incredible weekend specials" can make the "long cab ride" worth it.

RITZ-CARLTON, CENTRAL PARK ✕ Ⓢ | 27 | 27 | 26 | 26 | $750

50 Central Park S., Manhattan; 212-308-9100; fax 212-207-8831; 800-241-3333; www.ritzcarlton.com; 213 rooms, 48 suites

Sink into this "serene enclave" in a "prime location" across from Central Park, where the "breathtaking" views from some rooms are as good as the "impeccable" service ("never wait for a cab, open a door or carry a bag"); "splurge for the best club level", and relish "fantastic" in-room touches such as telescopes, Bang & Olufsen stereos and flat-screen TVs; but it's the "excellent" Atelier (a post-*Survey* chef change to Alain Allegretti may outdate the above Dining score) and La Prairie spa that "make this hotel a must."

Royalton | 19 | 19 | 19 | 18 | $395

44 W. 44th St., Manhattan; 212-869-4400; fax 212-869-8965; 800-635-9013; www.morganshotelgroup.com; 169 rooms, 24 suites

It's all "sleek" and "glamorous" at this Times Square Morgans Hotel boutique with "ultracool" lobby furnishings, "tiny", "smartly designed" rooms and a publishing power scene in the restaurant 44; too bad this "epitome of '80s cool" is so "annoyingly dark" that you can't find your key, and the staff is "dripping with attitude."

70 Park Avenue | – | – | – | – | $519

70 Park Ave., Manhattan; 212-973-2400; fax 212-973-2401; www.70parkavenuehotel.com; 201 rooms, 4 suites

Finally, Kimpton comes to Manhattan with this Murray Hill style-setter designed by Jeffery Bilhuber; it boasts a lobby with a 14-ft.

limestone and sandstone fireplace, rooms with customized linens, distinctive artwork, 42-inch LCD flat-screen TVs and touchtone-screen telephones for ordering room service electronically (dog-friendly quarters feature gourmet treats and chew toys); business types will like the 17th-floor suite with wraparound terrace and chef Kevin Reilly's lobby-level Silverleaf Tavern.

Sherry-Netherland, The 24 | 25 | 22 | 21 | $465

781 Fifth Ave., Manhattan; 212-355-2800; fax 212-319-4306; 800-247-4377; www.sherrynetherland.com; 30 rooms, 23 suites

Loyalists love this "jewel" sparkling with "personal service" that includes "elevator operators in white gloves", "unbelievable amenities" (via Caswell Massey and Godiva), "fantastic views" of Central Park ("if you get the right room") and an interesting "power scene"; this must be "what it's like to be a millionaire" gush fans of this member of Small Luxury Hotels of the World.

60 Thompson 20 | 19 | 19 | 20 | $375

60 Thompson St., Manhattan; 212-431-0400; fax 212-431-0200; 877-431-0400; www.thompsonhotels.com; 98 rooms, 12 suites, 1 duplex

"Rub shoulders with the sexy" and "feel instantly cool" at this SoHo boutique where it's all about the "superb drinks" and "jammin' music" in the "loungey bar" (and guest-only rooftop deck); even if a few say the "cranky staff" is "full of itself" and they "had more room in their college dorm", they probably didn't have such "fabulous" marble baths and Fresh toiletries; P.S. the Thai eatery, Kittichai, gets "excellent" reviews.

Soho Grand Hotel 20 | 20 | 19 | 20 | $386

310 W. Broadway, Manhattan; 212-965-3000; fax 212-965-3200; 800-965-3000; www.sohogrand.com; 367 rooms, 2 penthouses

Hip, but "not so hip that it hurts", this "postmodern", pet-friendly Downtowner with a "phenomenal bar" has the right degree of "cool" to let you feel comfortable amid the "low couches, low lights" and limos; reviewers disagree on the grandness of rooms and service, however: quarters are either "chic" and "romantic" or "gloomy" "matchboxes" with "paper-thin" walls, and the staff is "friendly" or full of "attitude" if you aren't "glamorous"; good thing all agree that the "superb" SoHo location is the "real appeal."

ST. REGIS Ⓗ Ⓢ 27 | 28 | 24 | 25 | $760

2 E. 55th St., Manhattan; 212-753-4500; fax 212-787-3447; 800-759-7550; www.stregis.com; 221 rooms, 94 suites

So "this is how the other half lives" say awed admirers of this Midtown "gold standard" where the "gracious" staff includes private butlers who "take care of all your needs", the "regal" rooms include suites overlooking Fifth Avenue and the King Cole Bar is "one of the best" lounges in the city (it was voted the top hotel bar in our *NYC Nightlife Survey*); though some say the "ornate" "elegance" of this 1904 beaux arts beauty is "not for everyone", to many it's simply the "crème de la crème", "if you can afford it."

Swissôtel - The Drake Ⓢ 20 | 22 | 17 | 19 | $575

440 Park Ave., Manhattan; 212-421-0900; fax 212-371-4190; 800-637-9477; www.swissotel.com; 387 rooms, 108 suites

This "too-often-overlooked" Midtown East "jewel" is a "model business hotel" with "pristine", "comfy" rooms (though "quality can vary"), "refined" decor, a "delightful bar", "Swiss-like efficiency" and a "perfect location" (it's "a treat" to visit Fauchon next door); if you ignore the "mediocre" restaurant, you'll find a "solid" value.

Tribeca Grand Hotel 21 20 19 20 $379

2 Sixth Ave., Manhattan; 212-519-6600; fax 212-519-6700; 877-519-6600; www.tribecagrand.com; 203 rooms, 7 suites

Stay here "to be noticed" or to spot celebs advise admirers of the "hot bar scene" at this "stylish" pet-friendly TriBeCa boutique (sister to the Soho Grand); rooms are "modern", but on weekends "the music pumps" so loudly you'll think you're "sleeping in a club", and while "brunch is a must-do" as is the outdoor grill restaurant in warmer weather, demanding types sniff "you can't fool me – take away the fluff and there's an Embassy Suites underneath."

Trump International Hotel & Tower Ⓢ 24 24 26 24 $645

1 Central Park W., Manhattan; 212-299-1000; fax 212-299-1150; 888-448-7867; www.trumpintl.com; 167 suites

Apprentice acolytes and business types trumpet this Upper Westsider with a "marvelous" French restaurant, Jean Georges, (voted the top hotel dining spot in our *NYC Restaurant Survey*) and all the "golden" "glamour" you'd expect from The Donald; you "can't beat the Central Park view rooms" with "enormous closets" nor those with a kitchen ("they're more like apartments"), and "even if you're in jeans they treat you warmly"; plus, the "dream location" on Columbus Circle puts you across from the new Time Warner Center and six blocks from Lincoln Center.

WALDORF-ASTORIA & TOWERS Ⓗ Ⓢ 22 23 21 22 $599

301 Park Ave., Manhattan; 212-355-3000; fax 212-872-7272; 800-925-3673; www.waldorfastoria.com; 1175 rooms, 250 suites

The "timeless" art deco "charm" of this "grand" "old lady" isn't lost on her many "dazzled" defenders who declare "everyone should stay here once", particularly in the more exclusive Towers (like "living in a Fitzgerald novel"); the "formal service", "lovely lobby", "elegant rooms" and "fabulous Midtown location" is enough to win over many, but others find the main hotel "weary"; N.B. the Bull and Bear restaurant has finished a major renovation.

Westin New York 24 21 19 22 $399

270 W. 43rd St., Manhattan; 212-201-2700; fax 212-201-2701; 800-451-0455; www.westinny.com; 863 rooms, 27 suites

Times Square travelers tout the "huge", "modern" rooms with "fantastic" Hudson River views, "Heavenly beds", "super showers" and flat-screen TVs at this chainster whose "incredible renovation" resulted in "crisp", "chic" decor; food-lovers frown on the blah food and it's a "downer" to "pay for use of the fitness facility", but the "friendly front desk" and "location" are "selling points."

W New York Ⓢ 16 19 19 19 $429

541 Lexington Ave., Manhattan; 212-755-1200; fax 212-319-8344; 877-946-8357; www.whotels.com; 628 rooms, 60 suites

It's a toss-up as to whether you'll find this "stylish Midtown" outpost "one of the coolest hotels" ever or just "terminally hip" and "overhyped"; if you're "under 30", a "poser" or looking for a "sleek" bar scene with "celeb-spotting galore", then it "doesn't disappoint"; but if you tire of "wannabe models acting snooty", lighting so "dim" you "wonder what they're hiding" and "cubicle-size" rooms (don't "trip over the bed" when you enter) then "think twice" before checking in; N.B. check out the on-site Bliss spa.

W The Court | 22 | 22 | 17 | 19 | $549 |

130 E. 39th St., Manhattan; 212-685-1100; fax 212-889-0287; 877-946-8357; www.whotels.com; 166 rooms, 33 suites

"Much more spacious" than the W on Lexington say fans of this Murray Hill sister with "thankfully larger" (though still "shoebox"-size) quarters featuring "endless amenities" and "heavenly beds"; there's the expected "hopping bar", "dark lobby" and "clientele in black", but there's "less attitude" from the "good-looking staff"; hmm, maybe "overdone" hipness can be comfortable.

W Times Square Ⓢ | 21 | 20 | 21 | 21 | $429 |

1567 Broadway, Manhattan; 212-930-7400; fax 212-930-7500; 888-625-5144; www.whotels.com; 464 rooms, 43 suites

W worshipers dig the late-night "throbbing" scene at this four-year-old outpost where the "black clothes" and "beautiful people" are as plentiful as the "amazing drinks"; but "paper-thin walls" mean it's "as noisy inside as Times Square is outside", the "phone booth"–size bathrooms have showers without curtains, and the "aloof staff" scatters "attitude" everywhere; at least most can agree on Blue Fin restaurant for "fantastic" seafood.

W Union Square | 24 | 23 | 23 | 23 | $549 |

201 Park Ave. S., Manhattan; 212-253-9119; fax 212-253-9229; 877-946-8357; www.whotels.com; 254 rooms, 16 suites

An "awesome" Union Square location (don't miss the "great Farmer's Market" and lively Park scene) gives this property an "edge" over its Midtown siblings; there's still the requisite "too-hip bar" (Underbar) and a "cooler-than-thou" crowd in the lobby lounge (with floor-to-ceiling windows), but there's also an "exemplary staff", Todd English's "amazing" Olives restaurant and "larger than average" rooms, so this is the "best of the NYC" W bunch.

Westchester

CASTLE ON THE HUDSON, THE | 25 | 25 | 27 | 23 | $340 |

400 Benedict Ave., Tarrytown; 914-631-1980; fax 914-631-4612; 800-616-4487; www.castleonthehudson.com; 31 rooms, 5 suites

Castle connoisseurs say this small but "magical" Hudson River resort (a member of Small Luxury Hotels of the World) will take you "back in time" while treating you very well in the present, what with its "fantastic rooms", "attentive service", tennis and bocce courts and "spectacular Equus restaurant"; add a "creative landscape" and water views, and it equals a "romantic getaway for overworked NYers" – just be "sure to bring your wallet."

Renaissance Westchester | 20 | 20 | 17 | 21 | $239 |

80 W. Red Oak Ln., White Plains; 914-694-5400; fax 914-694-5616; 888-236-2427; www.renaissancehotels.com; 343 rooms, 7 suites

In an area with "limited choices", you can hit "a bull's-eye" at this "quiet" Westchester option (35 minutes from NYC); with a "lovely mountainous" setting, a "country-club" feel and "pleasant" rooms, it's suitable "for a corporate retreat", but the "standard coffee shop–type restaurant" could use a renaissance of its own.

North Carolina

Asheville

Greystone Inn, The Ⓗ Ⓢ ▽ 21 | 19 | 21 | 21 | $380

Greystone Ln., Lake Toxaway; 828-966-4700; fax 828-862-5689; 800-824-5766; www.greystoneinn.com; 33 rooms

"A touch of class in the mountains" yodel loyalists of this 90-year-old Swiss-style six-story country inn on Lake Toxaway, near Asheville, that was once the mansion home of local luminary Lucy Moltz and is now a "posh", all-meals-included retreat on the National Register of Historic Places; this getaway pampers guests with a full-service spa, a 20-acre Tom Fazio–designed golf course, tennis courts, a champagne cruise and antiques-filled rooms.

Grove Park Inn Resort & Spa, The Ⓗ Ⓢ 20 | 22 | 22 | 26 | $195

290 Macon Ave.; 828-252-2711; fax 828-253-7053; 800-438-5800; www.groveparkinn.com; 500 rooms, 10 suites

Catch the "old-world vibes" at this "very earthy", "classic" 1913 granite stone "beauty" set in an "idyllic location" overlooking the skyline and "romantic Blue Ridge Mountains"; "dining on the veranda is spectacular", plus there's a "great conference center" – yes, it "gets better with age, especially as they continue to add enjoyable amenities" like the "elaborate spa" and health club.

INN ON BILTMORE Ⓗ 27 | 24 | 25 | 26 | $309

1 Approach Rd.; 828-225-1660; fax 828-225-1629; 800-624-1575; www.biltmore.com; 205 rooms, 8 suites

"Blue Ridge heaven" is yours at this "grand hotel destination" with "world-class accommodations", the place to turn in "after your poor little legs have explored" George Vanderbilt's sprawling Biltmore estate and "your whole body needs pampering"; "you'll feel like a Vanderbilt" too with "to-die-for bedding", "outstanding food" and "European-style service", plus golf, health club facilities and an unusual round pool with "marvelous vistas."

RICHMOND HILL INN ✕ 25 | 26 | 27 | 23 | $255

87 Richmond Hill Dr.; 828-252-7313; fax 828-252-8726; 888-742-4536; www.richmondhillinn.com; 33 rooms, 3 suites

It's a "mountain paradise" sigh those smitten by the "homey perfection" of this "magical" inn near the Biltmore Estate; the "superb" on-site restaurant, Gabrielle's, serves "sublime" regional cuisine, the service "sure aims to please" and the "perennial gardens" and grounds are "immaculately maintained."

Swag, The – | – | – | – | $565

2300 Swag Rd., Waynesville; 828-926-0430; fax 828-926-2036; 800-789-7672; www.elegantsmallhotel.com; 10 rooms, 5 cabins

Get back in touch with nature at this "very special" "escape", a rustic "jewel" surrounded by 250 acres "literally next door" to the Great Smoky Mountains National Park; owner "Deener Matthews is wonderful" proclaim proponents who get in the swing of "paradise" with birding, hiking and relaxing in accommodations offering panoramic views; N.B. prices include all meals.

Chapel Hill

Carolina Inn, The Ⓗ 20 | 22 | 20 | 21 | $149

211 Pittsboro St.; 919-933-2001; fax 919-962-3400; 800-962-8519; www.carolinainn.com; 169 rooms, 15 suites

Has a place "in my Rolodex for unequaled Southern hospitality" admit acolytes of this circa-1924 plantation-style "grande dame" that's "on the National Register of Historic Places for obvious reasons"; "you can't beat the location" near the University of North Carolina (it's UNC-owned) "for a football weekend" when it attracts "lots of action in the Pine Room bar"; "rooms are cheerful", and that "chocolate-chip cookie upon arrival sure is nice."

FEARRINGTON HOUSE COUNTRY INN, THE 28 | 27 | 29 | 26 | $220

2000 Fearrington Village Ctr., Pittsboro; 919-542-2121; fax 919-542-4202; www.fearrington.com; 22 rooms, 11 suites

"A must if you're in the triangle", Relais & Châteaux's "little piece of heaven" on farmland dating back to the 1700s is "comfortably off the beaten track" of Chapel Hill and makes you "think you're in the English countryside"; a "pampering staff" sets the "lovely" stage for a "hospitable" stay, so "unwind luxuriously" in your antiques-filled room with heated towel racks, then head down for a "fantastic dinner" "topped off" with "mouthwatering chocolate soufflé"; P.S. "afternoon tea with goodies" and breakfast are included.

Siena Hotel 21 | 22 | 23 | 19 | $195

1505 E. Franklin St.; 919-929-4000; fax 919-968-8527; 800-223-7379; www.sienahotel.com; 79 rooms, 12 suites

An "oasis in the busy triangle" area, this "comfortable" "Carolina retreat" a mile and a half from Downtown offers European-style "luxury in an unlikely locale"; fans fall for the "wonderful rooms", many decorated with ornate gilded mirrors and marble-top desks, and "turndown service that's an added treat", but a few declare the decor has "a little too much flair"; P.S. the on-site Il Palio serves "some of the best Italian cuisine south of the Mason-Dixon line."

Washington Duke Inn 23 | 23 | 22 | 24 | $289

3001 Cameron Blvd., Durham; 919-490-0999; fax 919-688-0105; 800-443-3853; www.washingtondukeinn.com; 146 rooms, 7 suites

"Location is the prime asset" of this "entirely comfortable" "gem" just a "stone's throw from Duke's West campus"; expect "wonderful service" – along with a "handsome bar", "great restaurant" and "nicely appointed rooms" overlooking the "gorgeous golf course"; N.B. new rooms, a conference center and a pool were just added.

Charlotte

Ballantyne ▽ 24 | 24 | 18 | 28 | $259

10000 Ballantyne Commons Pkwy.; 704-248-4000; fax 704-248-4005; 866-248-4824; www.ballantyneresort.com; 200 rooms, 12 suites

"Shines with Southern hospitality" attest touters of this "sprawling", "impressive facility" in a "beautiful country-club setting" in South Charlotte; "everything is perfect", from the rooms decked out with damask curtains and marble baths to the "great" "full-service spa and up-to-date amenities" replete with an indoor grotto pool and his-and-hers saunas; an 18-hole golf course, private tennis lessons and loads of dining and lounge options, including the Veranda bar in the mahogany lobby, further explain why "people would want to vacation in the suburbs."

Park Hotel, The ▽ 21 | 23 | 20 | 19 | $169

2200 Rexford Rd.; 704-364-8220; fax 704-365-4712; 800-334-0331; www.theparkhotel.com; 188 rooms, 8 suites

"So what if it's not Downtown? great rooms", "top-notch service", a "sensible price" and an "ideal location near the outdoor shopping plaza" make this "intimate" South Park spot "quite attractive" to the business crowd, providing "all the amenities a traveler needs while away from home", from 25-inch TVs to residential-like furnishings; but the less-impressed find it "provincial" and a little too close to home stylewise.

Westin Charlotte 25 | 20 | 20 | 25 | $159

601 S. College St.; 704-375-2600; fax 704-375-2623; 800-937-8461; www.westin.com; 678 rooms, 22 suites

"Swanky", "hip, trendy" with a "location that's handy for strolling in Uptown", this John Portman–designed tower exemplifies modern luxury with its "contemporary exterior and understated interiors"; it's a "real find for those traveling to the Queen City", seducing admirers with a "dramatic, lofty lobby area", "elaborately furnished" rooms with "all the electronic toys" and an "amazing gym"; just a few feel that it's "lacking diningwise."

Outer Banks

Sanderling, The ▽ 24 | 24 | 22 | 25 | $254

1461 Duck Rd., Duck; 252-261-4111; fax 252-261-1352; 800-701-4111; www.thesanderling.com; 88 rooms, 4 villas

For a bit of "Cape Cod on the Outer Banks", head to this "elegant, small-scale resort in a remote location" with secluded beaches, "impeccable grounds", a full-service spa overlooking the Atlantic and Currituck Sound, plus three "gorgeous", cedar-shingled inns and oceanside villas equipped with kitchenettes and porches; dining options – including the restored historic Lifesaving Station, with its nautical memorabilia – are also worth dropping anchor for.

Pinehurst

Pinehurst Resort Ⓗ Ⓢ 20 | 23 | 21 | 27 | $158

1 Carolina Vista Dr.; 910-295-6811; fax 910-295-8503; 800-487-4653; www.pinehurst.com; 230 rooms, 25 suites, 30 villas, 40 condos

"Golf is king" at this "fabulous property" on "spectacular grounds" where the "courses provide the ultimate in variation"; for an "unmatched experience", stay in the historic Carolina hotel, restored Holly Inn, the Manor Inn or a villa and "enjoy a wonderful dinner" finished with a "cognac on the porch"; the "rejuvenating" spa gives the "non-golfing spouse an outlet" ("and bring your whites or no croquet for you!") – indeed, it has "so much charm you might forget" the "rooms are smaller than a putting green."

Ohio

Cincinnati

Cincinnatian Hotel, The ✗Ⓗ 23 | 24 | 23 | 22 | $148

601 Vine St.; 513-381-3000; fax 513-651-0256; 800-942-9000; www.cincinnatianhotel.com; 139 rooms, 7 suites

"The best hotel in Cincinnati" may be this "formal" 1882 grande dame Downtown, where the "polite" staff delivers "old-fashioned, honest service"; the "well-appointed rooms", while a bit "small" and "quaint", are "first class", and the "eclectic" cuisine at The Palace restaurant is "tops", so when you're "in Reds country", it's the only "place to go, dahling."

Hilton Cincinnati Netherland Plaza Ⓢ ▽ 18 | 21 | 19 | 21 | $224

35 W. Fifth St.; 513-421-9100; fax 513-421-4291; 800-774-1500; www.hilton.com; 461 rooms, 100 suites

Admirers of this "deco heaven", a 1931 hotel with a "great location near Fountain Square" and the Carew Tower mall Downtown appreciate the "exquisite artwork" in its "spectacular public areas" and a solid staff; too bad many of the "European-style rooms" "are minuscule."

Westin 20 | 19 | 15 | 20 | $239

21 E. Fifth St.; 513-621-7700; fax 513-852-5670; 888-625-5144; www.westin.com; 432 rooms, 18 suites

Business travelers make tracks to this Downtown hotel where the "airy" rooms have river views and "Heavenly beds" that "rock" (figuratively, of course); the "friendly staff" keeps things humming, and the 17th-floor pool, high-speed Internet access and Kinko's on-site (open 24 hours) please road warriors, too; still, the "shopping complex location" at Fountain Square feels a bit "antiseptic."

Cleveland

Hyatt Regency at the Arcade ⒽⓈ ▽ 22 | 18 | 16 | 21 | $179

420 Superior Ave.; 216-575-1234; fax 216-575-1690; 800-233-1234; www.hyatt.com; 293 rooms

Combining a "stunning" 1890 arcade, modeled after Milan's Vittorio Emanuele, with two contemporary towers, this "brilliant" conversion of "a Cleveland landmark" is "not your typical Hyatt"; with its "comfortable rooms", "upgraded gym" and WiFi access, it's a good choice for "business travelers", especially those who appreciate "a bit of character."

Renaissance ✗ ▽ 22 | 20 | 24 | 21 | $199

24 Public Sq.; 216-696-5600; fax 216-696-0432; 800-468-3571; www.renaissancehotels.com/CLEBR; 441 rooms, 49 suites

From the "superior Sans Souci restaurant" (serving modern Mediterranean fare) to the "terrific mahogany bar" and the "elegant lobby", this "old-world hotel" is "a beautiful setting from which to plan your adventures"; staffed by a "knowledgeable" crew, it's "conveniently located near the Downtown action", "adjacent to Tower City shopping", and while the rooms "could use some updating", many have views of Lake Erie.

Ritz-Carlton, The | 24 | 26 | 24 | 22 | $219 |

1515 W. Third St.; 216-623-1300; fax 216-623-1492; 800-241-3333; www.ritzcarlton.com; 180 rooms, 27 suites

With "amazing service", "elegant, understated" decor and first-rate New American fare in the Century Restaurant, this "classy" joint "never fails to impress" or to "live up to the Ritz reputation"; the Downtown location is handy for business, and when work is done, "afternoon tea is a wonderful pleasure", as is a swim in the indoor pool or a visit to the club-level lounge.

Walden Country Inn & Stables | – | – | – | – | $270 |

1119 Aurora Hudson Rd., Aurora; 330-562-5508; fax 330-562-8001; www.waldenco.com; 24 suites

For farmhouse luxe, head to this getaway 40 minutes from Downtown Cleveland where the modern buildings are set up around a 175-year-old barn and silo amid 1,000 picturesque acres; glass walls allow for lots of natural light and views of rolling fields and roaming horses (there's an equestrian center for riding), and a full lineup of en-suite spa services are available, as are tee times for the nearby Walden golf course; The Barn fine-dining, dinner-only restaurant features New American cuisine.

Grand Rapids

Kerr House | – | – | – | – | $695 |

17777 Beaver St.; 419-832-1733; fax 419-832-4303; www.thekerrhouse.com; 5 rooms

A full-service health spa in a Victorian-style B&B, this indulgent retreat in a small town southwest of Toledo pampers only six to eight guests at a time; after you start your day with breakfast in bed, massages, aerobics, workshops, yoga and more keep you busy till an all-natural candlelight dinner; no need to worry about dressing up – comfort's the key in this sybaritic setting.

Oklahoma

Bartlesville

Inn at Price Tower | – | – | – | – | $125 |

510 Dewey Ave.; 918-336-1000; fax 918-336-7117; 877-424-2424; www.pricetower.org; 18 rooms, 3 suites

"Dramatic two-story suites" and "renovated rooms" "pay homage" to Frank Lloyd Wright at this hotel housed in the only skyscraper that he ever designed; the guestrooms, located on the building's top seven floors, include platform beds, Internet access, views of the Oklahoma plains and turndown service; but critics are less than bowled over by the "claustrophobia-inducing bathrooms."

Oklahoma City

Waterford Marriott | ▽ 21 | 21 | 19 | 21 | $159 |

6300 Waterford Blvd.; 405-848-4782; fax 405-843-9161; 800-228-9290; www.marriott.com; 166 rooms, 31 suites

The "long overdue face-lift has begun" (to a tune of $4.8 million) at this "classy" hotel located in an "upscale" "suburban" area of

Oklahoma City, offering amenities such as 8,000 feet of meeting space, a "terrific health club" and an outdoor pool; now that the "shopworn" digs are being taken of, foodies suggest that the "restaurant needs help", too.

Oregon

Black Butte

Black Butte Ranch ▽ 20 | 21 | 21 | 27 | $130

12930 Hawks Beard, Black Butte Ranch; 541-595-6211; fax 541-595-6211; 800-452-7455; www.blackbutteranch.com; 126 condos

About 13 miles from the Hoodoo ski area, this "family-oriented" "vacation place" "has anything someone could hope for: peace, quiet, pools", tennis and a butte-ful restaurant showcasing "excellent food" and some of "the best mountain views ever"; "if you love the outdoors", it's "a great place to experience it" as the hiking and fishing on the "awesome grounds" are "fantastic", plus there are newly renovated on-site golf courses and more greens in the nearby town of Sisters.

Crater Lake National Park

Crater Lake Lodge Ⓗ – | – | – | – | $129

1211 Avenue C, White City; 541-830-8700; fax 541-830-8514; www.craterlakelodges.com; 17 lodges

Perched on the rim of Crater Lake, this 1920s lodge was completely rebuilt about 10 years ago and boasts unparalleled views of the water and the Cascade Mountain Range; the Great Hall still has an original stone fireplace, some of the rooms feature claw-foot tubs and Northwest fare is served in the main dining room.

Gleneden Beach

Salishan Lodge Ⓢ 23 | 22 | 22 | 23 | $159

7760 Hwy. 101 N.; 541-764-2371; fax 541-764-3510; 800-725-4742; www.salishan.com; 202 rooms, 3 suites

A "harmonious setting perfect for a getaway", this "secluded" spot "captures the best of the Oregon Coast" with "romantic fireplaces" in every room, "exceptional food and wine" and "the nicest staff you'll ever find"; putters also deem it a "golfer's paradise" boasting an "awesome", "uncrowded course" with old-growth timber or seaside bluffs at every turn; N.B. a multimillion-dollar renovation, including a new fitness center and spa, was finished post-*Survey.*

Gold Beach

Tu Tu' Tun Lodge ▽ 28 | 29 | 29 | 27 | $235

96550 N. Bank Rogue; 541-247-6664; fax 541-247-0672; 800-864-6357; www.tututun.com; 16 rooms, 2 suites, 2 houses

This is the "real Nature Channel" laud loyalists of this remote, "romantic", contemporary cedar-planked lodge on the banks of the Rogue River, seven miles inland from the ocean; "five-star" amenities "in the middle of the wilderness" await, including hot tubs, woodburning fireplaces and balconies with "great views", plus the "extremely helpful owners and staff" arrange "amazing" white-water boat trips, salmon fishing and hiking expeditions, so no one minds "no TVs in the rooms"; P.S. although "memorable even in the off-season" (November–April), the "awesome dining" room is only open during the peak months.

Hood River

Columbia Gorge Hotel 22 | 24 | 25 | 24 | $199

4000 Westcliff Dr.; 541-386-5566; fax 541-387-9141; 800-345-1921; www.columbiagorgehotel.com; 33 rooms, 4 suites

Boasting a "fairy-tale" setting on the Columbia River, this historic pet-friendly country inn an hour east of Portland "may be the most romantic spot for a hotel ever"; while opinions are split over the rooms – "beautifully decorated with huge, overstuffed beds" vs. a "bit smallish" – "you can't beat the views" of the garden and waterfall; indeed, "it's got location" "in spades", plus "the warmth of the staff is without equal", there's a complimentary nightly champagne and caviar social and a "mammoth" breakfast.

Mount Bachelor

Sunriver Resort 22 | 22 | 22 | 26 | $199

1 Center Dr., Sunriver; 541-593-1000; fax 541-593-5458; 800-801-8765; www.sunriver-resort.com; 128 rooms, 75 suites, 33 lodges

A "treat, pure and simple", "with so much to do anytime of the year", this "gorgeous" resort bordered by the Cascade Mountains boasts an "astounding view that makes you feel like you're a million miles away from the hustle-bustle"; accommodations range from deluxe lodge rooms to condos to vacation home rentals – "perfect for a family" – and "kids and parents love the activities", including skiing at Mt. Bachelor and horseback riding; a "fun little village" nearby adds to the appeal.

Mount Hood

Timberline Lodge 17 | 20 | 21 | 25 | $140

Hwy. 26, Timberline Lodge; 503-622-7979; fax 503-272-3311; 800-547-1406; www.timberlinelodge.com; 60 rooms

"How can you pull up" to this "rustic old lodge" at the base of Mt. Hood, the "cliffside" home of Bruno, the "charming host St. Bernard", and "not imagine" *The Shining,* which was partly shot on this "amazing" property's grounds (note: the "drive is not for the faint of heart"); "expect a camp feel and you'll have a wonderful experience" at this "atmospheric" National Historic Landmark with a three-story fireplace, "family-size rooms", "artisan detail work", a "staff that bends over backwards" and a "wonderful restaurant."

Portland

Avalon Hotel & Spa ∇ 23 | 24 | 21 | 25 | $169

455 SW Hamilton Ct.; 503-802-5800; fax 503-802-5820; 888-556-4402; www.avalonhotelandspa.com; 81 rooms, 18 suites

This "quiet little" modern boutique hotel, boasting a location on the river off the beaten path of Portland, features deluxe rooms along with one- and two-bedroom suites, all sporting panoramic views of the nature sanctuary across the Willamette (with Mt. Hood in the background); but sybarites suggest the hostelry's greatest asset is the "fabulous" spa.

Benson Hotel, The Ⓗ🐕🎮Ⓢ 20 23 22 19 $160

309 SW Broadway; 503-228-2000; fax 503-471-3920; 888-523-6766; www.bensonhotel.com; 280 rooms, 7 penthouses

"When a celeb" or a president pulls into Portland, "chances are they're staying at" this "hoity-toity" "granddaddy" Downtown landmark built by lumber baron Simon Benson and architect A.E. Doyle in 1912; even though it's pet-friendly, "nothing beats the ambiance" of the "beautifully restored" "gracious" lobby, with "magnificent wood paneling throughout", the "gigantic staircase" and the "terrific dining room"; if cynics find it's "riding on its historic-ness", most rejoin "the ol' legend lives on."

5th Avenue Suites Hotel Ⓗ🐕Ⓢ 24 24 21 21 $179

506 SW Washington; 503-222-0001; fax 503-222-0004; 888-207-2201; www.5thavenuesuites.com; 82 rooms, 139 suites

"Even if it were twice the price", this "pet-friendly" Kimpton Downtowner would still be among the "best places to stay in town" agree admirers who slap high fives in appreciation of this 1912 landmark's "good value", "delicious" buttercup and apricot decor and "gracious staff" (though service is "spotty" to some); there's a nightly wine tasting party, an on-site Aveda spa and dining at the Red Star Tavern next door.

Governor Hotel, The Ⓗ🎮 ∇ 20 19 21 18 $219

614 SW 11th Ave.; 503-224-3400; fax 503-241-2122; 800-554-3456; www.govhotel.com; 56 rooms, 44 suites

Although this "delightful", "well-furnished" address on the National Register of Historic Places turns heads for its "impressive" turn-of-the-century lobby, it "also offers surprisingly "comfortable" rooms for a circa-1909 hotel, complete with "wonderful balconies" offering Downtown views, "excellent service", a fitness center, the popular American bistro Jake's Grill and a great location for museums, shopping and attractions.

Heathman Hotel, The ✕Ⓗ🐕🎮 21 25 25 21 $169

1001 SW Broadway; 503-241-4100; fax 503-790-7111; 800-551-0011; www.heathmanhotel.com; 117 rooms, 33 suites

"You can't beat this old clubby" "classic" for food or ambiance or its "ideal" Downtown location next to the Portland Center for the Performing Arts; "rooms are compact", "but interesting", with the "feel of home away from home" thanks to a "terrific inventory of free in-room movies" and "French-press coffeemakers", while "service is wonderful or amateurish, but always heartfelt"; have a drink in the "happening" bar with live entertainment or head to the Heathman restaurant for "epicurean delights."

Hilton 18 20 17 19 $169

921 SW Sixth Ave.; 503-226-1611; fax 503-220-2565; www.hilton.com; 771 rooms, 11 suites

Guests are mixed about this "business travelers' hotel" that's "well situated for touring the main interests of Portland"; praise goes to the "very service-oriented" staff ("treated me as if I were a VIP and I'm not") and "top-of-the-line suites" – "get a room with a view of Pioneer Square"; but it can be "confusing" as there are "two separate towers, a block apart": the Executive Tower has "boutique-style accommodations" while the older building houses an "impressive fitness center" but rooms that "disappoint."

Lucia, Hotel ▽ 20 | 19 | 23 | 19 | $170
400 SW Broadway; 503-225-1717; fax 503-225-1919; 877-225-1717; 119 rooms, 8 suites
Arguably "the hippest hotel in Portland", Kimpton's "swank boutique" address makes a big impression despite its "tiny but well-equipped" accommodations with high-speed Internet access and "plush beds"; "the bathrooms are absurdly small" ("can barely wash your face"), and the rooms are dogged by mysterious "loud, mechanical noises" that suggest it may "still be working out the kinks"; still, it makes up for any shortcomings with Typhoon next door, a "great Thai" restaurant and "personable service."

RiverPlace Hotel 24 | 22 | 21 | 22 | $189
1510 SW Harbor Way; 503-228-3233; fax 503-295-6190; 800-227-1333; www.riverplacehotel.com; 74 rooms, 10 suites
This "subtly elegant" European-style hotel with a "perfect location" on Portland's waterfront overlooking the Willamette River, marina and residential neighborhood offers "very comfortable", "generously sized rooms" with oak and teak furniture and an accommodating "concierge that goes out of his way with directions"; P.S. new owners have completed a major "needed renovation" post-*Survey*, and have unveiled the new Three Degrees Restaurant with outdoor harborside dining.

Vintage Plaza, Hotel Ⓢ 21 | 21 | 20 | 18 | $169
422 SW Broadway; 503-228-1212; fax 503-417-3386; 800-263-2305; www.vintageplaza.com; 107 rooms, 9 suites
Bringing both "old-world charm" and a "wine-country vibe to Downtown Portland" (with "cute vineyard names on the rooms" and the free nightly vino tastings in the lobby), Kimpton's boutique business hotel, "just a block from city shopping", is a "fine place to stay"; "abundant delights" include "cozy" accommodations, replete with "huge bathrooms" outfitted with deep-soak tubs (observe the "unique starview rooms" with solarium windows), a "welcoming staff" and "casual dining" at Italian restaurant Pazzo.

Westin 23 | 20 | 16 | 19 | $299
750 SW Alder St.; 503-294-9000; fax 503-241-9565; 888-627-8401; www.westin.com; 188 rooms, 17 suites
"Feels more like a boutique hotel than a giant" chain agree admirers of this "dependable" Downtowner with rooms boasting those "cloudlike", "crowd-pleasing 'Heavenly' beds" and showers and unobstructed views of the city and the Willamette River; service that's "attentive to details" and a "perfect location" with "lots of activities within walking distance" make this Westin a "winner", even though a few find the food "merely adequate."

Pennsylvania

Bradford

Glendorn Ⓢ – | – | – | – | $495
1000 Glendorn Dr.; 814-362-6511; fax 814-368-9923; 800-843-8568; www.glendorn.com; 2 rooms, 2 suites, 7 cabins
Arriving at this "luxurious" Relais & Châteaux "Adirondack-style camp" on a former private estate is "like stepping into an enchanted

forest" (the Allegheny National Forest, to be exact); guests can "explore the streams", swim, bike, fish, skeet shoot, get a massage or "do nothing", and after an "incredible" meal, "retreat" to a suite or cabin with "pine-covered walls" and up to "three fireplaces."

Bucks County

EverMay On The Delaware ✕ 23 | 22 | 24 | 17 | $165

889 River Rd., Erwinna; 610-294-9100; fax 610-294-8249; 877-864-2365; www.evermay.com; 17 rooms, 1 suite

Promising "picturesque views of the Delaware River", this "delightful, quiet" "country inn" "takes you back in time", as do local antiquing sources; rooms are variably described as "comfortable" and "romantic" or "closetlike" and "outdated", but "gourmet" dining is a "highlight" as are the "pretty grounds", particularly in fall.

Farmington

NEMACOLIN WOODLANDS 26 | 24 | 23 | 28 | $315

1001 LaFayette Dr.; 724-329-8555; fax 724-329-6947; 800-422-2736; www.nemacolin.com; 308 rooms, 27 suites, 9 resort homes

"If you like outdoor activity", this western PA resort is a "top-notch" choice with "magnificent facilities" for all ages including golf, horseback riding, fly fishing and a "serene" spa; Chateau LaFayette is "the place to stay" among various lodgings, as is the newer Falling Rock Lodge, whose "cool, crisp" silhouette was inspired by Frank Lloyd Wright's nearby Fallingwater house; some call the dining "tops" and others "just average", but overall most say this one's a "treat."

Hershey

Hershey, The Hotel Ⓢ 22 | 24 | 23 | 25 | $329

100 Hotel Rd.; 717-533-2171; fax 717-534-8887; 800-437-7439; www.hersheypa.com; 222 rooms, 10 suites

"Drown yourself in chocolate as it's in everything" at this "old-fashioned" hotel tied to the Hershey Park but with so many on-site activities "it's like its own city"; among these are golf and the "wildly popular spa", where "you don't have to be a cocoa lover, but it does make the treatments more interesting"; while it's "great for families", it's also a "treat when kids aren't involved" since that unmistakable, "constant aroma is an aphrodisiac."

Philadelphia

FOUR SEASONS PHILADELPHIA ✕ Ⓢ 27 | 28 | 27 | 27 | $345

1 Logan Sq.; 215-963-1500; fax 215-963-9506; 866-516-1100; www.fourseasons.com; 356 rooms, 8 suites

Now "this is brotherly love" quip fans of the "class act" in Center City, where "VIP treatment" is the norm and even "children get toys when they check in"; epicures say the Fountain restaurant "beckons from afar" (it was voted No. 1 for Food, Decor and Service in our *Philadelphia Restaurant Survey*), and the spa wins fans as well.

Hilton Inn at Penn | 22 | 20 | 17 | 19 | $209

3600 Sansom St.; 215-222-0200; fax 215-222-4600; 800-445-8667; www.theinnatpenn.com; 236 rooms

"Not your typical Hilton", this hotel situated "on the U. Penn. campus" is an "attractive, convenient" base "for families visiting students" and is a "great spot for business meetings"; "airy" rooms add to the appeal, but dining that earns mixed marks and a location "too far from Rittenhouse and the Old City" are weaknesses.

Hyatt Regency Philadelphia at Penn's Landing 🔭 | 21 | 19 | 15 | 20 | $269

201 S. Christopher Columbus Blvd.; 215-928-1234; fax 215-521-6600; 800-233-1234; www.pennslanding.hyatt.com; 336 rooms, 10 suites

Located at Penn's Landing on the Delaware River, this "busy", "modern hotel" is "a bit out in the wind", but "if your business or personal agenda is here", you'll appreciate the "well-run" facilities, rooms with "magnificent views" and "great lobby bar" that's welcoming at night when the "waterfront is a ghost town."

Loews Philadelphia Ⓢ | 21 | 19 | 18 | 20 | $224

1200 Market St.; 215-627-1200; fax 215-231-7310; 800-235-6397; www.loewshotels.com; 545 rooms, 36 suites

"Modernist heaven" awaits in this hotel set in the former PSFS bank building whose "one-of-a-kind architecture" gives it "more of a boutique feel" than a chain affiliation warrants; although some find the decor "hard edged", take issue with having to "pay to use the pool and exercise equipment" and give service a mixed review, its location "across from the Convention Center" and "great business amenities" make it "a hip option for conventioneers."

Marriott Philadelphia | 19 | 19 | 17 | 20 | $249

1201 Market St.; 215-625-2900; fax 215-625-6000; 800-228-9290; www.marriott.com; 1332 rooms, 76 suites

If "Downtown Philly is where you want to stay", then this "massive" hotel connected to the Convention Center is a "solid, if unexciting", bet, offering "fair rates for the location", "comfy" rooms and a "long" lap pool; while on-site "dining options are limited", most feel the staff, including some of the "most efficient doormen", does a "consistent job for such a large hotel."

Omni Hotel at Independence Park 🔭 | 22 | 21 | 19 | 20 | $259

401 Chestnut St.; 215-925-0000; fax 215-925-1263; 800-843-6664; www.omnihotels.com; 147 rooms, 3 suites

"A tourist's dream come true", this "classy" "sleeper" is "terrific for both sightseeing and nightlife" thanks to its Society Hill location "one block from Independence Hall and in the center of Philly's hip restaurant revival"; it boasts a "small" but "beautiful interior" (think marble, chandeliers and flowers), "large, airy rooms" and "all the Park Avenue amenities", including "good dining" at Azalea.

Park Hyatt Philadelphia at the Bellevue ✕Ⓗ🔭Ⓢ | 23 | 25 | 23 | 24 | $320

Broad and Walnut Sts.; 215-893-1234; fax 215-732-8518; 800-233-1234; www.hyatt.com; 166 rooms, 16 suites

For "a taste of Versailles in Center City", "enter the realm of great elegance" that is this "glamorous" hotel in the "gracious" Bellevue "where you're greeted with champagne" by an "outstanding" staff; prepare to "be awed by the common spaces", the "delicious, breathtaking" Founders restaurant and the fitness facilities.

RITTENHOUSE HOTEL, THE ✕ 🏡 👪 Ⓢ | 27 | 26 | 26 | 24 | $400

210 W. Rittenhouse Sq.; 215-546-9000; fax 215-732-3364; 800-635-1042; www.rittenhousehotel.com; 87 rooms, 11 suites

Located "right on beautiful Rittenhouse Square", this "august" "oasis" is "everything you've ever wanted in a luxury hotel", which is why it's "a favorite among celebrities and the who's who of Philly"; "understated class rules", from the "elegant public spaces" and "huge" rooms "as warm and comfortable as the robes" (plus "slippers"!) to "fantastic restaurants" like the "adventurous" Lacroix (one of "the best in the city") and the "gracious" staff; cognoscenti caution, however, that it's "less friendly to kids."

Ritz-Carlton, Philadelphia ✕ Ⓗ 🏡 👪 Ⓢ | 25 | 25 | 24 | 25 | $300

10 Ave. of the Arts; 215-523-8000; fax 215-568-0942; 800-241-3333; www.ritzcarlton.com; 298 rooms, 32 suites, 1 penthouse

Housed in a "magnificently restored" bank building modeled after the Pantheon in Rome, this Center City "domed treasure" boasts a "soaring sunlit lobby" with "marble everywhere" (which means it can get "noisy" at times); "wonderful touches abound", from "warm cookies upon check-in" to "late drinks" in the Vault; the rooms are "well done, given the constraints" of renovation, so now "the only thing missing is a first-class fitness facility."

Sofitel Philadelphia 🏡 👪 | 24 | 23 | 21 | 22 | $300

120 S. 17th St.; 215-569-8300; fax 215-564-7452; www.sofitel.com; 207 rooms, 70 suites

"One of the better-kept secrets among high-end hotels", this "modern" locale "a block from Rittenhouse Square" offers "a touch of Paris in Philadelphia", with "wonderful" "French-influenced" "hospitality", as well as "great entertainment that includes a piano bar"; the "contemporary" accommodations are "fabulous" and the marble bathrooms are "even better", but both may be trumped by the prime location right "in the heart of an upscale shopping district."

Westin 🏡 | 23 | 21 | 18 | 20 | $359

99 S. 17th St.; 215-563-1600; fax 215-564-9559; 800-228-3000; www.westin.com; 273 rooms, 17 suites

"It's 1776 24/7" at this "lovely old hotel" in Center City, judging from its "well-appointed" lobby graced with "elegant" "period pieces"; it offers rooms with "truly heavenly" beds and showers, but some find it "too quiet", especially in the "slow" bar and restaurant where it's "like having dinner with your family after an argument."

Pittsburgh

Omni William Penn Ⓗ 👪 | 20 | 21 | 17 | 20 | $199

530 William Penn Pl.; 412-281-7100; fax 412-553-5252; 800-843-6664; www.omniwilliampenn.com; 473 rooms, 39 suites

Set in a historic building Downtown, this "noble" "grande dame" evokes a "bygone era" when "old-fashioned service", "tasteful and spacious" rooms and a "sparkling", "ornate lobby" were the norm; while some feel it's a little "past its prime", if not downright "tired", it "still has the charm of an earlier century."

Priory, The Ⓗ 🅱 — | — | — | — | $134

614 Pressley St.; 412-231-3338; fax 412-231-4838; 866-377-4679; www.thepriory.com; 21 rooms, 4 suites

"You won't have to take any vows" at this "unusual and fun" former monastery on the North Shore that's now a 24-room inn "in B&B dressing" (i.e. a "quaint" sitting room and library strewn with Edwardian antiques and full of nooks with skyline views); a serene courtyard and grand domed banquet hall (originally St. Mary's Church) enhance the "special setting", but if you start feeling a bit cloistered, a healthy dose of modernity can be found at the nearby Andy Warhol Museum.

Poconos

Deerfield Spa Ⓢ — | — | — | — | $574

650 Resica Falls Rd., East Stroudsburg; 570-223-0160; fax 570-223-8270; 800-852-4494; www.deerfieldspa.com; 20 rooms

There's "lot's to do" at this decidedly "non-chichi", "country"-style seasonal Poconos spa, from getting a facial or massage to joining an aerobics, aquatic karate, reflexology or astrology session; "healthy, delicious food" keeps energy levels up, so even those who joke it reminds them of "summer camp" concede it's "good for a quick getaway with the girls"; N.B. rates are based on a two-night minimum stay.

Skytop Lodge 17 | 23 | 19 | 25 | $435

1 Skytop, Skytop; 570-595-7401; fax 570-595-9618; 800-345-7759; www.skytop.com; 192 rooms, 27 suites

When you arrive at this "exquisite" "retreat" "in the Poconos", you may experience a "flashback to olden days when families traveled to all-inclusive mountain resorts"; with a full range of activities, including an "excellent golf course", "great trout-fishing stream" and hiking and cycling trails, it's easy to work up an appetite for the "old-fashioned" formal dinner hour; the decor may be "a bit dated", but "proper" service "more than makes up for" "some wear."

Puerto Rico

Fajardo

Las Casitas Village ▽ 26 | 22 | 21 | 27 | $494

1000 El Conquistador Ave.; 787-863-1000; 800-468-8365; www.wyndham.com; 67 casitas, 80 apartments, 90 villas

"With a clifftop view of the ocean to one side and the El Yunque rain forest on the other, the location is superb" agree admirers of this "hotel within a hotel" that's "more private than the larger adjacent property, El Conquistador", and 30 miles northwest of San Juan; it's "paradise", thanks to the Golden Door "spa that's a sanctuary", waterfront "villas that are a dream" and a "phenomenal staff eager to please"; still a few feel food and service are "hit-or-miss."

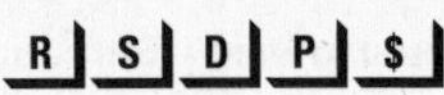

Las Croabas

Wyndham El Conquistador 22 | 21 | 20 | 25 | $413

1000 El Conquistador Ave.; 787-863-1000; fax 787-863-6586; 800-468-8365; www.wyndham.com; 750 rooms, 16 suites

"An absolute marvel of architecture built on a high cliff", this "self-contained" "golf destination" and "mega resort with breathtaking views" boasts "so many restaurants", a casino, "gorgeous pools" and "choices of treatments" at the Golden Door spa that it "could apply for statehood"; "pretend you're James Bond" (the last *Goldfinger* scene was filmed here) and "take the *funicular,* a fun ride to the base" to catch a ferry to the "beautiful beach" on private Palomino Island, which some consider a "perk" and others find the "one major drawback."

Rincon

Horned Dorset Primavera, The 25 | 27 | 27 | 20 | $850

Apartado 1132 ; 787-823-4030; fax 787-823-5580; 800-633-1857; www.horneddorset.com; 55 suites

"Once experienced, one can never get enough" of this Relais & Châteaux "peaceful" "hidden gem" two hours from San Juan on the west coast where "luxury and pampering in the old Caribbean"–style is on offer, from "incredible" service "almost invisible to the eye, but there when you need it" to "amazing rooms" and duplexes, some with private infinity pools, to "delicious food" at the Blue Room restaurant; if a few find it "without a decent beach", most "can't wait to go back", deeming it "ideal for honeymooners or anniversary celebrations."

San Juan

Caribe Hilton 19 | 19 | 19 | 21 | $225

Los Rosales St., San Geronimo Grounds; 787-721-0303; fax 787-724-6992; 800-774-1500; www.hilton.com; 605 rooms, 41 suites

"A reliable standby", this "beachfront" property "rocks" with a "stunning lobby", "private beach and central location" "perfectly sited to get the best ocean breeze"; the newer "tower rooms have magnificent views toward" Old San Juan, plus it's "fun to watch the cruise ships" and explore the "excellent pools", "beautiful grounds" and "bar overlooking the water"; but dissenters declare "service is minimal", a "beer sets you back as much as a room" and "it's a little remote from the life of" the city.

El Convento, Hotel Ⓗ 24 | 24 | 23 | 21 | $355

100 Cristo St., Old San Juan; 787-723-9020; fax 787-721-2877; 800-468-2779; www.elconvento.com; 63 rooms, 5 suites

"Once a convent, now a luxury hotel" with a "resident ghost" and a "wonderfully friendly staff", this "trip back in time" to the 17th century "lies at the elegant juncture of ancient and modern" in Old San Juan, "exuding a personality that pushes your vacation up a notch"; the four-story property boasts "huge rooms that ring a lovely courtyard", "happening" restaurants and a "lively tapas bar"; "if you're into history and not the beach", "it's the perfect home base" to "explore the old city and fortress."

Hyatt Dorado Beach 20 20 19 25 $549
Hwy. 693, Dorado; 787-796-1234; fax 787-796-2022; 800-233-1234; www.hyatt.com; 262 rooms, 18 casitas
"Roll out of bed and onto" the "gorgeous", "secluded beach" "with your coffee in hand" – yes, the oceanfront casitas "can't be beat for the ultimate in feeling like a millionaire" at this "beautiful vacation spot" built by "Laurence Rockefeller in the 1950s"; guests "love the waterslides", "swim-up bar", "super-lush freshwater pool longer than the Empire State Building", "breathtaking views" and four golf courses, including one that "weaves majestically through the lush, expansive property"; still, critics complain the "food lacks inspiration."

InterContinental 20 21 20 23 $399
5961 Isla Verde Ave.; 787-791-6100; fax 787-253-2510; 800-468-9076; www.interconti.com; 380 rooms, 22 suites
"In the center of the primary tourist area" "a stone's throw from" the airport and Old San Juan and "footsteps from a beautiful beach", this "convenient spot" in the Isla Verde district also entices with a "lovely pool area", "swim-up bar", "spacious rooms", a "small casino" and "access to a great steakhouse" (there's a "Ruth's Chris on premises"); still, a handful find "it just isn't anything special" and the "service is beyond amateur."

Paradisus Puerto Rico – – – – $420
Coco Beach; 787-809-1770; fax 787-657-1060; 800-336-3542; www.solmelia.com; 481 suites, 5 villas
Located 40 minutes from the airport and Old San Juan, this all-inclusive, set on a secluded beach near El Yunque National Rainforest, is surrounded by gardens; rooms are in 20 two-story bungalows, with marble baths and mahogany details, and if you opt for a Royal Service Suite you can choose your very own bedding and pillows; on-site activities include a golf course and a lagoon-style pool.

Ritz-Carlton, The 24 24 23 25 $329
6961 Ave. of the Governors, Carolina; 787-253-1700; 800-241-3333; www.ritzcarlton.com; 374 rooms, 42 suites
You can get off the airplane and onto the "spectacular powdery sand beach" "in 15 minutes" sigh travelers who find this "classic" "paradise" with "outstanding service" "great for a quick getaway"; "live like a king, if only for your stay" thanks to the "excellent food", a "picture-perfect swimming pool" with "plush chaise lounges", "sumptuous rooms", an "intimate casino", "well-maintained tennis courts" and a "top-notch" spa; but hard-to-please patrons "expected more pampering."

Westin Rio Mar 22 20 19 25 $425
6000 Rio Mar Blvd., Rio Grande; 787-888-6000; fax 787-888-6235; 888-627-8556; www.westinriomar.com; 600 rooms, 72 suites
"The location is perfect for a tour of the El Yunque rain forest" or if "you want sun and sand" say fans of this property with an on-site casino, golf courses that "make you cry tears of joy", a "lovely pool" and service that's "eager to help"; but contrarians carp it's "overrun with kids", "isolated", "food is spotty" and the "staff is unresponsive."

Wyndham El San Juan 20 | 22 | 23 | 25 | $346

6063 Isla Verde Ave., Carolina; 787-791-1000; fax 787-791-6985; 877-999-3223; www.wyndham.com; 382 rooms, 57 suites

The "showstopper lobby" of this "festive hotel" in the Isla Verde district is "where the party is at" – what a "see-and-be-seen scene" "with people decked out to impress", "excellent music", dancing and "an energy beating through that makes you feel the spirit of the land"; it's a "hot spot" prized for its "delightful casino", "variety of delicious restaurants", "grand service" and pools with swim-up bars; if a few el grouchos deem the quarters "mediocre", others retort "if you don't spend time in your room, this is the place."

Vieques

Martineau Bay Resort & Spa ▽ 27 | 21 | 14 | 25 | $656

(fka Wyndham Martineau Bay Resort & Spa)

State Rd. 200; 787-741-4100; fax 787-741-4171; 800-996-3426; www.martineaubayresorts.com; 138 rooms, 20 suites

Perhaps the "largest hotel on the island, but still much smaller than those on the mainland", this resort, which was taken over by the W hotel chain post-*Survey,* is set to undergo major renovations; you can still expect access to three "untouched beaches", "gorgeous tiled rooms", "great views", a full-service spa and a "relaxing atmosphere", but the cool quotient is destined to go up a few notches with the takeover.

Rhode Island

Block Island

1661 Inn & Hotel Manisses, The Ⓗ 20 | 23 | 23 | 20 | $235

1 Spring St.; 401-466-2421; fax 401-466-3162; 800-626-4773; www.blockislandresorts.com; 69 rooms

Exuding "islandy" "charm", this pair of lodgings augmented by cottages is a "destination for discriminating" guests (for Hotel Manisses, they must also be over 12); while some go for the year-round Inn's "million-dollar views from the veranda", others prefer the seasonal Hotel, overlooking its "small" quarters and fixating on the "wonderful" restaurant that "uses home-grown veggies" from its farm ("meet the animals", including llamas and emus).

Newport

CASTLE HILL INN & RESORT ✕Ⓗ 25 | 25 | 26 | 25 | $395

590 Ocean Ave.; 401-849-3800; fax 401-849-3838; 888-466-1355; www.castlehillinn.com; 15 rooms, 10 suites

Anchored by the residence of 19th-century naturalist Alexander Agassiz, this "exquisite" enclave with "amazing views" of Newport Harbor retains an "intimacy" that makes guests feel they're "visiting an elegant private home"; "quick-to-please" service "transports you back" to the Gilded Age, while "drinks on the patio", "great" on-site dining and "beautifully appointed rooms" with "heated floors" help "rekindle the romance" ("one sunset from the Turret Room suite and all seems right in the world").

Francis Malbone House Ⓗ | 23 | 24 | 20 | 19 | $245

392 Thames St.; 401-846-0392; fax 401-848-5956; 800-846-0392; www.malbone.com; 17 rooms, 3 suites

For those who aim to be "in the center of town versus on the water", this pair of "impeccably maintained" 18th-century homes transformed into an "upscale B&B" cultivates a "serene mood" "with no pretentious Newport attitude"; "perfectly appointed" accommodations complete with fireplaces, "fabulous breakfasts" in the "lovely courtyard", afternoon tea and a "caring staff" all make it a "joy to return to."

Vanderbilt Hall Hotel Ⓗ | – | – | – | – | $329

41 Mary St.; 401-846-6200; fax 401-846-0701; www.vanderbilthall.com; 36 rooms, 12 suites

Live as a robber baron in this early 1900s inn that was once the Newport Men's Social Club and was dedicated by Alfred Vanderbilt to his father, Cornelius; rooms are individually designed and activities include a billiards room, a fitness room with sauna and an American restaurant with a martini bar.

Providence

Providence, Hotel ✕Ⓗ | – | – | – | – | $289

311 Westminster St.; 401-861-8000; fax 401-861-8002; 800-861-8990; www.thehotelprovidence.com; 80 rooms, 16 suites

Providence has its first independent European-style boutique with this newcomer set in two 19th-century Classical-style buildings in historic Downtown; accommodations feature WiFi access, pillowtop beds, marble bathrooms, complimentary newspapers and in-room dining via the on-site Italian restaurant, L'Epicureo, which relocated here from Federal Hill; corporate cronies will congregate in 2,200 sq. ft. of meeting space.

Westin Ⓢ | 23 | 20 | 18 | 21 | $334

1 W. Exchange St.; 401-598-8000; fax 401-598-8200; 800-368-7764; www.westin.com; 360 rooms, 4 suites

"What could be cooler" than being "just a skywalk away from Providence Place" mall exclaim shoppers about this Downtown business hotel that is also "near nightlife"; "what it lacks in character it makes up for in amenities", including those "Heavenly beds that have earned their names"; although in-house dining's "so-so", the gym's "awesome" and the staff "goes out of its way to make you feel at home"; P.S. parents should book early or "don't count on a room for graduation week."

Westerly

Weekapaug Inn | – | – | – | – | $425

25 Spray Rock Rd.; 401-322-0301; fax 401-322-1016; 866-322-0301; www.weekapauginn.com; 61 rooms, 6 suites

Typifying "old New England at its best", this all-inclusive waterfront inn maintained by the Buffum family for more than a century is a "relaxing", "family-oriented" "getaway" with "no phones or TVs in the guestrooms" to distract from water sports and other outdoor activities; the dining room serves "amazing food" and is BYO only, and credit cards are not accepted, so bring your checkbook and leave the modern world behind.

South Carolina

Aiken

Willcox, The ▽ 27 | 25 | 25 | 21 | $175

100 S. Colleton Ave.; 803-648-1898; fax 803-648-6664; www.thewillcox.com; 15 rooms, 7 suites

Situated between Main Street and the "rolling green hills" of Hitchcock Woods, this "beautiful old" Relais & Châteaux mansion affords guests a "fantastic stay" in "one of the prettiest towns" around, right in the middle of horse breeding, hunting and polo country; the "friendly" staff is a "true reflection of Southern charm at its best" while the "lovely rooms, quiet atmosphere" and fitness center offer a respite from nearby golf and equestrian activities.

Charleston

CHARLESTON PLACE 25 | 25 | 26 | 25 | $479

205 Meeting St.; 843-722-4900; fax 843-722-0728; 800-611-5545; www.charlestonplacehotel.com; 400 rooms, 40 suites

"Decadence and old-world charm" unite at this "outstanding" hotel set "smack dab in the center of Charleston" that exudes such "class it feels like you should be dropped off at the entrance by horse and carriage"; the "perfect location" is an "excellent" jumping-off "place to explore the city's historic district" while the "exceptional dining" at Charleston Grill restaurant, "wonderful" "year-round rooftop pool" and a staff that treats you as if "you're a guest at their home" bespeak "totally unexpected luxury."

John Rutledge House Inn ▽ 27 | 25 | 15 | 24 | $265

116 Broad St.; 843-723-7999; fax 843-720-2615; 866-720-2609; www.charminginns.com; 16 rooms, 3 suites

Expect a "warm reception" at this former home of John Rutledge, one of the 55 signers of the Constitution, a "fine period" landmark in the Downtown historic district that lets you "step back in time"; the "carriage houses are very nice, but to get the real feel, stay in the main house", dating from 1763, with "big rooms" brimming with antiques; N.B. meals are served at the nearby Wentworth Mansion.

Market Pavilion Hotel – | – | – | – | $425

225 East Bay St.; 843-723-0500; fax 843-723-4320; 877-440-2250; www.marketpavilion.com; 61 rooms, 9 suites

Situated in the quaint center of Downtown, this boutique newcomer boasts dark-wood furniture, marble baths and old-world window treatments along with modern services like a dedicated concierge level, butler service, a rooftop cascading pool and the Pavilion Bar with sweeping views of Colonial Charleston; the on-site Grill 225 serves Continental fare and an elaborate Sunday brunch.

Mills House Hotel, The ▽ 18 | 22 | 18 | 19 | $369

115 Meeting St.; 843-577-2400; fax 843-722-0623; 800-874-9600; www.millshouse.com; 196 rooms, 19 suites

"Excellent service" is the backbone of this "unique" "hotel in the best part of the historic" district that "catches the mood" of the antebellum South ("if Rhett Butler had been real, he would have certainly been thrown out of here"); 21st-century touches like a pool with a view, Low Country fare at the restaurant and two lounges add to its allure "for a conference or weekend getaway"; if the rooms seem a "little tired", most feel that's "part of its charm."

Planters Inn 25 | 23 | 26 | 20 | $295

112 N. Market St.; 843-722-2345; fax 843-577-2125; 800-845-7082; www.plantersinn.com; 44 rooms, 20 suites

"Pure pleasure" opine proponents of Relais & Châteaux's "great little old luxury inn", an "elegant, understated", circa-1844 "oasis for a Charleston adventure"; it's "pitch perfect", from the "friendly service" and "charming rooms" decorated with museum period–style furnishings with fireplaces, Jacuzzis or piazzas overlooking the garden courtyard to the "wonderful" Peninsula Grill.

WENTWORTH MANSION ▽ 28 | 27 | 27 | 25 | $335

149 Wentworth St.; 843-853-1886; fax 843-720-5290; 888-466-1886; www.wentworthmansion.com; 14 family rooms, 7 suites

The "highest praise" goes to this Gilded Age "charmer", a member of Small Luxury Hotels of the World and the former home of cotton magnate Francis S. Rodgers, boasting mahogany and oak details, Tiffany windows and a "staff that treats you like visiting dignitaries"; every "fabulous" room is kitted out with a whirlpool bath and a gas fireplace, plus insiders advise a visit to the "amazing cupola", the Rodgers library for cordials and the "sublime" Circa 1886 eatery.

Wild Dunes Resort ▽ 25 | 22 | 20 | 25 | $190

5757 Palm Blvd., Isle of Palms; 843-886-6000; fax 843-886-2916; 888-778-1876; www.wilddunes.com; 93 rooms, 375 villas, 82 resort homes

Whether you're looking for the "perfect sunset", proximity to Charleston or a "breathtaking golf course" at a "fab hotel", this "wonderful escape" has "got it all" for both adults and kids; rooms depend on "where you stay inside the resort" – villas and homes accommodate larger parties, but the Boardwalk Inn is "very modern" – and recreational activities abound with biking and running trails, kayaking, a spa, two pools and the ocean.

WOODLANDS RESORT & INN 29 | 28 | 29 | 25 | $295

125 Parsons Rd., Summerville; 843-875-2600; fax 843-875-2603; 800-774-9999; www.woodlandsinn.com; 5 rooms, 13 suites, 1 cottage

While it's so "off the beaten path" "you may give up on finding it", this "wonderful" Relais & Châteaux resort a "long way from Charleston" "erases all doubts"; the "drive down between the majestic old trees takes you back in time" while the "gorgeous rooms", "world-class dinners" and activities like swimming, croquet and tennis make it "worth every penny"; this is "gracious living in the Low Country" so give in to the "total relaxation."

Hilton Head

Disney's Hilton Head Island Resort ▽ 27 | 25 | 15 | 25 | $275

22 Harbourside Ln., Hilton Head Island; 407-939-7540; www.disneyvacationclub.com; 123 villas

"Disney goes camping in the Low Country at this great family resort" with a "comfortably rustic feel" reminiscent of a hunting and fishing lodge on the "inland side of Hilton Head"; it's "quiet and relaxing" and yet there are "lots of activities for everybody", including golf and a "great pool", plus "the accommodations are spacious" and "tastefully" decorated; while "there are no real restaurants at the resort", there are "wonderful nearby choices."

Hilton Head Health Institute Ⓢ — | — | — | — | $342

14 Valencia Rd., Hilton Head Island; 843-785-3919; fax 843-686-5659; 800-292-2440; www.hhhealth.com; 21 cottages

"Don't expect to sit around and be pampered" at this "comfortable residence", where results-oriented guests head to "reform their habits and lose those extra 10 pounds"; you'll "literally be working your butt off" with personalized fitness and nutrition classes, and learning how to de-stress and reduce anxiety at the full-service spa.

Hilton Head Marriott Beach & Golf Resort 21 | 21 | 18 | 22 | $279

1 Hotel Circle, Oceanfront at Palmetto Dunes, Hilton Head Island; 843-686-8400; fax 843-785-2419; 800-295-5998; www.marriott.com; 476 rooms, 36 suites

The "great" outdoor pool, 25 tennis courts and "three golf courses within walking distance" are just a few of the activities on offer at this oceanfront high-rise resort 10 minutes from the airport; there's nothing like "watching the sunset from the beachside bar", plus the restaurants and "large rooms" "rarely disappoint", the staff is "friendly" and it's "convenient to all attractions"; but cynics sigh it's "lost its snap": "everything is adequate", but there's "nothing special."

Inn at Palmetto Bluff Ⓢ — | — | — | — | $450

19 Village Park Square, Bluffton; 843-706-6500; fax 843-706-6550; 866-706-6565; www.palmettobluffresort.com; 42 rooms, 8 suites, 17 houses

Set amid flowering gardens in South Carolina's Low Country near Savannah, this new Auberge Resort is a golfer's dream since it has an on-site Jack Nicklaus–designed course; but it's also a boon to those who fancy graceful design, pampering and excellent cuisine: modern cottages boast pinewood floors, vaulted ceilings, fireplaces and screened verandas, and there's a spa and three restaurants.

Sea Pines Resort Ⓢ ▽ 22 | 22 | 19 | 25 | $200

32 Greenwood Dr., Hilton Head Island; 843-785-3333; fax 843-842-1475; 888-807-6873; www.seapines.com; 60 rooms, 430 villas

There are "lots of pine trees and shade" around this "wonderful resort" comprised of the "quiet, relaxing" Inn at Harbour Town, villas and houses that you can rent; the hotel overlooks golf courses ("what a bed, what a view"), plus there are "excellent" activities for the family, including "nice boating", tennis, a "great little area of shops" and perhaps "some of the best beaches in the country"; N.B. a post-*Survey* $20-million renovation of the Inn, Harbour Town Grill and conference center may impact the above scores.

Westin 22 | 22 | 19 | 23 | $199

2 Grasslawn Ave., Hilton Head Island; 843-681-4000; fax 843-681-1096; 800-228-3000; www.westin.com; 290 rooms, 20 suites, 110 villas

You may "choose to spend your entire day at the hotel pools, bars, club lounge and restaurants" when you stay at this "marvelous" oceanside resort with "excellent facilities" and a kids' program; there are "so many accommodations" and "so many activities" to choose from, including golf, tennis and kayaking, not to mention the beach with "private cabanas for guests"; but a handful who "expected more" decry "smallish rooms."

Kiawah Island

Kiawah Island Resorts 21 | 22 | 20 | 26 | $279

12 Kiawah Beach Dr.; 843-768-2121; fax 843-768-6099; 800-576-1570; www.kiawahresort.com; 150 rooms, 8 suites, 600 villas, 60 houses

"Kiawah's a keeper" concur acolytes of this "lovely" island resort, an "excellent place to unwind", "stroll pristine beaches", bike along paths, tee-off at "great golf courses" and "get away from reality"; "respect for the natural habitat" mixed with a "gracious atmosphere", plus "lots of lodging choices" and restaurants mean "you can spend a week and never leave the grounds."

Sanctuary at Kiawah Island – | – | – | – | $625

1 Sanctuary Beach Dr.; 843-768-6000; fax 843-768-5150; 877-683-1234; www.thesanctuary.com; 236 rooms, 19 suites

Blessed with beaches, parks (including an Audubon sanctuary), golf courses and historic sites of all kinds as well as proximity to Charleston, Kiawah Island is the idyllic spot where this one-year-old resort blends right into its surroundings; while it resembles a rambling old plantation estate on the outside, the interior bespeaks a more contemporary elegance with marble showers, ocean views in the signature restaurant and a whirlpool in the spa.

Myrtle Beach

Breakers Resort ∇ 20 | 21 | 19 | 23 | $150

2006 N. Ocean Blvd.; 843-444-4444; fax 843-444-4444; 800-952-4507; www.breakers.com; 413 rooms, 200 suites

A "super place to bring the family, if you don't mind splurging a little", this "very spread out" high-rise resort with several options, including the newest Breakers Paradise Tower, is a "cut above the rest" when it comes to "Downtown beach hotels"; "kids love" the 418-ft. lazy river and the indoor and outdoor swimming pools, while parents appreciate the children's programs, poolside spa, golf courses within minutes and staff that "caters to all your needs."

Long Bay Resort – | – | – | – | $157

7200 N. Ocean Blvd.; 843-449-3361; fax 843-449-8297; 800-615-3313; www.longbayresort.com; 101 rooms, 90 suites, 100 condos

"What a life!" exclaim enthusiasts of this oceanfront resort on the north end of town where guests can make a splash in multiple pools, float down the lazy river or relax in "neat" accommodations ranging from condos to suites to rooms "huge" enough to fit mom, dad and two kids; the "very family-friendly" staff, "highly recommended" restaurant and proximity to golf courses galore make it "one of the best places to stay in Myrtle."

Myrtle Beach Marriott Resort Grande Dunes – | – | – | – | $239

8400 Costa Verde Dr.; 843-449-8880; fax 843-449-8669; 888-236-2427; www.marriott.com; 399 rooms, 6 suites

It's "really a new twist on Myrtle Beach" rave resort-goers about this "fabulous" oceanfront property rising above the Grand Dunes, a 2,200-acre plantation-style development, replete with "outstanding golf", tennis courts, a European spa and a palm tree–studded pool overlooking the Atlantic; the spacious rooms are done up in rich colors, and there are "very nice" dining options.

Pawleys Island

Litchfield Plantation ▽ 21 | 21 | 22 | 24 | $215

Kings River Rd.; 843-237-9121; fax 843-237-1041; 800-869-1410; www.litchfieldplantation.com; 11 rooms, 18 suites

An "excellent experience" that "takes you to another time", this coastal rice plantation dating back to the 1750s feels "like Tara" with 600 acres of "stunning grounds", a country inn graced with original features and a brick and stucco mansion with nearby championship golf courses; "unique rooms", "service that's anxious to please" and "exceptional dining" at the Carriage House make this Small Luxury Hotels of the World member even more "special."

Tennessee

Gatlinburg

Lodge at Buckberry Creek – | – | – | – | $265

961 Campbell Lead Rd.; 865-430-8030; fax 865-430-4659; 866-305-6343; www.buckberrylodge.com; 46 suites

Set on a roaring creek amid 26 acres of wooded, rolling hills in East Tennessee's Smoky Mountains, this all-suite lodge transports guest to the Adirondacks, even showcasing a few antiques from the region; owned by the McLean family for 50 years, it blends backcountry authenticity with concierge services, in-suite fireplaces and cozy couches and an on-site spa.

Memphis

Madison Hotel ▽ 25 | 25 | 24 | 24 | $220

79 Madison Ave.; 901-333-1200; fax 901-333-1299; 866-446-3674; www.madisonhotelmemphis.com; 74 rooms, 36 suites

"Thought I was in NYC" exclaim enthusiasts of this circa-1905 former bank building turned "edgy boutique" (and member of Small Luxury Hotels of the World) near the Beale Street entertainment district; the staff is "extremely helpful", the beds and Italian "linens are divine" and most quarters feature separate baths and showers and whirlpool or jet tubs, plus there is a "great view of the Mississippi from the rooftop terrace."

Peabody, The 20 | 23 | 23 | 23 | $235

149 Union Ave.; 901-529-4000; fax 901-529-3600; 800-732-2639; www.peabodymemphis.com; 455 rooms, 9 suites

"Quack, quack" – "who could resist staying at a hotel that has ducks marching through the lobby" and is sited "where the

Mississippi Delta begins" – yes, this circa-1850 "grand old dame of the South" draws flocks of fans who find it "charming" and "convenient to Downtown"; "friendly employees", two "good restaurants", "cocktails on the roof", "immaculate rooms", plus "a lobby straight out of a Cole Porter song" up the ante; P.S. an ongoing renovation may appease those who say it needs "an overhaul."

Nashville

Gaylord Opryland Ⓢ 19 | 18 | 17 | 22 | $189

2800 Opryland Dr.; 615-889-1000; fax 615-871-5728; 888-976-2000; www.gaylordopryland.com; 2681 rooms, 200 suites

"Bring comfortable shoes" to this glass-covered "Opryland centerpiece" so "gigantic" it feels like a "50-story hotel laid on its side" and so Southern that "charm oozes out of every inch"; "people-watch from your balcony overlooking the tropical gardens" and enjoy the "boats cruising the indoor river", 44-ft. waterfall, "great convention facilities" and Springdale Golf Club; but cynics are "overwhelmed" by the "labyrinth too unwieldy to navigate" and "Biosphere atmosphere"; N.B. a spa opened in 2005.

Hermitage Ⓗ Ⓢ ▽ 24 | 23 | 20 | 21 | $199

231 Sixth Ave. N.; 615-244-3121; fax 615-254-6909; 888-888-9414; www.thehermitagehotel.com; 119 rooms, 4 suites

Expect "infinite class: just about everything is done right" at this "luxurious", "beautifully renovated" Downtown hotel within walking distance of the Nashville Convention Center that's hosted a who's who of presidents and celebrities, from Al Capone to Greta Garbo; dating back to 1910 and named after Andrew Jackson's Hermitage estate, it's a study in "old-world charm", with "fabulous baths", "Irish linens", "superb service" and views of the skyline.

Loews Vanderbilt, Hotel 21 | 22 | 18 | 20 | $199

2100 West End Ave.; 615-320-1700; fax 615-320-5019; 800-336-3335; www.loewshotels.com; 315 rooms, 25 suites

"Run into music stars" in this recently renovated, "cosmopolitan hotel" that lends a "big-city feel to this C&W town"; an "energetic staff", "gigantic" rooms, "wonderful food"(at Ruth's Chris and Eat), plus a jukebox in the lobby add "lots of character" – and its "great location" across from "scenic Vanderbilt University" in the West End corridor ensures it's "often filled to capacity."

Renaissance Nashville Ⓢ ▽ 20 | 20 | 17 | 20 | $139

611 Commerce St.; 615-255-8400; fax 615-255-8202; 800-327-6618; www.marriott.com; 649 rooms, 24 suites

Enjoy "the fun and grit" of Music City and "service fit for a queen" at this Downtown property "in the center of everything" "near all the nightlife" and linked to the Nashville Conference Center; "you get more space" in the corner rooms, and there's a "club lounge with a city view", an "atrium with a nice kiosk for a quick breakfast" and a restaurant with "much better food" than years past.

Sheraton Music City Ⓢ ▽ 20 | 20 | 16 | 20 | $159

777 McGavok Pike; 615-885-2200; fax 615-231-1134; 888-625-5144; www.sheratonmusiccity.com; 369 rooms, 41 suites

"Suitable for business meetings" yet "away from the Downtown scene" and close to the airport, this "good alternative", which underwent an $8-million redo, boasts oversized rooms with sleigh beds and pillow-top mattresses, many with balconies or patios, and a "helpful" staff; with a "great buffet" as well as pools, tennis courts and a health club, it also works for a "weekend getaway."

Union Station, A Wyndham Historic Hotel ▽ 18 | 19 | 19 | 19 | $149

1001 Broadway; 615-726-1001; fax 615-248-3554; 800-822-4200; www.wyndham.com; 111 rooms, 12 suites

"All aboard for a very pleasurable experience" agree admirers who make tracks to this "wonderful historic property" in a railway station dating back to 1900 with 65-ft.-high vaulted ceilings and Tiffany stained-glass windows in the lobby; it's "great for those who want a non-hotel hotel" with "charming rooms", "excellent food" and "outstanding service"; but others blow off steam citing "rooms in need of updating" and a "poorly trained staff."

Walland

BLACKBERRY FARM 28 | 29 | 29 | 28 | $695

1471 W. Millers Cove Rd.; 865-380-2260; fax 865-681-7753; 800-648-2348; www.blackberryfarm.com; 44 rooms, 1 cottage, 11 houses

"Your wish is their command" at this "magical" Relais & Châteaux "paradise found" "deep in the Smoky Mountains" where "even the most workaholic mogul will relax"; "it's like going to a remote planet" where all that matters is luxuriating in "spacious cottages" with fireplaces and whirlpool baths, "watching sunsets from a rocking chair" and being pampered at the Aveda spa; John Fleer's Foothills fare, including "indescribable breakfasts", "picnic hampers filled each day with something better than the last" and "scrumptious dinners", is "over the edge in culinary comfort."

Texas

★ Tops in State

27 Mansion on Turtle Creek, *Dallas*
26 Four Seasons at Las Colinas, *Irving*
Four Seasons, *Houston*
25 Crescent Court, *Dallas*
St. Regis, *Houston*
Lake Austin Spa, *Austin*
Four Seasons, *Austin*
24 Westin La Cantera, *San Antonio*
Houstonian, *Houston*
Zaza, Hotel, *Dallas*
23 Adolphus, *Dallas*
Hyatt Regency Hill Country, *San Antonio*
Barton Creek, *Austin*
Lancaster, *Houston*

Austin

Barton Creek 22 | 23 | 21 | 26 | $310

8212 Barton Club Dr.; 512-329-4000; fax 512-329-4597; 800-336-6158; www.bartoncreek.com; 294 rooms, 6 suites

Par-tialists wonder "who needs heaven" when there's this "golfer's dream" of "four championship courses" "tucked away" in a "gorgeous" setting with "wonderful views of Texas Hill Country", "cactus and longhorn decorations everywhere", "large" rooms, an "amazing" fitness center and treatments like a mustard bath in the "fantastic" spa; duffers deride it as "nothing special", "a bit pricey" and "getting a little long in the tooth."

Driskill, The 23 23 22 23 $195

604 Brazos St.; 512-474-5911; fax 512-474-2214; 800-252-9367; www.driskillhotel.com; 165 rooms, 23 suites

There's "a sense of history so rich you can taste it" at this "quaint" "cattle baron heaven" and "grande dame of Austin hotels" "right in the heart of the action" on Sixth Street; although rooms are "small", the older ones are "individually decorated in period style" (complete with "ghosts"), and the whole hostelry is "much nicer since" "beautiful renovations"; throw in what may be "the best bar" in town ("look for the politicos in the evening") and you can see how "it doesn't wind up in country music lyrics for nothing."

Four Seasons 24 26 24 24 $305

98 San Jacinto Blvd.; 512-478-4500; fax 512-478-3117; 800-332-3442; www.fourseasons.com; 263 rooms, 28 suites

"Consistency is the theme" at this "usual class act" from the Four Seasons folks, offering "relaxed, genteel ambiance with Austin style", a "central location", "great rooms" with "luxurious beds", "outstanding customer service" and "fantastic public areas" (including a "bar overlooking the river and local bat colony"); it's recommended "for a romantic weekend escape" but the "star treatment" is also "extended to the youngest of travelers."

Hilton Austin ∇ 20 19 18 19 $179

500 E. Fourth St.; 512-482-8000; fax 512-469-0078; 800-774-1500; www.hilton.com; 720 rooms, 80 suites

A "newish convention hotel" with "a nice Texas touch" adjacent to the Austin Convention Center, this property has 60,000 sq. ft. of meeting space, an "excellent location" that's "close to everything" (including "sightseeing"), "decent" rooms with "nice decor" and views, steak-and-seafood dining in Finn & Porter restaurant and "friendly service"; still, scribes who submit it's "nothing special" utter, "um, it's a Hilton, just like all the others."

LAKE AUSTIN SPA RESORT 25 25 23 25 $700

1705 S. Quinlan Park Rd.; 512-372-7300; fax 512-266-1572; 800-847-5637; www.lakeaustin.com; 40 rooms, 1 suite, 3 cottages

"Forget your worries and rejuvenate your soul" at this "no-pressure", "pricey but relaxing" pet-friendly "getaway", a "very pleasant and well-organized" spot with a "charming location on" Lake Austin, a staff that "really cares", plenty of outdoor activities including 36 holes of golf and "delicious" "diet food that can fool you" (with a no-alcohol policy); a "major expansion" resulted in a "gorgeous" spa facility that "makes a stay here sublime."

Renaissance Austin ∇ 23 23 17 22 $179

9721 Arboretum Blvd.; 512-343-2626; fax 512-346-7953; 800-468-3571; www.renaissanceaustin.com; 433 rooms, 45 suites

The "huge atrium" makes for a "lovely setting" for industry gatherings at this "dependably" "good business hotel", with

60,000 sq. ft. of meeting spaces "within easy walking distance" of shopping and dining and "convenient" to several large corporate headquarters; an "incredible renovation" put the public facilities on par with the rooms, and the staff is as "pleasant" as ever.

Dallas/Ft. Worth

Adolphus, The ✕Ⓗ | 23 | 24 | 24 | 22 | $188

1321 Commerce St., Dallas; 214-742-8200; fax 214-651-3561; 800-221-9083; www.hoteladolphus.com; 400 rooms, 22 suites
A vision of beer baron Adolphus Busch, this "grand ol'" "Dallas beauty" "in the middle of a reviving Downtown" is "worth a visit" agree adherents who appreciate "old-world charm", "antiques", "huge flower arrangements" and "formal" dining in the French Room (voted No. 1 for Food, Decor and Service in our *Dallas Restaurant Survey*); moderates maintain it's a smidgen "stuffy"; P.S. those who fret about "faded splendor" may not be aware of the "great renovations" completed post-*Survey*.

Ashton Ⓗ | – | – | – | – | $260

610 Main St., Ft. Worth; 817-332-0100; fax 817-332-0110; 866-327-4866; www.theashtonhotel.com; 29 rooms, 10 suites
This "classy" member of Small Luxury Hotels of the World, a block from Sundance Square, is set in refurbished buildings listed on the National Register of Historic Places; awed admirers attest it's "a wonderful retreat" "trying very hard to live up to" the hotel's "promise", with draws including custom-designed furnishings, Frette linens and American bistro dining in Café Ashton.

CRESCENT COURT, HOTEL ✕Ⓢ | 25 | 26 | 24 | 26 | $380

400 Crescent Ct., Dallas; 214-871-3200; fax 214-871-3272; 888-767-3966; www.crescentcourt.com; 162 rooms, 29 suites
"Cushy", "classic" and "consistent", this uptown Crescent Complex "oasis" is both "ideal for business" and "a nice weekend escape", especially considering the "spectacular health club and spa" (with an "intriguing BBQ sauce treatment"), nearby "high-end shopping" and dining at the on-site Nobu outpost; this pet-friendly lap of "luxury" also offers "lavish amenities", a lobby with "more marble than a quarry", "tasteful" rooms and "top-notch service."

Fairmont Dallas | 20 | 21 | 19 | 20 | $239

1717 N. Akard St., Dallas; 214-720-2020; fax 214-720-5269; 800-441-1414; www.fairmont.com; 501 rooms, 50 suites
Boosters brag that this "big hotel with a big heart" is an "old yet graceful" "classic" with "comfy rooms" and a "fabulous" location providing "easy access to Dallas business centers" and "the arts district"; those who think it "tries hard" and only "sometimes succeeds" say it's "showing its age", with "tired rooms and lobby", "extremely slow elevators" and "average food."

FOUR SEASONS AT LAS COLINAS ✕Ⓢ | 26 | 26 | 24 | 28 | $325

4150 N. MacArthur Blvd., Irving; 972-717-0700; fax 972-717-2550; 800-332-3442; www.fourseasons.com; 342 rooms, 15 suites
"Everybody wins" at this "resortlike location" "a bit removed from everything" but "within minutes of the big city" that's like a

"luxurious business hotel crossed with an exclusive country club" ("indeed, everything is bigger in Texas") and features "some of the best golf", a "spectacular fitness facility", a "drop-dead gorgeous pool", an "Asian-inspired cafe on the green that's surprisingly sophisticated", "unbelievable service" and envy-inspiring rooms ("if only your casa were like their casitas").

Greenhouse, The Ⓢ — | — | — | — | $972

1171 107th St., Arlington; 817-640-4000; fax 817-649-0422; www.thegreenhousespa.net; 33 rooms, 2 suites

You'll "lose weight" and "never feel so pampered" in the process at this "boot camp" "for women only" nestled in a Southern-style mansion on the outskirts of Dallas, where "after a day of exercise and activity" you can get a "tuck-in massage before bed" in rooms whispering "luxury extraordinaire"; "delicious low-cal meals" are served on china "so beautiful you don't even see there's no food."

Magnolia Hotel Ⓗ ▽ 26 | 23 | 15 | 22 | $220

1401 Commerce St., Dallas; 214-915-6500; fax 214-253-0053; 888-915-1110; www.magnoliahotels.com; 200 rooms, 130 suites

"Stylish, minimalist rooms with cool photography", a "gorgeous lobby" and a "fun, hip, helpful staff" are housed in this "historic building" with "modern elegance" and "downtown cool", making it an "excellent place to stay" that's "nicer than your typical boutique hotel"; there's also a complimentary billiards room and "free cookies and milk at night."

MANSION ON TURTLE CREEK, THE 27 | 27 | 28 | 26 | $405

2821 Turtle Creek Blvd., Dallas; 214-559-2100; fax 214-528-4187; 888-767-3966; www.mansiononturtlecreek.com; 127 rooms, 16 suites

Expect a "luxury stay" at this "world-class hotel deep in the heart of Texas", a "distinctive destination" and "hallmark" "amid the serenity of Turtle Creek" delivering "pure elegance" and "well-appointed rooms", "over-the-top" service that "makes you feel like royalty" (there's a two-to-one staff-to-guest ratio) and "incredible" "haute" fare (modern Southwestern) from "world-famous chef Dean Fearing" – in short, the whole "sublime" experience is "worth every penny", maybe even more since the post-*Survey* takeover by Rosewood Hotels.

Melrose Hotel, The Ⓗ 21 | 22 | 19 | 19 | $289

3015 Oak Lawn Ave., Dallas; 214-521-5151; fax 214-521-2470; 800-635-7673; www.melrosehotel.com; 162 rooms, 22 suites

"Very loyal gay clientele mixes with very loyal old money" at this "classic", "old-fashioned European–style" hotel offering "a step back in time"; believers brag about "bright, airy" quarters that are "well appointed and cozy", "friendly service", "one of the coolest bars in Dallas" and a location that's "convenient to" "GLBT nightlife", but some raters recommend "seeing your room before you accept it" at this "dowager."

Omni Mandalay Hotel 24 | 22 | 19 | 22 | $229

221 E. Las Colinas Blvd., Irving; 972-556-0800; fax 972-556-0729; 800-843-6664; www.omnihotels.com; 325 rooms, 96 suites

"An alternative for a large conference" near Dallas/Ft. Worth Airport is this "very comfortable business meeting arena" with more than 22 event spaces, including "rooms as big as Texas" where conventioneers can bring bustle to a "quiet" "suburban" location; still, despite "consistently good service", some patrons pan this "converted Four Seasons" for being "a little tired."

Renaissance Worthington ▽ 23 | 24 | 19 | 23 | $239

200 Main St., Ft. Worth; 817-870-1000; fax 817-338-9176; 800-468-3571; www.renaissancehotels.com; 444 rooms, 30 suites

As the "respectful" staff will tell you, this hotel in a "great location" for families is "an easy stroll" to lots of shops, movies, restaurants and nightlife, and it's "close to the stockyards, the rodeo, museums" and other "things to do and see in the people-friendly cow town"; if the in-house dining and stores are "limited", at least the health club is "well equipped."

Westin Galleria 20 | 20 | 17 | 20 | $279

13340 Dallas Pkwy., Dallas; 972-934-9494; fax 975-851-2869; 888-625-5144; www.westin.com; 411 rooms, 21 suites

"If you have children old enough to shop, ice skate and hang out", "send them off while you take a rest" at this "old favorite" "for families" and their "unmaxed credit cards" situated inside the "luxe" Galleria mall; the staff is "always friendly" and Oceania is a "godsend" for upscale seafood, but despite the "new, much-hyped work-out facility", the "public spaces stuck in the '70s" and "small", "run-down" rooms have overnighters begging "please renovate."

Westin Stonebriar Resort Ⓢ 24 | 22 | 20 | 24 | $319

1549 Legacy Dr., Frisco; 972-668-8000; fax 972-668-8100; 888-627-8441; www.westinstonebriar.com; 288 rooms, 13 suites

"From the outside it doesn't appear to be much" but "on the inside they do a great job of making you forget you're in the middle of the Metroplex" just north of Dallas at this resort that "caters to golfers and business conferencers", with "good play on the Fazio course", a "small" but "fun pool" and "pleasant" if "too few" staffers; the gym might be "in a broom cupboard", but you'll get your workout in anyway, as the hotel is so "big", it's a "long walk to your room."

Wyndham Anatole Ⓢ 19 | 20 | 20 | 23 | $339

2201 Stemmons Frwy., Dallas; 214-748-1200; fax 214-761-7520; 800-822-4200; www.wyndham.com; 1600 rooms, 129 suites

Like Texas itself, this hotel is "huge!" – "the rooms are bigger than NYC apartments", and "you can get lost" trying to find yours along this "monster's" "rambling" hallways; there's a "great piano lounge", the "meals and the view from Nana Grill are among Dallas' best" and "acres" of parkland and a "huge pool" keep conference-goers' kids "fascinated"; still, with "too many conventioneers", "too institutional" a feel and "not enough staff", it's "like staying in a small country" – with a "disorganized" bureacracy.

Zaza, Hotel Ⓢ 27 | 22 | 23 | 23 | $359

2332 Leonard St., Dallas; 214-468-8399; fax 214-468-8397; 800-597-8399; www.hotelzaza.com; 152 suites

Za-lots are jazzed about this "happening" lodging that's "the closest thing you'll find to a boutique hotel in Dallas", with "the right combination of whimsy and decadence" in its "businessman-friendly" accommodations (it's also a "great choice for a romantic night away"); approvers attribute its "undeniable snob appeal" to the "high-end", "sexy suites" with "eclectic designer decor" and "hot scene" in the "rocking bar filled with hipsters", but skeptics note it's "not quite there" and wonder "what's all the hype for?"

Galveston

Galvez-Historic Wyndham Ⓗ 19 | 20 | 18 | 20 | $149

2024 Seawall Blvd.; 409-765-7721; fax 409-765-5780; 800-996-3426; www.wyndhamhotelgalvez.com; 219 rooms, 7 suites

Romantics rate this "lovely old hotel" opened in 1911 a "grand" "weekend getaway" destination "overlooking the Gulf of Mexico", with a "funky bar scene" and "quite good Sunday brunch"; phobes fault the "small" digs and dining that's "average overall."

Tremont House, A Wyndham Hotel Ⓗ 24 | 23 | 21 | 20 | $225

2300 Ship's Mechanic Row; 409-763-0300; fax 409-763-1539; 800-996-3426; www.wyndhamtremonthouse.com; 104 rooms, 15 suites

"It feels like stepping back into the early 1900s" at "the place to stay if you're not at the beach", a "beautiful hotel in a restored historic building near the waterfront" by the Strand; with "warming racks for towels", "high ceilings and beadboard walls" in rooms, this "relaxing" place "loaded with period charm" fits your vacation in Galveston "like a floral print shirt on a summer night."

Houston

Derek, Hotel 23 | 19 | 17 | 21 | $194

2525 W. Loop S.; 713-961-3000; fax 713-297-4392; www.hotelderek.com; 288 rooms, 26 suites

Surveyors say this "swanky, minimalist" boutique property where the "Wild West meets LA cool" in the Galleria area has "fantastic design", rooms housing "large baths and luxurious toiletries", a "see-and-be-seen" bar and "friendly staff" – just "don't expect anything normal because it tries to be different"; jaded journeyers jot that it's "average" with a "haughty" "attitude"; N.B. the restaurant, bistro moderne, opened post-*Survey*.

FOUR SEASONS ✕ Ⓢ 26 | 26 | 26 | 25 | $330

1300 Lamar St.; 713-650-1300; fax 713-652-6220; 800-332-3442; www.fourseasons.com; 289 rooms, 115 suites

"You forget that you're in" "humid, hectic Houston" at this "remarkable property" with "everything you love about the Four Seasons", including "fine accommodations" (with "impressive toiletries" and the "comfiest pillows"), "exemplary service", a "convenient Downtown location" for business, shopping and sports venues, and "great food from a very creative chef" in the American-Italian Quattro (plus a "hip bar" and "power breakfast scene"); N.B. a $10-million renovation has made it all the better.

Hilton Americas Houston ∇ 24 | 22 | 22 | 26 | $224

1600 Lamar St.; 713-739-8000; fax 713-739-8007; 800-774-1500; www.hilton.com; 1200 rooms

"Strikingly modern, minimalist decor frames a great close-up view of Downtown" at this "huge" pet-friendly property that's "more like a luxury hotel" than a business one, though it's connected to the

George R. Brown Convention Center and has "all the amenities" including "state-of-the-art meeting space", "hospitable service", a "great gym", "sublime" rooftop pool and "good steakhouse and bars"; still, a few holdouts hint that this "mega" facility is "shaking out the kinks."

Houstonian, The 23 | 25 | 22 | 27 | $315

111 N. Post Oak Ln.; 713-680-2626; fax 713-680-2992; 800-231-2759; www.houstonian.com; 280 rooms, 7 suites

This "stunning retreat" is "both elegant and country at the same time", rounding up the raves for it's "upscale, moneyed" feel, "fine rooms" with "tasteful decor", "first-rate service", "drop-dead unbelievable" "fitness center and spa", "lush landscaping" and "convenient location" just "minutes from Houston's urban Galleria district" – in short, "an excellent choice for travel" (if your kids are with you, check out The Bungalow for its extensive play areas).

Icon, Hotel – | – | – | – | $259

220 Main St.; 713-224-4266; fax 713-223-3223; www.hotelicon.com; 126 rooms, 9 suites

European opulence meets refined urban style at this Downtown hotel, where deep reds and browns with gold trimming add an old-school style; highlights include Jean-Georges Vongerichten's Bank eatery, Rande Gerber's first Texas venture, The Whiskey bar, and in-room amenities that include wall-mounted, 27-inch TVs.

InterContinental 22 | 21 | 18 | 22 | $249

2222 SW. Loop; 713-627-7600; fax 713-916-3327; 800-327-0200; www.interconti.com; 465 rooms, 20 suites

To some raters, this "well-appointed", pet-friendly property is "one of Houston's hippest" in a "location perfect for business or shopping" (one block from the Galleria), with "tasteful" decor, "huge meeting spaces", "comfortable linens and amenities", "good service" and a "lobby bar that's always hopping"; less impressed guests, however, are "underwhelmed."

Lancaster, The 23 | 24 | 24 | 21 | $270

701 Texas Ave.; 713-228-9500; fax 713-223-4528; 800-231-0336; www.lancaster.com; 83 rooms, 10 suites

"A charming English inn in the heart of Downtown", this "intimate and romantic" member of the Small Luxury Hotels of the World group is "super-handy for business, theater and opera", with "traditional" rooms that may be "small but have character", an "attentive staff" that has "pampering high on the agenda" and "great dining" in Bistro Lancaster, "a popular meet and greet place" with a "creative menu."

Omni Houston 20 | 23 | 23 | 22 | $369

4 Riverway; 713-871-8181; fax 713-871-0719; 800-843-6664; www.omnihotels.com; 335 rooms, 43 suites

"Whether for business or monkey business, this is a wonderful hotel" with grounds that make you feel "like you're staying in a park", though it's "right by the Galleria"; despite rooms that are "nothing special", it's "worth" a stay to dine at the New American eatery, Noe (opened post-*Survey*), to "relax" with a cocktail in one of the lounge's "big stuffed chairs" or to take a dip in the "lovely pool, if you don't mind the gawkers in the nearby office towers."

ST. REGIS | 26 | 26 | 24 | 24 | $430

1919 Briar Oaks Ln.; 713-840-7600; fax 713-840-8036; 877-787-3447; www.stregis.com; 177 rooms, 55 suites

"Shop awhile, rest awhile, repeat when necessary" is the prescription at this "elegant" balm of a hotel, where "top-notch service" is administered by a "staff that's quick to remedy any complaint"; there's "first-rate dining" and "exquisite" quarters graced with "live orchids", and the "peace" of this River Oaks location is preserved by new four-layer, noise-muffling windows.

Warwick, The | 19 | 20 | 19 | 18 | $239

5701 Main St.; 713-526-1991; fax 713-526-0359; www.warwickhotelhouston.com; 234 rooms, 74 suites

The "magnificent" "museum district location, sense of historical importance" and "spectacular city views" still draw discriminating guests to this "former grande dame" near a light rail station; it's "comfortable and inexpensive", but au courant clientele call it "unnecessarily old-fashioned", and snap just "try to find someone to help you when you need it"; N.B. new owners plan post-*Survey* renovations, including the addition of a spa.

Lajitas

Lajitas, the Ultimate Hideout | – | – | – | – | $315

HC 70, Box 400; 432-424-5000; fax 432-424-3277; 877-525-4827; www.lajitas.com; 87 rooms, 6 suites

A "personal golf cart picks you up at the private airstrip" and "takes you straight to the green" at this "fun getaway" on a 25,000-acre private estate "out in the middle of nowhere" in the "real Old West", where you'll need to "bring wads of cash" to enjoy its four different hotel settings, "eager" service, spa treatments, equestrian activities and cowboy-style fine dining; N.B. 2005 renovations included room additions and a pool expansion.

Marfa

Cibolo Creek Ranch | – | – | – | – | $450

HCR 67, Box 44; 432-229-3737; fax 432-229-3653; www.cibolocreekranch.com; 30 rooms, 2 suites

Travel back to 19th-century Texas without a time machine at this working longhorn ranch in the "lovely high desert climate" of the Chinati Mountains, where three historic forts were transformed into "a jewel of a destination" with traditional Mexican architecture, adobe fireplaces, wood-framed beds and no phones in the rooms; it's "worth every dime to the private-plane set", with a staff that "makes you feel like family" and three gourmet meals a day; N.B. activities include horseback riding, hunting and clay shooting.

San Antonio

Fairmount | ▽ 25 | 24 | 23 | 21 | $219

(fka Fairmount, A Wyndham Hotel)

401 S. Alamo St.; 210-224-8800; fax 210-475-0082; 800-996-3426; www.wyndham.com; 37 rooms, 19 suites

A "beautiful old hotel" "in the heart of Downtown" "within one block of the Riverwalk", this "historic landmark" is "not large so it's a little more personalized", with rooms featuring "big fluffy beds" and Southwestern/Continental dining (there's also "great Tex-Mex places within walking distance"); still, a slice of surveyors disclose it "does not show its age well"; N.B. an ownership change occurred post-*Survey*.

Hyatt Regency Hill Country | 22 | 23 | 21 | 27 | $328 |

9800 Hyatt Resort Dr.; 210-647-1234; fax 210-681-9681; 800-554-9288; www.hillcountry.hyatt.com; 445 rooms, 58 suites

Check into this "hill country" "home on the range in style", a "fun place to go with the family and for a corporate retreat" with "lodgelike" accommodations "surrounded by a championship golf course", outdoor activities including an "inner-tubing" "trip on the lazy river" and spa treatments that add to the "relaxing" atmosphere where you can "unwind without the pretension"; that said, some varmints veto the "mediocre rooms" and "food quality that can be lacking."

La Mansión del Rio | 22 | 23 | 23 | 22 | $319 |

112 College St.; 210-518-1000; fax 210-226-0389; 800-292-7300; www.lamansion.com; 332 rooms, 5 suites

"Quaint" and "picturesque", this pet-friendly "elegant and romantic" "old Spanish-style property" "on the Riverwalk" is "not your typical chain hotel"; while pleased pen pals posit it's "well worth a visit for business or pleasure" thanks to "nice, comfortable rooms" ("ask for a river view"), a "helpful staff" and "exciting" Regional American fare in Las Canarias restaurant, a "disappointed" few say it's "noisy" and "needs to be revamped."

Menger Hotel Ⓗ Ⓢ | 20 | 23 | 21 | 21 | $149 |

204 Alamo Plaza; 210-223-4361; fax 210-228-0022; 800-345-9285; www.historicmenger.com; 293 rooms, 22 suites

"Adventurous spirits" are "enchanted" by this "interesting" "hotel sensitive to its history", with "much memorabilia about its storied past", "lovely grounds" in a "prime location overlooking The Alamo", "old-fashioned service" and a "great bar"; wags warn "it was best when Teddy Roosevelt was here recruiting his Rough Riders", calling it a "dated", "glorified motel."

St. Anthony-Historic Wyndham Ⓗ | 21 | 23 | 21 | 21 | $219 |

300 E. Travis St.; 210-227-4392; fax 210-227-4391; 800-996-3426; www.wyndham.com; 314 rooms, 38 suites

"A traditional favorite with loads of class" a short stroll from the River Walk "right in the middle of the historic city", this "elegant" turn-of-the-century property has "always been gorgeous", but it now features "the amenities of today", including WiFi; "come hungry" for the "fantastic Sunday brunch", which you'll "love" snoozing off in a four-poster bed in a "sumptuous suite."

Valencia Riverwalk, Hotel | – | – | – | – | $299 |

150 E. Houston St.; 210-227-9700; fax 210-227-9701; 866-842-0100; www.hotelvalencia.com; 208 rooms, 5 suites

The emphasis is on style at this urban riverfront member of Small Luxury Hotels of the World, put together by hot LA designer Dodd Mitchell, where rooms are outfitted with plantation shutters, leather chairs and custom-made beds with faux mink designer throws; the chic look extends to its restaurant, with executive chef Jeffery Balfour stirring up New American–Spanish fare, and to Vbar, which draws crowds for tapas and waterfront views.

Watermark Hotel & Spa | – | – | – | – | $419
212 W. Crocket St.; 210-396-5800; fax 210-393-5813; 866-605-1212; www.watermarkhotel.com; 93 rooms, 6 suites
"Old West meets New Age" at this "location with a modern feel" that's making its mark on the River Walk; step across the lobby's mahogany floors and into your room featuring an urban-chic, iron four-poster bed and a marble bathroom with Jacuzzi; the facilities are "tidy" and "well maintained", and you can book a lavish, water-view suite adjoining the spa for private treatments for two.

Westin La Cantera | 26 | 23 | 21 | 28 | $339
16641 La Cantera Pkwy.; 210-558-6500; fax 210-558-2400; 888-937-8461; www.westinlacantera.com; 484 rooms, 24 suites, 11 casitas
With "palatial" grounds, this "fancy" "castle on a hill with sweeping views of the Texas Hill Country" is "one of the nicest" Lone Star State resorts for families; the "top-drawer" service and amenities include "impressive" rooms, "superb" restaurants, two "first-rate golf courses", "huge swimming pools", a "wonderful spa", kiddie camp and access via shuttle to nearby Six Flags Fiesta Texas.

Westin River Walk | 25 | 23 | 19 | 23 | $329
420 W. Market St.; 210-224-6500; fax 210-444-6000; 800-228-3000; www.westin.com/riverwalk; 433 rooms, 40 suites
"The good life" can be had amid the "breathtaking" "marble-faced public areas" at this chainster in a "quiet" River Walk location, and the "sleek, modern rooms" "don't let up from there"; neither does the "exemplary" staff whose "Southern hospitality" helps the "large" place "maintain a small feel", and if the dining isn't stellar, the chain's signature "beds and showers are."

The Woodlands

Marriott Woodlands Waterway | ▽ 24 | 24 | 19 | 24 | $149
1601 Lake Robbins Dr.; 281-367-9797; fax 281-681-5656; www.marriott.com; 329 rooms, 7 suites
"A beautiful resort with everything from golf to tennis to wooded areas", this "suburban convention hotel" is situated in the scenic, mile-long Woodlands Waterway with entertainment, shopping and dining about 30 miles from Houston ("farther from the metro area than desired"); rooms are "modern", service is "attentive" and there are two restaurants; N.B. a spa opens in November 2005.

U.S. Virgin Islands

St. Croix

Buccaneer, The | ▽ 22 | 21 | 20 | 24 | $340
Gallows Bay, Christiansted; 340-712-2100; fax 340-712-2105; 800-255-3881; www.thebuccaneer.com; 12 cottages, 2 suites, 3 houses
This "lovely family-run resort with a personal touch" and a "superb staff" is a "well-rounded" St. Croix property dating back to the

17th century exudes "subtle class"; fans are hooked on the "fabulous breakfast buffet", "terrific range of activities and sports options", including a spa, two pools and the "fun, easy golf course with great ocean views" as well as the "beautiful rooms", some with "window seats where you can snooze"; still, a few find it "disappointing" and "a hike from the main building to the beach."

Carambola Beach ▽ 20 | 17 | 17 | 22 | $350

Estate Davis Bay, Kingshill; 340-778-3800; fax 340-778-1682; 888-503-8760; www.carambolabeach.com; 150 rooms, 1 suite

"Finagle a waterside room and sleep with the crashing waves outside your window" at this "escape" on St. Croix's Davis Bay "nestled in the small but lush rain-forest area"; "it's a bit remote", with "minimalist, hutlike" rooms that are "romantic" ("because of the beautiful views and the feeling that we were the only people around") and a "challenging golf course"; a mystified few find "good bones" but a "lost treasure."

St. John

Caneel Bay 23 | 25 | 23 | 26 | $395

N. Shore Rd.; 340-776-6111; fax 340-693-8280; 888-767-3966; www.caneelbay.com; 166 cottages

"Exquisite old-world charm" and "unsurpassed serenity" mark this "sublime spot" in Virgin Islands National Park, an "expansive property" where "natural beauty prevails"; "escape to Utopia" with "seven amazing beaches that speak for themselves", offering "pristine" "white sand, crystal clear water" and "unbelievable snorkeling", plus "rooms are large and lux" (although without TVs and phones), service is "beyond expectations" and the food is "excellent" at the Turtle Bay Estate House and Equator Restaurant.

Westin 22 | 21 | 19 | 25 | $419

Great Cruz Bay; 340-693-8000; fax 340-779-4985; www.westin.com; 262 rooms, 7 suites, 96 villas, 13 townhouses

"An upscale version of the 'don't worry, be happy' vacation", this "primo" family "paradise" is "perfect" for "relaxing in a float, cocktail in hand" with "everything at your fingertips", from "plenty of diversions for kids" to a "beautiful but small beach"; "the private villas with pools are a great way to enjoy the resort without the hustle-bustle", plus the "gorgeous suites" and "nicely appointed rooms" offer "amenities beyond the expected"; if some "wish the dining was better, it's easy to get into town for good eats."

St. Thomas

Marriott Frenchman's Reef & Morning Star Beach Resort 20 | 20 | 18 | 23 | $475

5 Estate Bakkeroe; 340-776-8500; fax 340-715-6192; 800-228-9290; www.marriott.com; 453 rooms, 28 suites

It's an "environment equivalent to paradise" exclaim enthusiasts of this "friendly" "family destination" offering a "tremendous variety" of rooms, "excellent views" of the Charlotte Amalie Harbor, "convivial" dining options "overlooking the sea" and a "wonderful boat shuttle to town"; "rooms at Frenchman's Reef are large and well appointed" but "if you want the beach at your feet" – a "peaceful beach" too – "request the Morning Star resort"; if the less-captivated feel it's "somewhat dated", defenders say "it's not the Ritz – but you don't pay Ritz prices, either!"

Ritz-Carlton, The 26 | 25 | 23 | 25 | $545

6900 Great Bay; 340-775-3333; fax 340-775-4444; 800-241-3333; www.ritzcarlton.com; 148 rooms, 4 suites

"Away from the maddening crowds" on the east side of the island near the ferry to St. John, this "gorgeous beachfront" "treasure" valued for its "sophisticated Med flair", "great pool" and "lovely" gardens "goes beyond the lap of luxury", from a "staff that does everything but carry you on their backs" to "first-rate rooms"; "the world is a world away" thanks to the new "top-notch spa", "exceptional club level lounge" and "outstanding" fare.

Utah

Moab

Sorrel River Ranch Resort – | – | – | – | $249

Hwy. 128, Mile 17; 435-259-4642; fax 435-259-3016; 877-359-2715; www.sorrelriver.com; 55 suites

Blessed with a "picturesque, peaceful setting" overlooking the Colorado River and "red-rock beauty of Moab", this remote south Utah ranch (a member of Small Luxury Hotels of the World) offers luxurious suites and rooms outfitted with kitchenettes, porches and Western-style furniture; guests can venture to Arches and Canyonland National Parks, go white-water rafting, mountain biking or horseback riding, then dine at The River Grill restaurant.

Park City

Deer Valley Lodging ▽ 26 | 24 | 26 | 26 | $320

1375 Deer Valley Dr. S., Deer Valley; 435-649-4040; fax 435-658-3007; 800-453-3833; www.deervalleylodging.com; 593 rooms

Ski bunnies looking for "proximity to the slopes" give this lodging company a "gold medal" for its array of ski-in/ski-out hotels, condos, townhouses and private homes, plus "great service" and Bistro Toujours restaurant at The Chateaux at Silver Lake; but accommodations range from "amazing to not so", so be sure to ask for those outfitted with fireplaces, full kitchens and hot tubs.

GOLDENER HIRSCH INN ▽ 29 | 28 | 26 | 26 | $490

7570 Royal St. E.; 435-649-7770; fax 435-649-7901; 800-252-3373; www.goldenerhirschinn.com; 20 rooms, 2 penthouses

Blending European flavor with "convenient" ski-in/ski-out access to Deer Valley, this "very comfortable" Relais & Châteaux "Austrian dream" is full of "fanciful rooms" fitted with sculpted-wood balconies, Tyrolean hand-painted period furniture and Frette linens; "wonderful service" and "great food" at its contemporary American-Continental restaurant are available off-season too, when guests can hike, fly-fish or shop in Downtown Park City.

Park City, Hotel – | – | – | – | $699

2001 Park Ave.; 435-940-5000; fax 435-940-5001; 888-999-0098; www.hotelparkcity.com; 54 suites

This lodge-style Small Leading Hotels of the World affiliate is set amid the pines and aspens at the base of the Wasatch Mountains, about 35 minutes from Salt Lake City Airport; there's something for everyone with three ski resorts within five minutes, a year-round, heated outdoor pool, fireplaces and terraces in all suites, a world-class spa, a golf course and mountain vistas.

STEIN ERIKSEN LODGE 27 | 27 | 27 | 27 | $750

7700 Stein Way; 435-649-3700; fax 435-649-5825; 800-453-1302; www.steinlodge.com; 112 rooms, 58 suites

Former Olympic champ Stein Eriksen's "classy", adult-oriented resort is his "true gold-medal performance", where "every detail is attended to" from "hot chocolate in the locker room" and a concierge who "carries your skis to the slopes" to "excellent food"; even the "small" rooms come with jetted tubs, while some suites have wood-burning fireplaces and "balconies overlooking the mountains"; and though winter "prices are higher than the peaks", "summer is a bargain."

Salt Lake City

GRAND AMERICA HOTEL 27 | 25 | 22 | 26 | $269

555 S. Main St.; 801-258-6000; fax 801-596-6911; 800-621-4505; www.grandamerica.com; 380 rooms, 398 suites

"Wow" utter tongue-tied guests about this "plush" Downtown hotel that "far outclasses" its neighbors; "truly grand" describes both the staff "that seems to be everywhere and eager to assist you" and the "spectacular facilities" numbering a "relaxing" spa, fitness center, and indoor and outdoor pools; "fit for a king" or queen, the "opulent, spacious" guestrooms have "quality" sheets, imported furniture and "luxurious" marble baths, and many feature views of the Rockies.

Little America 20 | 22 | 15 | 19 | $119

500 S. Main St.; 801-596-5700; fax 801-596-5911; 800-453-9450; www.littleamerica.com; 850 rooms, 23 suites

With a "light rail station right in front for easy access" to Salt Lake City attractions, this "less ostentatious but hardly a poor cousin" to the Grand America is a "first choice" for families thanks to the indoor/outdoor pool and "spacious" standard rooms with living areas that make them "larger than most suites"; naysayers counter, it's "old and tired" with "ok" service.

Lodge at Snowbird ▽ 19 | 18 | 17 | 23 | $229

Hwy. 210, Little Cottonwood Canyon Rd., Snowbird; 801-933-2229; fax 801-933-2248; 800-232-9542; www.snowbird.com; 124 rooms

"Close mountain access makes up for the lack of style" at this circa-1970 and recently renovated condo complex comprising singles and studios, all of which have "views of the slopes" from private balconies (some with kitchens and fireplaces); a pool, hot tub and the nearby Cliff Lodge's "completely sybaritic" Cliff Spa offer opportunities to restore sore skiing muscles.

Monaco, Hotel ▽ 24 | 22 | 21 | 19 | $209

15 W. 200 S.; 801-595-0000; fax 801-532-8500; 800-805-1801; www.monaco-saltlakecity.com; 190 rooms, 35 suites

"You and your dog are treated like royalty" at this Kimpton Group "oasis of hip in the middle of Salt Lake City" that's so "pet-friendly" they'll even loan guests a goldfish for company; although "matchbox"-size, the rooms are a "funky" "change from the standard", and a "gracious" staff, full ski services, free neck massages and nightly wine tastings all add to the "inviting" vibe.

Snowbird Ski & Summer Resort Cliff Lodge & Spa ▽ 21 | 18 | 18 | 27 | $249

Little Cottonwood Canyon Rd., Snowbird; 801-933-2222; fax 801-933-2298; 800-232-9542; www.snowbird.com; 348 rooms, 21 suites, 54 condos

Thanks to ski-in/ski-out access, this "huge" "fortress" of a resort is among the "best places to stay at Snowbird simply because there's no hefty commute" to the slopes; "good rooms, fast service" and a "family-friendly atmosphere" are assets, as are the public spaces' "walls of glass offering impossible views" and a rooftop spa whose hot tub "overlooking the mountain" draws schussers to soak with "drinks in hand and snowflakes falling on your head."

Sundance ▽ 25 | 24 | 26 | 27 | $320

N. Fork Provo Canyon, Sundance; 801-225-4100; fax 801-226-1937; 800-892-1600; www.sundanceresort.com; 40 rooms, 70 suites, 12 houses

"Mr. Redford has preserved something special" at his "remote" place to "unwind", "enjoy the fluffy white stuff", hike, ride horses or kindle "romance" in "tastefully" "rustic" accommodations that include rooms, suites and homes "grouped along creeks that rush through the mountains"; gilding the lily is a "stunning staff that looks like it's imported from LA", a "fine" spa and "first-class" fare in the Tree Room and Foundry Grill, where "breakfast is the true winner."

St. George

Coyote Inn at Green Valley Spa – | – | – | – | $395

1871 W. Canyon View Dr.; 435-628-8060; fax 435-673-4084; 800-237-1068; www.greenvalleyspa.com; 46 suites

Surrounded by a dramatic desertscape, this exclusive fitness-oriented resort hosts a coterie of guests in its one- and two-bedroom adobe-style suites equipped with four-poster featherbeds, whirlpools, fireplaces and patios; highlights include hiking in Zion National Park, rock climbing, meditation, tennis, golf, swimming and aqua classes in six pools, a spa with loads of treatments, "excellent massages" and Native American–inspired therapies, and a restaurant serving gourmet South Beach Diet–type fare.

Vermont

Barnard

TWIN FARMS 29 | 29 | 28 | 27 | $1050

Stage Rd.; 802-234-9999; fax 802-234-9990; 800-894-6327; www.twinfarms.com; 4 rooms, 1 house, 11 cottages

"Nobody does it better" than this "spectacular" inn that earns a sky-high score for "sinfully indulgent" rooms in both the lodge and the main house (think raised hearth fireplaces, thick American quilts); catering to an "elite set" means "privacy respected", "meals expertly prepared" and "whatever else you could possibly want" in a country lodge; sure it's "expensive with a capital E", but it's worth every one of those "thousands of pennies."

Essex

Inn at Essex, The ▽ 21 | 22 | 25 | 19 | $269

70 Essex Way; 802-878-1100; fax 802-878-0063; 800-727-4295; www.vtculinaryresort.com; 103 rooms, 17 suites

It's no wonder the "dining is fantastic" at this "peaceful" country inn – meals are created by "future star chefs"/current students of the New England Culinary Institute; while decor is "Vermont kitsch" and service is "slow", you'll have "your own fireplace in winter", and golf, tennis and swimming in summer.

Lower Waterford

Rabbit Hill Inn Ⓗ Ⓢ – | – | – | – | $220

48 Lower Waterford Rd.; 802-748-5168; fax 802-748-8342; 800-762-8669; www.rabbithillinn.com; 15 suites, 4 rooms

The seasonal New American meals are "amazing" and the accommodations "incredible" at this rural country inn (established in 1795) that's "worth the high prices"; with a staff that "tries hard" to "treat you like family friends", fireplaces and double whirlpool tubs in most rooms and a "lovely location" in northeastern Vermont, this just might be the "most romantic place on the planet."

Mt. Snow

Inn at Sawmill Farm, The 25 | 26 | 26 | 22 | $450

7 Crosstown Road, West Dover; 802-464-8131; fax 802-464-1130; 800-493-1133; www.theinnatsawmillfarm.com; 17 rooms, 4 suites

An "unbelievable wine list" (nearly 1,300 wines) and "delicious" meals are the highlights of this "lovely little" "getaway" near Mt. Snow, but the "impeccable service" and "spectacular" individually decorated cottages with elaborate furnishings (no phones or TVs) are almost as good; with a "dreamy" setting for snowshoeing and cross-country skiing in winter, fly-fishing, tennis and canoeing in summer, it's no surprise that satisfied sojourners sigh "how can you go wrong?"

Shelburne

Inn at Shelburne Farms 24 | 25 | 26 | 23 | $270

1611 Harbor Rd.; 802-985-8498; fax 802-985-1233; www.shelburnefarms.org; 24 rooms, 2 cottages

"Shhh – it's quiet and we want it to stay that way" say soft-spoken sophists of this "atmospheric" working farm with a "heavenly" location on the shores of Lake Champlain that's "worth the drive and worth the cost"; the food is "fresh and organic", the "grounds are spectacular" and each room in the historic home is different – yes, it's all "truly an experience."

Smuggler's Notch

Smugglers' Notch Resort ▽ 20 | 20 | 14 | 24 | $307

4323 Vermont Rte. 108 S.; 802-644-8851; fax 802-644-5913; 800-451-8752; www.smuggs.com; 566 condos

You won't have to smuggle the kids to this "family-friendly" facility for a "wonderful affordable week away during any season" since it offers plenty of "activities for all ages" (fishing, biking, tennis, golf, skiing), "friendly service" and affordable rates; luckily you can stay at the base of the mountain in condos with kitchenettes, as there's "not much in the way of restaurants."

Stowe

Green Mountain Inn ▽ 19 | 20 | 18 | 18 | $229

18 Main St.; 802-253-7301; fax 802-253-5096; 800-253-7302; www.greenmountaininn.com; 86 rooms, 19 suites, 4 townhouses, 1 apartment

Fall foliage–lovers and skiers seeking a bed near Mt. Mansfield appreciate this historic inn that's "well situated on Main Street" where insiders suggest requesting rooms to the rear rather than the sometimes "noisy front" area; a "friendly staff", "heavenly" all-season outdoor pool and the "cozy" if not gourmet Whip Bar & Grill are all assets, and recently added annexes and renovations should hopefully quell complaints about the "need to update."

Stoweflake Mountain Resort ▽ 21 | 21 | 20 | 24 | $180

1746 Mountain Rd.; 802-253-7355; fax 802-253-6858; 800-253-2232; www.stoweflake.com; 152 rooms, 18 suites

There's "modern luxury" to be found in "a location where rugged is the norm" at this ski resort with an "outstanding" new 50,000-sq.-ft. spa featuring a hydrotherapy waterfall; the "hit-or-miss" dining focuses on organic ingredients and local products, and accommodations include rooms, suites, townhouse facilities with kitchens and "charming" fireplaces as well as a separate four-bedroom family house.

Topnotch at Stowe 17 | 21 | 20 | 24 | $390

4000 Mountain Rd.; 802-253-8585; fax 802-253-9263; 800-451-8686; www.topnotch-resort.com; 92 rooms, 7 suites, 35 townhouses

"Breathtaking views of the mountains" and a "lovely spa" that "exceeds expectations" are the highlights of this ski retreat with a "fantastic location" near the base of Stowe; there are "lots of activities inside and out", but "disappointing" rooms in need of an "overhaul" bring it all down a notch.

Trapp Family Lodge ▽ 20 | 21 | 20 | 22 | $555

700 Trapp Hill Rd.; 802-253-8511; fax 802-253-5740; 800-826-7000; www.trappfamily.com; 86 rooms, 12 suites, 100 houses, 8 villas

Nostalgics still like this Alpine-style ski resort from the Von Trapp Family (of *The Sound of Music* fame) with "yodel"-worthy views, a "beautiful" newer wing and "trails groomed for hiking", cross-country skiing and snowshoeing; but edelweiss-stompers snap "the legacy stuff is getting old", since this "factorylike" lodge is more of a "tourist Trapp" now.

Stratton Mountain

Equinox, The 22 | 23 | 21 | 25 | $372

3567 Main St., Manchester; 802-362-4700; fax 802-362-4861; 800-346-7625; www.equinoxresort.com; 150 rooms, 23 suites

With an "idyllic" setting among "sculpted gardens", this "beautifully restored" "classic New England inn" "has it all":

"fantastic service", a "romantic" restaurant, a "very private" separate residence (the Charles Orvis Inn), a "fabulous" new spa, "lots of activities" including falconry, golf, tennis, hiking and snowmobiling, and outlet shopping nearby; though finicky folks find the "food doesn't match the physical plant", it's a "winning combo" for most.

Sugarbush

Pitcher Inn, The ▽ 29 | 26 | 29 | 22 | $350

275 Main St., Warren; 802-496-6350; fax 802-496-6354; 888-867-4824; www.pitcherinn.com; 9 rooms, 2 suites

The "charmingly eclectic" accommodations ("tie a fly in the Trout Room", "sleep without detention in the School Room") and the "divine" cuisine pull patrons to this Relais & Châteaux inn nestled in a "quaint village"; the staff "knows what you want before you do" – be it "indulging" in the next-door spa or skiing at Sugarbush – and this is "one of the nicest places in the world" to do it.

Vergennes

Basin Harbor Club – | – | – | – | $250

4800 Basin Harbor Rd.; 802-475-2311; fax 802-475-6545; 800-622-4000; www.basinharbor.com; 200 rooms, 77 cottages

If you're looking for an "enjoyable" "old-fashioned family resort" that has "something for everyone", this historic "camp for grown-ups and kids" with a "super golf course" and "quiet" private cottages "right on Lake Champlain" is a "pretty" choice; the "plentiful" food is "fairly pedestrian" and activities like hayrides, bonfires and storytelling are "out of the 1950s", but that's perfect for "reunion" regulars (though "a bit stale" for others).

Woodstock

Quechee Inn at Marshland Farm Ⓗ ▽ 21 | 24 | 24 | 19 | $245

Quechee Main St., Quechee; 802-295-3133; 800-235-3133; www.quecheeinn.com; 22 rooms, 2 suites

A "quintessential Vermont inn", with a "romantic" "gourmet" restaurant and "cozy" quarters, this 19th-century former home (actually built in 1793) of the state's first lieutenant governor is "tucked away in a rural setting" where you can bike, canoe, cross-country ski, swim and visit the town ("a gem"); don't bother to keep in touch with the outside world, since there are "no phones in the rooms"; N.B. you can golf at the nearby private Quechee Club.

Woodstock Inn & Resort 19 | 21 | 20 | 21 | $264

14 The Green; 802-457-1100; fax 802-457-6699; 800-448-7900; www.woodstockinn.com; 134 rooms, 8 suites

Visitors get a "true New England experience" at this "serene" "old war-horse" "nestled in the land of covered bridges" where the "warm service", "cozy fireplace" and afternoon tea are treats on a wintery day; it's an "easy walk to Downtown shops", and there's a "surprisingly good fitness center" and golf course; but the rooms are merely "adequate" unless you "book a newer one."

Virginia

Charlottesville

Boar's Head Inn | 21 | 22 | 22 | 23 | $323 |

200 Ednam Dr.; 434-296-2181; fax 434-972-6024; 800-476-1988; www.boarsheadinn.com; 148 rooms, 11 suites

"Wahoowa!" cheer champions of this "gracious resort" owned by the University of Virginia, a "perfect weekend getaway" (that's also "good for corporate stays") in the "beautiful" "Appalachian foothills", convenient to area wineries, Monticello and other attractions; it boasts plenty of "fun amenities" – including the "spectacular" Birdwood golf course, a "terrific" sports club and an "excellent spa" – as well as an "outstanding restaurant" and "cottagelike rooms" that "ooze Southern charm."

KESWICK HALL AT MONTICELLO | 26 | 25 | 24 | 27 | $465 |

701 Club Dr., Keswick; 434-979-3440; fax 434-977-4171; 800-274-5391; www.keswick.com; 45 rooms, 3 suites

"Laura Ashley meets Thomas Jefferson" at this "wonderful" Orient-Express property "just outside Charlottesville" with "spacious rooms", "each with its own theme", and "outstanding grounds" that include a "relaxing, well-kept" Arnold Palmer signature golf course and a "nice spa"; gastronauts gush the "food alone is worth a visit", and with the opening of Fossett's, a 70-seat American regional, foodies can expect even more "superb dining."

200 South St. Inn Ⓗ | – | – | – | – | $150 |

200 South St.; 434-979-0200; fax 434-979-4463; 800-964-7008; www.southstreetinn.com; 16 rooms, 3 suites

Boasting an intriguing past as a girls' finishing school, and even a brothel, this two-floor B&B dating back to 1856 and comprised of two restored buildings now provides guests with antiques-filled rooms imbued with a timeless grace, along with canopy beds, fireplaces and whirlpool baths; the common library, patio and veranda where wine and cheese are served, and proximity to the University of Virginia and a pedestrian mall, add to its charms.

DC Metro Area

Goodstone Inn & Estate | – | – | – | – | $470 |

36205 Snake Hill Rd., Middleburg; 540-687-4645; fax 540-687-6115; 877-219-4663; www.goodstone.com; 9 rooms, 4 suites

Within this 265-acre historic estate in hunt and wine country, guests can stay in a room at one of the four former estate homes or rent the entire house; the Carriage House, the Dutch Cottage, the Spring House and the French Farm Cottage have all been recently restored and boast views of the Blue Ridge Mountains, and guests can take canoes on Goose Creek, go mountain biking or play a round of golf at nearby Stoneleigh Country Club.

MORRISON HOUSE | 25 | 26 | 27 | 20 | $399 |

116 S. Alfred St., Alexandria; 703-838-8000; fax 703-684-6283; 866-834-6628; www.morrisonhouse.com; 43 rooms, 3 suites

This Relais & Châteaux "hideaway in the city" is "perfect for a wedding night", but whether or not you're getting hitched, it's a "wonderful" "place to create memories", if not in the rooms with the "most comfortable beds", then during one of the "superbly prepared dinners"; with a "staff that makes you feel like a king", a "cozy bar" and a "country-house" ambiance, it adds a "breath of fresh luxury to the Old Town Alexandria experience."

Ritz-Carlton Pentagon City 25 | 25 | 24 | 24 | $399
1250 S. Hayes St., Arlington; 703-415-5000; fax 703-415-5061; 800-241-3333; www.ritzcarlton.com; 345 rooms, 21 suites
You can shop till you drop while staying at this "classy" Ritz-Carlton with "excellent access" to the "adjoining" "first-class" "fashion center", but don't overlook the "ambiance and charm", "extremely well-appointed" rooms, "delightful staff" and "amazing brunch."

RITZ-CARLTON TYSONS CORNER 26 | 25 | 25 | 25 | $359
1700 Tysons Blvd., McLean; 703-506-4300; fax 703-506-2694; 800-241-3333; www.ritzcarlton.com; 365 rooms, 33 suites
"Shopping, shopping and more shopping" is "reason enough to stay" at this "top-of-the-line" McLean property that's "attached to the ritziest mall in the area"; but many come to "relax in the opulence" of the "elegant surroundings", hang out on the "great club floor" and tuck into "the best dinner of your life" at Maestro's, voted No. 1 for Service in our *Washington, DC Restaurant Survey.*

Hot Springs

Homestead, The 23 | 26 | 22 | 27 | $275
Rte. 220 Main St.; 540-839-1766; fax 540-839-7670; 800-838-1766; www.thehomestead.com; 409 rooms, 18 suites
"Wonderful Southern hospitality" and "old Colonial charm" make this "destination resort" a "home away from home" (and "away from everything"), where "you could stay for a month and not be bored" thanks to "limitless activities" (including golf and fishing, a "top-notch equestrian center" and a "wonderful health spa"), not to mention "cozy hiding places", "fantastic rooms" and "fabulous food"; it's a bit "hard to get to", though."

Irvington

Tides Inn, The 21 | 25 | 21 | 25 | $325
480 King Carter Dr.; 804-438-5000; fax 804-438-5222; 800-843-3746; www.tidesinn.com; 84 rooms, 22 suites
"Bring the entire family" ("dogs, too!") to this "luxurious" resort in a "lovely setting right on Chesapeake Bay" for some "Southern charm with a nautical twist" (i.e. cruises on a 127-ft. private yacht, fishing, boating and kayaking); a few feel the facilities are a bit "tired", but most find nothing but smooth sailing in the "outstanding hospitality", "gorgeous rooms", "fantastic golf" and a spa.

Lansdowne

Lansdowne Resort 19 | 19 | 20 | 24 | $349
44050 Woodridge Pkwy.; 703-729-8400; fax 703-729-4096; 877-509-8400; www.lansdowneresort.com; 282 rooms, 14 suites
Surveyors are split over this "business-focused" property "close to DC" – pros find it ideal for "a weekend getaway" in a "beautiful

setting" where you're "pampered" "without pompousness" and can enjoy an "excellent golf course" and "fantastic food" to boot; foes who "don't golf" find it "serviceable" at best and a tad "pricey" for "disappointingly plain rooms" with "no personality"; N.B. post-*Survey* renovations have added a new outdoor pool and clubhouse.

Orange

Willow Grove Inn Ⓗ 🐾 🌲 — | — | — | — | $295

14079 Plantation Way; 540-672-5982; fax 540-672-3674; 800-949-1778; www.willowgroveinn.com; 5 rooms, 5 cottages

You don't have to be a former president or general to stay at this 18th-century country inn and former plantation that's listed on the National Register of Historic Places, but you'll stay in a room named after one; set amid 37 acres in the foothills of the Blue Ridge Mountains, it features accommodations with antique watercolor prints and heirloom quilts, gardens where hammocks sway, a lounge with a roaring fire and an on-site tavern.

Paris

Ashby Inn ✕ 🌲 ▽ 23 | 24 | 26 | 19 | $185

692 Federal St.; 540-592-3900; fax 540-592-3781; www.ashbyinn.com; 10 rooms

A "great place to come after a hard work week", this inn in a tiny village in hunt country delights diners and serenity seekers alike; the restaurant is the "place to be seen" for its "wonderful food" and regional "signature dishes", and the views of the Blue Ridge Mountains are "unsurpassed", making it "perfect for a wedding"; the rooms are decorated with 19th-century furniture, some with fireplaces, and the newer addition, a former schoolhouse, boasts four quarters with private porches.

Richmond

Jefferson Hotel, The ✕ Ⓗ 🐾 🌲 ⛳ 24 | 25 | 23 | 24 | $315

101 W. Franklin St.; 804-788-8000; fax 804-225-0334; 800-424-8014; www.jefferson-hotel.com; 228 rooms, 16 suites

You'll "step back in time" to a "more elegant era" as you walk through the "magnificent entrance" of this "grand hotel" with marble columns, a statue of the third U.S. president and a staircase right out of "*Gone With the Wind*"; a "helpful staff" even "offers to drive you to dinner" (within a three-mile radius), though many are happy with the "very good" on-site dining options, especially the "incredible Sunday brunch."

Washington

INN AT LITTLE WASHINGTON, THE ✕ 🌲 27 | 28 | 29 | 23 | $615

Main & Middle Sts.; 540-675-3800; fax 540-675-3100; 800-735-2478; www.theinnatlittlewashington.com; 10 rooms, 4 suites, 2 houses

"Perfection may be a bit costly", but "for a once-in-a-lifetime experience", fans tout this "fantastically flamboyant" Relais & Châteaux "slice of heaven" nestled between the Blue Ridge Mountains and Shenandoah Valley, "a must for the romantically minded" as well as for foodies who flock to the "world-class" Relais

Gourmand restaurant (voted No. 1 for Decor in our *Washington, DC Restaurant Survey*); expect "total pampering" from a "nearly clairvoyant" staff and "spectacularly decorated" lodgings.

White Post

L'Auberge Provençale ∇ 22 | 25 | 28 | 23 | $160

13630 Lord Fairfax Hwy.; 540-837-1375; fax 540-837-2004; 800-638-1702; www.laubergeprovencale.com; 10 rooms, 4 suites

Offering a taste of "Provence" in the middle of Virginia hunt country is this "first-rate" inn with a "fantastic" restaurant that's the setting for "lovely dinners" and "sumptuous breakfasts" using produce and herbs from the on-site garden; the rooms are "peaceful" as there are neither TVs nor phones, and the "staff couldn't be nicer."

Williamsburg

Kingsmill Resort 21 | 22 | 18 | 25 | $299

1010 Kingsmill Rd.; 757-253-1703; fax 757-253-8237; 800-832-5665; www.kingsmill.com; 243 rooms, 175 suites

"If golf is your game", duffers declare you'll feel right at home at this "wonderful resort" near Williamsburg with three "exceptional courses" as well as a slew of leisure activities, including swimming, tennis, fishing, biking and a "beautiful spa"; the staff is "friendly", and the "large rooms" outfitted with kitchens "are great for families", while business travelers dig the "superb conference facilities"; "a nice range of food offerings" appeals to all.

Williamsburg Colonial Houses 22 | 24 | 22 | 24 | $159

136 E. Francis St.; 757-229-1000; fax 757-565-8444; 800-447-8679; www.colonialwilliamsburg.org; 77 rooms

"All the romance of the 18th century" is preserved in these "unique and charming" restored Colonial houses in a historic area, and though the rooms are "small" and "rustic" and the "amenities are not the most luxurious", the "attentive staff is there in an instant" if you need them; foodies recommend "dinner at the taverns to complete the experience", and with "outstanding tennis facilities" and an "excellent golf course", athletic types can have the "best of both worlds."

WILLIAMSBURG INN 25 | 26 | 25 | 26 | $409

136 E. Francis St.; 757-220-7978; fax 757-565-8444; 800-447-8679; www.colonialwilliamsburg.com; 48 rooms, 14 suites

A "wonderful Colonial atmosphere" fills this "meticulously restored" "special place" that loyalists laud for its "unpretentious service", "beautiful rooms", "superb golf" and "outstanding food"; sure, "the price is shocking", but the "close proximity to the historic area" and the "gorgeous setting" make it one of the "coolest places in the nation."

Williamsburg Lodge 20 | 20 | 18 | 22 | $249

310 S. England St.; 757-229-1000; fax 757-565-8444; 800-447-8679; www.colonialwilliamsburg.org; 175 rooms

For families who "love history", this "reasonably priced" "alternative" to the more expensive Williamsburg Inn is near all the "olde sites", with an "informative and pleasant front desk staff" too; the "spacious" lodgings are "homey" and "dotted with folk art" and the "wonderful grounds" include a pool and golf course, but "don't expect excellent dining" since the restaurant is currently closed for renovations.

Washington

Blaine

Semiahmoo Resort ▽ 20 | 21 | 18 | 23 | $259

9565 Semiahmoo Pkwy.; 360-318-2000; fax 360-318-2087; 800-770-7992; www.semiahmoo.com; 186 rooms, 12 suites

Despite its "remote" location at the tip of a mile-long peninsula on Puget Sound, this "lovely" resort supplies plenty to do with "two wonderful golf courses", a "great spa", a marina and a "stunning" wildlife preserve; some critics carp that it's "corporate", but vets say if you "get an ocean view room" it "exceeds expectations."

Seattle

★ Tops in City

25 Fairmont Olympic
Willows Lodge
Bellevue Club
Grand Hyatt

24 Inn at Langley

Alexis Hotel 23 | 23 | 22 | 20 | $299

1007 First Ave.; 206-624-4844; fax 206-621-9009; 866-356-8894; www.alexishotel.com; 72 rooms, 37 suites

A "beautiful" Dale Chihuly sculpture in the lobby sets the tone at this "historic", "elegant" but "unpretentious" Kimpton property "near the harbor"; though some rooms are "wow" and others "not so wow", they boast "wonderful sheets and pillows" as well as "luxurious bathrooms"; service is "superb", the on-site Aveda day spa is "pampering" and the complimentary evening happy-hour is a "highlight."

BELLEVUE CLUB HOTEL 27 | 25 | 21 | 28 | $225

11200 SE Sixth St., Bellevue; 425-454-4424; fax 425-688-3197; 800-579-1110; www.bellevueclub.com; 64 rooms, 3 suites

One of the "best" boutiques around is this "tranquil" member of Small Luxury Hotels of the World, hailed for its "amazing" fitness facilities that are "larger than the hotel" including indoor/outdoor swimming pools, tennis courts and an "outstanding gym"; the "impressive" rooms feature "stunning accessories", the staff "takes care of the most minute details" and the restaurants serve "highly respectable cuisine."

Edgewater, The 20 | 20 | 19 | 20 | $270

Pier 67, 2411 Alaskan Way; 206-728-7000; fax 206-441-4119; 800-624-0670; www.edgewaterhotel.com; 230 rooms, 4 suites

"True to its name", this "gorgeous property" hangs over Elliott Bay and affords "outstanding views" of the Puget Sound (ask for a waterfront room) as well as a "cool, mountain-lodge feel"; the accommodations are "on the small side" but are "comfortable" with "lots of special touches", and the "public spaces are inviting"; though a few are edgy over the "variable" dining options, others point out "the Beatles stayed here" (in 1964), and that's "good enough for me."

FAIRMONT OLYMPIC 25 | 26 | 24 | 25 | $355

411 University St.; 206-621-1700; fax 206-623-2271; 800-821-8106; www.fairmont.com; 234 rooms, 216 suites

Even though Fairmont has taken over this former Four Seasons property, this "posh" "old-timer" in the "heart of the city" is "still a Seattle treasure" with "phenomenal" service including the "best concierge", "beautiful" rooms and a "knockout lobby"; it also boasts "one of the greatest indoor pools" and "excellent" restaurants; just a few fuss that it's "expensive."

Grand Hyatt Seattle 26 | 24 | 23 | 26 | $350

721 Pine St.; 206-774-1234; fax 206-774-6120; 800-223-1234; www.hyatt.com; 312 rooms, 113 suites

Loyalists "love everything" about this four-year-old lodging, from the "smartly" designed "high-tech" rooms with "incredible bathrooms" and "unbelievable" views of the Cascade and Olympic Mountains to the "eager-to-please staff" to the new Ruth's Chris steakhouse and brand-new spa; it may be "one of the best Hyatt properties" both "for a weekend getaway" and for business.

INN AT LANGLEY, THE 27 | 22 | 27 | 21 | $250

400 First St., Langley; 360-221-3033; fax 360-221-3033; www.innatlangley.com; 22 rooms, 2 suites, 2 cottages

Perhaps the "perfect romantic" getaway, this "picturesque" inn on the Puget Sound offers "fantastic", "memorable" multicourse meals from "stand-out" chef Matt Costello as well as "exceptional" rooms replete with fireplaces and "splendid" views; if you "book a treatment at the waterfront spa", you'll see why the wowed regard this as "one of the most relaxing places on earth."

Inn at the Market 24 | 24 | 21 | 20 | $210

86 Pine St.; 206-443-3600; fax 206-448-0631; 800-446-4484; www.innatthemarket.com; 60 rooms, 10 suites

"Steps from the famous" Pike Place Market, this "divine European-style", "small" boutique in an "unbeatable" location offers "charming" chambers with "comfortable" Temper-Pedic beds ("like sleeping on a cloud") and "amazing views"; the staff is "fabulous", the "beautiful rooftop garden" is a "nice place to lounge" and there's also "superb" French fare.

Marriott Waterfront ▽ 21 | 21 | 22 | 22 | $269

2100 Alaskan Way; 206-443-5000 ; fax 206-256-1100 ; 800-455-8254; www.marriott.com; 345 rooms, 13 suites

Supporters are swayed by the "amazing waterfront rooms with balconies" ("corner rooms are extra special"), "beautiful facilities", a "pleasant" staff and "delicious" food at Todd English's Fish Club at this newish property with a "quintessential Seattle location" that's "convenient to Pike Place Market"; doubters, however, detect a "high-end mall feel" and find the service "just average."

Mayflower Park Hotel ▽ 20 | 24 | 22 | 18 | $229

405 Olive Way; 206-623-8700; fax 206-382-6996; 800-426-5100; www.mayflowerpark.com; 152 rooms, 19 suites

With its "wonderful location" a stone's throw from shopping, dining and Pike Place Market and "fine" service from a "courteous" staff, this "established" independent connected to Westlake Center is a "real find" that supplies "amazing value"; the rooms are "small" but "comfortable", its restaurant, Andaluca, offers "excellent" Mediterranean fare and bar Oliver's is "one of the best in town."

Monaco, Hotel 23 | 23 | 22 | 22 | $299

1101 Fourth Ave.; 206-621-1770; fax 206-621-7779; 800-715-6513; www.monaco-seattle.com; 144 rooms, 45 suites

"Disneyland decor for adults" describes the "fantastically funky rooms" at this "delightful boutique" chain link on the site of an "old Pacific Northwest Bell office"; the "kind" staff provides "gracious" service, the "complimentary amenities" (a "wine hour for guests", goldfish in your room "if you're lonely") are "a nice touch", its "hip" restaurant, Sazarac, serves "tasty" Southern fare and its "central location" is "great for tourists."

Salish Lodge & Spa Ⓢ 26 | 23 | 24 | 25 | $529

6501 Railroad Ave., SE, Snoqualmie; 425-888-2556; fax 425-888-2533; 800-272-5474; www.salishlodge.com; 83 rooms, 4 suites

Even the tubs provide the "perfect getaway" at this "magnificent" "luxury inn" "set atop" the "gorgeous" Snoqualmie Falls (45 minutes from Downtown Seattle) where the "romantic" rooms feature fireplaces, Jacuzzis and a choice of 16 pillows; a meal in The Dining Room is "an experience you'll never forget", the "amazing" spa offers "world-class treatments" and the service is "top-notch"; even if the prices are as "lofty" as the "remarkable location", there's simply "nothing like it."

Sheraton Ⓢ 20 | 20 | 18 | 21 | $329

1400 Sixth Ave.; 206-621-9000; fax 206-621-8441; 800-325-3535; www.starwood.com; 828 rooms, 12 suites

"Comprehensive facilities", an "excellent location convenient to Downtown" and "spoiling" service from a "well-trained staff" make this "solid business hotel" "great for conferences"; the enclosed rooftop pool affords "beautiful views" and the rooms are "large" and "modern", but some grouse it's "not worth the money" and "needs updating."

Sorrento Hotel, The 22 | 23 | 23 | 20 | $275

900 Madison St.; 206-622-6400; fax 206-343-6155; 800-426-1265; www.hotelsorrento.com; 34 rooms, 40 suites

A "mahogany-lined lobby with a fireplace" is the prelude to a "great experience" at this "grande dame" that embodies "old-world charm"; the service is "warm", the Northwestern cuisine at the Hunt Club is "incredible" and the rooms, though "a tad small", feature the "finest quality linens."

Vintage Park, Hotel ▽ 23 | 21 | 20 | 18 | $249

1100 Fifth Ave.; 206-624-8000; fax 206-623-0568; 800-853-3914; www.hotelvintagepark.com; 125 rooms, 1 suite

Oenophiles exult in this "small", "lovely" vino-themed boutique that features tastings of "excellent" wines and chocolates, "stylish" accommodations and a "wonderful ambiance" throughout; the "remarkably fine" Italian restaurant, Tulio, "remains lively late into the evening", and though surveyors are split on the service ("helpful" vs. "indifferent"), most guests maintain this "treat" provides "good value."

Westin Seattle, The 22 21 20 21 $305
1900 Fifth Ave.; 206-728-1000; fax 206-728-2259; 888-625-5144; www.westin.com; 857 rooms, 34 suites
Located a "short walk to the Space Needle or nearly anywhere you want to go", this circular double-towered "flagship" also offers "wonderful views" of the harbor, "fabulous" beds in the "spacious" rooms and "consistent", "courteous service"; kids are treated to coloring books, bath toys and a "dial-a-bedtime-story" feature that's a "hit", and those who sniff the "old girl needs updating" may be appeased by recent renovations of the south annex and lobby.

WILLOWS LODGE Ⓢ 27 24 25 25 $195
14580 NE 145th St., Woodinville; 425-424-3900; 877-424-3930; www.willowslodge.com; 80 rooms, 6 suites
"Gorgeous" rooms with "NW-style decor" and "stand-out" amenities including fireplaces and a Jacuzzi are just the beginning at this "modern", "tranquil" six-year-old resort "close to wineries" and 20 minutes from Downtown Seattle; the "grounds are a joy", the spa is "wonderful" but the "crowning glory" may well be dinner at "amazing" New American restaurant Herbfarm (more casual fare is served at Barking Frog).

Woodmark Hotel on Lake Washington Ⓢ 24 23 20 22 $250
1200 Carillon Point, Kirkland; 425-822-3700; fax 425-822-3699; 800-822-3700; www.thewoodmark.com; 79 rooms, 21 suites
The "beautiful views" of Lake Washington "enchant you as you enjoy a fabulous afternoon tea" at this "wonderful" hotel "near Downtown Kirkland" where the standard rooms, though "smallish", are "cozy", service "attentive" and the "grounds well planted"; even if a few deride it as "dated" and warn you may "be part of someone else's wedding party", the "peaceful locale" and "good spa" make it a "great place to relax" 10 miles east of Seattle.

W Seattle 24 21 20 21 $354
1112 Fourth Ave.; 206-264-6000; fax 206-264-6100; 888-625-4988; www.whotels.com; 340 rooms, 86 suites
"Forget sightseeing and snuggle up" in a "fantastic bed" with "luxurious sheets" in your "swanky" room (the corner options are "unbeatable") at this "cooler-than-cool" chain link; when you emerge, hang in the "bustling", "New York-y" lounge or dine in the "innovative" Earth & Ocean restaurant with fellow "hipsters"; though the service is not as "sharp as the interior design" and the halls are "dark, dark, dark", most "can't wait to return."

Spokane

Lusso, Hotel – – – – $290
808 W. Sprague Ave.; 509-747-9750; fax 509-747-9751; 800-525-4800; www.slh.com/lusso/; 24 rooms, 14 suites
A "surprising oasis of Italian chic" between the Cascades and the Rockies, this "beautifully restored" villa-like retreat (a member of Small Luxury Hotels of the World) supplies a "great reason to go to Spokane"; "warm service", "European" touches like afternoon wine receptions, several restaurants and spacious rooms add to a "lovely" experience.

Stevenson

Skamania Lodge ▽ 21 22 20 27 $209

1131 SW Skamania Lodge Way; 509-427-7700; fax 509-427-2547; 800-221-7117; www.skamania.com; 243 rooms, 10 suites

With its "lodge feel", "wonderful location" 42 miles from Portland, Oregon, and "gorgeous views" of the Columbia River Gorge and Cascade Mountains, this "incredible spot" is as "relaxing as it gets", with a "terrific outdoor hot tub with waterfalls", rooms with original artwork and on-site golf; some find the Northwest fare "disappointing", but the "Sunday brunch is the best."

West Virginia

White Sulphur Springs

GREENBRIER, THE 25 28 26 28 $625

300 W. Main St.; 304-536-1110; fax 304-536-7854; 800-453-4858; www.greenbrier.com; 514 rooms, 136 houses, 33 suites

The "grande dame of getaways", this "oasis" in a "spectacular mountain setting" offers "impeccable", "white-glove service" and "mouthwatering" Continental-American cuisine in the "baroque opulence of the main dining room"; "you need 25 hours in a day" for all the activities, including bowling, a movie theater and "world-class spa", and though it's "pricey", "it's worth every penny"; N.B. the Cold War underground bunker is closed for renovations.

Wisconsin

Chetek

CANOE BAY 29 29 28 28 $325

Rte. 3, #28; 715-924-4594; fax 715-924-2078; www.canoebay.com; 12 cottages, 6 rooms, 1 villa

Set on 200-plus acres of "lush forestland" encompassing three private lakes, this kid-free Relais & Châteaux resort "near nothing" in northwestern Wisconsin is a "romantic" "oasis" for "resting and indulgence"; "bring a book and light a fire" in your room or "take a sunset canoe paddle and watch the beavers at work" before dining in the "impeccable" restaurant; such "pampering and seclusion" "does cost money", but wallet-watchers tip the "lodge is far more economical than the beautiful" cottages.

Kohler

AMERICAN CLUB, THE 26 26 26 28 $280

444 Highland Dr.; 920-457-8000; fax 920-457-0299; 800-344-2838; www.destinationkohler.com; 255 rooms

You can "take a whirlpool bath twice a day" at this "swank" "escape" north of Milwaukee as rooms come outfitted with "all the Kohler plumbing you could ever want"; alternately, partake of the "awesome spa" after a round on the "world-class" Blackwolf Run or Whistling Straights (the latter of which was voted the best course in the U.S. in our *America's Top Golf Courses Survey*); plus there's "great dining" and a staff that "satisfies every need."

Milwaukee

Hilton City Center ▽ 18 | 18 | 20 | 20 | $219

509 W. Wisconsin Ave.; 414-271-7250; fax 414-271-1039; 800-445-8667; www.hiltonmilwaukee.com; 720 rooms, 10 suites

Occupying a 1920s building, this chain link near the city center combines "old Milwaukee elegance with new millennium facilities" and has an "unbelievable indoor water park" that makes it "great for kids"; rooms are "pleasant" but "spartan", dining is "mediocre" and service swings between "attentive" and not, which is why some "only stay for the Hilton points."

Metro, Hotel ▽ 24 | 21 | 21 | 19 | $189

411 E. Mason St.; 414-272-1937; fax 414-223-1158; 877-638-7620; www.hotelmetro.com; 65 suites

Combining "Manhattan chic" with the "welcome and friendliness of Milwaukee", this "neat, little" boutique hotel is the "place to stay for trendy folks" who dig the "cool rooms", "whirlpool suites that can't be beat for romantic nights", "good contemporary American restaurant" and handy meeting space, all of which compensate for the lack of on-site facilities; N.B. a new saltwater pool and yoga center will be completed by the end of 2005.

Pfister Hotel, The 22 | 23 | 21 | 21 | $299

424 E. Wisconsin Ave.; 414-273-8222; fax 414-273-5025; 800-472-4403; www.thepfisterhotel.com; 225 rooms, 82 suites

Doing its part to "make those trips to cold Milwaukee bearable", this circa-1893 "landmark" "close to museums and shops" wows guests with its "grand old opulence", afternoon tea worthy of "white gloves", 23rd-floor bar, "fab" Sunday brunch and "friendly" staff; even if the ensemble is in need of a "face-lift", nostalgists still recommend staying in the "quirky but nicely appointed" old rooms because the "new ones are a bore."

Wyndham Milwaukee Center ▽ 19 | 19 | 17 | 20 | $179

139 E. Kilbourn Ave.; 414-276-8686; fax 414-276-8007; 800-996-3426; www.wyndham.com; 220 rooms

"If you want to be right in the heart of Milwaukee's theater district" and "near nightclub row", then this "elegant hotel" overseen by a "nice staff" is a "reliable" choice; with "simple yet pleasant" rooms and adequate meeting facilities, it's a "comfortable business hotel."

Wyoming

Jackson

AMANGANI 28 | 25 | 25 | 26 | $700

1535 NE Butte Rd.; 307-734-7333; fax 307-734-7332; 877-734-7333; www.amanresorts.com; 40 suites

"Aman-junkies" find "almost no faults" with this "impeccably designed", "very adult" "stone lodge set on a bluff overlooking the Tetons" and "reeking of quiet ultra wealth"; the "charismatic", "rustic"-"Zen" rooms are "huge with even bigger terraces", and assets include a "knowledgeable" staff, "great skiing", hiking, an "awesome pool" and well-stocked library; so even if you don't have a "loaded wallet", "go for dinner or the spas just to see the place."

FOUR SEASONS RESORT JACKSON HOLE ▽ 27 | 25 | 23 | 29 | $475

7680 Granite Loop Rd., Teton Village; 307-732-5600; fax 307-732-5601; 800-295-5281; www.fourseasons.com/jacksonhole; 122 rooms, 18 suites

"Rough it while being pampered" say those who relish the "ski concierge who warms your boots and relieves the burden of carrying your gear", "heated pools and hot tubs" and "top-notch spa" at this 2003 ski-in/ski-out resort "at the base of the Tetons"; if some find the ensemble "over the top for Jackson Hole's cowboy atmosphere", more praise the haute-Western aesthetic, "beautiful, homey rooms", children's programs and "stellar" staff.

Jackson Lake Lodge 18 | 21 | 18 | 22 | $173

US Hwy. 89 N., Moran; 307-543-3100; fax 307-543-3143; 800-628-9988; www.gtlc.com; 37 rooms, 348 cottages

Perched on a bluff overlooking Jackson Lake, this seasonal lodge (open mid-May–October) is a "terrific value for families" who praise the "relaxing" ambiance, "amazing views" and "very nice staff"; accommodations are "austere" – i.e. no TVs, radios or a/c – but "there's no real reason to spend much time in them" when "plentiful opportunities to see wildlife", fishing, horseback riding, float trips on Snake River and "fresh Teton air" await outdoors.

Jenny Lake Lodge 23 | 23 | 25 | 25 | $475

Inner Loop Rd., Moran; 307-733-4647; fax 307-543-3358; 800-628-9988; www.gtlc.com; 37 cabins

"Capturing the essence of the West", this Teton-side enclave of "very cozy cabins in the woods" caters to "people who love being one with nature but want to be comfortable and well fed"; highlights include the "friendly staff", the "elegant" restaurant whose American-French offerings are "worlds beyond typical National Park fare" and activities like horseback riding, biking, hiking and playing at the Jackson Hole Golf & Tennis Club.

Lost Creek Ranch – | – | – | – | $898

PO Box 95, Moose; 307-733-3435; fax 307-733-3435; www.lostcreek.com; 10 cabins

Located between Grand Teton National Park and Bridger-Teton National Forest (20 miles north of Jackson), this dude ranch has one- and two-bedroom cabins, all with porches, and a rustic lodge housing a communal living room, restaurant and fitness center; open only from May–October, it offers activities like horseback riding, skeet shooting, hiking and sightseeing expeditions and relaxing spa treatments (for an additional fee); N.B. per-night rates are based on a seven-night minimum in summer, three in fall.

Rusty Parrot Lodge ▽ 26 | 27 | 24 | 21 | $335

175 N. Jackson St.; 307-733-2000; fax 307-733-1422; 800-458-2004; www.rustyparrot.com; 30 rooms, 1 suite

"There's nothing rusty about this parrot" say fans of this Small Luxury Hotels member that has a "handy in-town location but still is quiet"; rooms containing wood-burning fireplaces and "your very own teddy bear to cuddle with" and the "helpful" staff make guests feel like they're "staying in a private home"; however, the "lovely" Wild Sage restaurant serving "out-of-this-world" communal breakfasts and the impressive spa remind them it's one tony address.

Snake River Lodge & Spa ▽ 23 | 23 | 21 | 25 | $439
7710 Granite Loop Rd., Teton Village; 307-732-6000; fax 307-732-6009; 866-975-7625; www.snakeriverlodge.com; 88 rooms, 40 suites
Winter or summer, this RockResort makes a "great home base in the Tetons" given its "comfy lobby", ski-in/ski-out convenience, "beautiful" lagoonlike pools and "super" multistory spa; while the "views aren't always the best", the "cozy" rooms have fireplaces and "local design accents", there's "good food" at Game Fish restaurant and the "friendly" staff "helps plan" your excursions.

Spring Creek Ranch ▽ 25 | 23 | 23 | 24 | $310
1800 Spirit Dance Rd.; 307-733-8833; fax 307-733-1524; 800-443-6139; www.springcreekranch.com; 125 rooms
"Unparalleled" views, "marvelous" inn rooms, condos or villas, with fireplaces and balconies, a pool and the "very good" Granary restaurant make this Grand Teton "base camp" "outstanding for families" or conferences; the "wonderful concierge schedules everything" from fly-fishing lessons to river-rafting, horseback and heli-skiing excursions, meaning pampered patrons don't have to "do a thing except make an occasional decision."

Wort Hotel ▽ 22 | 23 | 19 | 18 | $275
50 N. Glenwood St.; 307-733-2190; fax 307-733-2067; 800-322-2727; www.worthotel.com; 57 rooms, 3 suites
"Right in the heart of Jackson Hole" is this 1941 hotel that's listed on the National Register of Historic Places and whose spacious "cowboy-themed" accommodations come stocked with pine furniture and down comforters; a concierge helps fill in your schedule, there's a chophouse on-site and even day-trippers ought to sample the "great" live music and dancing at the Silver Dollar Bar, named for its 2,000-plus inlaid coins.

Yellowstone Nat'l Park

Lake Yellowstone Hotel 20 | 20 | 21 | 20 | $80
Lake Village Rd., Yellowstone National Park; 307-344-7311; fax 307-344-7456; www.travelyellowstone.com; 193 rooms, 1 suite, 102 cabins
"Step back in time" at this seasonal, "elegant" and recently refurbished hotel that's on the National Register of Historic Places; it "probably appeals to adults more than kids" with live "classical music at sunset beside Lake Yellowstone" filling in for the lack of TVs and radios (nor is there a/c); still, pros recommend "booking months ahead" to stay in the main lodge and "avoid the cabins."

Old Faithful Snow Lodge & Cabins ▽ 21 | 20 | 15 | 20 | $156
Old Faithful Bypass Rd., Yellowstone National Park; 307-344-7901; www.travelyellowstone.com; 100 rooms, 34 cabins
Although it lacks the history of the older hotels in Yellowstone, this 1999 timber construction "in the heart of the Old Faithful area" has "clean, cheery and spacious" Western-style rooms and cabins, all of which are typically sans radio, TV or a/c yet "a step above normal National Park lodging"; it's also one of the few local lodges open in winter, when it's accessible only by snowcoach and is a great base for cross-country skiing and snowshoeing.

Indexes

HOTEL TYPES

SPECIAL FEATURES

HOTEL TYPES

All-Inclusive

Arizona

Tucson
Canyon Ranch
Miraval Spa

California

Carmel Area
Seven Gables Inn
Los Angeles
Le Merigot Beach
Napa
Villagio Inn
Palm Springs Area
Two Bunch Palms
San Diego
Cal-a-Vie
Golden Door
San Francisco Bay Area
Albion River
Santa Barbara
Simpson House Inn
Solvang
Alisal Guest Ranch

Colorado

Clark
Home Ranch
Denver
C Lazy U Ranch

District of Columbia

Washington, DC
George

Florida

Miami
Doral Golf Resort
Tampa/St. Petersburg
Saddlebrook Resort

Georgia

Braselton
Château Élan
Georgia Coast
Lodge on Little St. Simons
Savannah
Ballastone Inn

Hawaii

Big Island
Kona Village Resort

Illinois

Gilman
Heartland Spa

Maine

Prouts Neck
Black Point Inn

Massachusetts

Deerfield
Deerfield Inn
Lenox
Canyon Ranch/Mass.

Michigan

Mackinac Island
Grand Hotel

Montana

Darby
Triple Creek Ranch

New Hampshire

Dixville Notch
Balsams

New York

Adirondacks
Elk Lake Lodge
Point
Catskills
Mohonk Mountain Hse.
New Age Health Spa
Cooperstown
Otesaga

North Carolina

Asheville
Greystone Inn
Pinehurst
Pinehurst Resort

Ohio

Grand Rapids
Kerr House

Oregon

Hood River
Columbia Gorge

Pennsylvania

Bradford
Glendorn
Pittsburgh
Priory
Poconos
Deerfield Spa
Skytop Lodge

Puerto Rico

San Juan
Paradisus Puerto Rico

Rhode Island
Block Island
1661 Inn
Westerly
Weekapaug Inn
South Carolina
Aiken
Willcox
Hilton Head
Hilton Head Health Inst.
Pawleys Island
Litchfield Plantation
Tennessee
Walland
Blackberry Farm
Texas
Austin
Lake Austin Spa
Dallas/Ft. Worth
Greenhouse
Utah
Salt Lake City
Sundance
St. George
Coyote Inn/Spa
Vermont
Barnard
Twin Farms
Virginia
Irvington
Tides Inn
Orange
Willow Grove Inn

Beach Resort

Alabama
Point Clear
Marriott Grand
California
Carmel Area
Bernardus Lodge
Casa Palmero
Monterey Plaza
Post Ranch Inn
Dana Point
Marriott Laguna Cliffs
Ritz-Carlton Laguna Niguel
St. Regis Monarch Beach
Huntington Beach
Hyatt Huntington Beach
Laguna Beach
Montage Resort
Surf & Sand Resort
Lake Tahoe Area
PlumpJack Squaw Valley
Los Angeles
Casa Del Mar
Disney Grand Calif.
Le Merigot Beach
Loews Santa Monica
San Diego
del Coronado
Four Seasons Aviara
Grande Colonial
Hilton La Jolla Torrey Pines
La Costa
Lodge at Torrey Pines
Loews Coronado Bay
Marriott Coronado Is.
San Francisco Bay Area
Casa Madrona
Santa Barbara
Bacara Resort
Four Seasons Santa Barbara
Florida
Amelia Island
Amelia Is. Plantation
Ritz-Carlton
Destin
Hilton Sandestin Beach
Ft. Lauderdale
Boca Raton Resort
Lago Mar Resort
Marriott Harbor Beach
Westin Diplomat Resort
Ft. Myers
Casa Ybel Resort
Sanibel Harbour Resort
Hutchinson Island
Hutchinson Is. Marriott
Jacksonville
Lodge & Club
Ponte Vedra Inn
Keys
Cheeca Lodge
Hawk's Cay Resort
Hilton Key West
Hyatt Key West
Little Palm Island
Pier House Resort
Sunset Key Cottages
Wyndham Casa Marina
Miami
Delano
Doral Golf Resort

Eden Roc
Fairmont Turnberry Isle
Fisher Island
Loews Miami Beach
Pritikin Longevity Center & Spa
Ritz-Carlton Key Biscayne
Ritz-Carlton South Beach
Sonesta Key Biscayne
Naples
Hyatt Coconut Point
La Playa Beach/Resort
Marco Beach Resort
Marco Island Marriott
Registry Resort
Ritz-Carlton Naples
Orlando
Disney Beach Club
Disney Grand Floridian
Disney Polynesian
Disney Yacht Club
Walt Disney Dolphin
Walt Disney Swan
Palm Beach
Breakers
PGA National Resort
Ritz-Carlton Palm Beach
Sandestin
Sandestin
Santa Rosa Beach
Water Color Inn
Sarasota
Captiva Beach Resort
Colony Beach
Resort at Longboat Key
Ritz-Carlton
St. Augustine
Renaissance/World Golf Village
Tampa/St. Petersburg
Belleview Biltmore
Clearwater Beach Marriott
Don CeSar Beach
Renaissance Vinoy
Vero Beach
Disney Vero Beach

Georgia

Georgia Coast
Cloister
Jekyll Island Club
King & Prince Resort
Lodge at Sea Island

Hawaii

Big Island
Fairmont Orchid
Four Seasons Hualalai
Hapuna Beach Prince
Hilton Waikoloa Vlg.
Kona Village Resort
Mauna Kea Beach
Mauna Lani Bay
Waikoloa Beach Marriott
Kauai
Grand Hyatt Kauai
Hanalei Bay Resort
Marriott Kauai Resort
Princeville Resort
Lanai
Manele Bay Hotel
Maui
Fairmont Kea Lani
Four Seasons/Wailea
Grand Wailea Resort
Hyatt
Kapalua Bay Hotel
Kapalua Villas
Ritz-Carlton Kapalua
Sheraton Maui
Westin Maui
Oahu
Hilton Hawaiian Vlg.
JW Marriott Ihilani
Kahala Mandarin Oriental
Marriott Waikiki Beach

Maine

Cape Elizabeth
Inn by the Sea
Kennebunkport
Cliff House
White Barn Inn
Prouts Neck
Black Point Inn
Rockport
Samoset Resort

Maryland

Cambridge
Hyatt Chesapeake Bay

Massachusetts

Cape Cod & The Islands
Chatham Bars Inn
Ocean Edge Resort
Wequassett Inn

Michigan
Bay Harbor
Inn at Bay Harbor
Mackinac Island
Grand Hotel
Mississippi
Biloxi
Beau Rivage
Missouri
Osage Beach
Tan Tar A Resort
New Jersey
Atlantic City
Trump Taj Mahal
New York
Long Island
Gurney's Inn
North Carolina
Outer Banks
Sanderling
Pinehurst
Pinehurst Resort
Oregon
Gleneden Beach
Salishan Lodge
Puerto Rico
Fajardo
Las Casitas Village
Las Croabas
Wyndham El Conquistador
San Juan
Caribe Hilton
Hyatt Dorado Beach
InterContinental
Paradisus Puerto Rico
Westin Rio Mar
Wyndham El San Juan
Rhode Island
Newport
Castle Hill Inn
Westerly
Weekapaug Inn
South Carolina
Charleston
Wild Dunes Resort
Woodlands Resort
Hilton Head
Disney Hilton Head Is.
Hilton Head Marriott Beach
Sea Pines Resort
Westin
Kiawah Island
Kiawah Island Resorts
Myrtle Beach
Myrtle Beach Marriott
U.S. Virgin Islands
St. Croix
Buccaneer
Carambola Beach
St. John
Caneel Bay
Westin
St. Thomas
Marriott Frenchman Reef
Ritz-Carlton
Vermont
Vergennes
Basin Harbor Club
Virginia
Irvington
Tides Inn
Washington
Blaine
Semiahmoo Resort
Wisconsin
Kohler
American Club

Bed & Breakfast/Inn

Arizona
Phoenix/Scottsdale
Hermosa Inn
Prescott
Hassayampa Inn
Sedona
Canyon Villa
L'Auberge de Sedona
Tucson
Arizona Inn
Hacienda del Sol
California
Carmel Area
Centrella
Cobblestone Inn
Cypress Inn
Green Gables Inn
Inn at Depot Hill
L'Auberge Carmel
Mission Ranch
Seven Gables Inn
Spindrift Inn
Tickle Pink Inn

Eureka
Carter House
Inverness
Manka Inverness Lodge
Lake Tahoe Area
PlumpJack Squaw Valley
Los Angeles
Maison 140
Mendocino
Stanford Inn by the Sea
Napa
Auberge du Soleil
Carneros Inn
Inn at Southbridge
Milliken Creek Inn
Vintage Inn
Palm Springs Area
Willows Historic Palm Springs
San Diego
Inn at Rancho Santa Fe
L'Auberge Del Mar
San Francisco Bay Area
Albion River
Archbishop's Mansion
Inn Above Tide
Petite Auberge
Vintners Inn
White Swan Inn
San Luis Obispo
Apple Farm
Santa Barbara
El Encanto
Simpson House Inn
Solvang
Fess Parker's
Sonoma
Applewood Inn
Gaige House Inn
Honor Mansion
Kenwood Inn
Madrona Manor
St. Orres
Whale Watch Inn
South Bay
Seal Cove Inn

Colorado

Beaver Creek
Inn at Beaver Creek
Colorado Springs
Cliff House/Pikes Peak
Snowmass
Stonebridge Inn
Telluride
Ice House Lodge
Inn at Lost Creek

Connecticut

Greenwich
Homestead Inn
Mystic
Inn at Mystic
New Preston
Boulders Inn
Old Saybrook
Saybrook Point Inn
Washington
Mayflower Inn
Westport
Inn at National Hall

Delaware

Wilmington
Inn at Montchanin

District of Columbia

Washington, DC
Morrison-Clark Inn

Florida

Keys
Gardens
Tampa/St. Petersburg
Chalet Suzanne Inn

Georgia

Georgia Coast
Lodge at Sea Island
Savannah
Ballastone Inn
Gastonian
Mulberry Inn
River Street Inn

Kansas

Wichita
Inn at the Park

Louisiana

New Orleans
Maison de Ville
White Castle
Nottoway Plantation

Maine

Brunswick
Captain Daniel Stone
Cape Elizabeth
Inn by the Sea

Freeport
Harraseeket Inn
Kennebunkport
Captain Lord Mansion
Cliff House
White Barn Inn
Mount Desert Island
Asticou Inn
Prouts Neck
Black Point Inn
York Harbor
York Harbor Inn

Maryland
Baltimore
Admiral Fell
Antrim 1844

Massachusetts
Boston
Beacon Hill
Jacob Hill Inn
Cape Cod & The Islands
Century House
Charlotte Inn
Chatham Bars Inn
Dan'l Webster Inn
Wauwinet
Wequassett Inn
White Elephant
Deerfield
Deerfield Inn
Rockport
Emerson Inn
Williamstown
Orchards

Michigan
Bay Harbor
Inn at Bay Harbor

Minnesota
Minneapolis/St. Paul
Nicollet Island Inn

Mississippi
Natchez
Monmouth Plantation

New Hampshire
Plainfield
Home Hill

New Jersey
Bernardsville
Bernards Inn
Cape May
Congress Hall
Inn of Cape May
Virginia
Spring Lake
Normandy Inn

New Mexico
Santa Fe
Inn of the Anasazi
Inn of the Five Graces
Inn on the Alameda

New York
Adirondacks
Elk Lake Lodge
Friends Lake Inn
Mirror Lake Inn
Point
Hudson Valley
Beekman Arms
Inn at Bullis Hall
Le Chambord
Old Drovers Inn
Roselawn
New York City
Inn at Irving Place

North Carolina
Asheville
Greystone Inn
Richmond Hill Inn
Swag

Ohio
Cleveland
Walden Country Inn

Oregon
Gold Beach
Tu Tu' Tun Lodge
Hood River
Columbia Gorge

Pennsylvania
Bucks County
EverMay/Delaware

Rhode Island
Block Island
1661 Inn
Newport
Castle Hill Inn
Francis Malbone Hse.
Westerly
Weekapaug Inn

South Carolina
Charleston
John Rutledge House
Planters Inn
Wentworth Mansion

Pawleys Island
Litchfield Plantation

Texas

Austin
Barton Creek

Utah

Park City
Goldener Hirsch Inn

Vermont

Essex
Inn at Essex

Lower Waterford
Rabbit Hill Inn

Mt. Snow
Inn at Sawmill Farm

Shelburne
Inn at Shelburne Farms

Stowe
Green Mountain Inn

Stratton Mountain
Equinox

Sugarbush
Pitcher Inn

Woodstock
Quechee Inn

Virginia

Charlottesville
200 South St. Inn

DC Metro Area
Goodstone Inn
Morrison House

Orange
Willow Grove Inn

Paris
Ashby Inn

Washington
Inn at Little Washington

White Post
L'Auberge Provençale

Williamsburg
Williamsburg Colonial

Washington

Seattle
Inn at Langley
Inn at the Market
Willows Lodge

Wisconsin

Chetek
Canoe Bay

Wyoming

Jackson
Lost Creek Ranch

Boutique

Arizona

Tucson
Hacienda del Sol
Lodge/Ventana Canyon

Arkansas

Little Rock
Capital Hotel

California

Carmel Area
Casa Palmero
La Playa
Pacific

Los Angeles
Argyle
Chateau Marmont
Farmer's Daughter
Le Merigot Beach
Maison 140
Mosaic
Viceroy
W Westwood
Wyndham Bel Age

Napa
Auberge du Soleil
Napa River Inn

Palm Springs Area
Ballantines

San Diego
Grande Colonial
Inn at Rancho Santa Fe
L'Auberge Del Mar
Parisi
Rancho Valencia
Solamar

San Francisco Bay Area
Adagio
Argonaut
Clift
Griffon
Huntington
Hyatt Vineyard Creek
Inn Above Tide
Majestic
Palomar
Petite Auberge
Serrano Hotel
Stanford Court
Vintners Inn
White Swan Inn
W San Francisco

San Jose
De Anza
Santa Barbara
Andalucia
El Encanto
Montecito Inn
San Ysidro Ranch
Upham
Solvang
Fess Parker's
Sonoma
Healdsburg
South Bay
Cypress Hotel
Garden Court
Yosemite
Château du Sureau

Colorado

Aspen
Jerome
Sky
Colorado Springs
Cliff House/Pikes Peak
Denver
Boulderado
Monaco
Oxford
Teatro
Telluride
Telluride

Connecticut

Greenwich
Delamar
Hyatt
Hartford
Goodwin

District of Columbia

Washington, DC
George
Helix
Jefferson
Madera
Monaco
Rouge

Florida

Ft. Lauderdale
Pillars/New River Sound
Keys
Gardens
Marquesa
Miami
Astor
Circa 39
Grove Isle Club
Hotel, The
Mayfair
Mutiny
Omni Colonnade
Raleigh
Shore Club
Victor
Wyndham Grand Bay
Palm Beach
Brazilian Court
Chesterfield
Colony
Santa Rosa Beach
Water Color Inn
Sarasota
Captiva Beach Resort
St. Augustine
Casa Monica

Georgia

Atlanta
W Atlanta
Georgia Coast
Lodge on Little St. Simons
Savannah
Mansion on Forsyth Park
River Street Inn

Hawaii

Oahu
W Honolulu - Diamond Head

Illinois

Chicago
Burnham
Hard Rock Chicago
Monaco
Omni Ambassador E.
Park Hyatt
Sutton Place
Whitehall

Louisiana

New Orleans
International House
Maison de Ville
Maison Dupuy
Maison Orleans
Monaco
Soniat House
W French Quarter

Maryland
St. Michaels
Inn at Perry Cabin
Massachusetts
Boston
Beacon Hill
Eliot
XV Beacon
Lenox
Marlowe
Onyx Hotel
Lenox
Blantyre
Wheatleigh
Michigan
Detroit
Royal Park
Minnesota
Minneapolis/St. Paul
Sofitel
Missouri
Kansas City
Phillips
Raphael
Nevada
Las Vegas
Hard Rock
New York
Buffalo
Mansion on Delaware
Hudson Valley
Inn at Bullis Hall
Long Island
American
New York City
Algonquin
Benjamin
Blakely
Bryant Park
Chambers
City Club
Elysée
Gansevoort
Hudson
Iroquois
Kitano
Library
Lowell
Maritime
Mercer
Muse
Park South
Royalton
70 Park Ave.
Sherry-Netherland
60 Thompson
Soho Grand Hotel
Tribeca Grand Hotel
Westchester
Castle on the Hudson
North Carolina
Chapel Hill
Siena
Charlotte
Park Hotel
Ohio
Cincinnati
Cincinnatian
Oklahoma
Oklahoma City
Waterford Marriott
Oregon
Hood River
Columbia Gorge
Portland
Avalon
5th Ave. Suites
Governor
Heathman Hotel
Lucia, Hotel
RiverPlace
Vintage Plaza
Westin
Pennsylvania
Philadelphia
Hilton Inn at Penn
Rittenhouse
Sofitel Philadelphia
Pittsburgh
Omni William Penn
Priory
Puerto Rico
Rincon
Horned Dorset
South Carolina
Aiken
Willcox
Charleston
Market Pavilion
Mills House
Planters Inn

Tennessee
Memphis
Madison
Nashville
Union Station
Texas
Dallas/Ft. Worth
Ashton
Mansion on Turtle Creek
Zaza, Hotel
Galveston
Tremont House
Houston
Lancaster
San Antonio
Valencia Riverwalk
Utah
Park City
Park City
Salt Lake City
Monaco
Virginia
Charlottesville
Keswick Hall
DC Metro Area
Morrison House
Washington
Seattle
Alexis
Bellevue Club
Edgewater
Inn at the Market
Mayflower Park
Monaco
Sorrento
Vintage Park
Spokane
Lusso
Wisconsin
Milwaukee
Metro
Wyoming
Jackson
Rusty Parrot Lodge
Wort Hotel

Condominium

California
Napa
Silverado
Colorado
Beaver Creek
Charter/Beaver Creek
Snowmass
Snowmass Club
Telluride
Wyndham Peaks
Florida
Miami
Conrad Miami
Fisher Island
Sandestin
Sandestin
Hawaii
Maui
Kapalua Villas
Idaho
Sun Valley
Sun Valley Lodge
Illinois
Chicago
Ritz-Carlton
Massachusetts
Boston
Four Seasons
Montana
Big Sky
Big Sky Resort
New York
Adirondacks
Elk Lake Lodge
South Carolina
Hilton Head
Sea Pines Resort
Myrtle Beach
Long Bay Resort
Utah
Park City
Deer Valley Lodging
Salt Lake City
Lodge at Snowbird
Vermont
Smuggler's Notch
Smugglers' Notch
Wyoming
Jackson
Four Seasons Jackson Hole
Spring Creek Ranch

Convention

Alaska
Anchorage
Captain Cook
Arizona
Phoenix/Scottsdale
Hyatt/Gainey Ranch
James

JW Marriott Desert Ridge
Phoenician
Pointe South Mountain
Ritz-Carlton
Wyndham Buttes
Tucson
Hilton El Conquistador
Westin La Paloma

California

Lake Tahoe Area
Resort at Squaw Creek
Los Angeles
Century Plaza
Loews Santa Monica
Newport Beach
Fairmont Newport Beach
Sacramento
Sheraton Grand
San Diego
Hilton La Jolla Torrey Pines
Loews Coronado Bay
Manchester Gr. Hyatt
Marriott San Diego
Marriott Del Mar
San Francisco Bay Area
Hyatt Vineyard Creek
Mandarin Oriental
Nikko
Omni
San Jose
Fairmont San Jose
Sonoma
MacArthur Place

Colorado

Colorado Springs
Broadmoor
Denver
C Lazy U Ranch
Inverness

Connecticut

Old Saybrook
Saybrook Point Inn

District of Columbia

Washington, DC
Fairmont Washington
Grand Hyatt
Willard InterContinental

Florida

Destin
Hilton Sandestin Beach
Ft. Lauderdale
Boca Raton Resort
Westin Diplomat Resort
Miami
Biltmore/Coral Gables
Hyatt Coral Gables
InterContinental Miami
JW Marriott Miami
Loews Miami Beach
Orlando
Gaylord Palms
Hyatt Grand Cypress
Loews Portofino Bay
Marriott Orlando
Peabody Orlando
Royal Pacific Resort
Walt Disney Dolphin
Walt Disney Swan
Palm Beach
Colony
St. Augustine
Renaissance/World Golf Village
Tampa/St. Petersburg
Don CeSar Beach

Georgia

Atlanta
Westin Peachtree Plaza

Idaho

Sun Valley
Sun Valley Lodge

Illinois

Chicago
Fairmont Chicago
Hilton Chicago
Ritz-Carlton
Sheraton Chicago

Indiana

Indianapolis
Westin

Kansas

Overland Park
Sheraton Overland Pk.

Louisiana

New Orleans
InterContinental
Omni Royal Orleans
Wyndham/Canal Place

Maine

Rockport
Samoset Resort

Maryland
Baltimore
Hyatt
Marriott Waterfront
Cambridge
Hyatt Chesapeake Bay
Massachusetts
Boston
Marriott Copley Pl.
Westin Copley Pl.
Mississippi
Biloxi
Beau Rivage
Missouri
Branson
Chateau on the Lake
St. Louis
Renaissance Grand
Montana
Big Sky
Big Sky Resort
Nevada
Las Vegas
Mandalay Bay Hotel
Paris Las Vegas
Venetian Hotel
New York
Catskills
Mohonk Mountain Hse.
Long Island
Gurney's Inn
New York City
Marriott Marquis
North Carolina
Charlotte
Westin Charlotte
Outer Banks
Sanderling
Pennsylvania
Philadelphia
Loews Philadelphia
Marriott
Pittsburgh
Omni William Penn
Poconos
Skytop Lodge
Puerto Rico
Fajardo
Las Casitas Village
San Juan
Caribe Hilton
Rhode Island
Providence
Westin
South Carolina
Hilton Head
Sea Pines Resort
Westin
Myrtle Beach
Myrtle Beach Marriott
Tennessee
Nashville
Gaylord Opryland
Renaissance Nashville
Sheraton Music City
Texas
Austin
Hilton Austin
Renaissance Austin
Dallas/Ft. Worth
Omni Mandalay
Wyndham Anatole
Houston
Hilton Americas Houston
The Woodlands
Marriott Woodlands
U.S. Virgin Islands
St. Thomas
Marriott Frenchman Reef
Utah
Park City
Stein Eriksen Lodge
Salt Lake City
Grand America
Little America
Snowbird
Vermont
Vergennes
Basin Harbor Club
Virginia
Hot Springs
Homestead
Lansdowne
Lansdowne Resort
Washington
Seattle
Sheraton
Westin Seattle
Stevenson
Skamania Lodge
West Virginia
White Sulphur Springs
Greenbrier

Wyoming
Jackson
Spring Creek Ranch

Destination Spa

Arizona
Phoenix/Scottsdale
Phoenician
Tucson
Canyon Ranch
Miraval Spa
California
Laguna Beach
Montage Resort
Lake Tahoe Area
Nakoma Resort
Palm Springs Area
Two Bunch Palms
San Diego
Cal-a-Vie
Golden Door
L'Auberge Del Mar
Santa Barbara
Bacara Resort
Colorado
Aspen
Lodge & Spa/Cordillera
Connecticut
Norwich
Spa at Norwich Inn
Old Saybrook
Saybrook Point Inn
Hawaii
Big Island
Four Seasons Hualalai
Maui
Four Seasons/Wailea
Grand Wailea Resort
Oahu
JW Marriott Ihilani
Idaho
Coeur d'Alene
Coeur d'Alene
Illinois
Gilman
Heartland Spa
Massachusetts
Lenox
Canyon Ranch/Mass.
Montana
Pray
Chico Hot Springs
Nevada
Las Vegas
Venetian Hotel
New Mexico
Santa Fe
Houses of the Moon
New York
Catskills
Mirbeau Inn
New Age Health Spa
Long Island
Gurney's Inn
Ohio
Grand Rapids
Kerr House
Pennsylvania
Poconos
Deerfield Spa
Puerto Rico
Fajardo
Las Casitas Village
South Carolina
Hilton Head
Hilton Head Health Inst.
Texas
Austin
Lake Austin Spa
Dallas/Ft. Worth
Greenhouse
San Antonio
Hyatt Hill Country
Utah
St. George
Coyote Inn/Spa
Virginia
Hot Springs
Homestead
West Virginia
White Sulphur Springs
Greenbrier
Wyoming
Jackson
Snake River Lodge

Golf Resort

Alabama
Birmingham
Renaissance Ross Bridge Golf
Point Clear
Marriott Grand

Arizona

Phoenix/Scottsdale
Arizona Biltmore
Boulders
Fairmont Scottsdale
Four Seasons Scottsdale
Hyatt/Gainey Ranch
JW Marriott Camelback
JW Marriott Desert Ridge
Phoenician
Pointe Hilton Squaw Peak
Pointe Hilton Tapatio Cliffs
Pointe South Mountain
Sheraton Wild Horse

Sedona
Enchantment Resort
Hilton Sedona Resort
L'Auberge de Sedona

Tucson
Hilton El Conquistador
Lodge/Ventana Canyon
Loews Ventana Canyon
Starr Pass Resort
Westin La Paloma
Westward Look Resort

California

Carmel Area
Carmel Valley Ranch
Casa Palmero
Inn at Spanish Bay
Lodge/Pebble Beach
Quail Lodge
Stonepine

Dana Point
St. Regis Monarch Beach

Lake Tahoe Area
Nakoma Resort
Resort at Squaw Creek

Los Angeles
Rancho Bernardo Inn

Napa
Meadowood
Silverado

Palm Springs Area
Hyatt Grand Champions
La Quinta Resort
Marriott Desert Springs
Marriott Rancho Las Palmas
Renaissance Esmeralda
Westin Mission Hills

San Diego
Barona Valley Ranch
Four Seasons Aviara
Hilton La Jolla Torrey Pines
La Casa del Zorro
La Costa
Lodge at Torrey Pines

San Jose
Lodge at Cordevalle

Santa Barbara
Bacara Resort

Solvang
Alisal Guest Ranch

Sonoma
Fairmont Sonoma Mission

South Bay
Ritz-Carlton Half Moon Bay

Colorado

Aspen
Lodge & Spa/Cordillera
Ritz-Carlton, Bachelor Gulch

Beaver Creek
Beaver Creek Lodge
Charter/Beaver Creek
Park Hyatt

Colorado Springs
Broadmoor

Denver
Omni Interlocken

Keystone
Keystone Resort

Snowmass
Snowmass Club

Telluride
Telluride
Wyndham Peaks

Vail
Sonnenalp

Florida

Amelia Island
Amelia Is. Plantation
Ritz-Carlton

Destin
Hilton Sandestin Beach

Ft. Lauderdale
Boca Raton Resort
Westin Diplomat Resort

Hutchinson Island
Hutchinson Is. Marriott

Jacksonville
Ponte Vedra Inn

Keys
Cheeca Lodge
Miami
Doral Golf Resort
Fairmont Turnberry Isle
Fisher Island
Naples
Hyatt Coconut Point
La Playa Beach/Resort
Marco Island Marriott
Ritz-Carlton Golf
Ritz-Carlton Naples
Orlando
Disney Grand Floridian
Gaylord Palms
Hyatt Grand Cypress
Marriott Orlando
Renaissance SeaWorld
Ritz-Carlton Orlando
Villas of Grand Cypress
Walt Disney Swan
Wyndham Palace
Palm Beach
Breakers
PGA National Resort
Sandestin
Sandestin
Sarasota
Resort at Longboat Key
St. Augustine
Renaissance/World Golf Village
Tampa/St. Petersburg
Belleview Biltmore
Renaissance Vinoy
Saddlebrook Resort

Georgia

Atlanta
Barnsley Gardens
Braselton
Château Élan
Georgia Coast
Cloister
Jekyll Island Club
King & Prince Resort
Lodge at Sea Island
Lake Oconee
Ritz-Carlton Reynolds
Savannah
Westin Savannah Harbor

Hawaii

Big Island
Fairmont Orchid
Four Seasons Hualalai
Hapuna Beach Prince
Hilton Waikoloa Vlg.
Mauna Kea Beach
Mauna Lani Bay
Waikoloa Beach Marriott
Kauai
Grand Hyatt Kauai
Marriott Kauai Resort
Princeville Resort
Lanai
Lodge at Koele
Manele Bay Hotel
Maui
Fairmont Kea Lani
Four Seasons/Wailea
Grand Wailea Resort
Hyatt
Kapalua Bay Hotel
Kapalua Villas
Ritz-Carlton Kapalua
Sheraton Maui
Westin Maui
Oahu
JW Marriott Ihilani
Kahala Mandarin Oriental

Idaho

Coeur d'Alene
Coeur d'Alene
Sun Valley
Sun Valley Lodge

Illinois

Galena
Eagle Ridge Resort

Maine

Prouts Neck
Black Point Inn
Rockport
Samoset Resort

Maryland

Cambridge
Hyatt Chesapeake Bay

Massachusetts

Cape Cod & The Islands
Ocean Edge Resort
Wequassett Inn
Lenox
Cranwell Resort

Michigan

Bay Harbor
Inn at Bay Harbor
Mackinac Island
Grand Hotel

Mississippi
Biloxi
Beau Rivage
Missouri
Osage Beach
Tan Tar A Resort
Nevada
Incline Village
Hyatt Resort
Las Vegas
Hyatt Lake Resort
Ritz-Carlton, Lake Las Vegas
New Hampshire
Bretton Woods
Mount Washington
Dixville Notch
Balsams
New Jersey
Atlantic City
Seaview Marriott Resort
New Mexico
Albuquerque
Hyatt Tamaya
Santa Fe
Bishop's Lodge
New York
Adirondacks
Point
Sagamore
Catskills
Mohonk Mountain Hse.
Cooperstown
Otesaga
North Carolina
Asheville
Grove Park Inn Resort
Inn on Biltmore
Charlotte
Ballantyne
Outer Banks
Sanderling
Pinehurst
Pinehurst Resort
Oregon
Black Butte
Black Butte Ranch
Gleneden Beach
Salishan Lodge
Pennsylvania
Farmington
Nemacolin Woodlands
Hershey
Hershey
Poconos
Skytop Lodge
Puerto Rico
Fajardo
Las Casitas Village
Las Croabas
Wyndham El Conquistador
San Juan
Hyatt Dorado Beach
Paradisus Puerto Rico
Westin Rio Mar
South Carolina
Charleston
Wild Dunes Resort
Hilton Head
Disney Hilton Head Is.
Hilton Head Marriott Beach
Inn at Palmetto Bluff
Sea Pines Resort
Westin
Kiawah Island
Kiawah Island Resorts
Sanctuary/Kiawah Is.
Myrtle Beach
Myrtle Beach Marriott
Tennessee
Nashville
Gaylord Opryland
Texas
Austin
Barton Creek
Dallas/Ft. Worth
Four Seasons/Las Colinas
Westin Stonebriar
Lajitas
Lajitas
San Antonio
Hyatt Hill Country
Westin La Cantera
U.S. Virgin Islands
St. Croix
Buccaneer
Carambola Beach
Utah
St. George
Coyote Inn/Spa
Vermont
Essex
Inn at Essex

Stowe
Stoweflake Mtn. Resort
Stratton Mountain
Equinox
Vergennes
Basin Harbor Club
Woodstock
Woodstock Inn
Virginia
Charlottesville
Boar's Head Inn
Irvington
Tides Inn
Lansdowne
Lansdowne Resort
Williamsburg
Kingsmill Resort
Washington
Blaine
Semiahmoo Resort
Stevenson
Skamania Lodge
West Virginia
White Sulphur Springs
Greenbrier
Wisconsin
Kohler
American Club
Wyoming
Jackson
Jackson Lake Lodge
Spring Creek Ranch

Ski Resort

Alaska
Girdwood
Alyeska Prince
California
Lake Tahoe Area
Nakoma Resort
PlumpJack Squaw Valley
Resort at Squaw Creek
Yosemite
Tenaya Lodge
Colorado
Aspen
Little Nell
Lodge & Spa/Cordillera
Ritz-Carlton, Bachelor Gulch
St. Regis
Beaver Creek
Beaver Creek Lodge
Charter/Beaver Creek
Inn at Beaver Creek
Park Hyatt
Keystone
Keystone Resort
Montrose
Elk Mountain Resort
Steamboat Springs
Steamboat Grand
Telluride
Ice House Lodge
Inn at Lost Creek
Telluride
Wyndham Peaks
Vail
Lodge at Vail
Sonnenalp
Vail Cascade Resort
Idaho
Sun Valley
Sun Valley Lodge
Illinois
Galena
Eagle Ridge Resort
Maine
Cape Elizabeth
Inn by the Sea
Kennebunkport
White Barn Inn
Prouts Neck
Black Point Inn
Rockport
Samoset Resort
Massachusetts
Lenox
Canyon Ranch/Mass.
Cranwell Resort
Montana
Big Sky
Big Sky Resort
Darby
Triple Creek Ranch
Pray
Chico Hot Springs
Whitefish
Grouse Mtn. Lodge

Nevada
Incline Village
Hyatt Resort

New Hampshire
Bretton Woods
Mount Washington
Dixville Notch
Balsams

New Mexico
Santa Fe
La Posada/Santa Fe
Taos
El Monte Sagrado

New York
Adirondacks
Mirror Lake Inn
Point
Sagamore
Catskills
Mirbeau Inn
Mohonk Mountain Hse.

Oregon
Black Butte
Black Butte Ranch
Crater Lake National Park
Crater Lake Lodge

Pennsylvania
Farmington
Nemacolin Woodlands
Hershey
Hershey
Poconos
Skytop Lodge

Utah
Park City
Deer Valley Lodging
Goldener Hirsch Inn
Stein Eriksen Lodge
Salt Lake City
Lodge at Snowbird
Snowbird
Sundance

Vermont
Smuggler's Notch
Smugglers' Notch
Stowe
Green Mountain Inn
Stoweflake Mtn. Resort
Topnotch at Stowe
Trapp Family Lodge
Stratton Mountain
Equinox

Washington
Seattle
Salish Lodge

Wisconsin
Kohler
American Club

Wyoming
Jackson
Four Seasons Jackson Hole
Snake River Lodge
Spring Creek Ranch

SPECIAL FEATURES

(Indexes list the best in each category.)

Additions

Alabama

Birmingham

Renaissance Ross Bridge Golf

Arizona

Tucson

Starr Pass Resort

California

Carmel Area

Casa Palmero

L'Auberge Carmel

Napa

Calistoga Ranch

Napa River Inn

Palm Springs Area

Le Parker Méridien

Morongo Casino

Smoke Tree Ranch

San Diego

Solamar

San Francisco Bay Area

Griffon

Vitale

San Jose

Lodge at Cordevalle

Santa Barbara

Andalucia

Colorado

Montrose

Elk Mountain Resort

Florida

Ft. Myers

Sanibel Harbour Resort

Miami

Bentley Beach

Circa 39

Conrad Miami

Victor

Georgia

Atlanta

Indigo

InterCont. Buckhead

Georgia Coast

King & Prince Resort

Savannah

Mansion on Forsyth Park

Louisiana

New Orleans

Monteleone

Maryland

Baltimore

Antrim 1844

Massachusetts

Boston

Jacob Hill Inn

Cape Cod & The Islands

Century House

Michigan

Detroit

Royal Park

Montana

Missoula

Resort at Paws Up

Nevada

Las Vegas

Renaissance Las Vegas

Wynn Las Vegas

New Hampshire

Plainfield

Home Hill

New Jersey

Atlantic City

Tropicana

Trump Plaza

Trump Taj Mahal

New Mexico

Santa Fe

Inn of the Five Graces

New York

Adirondacks

Whiteface Lodge

Hudson Valley

Inn at Bullis Hall

Ohio

Cleveland

Walden Country Inn

Oregon

Crater Lake National Park

Crater Lake Lodge

Puerto Rico
San Juan
Paradisus Puerto Rico
Rhode Island
Newport
Vanderbilt Hall
Providence
Providence
South Carolina
Charleston
Market Pavilion
Hilton Head
Inn at Palmetto Bluff
Tennessee
Gatlinburg
Lodge at Buckberry Creek
Texas
Houston
Icon
San Antonio
Valencia Riverwalk
Utah
Park City
Park City
Vermont
Vergennes
Basin Harbor Club
Virginia
DC Metro Area
Goodstone Inn
Orange
Willow Grove Inn

Beautiful Grounds

Arizona
Phoenix/Scottsdale
Arizona Biltmore
Boulders
Four Seasons Scottsdale
Hyatt/Gainey Ranch
JW Marriott Desert Ridge
Phoenician
Tucson
Arizona Inn
Loews Ventana Canyon
Starr Pass Resort
California
Carmel Area
Bernardus Lodge
Carmel Valley Ranch
Inn at Spanish Bay
Lodge/Pebble Beach
Post Ranch Inn
Quail Lodge
Dana Point
Ritz-Carlton Laguna Niguel
Huntington Beach
Hyatt Huntington Beach
Laguna Beach
Montage Resort
Los Angeles
Bel-Air, Hotel
Casa Del Mar
Rancho Bernardo Inn
Ritz-Carlton Huntington
Shutters on the Beach
Napa
Auberge du Soleil
Calistoga Ranch
Meadowood
Villagio Inn
Palm Springs Area
Marriott Desert Springs
Smoke Tree Ranch
Westin Mission Hills
San Diego
Barona Valley Ranch
del Coronado
Four Seasons Aviara
Inn at Rancho Santa Fe
La Costa
Lodge at Torrey Pines
Rancho Valencia
San Francisco Bay Area
Clift
Santa Barbara
Bacara Resort
El Encanto
Four Seasons Santa Barbara
Sonoma
Gaige House Inn
Kenwood Inn
MacArthur Place
Madrona Manor
South Bay
Ritz-Carlton Half Moon Bay
Stanford Park
Yosemite
Ahwahnee
Château du Sureau
Colorado
Montrose
Elk Mountain Resort

Delaware
Wilmington
Inn at Montchanin
Florida
Palm Beach
Breakers
Tampa/St. Petersburg
Grand Hyatt Tampa Bay
Hyatt Tampa Bay
Georgia
Atlanta
Barnsley Gardens
Braselton
Château Élan
Georgia Coast
Jekyll Island Club
Lodge at Sea Island
Lodge on Little St. Simons
Lake Oconee
Ritz-Carlton Reynolds
Hawaii
Big Island
Fairmont Orchid
Four Seasons Hualalai
Mauna Kea Beach
Waikoloa Beach Marriott
Kauai
Grand Hyatt Kauai
Princeville Resort
Lanai
Lodge at Koele
Manele Bay Hotel
Maui
Four Seasons/Wailea
Grand Wailea Resort
Hana-Maui
Ritz-Carlton Kapalua
Oahu
Hilton Hawaiian Vlg.
JW Marriott Ihilani
Kahala Mandarin Oriental
Idaho
Coeur d'Alene
Coeur d'Alene
Massachusetts
Cape Cod & The Islands
Wequassett Inn
Lenox
Blantyre
Cranwell Resort
Wheatleigh
Michigan
Bay Harbor
Inn at Bay Harbor
Mississippi
Natchez
Monmouth Plantation
New York
Adirondacks
Mirror Lake Inn
Point
Sagamore
Westchester
Castle on the Hudson
Ohio
Cleveland
Walden Country Inn
Pennsylvania
Bradford
Glendorn
Bucks County
EverMay/Delaware
Farmington
Nemacolin Woodlands
Puerto Rico
Vieques
Martineau Bay Resort
South Carolina
Charleston
Woodlands Resort
Pawleys Island
Litchfield Plantation
Tennessee
Gatlinburg
Lodge at Buckberry Creek
Texas
Austin
Barton Creek
Lake Austin Spa
San Antonio
Hyatt Hill Country
U.S. Virgin Islands
St. Croix
Carambola Beach
St. John
Caneel Bay
St. Thomas
Marriott Frenchman Reef
Virginia
Hot Springs
Homestead
Irvington
Tides Inn

West Virginia
White Sulphur Springs
Greenbrier
Wyoming
Jackson
Four Seasons Jackson Hole
Snake River Lodge
Spring Creek Ranch

Butlers

Arizona
Phoenix/Scottsdale
Boulders
Ritz-Carlton
California
Dana Point
St. Regis Monarch Beach
Palm Springs Area
Hyatt Grand Champions
San Francisco Bay Area
Pan Pacific SF
Yosemite
Château du Sureau
Connecticut
Uncasville
Mohegan Sun
District of Columbia
Washington, DC
St. Regis
Florida
Ft. Lauderdale
Boca Raton Resort
Palm Beach
Ritz-Carlton Palm Beach
Georgia
Atlanta
Ritz-Carlton Buckhead
Georgia Coast
Cloister
Lodge at Sea Island
Hawaii
Maui
Ritz-Carlton Kapalua
Massachusetts
Boston
Ritz-Carlton, Boston
Ritz-Carlton Boston Common
Lenox
Wheatleigh
Missouri
St. Louis
Ritz-Carlton
Nevada
Las Vegas
Ritz-Carlton, Lake Las Vegas
New Jersey
Atlantic City
Trump Taj Mahal
New Mexico
Santa Fe
Eldorado
New York
New York City
Millennium UN Plaza
70 Park Ave.
Puerto Rico
Fajardo
Las Casitas Village
Texas
Houston
St. Regis
Vermont
Stratton Mountain
Equinox
Virginia
DC Metro Area
Morrison House
Washington
Seattle
Alexis

Casinos

California
Palm Springs Area
Morongo Casino
San Diego
Barona Valley Ranch
Connecticut
Ledyard
Foxwoods Resort
Uncasville
Mohegan Sun
Florida
Ft. Lauderdale
Seminole Hard Rock
Louisiana
New Orleans
Wyndham/Canal Place
Mississippi
Biloxi
Beau Rivage
Missouri
St. Louis
Roberts Mayfair

Nevada
Incline Village
Hyatt Resort
Las Vegas
Bellagio Hotel
Caesars Palace
Green Valley Ranch
Hard Rock
Hyatt Lake Resort
JW Marriott Las Vegas
Mandalay Bay Hotel
MGM Grand Hotel
Mirage Hotel
Palms Casino Hotel
Paris Las Vegas
Rio All-Suite Hotel & Casino
Venetian Hotel
Wynn Las Vegas
New Jersey
Atlantic City
Bally's
Borgata Hotel
Caesars Atlantic City
Sands
Tropicana
Trump Marina
Trump Plaza
Trump Taj Mahal
New Mexico
Albuquerque
Hyatt Tamaya
Puerto Rico
Fajardo
Las Casitas Village
Las Croabas
Wyndham El Conquistador
San Juan
InterContinental
Paradisus Puerto Rico
Ritz-Carlton
Westin Rio Mar
Wyndham El San Juan

Children Not Recommended

(Call to confirm policy)
Arizona
Tucson
Canyon Ranch
Miraval Spa
California
Carmel Area
Cypress Inn
Inn at Depot Hill
L'Auberge Carmel
Post Ranch Inn
Seven Gables Inn
Stonepine
Ventana Inn
Napa
Auberge du Soleil
Milliken Creek Inn
Mount View
Palm Springs Area
Ballantines
Two Bunch Palms
San Diego
Cal-a-Vie
Golden Door
L'Auberge Del Mar
Sonoma
Gaige House Inn
Honor Mansion
Kenwood Inn
Yosemite
Château du Sureau
Connecticut
Greenwich
Homestead Inn
New Preston
Boulders Inn
Washington
Mayflower Inn
Delaware
Wilmington
Inn at Montchanin
Florida
Keys
Gardens
Little Palm Island
Marquesa
Miami
Grove Isle Club
Ritz-Carlton Coconut Grove
Shore Club
Tampa/St. Petersburg
Belleview Biltmore
Georgia
Georgia Coast
Lodge on Little St. Simons
Savannah
Gastonian
Illinois
Gilman
Heartland Spa

Louisiana
New Orleans
Maison de Ville
Soniat House
Maine
Kennebunkport
Captain Lord Mansion
White Barn Inn
Massachusetts
Boston
Jacob Hill Inn
Cape Cod & The Islands
Charlotte Inn
Dan'l Webster Inn
Wauwinet
Lenox
Blantyre
Canyon Ranch/Mass.
Wheatleigh
Mississippi
Natchez
Monmouth Plantation
Montana
Big Sky
Big Sky Resort
Darby
Triple Creek Ranch
New Hampshire
Plainfield
Home Hill
New York
Adirondacks
Friends Lake Inn
Lake Placid Lodge
Point
Catskills
Kate's Lazy Meadow
New Age Health Spa
Hudson Valley
Le Chambord
Old Drovers Inn
New York City
Inn at Irving Place
60 Thompson
Oregon
Hood River
Columbia Gorge
Pennsylvania
Bucks County
EverMay/Delaware
Philadelphia
Loews Philadelphia
Puerto Rico
Rincon
Horned Dorset
Rhode Island
Newport
Francis Malbone Hse.
Providence
Westin
South Carolina
Pawleys Island
Litchfield Plantation
Tennessee
Walland
Blackberry Farm
Texas
Austin
Lake Austin Spa
Dallas/Ft. Worth
Greenhouse
Utah
St. George
Coyote Inn/Spa
Vermont
Barnard
Twin Farms
Virginia
Paris
Ashby Inn
White Post
L'Auberge Provençale
Washington
Seattle
Inn at Langley
Wisconsin
Chetek
Canoe Bay
Wyoming
Jackson
Wort Hotel

City Views

California
Los Angeles
Century Plaza
Four Seasons Bev. Hills
Loews Beverly Hills
Millennium Biltmore
Peninsula Beverly Hills
Wyndham Bel Age

San Diego

San Diego
Marriott San Diego
W San Diego
San Francisco Bay Area
Argent
Clift
Four Seasons San Fran.
Huntington
Mandarin Oriental
Mark Hopkins

District of Columbia

Washington, DC
Four Seasons
Grand Hyatt
Park Hyatt
Ritz-Carlton

Florida

Miami
Conrad Miami
Mutiny
Omni Colonnade

Georgia

Atlanta
Georgian Terrace
InterCont. Buckhead
Ritz-Carlton

Illinois

Chicago
Burnham
Four Seasons
Sheraton Chicago
Sofitel Chic. Water Tower

Louisiana

New Orleans
Loews New Orleans
Monteleone
Windsor Court

Massachusetts

Boston
Commonwealth
Marlowe
Ritz-Carlton, Boston
Westin Copley Pl.

Minnesota

Minneapolis/St. Paul
Marquette

Nevada

Las Vegas
Bellagio Hotel
Four Seasons Las Vegas
Palms Casino Hotel
Renaissance Las Vegas
Venetian Hotel

New York

New York City
Dream Hotel
Four Seasons
Gansevoort
Helmsley Park Lane
Mandarin Oriental
Mark
Michelangelo
Millenium Hilton
New York Palace
Peninsula
Pierre New York
Rihga Royal
Ritz-Carlton, Battery Pk.
Ritz-Carlton, Central Park
Trump International

Oklahoma

Bartlesville
Inn at Price Tower

Oregon

Portland
Benson
Governor

Pennsylvania

Philadelphia
Four Seasons Phila.
Sofitel Philadelphia

South Carolina

Charleston
Market Pavilion

Tennessee

Nashville
Hermitage
Loews Vanderbilt
Renaissance Nashville

Texas

Austin
Hilton Austin
Dallas/Ft. Worth
Adolphus
Zaza, Hotel
Houston
Derek
Hilton Americas Houston
Icon
InterContinental
St. Regis

San Antonio
Menger
Valencia Riverwalk
Watermark

Utah

Salt Lake City
Grand America
Little America

Virginia

DC Metro Area
Morrison House

Washington

Seattle
Alexis
Fairmont Olympic
Grand Hyatt
Mayflower Park
Sheraton
W Seattle

Wisconsin

Milwaukee
Pfister Hotel
Wyndham Milwaukee

Cottages/Villas

Arizona

Phoenix/Scottsdale
Boulders
CopperWynd
Fairmont Scottsdale
Hermosa Inn
Phoenician
Royal Palms

Sedona
L'Auberge de Sedona

California

Carmel Area
La Playa
Mission Ranch
Post Ranch Inn
Quail Lodge
Tickle Pink Inn
Ventana Inn

Eureka
Carter House

Lake Tahoe Area
Nakoma Resort

Los Angeles
Chateau Marmont
Peninsula Beverly Hills
Ritz-Carlton Huntington

Napa
Auberge du Soleil
Calistoga Ranch
Carneros Inn
Mount View

Palm Springs Area
Hyatt Grand Champions
Le Parker Méridien
Smoke Tree Ranch
Two Bunch Palms
Viceroy Palm Springs

San Diego
del Coronado
Inn at Rancho Santa Fe
La Valencia

San Francisco Bay Area
Albion River

Santa Barbara
El Encanto
Four Seasons Santa Barbara
Upham

Sonoma
Gaige House Inn
MacArthur Place
St. Orres

Yosemite
Ahwahnee
Château du Sureau

Colorado

Montrose
Elk Mountain Resort

Snowmass
Snowmass Club

Connecticut

Norwich
Spa at Norwich Inn

Florida

Amelia Island
Amelia Is. Plantation

Ft. Lauderdale
Boca Raton Resort

Keys
Gardens
Hawk's Cay Resort
Sunset Key Cottages

Miami
Fisher Island

Naples
Registry Resort

Orlando
Villas of Grand Cypress

Palm Beach
Colony
PGA National Resort
Sandestin
Sandestin
Santa Rosa Beach
Water Color Inn
Sarasota
Captiva Beach Resort
Georgia
Atlanta
Barnsley Gardens
Braselton
Château Élan
Georgia Coast
Jekyll Island Club
King & Prince Resort
Lake Oconee
Ritz-Carlton Reynolds
Hawaii
Big Island
Four Seasons Hualalai
Maui
Fairmont Kea Lani
Hana-Maui
Kapalua Bay Hotel
Kapalua Villas
Louisiana
New Orleans
Maison de Ville
Maison Dupuy
Soniat House
Massachusetts
Cape Cod & The Islands
Ocean Edge Resort
Wauwinet
White Elephant
Lenox
Blantyre
Nevada
Incline Village
Hyatt Resort
Las Vegas
Bellagio Hotel
MGM Grand Hotel
New Hampshire
Plainfield
Home Hill
New York
Adirondacks
Elk Lake Lodge
Catskills
Mirbeau Inn
Mohonk Mountain Hse.
Long Island
Gurney's Inn
North Carolina
Outer Banks
Sanderling
Pinehurst
Pinehurst Resort
Puerto Rico
Fajardo
Las Casitas Village
San Juan
Paradisus Puerto Rico
South Carolina
Charleston
Wild Dunes Resort
Woodlands Resort
Hilton Head
Disney Hilton Head Is.
Hilton Head Health Inst.
Sea Pines Resort
Westin
Kiawah Island
Kiawah Island Resorts
Tennessee
Walland
Blackberry Farm
Texas
Austin
Lake Austin Spa
U.S. Virgin Islands
St. Croix
Buccaneer
St. John
Caneel Bay
Westin
Vermont
Barnard
Twin Farms
Shelburne
Inn at Shelburne Farms
Stowe
Trapp Family Lodge
Vergennes
Basin Harbor Club
Virginia
Orange
Willow Grove Inn

Washington
Seattle
Inn at Langley
Wisconsin
Chetek
Canoe Bay
Wyoming
Jackson
Jackson Lake Lodge

Dramatic Design

Arizona
Phoenix/Scottsdale
Arizona Biltmore
California
Carmel Area
Post Ranch Inn
Los Angeles
Maison 140
Mondrian
Raffles L'Ermitage
Viceroy
Palm Springs Area
Viceroy Palm Springs
San Francisco Bay Area
Argonaut
Clift
Palomar
Santa Barbara
Andalucia
Sonoma
Healdsburg
St. Orres
Yosemite
Ahwahnee
Colorado
Aspen
Sky
Colorado Springs
Broadmoor
Connecticut
Greenwich
Delamar
Homestead Inn
District of Columbia
Washington, DC
Helix
Madera
Ritz-Carlton, Georgetown
Rouge
Florida
Miami
Biltmore/Coral Gables
Delano
Shore Club
Victor
Georgia
Lake Oconee
Ritz-Carlton Reynolds
Hawaii
Big Island
Hilton Waikoloa Vlg.
Kona Village Resort
Lanai
Lodge at Koele
Illinois
Chicago
Burnham
Monaco
Park Hyatt
Sofitel Chic. Water Tower
Massachusetts
Boston
XV Beacon
Marlowe
Nine Zero
Michigan
Traverse City
Great Wolf Lodge
Minnesota
Minneapolis/St. Paul
Graves 601
Montana
Missoula
Resort at Paws Up
Nevada
Las Vegas
Bellagio Hotel
Paris Las Vegas
Ritz-Carlton, Lake Las Vegas
Venetian Hotel
New Mexico
Santa Fe
Inn of the Anasazi
Inn of the Five Graces
New York
Adirondacks
Lake Placid Lodge
New York City
Hudson
Maritime
Ohio
Cleveland
Hyatt/Arcade
Walden Country Inn

Oklahoma
Bartlesville
Inn at Price Tower
Oregon
Portland
Lucia, Hotel
Pennsylvania
Philadelphia
Loews Philadelphia
Ritz-Carlton
Tennessee
Gatlinburg
Lodge at Buckberry Creek
Texas
Dallas/Ft. Worth
Crescent Court
Zaza, Hotel
Marfa
Cibolo Creek Ranch
San Antonio
Valencia Riverwalk
Utah
Park City
Goldener Hirsch Inn
Wisconsin
Chetek
Canoe Bay
Wyoming
Jackson
Amangani
Four Seasons Jackson Hole
Yellowstone Nat'l Park
Old Faithful Snow Lodge

Fireplaces

(In-room)
Alabama
Birmingham
Renaissance Ross Bridge Golf
Alaska
Anchorage
Millennium Anchorage
Fairbanks
Pikes Waterfront Lodge
Arizona
Phoenix/Scottsdale
Boulders
CopperWynd
Fairmont Scottsdale
Four Seasons Scottsdale
Hermosa Inn
Hyatt/Gainey Ranch
Royal Palms
Sedona
Canyon Villa
Enchantment Resort
Hilton Sedona Resort
L'Auberge de Sedona
Tucson
Arizona Inn
Hacienda del Sol
Hilton El Conquistador
Loews Ventana Canyon
Miraval Spa
Starr Pass Resort
California
Carmel Area
Bernardus Lodge
Casa Palmero
Centrella
Cobblestone Inn
Inn at Depot Hill
Inn at Spanish Bay
Lodge/Pebble Beach
Mission Ranch
Pacific
Post Ranch Inn
Quail Lodge
Spindrift Inn
Stonepine
Ventana Inn
Dana Point
St. Regis Monarch Beach
Inverness
Manka Inverness Lodge
Laguna Beach
Surf & Sand Resort
Lake Tahoe Area
Nakoma Resort
Los Angeles
Bel-Air, Hotel
Beverly Hills
Chateau Marmont
Loews Santa Monica
Peninsula Beverly Hills
Ritz-Carlton Huntington
Mendocino
Stanford Inn by the Sea
Napa
Auberge du Soleil
Calistoga Ranch
Carneros Inn

La Résidence
Meadowood
Milliken Creek Inn
Napa River Inn
Napa Valley Lodge

Palm Springs Area
Hyatt Grand Champions
La Quinta Resort
Le Parker Méridien
Smoke Tree Ranch
Willows Historic Palm Springs

San Diego
Inn at Rancho Santa Fe
La Casa del Zorro
Loews Coronado Bay
Rancho Valencia

San Francisco Bay Area
Albion River
Archbishop's Mansion
Casa Madrona
Fairmont San Francisco
Hyatt Vineyard Creek
Inn Above Tide
Lafayette Park
Majestic
Petite Auberge
White Swan Inn

San Jose
De Anza
Lodge at Cordevalle

San Luis Obispo
Apple Farm

Santa Barbara
Bacara Resort
El Encanto
Four Seasons Santa Barbara
Montecito Inn
San Ysidro Ranch
Simpson House Inn

Solvang
Alisal Guest Ranch
Fess Parker's

Sonoma
Applewood Inn
Bodega Bay Lodge
Fairmont Sonoma Mission
Gaige House Inn
Honor Mansion
Kenwood Inn
MacArthur Place
Madrona Manor
Whale Watch Inn

South Bay
Ritz-Carlton Half Moon Bay
Seal Cove Inn

Yosemite
Ahwahnee
Château du Sureau

Colorado

Aspen
Jerome
Little Nell
Ritz-Carlton, Bachelor Gulch
St. Regis

Beaver Creek
Beaver Creek Lodge
Charter/Beaver Creek
Park Hyatt

Colorado Springs
Broadmoor
Cliff House/Pikes Peak

Denver
C Lazy U Ranch

Keystone
Keystone Resort

Montrose
Elk Mountain Resort

Snowmass
Snowmass Club

Steamboat Springs
Steamboat Grand

Telluride
Inn at Lost Creek
Telluride

Vail
Vail Cascade Resort

Connecticut

Norwich
Spa at Norwich Inn

Old Saybrook
Saybrook Point Inn

Delaware

Wilmington
Inn at Montchanin

District of Columbia

Washington, DC
Jefferson
Monaco
Ritz-Carlton, Georgetown

Florida

Jacksonville
Lodge & Club

Orlando
Villas of Grand Cypress

Georgia
Atlanta
Barnsley Gardens
InterCont. Buckhead
Georgia Coast
Jekyll Island Club
King & Prince Resort
Lodge at Sea Island
Savannah
Ballastone Inn
Gastonian
Idaho
Ketchum
Knob Hill Inn
Kansas
Wichita
Inn at the Park
Maine
Cape Elizabeth
Inn by the Sea
Kennebunkport
Cliff House
Maryland
Baltimore
Antrim 1844
Cambridge
Hyatt Chesapeake Bay
Massachusetts
Boston
Fairmont Copley Plaza
Jacob Hill Inn
Jurys
Lenox
Ritz-Carlton, Boston
Cape Cod & The Islands
Charlotte Inn
Lenox
Wheatleigh
Michigan
Bay Harbor
Inn at Bay Harbor
Detroit
Royal Park
Missouri
Osage Beach
Tan Tar A Resort
Montana
Darby
Triple Creek Ranch
Pray
Chico Hot Springs
New Hampshire
Bretton Woods
Mount Washington
New Jersey
Atlantic City
Trump Marina
Trump Taj Mahal
Spring Lake
Normandy Inn
New Mexico
Santa Fe
Bishop's Lodge
Houses of the Moon
Inn of the Anasazi
Inn of the Five Graces
New York
Adirondacks
Friends Lake Inn
Mirror Lake Inn
Sagamore
Whiteface Lodge
Catskills
Mohonk Mountain Hse.
Cooperstown
Otesaga
Hudson Valley
Inn at Bullis Hall
Old Drovers Inn
Roselawn
Long Island
Garden City
New York City
Lowell
Mercer
Royalton
70 Park Ave.
North Carolina
Asheville
Swag
Ohio
Cincinnati
Cincinnatian
Oregon
Black Butte
Black Butte Ranch
Gold Beach
Tu Tu' Tun Lodge
Hood River
Columbia Gorge
Portland
Avalon
Benson

Pennsylvania
Bradford
Glendorn
Farmington
Nemacolin Woodlands
Poconos
Skytop Lodge
Rhode Island
Newport
Castle Hill Inn
Francis Malbone Hse.
South Carolina
Aiken
Willcox
Charleston
Planters Inn
Wentworth Mansion
Woodlands Resort
Hilton Head
Inn at Palmetto Bluff
Tennessee
Gatlinburg
Lodge at Buckberry Creek
Walland
Blackberry Farm
Texas
Austin
Lake Austin Spa
Utah
Moab
Sorrel River Ranch
Park City
Deer Valley Lodging
Park City
Stein Eriksen Lodge
Salt Lake City
Lodge at Snowbird
Snowbird
Sundance
Vermont
Barnard
Twin Farms
Essex
Inn at Essex
Lower Waterford
Rabbit Hill Inn
Smuggler's Notch
Smugglers' Notch
Stowe
Stoweflake Mtn. Resort
Topnotch at Stowe
Trapp Family Lodge
Stratton Mountain
Equinox
Sugarbush
Pitcher Inn
Woodstock
Woodstock Inn
Virginia
Charlottesville
200 South St. Inn
DC Metro Area
Goodstone Inn
Orange
Willow Grove Inn
Paris
Ashby Inn
Washington
Blaine
Semiahmoo Resort
Seattle
Alexis
Bellevue Club
Edgewater
Inn at Langley
Willows Lodge
Stevenson
Skamania Lodge
Wisconsin
Chetek
Canoe Bay
Milwaukee
Metro
Wyoming
Jackson
Four Seasons Jackson Hole
Lost Creek Ranch
Rusty Parrot Lodge
Snake River Lodge
Spring Creek Ranch

Fishing

Alabama
Point Clear
Marriott Grand
Alaska
Glacier Bay
Glacier Bay Lodge
Arizona
Phoenix/Scottsdale
Hermosa Inn
Sedona
L'Auberge de Sedona

California

Carmel Area
Bernardus Lodge
Dana Point
Marriott Laguna Cliffs
Ritz-Carlton Laguna Niguel
Inverness
Manka Inverness Lodge
Laguna Beach
Montage Resort
Lake Tahoe Area
Resort at Squaw Creek
Los Angeles
Le Merigot Beach
Ritz-Carlton Marina del Rey
San Diego
del Coronado
Hilton La Jolla Torrey Pines
Loews Coronado Bay
Manchester Gr. Hyatt
San Francisco Bay Area
Argonaut
Inn Above Tide
Santa Barbara
Four Seasons Santa Barbara
Montecito Inn
San Ysidro Ranch
Solvang
Alisal Guest Ranch
Sonoma
Applewood Inn
South Bay
Ritz-Carlton Half Moon Bay
Yosemite
Ahwahnee
Château du Sureau

Colorado

Aspen
Jerome
Lodge & Spa/Cordillera
St. Regis
Beaver Creek
Park Hyatt
Clark
Home Ranch
Montrose
Elk Mountain Resort
Steamboat Springs
Steamboat Grand
Telluride
Telluride
Wyndham Peaks
Vail
Lodge at Vail
Vail Cascade Resort

Connecticut

Mystic
Inn at Mystic
New Preston
Boulders Inn

Florida

Amelia Island
Amelia Is. Plantation
Ritz-Carlton
Destin
Hilton Sandestin Beach
Ft. Lauderdale
Boca Raton Resort
Marriott Harbor Beach
Pillars/New River Sound
Ft. Myers
Casa Ybel Resort
Sanibel Harbour Resort
Hutchinson Island
Hutchinson Is. Marriott
Jacksonville
Ponte Vedra Inn
Keys
Cheeca Lodge
Hawk's Cay Resort
Hilton Key West
Little Palm Island
Ocean Reef Club
Sunset Key Cottages
Wyndham Casa Marina
Miami
Doral Golf Resort
Fairmont Turnberry Isle
Fisher Island
Grove Isle Club
Mayfair
Ritz-Carlton Key Biscayne
Ritz-Carlton South Beach
Naples
Hyatt Coconut Point
La Playa Beach/Resort
Marco Beach Resort
Marco Island Marriott
Registry Resort
Ritz-Carlton Naples
Orlando
Disney Grand Floridian
Disney Polynesian

Disney Yacht Club
Ritz-Carlton Orlando
Villas of Grand Cypress
Walt Disney Swan
Westin Grand Bohemian

Palm Beach
Brazilian Court
Breakers
Four Seasons
Ritz-Carlton Palm Beach

Sandestin
Sandestin

Santa Rosa Beach
Water Color Inn

Sarasota
Captiva Beach Resort
Colony Beach

Tampa/St. Petersburg
Chalet Suzanne Inn
Don CeSar Beach
Renaissance Vinoy
Saddlebrook Resort

Vero Beach
Disney Vero Beach

Georgia

Atlanta
Barnsley Gardens

Georgia Coast
Cloister
Jekyll Island Club
King & Prince Resort
Lodge at Sea Island
Lodge on Little St. Simons

Lake Oconee
Ritz-Carlton Reynolds

Hawaii

Big Island
Four Seasons Hualalai
Kona Village Resort
Mauna Kea Beach
Waikoloa Beach Marriott

Kauai
Marriott Kauai Resort

Maui
Fairmont Kea Lani
Four Seasons/Wailea
Hyatt
Kapalua Bay Hotel
Kapalua Villas
Sheraton Maui

Oahu
Hyatt Regency Waikiki

Idaho

Coeur d'Alene
Coeur d'Alene

Illinois

Galena
Eagle Ridge Resort

Maine

Cape Elizabeth
Inn by the Sea

Kennebunkport
Cliff House

Prouts Neck
Black Point Inn

York Harbor
York Harbor Inn

Maryland

Baltimore
Loews Annapolis

Cambridge
Hyatt Chesapeake Bay

St. Michaels
Inn at Perry Cabin

Massachusetts

Cape Cod & The Islands
Century House
Charlotte Inn
Chatham Bars Inn
Ocean Edge Resort
Wauwinet

Lenox
Cranwell Resort

Michigan

Detroit
Royal Park

Mississippi

Natchez
Monmouth Plantation

Missouri

Branson
Chateau on the Lake

Osage Beach
Tan Tar A Resort

Montana

Big Sky
Big Sky Resort

Darby
Triple Creek Ranch

Missoula
Resort at Paws Up

Whitefish
Grouse Mtn. Lodge

Nevada

Las Vegas
Hyatt Lake Resort
JW Marriott Las Vegas
Ritz-Carlton, Lake Las Vegas

New Hampshire

Dixville Notch
Balsams

New Mexico

Santa Fe
Bishop's Lodge

Taos
El Monte Sagrado

New York

Adirondacks
Elk Lake Lodge
Friends Lake Inn
Lake Placid Lodge
Mirror Lake Inn
Point
Sagamore
Whiteface Lodge

Catskills
Kate's Lazy Meadow
Mirbeau Inn
Mohonk Mountain Hse.

Cooperstown
Otesaga

Hudson Valley
Old Drovers Inn

Long Island
American
Gurney's Inn

Oklahoma

Bartlesville
Inn at Price Tower

Oregon

Black Butte
Black Butte Ranch

Crater Lake National Park
Crater Lake Lodge

Gold Beach
Tu Tu' Tun Lodge

Hood River
Columbia Gorge

Pennsylvania

Bradford
Glendorn

Farmington
Nemacolin Woodlands

Poconos
Skytop Lodge

Puerto Rico

Fajardo
Las Casitas Village

Las Croabas
Wyndham El Conquistador

Rincon
Horned Dorset

San Juan
Hyatt Dorado Beach
InterContinental
Paradisus Puerto Rico

Vieques
Martineau Bay Resort

Rhode Island

Newport
Castle Hill Inn

South Carolina

Charleston
Charleston Place
Planters Inn
Wild Dunes Resort

Hilton Head
Inn at Palmetto Bluff
Sea Pines Resort
Westin

Tennessee

Gatlinburg
Lodge at Buckberry Creek

Walland
Blackberry Farm

Texas

Austin
Lake Austin Spa

Galveston
Galvez-Historic Wyndham
Tremont House

Marfa
Cibolo Creek Ranch

U.S. Virgin Islands

St. John
Westin

St. Thomas
Marriott Frenchman Reef

Utah

Park City
Deer Valley Lodging
Goldener Hirsch Inn
Park City
Stein Eriksen Lodge

Salt Lake City
Snowbird
Sundance

Vermont

Barnard
Twin Farms
Lower Waterford
Rabbit Hill Inn
Mt. Snow
Inn at Sawmill Farm
Smuggler's Notch
Smugglers' Notch
Stowe
Green Mountain Inn
Stratton Mountain
Equinox
Sugarbush
Pitcher Inn
Vergennes
Basin Harbor Club
Woodstock
Quechee Inn
Woodstock Inn

Virginia

Charlottesville
Boar's Head Inn
Keswick Hall
Hot Springs
Homestead
Irvington
Tides Inn
Washington
Inn at Little Washington
Williamsburg
Kingsmill Resort

Washington

Blaine
Semiahmoo Resort
Seattle
Edgewater
Salish Lodge
Woodmark/Lake Wash.

West Virginia

White Sulphur Springs
Greenbrier

Wisconsin

Chetek
Canoe Bay

Wyoming

Jackson
Four Seasons Jackson Hole
Jackson Lake Lodge
Jenny Lake Lodge
Spring Creek Ranch
Yellowstone Nat'l Park
Lake Yellowstone

Hiking/Walking Trails

Alaska

Denali
Mt. McKinley Princess

Arizona

Phoenix/Scottsdale
JW Marriott Desert Ridge
Pointe Hilton Squaw Peak
Pointe South Mountain
Sanctuary/Camelback Mtn.
Tucson
Canyon Ranch
Lodge/Ventana Canyon
Loews Ventana Canyon
Miraval Spa

California

Carmel Area
Carmel Valley Ranch
Inn at Spanish Bay
Lodge/Pebble Beach
Lake Tahoe Area
Nakoma Resort
Resort at Squaw Creek
Napa
Auberge du Soleil
Palm Springs Area
La Quinta Resort
Marriott Rancho Las Palmas
Two Bunch Palms
Westin Mission Hills
San Diego
Cal-a-Vie
Golden Door
Hilton La Jolla Torrey Pines
Lodge at Torrey Pines
Marriott Coronado Is.
Santa Barbara
Bacara Resort
San Ysidro Ranch
Yosemite
Ahwahnee
Château du Sureau
Tenaya Lodge

Colorado

Clark
Home Ranch

Colorado Springs
Broadmoor
Cliff House/Pikes Peak
Denver
Omni Interlocken
Keystone
Keystone Resort
Telluride
Telluride
Wyndham Peaks
Vail
Lodge at Vail
Sonnenalp
Vail Cascade Resort
Florida
Amelia Island
Amelia Is. Plantation
Naples
La Playa Beach/Resort
Hawaii
Big Island
Hilton Waikoloa Vlg.
Mauna Lani Bay
Kauai
Princeville Resort
Maui
Hana-Maui
Ritz-Carlton Kapalua
Molokai
Molokai Ranch
Massachusetts
Cape Cod & The Islands
Ocean Edge Resort
Lenox
Blantyre
Canyon Ranch/Mass.
Montana
Darby
Triple Creek Ranch
New Hampshire
Bretton Woods
Mount Washington
New Mexico
Taos
El Monte Sagrado
New York
Adirondacks
Friends Lake Inn
Mirror Lake Inn
Point
Catskills
Mirbeau Inn
Mohonk Mountain Hse.
New Age Health Spa
Oregon
Black Butte
Black Butte Ranch
Gleneden Beach
Salishan Lodge
Gold Beach
Tu Tu' Tun Lodge
Pennsylvania
Bradford
Glendorn
Poconos
Deerfield Spa
Skytop Lodge
South Carolina
Charleston
Wild Dunes Resort
Hilton Head
Hilton Head Health Inst.
Hilton Head Marriott Beach
Texas
Austin
Lake Austin Spa
San Antonio
Hyatt Hill Country
Utah
Moab
Sorrel River Ranch
Park City
Deer Valley Lodging
Salt Lake City
Sundance
St. George
Coyote Inn/Spa
Vermont
Stowe
Stoweflake Mtn. Resort
Topnotch at Stowe
Trapp Family Lodge
Washington
Blaine
Semiahmoo Resort
West Virginia
White Sulphur Springs
Greenbrier
Wisconsin
Chetek
Canoe Bay

Kohler
American Club
Wyoming
Jackson
Lost Creek Ranch
Snake River Lodge
Yellowstone Nat'l Park
Lake Yellowstone

Historic Interest

Arizona
Grand Canyon
El Tovar
Phoenix/Scottsdale
Arizona Biltmore
Wigwam Resort
Prescott
Hassayampa Inn
Tucson
Arizona Inn
Hacienda del Sol
Arkansas
Little Rock
Capital Hotel
California
Carmel Area
La Playa
L'Auberge Carmel
Seven Gables Inn
Eureka
Carter House
Los Angeles
Argyle
Bel-Air, Hotel
Beverly Hills
Millennium Biltmore
Napa
Napa River Inn
Palm Springs Area
La Quinta Resort
Smoke Tree Ranch
Willows Historic Palm Springs
Riverside
Mission Inn
San Diego
del Coronado
La Valencia
San Francisco Bay Area
Archbishop's Mansion
Huntington
Majestic
Mark Hopkins
Palace
Santa Barbara
Four Seasons Santa Barbara
Sonoma
Applewood Inn
Yosemite
Ahwahnee
Colorado
Colorado Springs
Cliff House/Pikes Peak
Denver
Boulderado
Brown Palace
Oxford
Connecticut
Greenwich
Homestead Inn
Hartford
Goodwin
Westport
Inn at National Hall
Delaware
Wilmington
du Pont
Inn at Montchanin
District of Columbia
Washington, DC
Hay-Adams
Morrison-Clark Inn
Renaissance Mayflower
Watergate
Willard InterContinental
Florida
Ft. Lauderdale
Boca Raton Resort
Keys
Gardens
Marquesa
Wyndham Casa Marina
Miami
Biltmore/Coral Gables
Eden Roc
Fisher Island
Palm Beach
Brazilian Court
Breakers
St. Augustine
Casa Monica
Tampa/St. Petersburg
Belleview Biltmore
Don CeSar Beach
Renaissance Vinoy

Georgia

Atlanta

Georgian Terrace

Georgia Coast

Jekyll Island Club

King & Prince Resort

Savannah

Ballastone Inn

Gastonian

Mansion on Forsyth Park

Hawaii

Oahu

Royal Hawaiian

Sheraton Moana Surfrider

Illinois

Chicago

Burnham

Deer Path Inn

Drake

InterContinental

Omni Ambassador E.

Palmer House Hilton

Whitehall

Indiana

Indianapolis

Canterbury Hotel

Kansas

Wichita

Inn at the Park

Kentucky

Louisville

Camberley Brown

Seelbach Hilton

Louisiana

New Orleans

Bourbon Orleans

Fairmont

Maison de Ville

Monteleone

Soniat House

White Castle

Nottoway Plantation

Maine

Bar Harbor

Bar Harbor Inn

Brunswick

Captain Daniel Stone

Mount Desert Island

Asticou Inn

Prouts Neck

Black Point Inn

York Harbor

York Harbor Inn

Maryland

Baltimore

Admiral Fell

Antrim 1844

Massachusetts

Boston

Fairmont Copley Plaza

Jacob Hill Inn

Jurys

Cape Cod & The Islands

Century House

Dan'l Webster Inn

Deerfield

Deerfield Inn

Lenox

Blantyre

Cranwell Resort

Wheatleigh

Rockport

Emerson Inn

Michigan

Detroit

Dearborn Inn

Grand Rapids

Amway Grand Plaza

Mackinac Island

Grand Hotel

Mississippi

Natchez

Monmouth Plantation

Missouri

Kansas City

Phillips

St. Louis

Hyatt

Roberts Mayfair

New Hampshire

Bretton Woods

Mount Washington

Dixville Notch

Balsams

Plainfield

Home Hill

New Jersey

Bernardsville

Bernards Inn

Cape May

Congress Hall

Inn of Cape May

Virginia

Spring Lake
Normandy Inn
New Mexico
Santa Fe
La Posada/Santa Fe
New York
Buffalo
Mansion on Delaware
Catskills
Mohonk Mountain Hse.
Cooperstown
Otesaga
Hudson Valley
Beekman Arms
Inn at Bullis Hall
Le Chambord
Old Drovers Inn
Long Island
American
New York City
Algonquin
Elysée
Inn at Irving Place
Maritime
New York Palace
St. Regis
Waldorf-Astoria
North Carolina
Asheville
Greystone Inn
Grove Park Inn Resort
Inn on Biltmore
Chapel Hill
Carolina Inn
Pinehurst
Pinehurst Resort
Ohio
Cincinnati
Cincinnatian
Cleveland
Hyatt/Arcade
Walden Country Inn
Oklahoma
Bartlesville
Inn at Price Tower
Oregon
Crater Lake National Park
Crater Lake Lodge
Hood River
Columbia Gorge
Mount Hood
Timberline Lodge
Portland
Benson
5th Ave. Suites
Governor
Heathman Hotel
Pennsylvania
Philadelphia
Park Hyatt Phila./Bellevue
Ritz-Carlton
Pittsburgh
Omni William Penn
Priory
Puerto Rico
San Juan
El Convento
Hyatt Dorado Beach
Rhode Island
Block Island
1661 Inn
Newport
Castle Hill Inn
Francis Malbone Hse.
Vanderbilt Hall
Providence
Providence
South Carolina
Charleston
John Rutledge House
Planters Inn
Wentworth Mansion
Pawleys Island
Litchfield Plantation
Tennessee
Memphis
Madison
Peabody
Nashville
Hermitage
Union Station
Texas
Austin
Driskill
Dallas/Ft. Worth
Adolphus
Ashton
Magnolia
Melrose
Galveston
Galvez-Historic Wyndham
Tremont House
Houston
Warwick

Marfa
Cibolo Creek Ranch
San Antonio
Fairmount
Menger
St. Anthony
Vermont
Lower Waterford
Rabbit Hill Inn
Stowe
Green Mountain Inn
Trapp Family Lodge
Stratton Mountain
Equinox
Vergennes
Basin Harbor Club
Woodstock
Quechee Inn
Virginia
Charlottesville
Boar's Head Inn
Keswick Hall
200 South St. Inn
DC Metro Area
Goodstone Inn
Orange
Willow Grove Inn
Richmond
Jefferson
Williamsburg
Williamsburg Colonial
Williamsburg Inn
Washington
Seattle
Alexis
Inn at Langley
Wisconsin
Milwaukee
Pfister Hotel
Wyoming
Jackson
Jenny Lake Lodge
Wort Hotel
Yellowstone Nat'l Park
Lake Yellowstone

Island Settings

Alaska
Aleutian Islands
Grand Aleutian
California
San Diego
del Coronado
Loews Coronado Bay
Marriott Coronado Is.
Florida
Amelia Island
Amelia Is. Plantation
Ritz-Carlton
Ft. Myers
Casa Ybel Resort
Keys
Cheeca Lodge
Hawk's Cay Resort
Hilton Key West
Hyatt Key West
Little Palm Island
Marquesa
Ocean Reef Club
Pier House Resort
Sheraton Suites Key West
Sunset Key Cottages
Miami
Fisher Island
Grove Isle Club
Ritz-Carlton Key Biscayne
Naples
Marco Beach Resort
Marco Island Marriott
Palm Beach
Brazilian Court
Sarasota
Colony Beach
Vero Beach
Disney Vero Beach
Georgia
Georgia Coast
Cloister
Jekyll Island Club
Lodge at Sea Island
Lodge on Little St. Simons
Hawaii
Big Island
Fairmont Orchid
Four Seasons Hualalai
Hapuna Beach Prince
Hilton Waikoloa Vlg.
Kona Village Resort
Mauna Kea Beach
Mauna Lani Bay
Kauai
Grand Hyatt Kauai
Hanalei Bay Resort
Marriott Kauai Resort
Princeville Resort
Lanai
Manele Bay Hotel

Maui
Fairmont Kea Lani
Grand Wailea Resort
Hana-Maui
Hyatt
Kapalua Bay Hotel
Kapalua Villas
Ritz-Carlton Kapalua
Sheraton Maui
Westin Maui
Molokai
Molokai Ranch
Oahu
Halekulani
Hawaii Prince Waikiki
JW Marriott Ihilani
Kahala Mandarin Oriental
Royal Hawaiian
Sheraton Moana Surfrider
W Honolulu - Diamond Head

Maine
Mount Desert Island
Asticou Inn

Massachusetts
Cape Cod & The Islands
Century House
Charlotte Inn
Harbor View
Wauwinet

Michigan
Mackinac Island
Grand Hotel

New Hampshire
Newcastle
Wentworth by the Sea

New York
Long Island
American
Gurney's Inn

North Carolina
Outer Banks
Sanderling

Puerto Rico
Fajardo
Las Casitas Village
Las Croabas
Wyndham El Conquistador
Rincon
Horned Dorset
San Juan
El Convento
Hyatt Dorado Beach
Ritz-Carlton
Westin Rio Mar
Vieques
Martineau Bay Resort

Rhode Island
Block Island
1661 Inn

South Carolina
Charleston
Wild Dunes Resort
Hilton Head
Disney Hilton Head Is.
Hilton Head Health Inst.
Sea Pines Resort
Kiawah Island
Kiawah Island Resorts

Texas
Galveston
Tremont House

U.S. Virgin Islands
St. Croix
Buccaneer
Carambola Beach
St. John
Caneel Bay
Westin
St. Thomas
Marriott Frenchman Reef
Ritz-Carlton

Washington
Seattle
Inn at Langley

Mountain Settings/ Views

Alaska
Girdwood
Alyeska Prince
Wrangell-St. Elias Nat'l Park
Copper River Princess

Arizona
Phoenix/Scottsdale
Boulders
Hyatt/Gainey Ranch
JW Marriott Desert Ridge
Pointe Hilton Squaw Peak
Ritz-Carlton
Sedona
Enchantment Resort
L'Auberge de Sedona

Tucson
Canyon Ranch
Hacienda del Sol
Loews Ventana Canyon

California
Carmel Area
Bernardus Lodge
Quail Lodge
Lake Tahoe Area
Nakoma Resort
Palm Springs Area
Lodge/Rancho Mirage
Smoke Tree Ranch
Santa Barbara
San Ysidro Ranch
South Bay
Ritz-Carlton Half Moon Bay
Yosemite
Château du Sureau

Colorado
Aspen
Little Nell
St. Regis
Beaver Creek
Beaver Creek Lodge
Charter/Beaver Creek
Park Hyatt
Colorado Springs
Cliff House/Pikes Peak
Denver
C Lazy U Ranch
Keystone
Keystone Resort
Montrose
Elk Mountain Resort
Snowmass
Stonebridge Inn
Steamboat Springs
Steamboat Grand
Telluride
Inn at Lost Creek
Telluride

Massachusetts
Lenox
Cranwell Resort

Missouri
Branson
Chateau on the Lake

Montana
Big Sky
Big Sky Resort
Darby
Triple Creek Ranch
Whitefish
Grouse Mtn. Lodge

New Hampshire
Dixville Notch
Balsams

New Mexico
Taos
El Monte Sagrado

New York
Adirondacks
Elk Lake Lodge
Catskills
Mohonk Mountain Hse.

North Carolina
Asheville
Swag

Oregon
Crater Lake National Park
Crater Lake Lodge

Pennsylvania
Farmington
Nemacolin Woodlands
Poconos
Skytop Lodge

Tennessee
Gatlinburg
Lodge at Buckberry Creek
Walland
Blackberry Farm

Utah
Park City
Deer Valley Lodging
Park City
Stein Eriksen Lodge
Salt Lake City
Grand America
Little America
Lodge at Snowbird
Snowbird
Sundance

Vermont
Barnard
Twin Farms
Essex
Inn at Essex
Lower Waterford
Rabbit Hill Inn

Stowe
Stoweflake Mtn. Resort
Topnotch at Stowe
Virginia
White Post
L'Auberge Provençale
West Virginia
White Sulphur Springs
Greenbrier
Wyoming
Jackson
Four Seasons Jackson Hole
Jackson Lake Lodge
Spring Creek Ranch

No TVs/Phones
(In-room)
California
Carmel Area
Seven Gables Inn
Inverness
Manka Inverness Lodge
Solvang
Alisal Guest Ranch
Sonoma
St. Orres
Whale Watch Inn
Colorado
Clark
Home Ranch
Denver
C Lazy U Ranch
Florida
Keys
Little Palm Island
Georgia
Georgia Coast
Lodge on Little St. Simons
Hawaii
Big Island
Kona Village Resort
Illinois
Gilman
Heartland Spa
Maryland
Baltimore
Antrim 1844
New York
Adirondacks
Point
Catskills
New Age Health Spa
Hudson Valley
Old Drovers Inn
Ohio
Grand Rapids
Kerr House
Oregon
Crater Lake National Park
Crater Lake Lodge
Pennsylvania
Poconos
Deerfield Spa
Rhode Island
Westerly
Weekapaug Inn
Texas
Marfa
Cibolo Creek Ranch
U.S. Virgin Islands
St. John
Caneel Bay
Vermont
Lower Waterford
Rabbit Hill Inn
Virginia
Orange
Willow Grove Inn
Paris
Ashby Inn
White Post
L'Auberge Provençale

Offbeat/Funky
Arkansas
Little Rock
Peabody Little Rock
California
Los Angeles
Chateau Marmont
Farmer's Daughter
Maison 140
Mondrian
Napa
Carneros Inn
Palm Springs Area
Viceroy Palm Springs
San Diego
Solamar
San Francisco Bay Area
Casa Madrona
Monaco

Palomar
Rex
Serrano Hotel
San Jose
De Anza
Sonoma
St. Orres
South Bay
Stanford Park
Colorado
Aspen
Sky
Denver
Monaco
Teatro
Connecticut
Greenwich
Homestead Inn
District of Columbia
Washington, DC
George
Helix
Madera
Monaco
Rouge
Sofitel Lafayette Square
Florida
Ft. Lauderdale
Seminole Hard Rock
Miami
Delano
Hotel, The
Mayfair
Hawaii
Big Island
Kona Village Resort
Maui
Hana-Maui
Molokai
Molokai Ranch
Illinois
Chicago
House of Blues
Monaco
W Lakeshore
Louisiana
New Orleans
International House
Le Pavillon
Monaco
Massachusetts
Boston
Hotel @ MIT
Marlowe
Nine Zero
Minnesota
Minneapolis/St. Paul
Graves 601
Missouri
St. Louis
Hyatt
Nevada
Las Vegas
Hard Rock
Rio All-Suite Hotel & Casino
New York
New York City
Hudson
Library
Maritime
Mercer
Paramount
Royalton
Oregon
Portland
Lucia, Hotel
Puerto Rico
San Juan
Caribe Hilton
Tennessee
Nashville
Union Station
Texas
Austin
Driskill
Dallas/Ft. Worth
Magnolia
Houston
Derek
San Antonio
Menger
Vermont
Stowe
Trapp Family Lodge
Sugarbush
Pitcher Inn
Washington
Seattle
Monaco
Wisconsin
Milwaukee
Metro

Power Scenes

Arkansas
Little Rock
Capital Hotel

California
Carmel Area
Casa Palmero
Los Angeles
Bel-Air, Hotel
Beverly Hills
Chateau Marmont
Four Seasons Bev. Hills
Maison 140
Mondrian
Park Hyatt
Peninsula Beverly Hills
Raffles L'Ermitage
Regent Beverly Wilshire
San Diego
W San Diego
San Francisco Bay Area
Clift
Four Seasons San Fran.
Mandarin Oriental
Pan Pacific SF
Ritz-Carlton
San Jose
Fairmont San Jose

Colorado
Aspen
Jerome
Little Nell
Lodge & Spa/Cordillera
St. Regis
Denver
Brown Palace
Teatro
Westin Tabor Ctr.

Delaware
Wilmington
du Pont

District of Columbia
Washington, DC
Four Seasons
Hay-Adams
Jefferson
Madison
Renaissance Mayflower
Ritz-Carlton
Ritz-Carlton, Georgetown
Willard InterContinental

Florida
Miami
Circa 39
Victor
Naples
Ritz-Carlton Naples

Georgia
Atlanta
Four Seasons
Ritz-Carlton Buckhead
Georgia Coast
Cloister

Hawaii
Oahu
Halekulani
Hilton Hawaiian Vlg.
JW Marriott Ihilani
Kahala Mandarin Oriental
W Honolulu - Diamond Head

Illinois
Chicago
Four Seasons
Park Hyatt
Peninsula
Ritz-Carlton

Louisiana
New Orleans
Windsor Court
W New Orleans

Massachusetts
Boston
Boston Harbor
XV Beacon
Four Seasons
Langham Hotel
Ritz-Carlton, Boston
Ritz-Carlton Boston Common
Cape Cod & The Islands
Wauwinet

Michigan
Detroit
Townsend

Minnesota
Minneapolis/St. Paul
Graves 601

Nevada
Las Vegas
Bellagio Hotel
Palms Casino Hotel

New York
Adirondacks
Point
Long Island
Garden City

New York City
Carlyle
Essex House
Four Seasons
Le Parker Méridien
Mandarin Oriental
Maritime
New York Palace
Peninsula
Ritz-Carlton, Battery Pk.
Royalton
Sherry-Netherland
Trump International
Waldorf-Astoria

Oregon
Portland
Benson
Heathman Hotel

Pennsylvania
Philadelphia
Park Hyatt Phila./Bellevue
Rittenhouse
Ritz-Carlton

Texas
Austin
Driskill
Dallas/Ft. Worth
Adolphus
Mansion on Turtle Creek
Houston
Derek
Four Seasons
Houstonian

Virginia
DC Metro Area
Ritz-Carlton Pentagon City
Richmond
Jefferson

Private Balcony

(In all rooms)

Arizona
Phoenix/Scottsdale
Boulders
CopperWynd
Fairmont Scottsdale
Four Seasons Scottsdale
Hermosa Inn
Hyatt/Gainey Ranch
JW Marriott Camelback
JW Marriott Desert Ridge
Phoenician
Pointe Hilton Squaw Peak
Pointe South Mountain
Sanctuary/Camelback Mtn.
Sheraton Wild Horse
Wigwam Resort
Sedona
Enchantment Resort
Hilton Sedona Resort
L'Auberge de Sedona
Tucson
Hilton El Conquistador
Lodge/Ventana Canyon
Loews Ventana Canyon
Westin La Paloma
Westward Look Resort

California
Carmel Area
Bernardus Lodge
Carmel Valley Ranch
Highlands Inn
Inn at Depot Hill
Lodge/Pebble Beach
Pacific
Post Ranch Inn
Ventana Inn
Dana Point
Ritz-Carlton Laguna Niguel
St. Regis Monarch Beach
Huntington Beach
Hyatt Huntington Beach
Laguna Beach
Montage Resort
Surf & Sand Resort
Lake Tahoe Area
Nakoma Resort
Los Angeles
Century Plaza
Four Seasons Bev. Hills
Loews Beverly Hills
Loews Santa Monica
Millennium Biltmore
Park Hyatt
Raffles L'Ermitage
Ritz-Carlton Marina del Rey
Wyndham Bel Age
Napa
Auberge du Soleil
La Résidence
Meadowood
Milliken Creek Inn

Napa Valley Lodge
Silverado
Vintage Inn
Newport Beach
Four Seasons
Palm Springs Area
Ballantines
Hyatt Grand Champions
Marriott Desert Springs
Marriott Rancho Las Palmas
Renaissance Esmeralda
Westin Mission Hills
San Diego
Cal-a-Vie
Golden Door
Hilton La Jolla Torrey Pines
La Casa del Zorro
L'Auberge Del Mar
Loews Coronado Bay
Rancho Valencia
Westgate
San Francisco Bay Area
Vintners Inn
Santa Barbara
Bacara Resort
Sonoma
Bodega Bay Lodge
Yosemite
Château du Sureau
Colorado
Beaver Creek
Beaver Creek Lodge
Snowmass
Snowmass Club
Telluride
Ice House Lodge
Telluride
Florida
Amelia Island
Amelia Is. Plantation
Ritz-Carlton
Destin
Hilton Sandestin Beach
Hutchinson Island
Hutchinson Is. Marriott
Jacksonville
Lodge & Club
Ponte Vedra Inn
Keys
Gardens
Hyatt Key West
Little Palm Island
Sunset Key Cottages
Miami
Fairmont Turnberry Isle
Grove Isle Club
Mandarin Oriental
Mayfair
Pritikin Longevity Center & Spa
Ritz-Carlton Coconut Grove
Sonesta Key Biscayne
Wyndham Grand Bay
Naples
Hyatt Coconut Point
La Playa Beach/Resort
Marco Beach Resort
Marco Island Marriott
Registry Resort
Ritz-Carlton Golf
Ritz-Carlton Naples
Orlando
Disney's Animal Kingdom
Disney Beach Club
Disney's BoardWalk
Disney Grand Floridian
Disney Wilderness
Disney Yacht Club
Marriott Orlando
Ritz-Carlton Orlando
Villas of Grand Cypress
Walt Disney Swan
Palm Beach
Four Seasons
PGA National Resort
Ritz-Carlton Palm Beach
Santa Rosa Beach
Water Color Inn
Sarasota
Resort at Longboat Key
Ritz-Carlton
Tampa/St. Petersburg
Clearwater Beach Marriott
Saddlebrook Resort
Georgia
Atlanta
Barnsley Gardens
W Atlanta
Lake Oconee
Ritz-Carlton Reynolds
Hawaii
Big Island
Fairmont Orchid

Four Seasons Hualalai
Hapuna Beach Prince
Hilton Waikoloa Vlg.
Kona Village Resort
Mauna Kea Beach
Mauna Lani Bay
Waikoloa Beach Marriott
Kauai
Grand Hyatt Kauai
Hanalei Bay Resort
Lanai
Lodge at Koele
Manele Bay Hotel
Maui
Fairmont Kea Lani
Four Seasons/Wailea
Grand Wailea Resort
Kapalua Bay Hotel
Kapalua Villas
Ritz-Carlton Kapalua
Sheraton Maui
Westin Maui
Oahu
Halekulani
Hilton Hawaiian Vlg.
Hyatt Regency Waikiki
JW Marriott Ihilani
W Honolulu - Diamond Head

Idaho
Ketchum
Knob Hill Inn

Maine
Bar Harbor
Bar Harbor Inn
Cape Elizabeth
Inn by the Sea
Rockport
Samoset Resort

Maryland
Cambridge
Hyatt Chesapeake Bay

Massachusetts
Boston
Millennium Bostonian
Cape Cod & The Islands
Ocean Edge Resort
Wequassett Inn

Michigan
Traverse City
Great Wolf Lodge

Missouri
Kansas City
Fairmont Kansas City

Nevada
Las Vegas
Hard Rock
JW Marriott Las Vegas

New Mexico
Albuquerque
Hyatt Tamaya
Santa Fe
Houses of the Moon
Taos
El Monte Sagrado

North Carolina
Chapel Hill
Siena
Outer Banks
Sanderling

Oregon
Gleneden Beach
Salishan Lodge
Gold Beach
Tu Tu' Tun Lodge
Mount Bachelor
Sunriver Resort

Puerto Rico
Fajardo
Las Casitas Village
Rincon
Horned Dorset
San Juan
Caribe Hilton
Hyatt Dorado Beach
InterContinental
Westin Rio Mar
Vieques
Martineau Bay Resort

South Carolina
Hilton Head
Hilton Head Marriott Beach
Sea Pines Resort
Westin
Kiawah Island
Kiawah Island Resorts

Tennessee
Nashville
Sheraton Music City

Texas
Dallas/Ft. Worth
Crescent Court

Four Seasons/Las Colinas
Mansion on Turtle Creek
Westin Galleria
Westin Stonebriar

U.S. Virgin Islands

St. Croix
Buccaneer
Carambola Beach

St. John
Caneel Bay
Westin

Utah

Moab
Sorrel River Ranch

Salt Lake City
Grand America
Lodge at Snowbird

St. George
Coyote Inn/Spa

Virginia

Williamsburg
Kingsmill Resort

Washington

Seattle
Inn at Langley
Willows Lodge

Wisconsin

Chetek
Canoe Bay

Kohler
American Club

Wyoming

Jackson
Amangani
Four Seasons Jackson Hole
Jenny Lake Lodge
Spring Creek Ranch

Remote

Alabama

Birmingham
Renaissance Ross Bridge Golf

Alaska

Aleutian Islands
Grand Aleutian

Anchorage
Millennium Anchorage

Denali
Mt. McKinley Princess

Glacier Bay
Glacier Bay Lodge

Wrangell-St. Elias Nat'l Park
Copper River Princess

Arizona

Phoenix/Scottsdale
JW Marriott Camelback
JW Marriott Desert Ridge

Sedona
Los Abrigados

California

Carmel Area
Highlands Inn
L'Auberge Carmel

Lake Tahoe Area
Resort at Squaw Creek

Napa
Auberge du Soleil
Inn at Southbridge
Milliken Creek Inn

Palm Springs Area
La Quinta Resort
Marriott Rancho Las Palmas
Westin Mission Hills

San Diego
Cal-a-Vie

San Jose
Lodge at Cordevalle

Sonoma
St. Orres

Yosemite
Ahwahnee
Château du Sureau
Tenaya Lodge

Colorado

Clark
Home Ranch

Denver
C Lazy U Ranch

Telluride
Inn at Lost Creek
Telluride

Florida

Orlando
Ritz-Carlton Orlando

Tampa/St. Petersburg
Clearwater Beach Marriott

Georgia

Braselton
Château Élan

Idaho

Sun Valley
Sun Valley Lodge

Montana
Darby
Triple Creek Ranch
Missoula
Resort at Paws Up
Oregon
Black Butte
Black Butte Ranch
Gleneden Beach
Salishan Lodge
Pennsylvania
Farmington
Nemacolin Woodlands
South Carolina
Hilton Head
Inn at Palmetto Bluff
Texas
Houston
Omni Houston
Marfa
Cibolo Creek Ranch
San Antonio
Hyatt Hill Country
Utah
St. George
Coyote Inn/Spa
Vermont
Lower Waterford
Rabbit Hill Inn
Sugarbush
Pitcher Inn
Vergennes
Basin Harbor Club
Woodstock
Quechee Inn
Wisconsin
Kohler
American Club
Wyoming
Jackson
Amangani
Jenny Lake Lodge
Spring Creek Ranch
Yellowstone Nat'l Park
Old Faithful Snow Lodge

Romantic

Arizona
Phoenix/Scottsdale
Royal Palms
Sanctuary/Camelback Mtn.
Sedona
L'Auberge de Sedona
California
Carmel Area
Bernardus Lodge
Carmel Valley Ranch
Highlands Inn
Inn at Spanish Bay
La Playa
L'Auberge Carmel
Quail Lodge
Seven Gables Inn
Tickle Pink Inn
Ventana Inn
Los Angeles
Bel-Air, Hotel
Beverly Hills
Shutters on the Beach
Napa
Auberge du Soleil
Meadowood
Milliken Creek Inn
Silverado
Villagio Inn
San Diego
Inn at Rancho Santa Fe
La Costa
L'Auberge Del Mar
La Valencia
Rancho Valencia
San Francisco Bay Area
Casa Madrona
Claremont Resort
Inn Above Tide
Vintners Inn
Westin St. Francis
White Swan Inn
Santa Barbara
Andalucia
El Encanto
Four Seasons Santa Barbara
San Ysidro Ranch
Sonoma
Bodega Bay Lodge
Healdsburg
Kenwood Inn
Whale Watch Inn
Yosemite
Château du Sureau
Colorado
Aspen
Little Nell
Lodge & Spa/Cordillera

Denver
Boulderado
Oxford
Vail
Sonnenalp
Connecticut
Washington
Mayflower Inn
Westport
Inn at National Hall
Florida
Ft. Lauderdale
Pillars/New River Sound
Keys
Gardens
Little Palm Island
Marquesa
Miami
Grove Isle Club
Mayfair
St. Augustine
Casa Monica
Georgia
Lake Oconee
Ritz-Carlton Reynolds
Savannah
Ballastone Inn
Hawaii
Big Island
Fairmont Orchid
Four Seasons Hualalai
Kona Village Resort
Kauai
Princeville Resort
Lanai
Lodge at Koele
Maui
Four Seasons/Wailea
Hana-Maui
Oahu
Royal Hawaiian
Sheraton Moana Surfrider
Idaho
Ketchum
Knob Hill Inn
Illinois
Chicago
Deer Path Inn
Drake

Louisiana
New Orleans
Maison de Ville
Soniat House
Maine
Kennebunkport
White Barn Inn
Maryland
St. Michaels
Inn at Perry Cabin
Massachusetts
Boston
Marlowe
Cape Cod & The Islands
Charlotte Inn
Lenox
Wheatleigh
Mississippi
Natchez
Monmouth Plantation
New Jersey
Cape May
Inn of Cape May
New Mexico
Santa Fe
Inn of the Five Graces
New York
Adirondacks
Point
New York City
Algonquin
Carlyle
Inn at Irving Place
Lowell
Westchester
Castle on the Hudson
North Carolina
Asheville
Grove Park Inn Resort
Outer Banks
Sanderling
Pennsylvania
Bradford
Glendorn
Bucks County
EverMay/Delaware
Puerto Rico
Rincon
Horned Dorset

Tennessee
Walland
Blackberry Farm
Texas
Galveston
Galvez-Historic Wyndham
Houston
Lancaster
San Antonio
La Mansión del Rio
U.S. Virgin Islands
St. Croix
Buccaneer
St. John
Caneel Bay
Utah
Park City
Goldener Hirsch Inn
Vermont
Barnard
Twin Farms
Mt. Snow
Inn at Sawmill Farm
Sugarbush
Pitcher Inn
Virginia
Charlottesville
Boar's Head Inn
DC Metro Area
Morrison House
Washington
Inn at Little Washington
White Post
L'Auberge Provençale
Washington
Seattle
Inn at Langley
Sorrento
Wisconsin
Chetek
Canoe Bay

Sailing

Alabama
Point Clear
Marriott Grand
California
Carmel Area
Bernardus Lodge
Dana Point
Marriott Laguna Cliffs
Ritz-Carlton Laguna Niguel
Inverness
Manka Inverness Lodge
Laguna Beach
Montage Resort
Los Angeles
Le Merigot Beach
Ritz-Carlton Marina del Rey
San Diego
del Coronado
Hilton La Jolla Torrey Pines
Loews Coronado Bay
Manchester Gr. Hyatt
Marriott San Diego
San Francisco Bay Area
Argonaut
Inn Above Tide
Santa Barbara
Four Seasons Santa Barbara
Montecito Inn
San Ysidro Ranch
Solvang
Alisal Guest Ranch
South Bay
Ritz-Carlton Half Moon Bay
Colorado
Steamboat Springs
Steamboat Grand
Connecticut
Mystic
Inn at Mystic
New Preston
Boulders Inn
Florida
Amelia Island
Ritz-Carlton
Destin
Hilton Sandestin Beach
Ft. Lauderdale
Atlantic
Boca Raton Resort
Marriott Harbor Beach
Pillars/New River Sound
Ft. Myers
Sanibel Harbour Resort
Hutchinson Island
Hutchinson Is. Marriott
Jacksonville
Ponte Vedra Inn
Keys
Cheeca Lodge
Hawk's Cay Resort

Hilton Key West
Hyatt Key West
Little Palm Island
Ocean Reef Club
Sunset Key Cottages
Miami
Fairmont Turnberry Isle
Fisher Island
Grove Isle Club
Mayfair
Ritz-Carlton Key Biscayne
Ritz-Carlton South Beach
Sonesta Key Biscayne
Naples
Hyatt Coconut Point
La Playa Beach/Resort
Marco Beach Resort
Marco Island Marriott
Registry Resort
Ritz-Carlton Naples
Orlando
Disney Grand Floridian
Disney Polynesian
Hyatt Grand Cypress
Villas of Grand Cypress
Walt Disney Swan
Westin Grand Bohemian
Palm Beach
Brazilian Court
Four Seasons
Ritz-Carlton Palm Beach
Sandestin
Sandestin
Santa Rosa Beach
Water Color Inn
Sarasota
Captiva Beach Resort
Colony Beach
Resort at Longboat Key
Tampa/St. Petersburg
Clearwater Beach Marriott
Don CeSar Beach
Renaissance Vinoy
Vero Beach
Disney Vero Beach

Georgia

Georgia Coast
Cloister
Jekyll Island Club
King & Prince Resort
Lodge at Sea Island
Lodge on Little St. Simons
Lake Oconee
Ritz-Carlton Reynolds

Hawaii

Big Island
Four Seasons Hualalai
Hilton Waikoloa Vlg.
Kona Village Resort
Mauna Kea Beach
Waikoloa Beach Marriott
Kauai
Marriott Kauai Resort
Maui
Fairmont Kea Lani
Four Seasons/Wailea
Grand Wailea Resort
Hyatt
Kapalua Bay Hotel
Kapalua Villas
Sheraton Maui
Oahu
Hyatt Regency Waikiki
JW Marriott Ihilani
Royal Hawaiian
Sheraton Moana Surfrider

Idaho

Coeur d'Alene
Coeur d'Alene

Maine

Bar Harbor
Bar Harbor Inn
Cape Elizabeth
Inn by the Sea
Kennebunkport
Cliff House
Prouts Neck
Black Point Inn
Rockport
Samoset Resort
York Harbor
York Harbor Inn

Maryland

Baltimore
Loews Annapolis
Cambridge
Hyatt Chesapeake Bay
St. Michaels
Inn at Perry Cabin

Massachusetts
Cape Cod & The Islands
Century House
Charlotte Inn
Chatham Bars Inn
Wauwinet
Wequassett Inn
Lenox
Cranwell Resort
Missouri
Branson
Chateau on the Lake
Osage Beach
Tan Tar A Resort
Montana
Whitefish
Grouse Mtn. Lodge
Nevada
Incline Village
Hyatt Resort
Las Vegas
Hyatt Lake Resort
Ritz-Carlton, Lake Las Vegas
New York
Adirondacks
Point
Sagamore
Catskills
Mirbeau Inn
Long Island
Gurney's Inn
Oregon
Hood River
Columbia Gorge
Puerto Rico
Fajardo
Las Casitas Village
Rincon
Horned Dorset
San Juan
Hyatt Dorado Beach
InterContinental
Paradisus Puerto Rico
Ritz-Carlton
Vieques
Martineau Bay Resort
Rhode Island
Newport
Castle Hill Inn
South Carolina
Charleston
Charleston Place
Planters Inn
Wild Dunes Resort
Hilton Head
Hilton Head Health Inst.
Inn at Palmetto Bluff
Sea Pines Resort
Westin
Texas
Galveston
Galvez-Historic Wyndham
Tremont House
U.S. Virgin Islands
St. Croix
Buccaneer
St. John
Caneel Bay
Westin
St. Thomas
Marriott Frenchman Reef
Utah
Park City
Deer Valley Lodging
Goldener Hirsch Inn
Vermont
Vergennes
Basin Harbor Club
Virginia
Irvington
Tides Inn
Washington
Blaine
Semiahmoo Resort
Seattle
Edgewater
Woodmark/Lake Wash.

Scuba/Snorkeling

California
Carmel Area
Bernardus Lodge
Inn at Spanish Bay
Dana Point
Marriott Laguna Cliffs
Laguna Beach
Montage Resort
Los Angeles
Le Merigot Beach

San Diego
del Coronado
Hilton La Jolla Torrey Pines
La Valencia
Manchester Gr. Hyatt
Santa Barbara
Montecito Inn
San Ysidro Ranch
Florida
Ft. Lauderdale
Boca Raton Resort
Marriott Harbor Beach
Pillars/New River Sound
Hutchinson Island
Hutchinson Is. Marriott
Keys
Cheeca Lodge
Hawk's Cay Resort
Hilton Key West
Hyatt Key West
Little Palm Island
Ocean Reef Club
Sunset Key Cottages
Wyndham Casa Marina
Miami
Fairmont Turnberry Isle
Fisher Island
Grove Isle Club
Mayfair
Ritz-Carlton Key Biscayne
Ritz-Carlton South Beach
Naples
La Playa Beach/Resort
Marco Beach Resort
Marco Island Marriott
Orlando
Westin Grand Bohemian
Palm Beach
Brazilian Court
Breakers
Four Seasons
Ritz-Carlton Palm Beach
Santa Rosa Beach
Water Color Inn
Sarasota
Captiva Beach Resort
Colony Beach
Tampa/St. Petersburg
Clearwater Beach Marriott
Don CeSar Beach
Renaissance Vinoy
Vero Beach
Disney Vero Beach
Georgia
Georgia Coast
Cloister
Lodge at Sea Island
Hawaii
Big Island
Fairmont Orchid
Four Seasons Hualalai
Hapuna Beach Prince
Hilton Waikoloa Vlg.
Kona Village Resort
Mauna Kea Beach
Mauna Lani Bay
Waikoloa Beach Marriott
Kauai
Grand Hyatt Kauai
Hanalei Bay Resort
Marriott Kauai Resort
Princeville Resort
Lanai
Manele Bay Hotel
Maui
Fairmont Kea Lani
Four Seasons/Wailea
Grand Wailea Resort
Hyatt
Kapalua Bay Hotel
Kapalua Villas
Ritz-Carlton Kapalua
Sheraton Maui
Westin Maui
Molokai
Molokai Ranch
Oahu
Hilton Hawaiian Vlg.
Hyatt Regency Waikiki
JW Marriott Ihilani
Kahala Mandarin Oriental
Royal Hawaiian
Sheraton Moana Surfrider
W Honolulu - Diamond Head
Idaho
Coeur d'Alene
Coeur d'Alene
Maine
Cape Elizabeth
Inn by the Sea
York Harbor
York Harbor Inn

Massachusetts
Cape Cod & The Islands
Century House
Harbor View
Missouri
Branson
Chateau on the Lake
New York
Adirondacks
Sagamore
Long Island
Gurney's Inn
Puerto Rico
Fajardo
Las Casitas Village
Las Croabas
Wyndham El Conquistador
Rincon
Horned Dorset
San Juan
Hyatt Dorado Beach
InterContinental
Paradisus Puerto Rico
Ritz-Carlton
Westin Rio Mar
Vieques
Martineau Bay Resort
Rhode Island
Newport
Castle Hill Inn
South Carolina
Charleston
Charleston Place
U.S. Virgin Islands
St. Croix
Buccaneer
Carambola Beach
St. John
Westin
St. Thomas
Marriott Frenchman Reef
Ritz-Carlton
Utah
Park City
Goldener Hirsch Inn
Virginia
Washington
Inn at Little Washington
Williamsburg
Kingsmill Resort

Spa Facilities
Alabama
Birmingham
Renaissance Ross Bridge Golf
Wynfrey
Point Clear
Marriott Grand
Alaska
Anchorage
Captain Cook
Girdwood
Alyeska Prince
Arizona
Phoenix/Scottsdale
Arizona Biltmore
Boulders
Caleo Resort & Spa
CopperWynd
Fairmont Scottsdale
Four Seasons Scottsdale
Hyatt/Gainey Ranch
JW Marriott Camelback
JW Marriott Desert Ridge
Phoenician
Pointe Hilton Squaw Peak
Pointe Hilton Tapatio Cliffs
Pointe South Mountain
Ritz-Carlton
Royal Palms
Sanctuary/Camelback Mtn.
Sheraton Wild Horse
Wigwam Resort
Wyndham Buttes
Sedona
Enchantment Resort
Hilton Sedona Resort
Los Abrigados
Tucson
Canyon Ranch
Hilton El Conquistador
Lodge/Ventana Canyon
Loews Ventana Canyon
Miraval Spa
Starr Pass Resort
Westin La Paloma
Westward Look Resort
California
Carmel Area
Bernardus Lodge
Casa Palmero
Inn at Spanish Bay

La Playa
Lodge/Pebble Beach
Monterey Plaza
Post Ranch Inn
Quail Lodge
Stonepine
Ventana Inn
Dana Point
Marriott Laguna Cliffs
Ritz-Carlton Laguna Niguel
St. Regis Monarch Beach
Huntington Beach
Hyatt Huntington Beach
Laguna Beach
Montage Resort
Surf & Sand Resort
Lake Tahoe Area
Nakoma Resort
Resort at Squaw Creek
Los Angeles
Argyle
Beverly Hills
Casa Del Mar
Century Plaza
Fairmont Miramar
Four Seasons Bev. Hills
Le Méridien/Bev. Hills
Le Merigot Beach
Loews Beverly Hills
Loews Santa Monica
Millennium Biltmore
Park Hyatt
Peninsula Beverly Hills
Raffles L'Ermitage
Rancho Bernardo Inn
Regent Beverly Wilshire
Ritz-Carlton Huntington
Ritz-Carlton Marina del Rey
Shutters on the Beach
W Westwood
Wyndham Bel Age
Mendocino
Stanford Inn by the Sea
Napa
Auberge du Soleil
Calistoga Ranch
Carneros Inn
Inn at Southbridge
Meadowood
Milliken Creek Inn
Mount View
Napa River Inn
Silverado
Villagio Inn
Vintage Inn
Newport Beach
Balboa Bay Club
Four Seasons
Palm Springs Area
Hyatt Grand Champions
La Quinta Resort
Le Parker Méridien
Lodge/Rancho Mirage
Marriott Desert Springs
Marriott Rancho Las Palmas
Morongo Casino
Renaissance Esmeralda
Two Bunch Palms
Viceroy Palm Springs
Westin Mission Hills
Riverside
Mission Inn
San Diego
Barona Valley Ranch
Cal-a-Vie
del Coronado
Four Seasons Aviara
Golden Door
Hilton La Jolla Torrey Pines
Hyatt La Jolla
Inn at Rancho Santa Fe
La Casa del Zorro
La Costa
L'Auberge Del Mar
La Valencia
Lodge at Torrey Pines
Loews Coronado Bay
Manchester Gr. Hyatt
Marriott San Diego
Marriott Coronado Is.
Westgate
W San Diego
San Francisco Bay Area
Casa Madrona
Claremont Resort
Fairmont San Francisco
Four Seasons San Fran.
Huntington
Hyatt Vineyard Creek
Lafayette Park
Monaco
Omni

Palace
Ritz-Carlton
Vintners Inn
Westin St. Francis
W San Francisco
San Jose
Fairmont San Jose
Lodge at Cordevalle
San Luis Obispo
Apple Farm
Santa Barbara
Bacara Resort
Four Seasons Santa Barbara
San Ysidro Ranch
Solvang
Fess Parker's
Sonoma
Bodega Bay Lodge
Fairmont Sonoma Mission
Healdsburg
Kenwood Inn
MacArthur Place
South Bay
Ritz-Carlton Half Moon Bay
Yosemite
Château du Sureau
Tenaya Lodge

Colorado

Aspen
Lodge & Spa/Cordillera
Ritz-Carlton, Bachelor Gulch
St. Regis
Beaver Creek
Beaver Creek Lodge
Charter/Beaver Creek
Park Hyatt
Colorado Springs
Broadmoor
Denver
Brown Palace
JW Marriott Denver
Monaco
Omni Interlocken
Oxford
Steamboat Springs
Steamboat Grand
Telluride
Inn at Lost Creek
Telluride
Wyndham Peaks
Vail
Sonnenalp
Vail Cascade Resort

Connecticut

Greenwich
Hyatt
Ledyard
Foxwoods Resort
Mystic
Mystic Marriott
New Preston
Boulders Inn
Norwich
Spa at Norwich Inn
Old Saybrook
Saybrook Point Inn
Uncasville
Mohegan Sun
Washington
Mayflower Inn

District of Columbia

Washington, DC
Fairmont Washington
Four Seasons
Mandarin Oriental
Ritz-Carlton, Georgetown

Florida

Amelia Island
Amelia Is. Plantation
Ritz-Carlton
Destin
Hilton Sandestin Beach
Ft. Lauderdale
Atlantic
Boca Raton Resort
Lago Mar Resort
Marriott Harbor Beach
Seminole Hard Rock
Westin Diplomat Resort
Ft. Myers
Sanibel Harbour Resort
Hutchinson Island
Hutchinson Is. Marriott
Jacksonville
Ponte Vedra Inn
Keys
Cheeca Lodge
Hawk's Cay Resort
Little Palm Island
Ocean Reef Club
Pier House Resort

Miami
Bentley Beach
Biltmore/Coral Gables
Conrad Miami
Delano
Doral Golf Resort
Eden Roc
Fairmont Turnberry Isle
Fisher Island
Four Seasons Miami
Grove Isle Club
JW Marriott Miami
Loews Miami Beach
Mandarin Oriental
Pritikin Longevity Center & Spa
Ritz-Carlton Coconut Grove
Ritz-Carlton Key Biscayne
Ritz-Carlton South Beach
Setai
Shore Club
Sonesta Key Biscayne
Victor
Naples
Hyatt Coconut Point
La Playa Beach/Resort
Marco Beach Resort
Marco Island Marriott
Registry Resort
Ritz-Carlton Naples
Orlando
Celebration
Disney Grand Floridian
Gaylord Palms
JW Marriott Orlando
Loews Portofino Bay
Marriott Orlando
Peabody Orlando
Ritz-Carlton Orlando
Walt Disney Dolphin
Wyndham Palace
Palm Beach
Brazilian Court
Breakers
Four Seasons
PGA National Resort
Ritz-Carlton Palm Beach
Sandestin
Sandestin
Santa Rosa Beach
Water Color Inn
Sarasota
Colony Beach
Ritz-Carlton
Tampa/St. Petersburg
Belleview Biltmore
Chalet Suzanne Inn
Don CeSar Beach
Renaissance Vinoy
Saddlebrook Resort

Georgia

Atlanta
Barnsley Gardens
InterCont. Buckhead
Braselton
Château Élan
Georgia Coast
Cloister
Lodge at Sea Island
Lake Oconee
Ritz-Carlton Reynolds
Savannah
Mansion on Forsyth Park
Westin Savannah Harbor

Hawaii

Big Island
Fairmont Orchid
Four Seasons Hualalai
Hapuna Beach Prince
Hilton Waikoloa Vlg.
Mauna Kea Beach
Mauna Lani Bay
Kauai
Grand Hyatt Kauai
Marriott Kauai Resort
Princeville Resort
Lanai
Manele Bay Hotel
Maui
Fairmont Kea Lani
Four Seasons/Wailea
Grand Wailea Resort
Hana-Maui
Hyatt
Ritz-Carlton Kapalua
Sheraton Maui
Westin Maui
Oahu
Halekulani
Hawaii Prince Waikiki
Hilton Hawaiian Vlg.
Hyatt Regency Waikiki

JW Marriott Ihilani
Kahala Mandarin Oriental
Marriott Waikiki Beach
Royal Hawaiian
Sheraton Moana Surfrider

Idaho

Coeur d'Alene
Coeur d'Alene

Sun Valley
Sun Valley Lodge

Illinois

Chicago
Fairmont Chicago
Four Seasons
Park Hyatt
Peninsula
Ritz-Carlton
W Lakeshore

Galena
Eagle Ridge Resort

Gilman
Heartland Spa

Kentucky

Louisville
Seelbach Hilton

Louisiana

New Orleans
Iberville Suites
International House
Maison Orleans
Monteleone
Ritz-Carlton
W French Quarter
Windsor Court

Maine

Kennebunkport
Cliff House
White Barn Inn

Maryland

Baltimore
Harbor Court
Marriott Waterfront

Cambridge
Hyatt Chesapeake Bay

Massachusetts

Boston
Boston Harbor
Charles
Four Seasons
Ritz-Carlton, Boston
Ritz-Carlton Boston Common
Royal Sonesta
Seaport Hotel

Cape Cod & The Islands
Chatham Bars Inn
Dan'l Webster Inn

Lenox
Blantyre
Canyon Ranch/Mass.
Cranwell Resort

Michigan

Bay Harbor
Inn at Bay Harbor

Mackinac Island
Grand Hotel

Traverse City
Great Wolf Lodge

Minnesota

Minneapolis/St. Paul
Grand Hotel
Graves 601

Mississippi

Biloxi
Beau Rivage

Missouri

Branson
Chateau on the Lake

Kansas City
Fairmont Kansas City

Osage Beach
Tan Tar A Resort

Montana

Big Sky
Big Sky Resort

Missoula
Resort at Paws Up

Pray
Chico Hot Springs

Nevada

Incline Village
Hyatt Resort

Las Vegas
Bellagio Hotel
Caesars Palace
Four Seasons Las Vegas
Green Valley Ranch
Hard Rock
Hyatt Lake Resort
JW Marriott Las Vegas
Mandalay Bay Hotel
MGM Grand Hotel
Mirage Hotel

Palms Casino Hotel
Paris Las Vegas
Rio All-Suite Hotel & Casino
Ritz-Carlton, Lake Las Vegas
Venetian Hotel
Wynn Las Vegas

New Hampshire

Bretton Woods
Mount Washington
Newcastle
Wentworth by the Sea

New Jersey

Atlantic City
Bally's
Borgata Hotel
Caesars Atlantic City
Sands
Seaview Marriott Resort
Tropicana
Trump Marina
Trump Plaza
Trump Taj Mahal
Cape May
Congress Hall
Short Hills
Hilton

New Mexico

Albuquerque
Hyatt Tamaya
Santa Fe
Bishop's Lodge
Eldorado
Houses of the Moon
La Posada/Santa Fe
Taos
El Monte Sagrado

New York

Adirondacks
Mirror Lake Inn
Sagamore
Whiteface Lodge
Catskills
Mirbeau Inn
Mohonk Mountain Hse.
New Age Health Spa
Long Island
Garden City
Gurney's Inn
New York City
Benjamin
Dream Hotel
Essex House
Four Seasons
Gansevoort
Le Parker Méridien
Mandarin Oriental
New York Palace
Peninsula
Ritz-Carlton, Battery Pk.
Ritz-Carlton, Central Park
St. Regis
Swissôtel/The Drake
Trump International
Waldorf-Astoria
W New York
W Times Square

North Carolina

Asheville
Greystone Inn
Grove Park Inn Resort
Charlotte
Ballantyne
Outer Banks
Sanderling
Pinehurst
Pinehurst Resort

Ohio

Cincinnati
Hilton Cincinnati Neth. Pl.
Cleveland
Hyatt/Arcade
Ritz-Carlton
Grand Rapids
Kerr House

Oklahoma

Oklahoma City
Waterford Marriott

Oregon

Gleneden Beach
Salishan Lodge
Hood River
Columbia Gorge
Mount Bachelor
Sunriver Resort
Portland
Avalon
Benson
5th Ave. Suites
Vintage Plaza

Pennsylvania

Bradford
Glendorn

Farmington
Nemacolin Woodlands
Hershey
Hershey
Philadelphia
Four Seasons Phila.
Loews Philadelphia
Park Hyatt Phila./Bellevue
Rittenhouse
Ritz-Carlton
Poconos
Deerfield Spa
Skytop Lodge

Puerto Rico

Fajardo
Las Casitas Village
Las Croabas
Wyndham El Conquistador
Rincon
Horned Dorset
San Juan
Caribe Hilton
Hyatt Dorado Beach
InterContinental
Paradisus Puerto Rico
Ritz-Carlton
Westin Rio Mar
Wyndham El San Juan
Vieques
Martineau Bay Resort

Rhode Island

Providence
Westin

South Carolina

Aiken
Willcox
Charleston
Charleston Place
Wentworth Mansion
Wild Dunes Resort
Woodlands Resort
Hilton Head
Hilton Head Health Inst.
Hilton Head Marriott Beach
Inn at Palmetto Bluff
Sea Pines Resort
Kiawah Island
Kiawah Island Resorts
Sanctuary/Kiawah Is.
Myrtle Beach
Breakers Resort
Myrtle Beach Marriott

Tennessee

Gatlinburg
Lodge at Buckberry Creek
Memphis
Peabody
Nashville
Gaylord Opryland
Hermitage
Renaissance Nashville
Sheraton Music City
Walland
Blackberry Farm

Texas

Austin
Barton Creek
Driskill
Four Seasons
Lake Austin Spa
Dallas/Ft. Worth
Crescent Court
Four Seasons/Las Colinas
Greenhouse
Westin Stonebriar
Wyndham Anatole
Zaza, Hotel
Houston
Four Seasons
Houstonian
Icon
St. Regis
Lajitas
Lajitas
San Antonio
Fairmount
Hyatt Hill Country
Menger
Watermark
Westin La Cantera
The Woodlands
Marriott Woodlands

U.S. Virgin Islands

St. Croix
Buccaneer
St. John
Caneel Bay
Westin

St. Thomas
Marriott Frenchman Reef
Ritz-Carlton
Utah
Moab
Sorrel River Ranch
Park City
Goldener Hirsch Inn
Park City
Stein Eriksen Lodge
Salt Lake City
Grand America
Snowbird
Sundance
St. George
Coyote Inn/Spa
Vermont
Barnard
Twin Farms
Lower Waterford
Rabbit Hill Inn
Stowe
Green Mountain Inn
Stoweflake Mtn. Resort
Topnotch at Stowe
Stratton Mountain
Equinox
Woodstock
Woodstock Inn
Virginia
Charlottesville
Boar's Head Inn
Keswick Hall
DC Metro Area
Ritz-Carlton Tysons Corner
Hot Springs
Homestead
Irvington
Tides Inn
Lansdowne
Lansdowne Resort
Williamsburg
Kingsmill Resort
Washington
Blaine
Semiahmoo Resort
Seattle
Alexis
Bellevue Club
Fairmont Olympic
Grand Hyatt
Inn at Langley
Salish Lodge
Sheraton
Willows Lodge
Woodmark/Lake Wash.
Stevenson
Skamania Lodge
West Virginia
White Sulphur Springs
Greenbrier
Wisconsin
Kohler
American Club
Wyoming
Jackson
Amangani
Four Seasons Jackson Hole
Lost Creek Ranch
Rusty Parrot Lodge
Snake River Lodge
Spring Creek Ranch

Spa Facilities: Diet/Nutrition

Alabama
Point Clear
Marriott Grand
Arizona
Phoenix/Scottsdale
Boulders
CopperWynd
Four Seasons Scottsdale
JW Marriott Camelback
Phoenician
Royal Palms
Sedona
Enchantment Resort
Los Abrigados
Tucson
Canyon Ranch
Hilton El Conquistador
Miraval Spa
California
Carmel Area
Casa Palmero
Quail Lodge
Dana Point
St. Regis Monarch Beach
Los Angeles
Le Merigot Beach
Loews Santa Monica

Napa
Silverado
Palm Springs Area
Hyatt Grand Champions
Marriott Desert Springs
Viceroy Palm Springs
San Diego
Cal-a-Vie
Golden Door
Hilton La Jolla Torrey Pines
La Costa
Loews Coronado Bay
Marriott Coronado Is.
San Francisco Bay Area
Claremont Resort
Omni
Santa Barbara
El Encanto
Four Seasons Santa Barbara
Sonoma
Fairmont Sonoma Mission

Colorado

Aspen
St. Regis
Beaver Creek
Park Hyatt
Colorado Springs
Broadmoor
Telluride
Wyndham Peaks
Vail
Sonnenalp

Connecticut

Norwich
Spa at Norwich Inn

District of Columbia

Washington, DC
Fairmont Washington

Florida

Destin
Hilton Sandestin Beach
Ft. Lauderdale
Marriott Harbor Beach
Seminole Hard Rock
Westin Diplomat Resort
Miami
Delano
Fairmont Turnberry Isle
Fisher Island
Pritikin Longevity Center & Spa
Ritz-Carlton Key Biscayne
Shore Club
Naples
Hyatt Coconut Point
Marco Island Marriott
Registry Resort
Orlando
Gaylord Palms
Ritz-Carlton Orlando
Palm Beach
Brazilian Court
Sarasota
Colony Beach
Tampa/St. Petersburg
Saddlebrook Resort

Georgia

Braselton
Château Élan
Georgia Coast
Cloister
Lodge at Sea Island
Lake Oconee
Ritz-Carlton Reynolds

Hawaii

Big Island
Fairmont Orchid
Four Seasons Hualalai
Hilton Waikoloa Vlg.
Mauna Lani Bay
Kauai
Grand Hyatt Kauai
Princeville Resort
Maui
Fairmont Kea Lani
Grand Wailea Resort
Kapalua Villas
Ritz-Carlton Kapalua
Westin Maui
Oahu
Hilton Hawaiian Vlg.
JW Marriott Ihilani
Royal Hawaiian

Illinois

Chicago
Peninsula
Ritz-Carlton
Gilman
Heartland Spa

Massachusetts

Boston
Boston Harbor

Lenox
Canyon Ranch/Mass.
Cranwell Resort

Minnesota
Minneapolis/St. Paul
Grand Hotel

Montana
Darby
Triple Creek Ranch

Nevada
Las Vegas
Green Valley Ranch
JW Marriott Las Vegas
MGM Grand Hotel
Ritz-Carlton, Lake Las Vegas
Venetian Hotel

New Jersey
Atlantic City
Seaview Marriott Resort
Short Hills
Hilton

New Mexico
Santa Fe
Bishop's Lodge

New York
Adirondacks
Mirror Lake Inn
Buffalo
Mansion on Delaware
Catskills
New Age Health Spa
Hudson Valley
Roselawn
Long Island
Gurney's Inn
New York City
Peninsula
Swissôtel/The Drake
W New York

North Carolina
Charlotte
Ballantyne

Ohio
Grand Rapids
Kerr House

Pennsylvania
Farmington
Nemacolin Woodlands
Poconos
Deerfield Spa

Puerto Rico
Fajardo
Las Casitas Village
Las Croabas
Wyndham El Conquistador

South Carolina
Hilton Head
Hilton Head Health Inst.
Kiawah Island
Sanctuary/Kiawah Is.

Tennessee
Nashville
Loews Vanderbilt

Texas
Austin
Barton Creek
Four Seasons
Dallas/Ft. Worth
Greenhouse
Wyndham Anatole
Houston
Houstonian

U.S. Virgin Islands
St. Thomas
Marriott Frenchman Reef

Utah
Park City
Stein Eriksen Lodge
St. George
Coyote Inn/Spa

Vermont
Stowe
Stoweflake Mtn. Resort
Topnotch at Stowe
Stratton Mountain
Equinox

Virginia
Charlottesville
Keswick Hall

Washington
Blaine
Semiahmoo Resort
Seattle
Bellevue Club

West Virginia
White Sulphur Springs
Greenbrier

Wisconsin
Kohler
American Club

Spa Facilities: Hydrotherapy

Alabama

Point Clear
Marriott Grand

Arizona

Phoenix/Scottsdale
Arizona Biltmore
Caleo Resort & Spa
Four Seasons Scottsdale
JW Marriott Desert Ridge
Royal Palms
Sanctuary/Camelback Mtn.
Sheraton Wild Horse

Sedona
Enchantment Resort
Hilton Sedona Resort

Tucson
Canyon Ranch
Hilton El Conquistador
Miraval Spa
Starr Pass Resort
Westin La Paloma

California

Carmel Area
Casa Palmero
Inn at Spanish Bay
Lodge/Pebble Beach
Monterey Plaza
Quail Lodge
Ventana Inn

Dana Point
St. Regis Monarch Beach

Huntington Beach
Hyatt Huntington Beach

Laguna Beach
Montage Resort

Lake Tahoe Area
Resort at Squaw Creek

Los Angeles
Beverly Hills
Loews Beverly Hills
Peninsula Beverly Hills
Ritz-Carlton Marina del Rey

Napa
Carneros Inn
Inn at Southbridge
Mount View
Silverado
Villagio Inn
Vintage Inn

Newport Beach
Balboa Bay Club

Palm Springs Area
Hyatt Grand Champions
La Quinta Resort
Le Parker Méridien
Marriott Desert Springs
Marriott Rancho Las Palmas
Morongo Casino
Renaissance Esmeralda
Two Bunch Palms
Viceroy Palm Springs
Westin Mission Hills

San Diego
Barona Valley Ranch
Cal-a-Vie
Four Seasons Aviara
Golden Door
Hilton La Jolla Torrey Pines
La Costa
L'Auberge Del Mar
Lodge at Torrey Pines
Marriott Coronado Is.

San Francisco Bay Area
Casa Madrona
Claremont Resort
Monaco

San Jose
Lodge at Cordevalle

Santa Barbara
Bacara Resort
Four Seasons Santa Barbara

Solvang
Fess Parker's

Sonoma
Fairmont Sonoma Mission
Kenwood Inn

South Bay
Ritz-Carlton Half Moon Bay

Colorado

Aspen
Ritz-Carlton, Bachelor Gulch
St. Regis

Beaver Creek
Charter/Beaver Creek
Park Hyatt

Colorado Springs
Broadmoor

Denver
Monaco

Steamboat Springs
Steamboat Grand
Telluride
Wyndham Peaks
Vail
Vail Cascade Resort

Connecticut

Greenwich
Hyatt
Ledyard
Foxwoods Resort
Mystic
Mystic Marriott
Norwich
Spa at Norwich Inn

District of Columbia

Washington, DC
Fairmont Washington
Mandarin Oriental

Florida

Amelia Island
Amelia Is. Plantation
Ft. Lauderdale
Boca Raton Resort
Marriott Harbor Beach
Seminole Hard Rock
Westin Diplomat Resort
Keys
Cheeca Lodge
Pier House Resort
Miami
Doral Golf Resort
Fairmont Turnberry Isle
Fisher Island
Four Seasons Miami
Mandarin Oriental
Ritz-Carlton Key Biscayne
Ritz-Carlton South Beach
Shore Club
Sonesta Key Biscayne
Victor
Naples
Hyatt Coconut Point
La Playa Beach/Resort
Marco Island Marriott
Ritz-Carlton Naples
Orlando
Gaylord Palms
Loews Portofino Bay
Marriott Orlando
Ritz-Carlton Orlando
Walt Disney Swan
Wyndham Palace
Sarasota
Colony Beach
Ritz-Carlton
Tampa/St. Petersburg
Belleview Biltmore
Renaissance Vinoy
Saddlebrook Resort

Georgia

Atlanta
Barnsley Gardens
Braselton
Château Élan
Georgia Coast
Cloister
Lake Oconee
Ritz-Carlton Reynolds
Savannah
Westin Savannah Harbor

Hawaii

Big Island
Hilton Waikoloa Vlg.
Waikoloa Beach Marriott
Maui
Fairmont Kea Lani
Four Seasons/Wailea
Grand Wailea Resort
Hana-Maui
Ritz-Carlton Kapalua
Sheraton Maui
Westin Maui
Oahu
Hilton Hawaiian Vlg.
Hyatt Regency Waikiki
JW Marriott Ihilani
Kahala Mandarin Oriental

Idaho

Coeur d'Alene
Coeur d'Alene
Sun Valley
Sun Valley Lodge

Illinois

Gilman
Heartland Spa

Louisiana

New Orleans
Iberville Suites
Maison Orleans
Monteleone
Ritz-Carlton

Maine
Kennebunkport
Cliff House
Rockport
Samoset Resort
Maryland
Cambridge
Hyatt Chesapeake Bay
Massachusetts
Boston
Millennium Bostonian
Ritz-Carlton, Boston
Seaport Hotel
Westin Copley Pl.
Lenox
Canyon Ranch/Mass.
Cranwell Resort
Minnesota
Minneapolis/St. Paul
Graves 601
Mississippi
Biloxi
Beau Rivage
Missouri
Osage Beach
Tan Tar A Resort
Montana
Big Sky
Big Sky Resort
Nevada
Incline Village
Hyatt Resort
Las Vegas
Bellagio Hotel
Caesars Palace
Green Valley Ranch
Hard Rock
JW Marriott Las Vegas
Mirage Hotel
Palms Casino Hotel
Paris Las Vegas
Rio All-Suite Hotel & Casino
Ritz-Carlton, Lake Las Vegas
New Jersey
Atlantic City
Bally's
Borgata Hotel
Seaview Marriott Resort
Trump Taj Mahal
Short Hills
Hilton
New Mexico
Santa Fe
Bishop's Lodge
Houses of the Moon
New York
Adirondacks
Mirror Lake Inn
Sagamore
Catskills
Mirbeau Inn
New Age Health Spa
Long Island
Gurney's Inn
New York City
Mandarin Oriental
Swissôtel/The Drake
Waldorf-Astoria
W New York
W Times Square
North Carolina
Asheville
Grove Park Inn Resort
Charlotte
Ballantyne
Outer Banks
Sanderling
Pinehurst
Pinehurst Resort
Ohio
Grand Rapids
Kerr House
Oregon
Mount Bachelor
Sunriver Resort
Portland
Vintage Plaza
Pennsylvania
Farmington
Nemacolin Woodlands
Hershey
Hershey
Poconos
Deerfield Spa
Puerto Rico
Fajardo
Las Casitas Village
Las Croabas
Wyndham El Conquistador
San Juan
Caribe Hilton
Hyatt Dorado Beach

Paradisus Puerto Rico
Westin Rio Mar
Wyndham El San Juan

Vieques

Martineau Bay Resort

South Carolina

Aiken

Willcox

Kiawah Island

Sanctuary/Kiawah Is.

Pawleys Island

Litchfield Plantation

Tennessee

Walland

Blackberry Farm

Texas

Austin

Barton Creek
Lake Austin Spa

Dallas/Ft. Worth

Crescent Court
Four Seasons/Las Colinas
Greenhouse

Houston

Four Seasons

Lajitas

Lajitas

San Antonio

Hyatt Hill Country
Watermark

Utah

Park City

Park City
Stein Eriksen Lodge

Salt Lake City

Lodge at Snowbird

St. George

Coyote Inn/Spa

Vermont

Barnard

Twin Farms

Stratton Mountain

Equinox

Virginia

Charlottesville

Boar's Head Inn

Hot Springs

Homestead

Irvington

Tides Inn

Washington

Blaine

Semiahmoo Resort

Seattle

Fairmont Olympic
Salish Lodge
Willows Lodge
Woodmark/Lake Wash.

West Virginia

White Sulphur Springs

Greenbrier

Wisconsin

Kohler

American Club

Wyoming

Jackson

Four Seasons Jackson Hole
Snake River Lodge

Spa Facilities: Meditation

Alabama

Point Clear

Marriott Grand

Arizona

Phoenix/Scottsdale

Boulders
CopperWynd
Fairmont Scottsdale
Four Seasons Scottsdale
JW Marriott Camelback
JW Marriott Desert Ridge
Phoenician
Royal Palms
Sanctuary/Camelback Mtn.
Sheraton Wild Horse

Sedona

Enchantment Resort

Tucson

Canyon Ranch
Loews Ventana Canyon
Miraval Spa

California

Carmel Area

Stonepine

Dana Point

St. Regis Monarch Beach

Los Angeles

Century Plaza
Le Merigot Beach
Loews Santa Monica
Ritz-Carlton Huntington

Napa
Meadowood
Palm Springs Area
Marriott Desert Springs
San Diego
Cal-a-Vie
Golden Door
Lodge at Torrey Pines
Loews Coronado Bay
San Francisco Bay Area
Claremont Resort
Fairmont San Francisco
San Jose
Lodge at Cordevalle
Santa Barbara
El Encanto
Sonoma
Fairmont Sonoma Mission

Colorado

Beaver Creek
Park Hyatt
Colorado Springs
Broadmoor
Denver
Teatro
Telluride
Wyndham Peaks
Vail
Sonnenalp

Connecticut

Norwich
Spa at Norwich Inn

Florida

Ft. Lauderdale
Boca Raton Resort
Marriott Harbor Beach
Westin Diplomat Resort
Keys
Little Palm Island
Miami
Delano
Doral Golf Resort
Fisher Island
Mandarin Oriental
Pritikin Longevity Center & Spa
Shore Club
Naples
Marco Island Marriott
Orlando
Ritz-Carlton Orlando
Tampa/St. Petersburg
Don CeSar Beach

Georgia

Georgia Coast
Cloister
Lodge at Sea Island
Lake Oconee
Ritz-Carlton Reynolds

Hawaii

Big Island
Fairmont Orchid
Four Seasons Hualalai
Hilton Waikoloa Vlg.
Mauna Kea Beach
Mauna Lani Bay
Waikoloa Beach Marriott
Maui
Grand Wailea Resort
Ritz-Carlton Kapalua
Oahu
JW Marriott Ihilani
Royal Hawaiian

Massachusetts

Lenox
Canyon Ranch/Mass.

Michigan

Mackinac Island
Grand Hotel

Nevada

Las Vegas
Caesars Palace
Green Valley Ranch
Mandalay Bay Hotel

New Jersey

Short Hills
Hilton

New Mexico

Santa Fe
Bishop's Lodge
La Posada/Santa Fe

New York

Catskills
Mohonk Mountain Hse.
New Age Health Spa
Long Island
Gurney's Inn
New York City
Peninsula

Pennsylvania

Farmington
Nemacolin Woodlands

Philadelphia
Rittenhouse
Ritz-Carlton

Puerto Rico
Fajardo
Las Casitas Village
Rincon
Horned Dorset
San Juan
Ritz-Carlton
Vieques
Martineau Bay Resort

South Carolina
Hilton Head
Hilton Head Health Inst.
Kiawah Island
Sanctuary/Kiawah Is.

Texas
Austin
Barton Creek
Lake Austin Spa
Dallas/Ft. Worth
Greenhouse
Zaza, Hotel
Houston
Houstonian
San Antonio
Menger
Watermark

U.S. Virgin Islands
St. John
Caneel Bay

Utah
Salt Lake City
Lodge at Snowbird
Snowbird
St. George
Coyote Inn/Spa

Vermont
Stowe
Stoweflake Mtn. Resort
Topnotch at Stowe
Stratton Mountain
Equinox

Washington
Blaine
Semiahmoo Resort

West Virginia
White Sulphur Springs
Greenbrier

Wisconsin
Kohler
American Club

Wyoming
Jackson
Amangani

Spa Facilities: Mineral Springs

California
Los Angeles
Casa Del Mar
Palm Springs Area
Two Bunch Palms
Sonoma
Fairmont Sonoma Mission

Colorado
Vail
Vail Cascade Resort

Florida
Miami
Pritikin Longevity Center & Spa
Naples
Marco Island Marriott
Ritz-Carlton Naples
Palm Beach
PGA National Resort

Nevada
Las Vegas
Hard Rock

New Mexico
Santa Fe
Houses of the Moon

New York
Long Island
Gurney's Inn
New York City
Swissôtel/The Drake

North Carolina
Asheville
Grove Park Inn Resort

Pennsylvania
Philadelphia
Rittenhouse

Puerto Rico
Fajardo
Las Casitas Village

South Carolina
Aiken
Willcox

Kiawah Island
Kiawah Island Resorts
Sanctuary/Kiawah Is.
Texas
Austin
Barton Creek
Vermont
Stowe
Stoweflake Mtn. Resort
Stratton Mountain
Equinox
Virginia
Hot Springs
Homestead
West Virginia
White Sulphur Springs
Greenbrier
Wisconsin
Kohler
American Club

Spa Facilities: Weight Loss

Arizona
Phoenix/Scottsdale
Boulders
CopperWynd
Four Seasons Scottsdale
JW Marriott Camelback
Sedona
Enchantment Resort
Tucson
Canyon Ranch
Miraval Spa
California
Dana Point
St. Regis Monarch Beach
Los Angeles
Loews Santa Monica
Palm Springs Area
Renaissance Esmeralda
San Diego
Golden Door
La Costa
L'Auberge Del Mar
Loews Coronado Bay
Marriott Coronado Is.
San Francisco Bay Area
Claremont Resort
Four Seasons San Fran.
Colorado
Aspen
Lodge & Spa/Cordillera
St. Regis
Colorado Springs
Broadmoor
Telluride
Wyndham Peaks
District of Columbia
Washington, DC
Fairmont Washington
Grand Hyatt
Florida
Ft. Lauderdale
Marriott Harbor Beach
Seminole Hard Rock
Miami
Doral Golf Resort
Fisher Island
Pritikin Longevity Center & Spa
Ritz-Carlton Key Biscayne
Naples
Hyatt Coconut Point
Marco Island Marriott
Tampa/St. Petersburg
Don CeSar Beach
Georgia
Georgia Coast
Lodge at Sea Island
Lake Oconee
Ritz-Carlton Reynolds
Hawaii
Big Island
Four Seasons Hualalai
Hilton Waikoloa Vlg.
Mauna Lani Bay
Maui
Grand Wailea Resort
Ritz-Carlton Kapalua
Oahu
JW Marriott Ihilani
Idaho
Sun Valley
Sun Valley Lodge
Massachusetts
Deerfield
Deerfield Inn
Lenox
Canyon Ranch/Mass.

Nevada
Las Vegas
Venetian Hotel
New Jersey
Short Hills
Hilton
New Mexico
Santa Fe
Bishop's Lodge
New York
Long Island
Gurney's Inn
New York City
Le Parker Méridien
North Carolina
Charlotte
Westin Charlotte
Ohio
Grand Rapids
Kerr House
Pennsylvania
Farmington
Nemacolin Woodlands
Philadelphia
Rittenhouse
Poconos
Deerfield Spa
Puerto Rico
Fajardo
Las Casitas Village
Las Croabas
Wyndham El Conquistador
San Juan
Ritz-Carlton
South Carolina
Hilton Head
Hilton Head Health Inst.
Kiawah Island
Sanctuary/Kiawah Is.
Texas
Austin
Four Seasons
Lake Austin Spa
Dallas/Ft. Worth
Greenhouse
Houston
Houstonian
Utah
Park City
Stein Eriksen Lodge
St. George
Coyote Inn/Spa
Vermont
Stowe
Stoweflake Mtn. Resort
Stratton Mountain
Equinox
Virginia
Charlottesville
Boar's Head Inn
Keswick Hall
Washington
Blaine
Semiahmoo Resort
West Virginia
White Sulphur Springs
Greenbrier
Wisconsin
Kohler
American Club

Spa Facilities: Women Only

(At certain times)

California
San Diego
Golden Door
Sonoma
Gaige House Inn
Colorado
Beaver Creek
Park Hyatt
Florida
Destin
Hilton Sandestin Beach
Ohio
Grand Rapids
Kerr House
South Carolina
Kiawah Island
Sanctuary/Kiawah Is.
Texas
Dallas/Ft. Worth
Greenhouse
Utah
Salt Lake City
Grand America
Vermont
Stowe
Stoweflake Mtn. Resort

Spa Facilities: Yoga

Alabama

Point Clear

Marriott Grand

Arizona

Phoenix/Scottsdale

Arizona Biltmore
Boulders
CopperWynd
Fairmont Scottsdale
Four Seasons Scottsdale
JW Marriott Camelback
JW Marriott Desert Ridge
Phoenician
Pointe Hilton Squaw Peak
Pointe South Mountain
Royal Palms
Sanctuary/Camelback Mtn.
Sheraton Wild Horse

Sedona

Enchantment Resort
L'Auberge de Sedona
Los Abrigados

Tucson

Canyon Ranch
Hilton El Conquistador
Lodge/Ventana Canyon
Loews Ventana Canyon
Miraval Spa
Westward Look Resort

California

Carmel Area

Casa Palmero
Post Ranch Inn
Quail Lodge
Stonepine
Ventana Inn

Dana Point

Ritz-Carlton Laguna Niguel
St. Regis Monarch Beach

Huntington Beach

Hyatt Huntington Beach

Laguna Beach

Montage Resort
Surf & Sand Resort

Lake Tahoe Area

Resort at Squaw Creek

Los Angeles

Bel-Air, Hotel
Le Merigot Beach
Loews Santa Monica
Peninsula Beverly Hills
Regent Beverly Wilshire
Ritz-Carlton Huntington
Ritz-Carlton Marina del Rey

Mendocino

Stanford Inn by the Sea

Napa

Auberge du Soleil
Meadowood
Villagio Inn
Vintage Inn

Newport Beach

Four Seasons

Palm Springs Area

Hyatt Grand Champions
La Quinta Resort
Marriott Desert Springs
Two Bunch Palms
Viceroy Palm Springs
Westin Mission Hills

San Diego

Cal-a-Vie
del Coronado
Four Seasons Aviara
Golden Door
Hilton La Jolla Torrey Pines
L'Auberge Del Mar
Lodge at Torrey Pines
Loews Coronado Bay
Rancho Valencia
Solamar
Westgate

San Francisco Bay Area

Claremont Resort
Four Seasons San Fran.
Huntington
Monaco
Vitale

San Jose

Lodge at Cordevalle

Santa Barbara

Bacara Resort
Four Seasons Santa Barbara
San Ysidro Ranch

Sonoma

Fairmont Sonoma Mission

South Bay

Ritz-Carlton Half Moon Bay

Colorado
Aspen
Lodge & Spa/Cordillera
Ritz-Carlton, Bachelor Gulch
St. Regis
Beaver Creek
Park Hyatt
Colorado Springs
Broadmoor
Denver
Oxford
Teatro
Keystone
Keystone Resort
Montrose
Elk Mountain Resort
Steamboat Springs
Steamboat Grand
Telluride
Inn at Lost Creek
Wyndham Peaks
Vail
Sonnenalp
Vail Cascade Resort
Connecticut
Norwich
Spa at Norwich Inn
Old Saybrook
Saybrook Point Inn
Washington
Mayflower Inn
District of Columbia
Washington, DC
Fairmont Washington
Four Seasons
Grand Hyatt
Madera
Mandarin Oriental
Florida
Amelia Island
Amelia Is. Plantation
Destin
Hilton Sandestin Beach
Ft. Lauderdale
Boca Raton Resort
Lago Mar Resort
Marriott Harbor Beach
Seminole Hard Rock
Westin Diplomat Resort
Ft. Myers
Sanibel Harbour Resort
Jacksonville
Ponte Vedra Inn
Keys
Cheeca Lodge
Little Palm Island
Miami
Biltmore/Coral Gables
Delano
Doral Golf Resort
Fairmont Turnberry Isle
Fisher Island
Four Seasons Miami
Mandarin Oriental
Pritikin Longevity Center & Spa
Raleigh
Ritz-Carlton Key Biscayne
Ritz-Carlton South Beach
Naples
Hyatt Coconut Point
La Playa Beach/Resort
Marco Island Marriott
Ritz-Carlton Naples
Orlando
Gaylord Palms
Ritz-Carlton Orlando
Palm Beach
Breakers
Four Seasons
Ritz-Carlton Palm Beach
Sandestin
Sandestin
Sarasota
Colony Beach
Resort at Longboat Key
Ritz-Carlton
Tampa/St. Petersburg
Don CeSar Beach
Renaissance Vinoy
Georgia
Braselton
Château Élan
Georgia Coast
Cloister
Lodge at Sea Island
Lake Oconee
Ritz-Carlton Reynolds
Savannah
Westin Savannah Harbor
Hawaii
Big Island
Fairmont Orchid

Four Seasons Hualalai
Hapuna Beach Prince
Hilton Waikoloa Vlg.
Mauna Kea Beach
Mauna Lani Bay
Waikoloa Beach Marriott
Kauai
Grand Hyatt Kauai
Marriott Kauai Resort
Lanai
Manele Bay Hotel
Maui
Fairmont Kea Lani
Four Seasons/Wailea
Grand Wailea Resort
Hana-Maui
Ritz-Carlton Kapalua
Westin Maui
Oahu
JW Marriott Ihilani

Idaho
Coeur d'Alene
Coeur d'Alene

Illinois
Chicago
Fairmont Chicago
House of Blues
Peninsula
Ritz-Carlton
Galena
Eagle Ridge Resort
Gilman
Heartland Spa

Louisiana
New Orleans
Loews New Orleans
Monaco
Wyndham/Canal Place

Maine
Rockport
Samoset Resort

Maryland
Baltimore
Harbor Court
Cambridge
Hyatt Chesapeake Bay

Massachusetts
Boston
Boston Harbor
Ritz-Carlton, Boston
Ritz-Carlton Boston Common
Lenox
Canyon Ranch/Mass.
Cranwell Resort

Minnesota
Minneapolis/St. Paul
Grand Hotel

Nevada
Las Vegas
Mandalay Bay Hotel
Ritz-Carlton, Lake Las Vegas
Venetian Hotel

New Hampshire
Bretton Woods
Mount Washington

New Jersey
Short Hills
Hilton

New Mexico
Albuquerque
Hyatt Tamaya
Santa Fe
Bishop's Lodge
La Posada/Santa Fe
Taos
El Monte Sagrado

New York
Adirondacks
Lake Placid Lodge
Mirror Lake Inn
Sagamore
Catskills
Mirbeau Inn
Mohonk Mountain Hse.
New Age Health Spa
Hudson Valley
Roselawn
Long Island
Gurney's Inn
New York City
Le Parker Méridien
Peninsula
Trump International

North Carolina
Charlotte
Westin Charlotte

Ohio
Grand Rapids
Kerr House

Pennsylvania
Farmington
Nemacolin Woodlands

Hershey
Hershey
Philadelphia
Park Hyatt Phila./Bellevue
Rittenhouse
Ritz-Carlton
Poconos
Deerfield Spa
Skytop Lodge

Puerto Rico
Fajardo
Las Casitas Village
Las Croabas
Wyndham El Conquistador
Rincon
Horned Dorset
San Juan
Caribe Hilton
Ritz-Carlton
Vieques
Martineau Bay Resort

Rhode Island
Providence
Westin

South Carolina
Charleston
Charleston Place
Wild Dunes Resort
Hilton Head
Hilton Head Health Inst.
Westin
Kiawah Island
Sanctuary/Kiawah Is.
Myrtle Beach
Myrtle Beach Marriott

Texas
Austin
Barton Creek
Lake Austin Spa
Dallas/Ft. Worth
Crescent Court
Four Seasons/Las Colinas
Greenhouse
Zaza, Hotel
Houston
Houstonian
San Antonio
Hyatt Hill Country
Watermark

U.S. Virgin Islands
St. John
Caneel Bay
Westin

Utah
Park City
Stein Eriksen Lodge
Salt Lake City
Lodge at Snowbird
Snowbird
Sundance
St. George
Coyote Inn/Spa

Vermont
Smuggler's Notch
Smugglers' Notch
Stowe
Stoweflake Mtn. Resort
Topnotch at Stowe
Trapp Family Lodge
Stratton Mountain
Equinox
Woodstock
Woodstock Inn

Virginia
Charlottesville
Boar's Head Inn
Keswick Hall
Lansdowne
Lansdowne Resort
Williamsburg
Kingsmill Resort
Williamsburg Inn

Washington
Blaine
Semiahmoo Resort
Seattle
Bellevue Club

West Virginia
White Sulphur Springs
Greenbrier

Wisconsin
Kohler
American Club

Wyoming
Jackson
Amangani
Four Seasons Jackson Hole
Snake River Lodge
Spring Creek Ranch

Super Deluxe

Arizona

Phoenix/Scottsdale
Boulders
Fairmont Scottsdale
Four Seasons Scottsdale
Phoenician
Ritz-Carlton
Sanctuary/Camelback Mtn.
Tucson
Canyon Ranch

California

Carmel Area
Casa Palmero
Inn at Spanish Bay
Lodge/Pebble Beach
Stonepine
Laguna Beach
Montage Resort
Los Angeles
Bel-Air, Hotel
Beverly Hills
Four Seasons Bev. Hills
Peninsula Beverly Hills
Raffles L'Ermitage
Regent Beverly Wilshire
Ritz-Carlton Huntington
Ritz-Carlton Marina del Rey
Shutters on the Beach
Napa
Auberge du Soleil
Calistoga Ranch
Milliken Creek Inn
Palm Springs Area
Lodge/Rancho Mirage
Viceroy Palm Springs
San Diego
Four Seasons Aviara
Golden Door
San Francisco Bay Area
Campton Place
Four Seasons San Fran.
Park Hyatt
Ritz-Carlton
Santa Barbara
Bacara Resort
Four Seasons Santa Barbara
Sonoma
Gaige House Inn
South Bay
Ritz-Carlton Half Moon Bay
Yosemite
Château du Sureau

Colorado

Aspen
Little Nell
Lodge & Spa/Cordillera
Ritz-Carlton, Bachelor Gulch
St. Regis
Colorado Springs
Broadmoor

Connecticut

Washington
Mayflower Inn
Westport
Inn at National Hall

District of Columbia

Washington, DC
Four Seasons
Ritz-Carlton
Ritz-Carlton, Georgetown
St. Regis

Florida

Amelia Island
Ritz-Carlton
Ft. Lauderdale
Boca Raton Resort
Keys
Little Palm Island
Miami
Biltmore/Coral Gables
Fairmont Turnberry Isle
Fisher Island
Four Seasons Miami
Grove Isle Club
Mandarin Oriental
Ritz-Carlton Coconut Grove
Naples
Ritz-Carlton Golf
Ritz-Carlton Naples
Orlando
Disney Grand Floridian
Ritz-Carlton Orlando
Palm Beach
Breakers
Four Seasons
Ritz-Carlton Palm Beach

Georgia

Atlanta
Four Seasons
Ritz-Carlton Buckhead

Lake Oconee
Ritz-Carlton Reynolds

Hawaii

Big Island
Fairmont Orchid
Four Seasons Hualalai
Mauna Kea Beach
Mauna Lani Bay

Kauai
Princeville Resort

Lanai
Lodge at Koele

Maui
Fairmont Kea Lani
Four Seasons/Wailea
Grand Wailea Resort
Ritz-Carlton Kapalua

Oahu
Halekulani
Kahala Mandarin Oriental

Illinois

Chicago
Four Seasons
Park Hyatt
Peninsula
Ritz-Carlton

Louisiana

New Orleans
Ritz-Carlton
Soniat House
Windsor Court

Maine

Kennebunkport
White Barn Inn

Maryland

St. Michaels
Inn at Perry Cabin

Massachusetts

Boston
XV Beacon
Four Seasons
Langham Hotel
Ritz-Carlton, Boston
Ritz-Carlton Boston Common

Cape Cod & The Islands
Wauwinet

Lenox
Blantyre

Michigan

Detroit
Ritz-Carlton

Minnesota

Minneapolis/St. Paul
Grand Hotel

Missouri

St. Louis
Ritz-Carlton

Montana

Darby
Triple Creek Ranch

Missoula
Resort at Paws Up

Nevada

Las Vegas
Bellagio Hotel
Four Seasons Las Vegas
JW Marriott Las Vegas
Ritz-Carlton, Lake Las Vegas

New Mexico

Santa Fe
Inn of the Anasazi

New York

Adirondacks
Mirror Lake Inn
Point

Hudson Valley
Inn at Bullis Hall

Long Island
Garden City

New York City
Carlyle
Four Seasons
Mark
Peninsula
Pierre New York
Plaza Athénée
Ritz-Carlton, Battery Pk.
Ritz-Carlton, Central Park
St. Regis
Trump International

North Carolina

Chapel Hill
Fearrington House

Ohio

Cleveland
Ritz-Carlton

Oklahoma

Bartlesville
Inn at Price Tower

Pennsylvania

Bradford
Glendorn

Philadelphia
Four Seasons Phila.
Rittenhouse
Ritz-Carlton
Puerto Rico
Fajardo
Las Casitas Village
Las Croabas
Wyndham El Conquistador
Rincon
Horned Dorset
San Juan
Ritz-Carlton
Wyndham El San Juan
South Carolina
Charleston
Market Pavilion
Planters Inn
Tennessee
Memphis
Peabody
Walland
Blackberry Farm
Texas
Austin
Four Seasons
Dallas/Ft. Worth
Adolphus
Crescent Court
Four Seasons/Las Colinas
Greenhouse
Mansion on Turtle Creek
Houston
Four Seasons
Omni Houston
St. Regis
San Antonio
La Mansión del Rio
U.S. Virgin Islands
St. John
Caneel Bay
St. Thomas
Ritz-Carlton
Utah
Park City
Goldener Hirsch Inn
Salt Lake City
Grand America
St. George
Coyote Inn/Spa
Vermont
Barnard
Twin Farms
Sugarbush
Pitcher Inn
Virginia
Charlottesville
Keswick Hall
Richmond
Jefferson
Washington
Inn at Little Washington
Washington
Seattle
Bellevue Club
Fairmont Olympic
West Virginia
White Sulphur Springs
Greenbrier
Wisconsin
Kohler
American Club
Wyoming
Jackson
Amangani
Four Seasons Jackson Hole
Rusty Parrot Lodge
Spring Creek Ranch

Swimming Pools, Private

Arizona
Phoenix/Scottsdale
Four Seasons Scottsdale
JW Marriott Desert Ridge
Sedona
Enchantment Resort
Tucson
Canyon Ranch
California
Carmel Area
Bernardus Lodge
Palm Springs Area
La Quinta Resort
Morongo Casino
San Diego
La Casa del Zorro
San Luis Obispo
Apple Farm
Santa Barbara
Four Seasons Santa Barbara
San Ysidro Ranch

Florida
Amelia Island
Amelia Is. Plantation
Ft. Lauderdale
Boca Raton Resort
Marriott Harbor Beach
Miami
Setai
Hawaii
Big Island
Mauna Lani Bay
Maui
Fairmont Kea Lani
Idaho
Coeur d'Alene
Coeur d'Alene
Illinois
Chicago
Fairmont Chicago
Maryland
Baltimore
Hyatt
Massachusetts
Cape Cod & The Islands
Wequassett Inn
Nevada
Las Vegas
Ritz-Carlton, Lake Las Vegas
New York
Cooperstown
Otesaga
Puerto Rico
Rincon
Horned Dorset
San Juan
Paradisus Puerto Rico
Texas
Houston
Four Seasons
San Antonio
Westin La Cantera
Utah
Park City
Deer Valley Lodging
Salt Lake City
Snowbird
Virginia
Williamsburg
Williamsburg Inn

Trendy Places

Arizona
Phoenix/Scottsdale
James
California
Carmel Area
Post Ranch Inn
Ventana Inn
Lake Tahoe Area
PlumpJack Squaw Valley
Los Angeles
Argyle
Bel-Air, Hotel
Beverly Hills
Casa Del Mar
Chateau Marmont
Farmer's Daughter
Maison 140
Mondrian
Peninsula Beverly Hills
Raffles L'Ermitage
Regent Beverly Wilshire
Shutters on the Beach
Sofitel
W Westwood
Napa
Auberge du Soleil
Palm Springs Area
Morongo Casino
Two Bunch Palms
Viceroy Palm Springs
San Diego
Golden Door
Solamar
W San Diego
San Francisco Bay Area
Argent
Clift
Four Seasons San Fran.
Griffon
Palomar
Vitale
W San Francisco
Sonoma
Healdsburg
Colorado
Aspen
Jerome
Little Nell
Lodge & Spa/Cordillera
Ritz-Carlton, Bachelor Gulch

Sky
St. Regis
Beaver Creek
Park Hyatt
Denver
Monaco
Oxford
Teatro
Connecticut
Greenwich
Homestead Inn
Norwich
Spa at Norwich Inn
Westport
Inn at National Hall
District of Columbia
Washington, DC
George
Helix
Monaco
Florida
Ft. Lauderdale
Atlantic
Miami
Astor
Circa 39
Delano
Hotel, The
Loews Miami Beach
Mandarin Oriental
Shore Club
Tides
Victor
Georgia
Atlanta
Indigo
Ritz-Carlton Buckhead
Hawaii
Big Island
Mauna Kea Beach
Lanai
Lodge at Koele
Oahu
Halekulani
Kahala Mandarin Oriental
W Honolulu - Diamond Head
Illinois
Chicago
House of Blues
Monaco
Park Hyatt
Peninsula
Sutton Place
W Lakeshore
Louisiana
New Orleans
International House
Monaco
W French Quarter
Windsor Court
W New Orleans
Massachusetts
Boston
XV Beacon
Nine Zero
Minnesota
Minneapolis/St. Paul
Graves 601
Nevada
Las Vegas
Bellagio Hotel
Hard Rock
Palms Casino Hotel
New Jersey
Atlantic City
Borgata Hotel
New York
New York City
Chambers
Gansevoort
Hudson
Mandarin Oriental
Maritime
Mercer
Royalton
60 Thompson
Soho Grand Hotel
W Union Square
Oklahoma
Bartlesville
Inn at Price Tower
Oregon
Portland
Heathman Hotel
Lucia, Hotel
Puerto Rico
Fajardo
Las Casitas Village
Texas
Dallas/Ft. Worth
Zaza, Hotel

Houston
Derek
San Antonio
Valencia Riverwalk
Utah
Salt Lake City
Monaco
Washington
Seattle
Monaco
W Seattle
Wisconsin
Milwaukee
Metro
Pfister Hotel
Wyoming
Jackson
Amangani
Four Seasons Jackson Hole
Rusty Parrot Lodge

Water Views

Alaska
Aleutian Islands
Grand Aleutian
Anchorage
Millennium Anchorage
Arizona
Phoenix/Scottsdale
Hyatt/Gainey Ranch
Sedona
L'Auberge de Sedona
California
Carmel Area
Casa Palmero
Cypress Inn
Green Gables Inn
Inn at Spanish Bay
La Playa
Lodge/Pebble Beach
Monterey Plaza
Spindrift Inn
Dana Point
Marriott Laguna Cliffs
St. Regis Monarch Beach
Huntington Beach
Hyatt Huntington Beach
Laguna Beach
Montage Resort
Surf & Sand Resort
Los Angeles
Casa Del Mar
Loews Santa Monica
Ritz-Carlton Huntington
Napa
Calistoga Ranch
Napa River Inn
Palm Springs Area
La Quinta Resort
Renaissance Esmeralda
San Diego
La Valencia
Lodge at Torrey Pines
Loews Coronado Bay
Marriott San Diego
Marriott Coronado Is.
Parisi
Westgate
San Francisco Bay Area
Albion River
Four Seasons San Fran.
Huntington
Inn Above Tide
Mandarin Oriental
Mark Hopkins
Nikko
Omni
Pan Pacific SF
Ritz-Carlton
Vitale
San Luis Obispo
Apple Farm
Santa Barbara
Andalucia
Bacara Resort
El Encanto
Four Seasons Santa Barbara
San Ysidro Ranch
Sonoma
Gaige House Inn
Whale Watch Inn
South Bay
Ritz-Carlton Half Moon Bay
Yosemite
Château du Sureau
Connecticut
Greenwich
Delamar
Old Saybrook
Saybrook Point Inn

Washington
Mayflower Inn
District of Columbia
Washington, DC
Ritz-Carlton, Georgetown
Florida
Amelia Island
Amelia Is. Plantation
Ritz-Carlton
Destin
Hilton Sandestin Beach
Ft. Lauderdale
Atlantic
Boca Raton Resort
Hutchinson Island
Hutchinson Is. Marriott
Jacksonville
Lodge & Club
Keys
Hilton Key West
Hyatt Key West
Sheraton Suites Key West
Sunset Key Cottages
Wyndham Casa Marina
Miami
Bentley Beach
Biltmore/Coral Gables
Conrad Miami
Eden Roc
Fisher Island
Four Seasons Miami
InterContinental Miami
JW Marriott Miami
Loews Miami Beach
Mutiny
Pritikin Longevity Center & Spa
Raleigh
Ritz-Carlton Key Biscayne
Ritz-Carlton South Beach
Setai
Victor
Wyndham Grand Bay
Naples
La Playa Beach/Resort
Marco Beach Resort
Marco Island Marriott
Ritz-Carlton Naples
Orlando
Loews Portofino Bay
Ritz-Carlton Orlando
Royal Pacific Resort
Villas of Grand Cypress
Wyndham Palace
Palm Beach
Breakers
Colony
Sandestin
Sandestin
Santa Rosa Beach
Water Color Inn
Sarasota
Ritz-Carlton
Tampa/St. Petersburg
Belleview Biltmore
Clearwater Beach Marriott
Don CeSar Beach
Georgia
Georgia Coast
Jekyll Island Club
King & Prince Resort
Lodge at Sea Island
Lake Oconee
Ritz-Carlton Reynolds
Savannah
River Street Inn
Westin Savannah Harbor
Hawaii
Big Island
Fairmont Orchid
Maui
Grand Wailea Resort
Kapalua Villas
Sheraton Maui
Molokai
Molokai Ranch
Oahu
Hilton Hawaiian Vlg.
Marriott Waikiki Beach
Waikiki Parc
W Honolulu - Diamond Head
Illinois
Chicago
Hard Rock Chicago
Hilton Chicago
Monaco
71, Hotel
Sheraton Chicago
Galena
Eagle Ridge Resort

Louisiana
New Orleans
Loews New Orleans
Monteleone
Windsor Court
W New Orleans
Wyndham/Canal Place
White Castle
Nottoway Plantation
Maine
York Harbor
York Harbor Inn
Maryland
Baltimore
Marriott Waterfront
Cambridge
Hyatt Chesapeake Bay
Massachusetts
Boston
Ritz-Carlton Boston Common
Rockport
Emerson Inn
Michigan
Detroit
Royal Park
Grand Rapids
Amway Grand Plaza
Minnesota
Minneapolis/St. Paul
Nicollet Island Inn
Montana
Darby
Triple Creek Ranch
Missoula
Resort at Paws Up
Nevada
Las Vegas
Ritz-Carlton, Lake Las Vegas
New Jersey
Atlantic City
Seaview Marriott Resort
Tropicana
Trump Marina
Trump Plaza
Trump Taj Mahal
Cape May
Congress Hall
New York
Adirondacks
Friends Lake Inn
Whiteface Lodge
Hudson Valley
Beekman Arms
Roselawn
Long Island
Gurney's Inn
New York City
Millenium Hilton
Westin New York
North Carolina
Outer Banks
Sanderling
Oregon
Crater Lake National Park
Crater Lake Lodge
Gold Beach
Tu Tu' Tun Lodge
Hood River
Columbia Gorge
Portland
Avalon
Pennsylvania
Bucks County
EverMay/Delaware
Philadelphia
Hyatt Philadelphia
Poconos
Skytop Lodge
Puerto Rico
Fajardo
Las Casitas Village
Rincon
Horned Dorset
San Juan
Caribe Hilton
InterContinental
Paradisus Puerto Rico
Ritz-Carlton
Wyndham El San Juan
Vieques
Martineau Bay Resort
Rhode Island
Block Island
1661 Inn
Newport
Castle Hill Inn
South Carolina
Charleston
Wild Dunes Resort
Hilton Head
Hilton Head Marriott Beach
Inn at Palmetto Bluff

Kiawah Island
Sanctuary/Kiawah Is.
Myrtle Beach
Breakers Resort
Long Bay Resort
Myrtle Beach Marriott
Pawleys Island
Litchfield Plantation

Tennessee
Memphis
Madison
Peabody

Texas
Austin
Lake Austin Spa
Galveston
Galvez-Historic Wyndham
San Antonio
Valencia Riverwalk
Watermark

U.S. Virgin Islands
St. Croix
Buccaneer
Carambola Beach
St. John
Westin

Utah
Park City
Park City

Vermont
Shelburne
Inn at Shelburne Farms
Stowe
Topnotch at Stowe

Virginia
Irvington
Tides Inn

Washington
Blaine
Semiahmoo Resort
Seattle
Alexis
Fairmont Olympic
Grand Hyatt
Inn at Langley
Inn at the Market
Salish Lodge
W Seattle
Stevenson
Skamania Lodge

Wisconsin
Chetek
Canoe Bay
Milwaukee
Pfister Hotel
Wyndham Milwaukee

Wyoming
Jackson
Four Seasons Jackson Hole
Jackson Lake Lodge
Yellowstone Nat'l Park
Lake Yellowstone

Alphabetical Index

Listings followed by (C) are chains.